This Bible belongs to:

Given by:

Date:

Occasion:

"GIVE YOURSELF TO GOD AS THE KIND OF PERSON HE WILL APPROVE."
2 TIMOTHY 2:15

explore

THE COMPLETE NEW TESTAMENT

NCV
NEW CENTURY VERSION

NELSON BIBLES
A Division of Thomas Nelson Publishers
Since 1798
www.thomasnelson.com

explore

THE COMPLETE NEW TESTAMENT

Writing services managed by Sanford Communications, Inc.
Art Direction: Jami Anderson
Page Design and Layout: Anderson Thomas Design
Cover Design: Anderson Thomas Design
Contributors: David Sanford, Mike Umlandt, Elizabeth Honeycutt, Beyth Hogue, Elizabeth Jones, Brian Boys, Damon Evans, Marty Trammell, Michael Walt, Mike Hamel, Rebekah Clark, Shawna Sanford, Tony Johnson

TABLE OF CONTENTS

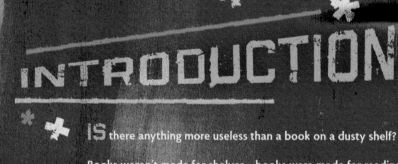

INTRODUCTION

IS there anything more useless than a book on a dusty shelf?

Books weren't made for shelves—books were made for reading. Some authors spend their entire lives writing one book. Their hope? That someone will actually read their book, get something from it, and then pass it along to someone else.

Suppose you have written a book. One day on the bus, the passenger sitting next to you pulls your book from his backpack. You're so excited—someone is actually reading your work!

You don't say anything, but as you watch him read page 17, you're dying to say, "Slow down and read the next page carefully—there's something really important you don't want to miss."

After all, no one knows the book like you do. You wrote it!

Well, God is the author of a Book—the Bible. He used many humans to actually write the words, but God is the author. No one knows the Book like God does. If you ask him, God will help you understand its powerful truths.

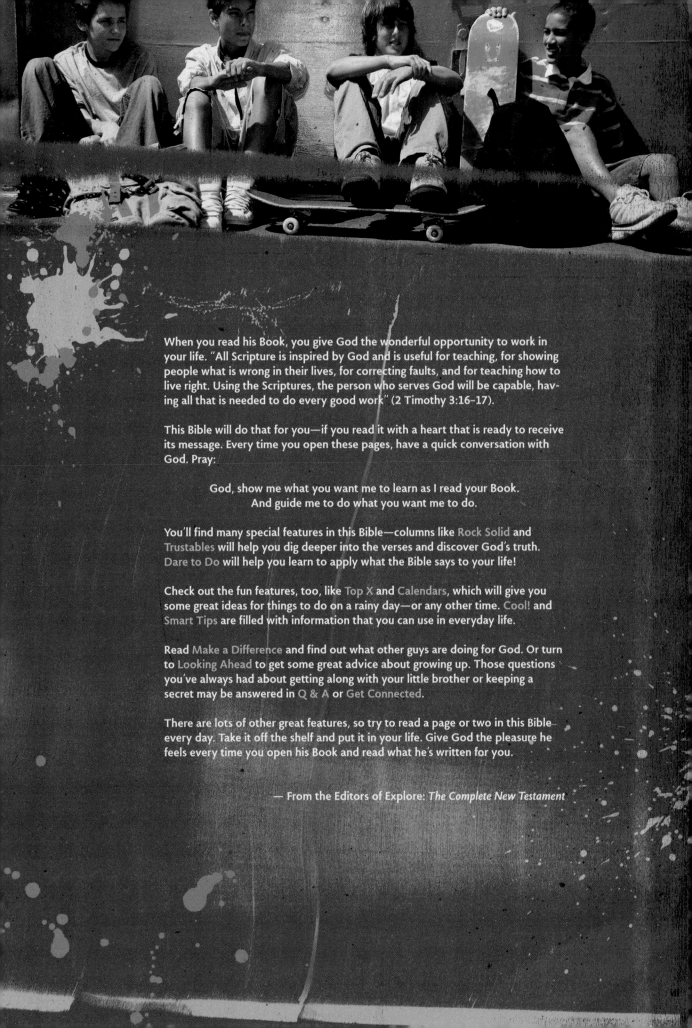

When you read his Book, you give God the wonderful opportunity to work in your life. "All Scripture is inspired by God and is useful for teaching, for showing people what is wrong in their lives, for correcting faults, and for teaching how to live right. Using the Scriptures, the person who serves God will be capable, having all that is needed to do every good work" (2 Timothy 3:16–17).

This Bible will do that for you—if you read it with a heart that is ready to receive its message. Every time you open these pages, have a quick conversation with God. Pray:

God, show me what you want me to learn as I read your Book.
And guide me to do what you want me to do.

You'll find many special features in this Bible—columns like Rock Solid and Trustables will help you dig deeper into the verses and discover God's truth. Dare to Do will help you learn to apply what the Bible says to your life!

Check out the fun features, too, like Top X and Calendars, which will give you some great ideas for things to do on a rainy day—or any other time. Cool! and Smart Tips are filled with information that you can use in everyday life.

Read Make a Difference and find out what other guys are doing for God. Or turn to Looking Ahead to get some great advice about growing up. Those questions you've always had about getting along with your little brother or keeping a secret may be answered in Q & A or Get Connected.

There are lots of other great features, so try to read a page or two in this Bible—every day. Take it off the shelf and put it in your life. Give God the pleasure he feels every time you open his Book and read what he's written for you.

— From the Editors of Explore: *The Complete New Testament*

A NOTE ABOUT THE NEW CENTURY VERSION®

God never intended the Bible to be too difficult for his people. To make sure God's message was clear, the authors of the Bible recorded God's word in familiar everyday language. These books brought a message that the original readers could understand. These first readers knew that God spoke through these books. Down through the centuries, many people wanted a Bible so badly that they copied different Bible books by hand!

Today, now that the Bible is readily available, many Christians do not regularly read it. Many feel that the Bible is too hard to understand or irrelevant to life.

The New Century Version captures the clear and simple message that the very first readers understood. This version presents the Bible as God intended it: clear and dynamic.

A team of scholars from the World Bible Translation Center worked together with twenty-one other experienced Bible scholars from all over the world to translate the text directly from the best available Greek and Hebrew texts. You can trust that this Bible accurately presents God's Word as it came to us in the original languages.

Translators kept sentences short and simple. They avoided difficult words and worked to make the text easier to read. They used modern terms for places and measurements. And they put figures of speech and idiomatic expressions ("he was gathered to his people") in language that even children understand ("he died").

Following the tradition of other English versions, the New Century Version indicates the divine name, *Yahweh*, by putting LORD, and sometimes GOD, in capital letters. This distinguishes it from *Adonai*, another Hebrew word that is translated Lord.

We acknowledge the infallibility of God's Word and yet our own frailty. We pray that God will use this Bible to help you understand his rich truth for yourself. To God be the glory.

—THE PUBLISHER

the NEW testament

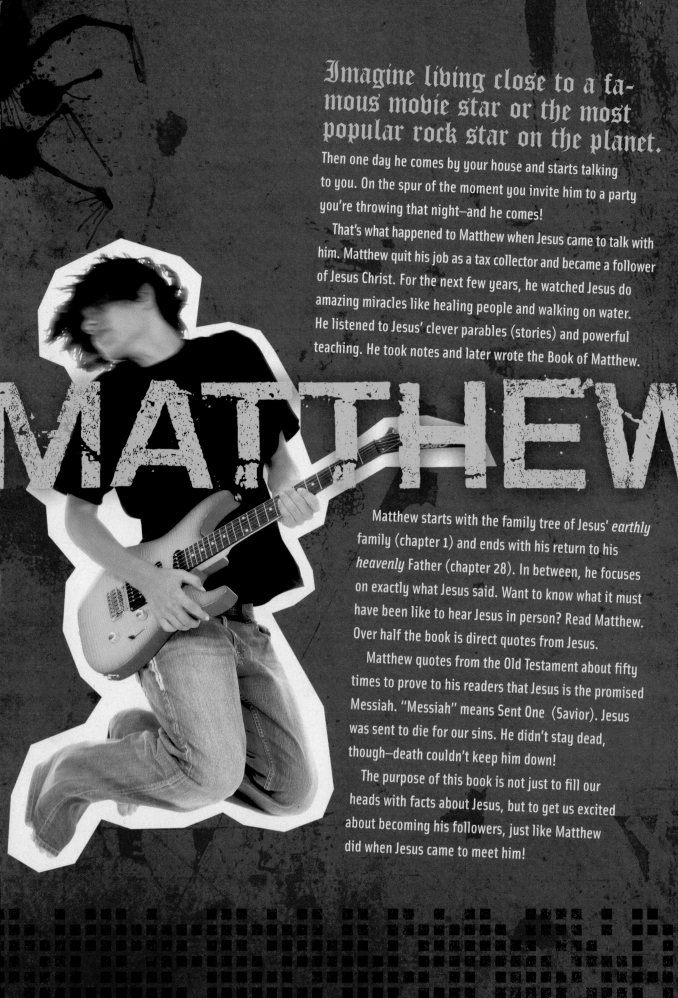

Imagine living close to a famous movie star or the most popular rock star on the planet.

Then one day he comes by your house and starts talking to you. On the spur of the moment you invite him to a party you're throwing that night—and he comes!

That's what happened to Matthew when Jesus came to talk with him. Matthew quit his job as a tax collector and became a follower of Jesus Christ. For the next few years, he watched Jesus do amazing miracles like healing people and walking on water. He listened to Jesus' clever parables (stories) and powerful teaching. He took notes and later wrote the Book of Matthew.

MATTHEW

Matthew starts with the family tree of Jesus' *earthly* family (chapter 1) and ends with his return to his *heavenly* Father (chapter 28). In between, he focuses on exactly what Jesus said. Want to know what it must have been like to hear Jesus in person? Read Matthew. Over half the book is direct quotes from Jesus.

Matthew quotes from the Old Testament about fifty times to prove to his readers that Jesus is the promised Messiah. "Messiah" means Sent One (Savior). Jesus was sent to die for our sins. He didn't stay dead, though—death couldn't keep him down!

The purpose of this book is not just to fill our heads with facts about Jesus, but to get us excited about becoming his followers, just like Matthew did when Jesus came to meet him!

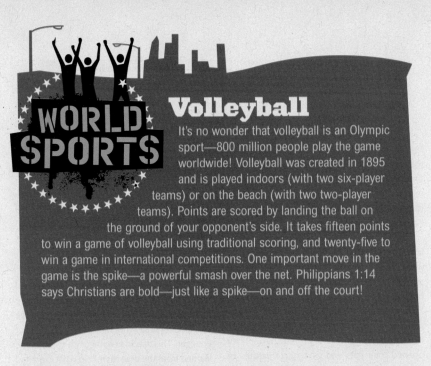

Volleyball

It's no wonder that volleyball is an Olympic sport—800 million people play the game worldwide! Volleyball was created in 1895 and is played indoors (with two six-player teams) or on the beach (with two two-player teams). Points are scored by landing the ball on the ground of your opponent's side. It takes fifteen points to win a game of volleyball using traditional scoring, and twenty-five to win a game in international competitions. One important move in the game is the spike—a powerful smash over the net. Philippians 1:14 says Christians are bold—just like a spike—on and off the court!

THE FAMILY HISTORY OF JESUS

1 This is the family history of Jesus Christ. He came from the family of David, and David came from the family of Abraham.

[2]Abraham was the father" of Isaac.
Isaac was the father of Jacob.
Jacob was the father of Judah and his brothers.
[3]Judah was the father of Perez and Zerah. (Their mother was Tamar.)
Perez was the father of Hezron.
Hezron was the father of Ram.
[4]Ram was the father of Amminadab.
Amminadab was the father of Nahshon.
Nahshon was the father of Salmon.
[5]Salmon was the father of Boaz. (Boaz's mother was Rahab.)
Boaz was the father of Obed. (Obed's mother was Ruth.)
Obed was the father of Jesse.
[6]Jesse was the father of King David.
David was the father of Solomon. (Solomon's mother had been Uriah's wife.)
[7]Solomon was the father of Rehoboam.
Rehoboam was the father of Abijah.
Abijah was the father of Asa."
[8]Asa was the father of Jehoshaphat.
Jehoshaphat was the father of Jehoram.
Jehoram was the ancestor of Uzziah.
[9]Uzziah was the father of Jotham.
Jotham was the father of Ahaz.
Ahaz was the father of Hezekiah.
[10]Hezekiah was the father of Manasseh.
Manasseh was the father of Amon.
Amon was the father of Josiah.
[11]Josiah was the grandfather of Jehoiachin" and his brothers.

(This was at the time that the people were taken to Babylon.)
[12]After they were taken to Babylon:
Jehoiachin was the father of Shealtiel.
Shealtiel was the grandfather of Zerubbabel.
[13]Zerubbabel was the father of Abiud.
Abiud was the father of Eliakim.
Eliakim was the father of Azor.
[14]Azor was the father of Zadok.
Zadok was the father of Akim.
Akim was the father of Eliud.
[15]Eliud was the father of Eleazar.
Eleazar was the father of Matthan.
Matthan was the father of Jacob.
[16]Jacob was the father of Joseph.
Joseph was the husband of Mary, and Mary was the mother of Jesus.
Jesus is called the Christ.

[17]So there were fourteen generations from Abraham to David. And there were fourteen generations from David until the people were taken to Babylon. And there were fourteen generations from the time when the people were taken to Babylon until Christ was born.

THE BIRTH OF JESUS CHRIST

[18]This is how the birth of Jesus Christ came about. His mother Mary was engaged" to marry Joseph, but before they married, she learned she was pregnant by the power of the Holy Spirit. [19]Because Mary's husband, Joseph, was a good man, he did not want to disgrace her in public, so he planned to divorce her secretly.

[20]While Joseph thought about these things, an angel of the Lord came to him in a dream. The angel said, "Joseph, descendant of David, don't be afraid to take Mary as your wife, because the baby in her is from the Holy Spirit. [21]She will give birth to a son, and you will name him Jesus," because he will save his people from their sins."

[22]All this happened to bring about what the Lord had said through the prophet: [23]"The

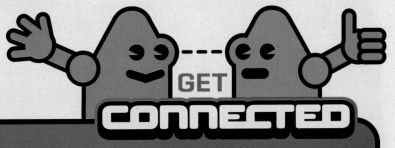

GET CONNECTED

FORGIVENESS

Have you ever had to say "I'm sorry" for something you did? It's *not* the easiest thing to do. Ignoring the problem and the person is much easier. But Jesus told his followers (that includes us!) that we should "go and make peace" with others before we even think about worshiping God (Matthew 5:24).

It takes guts, but an "I'm sorry" separates the men from the boys and often fixes a friendship. When you make peace, you have the advantage of a clear conscience, and your friends will see that you have what it takes to do what's right!

1:2 father "Father" in Jewish lists of ancestors can sometimes mean grandfather or more distant relative. **1:7 Asa** Some Greek copies read "Asaph," another name for Asa (see 1 Chronicles 3:10). **1:11 Jehoiachin** The Greek reads "Jeconiah," another name for Jehoiachin (see 2 Kings 24:6 and 1 Chronicles 3:16). **1:18 engaged** For the Jewish people an engagement was a lasting agreement, which could only be broken by a divorce. If a bride-to-be was unfaithful, it was considered adultery, and she could be put to death. **1:21 Jesus** The name "Jesus" means "salvation."

virgin will be pregnant. She will have a son, and they will name him Immanuel,"[n] which means "God is with us."

[24]When Joseph woke up, he did what the Lord's angel had told him to do. Joseph took Mary as his wife, [25]but he did not have sexual relations with her until she gave birth to the son. And Joseph named him Jesus.

WISE MEN COME TO VISIT JESUS

2 Jesus was born in the town of Bethlehem in Judea during the time when Herod was king. When Jesus was born, some wise men from the east came to Jerusalem. [2]They asked, "Where is the baby who was born to be the king of the Jews? We saw his star in the east and have come to worship him."

[3]When King Herod heard this, he was troubled, as were all the people in Jerusalem. [4]Herod called a meeting of all the leading priests and teachers of the law and asked them where the Christ would be born. [5]They answered, "In the town of Bethlehem in Judea. The prophet wrote about this in the Scriptures:

[6]'But you, Bethlehem, in the land of Judah,
    are not just an insignificant village in
        Judah.
    A ruler will come from you
        who will be like a shepherd for my
            people Israel.' "   *Micah 5:2*

[7]Then Herod had a secret meeting with the wise men and learned from them the exact time they first saw the star. [8]He sent the wise men to Bethlehem, saying, "Look carefully for the child. When you find him, come tell me so I can worship him too."

[9]After the wise men heard the king, they left. The star that they had seen in the east went before them until it stopped above the place where the child was. [10]When the wise men saw the star, they were filled with joy. [11]They came to the house where the child was and saw him with his mother, Mary, and they bowed down and worshiped him. They opened their gifts and gave him treasures of gold, frankincense, and myrrh. [12]But God warned the wise men in a dream not to go back to Herod, so they returned to their own country by a different way.

JESUS' PARENTS TAKE HIM TO EGYPT

[13]After they left, an angel of the Lord came to Joseph in a dream and said, "Get up! Take the child and his mother and escape to Egypt, because Herod is starting to look for the child so he can kill him. Stay in Egypt until I tell you to return."

[14]So Joseph got up and left for Egypt during the night with the child and his mother. [15]And Joseph stayed in Egypt until Herod died. This happened to bring about what the Lord had said through the prophet: "I called my son out of Egypt."[n]

HEROD KILLS THE BABY BOYS

[16]When Herod saw that the wise men had tricked him, he was furious. So he gave an order to kill all the baby boys in Bethlehem and in the surrounding area who were two years old or younger. This was in keeping with the time he learned from the wise men. [17]So what God had said through the prophet Jeremiah came true:
[18]"A voice was heard in Ramah
    of painful crying and deep sadness:
    Rachel crying for her children.
    She refused to be comforted,
        because her children are dead."
                        Jeremiah 31:15

JOSEPH AND MARY RETURN

[19]After Herod died, an angel of the Lord spoke to Joseph in a dream while he was in Egypt. [20]The angel said, "Get up! Take the child and his mother and go to the land of Israel, because the people who were trying to kill the child are now dead."

[21]So Joseph took the child and his mother and went to Israel. [22]But he heard that Archelaus was now king in Judea since his father Herod had died. So Joseph was afraid to go there. After being warned in a dream, he went to the area of Galilee, [23]to a town called Nazareth, and lived there. And so what God had said through the prophets came true: "He will be called a Nazarene."[n]

THE WORK OF JOHN THE BAPTIST

3 About that time John the Baptist began preaching in the desert area of Judea. [2]John said, "Change your hearts and lives because the kingdom of heaven is near." [3]John the Baptist is the one Isaiah the prophet was talking about when he said:
    "This is a voice of one
        who calls out in the desert:
    'Prepare the way for the Lord.
        Make the road straight for him.' "
                            Isaiah 40:3

ROCK SOLID

Matthew 3:2

You can change the world.

Yeah, you think, *I've heard that one before, but you don't know me.*

"You can change the world" is a great-sounding slogan. When we honestly take a look at our lives, though, we realize it's hard enough to change what we don't like about ourselves, let alone to change the world.

You really can't change the world…but *God* can, and he wants to use you!

God can change anything he wants to change. After all, he created everything. And he gave the Holy Spirit to everyone who believes in him. So if you've believed in him, you have the Holy Spirit, who is God, living in you! The one with the power to speak the universe into existence is the one who is living in you!

John the Baptist wasn't rich or famous. Yet from an early age, he was used by God to urge people to change their hearts and lives (Matthew 3:2). Many people said "yes," preparing the way for Jesus Christ's public ministry.

You can do amazing things when you trust our powerful and loving God to work through you.

BIBLE SUPERHEROES

John the Baptist
See Matthew 3; 14:1-12.

John the Baptist is famous for eating grasshoppers, wandering around in the desert, and losing his head. John was like his cousin Jesus—an angel predicted his birth, name, and ministry before his mom was even pregnant!

John's dad was a priest, but John never served in the Temple. Instead, he cleared the way for Jesus' ministry by telling people to give up sinning. He didn't care what others thought of him and it ended up costing his life. There's never been another man like John the Baptist.

God had specific plans for John's short but thrilling life. People probably thought he was weird—he sure looked like it! But his life was different for a purpose; he was living the life God had planned for him. Different can be best if you're following God!

[4] John's clothes were made from camel's hair, and he wore a leather belt around his waist. For food, he ate locusts and wild honey. [5] Many people came from Jerusalem and Judea and all the area around the Jordan River to hear John. [6] They confessed their sins, and he baptized them in the Jordan River.

[7] Many of the Pharisees and Sadducees came to the place where John was baptizing people. When John saw them, he said, "You are snakes! Who warned you to run away from God's coming punishment? [8] Do the things that show you really have changed your hearts and lives. [9] And don't think you can say to yourselves, 'Abraham is our father.' I tell you that God could make children for Abraham from these rocks. [10] The ax is now ready to cut down the trees, and every tree that does not produce good fruit will be cut down and thrown into the fire.[n]

[11] "I baptize you with water to show that your hearts and lives have changed. But there is one coming after me who is greater than I am, whose sandals I am not good enough to carry. He will baptize you with the Holy Spirit and fire. [12] He will come ready to clean the grain, separating the good grain from the chaff. He will put the good part of the grain into his barn, but he will burn the chaff with a fire that cannot be put out."[n]

JESUS IS BAPTIZED BY JOHN

[13] At that time Jesus came from Galilee to the Jordan River and wanted John to baptize him. [14] But John tried to stop him, saying, "Why do you come to me to be baptized? I need to be baptized by you!"

[15] Jesus answered, "Let it be this way for now. We should do all things that are God's will." So John agreed to baptize Jesus.

[16] As soon as Jesus was baptized, he came up out of the water. Then heaven opened, and he saw God's Spirit coming down on him like a dove. [17] And a voice from heaven said, "This is my Son, whom I love, and I am very pleased with him."

THE TEMPTATION OF JESUS

[4] Then the Spirit led Jesus into the desert to be tempted by the devil. [2] Jesus fasted for forty days and nights. After this, he was very hungry. [3] The devil came to Jesus to tempt him, saying, "If you are the Son of God, tell these rocks to become bread."

[4] Jesus answered, "It is written in the Scriptures, 'A person lives not on bread alone, but by everything God says.' "[n]

[5] Then the devil led Jesus to the holy city of Jerusalem and put him on a high place of the Temple. [6] The devil said, "If you are the Son of God, jump down, because it is written in the Scriptures:

'He has put his angels in charge of you.
   They will catch you in their hands
so that you will not hit your foot on a rock.' "

Psalm 91:11–12

[7] Jesus answered him, "It also says in the Scriptures, 'Do not test the Lord your God.' "[n]

[8] Then the devil led Jesus to the top of a very high mountain and showed him all the kingdoms of the world and all their splendor. [9] The devil said, "If you will bow down and worship me, I will give you all these things."

[10] Jesus said to the devil, "Go away from me, Satan! It is written in the Scriptures, 'You must worship the Lord your God and serve only him.' "[n]

[11] So the devil left Jesus, and angels came and took care of him.

JESUS BEGINS WORK IN GALILEE

[12] When Jesus heard that John had been put in prison, he went back to Galilee. [13] He left Nazareth and went to live in Capernaum, a town near Lake Galilee, in the area near Zebulun and Naphtali. [14] Jesus did this to bring about what the prophet Isaiah had said:

[15] "Land of Zebulun and land of Naphtali
   along the sea,
beyond the Jordan River.

DID YOU KNOW?

82% of boys think their parents' opinion is important.

Tween Audience Analysis Profile, The Health Communication Unit, 2004.

This is Galilee where the non-Jewish
people live.
[16] These people who live in darkness
will see a great light.
They live in a place covered with the
shadows of death,
but a light will shine on them."

Isaiah 9:1–2

JESUS CHOOSES SOME FOLLOWERS

[17] From that time Jesus began to preach,
saying, "Change your hearts and lives, because
the kingdom of heaven is near."

[18] As Jesus was walking by Lake Galilee, he
saw two brothers, Simon (called Peter) and his
brother Andrew. They were throwing a net
into the lake because they were fishermen.
[19] Jesus said, "Come follow me, and I will make
you fish for people." [20] So Simon and Andrew
immediately left their nets and followed him.

[21] As Jesus continued walking by Lake
Galilee, he saw two other brothers, James and
John, the sons of Zebedee. They were in a
boat with their father Zebedee, mending their
nets. Jesus told them to come with him. [22] Immediately they left the boat and their father,
and they followed Jesus.

JESUS TEACHES AND HEALS PEOPLE

[23] Jesus went everywhere in Galilee, teaching
in the synagogues, preaching the Good News

DID YOU KNOW?

**Most parents
and kids talk
together less
than an hour
a day.**

Philips' "Let's Connect" Family Communicating
Survey.

about the kingdom of heaven, and healing all the
people's diseases and sicknesses. [24] The news
about Jesus spread all over Syria, and people
brought all the sick to him. They were suffering
from different kinds of diseases. Some were in
great pain, some had demons, some were
epileptics,* and some were paralyzed. Jesus
healed all of them. [25] Many people from Galilee,

the Ten Towns," Jerusalem, Judea, and the land
across the Jordan River followed him.

JESUS TEACHES THE PEOPLE

5 When Jesus saw the crowds, he went up
on a hill and sat down. His followers came
to him, [2] and he began to teach them, saying:
[3] "They are blessed who realize their spiritual
poverty,
for the kingdom of heaven belongs to
them.
[4] They are blessed who grieve,
for God will comfort them.
[5] They are blessed who are humble,
for the whole earth will be theirs.
[6] They are blessed who hunger and thirst
after justice,
for they will be satisfied.
[7] They are blessed who show mercy to
others,
for God will show mercy to them.
[8] They are blessed whose thoughts are pure,
for they will see God.
[9] They are blessed who work for peace,
for they will be called God's children.
[10] They are blessed who are persecuted for
doing good,
for the kingdom of heaven belongs to
them.
[11] "People will insult you and hurt you.
They will lie and say all kinds of evil things

trustables

Matthew 3:17

Don't make eye contact.
Stay calm and keep your knees from knocking
together.

These thoughts may cross your mind when you get
in trouble with your parents. You broke a family rule,
and now there's a break in your relationship with
them. You have to be punished. You're busted.

This is what happened to us in our relationship
with God. We broke his rules; we sinned; and now
we're busted. Only being busted for sinning against
God means we have broken our relationship with
him, and we can't fix it.

Thankfully, Jesus Christ made a way for us to be

friends with God again. He paid the penalty that sin
brought to our lives, which is spiritual death. Christ
died for our sins on a cross and rose again three days
later. Now, instead of death because of our sins, we
can have life in Jesus Christ, God's Son.

How amazing that God loves us because of his
great love for Jesus. Imagine hearing what happened
when Jesus was baptized: "And a voice from heaven
said, 'This is my Son, whom I love, and I am very
pleased with him'" (Matthew 3:17).

God's Son, Jesus Christ, is the one and only
way back to the Father. Make sure you trust in him
for salvation.

⭐ **4:24 epileptics** People with a disease that causes them sometimes to lose control of their bodies and maybe faint, shake strongly, or not be able to move.   **4:25 Ten Towns** In Greek, called "Decapolis." It
was an area east of Lake Galilee that once had ten main towns.

about you because you follow me. But when they do, you will be blessed. [12]Rejoice and be glad, because you have a great reward waiting for you in heaven. People did the same evil things to the prophets who lived before you.

YOU ARE LIKE SALT AND LIGHT

[13]"You are the salt of the earth. But if the salt loses its salty taste, it cannot be made salty again. It is good for nothing, except to be thrown out and walked on.

[14]"You are the light that gives light to the world. A city that is built on a hill cannot be hidden. [15]And people don't hide a light under a bowl. They put it on a lampstand so the light shines for all the people in the house. [16]In the same way, you should be a light for other people. Live so that they will see the good things you do and will praise your Father in heaven.

THE IMPORTANCE OF THE LAW

[17]"Don't think that I have come to destroy the law of Moses or the teaching of the prophets. I have not come to destroy them but to bring about what they said. [18]I tell you the truth, nothing will disappear from the law until heaven and earth are gone. Not even the smallest letter or the smallest part of a letter will be lost until everything has happened. [19]Whoever refuses to obey any command and teaches other people not to obey that command will be the least important in the kingdom of heaven. But whoever obeys the commands and teaches other people to obey them will be great in the kingdom of heaven. [20]I tell you that if you are no more obedient than the teachers of the law and the Pharisees, you will never enter the kingdom of heaven.

JESUS TEACHES ABOUT ANGER

[21]"You have heard that it was said to our people long ago, 'You must not murder anyone.'" Anyone who murders another will be judged.' [22]But I tell you, if you are angry with a brother or sister," you will be judged. If you say bad things to a brother or sister, you will be judged by the council. And if you call someone a fool, you will be in danger of the fire of hell.

[23]"So when you offer your gift to God at the altar, and you remember that your brother or sister has something against you, [24]leave your gift there at the altar. Go and make peace with that person, and then come and offer your gift.

[25]"If your enemy is taking you to court, become friends quickly, before you go to court. Otherwise, your enemy might turn you over to the judge, and the judge might give you to a guard to put you in jail. [26]I tell you the truth, you will not leave there until you have paid everything you owe.

JESUS TEACHES ABOUT SEXUAL SIN

[27]"You have heard that it was said, 'You must not be guilty of adultery.'" [28]But I tell you that if anyone looks at a woman and wants to sin sexually with her, in his mind he has already done that sin with the woman. [29]If your right eye causes you to sin, take it out and throw it away. It is better to lose one part of your body than to have your whole body thrown into hell. [30]If your right hand causes you to sin, cut it off and throw it away. It is better to lose one part of your body than for your whole body to go into hell.

JESUS TEACHES ABOUT DIVORCE

[31]"It was also said, 'Anyone who divorces his wife must give her a written divorce paper.'"

Matthew 5:13

Saltine crackers go great with everything! Soup, cheese, peanut butter…I could eat a whole package in one sitting!

Did you know they make "salt-free" saltines? Could anything be more ridiculous? It's not even a "saltine" anymore. It's just a "tine." And the taste? Well, cardboard comes to mind. Nothing you'd want to spend much time stuffing your face with, trust me. Salt is the key!

The Bible says in Matthew 5:13 that Christians are the "salt of the earth." That's saying a lot. It means that Christians are supposed to give the world a taste of what God is like. Christians should bring pizzazz to life on earth. That means families that get along. That means fun gatherings and celebrations (woo-hoo, party!). That means making people around you feel important and appreciated.

Sometimes it seems like we are making "Christ-free" Christians just like they are making "salt-free" saltines. Bland. Lifeless. Only interested in themselves. And if they aren't like Jesus Christ, it probably means they aren't Christians at all. They're just "ians."

So go for it! Sprinkle a healthy dose of "Christ" into your life and give the world a real taste of God's goodness.

Q: How should I deal with bullies?

A: First of all, let your parents know if you feel in danger. They can work with your teachers and principal to make sure you don't get hurt. If you see someone getting picked on, stand up for him, but stay safe by telling a teacher what's going on. Most importantly, pray that God will help the bullies understand that what they are doing is not right.

Q: Are there any famous Christian athletes?

A: Yes, throughout time there have been many Christian men and women who have been the best in their sports. Eric Liddell was a Scottish track star of the early 1900s who felt God had made him to run. At the Olympics, when he found out that his strongest event (100 meters) would be run on Sunday, he withdrew. Instead, he ran the 400 meters...and still won the gold! Later, he went to China as a missionary where he spread the Good News under very harsh conditions.

Q: How do I tell if I really love Jesus?

A: The kind of love we should have for Jesus isn't just a feeling, but a decision to make him first in our lives. Jesus said that if we love him, then we'll obey his commandments (John 14:15). Nobody can obey Jesus perfectly, but if we love him we will try. If you love Jesus, you will want your life to make him happy.

---

[32]But I tell you that anyone who divorces his wife forces her to be guilty of adultery. The only reason for a man to divorce his wife is if she has sexual relations with another man. And anyone who marries that divorced woman is guilty of adultery.

MAKE PROMISES CAREFULLY

[33]"You have heard that it was said to our people long ago, 'Don't break your promises, but keep the promises you make to the Lord.'[n] [34]But I tell you, never swear an oath. Don't swear an oath using the name of heaven, because heaven is God's throne. [35]Don't swear an oath using the name of the earth, because the earth belongs to God. Don't swear an oath using the name of Jerusalem, because that is the city of the great King. [36]Don't even swear by your own head, because you cannot make one hair on your head become white or black. [37]Say only yes if you mean yes, and no if you mean no. If you say more than yes or no, it is from the Evil One.

DON'T FIGHT BACK

[38]"You have heard that it was said, 'An eye for an eye, and a tooth for a tooth.'[n] [39]But I tell you, don't stand up against an evil person. If someone slaps you on the right cheek, turn to him the other cheek also. [40]If someone wants to sue you in court and take your shirt, let him have your coat also. [41]If someone forces you to go with him one mile, go with him two miles. [42]If a person asks you for something, give it to him. Don't refuse to give to someone who wants to borrow from you.

LOVE ALL PEOPLE

[43]"You have heard that it was said, 'Love your neighbor'[n] and hate your enemies.' [44]But I say to you, love your enemies. Pray for those who hurt you."[n] [45]If you do this, you will be true children of your Father in heaven. He causes the sun to rise on good people and on evil people, and he sends rain to those who do right and to those who do wrong. [46]If you love only the people who love you, you will get no reward. Even the tax collectors do that. [47]And if you are nice only to your friends, you are no better than other people. Even those who don't know God are nice to their friends. [48]So you must be perfect, just as your Father in heaven is perfect.

JESUS TEACHES ABOUT GIVING

6 "Be careful! When you do good things, don't do them in front of people to be seen by them. If you do that, you will have no reward from your Father in heaven.

[2]"When you give to the poor, don't be like the hypocrites. They blow trumpets in the synagogues and on the streets so that people will see them and honor them. I tell you the truth, those hypocrites already have their full reward. [3]So when you give to the poor, don't let anyone know what you are doing. [4]Your giving should be done in secret. Your Father can see what is done in secret, and he will reward you.

JESUS TEACHES ABOUT PRAYER

[5]"When you pray, don't be like the hypocrites. They love to stand in the synagogues and on the street corners and pray so people will see them. I tell you the truth, they already have their full reward. [6]When you pray, you should go into your room and close the door and pray to your Father who cannot be seen. Your Father can see what is done in secret, and he will reward you.

 5:33 'Don't . . . Lord.' This refers to Leviticus 19:12; Numbers 30:2; Deuteronomy 23:21.   **5:38 'An eye . . . tooth.'** Quotation from Exodus 21:24; Leviticus 24:20; Deuteronomy 19:21.   **5:43 'Love your neighbor'** Quotation from Leviticus 19:18.   **5:44 you** Some Greek copies continue, "Bless those who curse you, do good to those who hate you." Compare Luke 6:28.

7"And when you pray, don't be like those people who don't know God. They continue saying things that mean nothing, thinking that God will hear them because of their many words. 8Don't be like them, because your Father knows the things you need before you ask him. 9So when you pray, you should pray like this:

'Our Father in heaven,
may your name always be kept holy.
10May your kingdom come
and what you want be done,
    here on earth as it is in heaven.
11Give us the food we need for each day.
12Forgive us for our sins,
    just as we have forgiven those who
        sinned against us.
13And do not cause us to be tempted,
    but save us from the Evil One.' [The
        kingdom, the power, and the glory
        are yours forever. Amen.]"

14Yes, if you forgive others for their sins, your Father in heaven will also forgive you for your sins. 15But if you don't forgive others, your Father in heaven will not forgive your sins.

JESUS TEACHES ABOUT WORSHIP

16"When you fast," don't put on a sad face like the hypocrites. They make their faces look sad to show people they are fasting. I tell you the truth, those hypocrites already have their full reward. 17So when you fast, comb your hair and wash your face. 18Then people will not know that you are fasting, but your Father, whom you cannot see, will see you. Your Father sees what is done in secret, and he will reward you.

GOD IS MORE IMPORTANT THAN MONEY

19"Don't store treasures for yourselves here on earth where moths and rust will destroy them and thieves can break in and steal them. 20But store your treasures in heaven where they cannot be destroyed by moths or rust and where thieves cannot break in and steal them. 21Your heart will be where your treasure is.

22"The eye is a light for the body. If your eyes are good, your whole body will be full of light. 23But if your eyes are evil, your whole body will be full of darkness. And if the only light you have is really darkness, then you have the worst darkness.

24"No one can serve two masters. The person will hate one master and love the other, or will follow one master and refuse to follow the other. You cannot serve both God and worldly riches.

DON'T WORRY

25"So I tell you, don't worry about the food or drink you need to live, or about the clothes you need for your body. Life is more than food, and the body is more than clothes. 26Look at the birds in the air. They don't plant or harvest or store food in barns, but your heavenly Father feeds them. And you know that you are worth much more than the birds. 27You cannot add any time to your life by worrying about it.

28"And why do you worry about clothes? Look at how the lilies in the field grow. They don't work or make clothes for themselves. 29But I tell you that even Solomon with his riches was not dressed as beautifully as one of these flowers. 30God clothes the grass in the field, which is alive today but tomorrow is thrown into the fire. So you can be even more sure that God will clothe you. Don't have so little faith! 31Don't worry and say, 'What will we eat?' or 'What will we drink?' or 'What will we wear?' 32The people who don't know God keep trying to get these things, and your Father in heaven knows you need them. 33Seek first God's kingdom and what God wants. Then all your other needs will be met as well. 34So don't worry about tomorrow, because tomorrow will have its own worries. Each day has enough trouble of its own.

BE CAREFUL ABOUT JUDGING OTHERS

7 "Don't judge others, or you will be judged. 2You will be judged in the same way that you judge others, and the amount you give to others will be given to you.

3"Why do you notice the little piece of dust in your friend's eye, but you don't notice the big piece of wood in your own eye? 4How can you say to your friend, 'Let me take that little piece of dust out of your eye'? Look at yourself! You still have that big piece of wood in your own eye. 5You hypocrite! First, take the wood out of your own eye. Then you will see clearly to take the dust out of your friend's eye.

6"Don't give holy things to dogs, and don't throw your pearls before pigs. Pigs will only trample on them, and dogs will turn to attack you.

ROCK SOLID

Matthew 6:25

Has your family ever experienced a tough time financially? You could probably tell that your mom or dad was worried about having enough money to make it through the month.

Jesus talked to people about this when he was on earth. He said, "Don't worry." And he didn't stop there. "Don't worry about the food or drink you need to live, or about the clothes you need for your body" (Matthew 6:25).

There may be times when you have to go without extras like new video games. But God will make sure you have clothes to wear and food to eat. He promised!

If you don't know where your next meal is going to come from or how your parents are going to pay the bills, don't worry. Instead, simply pray, "God, you promised to take care of me and I believe you." You can be sure that he will take care of everything you need.

6:13 **The . . . Amen.** Some Greek copies do not contain the bracketed text.   6:16 **fast** The people would give up eating for a special time of prayer and worship to God. It was also done to show sadness and disappointment.

ASK GOD FOR WHAT YOU NEED

[7]"Ask, and God will give to you. Search, and you will find. Knock, and the door will open for you. [8]Yes, everyone who asks will receive. Everyone who searches will find. And everyone who knocks will have the door opened.

[9]"If your children ask for bread, which of you would give them a stone? [10]Or if your children ask for a fish, would you give them a snake? [11]Even though you are bad, you know how to give good gifts to your children. How much more your heavenly Father will give good things to those who ask him!

THE MOST IMPORTANT RULE

[12]"Do to others what you want them to do to you. This is the meaning of the law of Moses and the teaching of the prophets.

THE WAY TO HEAVEN IS HARD

[13]"Enter through the narrow gate. The gate is wide and the road is wide that leads to hell, and many people enter through that gate. [14]But the gate is small and the road is narrow that leads to true life. Only a few people find that road.

PEOPLE KNOW YOU BY YOUR ACTIONS

[15]"Be careful of false prophets. They come to you looking gentle like sheep, but they are really dangerous like wolves. [16]You will know these people by what they do. Grapes don't come from thornbushes, and figs don't come from thorny weeds. [17]In the same way,

DID YOU KNOW?

Nearly 40% of preteens go online every day.

Laboratory Research on Tweens by Creative Consumer Concepts

every good tree produces good fruit, but a bad tree produces bad fruit. [18]A good tree cannot produce bad fruit, and a bad tree cannot produce good fruit. [19]Every tree that does not produce good fruit is cut down and thrown into the fire. [20]In the same way, you will know these false prophets by what they do.

[21]"Not all those who say 'You are our Lord' will enter the kingdom of heaven. The only people who will enter the kingdom of heaven are those who do what my Father in heaven wants. [22]On the last day many people will say to me, 'Lord, Lord, we spoke for you, and through you we forced out demons and did many miracles.' [23]Then I will tell them clearly, 'Get away from me, you who do evil. I never knew you.'

TWO KINDS OF PEOPLE

[24]"Everyone who hears my words and obeys them is like a wise man who built his house on rock. [25]It rained hard, the floods came, and the winds blew and hit that house. But it did not fall, because it was built on rock. [26]Everyone who hears my words and does not obey them is like a foolish man who built his house on sand. [27]It rained hard, the floods came, and the winds blew and hit that house, and it fell with a big crash."

[28]When Jesus finished saying these things, the people were amazed at his teaching, [29]because he did not teach like their teachers of the law. He taught like a person who had authority.

JESUS HEALS A SICK MAN

8 When Jesus came down from the hill, great crowds followed him. [2]Then a man with a skin disease came to Jesus. The man bowed down before him and said, "Lord, you can heal me if you will."

[3]Jesus reached out his hand and touched the man and said, "I will. Be healed!" And immediately the man was healed from his disease. [4]Then Jesus said to him, "Don't tell anyone about this. But go and show yourself to the priest[*] and offer the gift Moses commanded[*] for people who are made well. This will show the people what I have done."

COOL!

Extreme Sports

Do you like extreme sports? Here's one for you— fishing. That's right, fishing! Professional fishermen have the highest on-the-job death rate of any in the world. Definitely *not* a career for weenies.

Peter, Andrew, James, and John were fishermen before Jesus called them to become followers. These guys knew what it meant to take risks. Maybe that's why Jesus chose them.

Following Christ was also risky. At least three of these four men died for their faith, as did many of the early believers. Even today, people in some countries are still killed for being Christians. Definitely *not* a faith for wimps.

JESUS HEALS A SOLDIER'S SERVANT

[5]When Jesus entered the city of Capernaum, an army officer came to him, begging for help. [6]The officer said, "Lord, my servant is at home in bed. He can't move his body and is in much pain."

[7]Jesus said to the officer, "I will go and heal him."

[8]The officer answered, "Lord, I am not worthy for you to come into my house. You only need to command it, and my servant will be healed. [9]I, too, am a man under the authority of others, and I have soldiers under my command. I tell one soldier, 'Go,' and he goes. I tell another soldier, 'Come,' and he comes. I say to my servant, 'Do this,' and my servant does it."

[10]When Jesus heard this, he was amazed. He said to those who were following him, "I tell you the truth, this is the greatest faith I have found, even in Israel. [11]Many people will come from the east and from the west and will sit and eat with Abraham, Isaac, and Jacob in the kingdom of heaven. [12]But those people who should be in the kingdom will be thrown outside into the darkness, where people will cry and grind their teeth with pain."

[13]Then Jesus said to the officer, "Go home. Your servant will be healed just as you believed he would." And his servant was healed that same hour.

JESUS HEALS MANY PEOPLE

[14]When Jesus went to Peter's house, he saw that Peter's mother-in-law was sick in bed with a fever. [15]Jesus touched her hand, and the fever left her. Then she stood up and began to serve Jesus.

[16]That evening people brought to Jesus many who had demons. Jesus spoke and the demons left them, and he healed all the sick. [17]He did these things to bring about what Isaiah the prophet had said:

"He took our suffering on him
and carried our diseases."   *Isaiah 53:4*

PEOPLE WANT TO FOLLOW JESUS

[18]When Jesus saw the crowd around him, he told his followers to go to the other side of the lake. [19]Then a teacher of the law came to Jesus and said, "Teacher, I will follow you any place you go."

[20]Jesus said to him, "The foxes have holes to live in, and the birds have nests, but the Son of Man has no place to rest his head."

[21]Another man, one of Jesus' followers, said to him, "Lord, first let me go and bury my father."

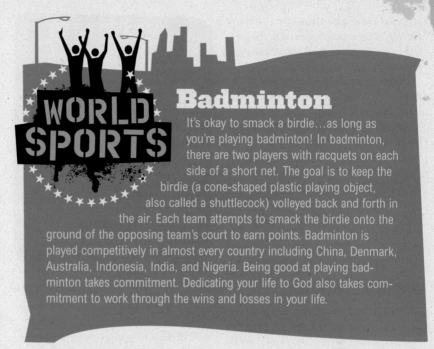

Badminton

It's okay to smack a birdie…as long as you're playing badminton! In badminton, there are two players with racquets on each side of a short net. The goal is to keep the birdie (a cone-shaped plastic playing object, also called a shuttlecock) volleyed back and forth in the air. Each team attempts to smack the birdie onto the ground of the opposing team's court to earn points. Badminton is played competitively in almost every country including China, Denmark, Australia, Indonesia, India, and Nigeria. Being good at playing badminton takes commitment. Dedicating your life to God also takes commitment to work through the wins and losses in your life.

[22]But Jesus told him, "Follow me, and let the people who are dead bury their own dead."

JESUS CALMS A STORM

[23]Jesus got into a boat, and his followers went with him. [24]A great storm arose on the lake so that waves covered the boat, but Jesus was sleeping. [25]His followers went to him and woke him, saying, "Lord, save us! We will drown!"

[26]Jesus answered, "Why are you afraid? You don't have enough faith." Then Jesus got up and gave a command to the wind and the waves, and it became completely calm.

[27]The men were amazed and said, "What kind of man is this? Even the wind and the waves obey him!"

JESUS HEALS TWO MEN WITH DEMONS

[28]When Jesus arrived at the other side of the lake in the area of the Gadarene[n] people, two men who had demons in them met him. These men lived in the burial caves and were so dangerous that people could not use the road by those caves. [29]They shouted, "What do you want with us, Son of God? Did you come here to torture us before the right time?"

[30]Near that place there was a large herd of pigs feeding. [31]The demons begged Jesus, "If you make us leave these men, please send us into that herd of pigs."

[32]Jesus said to them, "Go!" So the demons left the men and went into the pigs. Then the whole herd rushed down the hill into the lake and were drowned. [33]The herdsmen ran away and went into town, where they told about all of this and what had happened to the men who had demons. [34]Then the whole town went out to see Jesus. When they saw him, they begged him to leave their area.

JESUS HEALS A PARALYZED MAN

9 Jesus got into a boat and went back across the lake to his own town. [2]Some people brought to Jesus a man who was

DID YOU KNOW?

Kids spend 11 hours a week listening to music.

Laboratory Research on Tweens by Creative Consumer Concepts

paralyzed and lying on a mat. When Jesus saw the faith of these people, he said to the paralyzed man, "Be encouraged, young man. Your sins are forgiven."

[3]Some of the teachers of the law said to themselves, "This man speaks as if he were God. That is blasphemy!"[n]

[4]Knowing their thoughts, Jesus said, "Why are you thinking evil thoughts? [5]Which is easier: to say, 'Your sins are forgiven,' or to tell him, 'Stand up and walk'? [6]But I will prove to you that the Son of Man has authority on earth to forgive sins." Then Jesus said to the paralyzed man, "Stand up, take your mat, and go home." [7]And the man stood up and went home. [8]When the people saw this, they were amazed and praised God for giving power like this to human beings.

JESUS CHOOSES MATTHEW

[9]When Jesus was leaving, he saw a man named Matthew sitting in the tax collector's booth. Jesus said to him, "Follow me," and he stood up and followed Jesus.

[10]As Jesus was having dinner at Matthew's house, many tax collectors and "sinners" came and ate with Jesus and his followers. [11]When the Pharisees saw this, they asked Jesus' followers, "Why does your teacher eat with tax collectors and sinners?"

[12]When Jesus heard them, he said, "It is

DID YOU KNOW?

81% of boys believe their parents trust them.

Tween Audience Analysis Profile, The Health Communication Unit, 2004.

not the healthy people who need a doctor, but the sick. [13]Go and learn what this means: 'I want kindness more than I want animal sacrifices.'[n] I did not come to invite good people but to invite sinners."

JESUS' FOLLOWERS ARE CRITICIZED

[14]Then the followers of John[n] came to Jesus and said, "Why do we and the Pharisees often fast[n] for a certain time, but your followers don't?"

[15]Jesus answered, "The friends of the bridegroom are not sad while he is with them. But the time will come when the bridegroom will be taken from them, and then they will fast.

[16]"No one sews a patch of unshrunk cloth over a hole in an old coat. If he does, the patch will shrink and pull away from the coat, making the hole worse. [17]Also, people never pour new wine into old leather bags. Otherwise, the bags will break, the wine will spill, and the wine bags will be ruined. But people always pour new wine into new wine bags. Then both will continue to be good."

JESUS GIVES LIFE TO A DEAD GIRL AND HEALS A SICK WOMAN

[18]While Jesus was saying these things, a leader of the synagogue came to him. He bowed down before Jesus and said, "My daughter has just died. But if you come and lay your hand on her, she will live again." [19]So Jesus and his followers stood up and went with the leader.

[20]Then a woman who had been bleeding for twelve years came behind Jesus and touched the edge of his coat. [21]She was thinking, "If I can just touch his clothes, I will be healed."

[22]Jesus turned and saw the woman and said, "Be encouraged, dear woman. You are

trustables

Matthew 9:37–38

Have you thought about what your first job will be? Maybe you'll flip burgers. Maybe you'll deliver newspapers. There's good money in mowing lawns! No matter what kind of job you have, you're lucky to have it! There are always more workers to go around than there are jobs to give them. That's why the world has unemployment and people out of work.

In God's business, it's exactly the opposite. Jesus says, "There are many people to harvest but only a few workers to help harvest them" (Matthew 9:37). When Jesus talks about a "harvest," he is talking about saving people from hell and giving them a place in heaven forever.

Look around you. Many of the people you see desperately need to be "harvested." They are aching for God's love and forgiveness. Unfortunately, there are not enough "workers" to handle the workload. So what can be done?

God's answer to this problem is prayer. "Pray to the Lord…that he will send more workers," he says. Have you prayed about what your job for Jesus might be? One thing you can be sure of: if you are willing to help Jesus in "harvesting" people for heaven, you'll never run out of work! Instead, you'll be doing the most important job on earth.

9:3 blasphemy Saying things against God or not showing respect for God. **9:13 'I want . . . sacrifices.'** Quotation from Hosea 6:6. **9:14 John** John the Baptist, who preached to people about Christ's coming (Matthew 3, Luke 3). **9:14 fast** The people would give up eating for a special time of prayer and worship to God. It was also done to show sadness and disappointment.

January

1 *New Year's Day*—Write three goals for this year; ask God to help you stick to them.

2

3 Pray for a person of influence: it's actor Mel Gibson's birthday today.

4

5 Pray for a person of influence: musician Marilyn Manson's birthday is today.

6

7 Reread your favorite Bible verse today!

8

9 If you have a stepdad, thank him for being in your life!

10

11 It's *"Step in a Puddle and Splash Your Friend Day."* Watch out—you might get wet!

12

13

14 Pray for a person of influence: rapper LL Cool J has a birthday today.

15

16 Talk your family into Mexican grub tonight—it's *"Hot and Spicy Food Day"*!

17

18 How are you doing on your New Year's resolutions? Pray for God's help.

19

20

21 Stonewall Jackson was born today—more than 150 years ago!

22

23 Today is *"Measure Your Feet Day."* Why? Good question . . .

24 Pray for a person of influence: actress Mischa Barton will open birthday presents today.

25 Read your favorite verse again—what is God telling you?

26 Pray for a person of influence: it's former hockey star Wayne Gretzky's birthday.

27

28

29

30

31 The next time you hear sirens, pray for the people in the emergency vehicles.

"Touchdown!"

Every year in Salem, Oregon, tweens Justin, Chris, and Josh pass out flags, set up a scorer's table, choose team names, and write funny player introductions for the neighborhood flag football Souper Bowl. Dad's the referee, and Mom operates the video camera.

The annual event attracts neighborhood kids for the competition and gives them a chance to star in the Souper Bowl DVD. But halftime, with soup and a Good News message, is the real highlight. Over the years, four participants in the event have come to know Jesus' love.

If you have friends in your neighborhood, get them together and see if you can come up with some fun ideas to provide a simple and fun way of shining your light to your neighbors. You could host a flag football game like Justin, Chris, and Josh, or you could have a giant water balloon fight or a mini Olympics competition.

Whatever you decide, pray and ask God to help you use it to tell others about the good news of Jesus!

house, Jesus went into the girl's room and took hold of her hand, and she stood up. [26]The news about this spread all around the area.

JESUS HEALS MORE PEOPLE

[27]When Jesus was leaving there, two blind men followed him. They cried out, "Have mercy on us, Son of David!"

[28]After Jesus went inside, the blind men went with him. He asked the men, "Do you believe that I can make you see again?"

They answered, "Yes, Lord."

[29]Then Jesus touched their eyes and said, "Because you believe I can make you see again, it will happen." [30]Then the men were able to see. But Jesus warned them strongly, saying, "Don't tell anyone about this." [31]But the blind men left and spread the news about Jesus all around that area.

[32]When the two men were leaving, some people brought another man to Jesus. This man could not talk because he had a demon in him. [33]After Jesus forced the demon to leave the man, he was able to speak. The crowd was amazed and said, "We have never seen anything like this in Israel."

[34]But the Pharisees said, "The prince of demons is the one that gives him power to force demons out."

[35]Jesus traveled through all the towns and villages, teaching in their synagogues, preaching the Good News about the kingdom, and healing all kinds of diseases and sicknesses. [36]When he saw the crowds, he felt sorry for them because they were hurting and helpless, like sheep without a shepherd. [37]Jesus said to his followers, "There are many people to harvest but only a few workers to help harvest them. [38]Pray to the Lord, who owns the harvest, that he will send more workers to gather his harvest."[n]

JESUS SENDS OUT HIS APOSTLES

10 Jesus called his twelve followers together and gave them authority to drive out evil spirits and to heal every kind of disease and sickness. [2]These are the names of the twelve apostles: Simon (also called Peter) and his brother Andrew; James son of Zebedee, and his brother John; [3]Philip and Bartholomew; Thomas and Matthew, the tax collector; James son of Alphaeus, and Thaddaeus; [4]Simon the Zealot and Judas Iscariot, who turned against Jesus.

[5]Jesus sent out these twelve men with the following order: "Don't go to the non-Jewish people or to any town where the Samaritans

live. [6]But go to the people of Israel, who are like lost sheep. [7]When you go, preach this: 'The kingdom of heaven is near.' [8]Heal the sick, raise the dead to life again, heal those who have skin diseases, and force demons out of people. I give you these powers freely, so help other people freely. [9]Don't carry any money with you—gold or silver or copper. [10]Don't carry a bag or extra clothes or sandals or a walking stick. Workers should be given what they need.

DID YOU KNOW?

57% of 10- to 12-year-olds consider family the most important thing in their lives.

Tween Audience Analysis Profile, The Health Communication Unit, 2004.

[11]"When you enter a city or town, find some worthy person there and stay in that home until you leave. [12]When you enter that home, say, 'Peace be with you.' [13]If the people there welcome you, let your peace stay there. But if they don't welcome you, take back the peace you wished for them. [14]And if a home or town refuses to welcome you or listen to you, leave that place and shake its dust off your feet."[n] [15]I tell you the truth, on the Judgment Day it will be better for the towns of Sodom and Gomorrah[n] than for the people of that town.

JESUS WARNS HIS APOSTLES

[16]"Listen, I am sending you out like sheep among wolves. So be as clever as snakes and as innocent as doves. [17]Be careful of people, because they will arrest you and take you to court and whip you in their synagogues. [18]Because of me you will be taken to stand before governors and kings, and you will tell them and the non-Jewish people about me. [19]When you are arrested, don't worry about what to say or

made well because you believed." And the woman was healed from that moment on.

[23]Jesus continued along with the leader and went into his house. There he saw the funeral musicians and many people crying. [24]Jesus said, "Go away. The girl is not dead, only asleep." But the people laughed at him. [25]After the crowd had been thrown out of the

how to say it. At that time you will be given the things to say. ²⁰It will not really be you speaking but the Spirit of your Father speaking through you.

²¹"Brothers will give their own brothers to be killed, and fathers will give their own children to be killed. Children will fight against their own parents and have them put to death. ²²All people will hate you because you follow me, but those people who keep their faith until the end will be saved. ²³When you are treated badly in one city, run to another city. I tell you the truth, you will not finish going through all the cities of Israel before the Son of Man comes.

²⁴"A student is not better than his teacher, and a servant is not better than his master. ²⁵A student should be satisfied to become like his teacher; a servant should be satisfied to become like his master. If the head of the family is called Beelzebul, then the other members of the family will be called worse names!

FEAR GOD, NOT PEOPLE

²⁶"So don't be afraid of those people, because everything that is hidden will be shown. Everything that is secret will be made known. ²⁷I tell you these things in the dark, but I want you to tell them in the light. What you hear whispered in your ear you should shout from the housetops. ²⁸Don't be afraid of people, who can kill the body but cannot kill the soul. The only one you should fear is the one who can destroy the soul and the body in hell. ²⁹Two sparrows cost only a penny, but not even one of them can die without your Father's knowing it. ³⁰God even knows how many hairs are on your head. ³¹So don't be afraid. You are worth much more than many sparrows.

TELL PEOPLE ABOUT YOUR FAITH

³²"All those who stand before others and say they believe in me, I will say before my Father in heaven that they belong to me. ³³But all who stand before others and say they do not believe in me, I will say before my Father in heaven that they do not belong to me.

³⁴"Don't think that I came to bring peace to the earth. I did not come to bring peace, but a sword. ³⁵I have come so that

'a son will be against his father,
  a daughter will be against her mother,
a daughter-in-law will be against her
    mother-in-law.
³⁶ A person's enemies will be members of
    his own family.'   *Micah 7:6*

³⁷"Those who love their father or mother more than they love me are not worthy to be my followers. Those who love their son or daughter more than they love me are not worthy to be my followers. ³⁸Whoever is not willing to carry the cross and follow me is not worthy of me. ³⁹Those who try to hold on to their lives will give up true life. Those who give up their lives for me will hold on to true life. ⁴⁰Whoever accepts you also accepts me, and whoever accepts me also accepts the One who sent me. ⁴¹Whoever meets a prophet and accepts him will receive the reward of a prophet. And whoever accepts a good person because that person is good will receive the reward of a good person. ⁴²Those who give one of these little ones a cup of cold water because they are my followers will truly get their reward."

JESUS AND JOHN THE BAPTIST

11 After Jesus finished telling these things to his twelve followers, he left there and went to the towns in Galilee to teach and preach.

²John the Baptist was in prison, but he heard about what the Christ was doing. So John sent some of his followers to Jesus. ³They asked him, "Are you the One who is to come, or should we wait for someone else?"

⁴Jesus answered them, "Go tell John what you hear and see: ⁵The blind can see, the crippled can walk, and people with skin diseases are healed. The deaf can hear, the dead are raised to life, and the Good News is preached to the poor. ⁶Those who do not stumble in their faith because of me are blessed."

⁷As John's followers were leaving, Jesus began talking to the people about John. Jesus said, "What did you go out into the desert to see? A reedⁿ blown by the wind? ⁸What did you go out to see? A man dressed in fine

ROCK SOLID

Matthew 10:29-31

Do you have a hard time believing that God gives a rip about you? *Why should he?* you might think. *He's way up there somewhere and has important things to do like making sure that Pluto doesn't run into Neptune and that no one blows up the world.*

Think again. Jesus says, "Two sparrows cost only a penny, but not even one of them can die without your Father's knowing it" (Matthew 10:29). When you're sitting in your living room and hear a loud *thump* from another bird that didn't see the glass, remember that God knew about it—even though it was just a bird. If God cares about birds, he definitely cares about you!

Jesus says, "God even knows how many hairs are on your head" (Matthew 10:30). Who would take the time to count your hair? God would. He knows every tiny detail about you and nothing escapes his attention.

Even though God is watching out for the big stuff, like planets and presidents, he's also keeping track of every little bird, every hair on your head, and your whole life. God cares so much about you and he knows you better than you know yourself.

Next time you see a bird, remember that "you are worth much more than many sparrows" to God.

⭐ **11:7 reed** It means that John was not ordinary or weak like grass blown by the wind.

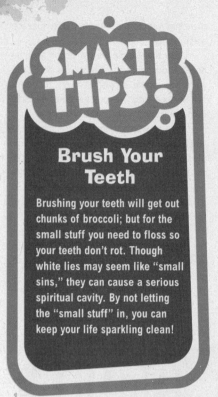

SMART TIPS!

Brush Your Teeth

Brushing your teeth will get out chunks of broccoli; but for the small stuff you need to floss so your teeth don't rot. Though white lies may seem like "small sins," they can cause a serious spiritual cavity. By not letting the "small stuff" in, you can keep your life sparkling clean!

clothes? No, those who wear fine clothes live in kings' palaces. [9]So why did you go out? To see a prophet? Yes, and I tell you, John is more than a prophet. [10]This was written about him:

'I will send my messenger ahead of you,
    who will prepare the way for you.'

Malachi 3:1

[11]I tell you the truth, John the Baptist is greater than any other person ever born, but even the least important person in the kingdom of heaven is greater than John. [12]Since the time John the Baptist came until now, the kingdom of heaven has been going forward in strength, and people have been trying to take it by force. [13]All the prophets and the law of Moses told about what would happen until the time John came. [14]And if you will believe what they said, you will believe that John is Elijah, whom they said would come. [15]Let those with ears use them and listen!

[16]"What can I say about the people of this time? What are they like? They are like children sitting in the marketplace, who call out to each other,

[17]'We played music for you, but you did
        not dance;
    we sang a sad song, but you did not cry.'

[18]John came and did not eat or drink like other people. So people say, 'He has a demon.' [19]The Son of Man came, eating and drinking, and people say, 'Look at him! He eats too much and drinks too much wine, and he is a friend of tax collectors and sinners.' But wisdom is proved to be right by what she does."

JESUS WARNS UNBELIEVERS

[20]Then Jesus criticized the cities where he did most of his miracles, because the people did not change their lives and stop sinning. [21]He said, "How terrible for you, Korazin! How terrible for you, Bethsaida! If the same miracles I did in you had happened in Tyre and Sidon," those people would have changed their lives a long time ago. They would have worn rough cloth and put ashes on themselves to show they had changed. [22]But I tell you, on the Judgment Day it will be better for Tyre and Sidon than for you. [23]And you, Capernaum," will you be lifted up to heaven? No, you will be thrown down to the depths. If the miracles I did in you had happened in Sodom," its people would have stopped sinning, and it would still be a city today. [24]But I tell you, on the Judgment Day it will be better for Sodom than for you."

JESUS OFFERS REST TO PEOPLE

[25]At that time Jesus said, "I praise you, Father, Lord of heaven and earth, because you have hidden these things from the people who are wise and smart. But you have shown them to those who are like little children. [26]Yes, Father, this is what you really wanted.

[27]"My Father has given me all things. No one knows the Son, except the Father. And no one knows the Father, except the Son and those whom the Son chooses to tell. [28]Come to me, all of you who are tired and have heavy loads, and I will give you rest. [29]Accept my teachings and learn from me, because I am gentle and humble in spirit, and you will find rest for your lives. [30]The burden that I ask you to accept is easy; the load I give you to carry is light."

JESUS IS LORD OF THE SABBATH

12 At that time Jesus was walking through some fields of grain on a Sabbath day. His followers were hungry, so they began to pick the grain and eat it. [2]When the Pharisees saw this, they said to Jesus, "Look! Your followers are doing what is unlawful to do on the Sabbath day."

[3]Jesus answered, "Have you not read what David did when he and the people with him were hungry? [4]He went into God's house, and he and those with him ate the holy bread, which was lawful only for priests to eat. [5]And have you not read in the law of Moses that on every Sabbath day the priests in the Temple break this law about the Sabbath day? But the priests are not wrong for doing that. [6]I tell you that there is something here that is greater than the Temple. [7]The Scripture says, 'I want kindness more than I want animal sacrifices.'" You don't really know what those words mean. If you understood them, you would not judge those who have done nothing wrong.

dare to do

Matthew 6:1
Read It: Do good deeds to please God, not so that other people will see you do them.
Do It: Don't brag about yourself when you do something good. If you help someone out today, God will see what you do and be pleased with you.

Matthew 6:6
Read It: Don't use your prayers to "show off."
Do It: If you are praying out loud, don't worry how it sounds to other people. You are talking to God, so focus on him.

Matthew 6:14
Read It: Forgive people when they hurt you, and God will forgive you.
Do It: Is there anyone you are mad at? If so, you should work on letting go of your anger and making peace with that person.

11:21 Tyre and Sidon Towns where wicked people lived.   **11:21, 23 Korazin . . . Bethsaida . . . Capernaum** Towns by Lake Galilee where Jesus preached to the people.   **11:23 Sodom** A city that God destroyed because the people were so evil.   **12:7 'I . . . sacrifices.'** Quotation from Hosea 6:6.

[8]"So the Son of Man is Lord of the Sabbath day."

JESUS HEALS A MAN'S HAND

[9]Jesus left there and went into their synagogue, [10]where there was a man with a crippled hand. They were looking for a reason to accuse Jesus, so they asked him, "Is it right to heal on the Sabbath day?"[n]

[11]Jesus answered, "If any of you has a sheep, and it falls into a ditch on the Sabbath day, you will help it out of the ditch. [12]Surely a human being is more important than a sheep. So it is lawful to do good things on the Sabbath day."

[13]Then Jesus said to the man with the crippled hand, "Hold out your hand." The man held out his hand, and it became well again, like the other hand. [14]But the Pharisees left and made plans to kill Jesus.

JESUS IS GOD'S CHOSEN SERVANT

[15]Jesus knew what the Pharisees were doing, so he left that place. Many people followed him, and he healed all who were sick. [16]But Jesus warned the people not to tell who he was. [17]He did these things to bring about what Isaiah the prophet had said:
[18]"Here is my servant whom I have chosen.
I love him, and I am pleased with him.
I will put my Spirit upon him,
and he will tell of my justice to all people.
[19]He will not argue or cry out;
no one will hear his voice in the streets.
[20]He will not break a crushed blade of grass
or put out even a weak flame
until he makes justice win the victory.
[21]   In him will the non-Jewish people find hope."   *Isaiah 42:1–4*

JESUS' POWER IS FROM GOD

[22]Then some people brought to Jesus a man who was blind and could not talk, because he had a demon. Jesus healed the man so that he could talk and see. [23]All the people were amazed and said, "Perhaps this man is the Son of David!"

[24]When the Pharisees heard this, they said, "Jesus uses the power of Beelzebul, the ruler of demons, to force demons out of people."

[25]Jesus knew what the Pharisees were thinking, so he said to them, "Every kingdom that is divided against itself will be destroyed. And any city or family that is divided against itself will not continue. [26]And if Satan forces out himself, then Satan is divided against himself,

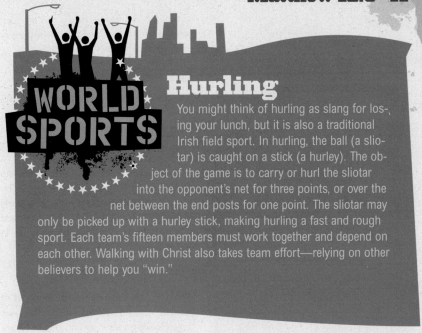

Hurling

You might think of hurling as slang for losing your lunch, but it is also a traditional Irish field sport. In hurling, the ball (a sliotar) is caught on a stick (a hurley). The object of the game is to carry or hurl the sliotar into the opponent's net for three points, or over the net between the end posts for one point. The sliotar may only be picked up with a hurley stick, making hurling a fast and rough sport. Each team's fifteen members must work together and depend on each other. Walking with Christ also takes team effort—relying on other believers to help you "win."

and his kingdom will not continue. [27]You say that I use the power of Beelzebul to force out demons. If that is true, then what power do your people use to force out demons? So they will be your judges. [28]But if I use the power of God's Spirit to force out demons, then the kingdom of God has come to you.

[29]"If anyone wants to enter a strong person's house and steal his things, he must first tie up the strong person. Then he can steal the things from the house.

[30]"Whoever is not with me is against me. Whoever does not work with me is working against me. [31]So I tell you, people can be forgiven

83% of kids say it's cool to be smart.

OnMission.com. "What's a Tween?" by Dr. Mary Manz Simon.

for every sin and everything they say against God. But whoever speaks against the Holy Spirit will not be forgiven. [32]Anyone who speaks against the Son of Man can be forgiven, but anyone who speaks against the Holy Spirit will not be forgiven, now or in the future.

PEOPLE KNOW YOU BY YOUR WORDS

[33]"If you want good fruit, you must make the tree good. If your tree is not good, it will have bad fruit. A tree is known by the kind of fruit it produces. [34]You snakes! You are evil people, so how can you say anything good? The mouth speaks the things that are in the heart. [35]Good people have good things in their hearts, and so they say good things. But evil people have evil in their hearts, so they say evil things. [36]And I tell you that on the Judgment Day people will be responsible for every careless thing they have said. [37]The words you have said will be used to judge you. Some of your words will prove you right, but some of your words will prove you guilty."

THE PEOPLE ASK FOR A MIRACLE

[38]Then some of the Pharisees and teachers of the law answered Jesus, saying, "Teacher, we want to see you work a miracle as a sign."

[39]Jesus answered, "Evil and sinful people are the ones who want to see a miracle for a sign. But no sign will be given to them, except the sign of the prophet Jonah. [40]Jonah was in the stomach of the big fish for three days and three nights. In the same way, the Son of Man will be in the grave three days and three nights. [41]On the Judgment Day the people from Nineveh[n]

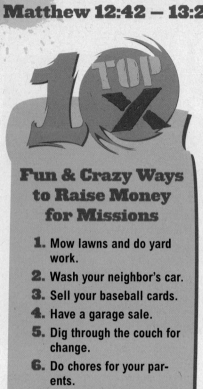

Fun & Crazy Ways to Raise Money for Missions

1. Mow lawns and do yard work.
2. Wash your neighbor's car.
3. Sell your baseball cards.
4. Have a garage sale.
5. Dig through the couch for change.
6. Do chores for your parents.
7. Baby-sit your cousins.
8. Hire yourself out as a "slave for a day."
9. Ask your grandma to sponsor you as a runner for a fund-raiser.
10. Walk the neighborhood dogs.

will stand up with you people who live now, and they will show that you are guilty. When Jonah preached to them, they were sorry and changed their lives. And I tell you that someone greater than Jonah is here. [42]On the Judgment Day, the Queen of the South[n] will stand up with you people who live today. She will show that you are guilty, because she came from far away to listen to Solomon's wise teaching. And I tell you that someone greater than Solomon is here.

PEOPLE TODAY ARE FULL OF EVIL

[43]"When an evil spirit comes out of a person, it travels through dry places, looking for a place to rest, but it doesn't find it. [44]So the spirit says, 'I will go back to the house I left.' When the spirit comes back, it finds the house still empty, swept clean, and made neat. [45]Then the evil spirit goes out and brings seven other spirits even more evil than it is, and they go in and live there. So the person has even

more trouble than before. It is the same way with the evil people who live today."

JESUS' TRUE FAMILY

[46]While Jesus was talking to the people, his mother and brothers stood outside, trying to find a way to talk to him. [47]Someone told Jesus, "Your mother and brothers are standing outside, and they want to talk to you."[n]

[48]He answered, "Who is my mother? Who are my brothers?" [49]Then he pointed to his followers and said, "Here are my mother and my brothers. [50]My true brother and sister and mother are those who do what my Father in heaven wants."

A STORY ABOUT PLANTING SEED

13 That same day Jesus went out of the house and sat by the lake. [2]Large crowds gathered around him, so he got into a boat and sat down, while the people stood on the shore. [3]Then Jesus used stories to teach them many things. He said: "A farmer went out to plant his seed. [4]While he was planting, some seed fell by the road, and the birds came and ate it all up. [5]Some seed fell on rocky ground, where there wasn't much dirt. That seed grew very fast, because the ground was not deep. [6]But when the sun rose, the plants dried up, because they did not have deep roots. [7]Some other seed fell among thorny weeds, which grew and choked the good plants. [8]Some other seed fell on good ground where it grew and produced a crop. Some plants made a hundred times more, some made sixty times more, and some made thirty times more. [9]Let those with ears use them and listen."

WHY JESUS USED STORIES TO TEACH

[10]The followers came to Jesus and asked, "Why do you use stories to teach the people?"

[11]Jesus answered, "You have been chosen to know the secrets about the kingdom of heaven, but others cannot know these secrets. [12]Those who have understanding will be given more, and they will have all they need. But those who do not have understanding, even what they have will be taken away from them. [13]This is why I use stories to teach the people: They see, but they don't really see. They hear, but they don't really hear or understand. [14]So they show that the things Isaiah said about them are true:

'You will listen and listen, but you will not understand.
    You will look and look, but you will not learn.

[15]For the minds of these people have become stubborn.
    They do not hear with their ears,
    and they have closed their eyes.
Otherwise they might really understand
    what they see with their eyes
    and hear with their ears.
They might really understand in their minds
    and come back to me and be healed.'
                                        Isaiah 6:9–10

[16]But you are blessed, because you see with your eyes and hear with your ears. [17]I tell you the truth, many prophets and good people wanted to see the things that you now see, but they did not see them. And they wanted to hear the things that you now hear, but they did not hear them.

JESUS EXPLAINS THE SEED STORY

[18]"So listen to the meaning of that story about the farmer. [19]What is the seed that fell by the road? That seed is like the person who hears the message about the kingdom but does not understand it. The Evil One comes and takes away what was planted in that person's heart. [20]And what is the seed that fell on rocky ground? That seed is like the person who hears the teaching and quickly accepts it with joy. [21]But he does not let the teaching go deep into his life, so he keeps it only a short time. When trouble or persecution comes because of the teaching he accepted, he quickly gives up. [22]And what is the seed that fell among the thorny weeds? That seed is like the person who hears the teaching but lets worries about this life and the temptation of wealth stop that teaching from grow-

DID YOU KNOW?

20% of students feel that teachers expect too much.

Tween Audience Analysis Profile, The Health Communication Unit, 2004.

ing. So the teaching does not produce fruit" in that person's life. [23] But what is the seed that fell on the good ground? That seed is like the person who hears the teaching and understands it. That person grows and produces fruit, sometimes a hundred times more, sometimes sixty times more, and sometimes thirty times more."

A STORY ABOUT WHEAT AND WEEDS

[24] Then Jesus told them another story: "The kingdom of heaven is like a man who planted good seed in his field. [25] That night, when everyone was asleep, his enemy came and planted weeds among the wheat and then left. [26] Later, the wheat sprouted and the heads of grain grew, but the weeds also grew. [27] Then the man's servants came to him and said, 'You planted good seed in your field. Where did the weeds come from?' [28] The man answered, 'An enemy planted weeds.' The servants asked, 'Do you want us to pull up the weeds?' [29] The man answered, 'No, because when you pull up the weeds, you might also pull up the wheat. [30] Let the weeds and the wheat grow together until the harvest time. At harvest time I will tell the workers, "First gather the weeds and tie them together to be burned. Then gather the wheat and bring it to my barn." ' "

STORIES OF MUSTARD SEED AND YEAST

[31] Then Jesus told another story: "The kingdom of heaven is like a mustard seed that a man planted in his field. [32] That seed is the smallest of all seeds, but when it grows, it is one of the largest garden plants. It becomes big enough for the wild birds to come and build nests in its branches."

[33] Then Jesus told another story: "The kingdom of heaven is like yeast that a woman took and hid in a large tub of flour until it made all the dough rise."

[34] Jesus used stories to tell all these things to the people; he always used stories to teach them. [35] This is as the prophet said:

"I will speak using stories;
I will tell things that have been secret
since the world was made."

Psalm 78:2

JESUS EXPLAINS ABOUT THE WEEDS

[36] Then Jesus left the crowd and went into the house. His followers came to him and said, "Explain to us the meaning of the story about the weeds in the field."

[37] Jesus answered, "The man who planted the good seed in the field is the Son of Man. [38] The field is the world, and the good seed are all of God's children who belong to the kingdom. The weeds are those people who belong to the Evil One. [39] And the enemy who planted the bad seed is the devil. The harvest time is the end of the age, and the workers who gather are God's angels.

[40] Just as the weeds are pulled up and burned in the fire, so it will be at the end of the age. [41] The Son of Man will send out his angels, and they will gather out of his kingdom all who cause sin and all who do evil. [42] The angels will throw them into the blazing furnace, where the people will cry and grind their teeth with pain. [43] Then the good people will shine like the sun in the kingdom of their Father. Let those with ears use them and listen.

STORIES OF A TREASURE AND A PEARL

[44] "The kingdom of heaven is like a treasure hidden in a field. One day a man found the treasure, and then he hid it in the field again. He was so happy that he went and sold everything he owned to buy that field.

[45] "Also, the kingdom of heaven is like a man looking for fine pearls. [46] When he found a very valuable pearl, he went and sold everything he had and bought it.

A STORY OF A FISHING NET

[47] "Also, the kingdom of heaven is like a net that was put into the lake and caught many different kinds of fish. [48] When it was full, the

ROCK SOLID

Matthew 13:44

You may think there are enough rules in your life yet, but here's one more. In fact, Paul in Philippians 4:4 gives this rule as a command: "Be full of joy!"

Jesus loved talking about happiness and joy. He said, "The kingdom of heaven is like a treasure hidden in a field. One day a man found the treasure, and then he hid it in the field again. He was so happy that he went and sold everything he owned to buy that field" (Matthew 13:44). That's how happy every follower of Jesus Christ should be.

Of all people on the earth, Christians should be full of joy! But a lot of them fail to obey this command. Although they say that deep down in their hearts they have joy, apparently it's so deep that they can't find it. Don't follow their example.

Instead, explode with feelings of great happiness in Jesus. God wants you to be extremely happy in his Son, which is great news because you want to be happy, too. Thankfully, these two desires go together.

So obey the rules: Be full of joy!

⭐ **13:22 produce fruit** To produce fruit means to have in your life the good things God wants.

COOL!

Iraq in the Bible

The country with more Bible history and prophecy tied to it than any place except Israel is...Iraq. In the Bible it's known as "Shinar," "Mesopotamia," or "Babylon." Here are some famous things that happened in the modern country of Iraq:

★ The Tower of Babel was built.
★ Jonah preached in Nineveh (Iraq).
★ The Babylonians (from Iraq) conquered Jerusalem.
★ Daniel was in the lions' den.
★ Peter preached the Good News.

When you hear about Iraq in the news, remember to pray for this famous country from the Bible.

fishermen pulled the net to the shore. They sat down and put all the good fish in baskets and threw away the bad fish. ⁴⁹It will be this way at the end of the age. The angels will come and separate the evil people from the good people. ⁵⁰The angels will throw the evil people into the blazing furnace, where people will cry and grind their teeth with pain."

⁵¹Jesus asked his followers, "Do you understand all these things?"

They answered, "Yes, we understand."

⁵²Then Jesus said to them, "So every teacher of the law who has been taught about the kingdom of heaven is like the owner of a house. He brings out both new things and old things he has saved."

JESUS GOES TO HIS HOMETOWN

⁵³When Jesus finished teaching with these stories, he left there. ⁵⁴He went to his hometown and taught the people in the synagogue, and they were amazed. They said, "Where did this man get this wisdom and this power to do miracles? ⁵⁵He is just the son of a carpenter. His mother is Mary, and his brothers are James, Joseph, Simon, and Judas. ⁵⁶And all his sisters are here with us. Where then does this man get all these things?" ⁵⁷So the people were upset with Jesus.

But Jesus said to them, "A prophet is honored everywhere except in his hometown and in his own home."

⁵⁸So he did not do many miracles there because they had no faith.

HOW JOHN THE BAPTIST WAS KILLED

14 At that time Herod, the ruler of Galilee, heard the reports about Jesus. ²So he said to his servants, "Jesus is John the Baptist, who has risen from the dead. That is why he can work these miracles."

³Sometime before this, Herod had arrested John, tied him up, and put him into prison. Herod did this because of Herodias, who had been the wife of Philip, Herod's brother. ⁴John had been telling Herod, "It is not lawful for you to be married to Herodias." ⁵Herod wanted to kill John, but he was afraid of the people, because they believed John was a prophet.

⁶On Herod's birthday, the daughter of Herodias danced for Herod and his guests, and she pleased him. ⁷So he promised with an oath to give her anything she wanted. ⁸Herodias told her daughter what to ask for, so she said to Herod, "Give me the head of John the Baptist here on a platter." ⁹Although King Herod was

very sad, he had made a promise, and his dinner guests had heard him. So Herod ordered that what she asked for be done. ¹⁰He sent soldiers to the prison to cut off John's head. ¹¹And they brought it on a platter and gave it to the girl, and she took it to her mother. ¹²John's followers came and got his body and buried it. Then they went and told Jesus.

MORE THAN FIVE THOUSAND FED

¹³When Jesus heard what had happened to John, he left in a boat and went to a lonely place by himself. But the crowds heard about it and followed him on foot from the towns. ¹⁴When he arrived, he saw a great crowd waiting. He felt sorry for them and healed those who were sick.

¹⁵When it was evening, his followers came to him and said, "No one lives in this place, and it is already late. Send the people away so they can go to the towns and buy food for themselves."

¹⁶But Jesus answered, "They don't need to go away. You give them something to eat."

¹⁷They said to him, "But we have only five loaves of bread and two fish."

¹⁸Jesus said, "Bring the bread and the fish to me." ¹⁹Then he told the people to sit down on the grass. He took the five loaves and the

two fish and, looking to heaven, he thanked God for the food. Jesus divided the bread and gave it to his followers, who gave it to the people. [20]All the people ate and were satisfied. Then the followers filled twelve baskets with the leftover pieces of food. [21]There were about five thousand men there who ate, not counting women and children.

JESUS WALKS ON THE WATER

[22]Immediately Jesus told his followers to get into the boat and go ahead of him across the lake. He stayed there to send the people home. [23]After he had sent them away, he went by himself up into the hills to pray. It was late, and Jesus was there alone. [24]By this time, the boat was already far away from land. It was being hit by waves, because the wind was blowing against it.

[25]Between three and six o'clock in the morning, Jesus came to them, walking on the water. [26]When his followers saw him walking on the water, they were afraid. They said, "It's a ghost!" and cried out in fear.

[27]But Jesus quickly spoke to them, "Have courage! It is I. Do not be afraid."

[28]Peter said, "Lord, if it is really you, then command me to come to you on the water."

[29]Jesus said, "Come."

And Peter left the boat and walked on the water to Jesus. [30]But when Peter saw the wind and the waves, he became afraid and began to sink. He shouted, "Lord, save me!"

[31]Immediately Jesus reached out his hand and caught Peter. Jesus said, "Your faith is small. Why did you doubt?"

[32]After they got into the boat, the wind became calm. [33]Then those who were in the boat worshiped Jesus and said, "Truly you are the Son of God!"

[34]When they had crossed the lake, they came to shore at Gennesaret. [35]When the people there recognized Jesus, they told people all around there that Jesus had come, and they brought all their sick to him. [36]They begged Jesus to let them touch just the edge of his coat, and all who touched it were healed.

OBEY GOD'S LAW

15 Then some Pharisees and teachers of the law came to Jesus from Jerusalem. They asked him, [2]"Why don't your followers obey the unwritten laws which have been handed down to us? They don't wash their hands before they eat."

[3]Jesus answered, "And why do you refuse to obey God's command so that you can follow your own teachings? [4]God said, 'Honor your father and your mother,'" and 'Anyone who says cruel things to his father or mother must be put to death.'" [5]But you say a person can tell his father or mother, 'I have something I could use to help you, but I have given it to God already.' [6]You teach that person not to honor his father or his mother. You rejected what God said for the sake of your own rules. [7]You are hypocrites! Isaiah was right when he said about you:

[8]'These people show honor to me with
    words,
but their hearts are far from me.
[9]Their worship of me is worthless.
    The things they teach are nothing but
      human rules.'"   *Isaiah 29:13*

[10]After Jesus called the crowd to him, he said, "Listen and understand what I am saying. [11]It is not what people put into their mouths that makes them unclean. It is what comes out of their mouths that makes them unclean."

[12]Then his followers came to him and asked, "Do you know that the Pharisees are angry because of what you said?"

[13]Jesus answered, "Every plant that my Father in heaven has not planted himself will be pulled up by the roots. [14]Stay away from the Pharisees; they are blind leaders." And if a blind person leads a blind person, both will fall into a ditch."

[15]Peter said, "Explain the example to us."

[16]Jesus said, "Do you still not understand? [17]Surely you know that all the food that enters the mouth goes into the stomach and then

trustables

Matthew 15:4

Throughout the Bible we're told, "Honor your father and your mother" (Matthew 15:4). Maybe you're thinking, *You don't know my parents!* True, but the Bible doesn't say to obey them only if they're cool.

Rebelling against your parents is like rebelling against God. In fact, it *is* an act of rebellion against one of God's Ten Commandments. Nothing could be more foolish.

The Bible says to obey your parents because it's important to God and good for you. You should always obey your parents. Of course, that's assuming they never ask you to do something against God's desires or the law of the land.

Our relationship with our parents is a great tool to teach us how to relate to God our heavenly Father. Your parents aren't perfect like God is, but they have experienced more in life than you have. (Ask your mom or dad if they can remember life before microwave ovens, video games, and the Internet.)

If we can't obey our own parents who we can see, hear, and touch, then how will we ever learn to obey our heavenly Father who we cannot touch, hear, or see?

"What's in it for me?" you ask. If you honor your parents, the Bible promises you will live longer and happier!

15:4 'Honor . . . mother.' Quotation from Exodus 20:12; Deuteronomy 5:16.   **15:4** 'Anyone . . . death.' Quotation from Exodus 21:17.   **15:14 leaders** Some Greek copies continue, "of blind people."

goes out of the body. [18]But what people say with their mouths comes from the way they think; these are the things that make people unclean. [19]Out of the mind come evil thoughts, murder, adultery, sexual sins, stealing, lying, and speaking evil of others. [20]These things make people unclean; eating with unwashed hands does not make them unclean."

JESUS HELPS A NON-JEWISH WOMAN

[21]Jesus left that place and went to the area of Tyre and Sidon. [22]A Canaanite woman from that area came to Jesus and cried out, "Lord, Son of David, have mercy on me! My daughter has a demon, and she is suffering very much."

[23]But Jesus did not answer the woman. So his followers came to Jesus and begged him, "Tell the woman to go away. She is following us and shouting."

[24]Jesus answered, "God sent me only to the lost sheep, the people of Israel."

[25]Then the woman came to Jesus again and bowed before him and said, "Lord, help me!"

[26]Jesus answered, "It is not right to take the children's bread and give it to the dogs."

[27]The woman said, "Yes, Lord, but even the dogs eat the crumbs that fall from their masters' table."

[28]Then Jesus answered, "Woman, you have great faith! I will do what you asked." And at that moment the woman's daughter was healed.

JESUS HEALS MANY PEOPLE

[29]After leaving there, Jesus went along the shore of Lake Galilee. He went up on a hill and sat there.

[30]Great crowds came to Jesus, bringing with them the lame, the blind, the crippled, those who could not speak, and many others. They put them at Jesus' feet, and he healed them. [31]The crowd was amazed when they saw that people who could not speak before were now able to speak. The crippled were made strong. The lame could walk, and the blind could see. And they praised the God of Israel for this.

MORE THAN FOUR THOUSAND FED

[32]Jesus called his followers to him and said, "I feel sorry for these people, because they have already been with me three days, and they have nothing to eat. I don't want to send them away hungry. They might faint while going home."

[33]His followers asked him, "How can we get enough bread to feed all these people? We are far away from any town."

[34]Jesus asked, "How many loaves of bread do you have?"

They answered, "Seven, and a few small fish."

[35]Jesus told the people to sit on the ground. [36]He took the seven loaves of bread and the fish and gave thanks to God. Then he divided the food and gave it to his followers, and they gave it to the people. [37]All the people ate and were satisfied. Then his followers filled seven baskets with the leftover pieces of food. [38]There were about four thousand men there who ate, besides women and children. [39]After sending the people home, Jesus got into the boat and went to the area of Magadan.

THE LEADERS ASK FOR A MIRACLE

16 The Pharisees and Sadducees came to Jesus, wanting to trick him. So they asked him to show them a miracle from God.

[2]Jesus answered," "At sunset you say we will have good weather, because the sky is red. [3]And in the morning you say that it will be a rainy day, because the sky is dark and red. You

Q&A

Q: What's the big deal about obeying the law, especially the stupid rules?

A: It's tempting to break the law when you disagree with the rule or you don't think you'll get caught. But this is not what God wants. The Bible tells us to obey the laws of our government (Titus 3:1). In extreme cases, Christians have disobeyed the law when it violated God's law. They were willing to suffer the punishment for it.

Q: What's one thing a Christian should do every day?

A: You should pray. Every Christian is in a relationship with God. If we don't talk with him every day, we won't grow closer to him. When you pray, you should thank God for what he's done for you, ask his forgiveness for any sins you've committed, and ask him to help the people you know—especially those people who are going through some kind of trouble or don't know him (James 5:13–16).

Q: Why do they always check the oil in car engines?

A: Plenty of oil is needed to keep your car from being ruined. A car engine has a lot of metal parts that get hot and rub together. The oil pump constantly squirts oil into these parts to keep them from grinding into each other. If you run a car for even a minute without oil, you'll wreck the engine. Just as an engine needs oil to run smoothly, you need regular communion with God to keep your life running smoothly.

see these signs in the sky and know what they mean. In the same way, you see the things that I am doing now, but you don't know their meaning. [4]Evil and sinful people ask for a miracle as a sign, but they will not be given any sign, except the sign of Jonah."[n] Then Jesus left them and went away.

GUARD AGAINST WRONG TEACHINGS

[5]Jesus' followers went across the lake, but they had forgotten to bring bread. [6]Jesus said to them, "Be careful! Beware of the yeast of the Pharisees and the Sadducees."

[7]His followers discussed the meaning of this, saying, "He said this because we forgot to bring bread."

[8]Knowing what they were talking about, Jesus asked them, "Why are you talking about not having bread? Your faith is small. [9]Do you still not understand? Remember the five loaves of bread that fed the five thousand? And remember that you filled many baskets with the leftovers? [10]Or the seven loaves of bread that fed the four thousand and the many baskets you filled then also? [11]I was not talking to you about bread. Why don't you understand that? I am telling you to beware of the yeast of the Pharisees and the Sadducees." [12]Then the followers understood that Jesus was not telling them to beware of the yeast used in bread but to beware of the teaching of the Pharisees and the Sadducees.

PETER SAYS JESUS IS THE CHRIST

[13]When Jesus came to the area of Caesarea Philippi, he asked his followers, "Who do people say the Son of Man is?"

[14]They answered, "Some say you are John the Baptist. Others say you are Elijah, and still others say you are Jeremiah or one of the prophets."

[15]Then Jesus asked them, "And who do you say I am?"

[16]Simon Peter answered, "You are the Christ, the Son of the living God."

[17]Jesus answered, "You are blessed, Simon son of Jonah, because no person taught you that. My Father in heaven showed you who I am. [18]So I tell you, you are Peter." On this rock I will build my church, and the power of death will not be able to defeat it. [19]I will give you the keys of the kingdom of heaven; the things you don't allow on earth will be the things that God does not allow, and the things you allow on earth will be the things that God allows." [20]Then Jesus warned his followers not to tell anyone he was the Christ.

JESUS SAYS THAT HE MUST DIE

[21]From that time on Jesus began telling his followers that he must go to Jerusalem, where the Jewish elders, the leading priests, and the teachers of the law would make him suffer many things. He told them he must be killed and then be raised from the dead on the third day.

[22]Peter took Jesus aside and told him not to talk like that. He said, "God save you from those things, Lord! Those things will never happen to you!"

[23]Then Jesus said to Peter, "Go away from me, Satan!" You are not helping me! You don't care about the things of God, but only about the things people think are important."

[24]Then Jesus said to his followers, "If people want to follow me, they must give up the things they want. They must be willing even to give up their lives to follow me. [25]Those who want to save their lives will give up true life, and those who give up their lives for me will have true life. [26]It is worthless to have the whole world if they lose their souls. They could never pay enough to buy back their souls. [27]The Son of Man will come again with his Father's glory and with his angels. At that time, he will reward them for what they have done. [28]I tell you the truth, some people standing here will see the Son of Man coming with his kingdom before they die."

JESUS TALKS WITH MOSES AND ELIJAH

17 Six days later, Jesus took Peter, James, and John, the brother of James, up on a high mountain by themselves. [2]While they watched, Jesus' appearance was changed; his face became bright like the sun, and his clothes became white as light. [3]Then

DID YOU KNOW?

22% of kids worry that their parents might divorce.

Steinberg 157

TOP 10

Things You Should Never Put in Your Nose

1. A pencil
2. M&Ms
3. An insect
4. Your friend's finger
5. A straw
6. Milk
7. A spaghetti noodle
8. Worms
9. Marbles
10. Your toe

Moses and Elijah" appeared to them, talking with Jesus.

[4]Peter said to Jesus, "Lord, it is good that we are here. If you want, I will put up three tents here—one for you, one for Moses, and one for Elijah."

[5]While Peter was talking, a bright cloud covered them. A voice came from the cloud and said, "This is my Son, whom I love, and I am very pleased with him. Listen to him!"

[6]When his followers heard the voice, they were so frightened they fell to the ground. [7]But Jesus went to them and touched them and said, "Stand up. Don't be afraid." [8]When they looked up, they saw Jesus was now alone.

[9]As they were coming down the mountain, Jesus commanded them not to tell anyone about what they had seen until the Son of Man had risen from the dead.

[10]Then his followers asked him, "Why do the teachers of the law say that Elijah must come first?"

[11]Jesus answered, "They are right to say that Elijah is coming and that he will make everything the way it should be. [12]But I tell you that Elijah has already come, and they did not recognize

---

 16:4 sign of Jonah Jonah's three days in the fish are like Jesus' three days in the tomb. The story about Jonah is in the Book of Jonah.   **16:18 Peter** The Greek name "Peter," like the Aramaic name "Cephas," means "rock."   **16:23 Satan** Name for the devil, meaning "the enemy." Jesus means that Peter was talking like Satan.   **17:3 Moses and Elijah** Two of the most important Jewish leaders in the past. God had given Moses the Law, and Elijah was an important prophet.

him. They did to him whatever they wanted to do. It will be the same with the Son of Man; those same people will make the Son of Man suffer." [13]Then the followers understood that Jesus was talking about John the Baptist.

JESUS HEALS A SICK BOY

[14]When Jesus and his followers came back to the crowd, a man came to Jesus and bowed before him. [15]The man said, "Lord, have mercy on my son. He has epilepsy[n] and is suffering very much, because he often falls into the fire or into the water. [16]I brought him to your followers, but they could not cure him."

[17]Jesus answered, "You people have no faith, and your lives are all wrong. How long must I put up with you? How long must I continue to be patient with you? Bring the boy here." [18]Jesus commanded the demon inside the boy. Then the demon came out, and the boy was healed from that time on.

[19]The followers came to Jesus when he was alone and asked, "Why couldn't we force the demon out?"

[20]Jesus answered, "Because your faith is too small. I tell you the truth, if your faith is as big as a mustard seed, you can say to this mountain, 'Move from here to there,' and it will move. All things will be possible for you. [[21]That kind of spirit comes out only if you use prayer and fasting.]"[n]

JESUS TALKS ABOUT HIS DEATH

[22]While Jesus' followers were gathering in Galilee, he said to them, "The Son of Man will be handed over to people, [23]and they

60% of kids have their own computer.

Shopping In America Survey, April 2005. "What's in the Bag for Tween Shoppers."

will kill him. But on the third day he will be raised from the dead." And the followers were filled with sadness.

JESUS TALKS ABOUT PAYING TAXES

[24]When Jesus and his followers came to Capernaum, the men who collected the Temple tax came to Peter. They asked, "Does your teacher pay the Temple tax?"

[25]Peter answered, "Yes, Jesus pays the tax." Peter went into the house, but before he could speak, Jesus said to him, "What do you think? The kings of the earth collect different kinds of taxes. But who pays the taxes—the king's children or others?"

[26]Peter answered, "Other people pay the taxes."

Jesus said to Peter, "Then the children of the king don't have to pay taxes. [27]But we don't want to upset these tax collectors. So go to the lake and fish. After you catch the first fish, open its mouth and you will find a coin. Take that coin and give it to the tax collectors for you and me."

WHO IS THE GREATEST?

18 At that time the followers came to Jesus and asked, "Who is greatest in the kingdom of heaven?"

[2]Jesus called a little child to him and stood the child before his followers. [3]Then he said, "I tell you the truth, you must change and become like little children. Otherwise, you will never enter the kingdom of heaven. [4]The greatest person in the kingdom of heaven is the one who makes himself humble like this child.

[5]"Whoever accepts a child in my name accepts me. [6]If one of these little children believes in me, and someone causes that child to sin, it would be better for that person to have a large stone tied around the neck and be drowned in the sea. [7]How terrible for the people of the world because of the things that cause them to sin. Such things will happen, but how terrible for the one who causes them to happen! [8]If your hand or your foot causes you to sin, cut it off and throw it away. It is better for you to lose part of your body and live for-

Jesus on Prayer

When Jesus prayed in private, he sometimes went all night. But when he prayed in public, his prayers were very short (Luke 10:21; John 12:28).

When Jesus taught his followers to pray, he kept it simple. Check out the Lord's Prayer in Matthew 6:9–13.

Jesus also gave his followers two privileges that people didn't have before:

★ addressing God as "Father" (Jesus used the word *Abba*, meaning "Daddy"), and
★ using Jesus' name when we pray.

Praying to the Father in the name of the Son is what makes Christian prayer unique.

17:15 epilepsy A disease that causes a person sometimes to lose control of his body and maybe faint, shake strongly, or not be able to move.　　**17:21 That . . . fasting.** Some Greek copies do not contain the bracketed text.

ever than to have two hands and two feet and be thrown into the fire that burns forever. [9]If your eye causes you to sin, take it out and throw it away. It is better for you to have only one eye and live forever than to have two eyes and be thrown into the fire of hell.

A LOST SHEEP

[10]"Be careful. Don't think these little children are worth nothing. I tell you that they have angels in heaven who are always with my Father in heaven. [[11]The Son of Man came to save lost people.][n]

[12]"If a man has a hundred sheep but one of the sheep gets lost, he will leave the other ninety-nine on the hill and go to look for the lost sheep. [13]I tell you the truth, if he finds it he is happier about that one sheep than about the ninety-nine that were never lost. [14]In the same way, your Father in heaven does not want any of these little children to be lost.

WHEN A PERSON SINS AGAINST YOU

[15]"If your fellow believer sins against you,[n] go and tell him in private what he did wrong. If he listens to you, you have helped that person to be your brother or sister again. [16]But if he refuses to listen, go to him again and take one or two other people with you. 'Every case may be proved by two or three witnesses.'[n] [17]If he refuses to listen to them, tell the church. If he refuses to listen to the church, then treat him like a person who does not believe in God or like a tax collector.

[18]"I tell you the truth, the things you don't allow on earth will be the things God does not allow. And the things you allow on earth will be the things that God allows.

[19]"Also, I tell you that if two of you on earth agree about something and pray for it, it will be done for you by my Father in heaven. [20]This is true because if two or three people come together in my name, I am there with them."

AN UNFORGIVING SERVANT

[21]Then Peter came to Jesus and asked, "Lord, when my fellow believer sins against me, how many times must I forgive him? Should I forgive him as many as seven times?"

[22]Jesus answered, "I tell you, you must forgive him more than seven times. You must forgive him even if he wrongs you seventy times seven.

[23]"The kingdom of heaven is like a king who decided to collect the money his servants owed him. [24]When the king began to collect his money, a servant who owed him several million dollars was brought to him. [25]But the servant did not have enough money to pay his master, the king. So the master ordered that everything the servant owned should be sold, even the servant's wife and children. Then the money would be used to pay the king what the servant owed.

[26]"But the servant fell on his knees and begged, 'Be patient with me, and I will pay you everything I owe.' [27]The master felt sorry for his servant and told him he did not have to pay it back. Then he let the servant go free.

[28]"Later, that same servant found another servant who owed him a few dollars. The servant grabbed him around the neck and said, 'Pay me the money you owe me!'

[29]"The other servant fell on his knees and begged him, 'Be patient with me, and I will pay you everything I owe.'

[30]"But the first servant refused to be patient. He threw the other servant into prison until he could pay everything he owed. [31]When the other servants saw what had happened, they were very sorry. So they went and told their master all that had happened.

[32]"Then the master called his servant in and said, 'You evil servant! Because you begged me to forget what you owed, I told you that you did not have to pay anything. [33]You should have showed mercy to that other servant, just as I showed mercy to you.' [34]The master was very angry and put the servant in prison to be punished until he could pay everything he owed.

[35]"This king did what my heavenly Father will do to you if you do not forgive your brother or sister from your heart."

JESUS TEACHES ABOUT DIVORCE

19 After Jesus said all these things, he left Galilee and went into the area of Judea on the other side of the Jordan River. [2]Large crowds followed him, and he healed them there.

[3]Some Pharisees came to Jesus and tried to trick him. They asked, "Is it right for a man to divorce his wife for any reason he chooses?"

[4]Jesus answered, "Surely you have read in the Scriptures: When God made the world, 'he made them male and female.'[n] [5]And God said, 'So a man will leave his father and mother and be united with his wife, and the two will become one body.'[n] [6]So there are not two, but one. God has joined the two together, so no one should separate them."

[7]The Pharisees asked, "Why then did Moses give a command for a man to divorce his wife by giving her divorce papers?"

ROCK SOLID

Matthew 18:21-35

Have you ever lost a bet with a friend? Man, that stinks! Have you ever had a friend say, "Don't worry about it," and not make you pay up? What a relief! We call this kind of action *mercy*.

Mercy is a powerful thing. It should change you and make you more merciful yourself. In other words, if a friend lets you off the hook over a bet, you shouldn't go and make someone pay when they lose a bet to you.

Take the story in Matthew 18, for instance, where a servant owed his king millions of dollars. He begged for mercy and the king granted it and wiped away his debt. Later, the servant ran across someone who owed him a few bucks. Instead of showing mercy, he forced the guy to cough up the money. What nerve! When the king found out about this, he locked the servant up until he could pay all of his debt.

Now instead of money, let's talk about showing mercy when someone offends you. Do you let them off the hook very easily? If we don't, we are doing exactly what the servant in the story did. God has forgiven us for everything we've done to offend him. Shouldn't we be willing and able to forgive the small things others do to us?

Don't you just love the last day of school? The promise of freedom waves its flag in your face as your mind begins to skateboard through all your summer plans. "OK, you have the rest of the day to sign year-books!" your favorite teacher says.

David from Seattle, Washington, looks forward to this part of the day. A lot of his friends have trouble coming up with what to write in the year-book. But David discovered that yearbook signing day is a perfect time to help his friends think, at least a little, about God. Here are some of the things David jotted down in his friends' yearbooks:

"You have a great voice," "I still remember that tackle you made," or "That was the coolest art project in class." Then he wrote a favorite Bible verse and included where it's found (in case his friend decided to actually look it up that summer).

God used those sentences to shine his light. You can use yearbook signing day—or any other day—to make a difference, too. Find a Bible verse that you like, and when someone asks you to sign something, write it down, too!

[8] Jesus answered, "Moses allowed you to divorce your wives because you refused to accept God's teaching, but divorce was not allowed in the beginning. [9] I tell you that anyone who divorces his wife and marries another woman is guilty of adultery.[n] The only reason for a man to divorce his wife is if his wife has sexual relations with another man."

[10] The followers said to him, "If that is the only reason a man can divorce his wife, it is better not to marry."

[11] Jesus answered, "Not everyone can accept this teaching, but God has made some able to accept it. [12] There are different reasons why some men cannot marry. Some men were born without the ability to become fathers. Others were made that way later in life by other people. And some men have given up marriage because of the kingdom of heaven. But the person who can marry should accept this teaching about marriage."[n]

JESUS WELCOMES CHILDREN

[13] Then the people brought their little children to Jesus so he could put his hands on them[n] and pray for them. His followers told them to stop, [14] but Jesus said, "Let the little children come to me. Don't stop them, because the kingdom of heaven belongs to people who are like these children." [15] After Jesus put his hands on the children, he left there.

A RICH YOUNG MAN'S QUESTION

[16] A man came to Jesus and asked, "Teacher, what good thing must I do to have life forever?"

[17] Jesus answered, "Why do you ask me about what is good? Only God is good. But if you want to have life forever, obey the commands."

[18] The man asked, "Which commands?"

Jesus answered, " 'You must not murder anyone; you must not be guilty of adultery; you must not steal; you must not tell lies about your neighbor; [19] honor your father and mother;[n] and love your neighbor as you love yourself.' "[n]

[20] The young man said, "I have obeyed all these things. What else do I need to do?"

[21] Jesus answered, "If you want to be perfect, then go and sell your possessions and give the money to the poor. If you do this, you will have treasure in heaven. Then come and follow me."

[22] But when the young man heard this, he left sorrowfully, because he was rich.

[23] Then Jesus said to his followers, "I tell you the truth, it will be hard for a rich person

to enter the kingdom of heaven. [24] Yes, I tell you that it is easier for a camel to go through the eye of a needle than for a rich person to enter the kingdom of God."

[25] When Jesus' followers heard this, they were very surprised and asked, "Then who can be saved?"

[26] Jesus looked at them and said, "For people this is impossible, but for God all things are possible."

[27] Peter said to Jesus, "Look, we have left everything and followed you. So what will we have?"

[28] Jesus said to them, "I tell you the truth, when the age to come has arrived, the Son of Man will sit on his great throne. All of you who

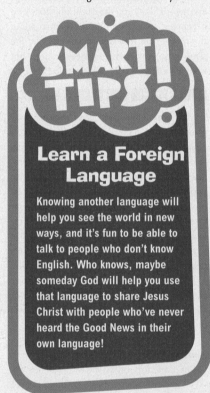

SMART TIPS!

Learn a Foreign Language

Knowing another language will help you see the world in new ways, and it's fun to be able to talk to people who don't know English. Who knows, maybe someday God will help you use that language to share Jesus Christ with people who've never heard the Good News in their own language!

followed me will also sit on twelve thrones, judging the twelve tribes of Israel. [29] And all those who have left houses, brothers, sisters, father, mother,[n] children, or farms to follow me will get much more than they left, and they will have life forever. [30] Many who are first now will be last in the future. And many who are last now will be first in the future.

A STORY ABOUT WORKERS

20 "The kingdom of heaven is like a person who owned some land. One morning, he went out very early to hire some people to work in his vineyard. [2] The man agreed to pay the workers one coin[n] for working

 19:9 adultery Some Greek copies continue, "And anyone who marries a divorced woman is guilty of adultery." Compare Matthew 5:32.   **19:12 But . . . marriage.** This may also mean, "The person who can accept this teaching about not marrying should accept it."   **19:13 put his hands on them** Showing that Jesus gave special blessings to these children.   **19:19 'You . . . mother.'** Quotation from Exodus 20:12–16; Deuteronomy 5:16–20.   **19:19 'love . . . yourself'** Quotation from Leviticus 19:18.   **19:29 mother** Some Greek copies continue, "or wife."   **20:2 coin** A Roman denarius. One coin was the average pay for one day's work.

that day. Then he sent them into the vineyard to work. ³About nine o'clock the man went to the marketplace and saw some other people standing there, doing nothing. ⁴So he said to them, 'If you go and work in my vineyard, I will pay you what your work is worth.' ⁵So they went to work in the vineyard. The man went out again about twelve o'clock and three o'clock and did the same thing. ⁶About five o'clock the man went to the marketplace again and saw others standing there. He asked them, 'Why did you stand here all day doing nothing?' ⁷They answered, 'No one gave us a job.' The man said to them, 'Then you can go and work in my vineyard.'

⁸"At the end of the day, the owner of the vineyard said to the boss of all the workers, 'Call the workers and pay them. Start with the last people I hired and end with those I hired first.'

⁹"When the workers who were hired at five o'clock came to get their pay, each received one coin. ¹⁰When the workers who were hired first came to get their pay, they thought they would be paid more than the others. But each one of them also received one coin. ¹¹When they got their coin, they complained to the man who owned the land. ¹²They said, 'Those people were hired last and worked only one hour. But you paid them the same as you paid us who worked hard all day in the hot sun.' ¹³But the man who owned the vineyard said to one of those workers, 'Friend, I am being fair to you. You agreed to work for one coin. ¹⁴So take your pay and go. I want to give the man who was hired last the same pay that I gave you. ¹⁵I can do what I want with my own money. Are you jealous because I am good to those people?'

¹⁶"So those who are last now will someday be first, and those who are first now will someday be last."

JESUS TALKS ABOUT HIS OWN DEATH

¹⁷While Jesus was going to Jerusalem, he took his twelve followers aside privately and said to them, ¹⁸"Look, we are going to Jerusalem. The Son of Man will be turned over to the leading priests and the teachers of the law, and they will say that he must die. ¹⁹They will give the Son of Man to the non-Jewish people to laugh at him and beat him with whips and crucify him. But on the third day, he will be raised to life again."

A MOTHER ASKS JESUS A FAVOR

²⁰Then the wife of Zebedee came to Jesus with her sons. She bowed before him and asked him to do something for her.

²¹Jesus asked, "What do you want?"

She said, "Promise that one of my sons will sit at your right side and the other will sit at your left side in your kingdom."

²²But Jesus said, "You don't understand what you are asking. Can you drink the cup that I am about to drink?"ⁿ

The sons answered, "Yes, we can."

²³Jesus said to them, "You will drink from my cup. But I cannot choose who will sit at my right or my left; those places belong to those for whom my Father has prepared them."

²⁴When the other ten followers heard this, they were angry with the two brothers. ²⁵Jesus called all the followers together and said, "You know that the rulers of the non-Jewish people love to show their power over the people. And their important leaders love to use all their authority. ²⁶But it should not be that way among you. Whoever wants to become great among you must serve the rest of you like a servant. ²⁷Whoever wants to become first among you must serve the rest of you like a slave. ²⁸In the same way, the Son of Man did not come to be served. He came to serve others and to give his life as a ransom for many people."

Q: Some of the guys in my class are really strong, and they have huge muscles! How can I be like that?

A: God gives every person a unique body. He created you just the way he wants you. As you grow, you will continue to develop strength and muscles, but remember that God thinks being strong spiritually is even more important. It's okay to work out and try to develop your muscles, but make sure you are working just as hard to be strong in your faith!

Q: How was life different in Bible times?

A: Living at that time would probably remind you of camping: no electricity, no hot water, no TV, no e-mail, no toilets, and no convenience stores. Life was much harder because there were no labor-saving devices (like dishwashers) and few medicines. If you had six kids, you were lucky to see three reach adulthood. People had to be tough to survive. In Bible times, family was very important. People were also better at inviting people into their homes and taking care of others.

Q: I'm new to our neighborhood. How can I get to know the other kids?

A: The best way to break the ice with the kids in your neighborhood is to go and introduce yourself. It might be a little awkward at first. But if you ask the neighborhood kids what they like doing for fun, you will be showing an interest in their lives. People always respond well to that!

20:22 drink . . . drink Jesus used the idea of drinking from a cup to ask if they could accept the same terrible things that would happen to him.

JESUS HEALS TWO BLIND MEN

[29]When Jesus and his followers were leaving Jericho, a great many people followed him. [30]Two blind men sitting by the road heard that Jesus was going by, so they shouted, "Lord, Son of David, have mercy on us!"

[31]The people warned the blind men to be quiet, but they shouted even more, "Lord, Son of David, have mercy on us!"

[32]Jesus stopped and said to the blind men, "What do you want me to do for you?"

[33]They answered, "Lord, we want to see."

[34]Jesus felt sorry for the blind men and touched their eyes, and at once they could see. Then they followed Jesus.

JESUS ENTERS JERUSALEM AS A KING

DID YOU KNOW?

29% of kids get an allowance.

Shopping In America Survey, April 2005. "What's in the Bag for Tween Shoppers."

21 As Jesus and his followers were coming closer to Jerusalem, they stopped at Bethphage at the hill called the Mount of Olives. From there Jesus sent two of his followers [2]and said to them, "Go to the town you can see there. When you enter it, you will quickly find a donkey tied there with its colt. Untie them and bring them to me. [3]If anyone asks you why you are taking the donkeys, say that the Master needs them, and he will send them at once."

[4]This was to bring about what the prophet had said:

[5]"Tell the people of Jerusalem,
'Your king is coming to you.
He is gentle and riding on a donkey,
  on the colt of a donkey.' "

Isaiah 62:11; Zechariah 9:9

[6]The followers went and did what Jesus told them to do. [7]They brought the donkey and the colt to Jesus and laid their coats on them, and Jesus sat on them. [8]Many people spread their coats on the road. Others cut branches from the trees and spread them on the road. [9]The people were walking ahead of Jesus and behind him, shouting,

"Praise" to the Son of David!
God bless the One who comes in the name
  of the Lord!   *Psalm 118:26*
Praise to God in heaven!"

[10]When Jesus entered Jerusalem, all the city was filled with excitement. The people asked, "Who is this man?"

[11]The crowd said, "This man is Jesus, the prophet from the town of Nazareth in Galilee."

JESUS GOES TO THE TEMPLE

[12]Jesus went into the Temple and threw out all the people who were buying and selling there. He turned over the tables of those who were exchanging different kinds of money, and he upset the benches of those who were selling doves. [13]Jesus said to all the people there, "It is written in the Scriptures, 'My Temple will be called a house for prayer.'" But you are changing it into a 'hideout for robbers.' "

[14]The blind and crippled people came to Jesus in the Temple, and he healed them. [15]The leading priests and the teachers of the law saw that Jesus was doing wonderful things and that the children were praising him in the Temple, saying, "Praise" to the Son of David."

trustables
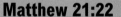

Matthew 21:22

King David was just a boy when he roughed up a bear and then fought with a lion. He wasn't even old enough to join the army when he took out Goliath. Hezekiah was only in his twenties when he began to lead a nation, and Samuel was dedicated to God's work by his mother as a baby. These Old Testament guys were great men for God even when they were young!

If God has put something in your heart to do that seems too big, too much, too hard for you, then remember the words of Jesus: "If you believe, you will get anything you ask for in prayer" (Matthew 21:22).

This promise isn't about asking for some cool new toy. Jesus is talking about asking for things *God* wants.

Prayer is not about you anyway. It's about what *God* can do in your life. What he can do is more than you could ever ask or think.

Your mom has not have left you at the Temple like Hannah left Samuel. And you may be thinking, *Well, I'm no king, either.* But some of the things God has planned for you are probably more than *you* can handle on your own.

So, the next time something big comes up, remember to talk with God. You will find you really *can* do anything because of him.

21:9, 15 Praise Literally, "Hosanna," a Hebrew word used at first in praying to God for help. At this time it was probably a shout of joy used in praising God or his Messiah.   **21:13 'My Temple . . . prayer.'** Quotation from Isaiah 56:7.   **21:13 'hideout for robbers'** Quotation from Jeremiah 7:11.

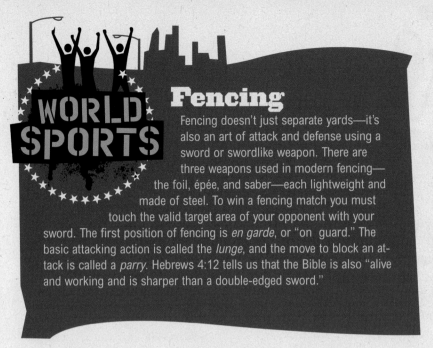

WORLD SPORTS

Fencing

Fencing doesn't just separate yards—it's also an art of attack and defense using a sword or swordlike weapon. There are three weapons used in modern fencing— the foil, épée, and saber—each lightweight and made of steel. To win a fencing match you must touch the valid target area of your opponent with your sword. The first position of fencing is *en garde*, or "on guard." The basic attacking action is called the *lunge*, and the move to block an attack is called a *parry*. Hebrews 4:12 tells us that the Bible is also "alive and working and is sharper than a double-edged sword."

All these things made the priests and the teachers of the law very angry.

16They asked Jesus, "Do you hear the things these children are saying?"

Jesus answered, "Yes. Haven't you read in the Scriptures, 'You have taught children and babies to sing praises'?"[n]

17Then Jesus left and went out of the city to Bethany, where he spent the night.

THE POWER OF FAITH

18Early the next morning, as Jesus was going back to the city, he became hungry. 19Seeing a fig tree beside the road, Jesus went to it, but there were no figs on the tree, only leaves. So Jesus said to the tree, "You will never again have fruit." The tree immediately dried up.

20When his followers saw this, they were amazed. They asked, "How did the fig tree dry up so quickly?"

21Jesus answered, "I tell you the truth, if you have faith and do not doubt, you will be able to do what I did to this tree and even more. You will be able to say to this mountain, 'Go, fall into the sea.' And if you have faith, it will happen. 22If you believe, you will get anything you ask for in prayer."

LEADERS DOUBT JESUS' AUTHORITY

23Jesus went to the Temple, and while he was teaching there, the leading priests and the elders of the people came to him. They said, "What authority do you have to do these things? Who gave you this authority?"

24Jesus answered, "I also will ask you a question. If you answer me, then I will tell you what authority I have to do these things. 25Tell me: When John baptized people, did that come from God or just from other people?"

They argued about Jesus' question, saying, "If we answer, 'John's baptism was from God,' Jesus will say, 'Then why didn't you believe him?' 26But if we say, 'It was from people,' we are afraid of what the crowd will do because they all believe that John was a prophet."

27So they answered Jesus, "We don't know."

Jesus said to them, "Then I won't tell you what authority I have to do these things.

A STORY ABOUT TWO SONS

28"Tell me what you think about this: A man had two sons. He went to the first son and said, 'Son, go and work today in my vineyard.' 29The son answered, 'I will not go.' But later the son changed his mind and went. 30Then the father went to the other son and said, 'Son, go and work today in my vineyard.' The son answered, 'Yes, sir, I will go and work,' but he did not go. 31Which of the two sons obeyed his father?"

The priests and leaders answered, "The first son."

Jesus said to them, "I tell you the truth, the tax collectors and the prostitutes will enter the kingdom of God before you do. 32John came to show you the right way to live. You did not believe him, but the tax collectors and prostitutes believed him. Even after seeing this, you still refused to change your ways and believe him.

A STORY ABOUT GOD'S SON

33"Listen to this story: There was a man who owned a vineyard. He put a wall around it and dug a hole for a winepress and built a tower. Then he leased the land to some farmers and left for a trip. 34When it was time for the grapes to be picked, he sent his servants to the farmers to get his share of the grapes. 35But the farmers grabbed the servants, beat one, killed another, and then killed a third servant with stones. 36So the man sent some other servants to the farmers, even more than he sent the first time. But the farmers did the same thing to the servants that they had done before. 37So the man decided to send his son to the farmers. He said, 'They will respect my

KNOW THE WORD!

TRINITY

Steam from hot cocoa, a roaring river, and a frozen pond all have something in common. They are all water, just in different forms.

In a similar way, God is *one* God in *three* persons: the Father, the Son (Jesus Christ), and the Holy Spirit. God is much more complicated than H_2O, but the illustration helps us understand the **Trinity**—the concept that there is only one God, yet we know him as Father God, Jesus, and the Holy Spirit.

Each person of the Trinity has a different place in our lives. The Holy Spirit lives within us. Jesus lives in heaven and speaks up for us before the Father.

The Trinity shows that God is too amazing for us to completely figure out!

21:16 'You . . . praises.' Quotation from the Septuagint (Greek) version of Psalm 8:2.

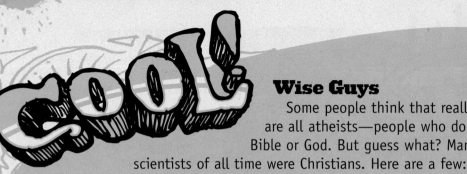

Wise Guys

Some people think that really smart people are all atheists—people who don't believe in the Bible or God. But guess what? Many of the greatest scientists of all time were Christians. Here are a few:

★ Charles Babbage (designed computers)
★ Francis Bacon (defined the scientific method)
★ Michael Faraday (developed electromagnetic field theory)
★ James Maxwell (formed the theory of light)
★ Samuel Morse (invented the telegraph)
★ Isaac Newton (discovered laws of physics)
★ Louis Pasteur (discovered germs)

These men believed God made everything, and they could see his order and beauty everywhere.

son.' ³⁸But when the farmers saw the son, they said to each other, 'This son will inherit the vineyard. If we kill him, it will be ours!' ³⁹Then the farmers grabbed the son, threw him out of the vineyard, and killed him. ⁴⁰So what will the owner of the vineyard do to these farmers when he comes?"

⁴¹The priests and leaders said, "He will surely kill those evil men. Then he will lease the vineyard to some other farmers who will give him his share of the crop at harvest time."

⁴²Jesus said to them, "Surely you have read this in the Scriptures:

'The stone that the builders rejected
    became the cornerstone.
The Lord did this,
    and it is wonderful to us.'

Psalm 118:22–23

⁴³"So I tell you that the kingdom of God will be taken away from you and given to people who do the things God wants in his kingdom. ⁴⁴The person who falls on this stone will be broken, and on whomever that stone falls, that person will be crushed."ⁿ

⁴⁵When the leading priests and the Pharisees heard these stories, they knew Jesus was talking about them. ⁴⁶They wanted to arrest him, but they were afraid of the people, because the people believed that Jesus was a prophet.

A STORY ABOUT A WEDDING FEAST

22 Jesus again used stories to teach them. He said, ²"The kingdom of heaven is like a king who prepared a wedding feast for his son. ³The king invited some people to the feast. When the feast was ready, the king sent his servants to tell the people, but they refused to come.

⁴"Then the king sent other servants, saying, 'Tell those who have been invited that my feast is ready. I have killed my best bulls and calves for the dinner, and everything is ready. Come to the wedding feast.'

⁵"But the people refused to listen to the servants and left to do other things. One went to work in his field, and another went to his business. ⁶Some of the other people grabbed the servants, beat them, and killed them. ⁷The king was furious and sent his army to kill the murderers and burn their city.

⁸"After that, the king said to his servants, 'The wedding feast is ready. I invited those people, but they were not worthy to come. ⁹So go to the street corners and invite everyone you find to come to my feast.' ¹⁰So the servants went into the streets and gathered all the people they could find, both good and bad. And the wedding hall was filled with guests.

¹¹"When the king came in to see the guests, he saw a man who was not dressed for a wedding. ¹²The king said, 'Friend, how were you allowed to come in here? You are not dressed for a wedding.' But the man said nothing. ¹³So the king told some servants, 'Tie this man's hands and feet. Throw him out into the darkness, where people will cry and grind their teeth with pain.'

¹⁴"Yes, many are invited, but only a few are chosen."

IS IT RIGHT TO PAY TAXES OR NOT?

¹⁵Then the Pharisees left that place and made plans to trap Jesus in saying something wrong. ¹⁶They sent some of their own followers and some people from the group called Herodians.ⁿ They said, "Teacher, we know that you are an honest man and that you teach the truth about God's way. You are not afraid of what other people think about you, because you pay no attention to who they are. ¹⁷So tell us what you think. Is it right to pay taxes to Caesar or not?"

¹⁸But knowing that these leaders were trying to trick him, Jesus said, "You hypocrites! Why are you trying to trap me? ¹⁹Show me a coin used for paying the tax." So the men

---

⭐ **21:44 The . . . crushed.** Some Greek copies do not have verse 44.   **22:16 Herodians** A political group that followed Herod and his family.

showed him a coin." ²⁰Then Jesus asked, "Whose image and name are on the coin?"

²¹The men answered, "Caesar's."

Then Jesus said to them, "Give to Caesar the things that are Caesar's, and give to God the things that are God's."

²²When the men heard what Jesus said, they were amazed and left him and went away.

SOME SADDUCEES TRY TO TRICK JESUS

²³That same day some Sadducees came to Jesus and asked him a question. (Sadducees believed that people would not rise from the dead.) ²⁴They said, "Teacher, Moses said if a married man dies without having children, his brother must marry the widow and have children for him. ²⁵Once there were seven brothers among us. The first one married and died. Since he had no children, his brother married the widow. ²⁶Then the second brother also died. The same thing happened to the third brother and all the other brothers. ²⁷Finally, the woman died. ²⁸Since all seven men had married her, when people rise from the dead, whose wife will she be?"

²⁹Jesus answered, "You don't understand, because you don't know what the Scriptures say, and you don't know about the power of God. ³⁰When people rise from the dead, they will not marry, nor will they be given to someone to marry. They will be like the angels in heaven. ³¹Surely you have read what God said to you about rising from the dead. ³²God said,

'I am the God of Abraham, the God of Isaac, and the God of Jacob.'ⁿ God is the God of the living, not the dead."

³³When the people heard this, they were amazed at Jesus' teaching.

THE MOST IMPORTANT COMMAND

³⁴When the Pharisees learned that the Sadducees could not argue with Jesus' answers to them, the Pharisees met together. ³⁵One Pharisee, who was an expert on the law of Moses, asked Jesus this question to test him: ³⁶"Teacher, which command in the law is the most important?"

³⁷Jesus answered, " 'Love the Lord your God with all your heart, all your soul, and all your mind.'ⁿ ³⁸This is the first and most important command. ³⁹And the second command is like the first: 'Love your neighbor as you love yourself.'ⁿ ⁴⁰All the law and the writings of the prophets depend on these two commands."

JESUS QUESTIONS THE PHARISEES

⁴¹While the Pharisees were together, Jesus asked them, ⁴²"What do you think about the Christ? Whose son is he?"

They answered, "The Christ is the Son of David."

⁴³Then Jesus said to them, "Then why did David call him 'Lord'? David, speaking by the power of the Holy Spirit, said,

⁴⁴'The Lord said to my Lord,
"Sit by me at my right side,

until I put your enemies under your
control." '   *Psalm 110:1*
⁴⁵David calls the Christ 'Lord,' so how can the Christ be his son?"

⁴⁶None of the Pharisees could answer Jesus' question, and after that day no one was brave enough to ask him any more questions.

JESUS ACCUSES SOME LEADERS

23 Then Jesus said to the crowds and to his followers, ²"The teachers of the law and the Pharisees have the authority to tell you what the law of Moses says. ³So you should obey and follow whatever they tell you, but their lives are not good examples for you to follow. They tell you to do things, but they themselves don't do them. ⁴They make strict rules and try to force people to obey them, but they are unwilling to help those who struggle under the weight of their rules.

⁵"They do good things so that other people will see them. They enlarge the little boxesⁿ holding Scriptures that they wear, and they make their special prayer clothes very long. ⁶Those Pharisees and teachers of the law love to have the most important seats at feasts and in the synagogues. ⁷They love people to greet them with respect in the marketplaces, and they love to have people call them 'Teacher.'

⁸"But you must not be called 'Teacher,' because you have only one Teacher, and you are all brothers and sisters together. ⁹And don't

---

Matthew 22:16–17

Cool new footwear, a Play Station, being the goof-off, or just trying to fit in—it's all about being liked. For many people, being liked is their highest ambition. The advertising on TV is all about things you can do to get people to like you more.

What's wrong with wanting people to like you?

A few days before they crucified Jesus, his enemies tried to trick him into angering the Roman authorities: "Teacher, we know that you are an honest man and that you teach the truth about God's way. You are not afraid of what other people think about you, because you pay no attention to who they are. So tell us what you think. Is it right to pay taxes to Caesar or not?" (Matthew 22:16–17). Jesus astounded them with his answer—an answer clearly designed to please God!

Are you a God-pleaser or a people-pleaser? Who's more important to you?

When you get your allowance, what do you spend it on? Are you envious of other kids because they're "cooler" than you? Do you beg your parents for a swimming pool so you can have a cooler house?

Try this today: each time you do something, ask yourself who you are doing it for. If you are not doing it for Jesus, you are serving the wrong master.

22:19 coin A Roman denarius. One coin was the average pay for one day's work.   **22:32 'I am . . . Jacob.'** Quotation from Exodus 3:6.   **22:37 'Love . . . mind.'** Quotation from Deuteronomy 6:5.
22:39 'Love . . . yourself.' Quotation from Leviticus 19:18.   **23:5 boxes** Small leather boxes containing four important Scriptures. Some Jews tied these to their foreheads and left arms, probably to show they were very religious.

call any person on earth 'Father,' because you have one Father, who is in heaven. [10]And you should not be called 'Master,' because you have only one Master, the Christ. [11]Whoever is your servant is the greatest among you. [12]Whoever makes himself great will be made humble. Whoever makes himself humble will be made great.

[13]"How terrible for you, teachers of the law and Pharisees! You are hypocrites! You close the door for people to enter the kingdom of heaven. You yourselves don't enter, and you stop others who are trying to enter. [[14]How terrible for you, teachers of the law and Pharisees. You are hypocrites. You take away widows' houses, and you say long prayers so that people will notice you. So you will have a worse punishment.][n]

[15]"How terrible for you, teachers of the law and Pharisees! You are hypocrites! You travel across land and sea to find one person who will change to your ways. When you find that person, you make him more fit for hell than you are.

[16]"How terrible for you! You guide the people, but you are blind. You say, 'If people swear by the Temple when they make a promise, that means nothing. But if they swear by the gold that is in the Temple, they must keep that promise.' [17]You are blind fools! Which is greater: the gold or the Temple that makes that gold holy? [18]And you say, 'If people swear by the altar when they make a promise, that means nothing. But if they swear by the gift on the altar, they must keep that promise.' [19]You are blind! Which is greater: the gift or the altar

that makes the gift holy? [20]The person who swears by the altar is really using the altar and also everything on the altar. [21]And the person who swears by the Temple is really using the Temple and also everything in the Temple. [22]The person who swears by heaven is also using God's throne and the One who sits on that throne.

[23]"How terrible for you, teachers of the law and Pharisees! You are hypocrites! You give to God one-tenth of everything you earn—even your mint, dill, and cumin.[n] But you don't obey the really important teachings of the law—justice, mercy, and being loyal. These are the things you should do, as well as those other things. [24]You guide the people, but you are blind! You are like a person who picks a fly out of a drink and then swallows a camel![n]

[25]"How terrible for you, teachers of the law and Pharisees! You are hypocrites! You wash the outside of your cups and dishes, but inside they are full of things you got by cheating others and by pleasing only yourselves. [26]Pharisees, you are blind! First make the inside of the cup clean, and then the outside of the cup can be truly clean.

[27]"How terrible for you, teachers of the law and Pharisees! You are hypocrites! You are like tombs that are painted white. Outside, those tombs look fine, but inside, they are full of the bones of dead people and all kinds of unclean things. [28]It is the same with you. People look at you and think you are good, but on the inside you are full of hypocrisy and evil.

[29]"How terrible for you, teachers of the law and Pharisees! You are hypocrites! You build tombs for the prophets, and you show honor to the graves of those who lived good lives. [30]You say, 'If we had lived during the time of our ancestors, we would not have helped them kill the prophets.' [31]But you give proof that you are descendants of those who murdered the prophets. [32]And you will complete the sin that your ancestors started.

[33]"You are snakes! A family of poisonous snakes! How are you going to escape God's judgment? [34]So I tell you this: I am sending to you prophets and wise men and teachers. Some of them you will kill and crucify. Some of them you will beat in your synagogues and chase from town to town. [35]So you will be guilty for the death of all the good people who have been killed on earth—from the murder of that good man Abel to the murder of Zechariah[n] son of Berakiah, whom you murdered between the Temple and the altar. [36]I tell you the truth, all of these things will happen to you people who are living now.

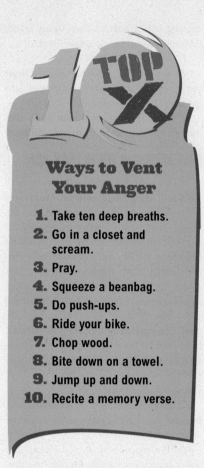

JESUS FEELS SORRY FOR JERUSALEM

[37]"Jerusalem, Jerusalem! You kill the prophets and stone to death those who are sent to you. Many times I wanted to gather your people as a hen gathers her chicks under her wings, but you did not let me. [38]Now your house will be left completely empty. [39]I tell you, you will not see me again until that time when you will say, 'God bless the One who comes in the name of the Lord.' "[n]

THE TEMPLE WILL BE DESTROYED

24 As Jesus left the Temple and was walking away, his followers came up to show him the Temple's buildings. [2]Jesus asked, "Do you see all these buildings? I tell you the truth, not one stone will be left on another. Every stone will be thrown down to the ground."

[3]Later, as Jesus was sitting on the Mount of Olives, his followers came to be alone with him. They said, "Tell us, when will these things happen? And what will be the sign that it is time for you to come again and for this age to end?"

[4]Jesus answered, "Be careful that no one fools you. [5]Many will come in my name, saying,

23:14 How . . . punishment. Some Greek copies do not contain the bracketed text.   **23:23 mint, dill, and cumin** Small plants grown in gardens and used for spices. Only very religious people would be careful enough to give a tenth of these plants.   **23:24 You . . . camel!** Meaning, "You worry about the smallest mistakes but commit the biggest sin."   **23:35 Abel . . . Zechariah** In the order of the books of the Hebrew Old Testament, the first and last men to be murdered.   **23:39 'God . . . Lord.'** Quotation from Psalm 118:26.

'I am the Christ,' and they will fool many people. [6]You will hear about wars and stories of wars that are coming, but don't be afraid. These things must happen before the end comes. [7]Nations will fight against other nations; kingdoms will fight against other kingdoms. There will be times when there is no food for people to eat, and there will be earthquakes in different places. [8]These things are like the first pains when something new is about to be born.

[9]"Then people will arrest you, hand you over to be hurt, and kill you. They will hate you because you believe in me. [10]At that time, many will lose their faith, and they will turn against each other and hate each other. [11]Many false prophets will come and cause many people to believe lies. [12]There will be more and more evil in the world, so most people will stop showing their love for each other. [13]But those people who keep their faith until the end will be saved. [14]The Good News about God's kingdom will be preached in all the world, to every nation. Then the end will come.

[15]"Daniel the prophet spoke about 'a blasphemous object that brings destruction.'" You will see this standing in the holy place." (You who read this should understand what it means.) [16]"At that time, the people in Judea should run away to the mountains. [17]If people are on the roofs" of their houses, they must not go down to get anything out of their houses. [18]If people are in the fields, they must not go back to get their coats. [19]At that time, how terrible it will be for women who are pregnant or have nursing babies! [20]Pray that it will not be winter or a Sabbath day when these things happen and you have to run away, [21]because at that time there will be much trouble. There will be more trouble than there has ever been since the beginning of the world until now, and nothing as bad will ever happen again. [22]God has decided to make that terrible time short. Otherwise, no one would go on living. But God will make that time short to help the people he has chosen. [23]At that time, someone might say to you, 'Look, there is the Christ!' Or another person might say, 'There he is!' But don't believe them. [24]False Christs and false prophets will come and perform great wonders and miracles. They will try to fool even the people God has chosen, if that is possible. [25]Now I have warned you about this before it happens.

[26]"If people tell you, 'The Christ is in the desert,' don't go there. If they say, 'The Christ is in the inner room,' don't believe it. [27]When the Son of Man comes, he will be seen by everyone, like lightning flashing from the east to the west. [28]Wherever the dead body is, there the vultures will gather.

[29]"Soon after the trouble of those days,

'the sun will grow dark,
    and the moon will not give its light.
The stars will fall from the sky.
    And the powers of the heavens will be
        shaken.'   *Isaiah 13:10; 34:4*

[30]"At that time, the sign of the Son of Man will appear in the sky. Then all the peoples of the world will cry. They will see the Son of Man coming on clouds in the sky with great power and glory. [31]He will use a loud trumpet to send his angels all around the earth, and they will gather his chosen people from every part of the world.

[32]"Learn a lesson from the fig tree: When its branches become green and soft and new leaves appear, you know summer is near. [33]In the same way, when you see all these things happening, you will know that the time is near, ready to come. [34]I tell you the truth, all these things will happen while the people of this time are still living. [35]Earth and sky will be destroyed, but the words I have said will never be destroyed.

WHEN WILL JESUS COME AGAIN?

[36]"No one knows when that day or time will be, not the angels in heaven, not even the Son." Only the Father knows. [37]When the Son of Man comes, it will be like what happened during Noah's time. [38]In those days before the flood, people were eating and drinking, marrying and giving their children to be married, until the day Noah entered the boat. [39]They knew nothing about what was happening until the flood came and destroyed them. It will be the same when the Son of Man comes. [40]Two men will be in the field. One will be taken, and the other will be left. [41]Two women will be grinding grain with a mill." One will be taken, and the other will be left.

[42]"So always be ready, because you don't know the day your Lord will come. [43]Remember this: If the owner of the house knew what time of night a thief was coming, the owner would watch and not let the thief break in. [44]So you also must be ready, because the Son of Man will come at a time you don't expect him.

[45]"Who is the wise and loyal servant that the master trusts to give the other servants

ROCK SOLID

Matthew 24:42

Surprise! Your life is over. Jesus just came back! Okay, not really. But that's exactly how it's going to happen. Just like that, life as we know it will all be over in a second.

Jesus says, "Always be ready, because you don't know the day your Lord will come" (Matthew 24:42).

How's your life right now? Stop reading for a second and think, *Am I ready for Jesus to come back today?*

Are you proud of the life you're living? Or is it time to get some things cleaned up?

Don't do things that you would be ashamed to have Jesus find you doing. What would it be like if Jesus showed up and you were in the middle of beating up a kid at school? On the other hand, what would it be like if Jesus showed up and caught you telling someone in your class how much Jesus loves him?

Jesus is going to come back to earth any day now. It's going to be a surprise, so it's not too early to get ready!

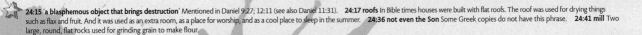
24:15 'a blasphemous object that brings destruction' Mentioned in Daniel 9:27; 12:11 (see also Daniel 11:31).   **24:17 roofs** In Bible times houses were built with flat roofs. The roof was used for drying things such as flax and fruit. And it was used as an extra room, as a place for worship, and as a cool place to sleep in the summer.   **24:36 not even the Son** Some Greek copies do not have this phrase.   **24:41 mill** Two large, round, flat rocks used for grinding grain to make flour.

their food at the right time? [46]When the master comes and finds the servant doing his work, the servant will be blessed. [47]I tell you the truth, the master will choose that servant to take care of everything he owns. [48]But suppose that evil servant thinks to himself, 'My master will not come back soon,' [49]and he begins to beat the other servants and eat and get drunk with others like him? [50]The master will come when that servant is not ready and is not expecting him. [51]Then the master will cut him in pieces and send him away to be with the hypocrites, where people will cry and grind their teeth with pain.

A STORY ABOUT TEN BRIDESMAIDS

25 "At that time the kingdom of heaven will be like ten bridesmaids who took their lamps and went to wait for the bridegroom. [2]Five of them were foolish and five were wise. [3]The five foolish bridesmaids took their lamps, but they did not take more oil for the lamps to burn. [4]The wise bridesmaids took their lamps and more oil in jars. [5]Because the bridegroom was late, they became sleepy and went to sleep.

[6]"At midnight someone cried out, 'The bridegroom is coming! Come and meet him!'

[7]Then all the bridesmaids woke up and got their lamps ready. [8]But the foolish ones said to the wise, 'Give us some of your oil, because our lamps are going out.' [9]The wise bridesmaids answered, 'No, the oil we have might not be enough for all of us. Go to the people who sell oil and buy some for yourselves.'

[10]"So while the five foolish bridesmaids went to buy oil, the bridegroom came. The bridesmaids who were ready went in with the bridegroom to the wedding feast. Then the door was closed and locked.

[11]"Later the others came back and said, 'Sir, sir, open the door to let us in.' [12]But the bridegroom answered, 'I tell you the truth, I don't want to know you.'

[13]"So always be ready, because you don't know the day or the hour the Son of Man will come.

A STORY ABOUT THREE SERVANTS

[14]"The kingdom of heaven is like a man who was going to another place for a visit. Before he left, he called for his servants and told them to take care of his things while he was gone. [15]He gave one servant five bags of gold, another servant two bags of gold, and a third servant one bag of gold, to each one as much

as he could handle. Then he left. [16]The servant who got five bags went quickly to invest the money and earned five more bags. [17]In the same way, the servant who had two bags invested them and earned two more. [18]But the servant who got one bag went out and dug a hole in the ground and hid the master's money.

[19]"After a long time the master came home and asked the servants what they did with his money. [20]The servant who was given five bags of gold brought five more bags to the master and said, 'Master, you trusted me to care for five bags of gold, so I used your five bags to earn five more.' [21]The master answered, 'You did well. You are a good and loyal servant. Because you were loyal with small things, I will let you care for much greater things. Come and share my joy with me.'

[22]"Then the servant who had been given two bags of gold came to the master and said, 'Master, you gave me two bags of gold to care for, so I used your two bags to earn two more.' [23]The master answered, 'You did well. You are a good and loyal servant. Because you were loyal with small things, I will let you care for much greater things. Come and share my joy with me.'

Q: Why do Christians have to go to church?

A: Christians need each other. Jesus didn't call people to believe in him and go it alone; he always called people to be part of his community—the church. He wants us to be baptized in front of this community and to take the Lord's Supper (Communion) together. The Bible tells us that it's wrong to stop going to church (Hebrews 10:25). If we stay away because we don't feel like going, we're harming ourselves and disobeying God.

Q: Why is it wrong to play violent video games if you're not going to go out and shoot people in the real world?

A: First-person shooter games make it fun to blow other people away. Even though you're not actually killing other people, the games cause you to fantasize about it. And it's not right to use other

people's suffering for entertainment (imaginary or not). The Bible says we're to fill our minds with what is good, honorable, and right (Philippians 4:8).

Q: Something always goes wrong on our family camping trips. Should I ask my dad to figure out another "family time" activity?

A: Part of the fun of camping is solving problems as a family. Where else will your family get time together with no TV, Internet, or phone to distract you? Besides, one of the best parts about camping is how it makes you appreciate your home when the trip is over.

²⁴"Then the servant who had been given one bag of gold came to the master and said, 'Master, I knew that you were a hard man. You harvest things you did not plant. You gather crops where you did not sow any seed. ²⁵So I was afraid and went and hid your money in the ground. Here is your bag of gold.' ²⁶The master answered, 'You are a wicked and lazy servant! You say you knew that I harvest things I did not plant and that I gather crops where I did not sow any seed. ²⁷So you should have put my gold in the bank. Then, when I came home, I would have received my gold back with interest.'

²⁸"So the master told his other servants, 'Take the bag of gold from that servant and give it to the servant who has ten bags of gold. ²⁹Those who have much will get more, and they will have much more than they need. But those who do not have much will have everything taken away from them.' ³⁰Then the master said, 'Throw that useless servant outside, into the darkness where people will cry and grind their teeth with pain.'

THE KING WILL JUDGE ALL PEOPLE

³¹"The Son of Man will come again in his great glory, with all his angels. He will be King and sit on his great throne. ³²All the nations of the world will be gathered before him, and he will separate them into two groups as a shepherd separates the sheep from the goats. ³³The Son of Man will put the sheep on his right and the goats on his left.

³⁴"Then the King will say to the people on his right, 'Come, my Father has given you his blessing. Receive the kingdom God has prepared for you since the world was made. ³⁵I was hungry, and you gave me food. I was thirsty, and you gave me something to drink. I was alone and away from home, and you invited me into your house. ³⁶I was without clothes, and you gave me something to wear. I was sick, and you cared for me. I was in prison, and you visited me.'

³⁷"Then the good people will answer, 'Lord, when did we see you hungry and give you food, or thirsty and give you something to drink? ³⁸When did we see you alone and away from home and invite you into our house? When did we see you without clothes and give you something to wear? ³⁹When did we see you sick or in prison and care for you?'

⁴⁰"Then the King will answer, 'I tell you the truth, anything you did for even the least of my people here, you also did for me.'

⁴¹"Then the King will say to those on his left, 'Go away from me. You will be punished. Go into the fire that burns forever that was prepared for the devil and his angels. ⁴²I was hungry, and you gave me nothing to eat. I was thirsty, and you gave me nothing to drink. ⁴³I was alone and away from home, and you did not invite me into your house. I was without clothes, and you gave me nothing to wear. I was sick and in prison, and you did not care for me.'

⁴⁴"Then those people will answer, 'Lord, when did we see you hungry or thirsty or alone and away from home or without clothes or sick or in prison? When did we see these things and not help you?'

⁴⁵"Then the King will answer, 'I tell you the truth, anything you refused to do for even the least of my people here, you refused to do for me.'

⁴⁶"These people will go off to be punished forever, but the good people will go to live forever."

THE PLAN TO KILL JESUS

26 After Jesus finished saying all these things, he told his followers, ²"You know that the day after tomorrow is the day of the Passover Feast. On that day the Son of Man will be given to his enemies to be crucified."

³Then the leading priests and the elders had a meeting at the palace of the high priest, named Caiaphas. ⁴At the meeting, they planned to set a trap to arrest Jesus and kill him. ⁵But they said, "We must not do it during the feast, because the people might cause a riot."

DID YOU KNOW?

88% of kids would rather be "a nice person" than be "rich."

Youth Intelligence and Nickelodeon—
Ypulse.com, June 11, 2004

PERFUME FOR JESUS' BURIAL

⁶Jesus was in Bethany at the house of Simon, who had a skin disease. ⁷While Jesus was there, a woman approached him with an alabaster jar filled with expensive perfume. She poured this perfume on Jesus' head while he was eating.

⁸His followers were upset when they saw the woman do this. They asked, "Why waste that perfume? ⁹It could have been sold for a great deal of money and the money given to the poor."

¹⁰Knowing what had happened, Jesus said, "Why are you troubling this woman? She did an excellent thing for me. ¹¹You will always have the poor with you, but you will not always have me. ¹²This woman poured perfume on my body to prepare me for burial. ¹³I tell you the truth, wherever the Good News is preached in all the world, what this woman has done will be told, and people will remember her."

JUDAS BECOMES AN ENEMY OF JESUS

¹⁴Then one of the twelve apostles, Judas Iscariot, went to talk to the leading priests. ¹⁵He said, "What will you pay me for giving Jesus to you?" And they gave him thirty silver coins. ¹⁶After that, Judas watched for the best time to turn Jesus in.

JESUS EATS THE PASSOVER MEAL

¹⁷On the first day of the Feast of Unleavened Bread, the followers came to Jesus. They said, "Where do you want us to prepare for you to eat the Passover meal?"

¹⁸Jesus answered, "Go into the city to a certain man and tell him, 'The Teacher says: "The chosen time is near. I will have the Passover with my followers at your house." ' " ¹⁹The followers did what Jesus told them to do, and they prepared the Passover meal.

²⁰In the evening Jesus was sitting at the table with his twelve followers. ²¹As they were eating, Jesus said, "I tell you the truth, one of you will turn against me."

²²This made the followers very sad. Each one began to say to Jesus, "Surely, Lord, I am not the one who will turn against you, am I?"

²³Jesus answered, "The man who has dipped his hand with me into the bowl is the one who will turn against me. ²⁴The Son of Man will die, just as the Scriptures say. But how terrible it will be for the person who hands the Son of Man over to be killed. It would be better for him if he had never been born."

²⁵Then Judas, who would give Jesus to his

enemies, said to Jesus, "Teacher, surely I am not the one, am I?"

Jesus answered, "Yes, it is you."

THE LORD'S SUPPER

[26] While they were eating, Jesus took some bread and thanked God for it and broke it. Then he gave it to his followers and said, "Take this bread and eat it; this is my body."

[27] Then Jesus took a cup and thanked God for it and gave it to the followers. He said, "Every one of you drink this. [28] This is my blood which is the new[n] agreement that God makes with his people. This blood is poured out for many to forgive their sins. [29] I tell you this: I will not drink of this fruit of the vine[n] again until that day when I drink it new with you in my Father's kingdom."

[30] After singing a hymn, they went out to the Mount of Olives.

JESUS' FOLLOWERS WILL LEAVE HIM

[31] Jesus told his followers, "Tonight you will all stumble in your faith on account of me, because it is written in the Scriptures:

'I will kill the shepherd,
and the sheep will scatter.' *Zechariah 13:7*

[32] But after I rise from the dead, I will go ahead of you into Galilee."

[33] Peter said, "Everyone else may stumble in their faith because of you, but I will not."

[34] Jesus said, "I tell you the truth, tonight before the rooster crows you will say three times that you don't know me."

[35] But Peter said, "I will never say that I don't know you! I will even die with you!" And all the other followers said the same thing.

JESUS PRAYS ALONE

[36] Then Jesus went with his followers to a place called Gethsemane. He said to them, "Sit here while I go over there and pray." [37] He took Peter and the two sons of Zebedee with him, and he began to be very sad and troubled. [38] He said to them, "My heart is full of sorrow, to the point of death. Stay here and watch with me."

[39] After walking a little farther away from them, Jesus fell to the ground and prayed, "My Father, if it is possible, do not give me this cup[n] of suffering. But do what you want, not what I want." [40] Then Jesus went back to his followers and found them asleep. He said to Peter, "You men could not stay awake with me for one hour? [41] Stay awake and pray for strength against temptation. The spirit wants to do what is right, but the body is weak."

[42] Then Jesus went away a second time and prayed, "My Father, if it is not possible for this painful thing to be taken from me, and if I must do it, I pray that what you want will be done." [43] Then he went back to his followers, and again he found them asleep, because their eyes were heavy. [44] So Jesus left them and went away and prayed a third time, saying the same thing.

[45] Then Jesus went back to his followers and said, "Are you still sleeping and resting? The time has come for the Son of Man to be handed over to sinful people. [46] Get up, we must go. Look, here comes the man who has turned against me."

JESUS IS ARRESTED

[47] While Jesus was still speaking, Judas, one of the twelve apostles, came up. With him were many people carrying swords and clubs who had been sent from the leading priests and the Jewish elders of the people. [48] Judas had planned to give them a signal, saying, "The man I kiss is Jesus. Arrest him." [49] At once Judas went to Jesus and said, "Greetings, Teacher!" and kissed him.

[50] Jesus answered, "Friend, do what you came to do."

Then the people came and grabbed Jesus and arrested him. [51] When that happened, one of Jesus' followers reached for his sword and pulled it out. He struck the servant of the high priest and cut off his ear.

[52] Jesus said to the man, "Put your sword back in its place. All who use swords will be killed with swords. [53] Surely you know I could ask my Father, and he would give me more than twelve armies of angels. [54] But it must happen this way to bring about what the Scriptures say."

[55] Then Jesus said to the crowd, "You came to get me with swords and clubs as if I were a criminal. Every day I sat in the Temple teaching, and you did not arrest me there. [56] But all these things have happened so that it will come about as the prophets wrote." Then all of Jesus' followers left him and ran away.

BIBLE SUPERHEROES

Matthew
See Matthew 9:9–13.

Matthew was a tax collector before he met Jesus. His job made him an outcast because he worked for the hated Romans. But Jesus looked past his reputation and saw his potential.

Matthew threw a party for Jesus and invited his rowdy friends. Jesus was excited, but the religious leaders were upset. Later, Jesus chose Matthew to be one of the twelve apostles.

None of Matthew's own words are recorded in Scripture; but he wasn't quiet about his faith. Many people think that he preached in faraway places such as Ethiopia and Egypt, where he was killed for believing in Jesus (martyred).

Do your friends know you are a follower of Jesus? Jesus can use you to bring the Good News to people near and far, just like he did with Matthew!

26:28 new Some Greek copies do not have this word. Compare Luke 22:20. **26:29 fruit of the vine** Product of the grapevine; this may also be translated "wine." **26:39 cup** Jesus is talking about the terrible things that will happen to him. Accepting these things will be very hard, like drinking a cup of something bitter.

JESUS BEFORE THE LEADERS

[57] Those people who arrested Jesus led him to the house of Caiaphas, the high priest, where the teachers of the law and the elders were gathered. [58] Peter followed far behind to the courtyard of the high priest's house, and he sat down with the guards to see what would happen to Jesus.

[59] The leading priests and the whole Jewish council tried to find something false against Jesus so they could kill him. [60] Many people came and told lies about him, but the council could find no real reason to kill him. Then two people came and said, [61] "This man said, 'I can destroy the Temple of God and build it again in three days.' "

[62] Then the high priest stood up and said to Jesus, "Aren't you going to answer? Don't you have something to say about their charges against you?" [63] But Jesus said nothing.

Again the high priest said to Jesus, "I command you by the power of the living God: Tell us if you are the Christ, the Son of God."

[64] Jesus answered, "Those are your words. But I tell you, in the future you will see the Son of Man sitting at the right hand of God, the Powerful One, and coming on clouds in the sky."

[65] When the high priest heard this, he tore his clothes and said, "This man has said things that are against God! We don't need any more witnesses; you all heard him say these things against God. [66] What do you think?"

The people answered, "He should die."

[67] Then the people there spat in Jesus' face and beat him with their fists. Others slapped him. [68] They said, "Prove to us that you are a prophet, you Christ! Tell us who hit you!"

PETER SAYS HE DOESN'T KNOW JESUS

[69] At that time, as Peter was sitting in the courtyard, a servant girl came to him and said, "You also were with Jesus of Galilee."

[70] But Peter said to all the people there that he was never with Jesus. He said, "I don't know what you are talking about."

[71] When he left the courtyard and was at the gate, another girl saw him. She said to the people there, "This man was with Jesus of Nazareth."

[72] Again, Peter said he was never with him, saying, "I swear I don't know this man Jesus!"

[73] A short time later, some people standing there went to Peter and said, "Surely you are one of those who followed Jesus. The way you talk shows it."

[74] Then Peter began to place a curse on himself and swear, "I don't know the man." At once, a rooster crowed. [75] And Peter remembered what Jesus had told him: "Before the rooster crows, you will say three times that you don't know me." Then Peter went outside and cried painfully.

JESUS IS TAKEN TO PILATE

27 Early the next morning, all the leading priests and elders of the people decided that Jesus should die. [2] They tied him, led him away, and turned him over to Pilate, the governor.

JUDAS KILLS HIMSELF

[3] Judas, the one who had given Jesus to his enemies, saw that they had decided to kill Jesus. Then he was very sorry for what he had done. So he took the thirty silver coins back to the priests and the leaders, [4] saying, "I sinned; I handed over to you an innocent man."

The leaders answered, "What is that to us? That's your problem, not ours."

[5] So Judas threw the money into the Temple. Then he went off and hanged himself.

[6] The leading priests picked up the silver coins in the Temple and said, "Our law does not allow us to keep this money with the Temple money, because it has paid for a man's death." [7] So they decided to use the coins to buy Potter's Field as a place to bury strangers who died in Jerusalem. [8] That is why that field is still called the Field of Blood. [9] So what Jeremiah the prophet had said came true: "They took thirty silver coins. That is how little the Israelites thought he was worth. [10] They used those thirty silver coins to buy the potter's field, as the Lord commanded me."[n]

PILATE QUESTIONS JESUS

[11] Jesus stood before Pilate the governor, and Pilate asked him, "Are you the king of the Jews?"

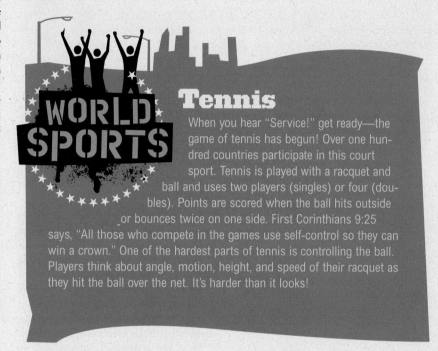

Tennis

When you hear "Service!" get ready—the game of tennis has begun! Over one hundred countries participate in this court sport. Tennis is played with a racquet and ball and uses two players (singles) or four (doubles). Points are scored when the ball hits outside or bounces twice on one side. First Corinthians 9:25 says, "All those who compete in the games use self-control so they can win a crown." One of the hardest parts of tennis is controlling the ball. Players think about angle, motion, height, and speed of their racquet as they hit the ball over the net. It's harder than it looks!

Jesus answered, "Those are your words."

[12] When the leading priests and the elders accused Jesus, he said nothing.

[13] So Pilate said to Jesus, "Don't you hear them accusing you of all these things?"

[14] But Jesus said nothing in answer to Pilate, and Pilate was very surprised at this.

PILATE TRIES TO FREE JESUS

[15] Every year at the time of Passover the governor would free one prisoner whom the people chose. [16] At that time there was a man in prison, named Barabbas,[n] who was known to be very bad. [17] When the people gathered at Pilate's house, Pilate said, "Whom do you want me to set free: Barabbas[n] or Jesus who is called the Christ?" [18] Pilate knew that they turned Jesus in to him because they were jealous.

[19] While Pilate was sitting there on the judge's seat, his wife sent this message to him: "Don't do anything to that man, because he is innocent. Today I had a dream about him, and it troubled me very much."

²⁰But the leading priests and elders convinced the crowd to ask for Barabbas to be freed and for Jesus to be killed.

²¹Pilate said, "I have Barabbas and Jesus. Which do you want me to set free for you?"

The people answered, "Barabbas."

²²Pilate asked, "So what should I do with Jesus, the one called the Christ?"

They all answered, "Crucify him!"

²³Pilate asked, "Why? What wrong has he done?"

But they shouted louder, "Crucify him!"

²⁴When Pilate saw that he could do nothing about this and that a riot was starting, he took some water and washed his hands" in front of the crowd. Then he said, "I am not guilty of this man's death. You are the ones who are causing it!"

²⁵All the people answered, "We and our children will be responsible for his death."

²⁶Then he set Barabbas free. But Jesus was beaten with whips and handed over to the soldiers to be crucified.

²⁷The governor's soldiers took Jesus into the governor's palace, and they all gathered around him. ²⁸They took off his clothes and put a red robe on him. ²⁹Using thorny branches, they made a crown, put it on his head, and put a stick in his right hand. Then the soldiers bowed before Jesus and made fun of him, saying, "Hail, King of the Jews!" ³⁰They spat on Jesus. Then they took his stick and began to beat him on the head. ³¹After they finished, the soldiers took off the robe and put his own clothes on him again. Then they led him away to be crucified.

JESUS IS CRUCIFIED

³²As the soldiers were going out of the city with Jesus, they forced a man from Cyrene, named Simon, to carry the cross for Jesus. ³³They all came to the place called Golgotha, which means the Place of the Skull. ³⁴The soldiers gave Jesus wine mixed with gall" to drink. He tasted the wine but refused to drink it. ³⁵When the soldiers had crucified him, they threw lots to decide who would get his clothes." ³⁶The soldiers sat there and continued watching him. ³⁷They put a sign above Jesus' head with a charge against him. It said: THIS IS JESUS, THE KING OF THE JEWS. ³⁸Two robbers were crucified beside Jesus, one on the right and the other on the left. ³⁹People walked by and insulted Jesus and shook their heads, ⁴⁰saying, "You said you could destroy the Temple and build it again in three days. So save yourself! Come down from that cross if you are really the Son of God!"

⁴¹The leading priests, the teachers of the law, and the Jewish elders were also making fun of Jesus. ⁴²They said, "He saved others, but he can't save himself! He says he is the king of Israel! If he is the king, let him come down now from the cross. Then we will believe in him. ⁴³He trusts in God, so let God save him now, if God really wants him. He himself said, 'I am the Son of God.' " ⁴⁴And in the same way, the robbers who were being crucified beside Jesus also insulted him.

JESUS DIES

⁴⁵At noon the whole country became dark, and the darkness lasted for three hours.

⁴⁶About three o'clock Jesus cried out in a loud voice, "Eli, Eli, lama sabachthani?" This means, "My God, my God, why have you abandoned me?"

⁴⁷Some of the people standing there who heard this said, "He is calling Elijah."

⁴⁸Quickly one of them ran and got a sponge and filled it with vinegar and tied it to a stick and gave it to Jesus to drink. ⁴⁹But the others said, "Don't bother him. We want to see if Elijah will come to save him."

⁵⁰But Jesus cried out again in a loud voice and died.

⁵¹Then the curtain in the Temple" was torn into two pieces, from the top to the bottom. Also, the earth shook and rocks broke apart. ⁵²The graves opened, and many of God's people who had died were raised from the dead. ⁵³They came out of the graves after Jesus was raised from the dead and went into the holy city, where they appeared to many people.

⁵⁴When the army officer and the soldiers guarding Jesus saw this earthquake and everything else that happened, they were very frightened and said, "He really was the Son of God!"

⁵⁵Many women who had followed Jesus from Galilee to help him were standing at a distance from the cross, watching. ⁵⁶Mary Magdalene, and Mary the mother of James and Joseph, and the mother of James and John were there.

JESUS IS BURIED

⁵⁷That evening a rich man named Joseph, a follower of Jesus from the town of Arimathea, came to Jerusalem. ⁵⁸Joseph went to Pilate and asked to have Jesus' body. So Pilate gave orders for the soldiers to give it to Joseph. ⁵⁹Then Joseph took the body and wrapped it in a clean linen cloth. ⁶⁰He put Jesus' body in a new tomb that he had cut out of a wall of rock, and he rolled a very large stone to block the entrance of the tomb. Then Joseph went away. ⁶¹Mary Magdalene and the other woman named Mary were sitting near the tomb.

THE TOMB OF JESUS IS GUARDED

⁶²The next day, the day after Preparation Day, the leading priests and the Pharisees went to Pilate. ⁶³They said, "Sir, we remember that while that liar was still alive he said, 'After three days I will rise from the dead.' ⁶⁴So give the order for the tomb to be guarded closely till the third day. Otherwise, his followers might come and steal the body and tell people that

27:24 washed his hands He did this as a sign to show that he wanted no part in what the people did. **27:34 gall** Probably a drink of wine mixed with drugs to help a person feel less pain. **27:35 clothes** Some Greek copies continue, "So what God said through the prophet came true, 'They divided my clothes among them, and they threw lots for my clothing.' " See Psalm 22:18. **27:51 curtain in the Temple** A curtain divided the Most Holy Place from the other part of the Temple. That was the special building in Jerusalem where God commanded the Jewish people to worship him.

he has risen from the dead. That lie would be even worse than the first one."

⁶⁵Pilate said, "Take some soldiers and go guard the tomb the best way you know." ⁶⁶So they all went to the tomb and made it safe from thieves by sealing the stone in the entrance and putting soldiers there to guard it.

JESUS RISES FROM THE DEAD

28 The day after the Sabbath day was the first day of the week. At dawn on the first day, Mary Magdalene and another woman named Mary went to look at the tomb.

²At that time there was a strong earthquake. An angel of the Lord came down from heaven, went to the tomb, and rolled the stone away from the entrance. Then he sat on the stone. ³He was shining as bright as lightning, and his clothes were white as snow. ⁴The soldiers guarding the tomb shook with fear because of the angel, and they became like dead men.

⁵The angel said to the women, "Don't be afraid. I know that you are looking for Jesus, who has been crucified. ⁶He is not here. He has risen from the dead as he said he would. Come and see the place where his body was. ⁷And go quickly and tell his followers, 'Jesus has risen from the dead. He is going into Galilee ahead of you, and you will see him there.' " Then the angel said, "Now I have told you."

⁸The women left the tomb quickly. They were afraid, but they were also very happy. They ran to tell Jesus' followers what had happened. ⁹Suddenly, Jesus met them and said, "Greetings." The women came up to him, took hold of his feet, and worshiped him. ¹⁰Then Jesus said to them, "Don't be afraid. Go and tell my followers to go on to Galilee, and they will see me there."

THE SOLDIERS REPORT TO THE LEADERS

¹¹While the women went to tell Jesus' followers, some of the soldiers who had been guarding the tomb went into the city to tell the leading priests everything that had happened. ¹²Then the priests met with the elders and made a plan. They paid the soldiers a large amount of money ¹³and said to them, "Tell the people that Jesus' followers came during the night and stole the body while you were asleep. ¹⁴If the governor hears about this, we will satisfy him and save you from trouble." ¹⁵So the soldiers kept the money and did as they were told. And that story is still spread among the people even today.

JESUS TALKS TO HIS FOLLOWERS

¹⁶The eleven followers went to Galilee to the mountain where Jesus had told them to go. ¹⁷On the mountain they saw Jesus and worshiped him, but some of them did not believe it was really Jesus. ¹⁸Then Jesus came to them and said, "All power in heaven and on earth is given to me. ¹⁹So go and make followers of all people in the world. Baptize them in the name of the Father and the Son and the Holy Spirit. ²⁰Teach them to obey everything that I have taught you, and I will be with you always, even until the end of this age."

Matthew 28:20

What a challenge! In Matthew 28:20, Jesus Christ tells his followers, "Teach them to obey everything that I have taught you, and I will be with you always, even until the end of this age." Fortunately, Jesus did all the hard work. He lived a perfect life, died in our place, and rose from the grave. Now he is asking those who believe in him to tell the world about him.

Okay, so you invited a friend to church, and he decided to join God's family, to become a Christian. Now what? Show him a new way to live. Helping your friend learn how to be a Christian is as easy as playing follow the leader. You follow Jesus, and your friend follows you.

You might be thinking, *What if I make a mistake?* No problem, you are not alone. Jesus is right there with you. He said he would be with us to the end. Show your friend what Jesus did by doing what Jesus did. If someone is sick, pray for that person. Be a friend to the friendless. Love your enemies. Give your life away to God and trust him for everything you need.

You aren't too young to lead your world. You can do it one friend at a time, and remember—Jesus is always with you!

Mark's is the earliest written account (Gospel) of Jesus.

It's short and to the point. It says Jesus is the Son of God and here's the proof: miracle after miracle—almost twenty of them—casting out demons, healing the sick, and raising the dead!

Mark skips over the first thirty years of Jesus' life and focuses on the few years between his baptism and his death and resurrection in Jerusalem.

His amazing miracles and powerful teaching made Jesus very popular with the people. That made him very *unpopular* with the religious rulers. They were jealous of his growing fame.

They couldn't stop him, so they decided to kill him. Jesus could have stopped their plans but he allowed them to kill him because it was part of God's plan. He explained to his followers that "the Son of Man did not come to be served. He came to serve others and to give his life as a ransom [payment for freedom] for many people" (Mark 10:45).

MARK

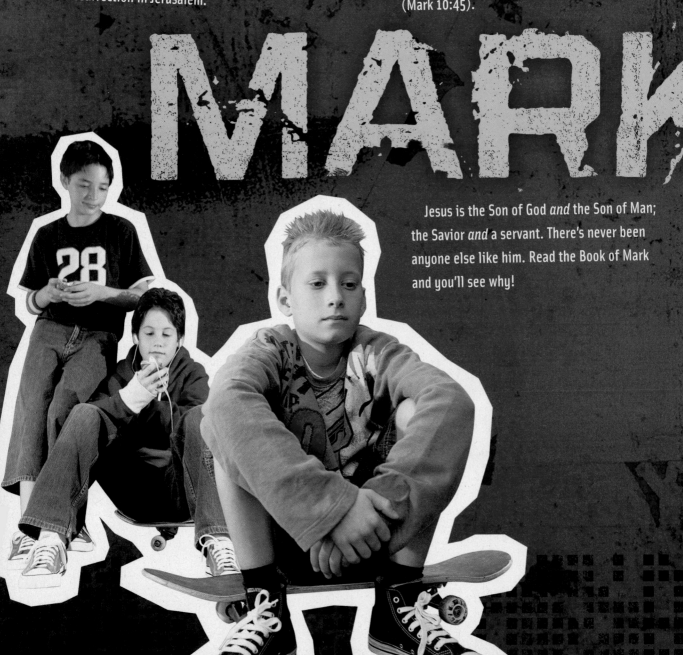

Jesus is the Son of God *and* the Son of Man; the Savior *and* a servant. There's never been anyone else like him. Read the Book of Mark and you'll see why!

JOHN PREPARES FOR JESUS

1 This is the beginning of the Good News about Jesus Christ, the Son of God,[n] [2]as the prophet Isaiah wrote:

"I will send my messenger ahead of you,
who will prepare your way."   *Malachi 3:1*

[3]"This is a voice of one
who calls out in the desert:
'Prepare the way for the Lord.
Make the road straight for him.'"

Isaiah 40:3

[4]John was baptizing people in the desert and preaching a baptism of changed hearts and lives for the forgiveness of sins. [5]All the people from Judea and Jerusalem were going out to him. They confessed their sins and were baptized by him in the Jordan River. [6]John wore clothes made from camel's hair, had a leather belt around his waist, and ate locusts and wild honey. [7]This is what John preached to the people: "There is one coming after me who is greater than I; I am not good enough even to kneel down and untie his sandals. [8]I baptize you with water, but he will baptize you with the Holy Spirit."

JESUS IS BAPTIZED

[9]At that time Jesus came from the town of Nazareth in Galilee and was baptized by John in the Jordan River. [10]Immediately, as Jesus was coming up out of the water, he saw heaven open. The Holy Spirit came down on him like a dove, [11]and a voice came from heaven: "You are my Son, whom I love, and I am very pleased with you."

[12]Then the Spirit sent Jesus into the desert. [13]He was in the desert forty days and was tempted by Satan. He was with the wild animals, and the angels came and took care of him.

JESUS CHOOSES SOME FOLLOWERS

[14]After John was put in prison, Jesus went into Galilee, preaching the Good News from God. [15]He said, "The right time has come. The kingdom of God is near. Change your hearts and lives and believe the Good News!"

[16]When Jesus was walking by Lake Galilee, he saw Simon[n] and his brother Andrew throwing a net into the lake because they were fishermen. [17]Jesus said to them, "Come follow me, and I will make you fish for people." [18]So Simon and Andrew immediately left their nets and followed him.

[19]Going a little farther, Jesus saw two more brothers, James and John, the sons of Zebedee. They were in a boat, mending their nets. [20]Jesus immediately called them, and they left their father in the boat with the hired workers and followed Jesus.

JESUS FORCES OUT AN EVIL SPIRIT

[21]Jesus and his followers went to Capernaum. On the Sabbath day he went to the synagogue and began to teach. [22]The people were amazed at his teaching, because he taught like a person who had authority, not like their teachers of the law. [23]Just then, a man was there in the synagogue who had an evil spirit in him. He shouted, [24]"Jesus of Nazareth! What do you want with us? Did you come to destroy us? I know who you are—God's Holy One!"

[25]Jesus commanded the evil spirit, "Be quiet! Come out of the man!" [26]The evil spirit shook the man violently, gave a loud cry, and then came out of him.

[27]The people were so amazed they asked each other, "What is happening here? This man is teaching something new, and with authority. He even gives commands to evil spirits, and they obey him." [28]And the news about Jesus spread quickly everywhere in the area of Galilee.

JESUS HEALS MANY PEOPLE

[29]As soon as Jesus and his followers left the synagogue, they went with James and John to the home of Simon[n] and Andrew. [30]Simon's mother-in-law was sick in bed with a fever, and the people told Jesus about her. [31]So Jesus went to her bed, took her hand, and helped her up. The fever left her, and she began serving them.

[32]That evening, after the sun went down, the people brought to Jesus all who were sick and had demons in them. [33]The whole town gathered at the door. [34]Jesus healed many who

Mark 1:12-13

Do you ever feel like no one understands you? Like you're all alone in the world?

Jesus knows exactly what you're going through. Why? Because when Jesus lived on this planet, God didn't keep him from going through hard times, having struggles, and being tempted. Like every human being, Jesus was tempted to sin.

The Bible tells us Jesus was tempted by Satan himself (Mark 1:12–13). You're only tempted in some ways, but Jesus experienced every temptation that exists. He can relate to you and to all people because he has been through all the hard things that come our way.

Feel lonely or misunderstood? Jesus understands. He knew what it was like to go for weeks in the desert all alone. Later, his followers were confused about who he was.

Have a problem with a relationship with a brother or sister? Jesus understands. His own brothers didn't believe in him. At one point, they thought he was out of his mind.

Jesus knows you perfectly and knows what you're going through. That's why he's such a wonderful Savior.

Talk to Jesus about everything you're facing. You won't surprise him, and he won't turn away from your call for help.

had different kinds of sicknesses, and he forced many demons to leave people. But he would not allow the demons to speak, because they knew who he was.

[35]Early the next morning, while it was still dark, Jesus woke and left the house. He went to a lonely place, where he prayed. [36]Simon and his friends went to look for Jesus. [37]When they found him, they said, "Everyone is looking for you!"

[38]Jesus answered, "We should go to other towns around here so I can preach there too. That is the reason I came." [39]So he went everywhere in Galilee, preaching in the synagogues and forcing out demons.

JESUS HEALS A SICK MAN

[40]A man with a skin disease came to Jesus. He fell to his knees and begged Jesus, "You can heal me if you will."

[41]Jesus felt sorry for the man, so he reached out his hand and touched him and said, "I will. Be healed!" [42]Immediately the disease left the man, and he was healed.

[43]Jesus told the man to go away at once, but he warned him strongly, [44]"Don't tell any-

one about this. But go and show yourself to the priest. And offer the gift Moses commanded for people who are made well." This will show the people what I have done." [45]The man left there, but he began to tell everyone that Jesus had healed him, and so he spread the news about Jesus. As a result, Jesus could not enter a town if people saw him. He stayed in places where nobody lived, but people came to him from everywhere.

JESUS HEALS A PARALYZED MAN

2 A few days later, when Jesus came back to Capernaum, the news spread that he was at home. [2]Many people gathered together so that there was no room in the house, not even outside the door. And Jesus was teaching them God's message. [3]Four people came, carrying a paralyzed man. [4]Since they could not get to Jesus because of the crowd, they dug a hole in the roof right above where he was speaking. When they got through, they lowered the mat with the paralyzed man on it. [5]When Jesus saw the faith of these people, he said to the paralyzed man, "Young man, your sins are forgiven."

[6]Some of the teachers of the law were sitting there, thinking to themselves, [7]"Why does this man say things like that? He is speaking as if he were God. Only God can forgive sins."

[8]Jesus knew immediately what these teachers of the law were thinking. So he said to them, "Why are you thinking these things? [9]Which is easier: to tell this paralyzed man, 'Your sins are forgiven,' or to tell him, 'Stand up. Take your mat and walk'? [10]But I will prove to you that the Son of Man has authority on earth to forgive sins." So Jesus said to the paralyzed man, [11]"I tell you, stand up, take your mat, and go home." [12]Immediately the paralyzed man stood up, took his mat, and walked out while everyone was watching him.

The people were amazed and praised God. They said, "We have never seen anything like this!"

[13]Jesus went to the lake again. The whole crowd followed him there, and he taught them. [14]While he was walking along, he saw a man named Levi son of Alphaeus, sitting in the tax collector's booth. Jesus said to him, "Follow me," and he stood up and followed Jesus.

[15]Later, as Jesus was having dinner at Levi's house, many tax collectors and "sinners" were eating there with Jesus and his followers. Many people like this followed Jesus. [16]When the teachers of the law who were Pharisees saw Jesus eating with the tax collectors and

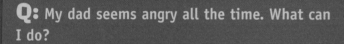

Q: Is heaven going to be like sitting in church all day long?

A: No; heaven is going to be more exciting than doing the thing you love best in the whole world. Your body and mind will be perfect. You and millions of other believers will get to see the God of the universe. And you will no longer be tempted to do wrong. Paul talks of a glimpse of heaven that was so incredibly good that he couldn't describe it (2 Corinthians 12:1–4).

Q: My dad seems angry all the time. What can I do?

A: Your dad may have stress at work or from something else that is making life tough for him. Before you do anything, pray for him. Ask God to help his situation and his reaction to it. Then go talk to your dad privately. Tell him you care about him and ask if there's anything you can do to help him. He may not want to admit to being angry, but knowing somebody appreciates him will help a lot.

Q: Why does my mom say it's so important to go outdoors?

A: So you don't turn into a slug! You probably need less time in front of the TV and more exercise. God created the whole outdoors so that we would see it and give him praise. It is good to get outside and take a look at God's amazing creation every once in a while.

"sinners," they asked his followers, "Why does he eat with tax collectors and sinners?"

[17]Jesus heard this and said to them, "It is not the healthy people who need a doctor, but the sick. I did not come to invite good people but to invite sinners."

JESUS' FOLLOWERS ARE CRITICIZED

[18]Now the followers of John[n] and the Pharisees often fasted[n] for a certain time. Some people came to Jesus and said, "Why do John's followers and the followers of the Pharisees often fast, but your followers don't?"

[19]Jesus answered, "The friends of the bridegroom do not fast while the bridegroom is still with them. As long as the bridegroom is with them, they cannot fast. [20]But the time will come when the bridegroom will be taken from them, and then they will fast.

[21]"No one sews a patch of unshrunk cloth over a hole in an old coat. Otherwise, the patch will shrink and pull away—the new patch will pull away from the old coat. Then the hole will be worse. [22]Also, no one ever pours new wine into old leather bags. Otherwise, the new wine will break the bags, and the wine will be ruined along with the bags. But new wine should be put into new leather bags."

JESUS IS LORD OF THE SABBATH

[23]One Sabbath day, as Jesus was walking through some fields of grain, his followers began to pick some grain to eat. [24]The Pharisees said to Jesus, "Why are your followers doing what is not lawful on the Sabbath day?"

[25]Jesus answered, "Have you never read what David did when he and those with him were hungry and needed food? [26]During the time of Abiathar the high priest, David went into God's house and ate the holy bread, which is lawful only for priests to eat. And David also gave some of the bread to those who were with him."

[27]Then Jesus said to the Pharisees, "The Sabbath day was made to help people; they were not made to be ruled by the Sabbath day. [28]So then, the Son of Man is Lord even of the Sabbath day."

JESUS HEALS A MAN'S HAND

3 Another time when Jesus went into a synagogue, a man with a crippled hand was there. [2]Some people watched Jesus closely to see if he would heal the man on the Sabbath day so they could accuse him.

[3]Jesus said to the man with the crippled hand, "Stand up here in the middle of everyone."

[4]Then Jesus asked the people, "Which is lawful on the Sabbath day: to do good or to do evil, to save a life or to kill?" But they said nothing to answer him.

[5]Jesus was angry as he looked at the people, and he felt very sad because they were stubborn. Then he said to the man, "Hold out your hand." The man held out his hand and it was healed. [6]Then the Pharisees left and began making plans with the Herodians[n] about a way to kill Jesus.

MANY PEOPLE FOLLOW JESUS

[7]Jesus left with his followers for the lake, and a large crowd from Galilee followed him. [8]Also many people came from Judea, from Jerusalem, from Idumea, from the lands across the Jordan River, and from the area of Tyre and Sidon. When they heard what Jesus was doing, many people came to him. [9]When Jesus saw the crowds, he told his followers to get a boat ready for him to keep people from crowding against him. [10]He had healed many people, so all the sick were pushing toward him to touch him. [11]When evil spirits saw Jesus, they fell down before him and shouted, "You are the Son of God!" [12]But Jesus strongly warned them not to tell who he was.

JESUS CHOOSES HIS TWELVE APOSTLES

[13]Then Jesus went up on a mountain and called to him those he wanted, and they came to him. [14]Jesus chose twelve and called them apostles.[n] He wanted them to be with him, and he wanted to send them out to preach [15]and to have the authority to force demons out of people. [16]These are the twelve men he chose: Simon (Jesus named him Peter), [17]James and John, the sons of Zebedee (Jesus named them Boanerges, which means "Sons of Thunder"), [18]Andrew, Philip, Bartholomew, Matthew, Thomas, James the son of Alphaeus, Thaddaeus, Simon the Zealot, [19]and Judas Iscariot, who later turned against Jesus.

SOME PEOPLE SAY JESUS HAS A DEVIL

[20]Then Jesus went home, but again a crowd gathered. There were so many people that Jesus and his followers could not eat. [21]When his family heard this, they went to get him because they thought he was out of his mind. [22]But the teachers of the law from Jerusalem were saying, "Beelzebul is living inside him! He uses power from the ruler of demons to force demons out of people."

[23]So Jesus called the people together and taught them with stories. He said, "Satan will

"MAKE A DIFFERENCE"

Losing stinks like the towel they use to wipe sweat off a basketball court. Doesn't God listen when you pray for a win before every game? Maybe God answers our prayers about winning a little differently than we ask because he has a different idea about what it means to "win." Sometimes God uses our losses to make a difference in the lives of our friends.

Meet Josh. After losing six games in a row, Josh found that the guys on his fifth grade Boys and Girls Club team were a lot less cocky. When they sat together at lunch they were forced by their losses to talk about more than sports.

Josh was able to turn the conversation to the fact that there is more to life than basketball. He was able to share Jesus Christ with friends who wouldn't have been as interested if their team had been winning.

Often when the losses are piling up, players are more open and honest. That's a perfect time to open your mouth and watch God make a difference—watch him turn losing into winning.

2:18 John John the Baptist, who preached to the Jewish people about Christ's coming (Mark 1:4–8).   **2:18 fasted** The people would give up eating for a special time of prayer and worship to God. It was also done to show sadness and disappointment.   **3:6 Herodians** A political group that followed Herod and his family.   **3:14 and called them apostles** Some Greek copies do not have this phrase.

COOL!

Shocking!

The electric eel (*Electrophorus electricus*) is the most shocking animal on Earth. The South American variety can grow to be ten feet long and give off 650 volts—more than enough to stun large prey, including humans!

The electric eel produces and stores electricity like a battery does. The eel has two opposite poles—its head and its tail—and voltage can flow from either end to the other.

God sure is creative—he must have gotten a *charge* out of making these shocking creatures!

---

not force himself out of people. ²⁴A kingdom that is divided cannot continue, ²⁵and a family that is divided cannot continue. ²⁶And if Satan is against himself and fights against his own people, he cannot continue; that is the end of Satan. ²⁷No one can enter a strong person's house and steal his things unless he first ties up the strong person. Then he can steal things from the house. ²⁸I tell you the truth, all sins that people do and all the things people say against God can be forgiven. ²⁹But anyone who speaks against the Holy Spirit will never be forgiven; he is guilty of a sin that continues forever."

³⁰Jesus said this because the teachers of the law said that he had an evil spirit inside him.

JESUS' TRUE FAMILY

³¹Then Jesus' mother and brothers arrived. Standing outside, they sent someone in to tell him to come out. ³²Many people were sitting around Jesus, and they said to him, "Your mother and brothers* are waiting for you outside."

³³Jesus asked, "Who are my mother and my brothers?" ³⁴Then he looked at those sitting around him and said, "Here are my mother and my brothers! ³⁵My true brother and sister and mother are those who do what God wants."

A STORY ABOUT PLANTING SEED

4 Again Jesus began teaching by the lake. A great crowd gathered around him, so he sat down in a boat near the shore. All the people stayed on the shore close to the water. ²Jesus taught them many things, using stories. He said, ³"Listen! A farmer went out to plant his seed. ⁴While he was planting, some seed fell by the road, and the birds came and ate it up. ⁵Some seed fell on rocky ground where there wasn't much dirt. That seed grew very fast, because the ground was not deep. ⁶But when the sun rose, the plants dried up because they did not have deep roots. ⁷Some other seed fell among thorny weeds, which grew and choked the good plants. So those plants did not produce a crop. ⁸Some other seed fell on good ground and began to grow. It got taller and produced a crop. Some plants made thirty times more, some made sixty times more, and some made a hundred times more."

⁹Then Jesus said, "Let those with ears use them and listen!"

JESUS TELLS WHY HE USED STORIES

¹⁰Later, when Jesus was alone, the twelve apostles and others around him asked him about the stories.

¹¹Jesus said, "You can know the secret about the kingdom of God. But to other people I tell everything by using stories ¹²so that:
'They will look and look, but they will not learn.
They will listen and listen, but they will not understand.

YOU SPEAK OUT!

Q: What does it mean to be a Christian?
A: "You have God in your heart and you tell other people about him." (Jonathan, 12)

Q: How do you deal with being angry?
A: "Usually I lie on my bed until somebody brings me food or tells me to buck up and clean my room, or until I just calm down." (Matthew, 11)

Q: What is the best part of being a Christian?
A: "Knowing that God is with me wherever I go." (Jon, 12)

 3:32 brothers Some Greek copies continue, "and sisters."

If they did learn and understand,
they would come back to me and be
forgiven.' "   Isaiah 6:9–10

JESUS EXPLAINS THE SEED STORY

[13]Then Jesus said to his followers, "Don't you understand this story? If you don't, how will you understand any story? [14]The farmer is like a person who plants God's message in people. [15]Sometimes the teaching falls on the road. This is like the people who hear the teaching of God, but Satan quickly comes and takes away the teaching that was planted in them. [16]Others are like the seed planted on rocky ground. They hear the teaching and quickly accept it with joy. [17]But since they don't allow the teaching to go deep into their lives, they keep it only a short time. When trouble or persecution comes because of the teaching they accepted, they quickly give up. [18]Others are like the seed planted among the thorny weeds. They hear the teaching, [19]but the worries of this life, the temptation of wealth, and many other evil desires keep the teaching from growing and producing fruit* in their lives. [20]Others are like the seed planted in the good ground. They hear the teaching and accept it. Then they grow and produce fruit—sometimes thirty times more, sometimes sixty times more, and sometimes a hundred times more."

USE WHAT YOU HAVE

[21]Then Jesus said to them, "Do you hide a lamp under a bowl or under a bed? No! You put the lamp on a lampstand. [22]Everything that is hidden will be made clear and every secret thing will be made known. [23]Let those with ears use them and listen!

[24]"Think carefully about what you hear. The way you give to others is the way God will give to you, but God will give you even more. [25]Those who have understanding will be given more. But those who do not have understanding, even what they have will be taken away from them."

39% of kids say Chinese is their favorite kind of food.

Center for Culinary Development. "Tween peeks."

JESUS USES A STORY ABOUT SEED

[26]Then Jesus said, "The kingdom of God is like someone who plants seed in the ground. [27]Night and day, whether the person is asleep or awake, the seed still grows, but the person does not know how it grows. [28]By itself the earth produces grain. First the plant grows, then the head, and then all the grain in the head. [29]When the grain is ready, the farmer cuts it, because this is the harvest time."

A STORY ABOUT MUSTARD SEED

[30]Then Jesus said, "How can I show you what the kingdom of God is like? What story can I use to explain it? [31]The kingdom of God is like a mustard seed, the smallest seed you plant in the ground. [32]But when planted, this seed grows and becomes the largest of all garden plants. It produces large branches, and the wild birds can make nests in its shade."

[33]Jesus used many stories like these to teach the crowd God's message—as much as they could understand. [34]He always used stories to teach them. But when he and his followers were alone, Jesus explained everything to them.

JESUS CALMS A STORM

[35]That evening, Jesus said to his followers, "Let's go across the lake." [36]Leaving the crowd behind, they took him in the boat just as he was. There were also other boats with them. [37]A very strong wind came up on the lake. The waves came over the sides and into the boat so that it

BIBLE SUPERHEROES

Rahab
See Joshua 2; 6.

Here's an Old Testament "rags to riches" story for you: Rahab went from being a prostitute to marrying into the family of God's people. She went on to become the great-grandmother of King David and the great-great- (times some!) grandmother of Jesus Christ (Matthew 1:5).

How did she manage this change? Faith. Faith is simply "belief that obeys." She believed that God was stronger than the walls of her city, so she hid two Jewish spies and helped them escape (read more about her faith in Hebrews 11:31).

Rahab lied to protect the spies. *Isn't that a sin?* you might wonder. Lying is never right, but in this special case, it wasn't a sin. It was necessary to save the men.

When it came to choosing sides, Rahab made the right choice.

⭐ **4:19 producing fruit** To produce fruit means to have in your life the good things God wants.

was already full of water. [38] Jesus was at the back of the boat, sleeping with his head on a cushion. His followers woke him and said, "Teacher, don't you care that we are drowning!"

[39] Jesus stood up and commanded the wind and said to the waves, "Quiet! Be still!" Then the wind stopped, and it became completely calm.

[40] Jesus said to his followers, "Why are you afraid? Do you still have no faith?"

[41] The followers were very afraid and asked each other, "Who is this? Even the wind and the waves obey him!"

A MAN WITH DEMONS INSIDE HIM

5 Jesus and his followers went to the other side of the lake to the area of the Gerasene[n] people. [2] When Jesus got out of the boat, instantly a man with an evil spirit came to him from the burial caves. [3] This man lived in the caves, and no one could tie him up, not even with a chain. [4] Many times peo-ple had used chains to tie the man's hands and feet, but he always broke them off. No one was strong enough to control him. [5] Day and night he would wander around the burial caves and on the hills, screaming and cutting himself with stones. [6] While Jesus was still far away, the man saw him, ran to him, and fell down before him.

[7] The man shouted in a loud voice, "What do you want with me, Jesus, Son of the Most High God? I command you in God's name not to torture me!" [8] He said this because Jesus was saying to him, "You evil spirit, come out of the man."

[9] Then Jesus asked him, "What is your name?"

He answered, "My name is Legion," be-cause we are many spirits." [10] He begged Jesus again and again not to send them out of that area.

[11] A large herd of pigs was feeding on a hill near there. [12] The demons begged Jesus, "Send us into the pigs; let us go into them." [13] So Jesus allowed them to do this. The evil spirits left the man and went into the pigs. Then the herd of pigs—about two thousand of them—rushed down the hill into the lake and were drowned.

[14] The herdsmen ran away and went to the town and to the countryside, telling everyone about this. So people went out to see what had happened. [15] They came to Jesus and saw the man who used to have the many evil spir-its, sitting, clothed, and in his right mind. And they were frightened. [16] The people who saw this told the others what had happened to the man who had the demons living in him, and they told about the pigs. [17] Then the people began to beg Jesus to leave their area.

[18] As Jesus was getting back into the boat, the man who was freed from the demons begged to go with him.

[19] But Jesus would not let him. He said, "Go home to your family and tell them how much the Lord has done for you and how he has had mercy on you." [20] So the man left and began to tell the people in the Ten Towns" about what Jesus had done for him. And everyone was amazed.

JESUS GIVES LIFE TO A DEAD GIRL AND HEALS A SICK WOMAN

[21] When Jesus went in the boat back to the other side of the lake, a large crowd gathered around him there. [22] A leader of the synagogue, named Jairus, came there, saw Jesus, and fell at his feet. [23] He begged Jesus, saying again and again, "My daughter is dying. Please come and put your hands on her so she will be healed and will live." [24] So Jesus went with him.

Things to Do at Church

1. Greet people before the service.

2. Pick up trash after the service.

3. Sing joyfully!

4. Draw a picture about the sermon while you're lis-tening.

5. Help out with younger kids' Sunday school classes.

6. Shoot baskets in the gym.

7. Pass out bulletins.

8. Be an usher or help with communion.

9. Sit with your friends (but don't whisper!)

10. Help older people back to their cars.

A large crowd followed Jesus and pushed very close around him. [25] Among them was a woman who had been bleeding for twelve years. [26] She had suffered very much from many doctors and had spent all the money she had, but instead of improving, she was getting worse. [27] When the woman heard about Jesus, she came up behind him in the crowd and touched his coat. [28] She thought, "If I can just touch his clothes, I will be healed." [29] Instantly her bleeding stopped, and she felt in her body that she was healed from her disease.

[30] At once Jesus felt power go out from him. So he turned around in the crowd and asked, "Who touched my clothes?"

[31] His followers said, "Look at how many people are pushing against you! And you ask, 'Who touched me?'"

[32] But Jesus continued looking around to see who had touched him. [33] The woman, knowing that she was healed, came and fell at Jesus' feet. Shaking with fear, she told him the

RESURRECTION (EASTER)

When you were younger, did you search for Easter eggs in your backyard? Many people "cele-brate" Easter without knowing what it's about! Easter is a Christian hol-iday that was first celebrated on the day that Jesus came back to life. His followers were amazed to see that Jesus was alive!

Every year, Christians around the world take time to remember the *Resurrection* (Jesus' victory over death when he came back to life). If he had stayed dead, we would have no hope. Jesus' rising from the dead is definitely reason to celebrate Easter each spring.

Jesus' rising from death was a huge show of God's power—the same power that will raise *us* from the dead when Jesus comes again!

⭐ **5:1 Gerasene** From Gerasa, an area southeast of Lake Galilee. The exact location is uncertain and some Greek copies read "Gergesene"; others read "Gadarene." **5:9 Legion** Means very many. A legion was about five thousand men in the Roman army. **5:20 Ten Towns** In Greek, called "Decapolis." It was an area east of Lake Galilee that once had ten main towns.

whole truth. [34]Jesus said to her, "Dear woman, you are made well because you believed. Go in peace; be healed of your disease."

[35]While Jesus was still speaking, some people came from the house of the synagogue leader. They said, "Your daughter is dead. There is no need to bother the teacher anymore."

[36]But Jesus paid no attention to what they said. He told the synagogue leader, "Don't be afraid; just believe."

[37]Jesus let only Peter, James, and John the brother of James go with him. [38]When they came to the house of the synagogue leader, Jesus found many people there making lots of noise and crying loudly. [39]Jesus entered the house and said to them, "Why are you crying and making so much noise? The child is not dead, only asleep." [40]But they laughed at him. So, after throwing them out of the house, Jesus took the child's father and mother and his three followers into the room where the child was. [41]Taking hold of the girl's hand, he said to her, "Talitha, koum!" (This means, "Young girl, I tell you to stand up!") [42]At once the girl stood right up and began walking. (She was twelve years old.) Everyone was completely amazed. [43]Jesus gave them strict orders not to tell people about this. Then he told them to give the girl something to eat.

JESUS GOES TO HIS HOMETOWN

6 Jesus left there and went to his hometown, and his followers went with him. [2]On the Sabbath day he taught in the synagogue. Many people heard him and were amazed, saying, "Where did this man get these teachings? What is this wisdom that has been given to him? And where did he get the power to do miracles? [3]He is just the carpenter, the son of Mary and the brother of James, Joseph, Judas, and Simon. And his sisters are here with us." So the people were upset with Jesus.

[4]Jesus said to them, "A prophet is honored everywhere except in his hometown and with his own people and in his own home." [5]So Jesus was not able to work any miracles there except to heal a few sick people by putting his hands on them. [6]He was amazed at how many people had no faith.

Then Jesus went to other villages in that area and taught. [7]He called his twelve followers together and got ready to send them out two by two and gave them authority over evil spirits. [8]This is what Jesus commanded them: "Take nothing for your trip except a walking stick. Take no bread, no bag, and no money in your pockets. [9]Wear sandals, but take only the clothes you are wearing. [10]When you enter a house, stay there until you leave that town. [11]If the people in a certain place refuse to welcome you or listen to you, leave that place. Shake its dust off your feet" as a warning to them."[n]

[12]So the followers went out and preached that people should change their hearts and lives. [13]They forced many demons out and put olive oil on many sick people and healed them.

HOW JOHN THE BAPTIST WAS KILLED

[14]King Herod heard about Jesus, because he was now well known. Some people said,[n] "He is John the Baptist, who has risen from the dead. That is why he can work these miracles."

[15]Others said, "He is Elijah."[n]

Other people said, "Jesus is a prophet, like the prophets who lived long ago."

[16]When Herod heard this, he said, "I killed John by cutting off his head. Now he has risen from the dead!"

[17]Herod himself had ordered his soldiers to arrest John and put him in prison in order to please his wife, Herodias. She had been the wife of Philip, Herod's brother, but then Herod had married her. [18]John had been telling Herod, "It is not lawful for you to be married to your brother's wife." [19]So Herodias hated John and wanted to kill him. But she couldn't, [20]because Herod was afraid of John and protected him. He knew John was a good and holy man. Also, though John's preaching always bothered him, he enjoyed listening to John.

[21]Then the perfect time came for Herodias to cause John's death. On Herod's birthday, he gave a dinner party for the most important government leaders, the commanders of his army, and the most important people in Galilee. [22]When the daughter of Herodias[n] came in and danced, she pleased Herod and the people eating with him.

So King Herod said to the girl, "Ask me for anything you want, and I will give it to you." [23]He promised her, "Anything you ask for I will give to you—up to half of my kingdom."

ROCK SOLID

Mark 5:36

Are you afraid to die? If so, have you ever asked yourself why? Is it the unknown? Or is it the fear of losing everything you have? It's not something many people think about unless they are terminally sick or skydiving with a sticky parachute!

But if you are a believer in Jesus Christ, and you know heaven awaits you, what's to be afraid of? As Jesus said, "Don't be afraid; just believe" (Mark 5:36). Those were his words to a religious leader whose twelve-year-old daughter had just died. What was more thrilling for that girl? Coming back to life? Or, years later, going to be with Jesus in heaven?

There's nothing wrong with wanting to live the longest life on earth that you can. But if we aren't excited about our eternal life in heaven, we must not be clear on what's in store.

Just think of the best vacation you can imagine. Now multiply that by a million and stretch it out forever. That's heaven! No pain. No death. No loss. Beauty. That's what we should be longing for!

So live your life to the fullest, but don't be so down on death.

6:11 Shake . . . feet A warning. It showed that they were rejecting these people.   **6:11 them** Some Greek copies continue, "I tell you the truth, on the Judgment Day it will be better for the towns of Sodom and Gomorrah than for the people of that town." See Matthew 10:15.   **6:14 Some people said** Some Greek copies read "He said."   **6:15 Elijah** A great prophet who spoke for God and who lived hundreds of years before Christ. See 1 Kings 17.   **6:22 When . . . Herodias** Some Greek copies read "When his daughter Herodias."

COOL!

You Are What You Spend For

Did you know that twenty-five million buyers between the ages of 8 and 13 represent a $335 billion market: their own money and the money their parents spend on them. What do they purchase? These are their top priorities according to "What a Tween Wants. . . Now: Market Research Experts Reveal What's New with This Important Demographic" by Erin E. Clack.

★ Clothes
★ Shoes and sneakers
★ Entertainment
★ Room decor and furniture
★ Makeup
★ Educational stuff (computer software, etc.)

Seventy-two percent of their buying decisions are made with the help of a parent. Twenty percent are made by the parent and 8 percent by the young buyer. Remember, how you spend money shows what's important to you. Every penny you have comes from God, so be sure to give him back some!

---

²⁴The girl went to her mother and asked, "What should I ask for?"

Her mother answered, "Ask for the head of John the Baptist."

²⁵At once the girl went back to the king and said to him, "I want the head of John the Baptist right now on a platter."

²⁶Although the king was very sad, he had made a promise, and his dinner guests had heard it. So he did not want to refuse what she asked. ²⁷Immediately the king sent a soldier to bring John's head. The soldier went and cut off John's head in the prison ²⁸and brought it back on a platter. He gave it to the girl, and the girl gave it to her mother. ²⁹When John's followers heard this, they came and got John's body and put it in a tomb.

MORE THAN FIVE THOUSAND FED

³⁰The apostles gathered around Jesus and told him about all the things they had done and taught. ³¹Crowds of people were coming and going so that Jesus and his followers did not even have time to eat. He said to them, "Come away by yourselves, and we will go to a lonely place to get some rest."

³²So they went in a boat by themselves to a lonely place. ³³But many people saw them leave and recognized them. So from all the towns they ran to the place where Jesus was going, and they got there before him. ³⁴When he arrived, he saw a great crowd waiting. He felt sorry for them, because they were like sheep without a shepherd. So he began to teach them many things.

³⁵When it was late in the day, his followers came to him and said, "No one lives in this place, and it is already very late. ³⁶Send the people away so they can go to the countryside and towns around here to buy themselves something to eat."

³⁷But Jesus answered, "You give them something to eat."

They said to him, "We would all have to work a month to earn enough money to buy that much bread!"

³⁸Jesus asked them, "How many loaves of bread do you have? Go and see."

When they found out, they said, "Five loaves and two fish."

³⁹Then Jesus told his followers to have the people sit in groups on the green grass. ⁴⁰So they sat in groups of fifty or a hundred. ⁴¹Jesus took the five loaves and two fish and, looking up to heaven, he thanked God for the food. He divided the bread and gave it to his followers for them to give to the people. Then he divided the two fish among them all. ⁴²All the people ate and were satisfied. ⁴³The followers filled twelve baskets with the leftover pieces of bread and fish. ⁴⁴There were five thousand men who ate.

JESUS WALKS ON THE WATER

⁴⁵Immediately Jesus told his followers to get into the boat and go ahead of him to Beth-

DID YOU KNOW?

There are over 312 million boys in the world!

U.S. Census Bureau. World population statistics.

saida across the lake. He stayed there to send the people home. [46]After sending them away, he went into the hills to pray.

[47]That night, the boat was in the middle of the lake, and Jesus was alone on the land. [48]He saw his followers struggling hard to row the boat, because the wind was blowing against them. Between three and six o'clock in the morning, Jesus came to them, walking on the water, and he wanted to walk past the boat. [49]But when they saw him walking on the water, they thought he was a ghost and cried out. [50]They all saw him and were afraid. But quickly Jesus spoke to them and said, "Have courage! It is I. Do not be afraid." [51]Then he got into the boat with them, and the wind became calm. The followers were greatly amazed. [52]They did not understand about the miracle of the five loaves, because their minds were closed.

[53]When they had crossed the lake, they came to shore at Gennesaret and tied the boat there. [54]When they got out of the boat, people immediately recognized Jesus. [55]They ran everywhere in that area and began to bring sick people on mats wherever they heard he was. [56]And everywhere he went—into towns, cities, or countryside—the people brought the sick to the marketplaces. They begged him to let them touch just the edge of his coat, and all who touched it were healed.

OBEY GOD'S LAW

7 When some Pharisees and some teachers of the law came from Jerusalem, they gathered around Jesus. [2]They saw that some of Jesus' followers ate food with hands that were not clean, that is, they hadn't washed them. [3](The Pharisees and all the Jews never eat before washing their hands in the way required by their unwritten laws. [4]And when they buy something in the market, they never eat it until they wash themselves in a special way. They also follow many other unwritten laws, such as the washing of cups, pitchers, and pots.")

[5]The Pharisees and the teachers of the law said to Jesus, "Why don't your followers obey the unwritten laws which have been handed down to us? Why do your followers eat their food with hands that are not clean?"

[6]Jesus answered, "Isaiah was right when he spoke about you hypocrites. He wrote,

'These people show honor to me with words,
    but their hearts are far from me.
[7]Their worship of me is worthless.
    The things they teach are nothing but
      human rules.'   *Isaiah 29:13*

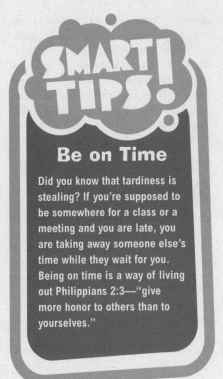

SMART TIPS!

Be on Time

Did you know that tardiness is stealing? If you're supposed to be somewhere for a class or a meeting and you are late, you are taking away someone else's time while they wait for you. Being on time is a way of living out Philippians 2:3—"give more honor to others than to yourselves."

[8]You have stopped following the commands of God, and you follow only human teachings."[n]

[9]Then Jesus said to them, "You cleverly ignore the commands of God so you can follow your own teachings. [10]Moses said, 'Honor your father and your mother,'[n] and 'Anyone who says cruel things to his father or mother must be put to death.'[n] [11]But you say a person can tell his father or mother, 'I have something I could use to help you, but it is Corban—a gift to God.' [12]You no longer let that person use that money for his father or his mother. [13]By your own rules, which you teach people, you are rejecting what God said. And you do many things like that."

[14]After Jesus called the crowd to him again, he said, "Every person should listen to me and understand what I am saying. [15]There is nothing people put into their bodies that makes them unclean. People are made unclean by the things that come out of them. [[16]Let those with ears use them and listen.]"[n]

[17]When Jesus left the people and went into the house, his followers asked him about this story. [18]Jesus said, "Do you still not understand? Surely you know that nothing that enters someone from the outside can make that person unclean. [19]It does not go into the mind, but into the stomach. Then it goes out of the body." (When Jesus said this, he meant that no longer was any food unclean for people to eat.)

[20]And Jesus said, "The things that come out of people are the things that make them unclean. [21]All these evil things begin inside people, in the mind: evil thoughts, sexual sins, stealing, murder, adultery, [22]greed, evil actions, lying, doing sinful things, jealousy, speaking evil of others, pride, and foolish living. [23]All these evil things come from inside and make people unclean."

JESUS HELPS A NON-JEWISH WOMAN

[24]Jesus left that place and went to the area around Tyre.[n] When he went into a house, he

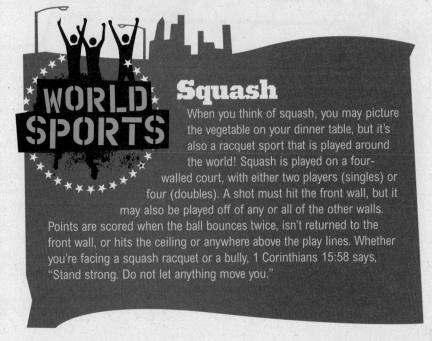

WORLD SPORTS

Squash

When you think of squash, you may picture the vegetable on your dinner table, but it's also a racquet sport that is played around the world! Squash is played on a four-walled court, with either two players (singles) or four (doubles). A shot must hit the front wall, but it may also be played off of any or all of the other walls. Points are scored when the ball bounces twice, isn't returned to the front wall, or hits the ceiling or anywhere above the play lines. Whether you're facing a squash racquet or a bully, 1 Corinthians 15:58 says, "Stand strong. Do not let anything move you."

7:4 pots Some Greek copies continue, "and dining couches."   **7:8 teachings** Some Greek copies continue, "You wash pitchers and jugs and do many other such things."   **7:10 'Honor . . . mother.'** Quotation from Exodus 20:12; Deuteronomy 5:16.   **7:10 'Anyone . . . death.'** Quotation from Exodus 21:17.   **7:16 Let . . . listen.** Some Greek copies do not contain the bracketed text.   **7:24 Tyre** Some Greek copies continue, "and Sidon."

did not want anyone to know he was there, but he could not stay hidden. [25]A woman whose daughter had an evil spirit in her heard that he was there. So she quickly came to Jesus and fell at his feet. [26]She was Greek, born in Phoenicia, in Syria. She begged Jesus to force the demon out of her daughter.

[27]Jesus told the woman, "It is not right to take the children's bread and give it to the dogs. First let the children eat all they want."

[28]But she answered, "Yes, Lord, but even the dogs under the table can eat the children's crumbs."

[29]Then Jesus said, "Because of your answer, you may go. The demon has left your daughter."

[30]The woman went home and found her daughter lying in bed; the demon was gone.

JESUS HEALS A DEAF MAN

[31]Then Jesus left the area around Tyre and went through Sidon to Lake Galilee, to the area of the Ten Towns.[n] [32]While he was there, some people brought a man to him who was deaf and could not talk plainly. The people begged Jesus to put his hand on the man to heal him.

[33]Jesus led the man away from the crowd, by himself. He put his fingers in the man's ears and then spit and touched the man's tongue. [34]Looking up to heaven, he sighed and said to the man, "Ephphatha!" (This means, "Be opened.") [35]Instantly the man was able to hear and to use his tongue so that he spoke clearly.

[36]Jesus commanded the people not to tell anyone about what happened. But the more he commanded them, the more they told about it. [37]They were completely amazed and said, "Jesus does everything well. He makes the deaf hear! And those who can't talk he makes able to speak."

MORE THAN FOUR THOUSAND PEOPLE FED

8 Another time there was a great crowd with Jesus that had nothing to eat. So Jesus called his followers and said, [2]"I feel sorry for these people, because they have already been with me for three days, and they have nothing to eat. [3]If I send them home hungry, they will faint on the way. Some of them live a long way from here."

[4]Jesus' followers answered, "How can we get enough bread to feed all these people? We are far away from any town."

[5]Jesus asked, "How many loaves of bread do you have?"

They answered, "Seven."

[6]Jesus told the people to sit on the ground. Then he took the seven loaves, gave thanks to God, and divided the bread. He gave the pieces to his followers to give to the people, and they did so. [7]The followers also had a few small fish. After Jesus gave thanks for the fish, he told his followers to give them to the people also. [8]All the people ate and were satisfied. Then his followers filled seven baskets with the leftover pieces of food. [9]There were about four thousand people who ate. After they had eaten, Jesus sent them home. [10]Then right away he got into a boat with his followers and went to the area of Dalmanutha.

THE LEADERS ASK FOR A MIRACLE

[11]The Pharisees came to Jesus and began to ask him questions. Hoping to trap him, they asked Jesus for a miracle from God. [12]Jesus sighed deeply and said, "Why do you people ask for a miracle as a sign? I tell you the truth, no sign will be given to you." [13]Then Jesus left the Pharisees and went in the boat to the other side of the lake.

GUARD AGAINST WRONG TEACHINGS

[14]His followers had only one loaf of bread with them in the boat; they had forgotten to bring more. [15]Jesus warned them, "Be careful! Beware of the yeast of the Pharisees and the yeast of Herod."

[16]His followers discussed the meaning of this, saying, "He said this because we have no bread."

[17]Knowing what they were talking about, Jesus asked them, "Why are you talking about not having bread? Do you still not see or understand? Are your minds closed? [18]You have

trustables

Mark 9:41

If you've ever watched a marathon, you know how important water is to runners. At every mile, a crowd of people stands holding cups of water in their outstretched arms. Runners take the cups in stride, downing half of it and dumping the rest over their heads. They toss the cups into the gutter and press on toward the finish line. The runners don't know these people. They're just strangers offering support and much-needed thirst quenching. They don't even expect a "thank you" or any kind of payment. Just doing it is reward enough.

There's a lesson taught in the Bible that talks about such gestures. Mark 9:41 says, "Whoever gives you a drink of water because you belong to the Christ will truly get his reward." Of course, a cup of water is just one example. It could be anything kind, compassionate, or giving: Making friends with the unpopular kids at school. Helping an elderly neighbor with yard work. Volunteering for a charity.

Don't worry about getting a "thank-you" or any kind of payment when you do these things. That's not the point. The point is seeing a need and meeting it. God is watching and keeping track. And someday when you reach the finish line of your life, your reward will be waiting.

7:31 Ten Towns In Greek, called "Decapolis." It was an area east of Lake Galilee that once had ten main towns.

JUST LEAVE ME ALONE!

Peter felt like all he did was work to make his parents and other people happy. He was tired and convinced that people were just using him. He wanted to scream, "Just leave me alone!"

Whenever you feel used or empty, check out what God has done for you by reading his Word. Peter did that, and the joy he got filled him back up—and made him want to keep doing good. The Bible tells us to "never become tired of doing good" (2 Thessalonians 3:13).

eyes, but you don't really see. You have ears, but you don't really listen. Remember when [19]I divided five loaves of bread for the five thousand? How many baskets did you fill with leftover pieces of food?"

They answered, "Twelve."

[20]"And when I divided seven loaves of bread for the four thousand, how many baskets did you fill with leftover pieces of food?"

They answered, "Seven."

[21]Then Jesus said to them, "Don't you understand yet?"

JESUS HEALS A BLIND MAN

[22]Jesus and his followers came to Bethsaida. There some people brought a blind man to Jesus and begged him to touch the man. [23]So Jesus took the blind man's hand and led him out of the village. Then he spit on the man's eyes and put his hands on the man and asked, "Can you see now?"

[24]The man looked up and said, "Yes, I see people, but they look like trees walking around."

[25]Again Jesus put his hands on the man's eyes. Then the man opened his eyes wide and they were healed, and he was able to see everything clearly. [26]Jesus told him to go home, saying, "Don't go into the town."[n]

PETER SAYS JESUS IS THE CHRIST

[27]Jesus and his followers went to the towns around Caesarea Philippi. While they were traveling, Jesus asked them, "Who do people say I am?"

[28]They answered, "Some say you are John the Baptist. Others say you are Elijah," and others say you are one of the prophets."

[29]Then Jesus asked, "But who do you say I am?"

Peter answered, "You are the Christ."

[30]Jesus warned his followers not to tell anyone who he was.

[31]Then Jesus began to teach them that the Son of Man must suffer many things and that he would be rejected by the Jewish elders, the leading priests, and the teachers of the law. He told them that the Son of Man must be killed and then rise from the dead after three days. [32]Jesus told them plainly what would happen. Then Peter took Jesus aside and began to tell him not to talk like that. [33]But Jesus turned and looked at his followers. Then he told Peter not to talk that way. He said, "Go away from me, Satan!" You don't care about the things of God, but only about things people think are important."

DID YOU KNOW?

95% of kids' parents set rules about watching TV.

"Meet the 'tweens: children between the ages of 8 and 12 are a key market segment," Forecast, Dec. 2002, by Alison Stein Wellner.

[34]Then Jesus called the crowd to him, along with his followers. He said, "If people want to follow me, they must give up the things they want. They must be willing even to give up their lives to follow me. [35]Those who want to save their lives will give up true life. But those who give up their lives for me and for the Good News will have true life. [36]It is worthless to have the whole world if they lose their souls. [37]They could never pay enough to buy back their souls. [38]The people who live now are living in a sinful and evil time. If people are ashamed of me and my teaching, the Son of Man will be ashamed of them when he comes with his Father's glory and with the holy angels."

9 Then Jesus said to the people, "I tell you the truth, some people standing here will see the kingdom of God come with power before they die."

JESUS TALKS WITH MOSES AND ELIJAH

[2]Six days later, Jesus took Peter, James, and John up on a high mountain by themselves. While they watched, Jesus' appearance was changed. [3]His clothes became shining white, whiter than any person could make them. [4]Then Elijah and Moses" appeared to them, talking with Jesus.

[5]Peter said to Jesus, "Teacher, it is good that we are here. Let us make three tents—one for you, one for Moses, and one for Elijah." [6]Peter did not know what to say, because he and the others were so frightened.

[7]Then a cloud came and covered them, and a voice came from the cloud, saying, "This is my Son, whom I love. Listen to him!"

 8:26 town Some Greek copies continue, "Don't even go and tell anyone in the town." **8:28 Elijah** A man who spoke for God and who lived hundreds of years before Christ. See 1 Kings 17. **8:33 Satan** Name for the devil meaning "the enemy." Jesus means that Peter was talking like Satan. **9:4 Elijah and Moses** Two of the most important Jewish leaders in the past. God had given Moses the Law, and Elijah was an important prophet.

[8]Suddenly Peter, James, and John looked around, but they saw only Jesus there alone with them.

[9]As they were coming down the mountain, Jesus commanded them not to tell anyone about what they had seen until the Son of Man had risen from the dead.

[10]So the followers obeyed Jesus, but they discussed what he meant about rising from the dead.

[11]Then they asked Jesus, "Why do the teachers of the law say that Elijah must come first?"

[12]Jesus answered, "They are right to say that Elijah must come first and make everything the way it should be. But why does the Scripture say that the Son of Man will suffer much and that people will treat him as if he were nothing? [13]I tell you that Elijah has already come. And people did to him whatever they wanted to do, just as the Scriptures said it would happen."

JESUS HEALS A SICK BOY

[14]When Jesus, Peter, James, and John came back to the other followers, they saw a great crowd around them and the teachers of the law arguing with them. [15]But as soon as the crowd saw Jesus, the people were surprised and ran to welcome him.

[16]Jesus asked, "What are you arguing about?"

[17]A man answered, "Teacher, I brought my son to you. He has an evil spirit in him that stops him from talking. [18]When the spirit attacks him, it throws him on the ground. Then my son foams at the mouth, grinds his teeth, and becomes very stiff. I asked your followers to force the evil spirit out, but they couldn't."

[19]Jesus answered, "You people have no faith. How long must I stay with you? How long must I put up with you? Bring the boy to me."

[20]So the followers brought him to Jesus. As soon as the evil spirit saw Jesus, it made the boy lose control of himself, and he fell down and rolled on the ground, foaming at the mouth.

[21]Jesus asked the boy's father, "How long has this been happening?"

The father answered, "Since he was very young. [22]The spirit often throws him into a fire or into water to kill him. If you can do anything for him, please have pity on us and help us."

[23]Jesus said to the father, "You said, 'If you can!' All things are possible for the one who believes."

[24]Immediately the father cried out, "I do believe! Help me to believe more!"

[25]When Jesus saw that a crowd was quickly gathering, he ordered the evil spirit, saying, "You spirit that makes people unable to hear or speak, I command you to come out of this boy and never enter him again!"

[26]The evil spirit screamed and caused the boy to fall on the ground again. Then the spirit came out. The boy looked as if he were dead, and many people said, "He is dead!" [27]But Jesus took hold of the boy's hand and helped him to stand up.

[28]When Jesus went into the house, his followers began asking him privately, "Why couldn't we force that evil spirit out?"

[29]Jesus answered, "That kind of spirit can only be forced out by prayer."[n]

JESUS TALKS ABOUT HIS DEATH

[30]Then Jesus and his followers left that place and went through Galilee. He didn't want anyone to know where he was, [31]because he was teaching his followers. He said to them, "The Son of Man will be handed over to people, and they will kill him. After three days, he

Q: Where did we get the word "church"?

A: It's from an ancient Greek word meaning "Lord's house." The early Christians didn't use the word "church" because they were meeting in each other's houses. Now we use the word to describe groups of Christians that regularly get together to worship God, learn about the Bible, and share their lives with other Christians. The church can also refer to all the believers all over the world.

Q: It doesn't really matter what you have faith in as long as you believe in something good, right?

A: What you believe in matters very much. If you believe that the Easter Bunny is going to take your family to Hawaii, your faith is sadly misplaced! What you believe in has to be true or you're in for a shock. Paul said that if Jesus didn't rise from the dead, then we're a bunch of pathetic people (1 Corinthians 15:17). He said this, of course, because he had met the risen Lord; he knew that his faith was in the right person.

Q: I don't like bowling because I'm not very good at it. But my grandpa likes to take us. Should I tell him how I feel?

A: If your grandpa really loves bowling, you should keep doing it because you love your grandpa. If he asks you directly how you like bowling, find a gentle way to tell him that it's not your favorite activity. He might be able to help you improve your skills, or he might be willing to try something new. True love always thinks of others first (1 Corinthians 13:5).

Clean Out the Junk

Rid your room of junk! Don't just push things under the bed, but go through everything and get rid of the trash. If you've got junk in your life, hiding it will never take care of the problem; you've got to get rid of it once and for all.

will rise from the dead." [32]But the followers did not understand what Jesus meant, and they were afraid to ask him.

WHO IS THE GREATEST?

[33]Jesus and his followers went to Capernaum. When they went into a house there, he asked them, "What were you arguing about on the road?" [34]But the followers did not answer, because their argument on the road was about which one of them was the greatest.

[35]Jesus sat down and called the twelve apostles to him. He said, "Whoever wants to be the most important must be last of all and servant of all."

[36]Then Jesus took a small child and had him stand among them. Taking the child in his arms, he said, [37]"Whoever accepts a child like this in my name accepts me. And whoever accepts me accepts the One who sent me."

ANYONE NOT AGAINST US IS FOR US

[38]Then John said, "Teacher, we saw someone using your name to force demons out of a person. We told him to stop, because he does not belong to our group."

[39]But Jesus said, "Don't stop him, because anyone who uses my name to do powerful things will not easily say evil things about me. [40]Whoever is not against us is with us. [41]I tell you the truth, whoever gives you a drink of water because you belong to the Christ will truly get his reward.

[42]"If one of these little children believes in me, and someone causes that child to sin, it would be better for that person to have a large stone tied around his neck and be drowned in the sea. [43]If your hand causes you to sin, cut it off. It is better for you to lose part of your body and live forever than to have two hands and go to hell, where the fire never goes out. [[44]In hell the worm does not die; the fire is never put out.]" [45]If your foot causes you to sin, cut it off. It is better for you to lose part of your body and to live forever than to have two feet and be thrown into hell. [[46]In hell the worm does not die; the fire is never put out.]" [47]If your eye causes you to sin, take it out. It is better for you to enter the kingdom of God with only one eye than to have two eyes and be thrown into hell. [48]In hell the worm does not die; the fire is never put out. [49]Every person will be salted with fire.

[50]"Salt is good, but if the salt loses its salty taste, you cannot make it salty again. So, be full of salt, and have peace with each other."

JESUS TEACHES ABOUT DIVORCE

10 Then Jesus left that place and went into the area of Judea and across the Jordan River. Again, crowds came to him, and he taught them as he usually did.

[2]Some Pharisees came to Jesus and tried to trick him. They asked, "Is it right for a man to divorce his wife?"

[3]Jesus answered, "What did Moses command you to do?"

[4]They said, "Moses allowed a man to write out divorce papers and send her away."[n]

[5]Jesus said, "Moses wrote that command for you because you were stubborn. [6]But when God made the world, 'he made them male and female.'[n] [7]'So a man will leave his father and mother and be united with his wife,'[n] [8]and the two will become one body.'[n] So there are not two, but one. [9]God has joined the two together, so no one should separate them."

[10]Later, in the house, his followers asked Jesus again about the question of divorce. [11]He answered, "Anyone who divorces his wife and marries another woman is guilty of adultery against her. [12]And the woman who divorces her husband and marries another man is also guilty of adultery."

JESUS ACCEPTS CHILDREN

[13]Some people brought their little children to Jesus so he could touch them, but his followers told them to stop. [14]When Jesus saw this, he was

ROCK SOLID

Mark 10:13–15

Remember going to see Santa at the mall when you were a little kid? Remember all the questions you began to ask as you got older? "Where are all the reindeer?" "How can Santa remember all these kids' requests?" "How can he be in two malls at one time?" "Why is that kid going down the escalator shouting 'Santa's not real! Santa's not real!' with that mall security guard running after him?" Eventually the questions drown out any belief in jolly ol' Saint Nick.

In Mark 10:15, Jesus says that "you must accept the kingdom of God as if you were a little child, or you will never enter it." Like the little kids in line to see Santa, we must be in awe of God's presence and fully trusting in his reality. Unlike Santa, however, Jesus is real!

Jesus and the Bible can stand up to all the hard questioning in the world. But some people spend their entire lives raising objections. They never get to the point where they make a solid decision to believe in Jesus. Faith is what God is looking for.

Without faith, no one can believe in Jesus and be saved. Without faith, you'll forever be like that kid at the mall shouting "Jesus isn't real!" as the escalator carries you down, farther away from the kingdom of God.

upset and said to them, "Let the little children come to me. Don't stop them, because the kingdom of God belongs to people who are like these children. ¹⁵I tell you the truth, you must accept the kingdom of God as if you were a little child, or you will never enter it." ¹⁶Then Jesus took the children in his arms, put his hands on them, and blessed them.

A RICH YOUNG MAN'S QUESTION

¹⁷As Jesus started to leave, a man ran to him and fell on his knees before Jesus. The man asked, "Good teacher, what must I do to have life forever?"

¹⁸Jesus answered, "Why do you call me good? Only God is good. ¹⁹You know the commands: 'You must not murder anyone. You must not be guilty of adultery. You must not steal. You must not tell lies about your neighbor. You must not cheat. Honor your father and mother.' "ⁿ

²⁰The man said, "Teacher, I have obeyed all these things since I was a boy."

²¹Jesus, looking at the man, loved him and said, "There is one more thing you need to do. Go and sell everything you have, and give the money to the poor, and you will have treasure in heaven. Then come and follow me."

²²He was very sad to hear Jesus say this, and he left sorrowfully, because he was rich.

²³Then Jesus looked at his followers and said, "How hard it will be for the rich to enter the kingdom of God!"

²⁴The followers were amazed at what Jesus said. But he said again, "My children, it is very hardⁿ to enter the kingdom of God! ²⁵It is easier for a camel to go through the eye of a needle than for a rich person to enter the kingdom of God."

²⁶The followers were even more surprised and said to each other, "Then who can be saved?"

²⁷Jesus looked at them and said, "For people this is impossible, but for God all things are possible."

²⁸Peter said to Jesus, "Look, we have left everything and followed you."

²⁹Jesus said, "I tell you the truth, all those who have left houses, brothers, sisters, mother, father, children, or farms for me and for the Good News ³⁰will get more than they left. Here in this world they will have a hundred times more homes, brothers, sisters, mothers, children, and fields. And with those things, they will also suffer for their belief. But in this age they will have life forever. ³¹Many who are first now will be last in the future. And many who are last now will be first in the future."

JESUS TALKS ABOUT HIS DEATH

³²As Jesus and the people with him were on the road to Jerusalem, he was leading the way. His followers were amazed, but others in the crowd who followed were afraid. Again Jesus took the twelve apostles aside and began to tell them what was about to happen in Jerusalem. ³³He said, "Look, we are going to Jerusalem. The Son of Man will be turned over to the leading priests and the teachers of the law. They will say that he must die, and they will turn him over to the non-Jewish people, ³⁴who will laugh at him and spit on him. They will beat him with whips and crucify him. But on the third day, he will rise to life again."

TWO FOLLOWERS ASK JESUS A FAVOR

³⁵Then James and John, sons of Zebedee, came to Jesus and said, "Teacher, we want to ask you to do something for us."

³⁶Jesus asked, "What do you want me to do for you?"

³⁷They answered, "Let one of us sit at your right side and one of us sit at your left side in your glory in your kingdom."

Q&A

Q: There seem to be some real losers at our church. Where are all the cool people?

A: People who come to church have admitted that they need help. If they had it "all together," they wouldn't need to depend on God. Paul told the Corinthian church that God chose them *because* they were unimportant in the world's eyes (1 Corinthians 1:26–28). Heaven is for people who know they can't make it on their own—even though the world might call them "losers." But in God's eyes, they are the coolest people on the planet—and his opinion is what really counts!

Q: I hate to study, and my teacher never notices when I cheat. Doesn't that make cheating okay?

A: You already know that cheating is wrong. Otherwise, you wouldn't try to hide it. But what's even worse than cheating is laziness. You didn't earn your talents and abilities. They were given to you by God, and one day he will ask you what you did with them. To explain this point, Jesus told the story of the three servants. Check it out in Matthew 25:14–30.

Q: Will God forgive me for being angry at him?

A: Yes. You know God is holy, and you know he will only do what's best and right. But when he allows something disappointing to happen, your anger will naturally flare up. In Jonah 4 (in the Old Testament), God's own prophet was furious with him, but God forgave him and gently pointed out where Jonah was wrong.

 10:19 'You . . . mother.' Quotation from Exodus 20:12–16; Deuteronomy 5:16–20.   **10:24 hard** Some Greek copies continue, "for those who trust in riches."

[38]Jesus said, "You don't understand what you are asking. Can you drink the cup that I must drink? And can you be baptized with the same kind of baptism that I must go through?"[n]

[39]They answered, "Yes, we can."

Jesus said to them, "You will drink the same cup that I will drink, and you will be baptized with the same baptism that I must go through. [40]But I cannot choose who will sit at my right or my left; those places belong to those for whom they have been prepared."

[41]When the other ten followers heard this, they began to be angry with James and John.

[42]Jesus called them together and said, "The other nations have rulers. You know that those rulers love to show their power over the people, and their important leaders love to use all their authority. [43]But it should not be that way among you. Whoever wants to become great among you must serve the rest of you like a servant. [44]Whoever wants to become the first among you must serve all of you like a slave. [45]In the same way, the Son of Man did not come to be served. He came to serve others and to give his life as a ransom for many people."

JESUS HEALS A BLIND MAN

[46]Then they came to the town of Jericho. As Jesus was leaving there with his followers and a great many people, a blind beggar named Bartimaeus son of Timaeus was sitting by the road. [47]When he heard that Jesus from Nazareth was walking by, he began to shout, "Jesus, Son of David, have mercy on me!"

[48]Many people warned the blind man to be quiet, but he shouted even more, "Son of David, have mercy on me!"

[49]Jesus stopped and said, "Tell the man to come here."

So they called the blind man, saying, "Cheer up! Get to your feet. Jesus is calling you." [50]The blind man jumped up, left his coat there, and went to Jesus.

[51]Jesus asked him, "What do you want me to do for you?"

The blind man answered, "Teacher, I want to see."

[52]Jesus said, "Go, you are healed because you believed." At once the man could see, and he followed Jesus on the road.

JESUS ENTERS JERUSALEM AS A KING

11 As Jesus and his followers were coming closer to Jerusalem, they came to the towns of Bethphage and Bethany near the Mount of Olives. From there Jesus sent two of his followers [2]and said to them, "Go to the

DID YOU KNOW?

39% of kids know friends or relatives who live in other countries.

Lindstrom, Martin. *BRANDchild: Remarkable insights into the minds of today's global kids and their relationships with brands,* p. 5.

town you can see there. When you enter it, you will quickly find a colt tied, which no one has ever ridden. Untie it and bring it here to me. [3]If anyone asks you why you are doing this, tell him its Master needs the colt, and he will send it at once."

[4]The followers went into the town, found a colt tied in the street near the door of a house, and untied it. [5]Some people were standing there and asked, "What are you doing? Why are you untying that colt?" [6]The followers answered the way Jesus told them to answer, and the people let them take the colt.

[7]They brought the colt to Jesus and put their coats on it, and Jesus sat on it. [8]Many people spread their coats on the road. Others cut branches in the fields and spread them on the road. [9]The people were walking ahead of Jesus and behind him, shouting,

"Praise God!
God bless the One who comes in the name
    of the Lord!   *Psalm 118:26*
[10]God bless the kingdom of our father
    David!
    That kingdom is coming!
Praise[n] to God in heaven!"

[11]Jesus entered Jerusalem and went into the Temple. After he had looked at everything, since it was already late, he went out to Bethany with the twelve apostles.

[12]The next day as Jesus was leaving Bethany, he became hungry. [13]Seeing a fig tree in leaf from far away, he went to see if it had any figs on it. But he found no figs, only leaves,

because it was not the right season for figs. [14]So Jesus said to the tree, "May no one ever eat fruit from you again." And Jesus' followers heard him say this.

JESUS GOES TO THE TEMPLE

[15]When Jesus returned to Jerusalem, he went into the Temple and began to throw out those who were buying and selling there. He turned over the tables of those who were exchanging different kinds of money, and he upset the benches of those who were selling doves. [16]Jesus refused to allow anyone to carry goods through the Temple courts. [17]Then he taught the people, saying, "It is written in the Scriptures, 'My Temple will be called a house for prayer for people from all nations.'[n] But you are changing God's house into a 'hideout for robbers.' "[n]

[18]The leading priests and the teachers of the law heard all this and began trying to find a way to kill Jesus. They were afraid of him, because all the people were amazed at his teaching. [19]That evening, Jesus and his followers[n] left the city.

THE POWER OF FAITH

[20]The next morning as Jesus was passing by with his followers, they saw the fig tree dry and dead, even to the roots. [21]Peter remembered the tree and said to Jesus, "Teacher, look! The fig tree you cursed is dry and dead!"

[22]Jesus answered, "Have faith in God. [23]I tell you the truth, you can say to this mountain, 'Go, fall into the sea.' And if you have no doubts in your mind and believe that what you say will happen, God will do it for you. [24]So I tell you to believe that you have received the things you ask for in prayer, and God will give them to you. [25]When you are praying, if you are angry with someone, forgive him so that your Father in heaven will also forgive your sins. [26]But if you don't forgive other people, then your Father in heaven will not forgive your sins.]"[n]

LEADERS DOUBT JESUS' AUTHORITY

[27]Jesus and his followers went again to Jerusalem. As Jesus was walking in the Temple, the leading priests, the teachers of the law, and the elders came to him. [28]They said to him, "What authority do you have to do these things? Who gave you this authority?"

[29]Jesus answered, "I will ask you one question. If you answer me, I will tell you what authority I have to do these things. [30]Tell me: When John baptized people, was that authority from God or just from other people?"

[31]They argued about Jesus' question, saying, "If we answer, 'John's baptism was from

10:38 Can you . . . through? Jesus was asking if they could suffer the same terrible things that would happen to him.   **11:10 Praise** Literally, "Hosanna," a Hebrew word used at first in praying to God for help, but at this time it was probably a shout of joy used in praising God or his Messiah.   **11:17 'My Temple . . . nations.'** Quotation from Isaiah 56:7.   **11:17 'hideout for robbers'** Quotation from Jeremiah 7:11.   **11:19 his followers** Some Greek copies mention only Jesus here.   **11:26 But . . . sins.** Some Greek copies do not contain the bracketed text.

God,' Jesus will say, 'Then why didn't you believe him?' ³²But if we say, 'It was from other people,' the crowd will be against us." (These leaders were afraid of the people, because all the people believed that John was a prophet.)

³³So they answered Jesus, "We don't know."

Jesus said to them, "Then I won't tell you what authority I have to do these things."

A STORY ABOUT GOD'S SON

12 Jesus began to use stories to teach the people. He said, "A man planted a vineyard. He put a wall around it and dug a hole for a winepress and built a tower. Then he leased the land to some farmers and left for a trip. ²When it was time for the grapes to be picked, he sent a servant to the farmers to get his share of the grapes. ³But the farmers grabbed the servant and beat him and sent him away empty-handed. ⁴Then the man sent another servant. They hit him on the head and showed no respect for him. ⁵So the man sent another servant, whom they killed. The man sent many other servants; the farmers beat some of them and killed others.

⁶"The man had one person left to send, his son whom he loved. He sent him last of all, saying, 'They will respect my son.'

⁷"But the farmers said to each other, 'This son will inherit the vineyard. If we kill him, it will be ours.' ⁸So they took the son, killed him, and threw him out of the vineyard.

DID YOU KNOW?

50% of preteens have divorced parents.

Lindstrom, Martin. BRANDchild: Remarkable insights into the minds of today's global kids and their relationships with brands, p. 11.

⁹"So what will the owner of the vineyard do? He will come and kill those farmers and will give the vineyard to other farmers. ¹⁰Surely you have read this Scripture:

'The stone that the builders rejected
  became the cornerstone.
¹¹The Lord did this,
  and it is wonderful to us.' "

Psalm 118:22–23

¹²The Jewish leaders knew that the story was about them. So they wanted to find a way to arrest Jesus, but they were afraid of the people. So the leaders left him and went away.

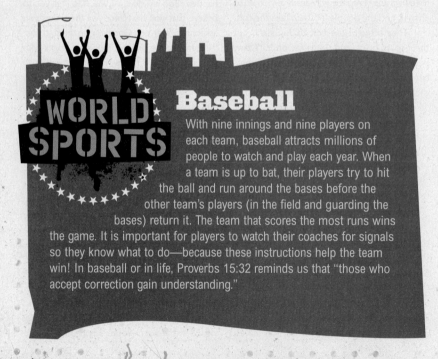

WORLD SPORTS

Baseball

With nine innings and nine players on each team, baseball attracts millions of people to watch and play each year. When a team is up to bat, their players try to hit the ball and run around the bases before the other team's players (in the field and guarding the bases) return it. The team that scores the most runs wins the game. It is important for players to watch their coaches for signals so they know what to do—because these instructions help the team win! In baseball or in life, Proverbs 15:32 reminds us that "those who accept correction gain understanding."

IS IT RIGHT TO PAY TAXES OR NOT?

¹³Later, the Jewish leaders sent some Pharisees and Herodians" to Jesus to trap him in saying something wrong. ¹⁴They came to him and said, "Teacher, we know that you are an honest man. You are not afraid of what other people think about you, because you pay no attention to who they are. And you teach the truth about God's way. Tell us: Is it right to pay taxes to Caesar or not? ¹⁵Should we pay them, or not?"

But knowing what these men were really trying to do, Jesus said to them, "Why are you trying to trap me? Bring me a coin to look at." ¹⁶They gave Jesus a coin, and he asked, "Whose image and name are on the coin?"

They answered, "Caesar's."

¹⁷Then Jesus said to them, "Give to Caesar the things that are Caesar's, and give to God the things that are God's." The men were amazed at what Jesus said.

SOME SADDUCEES TRY TO TRICK JESUS

¹⁸Then some Sadducees came to Jesus and asked him a question. (Sadducees believed that people would not rise from the dead.) ¹⁹They said, "Teacher, Moses wrote that if a man's brother dies, leaving a wife but no children, then that man must marry the widow and have children for his brother. ²⁰Once there were seven brothers. The first brother married and died, leaving no children. ²¹So the second brother married the widow, but he also died and had no children. The same thing happened with the third brother. ²²All seven brothers married her and died, and none of the brothers had any children. Finally the woman died too. ²³Since all seven brothers had married her, when people rise from the dead, whose wife will she be?"

²⁴Jesus answered, "Why don't you understand? Don't you know what the Scriptures say, and don't you know about the power of God? ²⁵When people rise from the dead, they will not marry, nor will they be given to someone to marry. They will be like the angels in heaven. ²⁶Surely you have read what God said about people rising from the dead. In the book in which Moses wrote about the burning bush," it says that God told Moses, 'I am the God of Abraham, the God of Isaac, and the God of Jacob.'ⁿ ²⁷God is the God of the living, not the dead. You Sadducees are wrong!"

THE MOST IMPORTANT COMMAND

²⁸One of the teachers of the law came and heard Jesus arguing with the Sadducees. Seeing that Jesus gave good answers to their questions, he asked Jesus, "Which of the commands is most important?"

February

1 Celebrate Black History Month—research Malcolm X today!

2

3 Martin Luther King Jr. inspired millions. Read his "I Have a Dream" speech.

4 It's "Thank a Mailperson Day." Leave a note clipped to your mailbox for the letter carrier.

6 What comes between you and God? Pray for strength to give it up this Lent season.

7 Pray for a person of influence: it's actor Ashton Kutcher's birthday.

8

9 Is your computer storing music, pictures, or other stuff that doesn't honor God? Delete that junk today.

10 Pray for a person of influence: snowboarder Ross Powers has a birthday today.

11 Pray for a person of influence: pro surfer Kelly Slater celebrates his birthday today.

13

14 Valentine's Day— Read 1 Corinthians 13 and pray for your future wife.

15

16 Make an effort to smile at unhappy-looking people—it's "Do a Grouch a Favor Day"!

17 Pray for a person of influence: it's actress Paris Hilton's birthday.

18 Pray about giving this BibleZine to a friend when you're done with it.

20 Bored? Make a list of 100 things you want to do in your lifetime.

22 Pray for God's influence as your government makes decisions for your country.

23 Pray for a person of influence: today is actress Dakota Fanning's birthday.

25 "Pistol Day"— Ask your parents to make sure any guns in your home are locked away.

26

27 Finish your research on Black History month by reading about Rosa Parks.

[29]Jesus answered, "The most important command is this: 'Listen, people of Israel! The Lord our God is the only Lord. [30]Love the Lord your God with all your heart, all your soul, all your mind, and all your strength.'[n] [31]The second command is this: 'Love your neighbor as you love yourself.'[n] There are no commands more important than these."

[32]The man answered, "That was a good answer, Teacher. You were right when you said God is the only Lord and there is no other God besides him. [33]One must love God with all his heart, all his mind, and all his strength. And one must love his neighbor as he loves himself. These commands are more important than all the animals and sacrifices we offer to God."

[34]When Jesus saw that the man answered him wisely, Jesus said to him, "You are close to the kingdom of God." And after that, no one was brave enough to ask Jesus any more questions.

[35]As Jesus was teaching in the Temple, he asked, "Why do the teachers of the law say that the Christ is the son of David? [36]David himself, speaking by the Holy Spirit, said:

'The Lord said to my Lord,
"Sit by me at my right side,
    until I put your enemies under your
        control." '   *Psalm 110:1*

[37]David himself calls the Christ 'Lord,' so how can the Christ be his son?" The large crowd listened to Jesus with pleasure.

[38]Jesus continued teaching and said, "Beware of the teachers of the law. They like to walk around wearing fancy clothes, and they love for people to greet them with respect in the marketplaces. [39]They love to have the most important seats in the synagogues and at feasts. [40]But they cheat widows and steal their houses and then try to make themselves look good by saying long prayers. They will receive a greater punishment."

TRUE GIVING

[41]Jesus sat near the Temple money box and watched the people put in their money. Many rich people gave large sums of money. [42]Then a poor widow came and put in two small copper coins, which were only worth a few cents.

[43]Calling his followers to him, Jesus said, "I tell you the truth, this poor widow gave more than all those rich people. [44]They gave only what they did not need. This woman is very poor, but she gave all she had; she gave all she had to live on."

THE TEMPLE WILL BE DESTROYED

13 As Jesus was leaving the Temple, one of his followers said to him, "Look, Teacher! How beautiful the buildings are! How big the stones are!"

[2]Jesus said, "Do you see all these great buildings? Not one stone will be left on another. Every stone will be thrown down to the ground."

[3]Later, as Jesus was sitting on the Mount of Olives, opposite the Temple, he was alone with Peter, James, John, and Andrew. They asked Jesus, [4]"Tell us, when will these things happen? And what will be the sign that they are going to happen?"

[5]Jesus began to answer them, "Be careful that no one fools you. [6]Many people will come in my name, saying, 'I am the One,' and they will fool many people. [7]When you hear about wars and stories of wars that are coming, don't be afraid. These things must happen before the end comes. [8]Nations will fight against other nations, and kingdoms against other kingdoms. There will be earthquakes in different places, and there will be times when there is no food for people to eat. These things are like the first pains when something new is about to be born.

[9]"You must be careful. People will arrest you and take you to court and beat you in their synagogues. You will be forced to stand before kings and governors, to tell them about me. This will happen to you because you follow me. [10]But before these things happen, the Good News must be told to all people. [11]When you are arrested and judged, don't worry ahead of time about what you should say. Say whatever is given you to say at that time, because it will not really be you speaking; it will be the Holy Spirit.

[12]"Brothers will give their own brothers to be killed, and fathers will give their own children to be killed. Children will fight against their own parents and cause them to be put to death. [13]All people will hate you because you follow me, but those people who keep their faith until the end will be saved.

[14]"You will see 'a blasphemous object that brings destruction'[n] standing where it should not be." (You who read this should understand what it means.) "At that time, the people in

ROCK SOLID

Mark 12:30-31

If you're a Christian, how do you let other people know it? There's nothing wrong with a T-shirt with a catchy slogan or your WWJD ("What Would Jesus Do?") wristband. You can carry a Bible with you nearly everywhere you go. You can pray before every meal. You can even make it a point to talk about your faith.

All of that is great, but Jesus didn't mention any of those things when he was speaking to his followers two or three days before he died on the cross. He said, "Love the Lord your God with all your heart, all your soul, all your mind, and all your strength" and "Love your neighbor as you love yourself" (Mark 12:30–31). That's pretty simple, although not always easy to do.

If people see that you love God and love people—at school, at church, in the neighborhood, and wherever else you go—they'll know you are a follower of Jesus Christ.

Talk about Jesus whenever you get a chance—but be sure to match your words with *love.*

12:29-30 'Listen . . . strength.' Quotation from Deuteronomy 6:4–5.   **12:31** 'Love . . . yourself.' Quotation from Leviticus 19:18.   **13:14** 'a blasphemous object that brings destruction' Mentioned in Daniel 9:27; 12:11 (cf. Daniel 11:31).

dating

Right now the girls you know are probably just your friends. (Or you might think *Girls? Eww, gross!*) But sooner or later you'll start to see that girls aren't just great as friends, and you might actually start liking one as more than that! What do you do then?

The role of dating can be confusing. People use the word "love" casually, and it seems like new couples are holding hands every week. You might wonder *What's the deal with dating?* Some young people date because they feel special knowing someone likes them. But many people date just because others are. Asking the girl you like out on a date isn't always the right way to handle your feelings for her. In fact, there are many reasons why doing things just as friends can usually be better. No matter what you decide to do, we're told in 1 Timothy 5:1–2 that you should treat girls like sisters, so "always treat them in a pure way."

Dating relationships before and during high school usually don't last very long. Your feelings can change quickly and so can everyone else's. Instead of getting your feelings hurt when the girl you like says "no thanks" to dating, save yourself the trouble and stick with friendship. Remember, there's nothing wrong with *not* dating!

Another alternative that many young people choose is group dating. Doing activities with a big group of friends can be lots of fun and takes the pressure off of trying to impress your crush. If you're unsure about what kinds of physical boundaries to have in a dating relationship, group dates are great, as well—with lots of people around you won't be tempted to try anything you (or your date) are uncomfortable with.

Dating is designed to help you get to know a person better when you're thinking about marriage. This is sometimes called *courtship*. Since most people don't get married in high school, try to save dating (or courtship) for when you're ready to get married. For now, just enjoy making and keeping great friends—with boys and girls!

trustables

Mark 14:36

God has a special promise for you. Ready? It's found in the words of Jesus the night before his crucifixion. He prayed, "Abba, Father! You can do all things" (Mark 14:36). God the Father is almighty. He is never too weak or far away to help us in our times of greatest need.

God is all-powerful, but he understands that even boys who seem to have endless energy eventually will get tired. He knows that you will get tired of doing good. Things happen every day that force you to choose how you will respond. Your Father who created you knows that no matter how hard you try, you will make mistakes; you will stumble, and even fall. And when you do, you can't just put in new batteries and march along like a little pink bunny playing your drum. You must rest.

God has more than physical rest in store for you. New challenges will greet you every day, and if you try to face them alone, you will fail. You need more than a good night's sleep; you need to trust the Lord and rely on his strength.

So get alone and pray to God. He will give you a mighty strength beyond your own abilities. Trust the Lord and become strong again!

Judea should run away to the mountains. [15]If people are on the roofs* of their houses, they must not go down or go inside to get anything out of their houses. [16]If people are in the fields, they must not go back to get their coats. [17]At that time, how terrible it will be for women who are pregnant or have nursing babies! [18]Pray that these things will not happen in winter, [19]because those days will be full of trouble. There will be more trouble than there has ever been since the beginning, when God made the world, until now, and nothing as bad will ever happen again. [20]God has decided to make that terrible time short. Otherwise, no one would go on living. But God will make that time short to help the people he has chosen. [21]At that time, someone might say to you, 'Look, there is the Christ!' Or another person might say, 'There he is!' But don't believe them. [22]False Christs and false prophets will come and perform great wonders and miracles. They will try to fool even the people God has chosen, if that is possible. [23]So be careful. I have warned you about all this before it happens.

[24]"During the days after this trouble comes,

'the sun will grow dark,
and the moon will not give its light.
[25]The stars will fall from the sky.
And the powers of the heavens will be shaken.'   *Isaiah 13:10; 34:4*

[26]"Then people will see the Son of Man coming in clouds with great power and glory. [27]Then he will send his angels all around the earth to gather his chosen people from every part of the earth and from every part of heaven.

[28]"Learn a lesson from the fig tree: When its branches become green and soft and new leaves appear, you know summer is near. [29]In the same way, when you see these things happening, you will know that the time is near, ready to come. [30]I tell you the truth, all these things will happen while the people of this time are still living. [31]Earth and sky will be destroyed, but the words I have said will never be destroyed.

[32]"No one knows when that day or time will be, not the angels in heaven, not even the Son. Only the Father knows. [33]Be careful! Always be ready,* because you don't know when that time will be. [34]It is like a man who goes on a trip. He leaves his house and lets his servants take care of it, giving each one a special job to do. The man tells the servant guarding the door always to be watchful. [35]So always be ready, because you don't know when the owner of the house will come back. It might be in the evening, or at midnight, or in the morning while it is still dark, or when the sun rises. [36]Always be ready. Otherwise he might come back suddenly and find you sleeping. [37]I

tell you this, and I say this to everyone: 'Be ready!' "

THE PLAN TO KILL JESUS

14 It was now only two days before the Passover and the Feast of Unleavened Bread. The leading priests and teachers of the law were trying to find a trick to arrest Jesus and kill him. [2]But they said, "We must not do it during the feast, because the people might cause a riot."

A WOMAN WITH PERFUME FOR JESUS

[3]Jesus was in Bethany at the house of Simon, who had a skin disease. While Jesus was eating there, a woman approached him with an alabaster jar filled with very expensive perfume, made of pure nard. She opened the jar and poured the perfume on Jesus' head.

[4]Some who were there became upset and said to each other, "Why waste that perfume? [5]It was worth a full year's work. It could have been sold and the money given to the poor." And they got very angry with the woman.

[6]Jesus said, "Leave her alone. Why are you troubling her? She did an excellent thing for me. [7]You will always have the poor with you, and you can help them anytime you want. But you will not always have me. [8]This woman did the only thing she could do for me; she poured perfume

---

⭐ **13:15 roofs** In Bible times houses were built with flat roofs. The roof was used for drying things such as flax and fruit. And it was used as an extra room, as a place for worship, and as a cool place to sleep in the summer.   **13:33 ready** Some Greek copies continue, "and pray."

on my body to prepare me for burial. [9]I tell you the truth, wherever the Good News is preached in all the world, what this woman has done will be told, and people will remember her."

JUDAS BECOMES AN ENEMY OF JESUS

[10]One of the twelve apostles, Judas Iscariot, went to talk to the leading priests to offer to hand Jesus over to them. [11]These priests were pleased about this and promised to pay Judas money. So he watched for the best time to turn Jesus in.

JESUS EATS THE PASSOVER MEAL

[12]It was now the first day of the Feast of Unleavened Bread when the Passover lamb was sacrificed. Jesus' followers said to him, "Where do you want us to go and prepare for you to eat the Passover meal?"

[13]Jesus sent two of his followers and said to them, "Go into the city and a man carrying a jar of water will meet you. Follow him. [14]When he goes into a house, tell the owner of the house, 'The Teacher says: "Where is my guest room in which I can eat the Passover meal with my followers?" ' [15]The owner will show you a large room upstairs that is furnished and ready. Prepare the food for us there."

[16]So the followers left and went into the city. Everything happened as Jesus had said, so they prepared the Passover meal.

[17]In the evening, Jesus went to that house with the twelve. [18]While they were all eating, Jesus said, "I tell you the truth, one of you will turn against me—one of you eating with me now."

[19]The followers were very sad to hear this. Each one began to say to Jesus, "I am not the one, am I?"

[20]Jesus answered, "It is one of the twelve— the one who dips his bread into the bowl with me. [21]The Son of Man will die, just as the Scriptures say. But how terrible it will be for the person who hands the Son of Man over to be killed. It would be better for him if he had never been born."

THE LORD'S SUPPER

[22]While they were eating, Jesus took some bread and thanked God for it and broke it. Then he gave it to his followers and said, "Take it; this is my body."

[23]Then Jesus took a cup and thanked God for it and gave it to the followers, and they all drank from the cup.

[24]Then Jesus said, "This is my blood which is the new" agreement that God makes with his people. This blood is poured out for many. [25]I tell you the truth, I will not drink of this fruit of the vine" again until that day when I drink it new in the kingdom of God."

[26]After singing a hymn, they went out to the Mount of Olives.

JESUS' FOLLOWERS WILL LEAVE HIM

[27]Then Jesus told the followers, "You will all stumble in your faith, because it is written in the Scriptures:

'I will kill the shepherd,
and the sheep will scatter.'

Zechariah 13:7

[28]But after I rise from the dead, I will go ahead of you into Galilee."

[29]Peter said, "Everyone else may stumble in their faith, but I will not."

[30]Jesus answered, "I tell you the truth, tonight before the rooster crows twice you will say three times you don't know me."

[31]But Peter insisted, "I will never say that I don't know you! I will even die with you!" And all the other followers said the same thing.

JESUS PRAYS ALONE

[32]Jesus and his followers went to a place called Gethsemane. He said to them, "Sit here while I pray." [33]Jesus took Peter, James, and John with him, and he began to be very sad and troubled. [34]He said to them, "My heart is full of sorrow, to the point of death. Stay here and watch."

[35]After walking a little farther away from them, Jesus fell to the ground and prayed that, if possible, he would not have this time of suffering. [36]He prayed, "Abba," Father! You can do all things. Take away this cup" of suffering. But do what you want, not what I want."

[37]Then Jesus went back to his followers and found them asleep. He said to Peter, "Simon, are you sleeping? Couldn't you stay awake with me for one hour? [38]Stay awake and pray for strength against temptation. The spirit wants to do what is right, but the body is weak."

BIBLE SUPERHEROES

James and Jude (Judas)
See Matthew 13:55; Jude 1.

How would you like to have Jesus for a big brother? Imagine how James and Jude felt. They were two of Jesus' younger siblings.

Growing up with a "perfect" brother must have been a real pain. How many times did they hear, "Why can't you be more like Jesus?" They certainly didn't believe him when he claimed to be God—they thought he was crazy! (Mark 3:21).

All that changed after Jesus rose from the dead. After that, the brothers decided to live for Jesus completely. James became a church leader and wrote the Book of James. Jude wrote the Book of Jude to encourage Jesus' followers.

The brothers could have bragged, but they never said, "I grew up with Jesus; my brother is God!" Instead, they called themselves "servants of Jesus" and lived for him.

14:24 new Some Greek copies do not have this word. Compare Luke 22:20.   **14:25 fruit of the vine** Product of the grapevine; this may also be translated "wine."   **14:36 Abba** Name that a Jewish child called his father.   **14:36 cup** Jesus is talking about the terrible things that will happen to him. Accepting these things will be very hard, like drinking a cup of something bitter.

Matthew 7:7
Read It: Ask God, and he will give you what you need.
Do It: Ask God for something you really need. Wait to see what his answer is.

Matthew 7:12
Read It: Do to others what you want them to do to you.
Do It: The next time you are with your family or friends, ask yourself, "Would I want them to do or say this to me?"

Matthew 7:20
Read It: You will know someone is a fake by what he does.
Do It: Don't always believe what people tell you. First, see if how they live matches what they say.

JESUS IS ARRESTED

[43]At once, while Jesus was still speaking, Judas, one of the twelve apostles, came up. With him were many people carrying swords and clubs who had been sent from the leading priests, the teachers of the law, and the Jewish elders.

[44]Judas had planned a signal for them, saying, "The man I kiss is Jesus. Arrest him and guard him while you lead him away." [45]So Judas went straight to Jesus and said, "Teacher!" and kissed him. [46]Then the people grabbed Jesus and arrested him. [47]One of his followers standing nearby pulled out his sword and struck the servant of the high priest and cut off his ear.

[48]Then Jesus said, "You came to get me with swords and clubs as if I were a criminal. [49]Every day I was with you teaching in the Temple, and you did not arrest me there. But all these things have happened to make the Scriptures come true." [50]Then all of Jesus' followers left him and ran away.

[51]A young man, wearing only a linen cloth, was following Jesus, and the people also grabbed him. [52]But the cloth he was wearing came off, and he ran away naked.

JESUS BEFORE THE LEADERS

[53]The people who arrested Jesus led him to the house of the high priest, where all the leading priests, the elders, and the teachers of the law were gathered. [54]Peter followed far behind and entered the courtyard of the high priest's house. There he sat with the guards, warming himself by the fire.

[55]The leading priests and the whole Jewish council tried to find something that Jesus had done wrong so they could kill him. But the council could find no proof of anything. [56]Many people came and told false things about him, but all said different things—none of them agreed.

[57]Then some people stood up and lied about Jesus, saying, [58]"We heard this man say, 'I will destroy this Temple that people made. And three days later, I will build another Temple not made by people.' " [59]But even the things these people said did not agree.

[60]Then the high priest stood before them and asked Jesus, "Aren't you going to answer? Don't you have something to say about their charges against you?" [61]But Jesus said nothing; he did not answer.

The high priest asked Jesus another question: "Are you the Christ, the Son of the blessed God?"

[62]Jesus answered, "I am. And in the future you will see the Son of Man sitting at the right hand of God, the Powerful One, and coming on clouds in the sky."

[63]When the high priest heard this, he tore his clothes and said, "We don't need any more witnesses! [64]You all heard him say these things against God. What do you think?"

They all said that Jesus was guilty and should die. [65]Some of the people there began to spit at Jesus. They blindfolded him and beat him with their fists and said, "Prove you are a prophet!" Then the guards led Jesus away and beat him.

PETER SAYS HE DOESN'T KNOW JESUS

[66]While Peter was in the courtyard, a servant girl of the high priest came there. [67]She saw Peter warming himself at the fire and looked closely at him.

Then she said, "You also were with Jesus, that man from Nazareth."

[68]But Peter said that he was never with Jesus. He said, "I don't know or understand what you are talking about." Then Peter left and went toward the entrance of the courtyard. And the rooster crowed."

[69]The servant girl saw Peter there, and again she said to the people who were standing nearby, "This man is one of those who followed Jesus." [70]Again Peter said that it was not true.

A short time later, some people were standing near Peter saying, "Surely you are one of those who followed Jesus, because you are from Galilee, too."

[71]Then Peter began to place a curse on himself and swear, "I don't know this man you're talking about!"

[72]At once, the rooster crowed the second time. Then Peter remembered what Jesus had told him: "Before the rooster crows twice, you will say three times that you don't know me." Then Peter lost control of himself and began to cry.

PILATE QUESTIONS JESUS

15 Very early in the morning, the leading priests, the elders, the teachers of the law, and all the Jewish council decided what to do with Jesus. They tied him, led him away, and turned him over to Pilate, the governor.

[2]Pilate asked Jesus, "Are you the king of the Jews?"

Jesus answered, "Those are your words."

[3]The leading priests accused Jesus of many things. [4]So Pilate asked Jesus another question,

[39]Again Jesus went away and prayed the same thing. [40]Then he went back to his followers, and again he found them asleep, because their eyes were very heavy. And they did not know what to say to him.

[41]After Jesus prayed a third time, he went back to his followers and said to them, "Are you still sleeping and resting? That's enough. The time has come for the Son of Man to be handed over to sinful people. [42]Get up, we must go. Look, here comes the man who has turned against me."

⭐ **14:68 And the rooster crowed.** Some Greek copies do not have this phrase.

"You can see that they are accusing you of many things. Aren't you going to answer?"

⁵But Jesus still said nothing, so Pilate was very surprised.

PILATE TRIES TO FREE JESUS

⁶Every year at the time of the Passover the governor would free one prisoner whom the people chose. ⁷At that time, there was a man named Barabbas in prison who was a rebel and had committed murder during a riot. ⁸The crowd came to Pilate and began to ask him to free a prisoner as he always did.

⁹So Pilate asked them, "Do you want me to free the king of the Jews?" ¹⁰Pilate knew that the leading priests had turned Jesus in to him because they were jealous. ¹¹But the leading priests had persuaded the people to ask Pilate to free Barabbas, not Jesus.

¹²Then Pilate asked the crowd again, "So what should I do with this man you call the king of the Jews?"

¹³They shouted, "Crucify him!"

¹⁴Pilate asked, "Why? What wrong has he done?"

But they shouted even louder, "Crucify him!"

¹⁵Pilate wanted to please the crowd, so he freed Barabbas for them. After having Jesus beaten with whips, he handed Jesus over to the soldiers to be crucified.

¹⁶The soldiers took Jesus into the governor's palace (called the Praetorium) and called all the other soldiers together. ¹⁷They put a purple robe on Jesus and used thorny branches to make a crown for his head. ¹⁸They began to call out to him, "Hail, King of the Jews!" ¹⁹The soldiers beat Jesus on the head many times with a stick. They spit on him and made fun of him by bowing on their knees and worshiping him. ²⁰After they finished, the soldiers took off the purple robe and put his own clothes on him again. Then they led him out of the palace to be crucified.

JESUS IS CRUCIFIED

²¹A man named Simon from Cyrene, the father of Alexander and Rufus, was coming from the fields to the city. The soldiers forced Simon to carry the cross for Jesus. ²²They led Jesus to the place called Golgotha, which means the Place of the Skull. ²³The soldiers tried to give Jesus wine mixed with myrrh to drink, but he refused. ²⁴The soldiers crucified Jesus and divided his clothes among themselves, throwing lots to decide what each soldier would get.

²⁵It was nine o'clock in the morning when they crucified Jesus. ²⁶There was a sign with this charge against Jesus written on it: THE KING OF THE JEWS. ²⁷They also put two robbers on crosses beside Jesus, one on the right, and the other on the left. [²⁸And the Scripture came true that says, "They put him with criminals."]ⁿ ²⁹People walked by and insulted Jesus and shook their heads, saying, "You said you could destroy the Temple and build it again in three days. ³⁰So save yourself! Come down from that cross!"

³¹The leading priests and the teachers of the law were also making fun of Jesus. They said to each other, "He saved other people, but he can't save himself. ³²If he is really the Christ, the king of Israel, let him come down now from the cross. When we see this, we will believe in him." The robbers who were being crucified beside Jesus also insulted him.

JESUS DIES

³³At noon the whole country became dark, and the darkness lasted for three hours. ³⁴At three o'clock Jesus cried in a loud voice, "Eloi, Eloi, lama sabachthani." This means, "My God, my God, why have you abandoned me?"

³⁵When some of the people standing there heard this, they said, "Listen! He is calling Elijah."

³⁶Someone there ran and got a sponge, filled it with vinegar, tied it to a stick, and gave it to Jesus to drink. He said, "We want to see if Elijah will come to take him down from the cross."

³⁷Then Jesus cried in a loud voice and died.

³⁸The curtain in the Templeⁿ was torn into two pieces, from the top to the bottom. ³⁹When the army officer who was standing in front of the cross saw what happened when Jesus died,ⁿ he said, "This man really was the Son of God!"

⁴⁰Some women were standing at a distance from the cross, watching; among them were Mary Magdalene, Salome, and Mary the mother of James and Joseph. (James was her youngest son.) ⁴¹These women had followed Jesus in Galilee and helped him. Many other

KNOW THE WORD!

SACRIFICE

If your sister lets you have the last chocolate chunk cookie, you could say that she "sacrificed" it for you—that she gave it up for your sake, or for your benefit.

When Christians talk about Jesus' *sacrifice*, they're referring to his life that he gave up for their benefit. Jesus is God. He didn't have to come to earth as a baby and grow up in an average family. He didn't have to spend several years teaching people how to please God. And he definitely didn't have to let people torture and kill him!

Jesus made the ultimate sacrifice. Why did he do it? Jesus sacrificed his rights so that anyone who believes in him can be forgiven and accepted as God's child.

 15:28 And . . . criminals." Some Greek copies do not contain the bracketed text, which quotes from Isaiah 53:12.   **15:38 curtain in the Temple** A curtain divided the Most Holy Place from the other part of the Temple. That was the special building in Jerusalem where God commanded the Jewish people to worship him.   **15:39 when Jesus died** Some Greek copies read "when Jesus cried out and died."

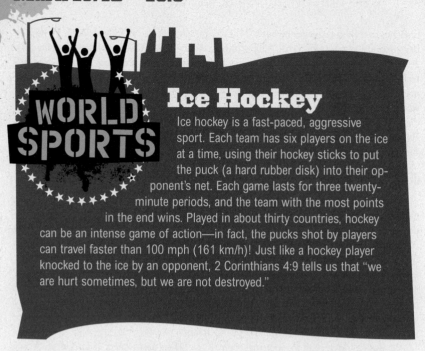

Ice Hockey

Ice hockey is a fast-paced, aggressive sport. Each team has six players on the ice at a time, using their hockey sticks to put the puck (a hard rubber disk) into their opponent's net. Each game lasts for three twenty-minute periods, and the team with the most points in the end wins. Played in about thirty countries, hockey can be an intense game of action—in fact, the pucks shot by players can travel faster than 100 mph (161 km/h)! Just like a hockey player knocked to the ice by an opponent, 2 Corinthians 4:9 tells us that "we are hurt sometimes, but we are not destroyed."

women were also there who had come with Jesus to Jerusalem.

JESUS IS BURIED

42 This was Preparation Day. (That means the day before the Sabbath day.) That evening, 43 Joseph from Arimathea was brave enough to go to Pilate and ask for Jesus' body. Joseph, an important member of the Jewish council, was one of the people who was waiting for the kingdom of God to come. 44 Pilate was amazed that Jesus would have already died, so he called the army officer who had guarded Jesus and asked him if Jesus had already died. 45 The officer told Pilate that he was dead, so Pilate told Joseph he could have the body. 46 Joseph bought some linen cloth, took the body down from the cross, and wrapped it in the linen. He put the body in a tomb that was cut out of a wall of rock. Then he rolled a very large stone to block the entrance of the tomb. 47 And Mary Magdalene and Mary the mother of Joseph saw the place where Jesus was laid.

JESUS RISES FROM THE DEAD

16 The day after the Sabbath day, Mary Magdalene, Mary the mother of James, and Salome bought some sweet-smelling spices to put on Jesus' body. 2 Very early on that day, the first day of the week, soon after sunrise, the women were on their way to the tomb. 3 They said to each other, "Who will roll away for us the stone that covers the entrance of the tomb?"

4 Then the women looked and saw that the stone had already been rolled away, even though it was very large. 5 The women entered the tomb and saw a young man wearing a white robe and sitting on the right side, and they were afraid.

6 But the man said, "Don't be afraid. You are looking for Jesus from Nazareth, who has been crucified. He has risen from the dead; he is not here. Look, here is the place they laid him. 7 Now go and tell his followers and Peter, 'Jesus is going into Galilee ahead of you, and you will see him there as he told you before.' "

8 The women were confused and shaking with fear, so they left the tomb and ran away. They did not tell anyone about what happened, because they were afraid.

———

Verses 9–20 are not included in some of the earliest surviving Greek copies of Mark.

SOME FOLLOWERS SEE JESUS

[9 After Jesus rose from the dead early on the first day of the week, he showed himself first to

COOL!

Famous Logos

The most famous company logo today is the Nike Swoosh. It was created in 1964 by Carolyn Davidson. She made it for a company called Blue Ribbon Sports, which later became Nike (and was only paid $35 for her creation!). The most famous Christian logos are the cross and the fish. The cross stands for the death of Jesus and the forgiveness of sins through his blood. But do you know what the fish (⌒) means? It was a secret code among early believers. The five letters in the Greek word for "fish" (ιχθυζ, ichthys) were the initials for "Jesus Christ, God's Son, Savior" (in Greek).

Mary Magdalene. One time in the past, he had forced seven demons out of her. [10]After Mary saw Jesus, she went and told his followers, who were very sad and were crying. [11]But Mary told them that Jesus was alive. She said that she had seen him, but the followers did not believe her.

[12]Later, Jesus showed himself to two of his followers while they were walking in the country, but he did not look the same as before. [13]These followers went back to the others and told them what had happened, but again, the followers did not believe them.

JESUS TALKS TO THE APOSTLES

[14]Later Jesus showed himself to the eleven apostles while they were eating, and he criticized them because they had no faith. They were stubborn and refused to believe those who had seen him after he had risen from the dead.

DID YOU KNOW?

11% of kids like vacations because they can ride elevators.

RAB Instant Background Report for Kids and Tweens Market.

[15]Jesus said to his followers, "Go everywhere in the world, and tell the Good News to everyone. [16]Anyone who believes and is baptized will be saved, but anyone who does not believe will be punished. [17]And those who believe will be able to do these things as proof: They will use my name to force out demons. They will speak in new languages." [18]They will pick up snakes and drink poison without being hurt. They will touch the sick, and the sick will be healed."

[19]After the Lord Jesus said these things to his followers, he was carried up into heaven, and he sat at the right side of God. [20]The followers went everywhere in the world and told the Good News to people, and the Lord helped them. The Lord proved that the Good News they told was true by giving them power to work miracles.]

16:17 languages This can also be translated "tongues."

Doctor Luke was a friend and traveling companion of the apostle Paul as he preached.

He saw thousands of people in many countries come to faith in Jesus Christ. Many of these people were non-Jews like Luke himself. They didn't know much about the Old Testament or God's plan for the world.

To help these new Christians—and those who would come after them—Luke wrote a history about Jesus and his followers. This Gospel is part one; the Book of Acts is part two.

Luke begins at the birth of Jesus, but spends most of his time telling what Jesus did between the time John baptized him and when he rose from the dead.

Luke wants his readers to know some important things about Jesus:

- How he reached out to non-Jews, showing his love for all
- How he cared for women, children, and the poor
- How he trusted in the Holy Spirit

Luke repeats many of Jesus' *parables*. These are simple "teaching stories" that help people understand Jesus' message. Some are world-famous now, like the stories of the good Samaritan (Luke 10:25–37) and the prodigal son (Luke 15:11–32).

Luke also tells us of many of Jesus' miracles, such as healing the sick and raising the dead. You can bet these amazing deeds got people's attention!

LUKE

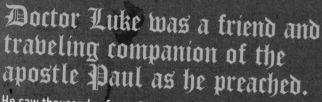

Luke wants to get *your* attention. He wants to introduce you to "the Son of Man [who] came to find lost people and save them" (19:10).

LUKE WRITES ABOUT JESUS' LIFE

1 Many have tried to report on the things that happened among us. [2]They have written the same things that we learned from others—the people who saw those things from the beginning and served God by telling people his message. [3]Since I myself have studied everything carefully from the beginning, most excellent[n] Theophilus, it seemed good for me to write it out for you. I arranged it in order, [4]to help you know that what you have been taught is true.

ZECHARIAH AND ELIZABETH

[5]During the time Herod ruled Judea, there was a priest named Zechariah who belonged to Abijah's group.[n] Zechariah's wife, Elizabeth, came from the family of Aaron. [6]Zechariah and Elizabeth truly did what God said was good. They did everything the Lord commanded and were without fault in keeping his law. [7]But they had no children, because Elizabeth could not have a baby, and both of them were very old.

[8]One day Zechariah was serving as a priest before God, because his group was on duty. [9]According to the custom of the priests, he was chosen by lot to go into the Temple of the Lord and burn incense. [10]There were a great many people outside praying at the time the incense was offered. [11]Then an angel of the Lord appeared to Zechariah, standing on the right side of the incense table. [12]When he saw the angel, Zechariah was startled and frightened. [13]But the angel said to him, "Zechariah, don't be afraid. God has heard your prayer. Your wife, Elizabeth, will give birth to a son, and you will name him John. [14]He will bring you joy and gladness, and many people will be happy because of his birth. [15]John will be a great man for the Lord. He will never drink wine or beer, and even from birth, he will be filled with the Holy Spirit. [16]He will help many people of Israel return to the Lord their God. [17]He will go before the Lord in spirit and power like Elijah. He will make peace between parents and their children and will bring those who are not obeying God back to the right way of thinking, to make a people ready for the coming of the Lord."

[18]Zechariah said to the angel, "How can I know that what you say is true? I am an old man, and my wife is old, too."

[19]The angel answered him, "I am Gabriel. I stand before God, who sent me to talk to you and to tell you this good news. [20]Now, listen! You will not be able to speak until the day

these things happen, because you did not believe what I told you. But they will really happen."

[21]Outside, the people were still waiting for Zechariah and were surprised that he was staying so long in the Temple. [22]When Zechariah came outside, he could not speak to them, and they knew he had seen a vision in the Temple. He could only make signs to them and remained unable to speak. [23]When his time of service at the Temple was finished, he went home.

[24]Later, Zechariah's wife, Elizabeth, became pregnant and did not go out of her house for five months. Elizabeth said, [25]"Look what the Lord has done for me! My people were ashamed[n] of me, but now the Lord has taken away that shame."

AN ANGEL APPEARS TO MARY

[26]During Elizabeth's sixth month of pregnancy, God sent the angel Gabriel to Nazareth, a town in Galilee, [27]to a virgin. She was engaged to marry a man named Joseph from the family of David. Her name was Mary. [28]The angel came to

Q&A

Q: Why is the church program never as good as what's on TV?

A: Maybe the church program doesn't appeal to you because it's not always easy to get and its message is not always popular. Are you up for the challenge? Anybody can flop down on the couch and watch TV. On the other hand, Jesus said that the way to heaven is narrow (Matthew 7:13–14). We go to church to remember the difficult thing Jesus did for us and to encourage each other to follow him. Every time you go to church you should come away feeling challenged to be a better person. TV won't always do that for you!

Q: All that girls care about is "who likes who." Why?

A: Not *all* girls feel that way. But girls in general are very different from boys. Guys care about *who can do the most pull-ups* or *who's the best at free throws*. Girls care more about relationships, like *who's most popular* and *who's best friends with who*. God made guys and girls different so that when a man and a woman get married, they can better help each other.

Q: Does the Bible say anything about junk food? I love to eat chips and candy!

A: Junk food tastes so good that you can eat it when you're not hungry. You sit down with a bag of chips in front of the TV and pretty soon it's gone! The empty calories are bad for you, but the worst part is that you can't stop eating. God is helping us become better people in all areas of our lives (Galatians 5:22–23). And that includes self-control with junk food.

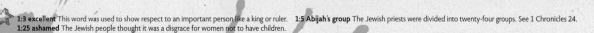

1:3 excellent This word was used to show respect to an important person like a king or ruler.   **1:5 Abijah's group** The Jewish priests were divided into twenty-four groups. See 1 Chronicles 24.
1:25 ashamed The Jewish people thought it was a disgrace for women not to have children.

Matthew 7:24
Read It: Obeying God's Word is like building your house on a rock.
Do It: If you want a Christian life that is strong, don't just read the Bible—make its teachings the foundation of your life.

Matthew 7:25
Read It: There are going to be a lot of really hard times in your life.
Do It: If you're going through a hard time, ask God to show you what he wants you to do.

Matthew 7:26
Read It: Not obeying God's Word is like building a house on the sand.
Do It: Things built on sand won't last. Build your "house on the rock" by reading the Bible and talking with God every day.

her and said, "Greetings! The Lord has blessed you and is with you."

²⁹But Mary was very startled by what the angel said and wondered what this greeting might mean.

³⁰The angel said to her, "Don't be afraid, Mary; God has shown you his grace. ³¹Listen! You will become pregnant and give birth to a son, and you will name him Jesus. ³²He will be great and will be called the Son of the Most High. The Lord God will give him the throne of King David, his ancestor. ³³He will rule over the people of Jacob forever, and his kingdom will never end."

³⁴Mary said to the angel, "How will this happen since I am a virgin?"

³⁵The angel said to Mary, "The Holy Spirit will come upon you, and the power of the Most High will cover you. For this reason the baby will be holy and will be called the Son of God. ³⁶Now Elizabeth, your relative, is also pregnant with a son though she is very old. Everyone thought she could not have a baby, but she has been pregnant for six months. ³⁷God can do anything!"

³⁸Mary said, "I am the servant of the Lord. Let this happen to me as you say!" Then the angel went away.

MARY VISITS ELIZABETH

³⁹Mary got up and went quickly to a town in the hills of Judea. ⁴⁰She came to Zechariah's house and greeted Elizabeth. ⁴¹When Eliza-beth heard Mary's greeting, the unborn baby inside her jumped, and Elizabeth was filled with the Holy Spirit. ⁴²She cried out in a loud voice, "God has blessed you more than any other woman, and he has blessed the baby to which you will give birth. ⁴³Why has this good thing happened to me, that the mother of my Lord comes to me? ⁴⁴When I heard your voice, the baby inside me jumped with joy. ⁴⁵You are blessed because you believed that what the Lord said to you would really happen."

MARY PRAISES GOD

⁴⁶Then Mary said,
"My soul praises the Lord;
⁴⁷   my heart rejoices in God my Savior,
⁴⁸because he has shown his concern for his
      humble servant girl.
   From now on, all people will say that I am
      blessed,
⁴⁹   because the Powerful One has done
         great things for me.
   His name is holy.
⁵⁰God will show his mercy forever and ever
      to those who worship and serve him.
⁵¹He has done mighty deeds by his power.
   He has scattered the people who are
      proud
      and think great things about themselves.
⁵²He has brought down rulers from their
         thrones
      and raised up the humble.
⁵³He has filled the hungry with good things
      and sent the rich away with nothing.
⁵⁴He has helped his servant, the people of
      Israel,
      remembering to show them mercy
⁵⁵as he promised to our ancestors,
      to Abraham and to his children
         forever."

GET CONNECTED

BELONGING

Have you noticed the "cool" people always belong to groups like the student council, the football team, or the choir? Have you ever wondered where you belong? Whenever you're feeling like you don't belong to anything exciting, remember that if you're a Christian, you belong to God's group (Ephesians 2:19). It's a group of forever friends all over the globe who will spend eternity together! Now, what could be better than that? So the next time you wonder where you belong, remember that you belong to the worldwide family of God!

[56]Mary stayed with Elizabeth for about three months and then returned home.

THE BIRTH OF JOHN

[57]When it was time for Elizabeth to give birth, she had a boy. [58]Her neighbors and relatives heard how good the Lord was to her, and they rejoiced with her.

[59]When the baby was eight days old, they came to circumcise him. They wanted to name him Zechariah because this was his father's name, [60]but his mother said, "No! He will be named John."

[61]The people said to Elizabeth, "But no one in your family has this name." [62]Then they made signs to his father to find out what he would like to name him.

[63]Zechariah asked for a writing tablet and wrote, "His name is John," and everyone was surprised. [64]Immediately Zechariah could talk again, and he began praising God. [65]All their neighbors became alarmed, and in all the mountains of Judea people continued talking about all these things. [66]The people who heard about them wondered, saying, "What will this child be?" because the Lord was with him.

ZECHARIAH PRAISES GOD

[67]Then Zechariah, John's father, was filled with the Holy Spirit and prophesied:

[68]"Let us praise the Lord, the God of Israel,
    because he has come to help his people
        and has given them freedom.

70% of kids think it's important to be involved in politics.

Trends & Tudes. Harris Interactive. October 2004.

[69]He has given us a powerful Savior
    from the family of God's servant David.
[70]He said that he would do this
    through his holy prophets who lived long ago:
[71]He promised he would save us from our enemies
    and from the power of all those who hate us.
[72]He said he would give mercy to our ancestors
    and that he would remember his holy promise.

[73]God promised Abraham, our father,
[74]   that he would save us from the power of our enemies
    so we could serve him without fear,
[75]being holy and good before God as long as we live.

[76]"Now you, child, will be called a prophet of the Most High God.
    You will go before the Lord to prepare his way.
[77]You will make his people know that they will be saved
    by having their sins forgiven.
[78]With the loving mercy of our God,
    a new day from heaven will dawn upon us.
[79]It will shine on those who live in darkness,
    in the shadow of death.
    It will guide us into the path of peace."

[80]And so the child grew up and became strong in spirit. John lived in the desert until the time when he came out to preach to Israel.

THE BIRTH OF JESUS

2 At that time, Augustus Caesar sent an order that all people in the countries under Roman rule must list their names in a register. [2]This was the first registration;* it was taken while Quirinius was governor of Syria. [3]And all went to their own towns to be registered.

[4]So Joseph left Nazareth, a town in Galilee, and went to the town of Bethlehem in Judea, known as the town of David. Joseph went there because he was from the family of David.

BIBLE SUPERHEROES

Abraham
See Genesis 17; 18; 22.

Abraham is one of the few men called the "friend" of God in the Old Testament. One reason for this is that when God told Abraham to leave his home and go to a strange land, Abraham obeyed.

Abraham means "father of many nations." He is the father of the Jews through his son Isaac, the father of the Arabs through his son Ishmael, and the spiritual "father" of all Christians through faith (Romans 4:16). All this from an old man with a wife who couldn't have kids!

Abraham wasn't blessed because he was perfect; he made some big mistakes. But he trusted God through good times and bad. His name appears about seventy times in the New Testament. He is a role model of the faith that pleases God. Like Abraham, you can be God's friend by obeying him!

[5]Joseph registered with Mary, to whom he was engaged[n] and who was now pregnant. [6]While they were in Bethlehem, the time came for Mary to have the baby, [7]and she gave birth to her first son. Because there were no rooms left in the inn, she wrapped the baby with pieces of cloth and laid him in a feeding trough.

SHEPHERDS HEAR ABOUT JESUS

[8]That night, some shepherds were in the fields nearby watching their sheep. [9]Then an angel of the Lord stood before them. The glory of the Lord was shining around them, and they became very frightened. [10]The angel said to them, "Do not be afraid. I am bringing you good news that will be a great joy to all the people. [11]Today your Savior was born in the town of David. He is Christ, the Lord. [12]This is how you will know him: You will find a baby wrapped in pieces of cloth and lying in a feeding box."

[13]Then a very large group of angels from heaven joined the first angel, praising God and saying:

[14]"Give glory to God in heaven,
and on earth let there be peace among
the people who please God."[n]

[15]When the angels left them and went back to heaven, the shepherds said to each other, "Let's go to Bethlehem. Let's see this thing that has happened which the Lord has told us about."

[16]So the shepherds went quickly and found Mary and Joseph and the baby, who was lying in a feeding trough. [17]When they had seen him, they told what the angels had said about this child. [18]Everyone was amazed at what the shepherds said to them. [19]But Mary treasured these things and continued to think about them. [20]Then the shepherds went back to their sheep, praising God and thanking him for everything they had seen and heard. It had been just as the angel had told them.

[21]When the baby was eight days old, he was circumcised and was named Jesus, the name given by the angel before the baby began to grow inside Mary.

JESUS IS PRESENTED IN THE TEMPLE

[22]When the time came for Mary and Joseph to do what the law of Moses taught about being made pure,[n] they took Jesus to Jerusalem to present him to the Lord. [23](It is written in the law of the Lord: "Every firstborn male shall be given to the Lord.")[n] [24]Mary and Joseph also went to offer a sacrifice, as the law of the Lord says: "You must sacrifice two doves or two young pigeons."[n]

SIMEON SEES JESUS

[25]In Jerusalem lived a man named Simeon who was a good man and godly. He was waiting for the time when God would take away Israel's sorrow, and the Holy Spirit was in him. [26]Simeon had been told by the Holy Spirit that he would not die before he saw the Christ promised by the Lord. [27]The Spirit led Simeon to the Temple. When Mary and Joseph brought the baby Jesus to the Temple to do what the law said they must do, [28]Simeon took the baby in his arms and thanked God:

KNOW THE WORD!

SIN

It's only three letters, but *sin* is an important word in the Bible that lots of people today do not understand. Sin is anything we do that makes God unhappy. If God asks you to do something (such as obey your parents) and you don't do it, then that's sin. If God tells you to *not* to do something (such as steal) and you do it, then that's also sin.

No one except Jesus has been able to live without sinning. So what can you do about the wrong things you've done?

Jesus died and rose from the dead to forgive your sin. You couldn't ever clear away your sin…but Jesus can! All you have to do is ask him to forgive you.

[29]"Now, Lord, you can let me, your servant,
die in peace as you said.
[30]With my own eyes I have seen your
salvation,
[31]   which you prepared before all people.
[32]It is a light for the non-Jewish people to see
and an honor for your people, the
Israelites."

[33]Jesus' father and mother were amazed at what Simeon had said about him. [34]Then Simeon blessed them and said to Mary, "God has chosen this child to cause the fall and rise of many in Israel. He will be a sign from God that many people will not accept [35]so that the thoughts of many will be made known. And the things that will happen will make your heart sad, too."

ANNA SEES JESUS

[36]There was a prophetess, Anna, from the family of Phanuel in the tribe of Asher. Anna was very old. She had once been married for seven years. [37]Then her husband died, and she was a widow for eighty-four years. Anna never left the Temple but worshiped God, going without food and praying day and night.

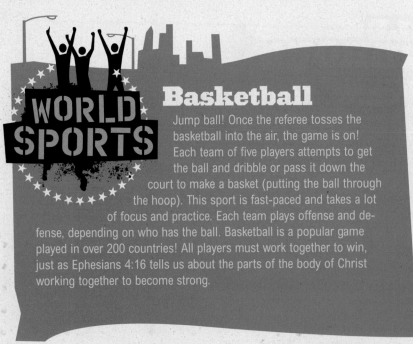

Basketball

Jump ball! Once the referee tosses the basketball into the air, the game is on! Each team of five players attempts to get the ball and dribble or pass it down the court to make a basket (putting the ball through the hoop). This sport is fast-paced and takes a lot of focus and practice. Each team plays offense and defense, depending on who has the ball. Basketball is a popular game played in over 200 countries! All players must work together to win, just as Ephesians 4:16 tells us about the parts of the body of Christ working together to become strong.

2:5 engaged For the Jewish people, an engagement was a lasting agreement. It could only be broken by divorce. **2:14 and . . . God** Some Greek copies read "and on earth let there be peace and goodwill among people." **2:22 pure** The Law of Moses said that forty days after a Jewish woman gave birth to a son, she must be cleansed by a ceremony at the Temple. Read Leviticus 12:2–8. **2:23 "Every . . . Lord."** Quotation from Exodus 13:2. **2:24 "You . . . pigeons."** Quotation from Leviticus 12:8.

[38]Standing there at that time, she thanked God and spoke about Jesus to all who were waiting for God to free Jerusalem.

JOSEPH AND MARY RETURN HOME

[39]When Joseph and Mary had done everything the law of the Lord commanded, they went home to Nazareth, their own town in Galilee. [40]The little child grew and became strong. He was filled with wisdom, and God's goodness was upon him.

JESUS AS A BOY

[41]Every year Jesus' parents went to Jerusalem for the Passover Feast. [42]When he was twelve years old, they went to the feast as they always did. [43]After the feast days were over, they started home. The boy Jesus stayed behind in Jerusalem, but his parents did not know it. [44]Thinking that Jesus was with them in the group, they traveled for a whole day. Then they began to look for him among their family and friends. [45]When they did not find him, they went back to Jerusalem to look for him there. [46]After three days they found Jesus sitting in the Temple with the teachers, listening to them and asking them questions. [47]All who heard him were amazed at his understanding and answers. [48]When Jesus' parents saw him, they were astonished. His mother said to him, "Son, why did you do this to us? Your father and I were very worried about you and have been looking for you."

[49]Jesus said to them, "Why were you looking for me? Didn't you know that I must be in my Father's house?" [50]But they did not understand the meaning of what he said.

[51]Jesus went with them to Nazareth and was obedient to them. But his mother kept in her mind all that had happened. [52]Jesus became wiser and grew physically. People liked him, and he pleased God.

THE PREACHING OF JOHN

3 It was the fifteenth year of the rule of Tiberius Caesar. These men were under Caesar: Pontius Pilate, the ruler of Judea; Herod, the ruler of Galilee; Philip, Herod's brother, the ruler of Iturea and Traconitis; and Lysanias, the ruler of Abilene. [2]Annas and Caiaphas were the high priests. At this time, the word of God came to John son of Zechariah in the desert. [3]He went all over the area around the Jordan River preaching a baptism of changed hearts and lives for the forgiveness of sins. [4]As it is written in the book of Isaiah the prophet:

"This is a voice of one
    who calls out in the desert:
'Prepare the way for the Lord.
    Make the road straight for him.
[5]Every valley should be filled in,
    and every mountain and hill should be made flat.
Roads with turns should be made straight,
    and rough roads should be made smooth.
[6]And all people will know about the
        salvation of God!' "   *Isaiah 40:3–5*

[7]To the crowds of people who came to be baptized by John, he said, "You are all snakes! Who warned you to run away from God's coming punishment? [8]Do the things that show you really have changed your hearts and lives. Don't begin to say to yourselves, 'Abraham is our father.' I tell you that God could make children for Abraham from these rocks. [9]The ax is now ready to cut down the trees, and every tree that does not produce good fruit will be cut down and thrown into the fire."[n]

[10]The people asked John, "Then what should we do?"

[11]John answered, "If you have two shirts, share with the person who does not have one. If you have food, share that also."

[12]Even tax collectors came to John to be baptized. They said to him, "Teacher, what should we do?"

[13]John said to them, "Don't take more taxes from people than you have been ordered to take."

[14]The soldiers asked John, "What about us? What should we do?"

John said to them, "Don't force people to give you money, and don't lie about them. Be satisfied with the pay you get."

[15]Since the people were hoping for the Christ to come, they wondered if John might be the one.

ROCK SOLID

Luke 3:18

Some of your friends come over for the afternoon and you hang out playing the latest version of Halo. You laugh and have a good time, and later you shoot some hoops and bum around the neighborhood. What have you gained?

When the day is over, what do you have from it? How is your life different? Could there be more to friends, more to life, than just hanging out?

Even when you're hanging out, you can be a follower of Jesus.

The Bible says, "John continued to preach the Good News, saying many other things to *encourage* the people" (Luke 3:18). He didn't suddenly start doing that as a grown man. God used him to encourage others when he was younger, too.

Every person needs friends who will be there to encourage him to keep on living for Jesus, day after day. So when you're hanging out with friends, don't let a whole afternoon go by where nothing meaningful is said. Use your words to help your friends get more excited about Jesus.

Decide now that you'll make encouragement a part of spending time with your friends. They need it, and so do you!

 3:9 The ax . . . fire. This means that God is ready to punish his people who do not obey him.

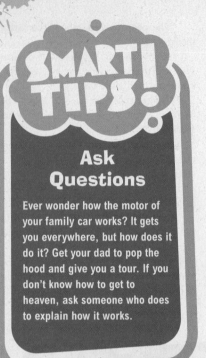

Ask Questions

Ever wonder how the motor of your family car works? It gets you everywhere, but how does it do it? Get your dad to pop the hood and give you a tour. If you don't know how to get to heaven, ask someone who does to explain how it works.

[16] John answered everyone, "I baptize you with water, but there is one coming who is greater than I am. I am not good enough to untie his sandals. He will baptize you with the Holy Spirit and fire. [17] He will come ready to clean the grain, separating the good grain from the chaff. He will put the good part of the grain into his barn, but he will burn the chaff with a fire that cannot be put out."[n] [18] And John continued to preach the Good News, saying many other things to encourage the people.

[19] But John spoke against Herod, the governor, because of his sin with Herodias, the wife of Herod's brother, and because of the many other evil things Herod did. [20] So Herod did something even worse: He put John in prison.

JESUS IS BAPTIZED BY JOHN

[21] When all the people were being baptized by John, Jesus also was baptized. While Jesus was praying, heaven opened [22] and the Holy Spirit came down on him in the form of a dove. Then a voice came from heaven, saying, "You are my Son, whom I love, and I am very pleased with you."

THE FAMILY HISTORY OF JESUS

[23] When Jesus began his ministry, he was about thirty years old. People thought that Jesus was Joseph's son.
Joseph was the son[n] of Heli.
[24] Heli was the son of Matthat.
Matthat was the son of Levi.
Levi was the son of Melki.
Melki was the son of Jannai.
Jannai was the son of Joseph.
[25] Joseph was the son of Mattathias.
Mattathias was the son of Amos.
Amos was the son of Nahum.
Nahum was the son of Esli.
Esli was the son of Naggai.
[26] Naggai was the son of Maath.
Maath was the son of Mattathias.
Mattathias was the son of Semein.

Semein was the son of Josech.
Josech was the son of Joda.
[27] Joda was the son of Joanan.
Joanan was the son of Rhesa.
Rhesa was the son of Zerubbabel.
Zerubbabel was the grandson of Shealtiel.
Shealtiel was the son of Neri.
[28] Neri was the son of Melki.
Melki was the son of Addi.
Addi was the son of Cosam.
Cosam was the son of Elmadam.
Elmadam was the son of Er.
[29] Er was the son of Joshua.
Joshua was the son of Eliezer.
Eliezer was the son of Jorim.
Jorim was the son of Matthat.
Matthat was the son of Levi.
[30] Levi was the son of Simeon.
Simeon was the son of Judah.
Judah was the son of Joseph.
Joseph was the son of Jonam.
Jonam was the son of Eliakim.
[31] Eliakim was the son of Melea.
Melea was the son of Menna.
Menna was the son of Mattatha.
Mattatha was the son of Nathan.
Nathan was the son of David.
[32] David was the son of Jesse.
Jesse was the son of Obed.
Obed was the son of Boaz.
Boaz was the son of Salmon.[n]
Salmon was the son of Nahshon.
[33] Nahshon was the son of Amminadab.
Amminadab was the son of Admin.
Admin was the son of Arni.
Arni was the son of Hezron.

COOL!

Jerusalem: City of Peace

"Jerusalem" means "City of Peace," but it's been fought over for centuries. King David conquered it more than 3,000 years ago; and the Jews have always cherished Jerusalem, especially because it's the site of God's holy Temple.

Christians honor Jerusalem because it's where Jesus died and rose again. Muslims value it because the Dome of the Rock is there—the third holiest place in Islam.

Christians and Muslims fought over Jerusalem during the Crusades. Jews and Palestinians fight over it today.

Only when Jesus returns to Jerusalem will it finally become the *real* City of Peace.

3:17 He will . . . out. This means that Jesus will come to separate good people from bad people, saving the good and punishing the bad.   **3:23 son** "Son" in Jewish lists of ancestors can sometimes mean grandson or more distant relative.   **3:32 Salmon** Some Greek copies read "Sala."

Hezron was the son of Perez.
Perez was the son of Judah.
[34]Judah was the son of Jacob.
Jacob was the son of Isaac.
Isaac was the son of Abraham.
Abraham was the son of Terah.
Terah was the son of Nahor.
[35]Nahor was the son of Serug.
Serug was the son of Reu.
Reu was the son of Peleg.
Peleg was the son of Eber.
Eber was the son of Shelah.
[36]Shelah was the son of Cainan.
Cainan was the son of Arphaxad.
Arphaxad was the son of Shem.
Shem was the son of Noah.
Noah was the son of Lamech.
[37]Lamech was the son of Methuselah.
Methuselah was the son of Enoch.
Enoch was the son of Jared.
Jared was the son of Mahalalel.
Mahalalel was the son of Kenan.
[38]Kenan was the son of Enosh.
Enosh was the son of Seth.
Seth was the son of Adam.
Adam was the son of God.

JESUS IS TEMPTED BY THE DEVIL

4 Jesus, filled with the Holy Spirit, returned from the Jordan River. The Spirit led Jesus into the desert [2]where the devil tempted Jesus for forty days. Jesus ate nothing during that time, and when those days were ended, he was very hungry.

[3]The devil said to Jesus, "If you are the Son of God, tell this rock to become bread."

[4]Jesus answered, "It is written in the Scriptures: 'A person does not live on bread alone.' "[n]

[5]Then the devil took Jesus and showed him all the kingdoms of the world in an instant. [6]The devil said to Jesus, "I will give you all these kingdoms and all their power and glory. It has all been given to me, and I can give it to anyone I wish. [7]If you worship me, then it will all be yours."

[8]Jesus answered, "It is written in the Scriptures: 'You must worship the Lord your God and serve only him.' "[n]

[9]Then the devil led Jesus to Jerusalem and put him on a high place of the Temple. He said to Jesus, "If you are the Son of God, jump down. [10]It is written in the Scriptures:

'He has put his angels in charge of you
    to watch over you.'   *Psalm 91:11*
[11]It is also written:
'They will catch you in their hands
    so that you will not hit your foot on a
        rock.' "   *Psalm 91:12*

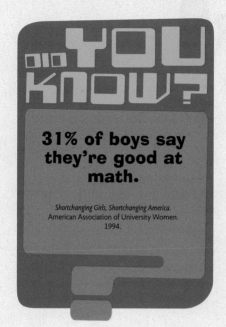

31% of boys say they're good at math.

Shortchanging Girls, Shortchanging America.
American Association of University Women.
1994.

[12]Jesus answered, "But it also says in the Scriptures: 'Do not test the Lord your God.' "[n]

[13]After the devil had tempted Jesus in every way, he left him to wait until a better time.

JESUS TEACHES THE PEOPLE

[14]Jesus returned to Galilee in the power of the Holy Spirit, and stories about him spread all through the area. [15]He began to teach in their synagogues, and everyone praised him.

[16]Jesus traveled to Nazareth, where he had grown up. On the Sabbath day he went to the synagogue, as he always did, and stood up to read. [17]The book of Isaiah the prophet was given to him. He opened the book and found the place where this is written:

[18]"The Lord has put his Spirit in me,
    because he appointed me to tell the
        Good News to the poor.
He has sent me to tell the captives they are
    free
and to tell the blind that they can see
    again.   *Isaiah 61:1*
God sent me to free those who have been
    treated unfairly   *Isaiah 58:6*
[19]   and to announce the time when the
        Lord will show his kindness."
                    Isaiah 61:2

[20]Jesus closed the book, gave it back to the assistant, and sat down. Everyone in the synagogue was watching Jesus closely. [21]He began to say to them, "While you heard these words just now, they were coming true!"

[22]All the people spoke well of Jesus and were amazed at the words of grace he spoke. They asked, "Isn't this Joseph's son?"

[23]Jesus said to them, "I know that you will tell me the old saying: 'Doctor, heal yourself.' You want to say, 'We heard about the things you did in Capernaum. Do those things here in your own town!' " [24]Then Jesus said, "I tell you the truth, a prophet is not accepted in his hometown. [25]But I tell you the truth, there were many widows in Israel during the time of Elijah. It did not rain in Israel for three and one-half years, and there was no food anywhere in the whole country. [26]But Elijah was sent to none of those widows, only to a widow in Zarephath, a town in Sidon. [27]And there were many with skin diseases living in Israel during

YOU SPEAK OUT!

Q: What is your favorite thing about church?
A: "When we have a special event." (Jacob, 11)

Q: Why should Christians go to church?
A: "Because we don't know everything about God and we can't help others if we are not willing to learn." (Curtis, 12)

Q: What's the craziest thing you've ever done?
A: "I brought my trampoline into the house and did a double front flip over the couch." (C.J., 11)

COOL!

Pagan Rome

Rome was the first modern city to reach a population of one million (around 5 B.C.). Many of these people were slaves. Many also became Christians after the message of Jesus Christ was preached there.

Evidence from the *catacombs*—underground burial chambers—shows there were a lot of Christians in Rome. Most of them were slaves.

Rome became a symbol of paganism and unbelief because some of her emperors killed Christians. But no matter how many Christians they killed, Rome couldn't stop the church from growing. Nothing can! (Matthew 16:18).

the time of the prophet Elisha. But none of them were healed, only Naaman, who was from the country of Syria."

28When all the people in the synagogue heard these things, they became very angry. 29They got up, forced Jesus out of town, and took him to the edge of the cliff on which the town was built. They planned to throw him off the edge, 30but Jesus walked through the crowd and went on his way.

JESUS FORCES OUT AN EVIL SPIRIT

31Jesus went to Capernaum, a city in Galilee, and on the Sabbath day, he taught the people. 32They were amazed at his teaching, because he spoke with authority. 33In the synagogue a man who had within him an evil spirit shouted in a loud voice, 34"Jesus of Nazareth! What do you want with us? Did you come to destroy us? I know who you are—God's Holy One!"

35Jesus commanded the evil spirit, "Be quiet! Come out of the man!" The evil spirit threw the man down to the ground before all the people and then left the man without hurting him.

36The people were amazed and said to each other, "What does this mean? With authority and power he commands evil spirits, and they come out." 37And so the news about Jesus spread to every place in the whole area.

JESUS HEALS MANY PEOPLE

38Jesus left the synagogue and went to the home of Simon." Simon's mother-in-law was sick with a high fever, and they asked Jesus to help her. 39He came to her side and commanded the fever to leave. It left her, and immediately she got up and began serving them.

40When the sun went down, the people brought those who were sick to Jesus. Putting his hands on each sick person, he healed every one of them. 41Demons came out of many people, shouting, "You are the Son of God." But Jesus commanded the demons and would not allow them to speak, because they knew Jesus was the Christ.

42At daybreak, Jesus went to a lonely place, but the people looked for him. When they found him, they tried to keep him from leaving. 43But Jesus said to them, "I must preach about God's kingdom to other towns, too. This is why I was sent."

44Then he kept on preaching in the synagogues of Judea."

JESUS' FIRST FOLLOWERS

5 One day while Jesus was standing beside Lake Galilee, many people were pressing all around him to hear the word of God. 2Jesus saw two boats at the shore of the lake. The fishermen had left them and were washing their nets. 3Jesus got into one of the boats, the one that belonged to Simon," and asked him to push off a little from the land. Then Jesus sat down and continued to teach the people from the boat.

4When Jesus had finished speaking, he said to Simon, "Take the boat into deep water, and put your nets in the water to catch some fish."

5Simon answered, "Master, we worked hard all night trying to catch fish, and we caught nothing. But you say to put the nets in the water, so I will." 6When the fishermen did as Jesus told them, they caught so many fish that the nets began to break. 7They called to their partners in the other boat to come and help them. They came and filled both boats so full that they were almost sinking.

8When Simon Peter saw what had happened, he bowed down before Jesus and said, "Go away from me, Lord. I am a sinful man!" 9He and the other fishermen were amazed at the many fish they caught, as were 10James and John, the sons of Zebedee, Simon's partners.

Jesus said to Simon, "Don't be afraid. From now on you will fish for people." 11When the men brought their boats to the shore, they left everything and followed Jesus.

JESUS HEALS A SICK MAN

12When Jesus was in one of the towns, there was a man covered with a skin disease. When he saw Jesus, he bowed before him and begged him, "Lord, you can heal me if you will."

13Jesus reached out his hand and touched the man and said, "I will. Be healed!" Immediately the disease disappeared. 14Then Jesus said, "Don't tell anyone about this, but go and show yourself to the priest" and offer a gift for your healing, as Moses commanded." This will show the people what I have done."

15But the news about Jesus spread even more. Many people came to hear Jesus and to be healed of their sicknesses, 16but Jesus often slipped away to be alone so he could pray.

4:38; 5:3 Simon Simon's other name was Peter. 4:44 Judea Some Greek copies read "Galilee." 5:14 show . . . priest The Law of Moses said a priest must say when a Jewish person with a skin disease was well. 5:14 Moses commanded Read about this in Leviticus 14:1–32.

JESUS HEALS A PARALYZED MAN

¹⁷One day as Jesus was teaching the people, the Pharisees and teachers of the law from every town in Galilee and Judea and from Jerusalem were there. The Lord was giving Jesus the power to heal people. ¹⁸Just then, some men were carrying on a mat a man who was paralyzed. They tried to bring him in and put him down before Jesus. ¹⁹But because there were so many people there, they could not find a way in. So they went up on the roof and lowered the man on his mat through the ceiling into the middle of the crowd right before Jesus. ²⁰Seeing their faith, Jesus said, "Friend, your sins are forgiven."

²¹The Jewish teachers of the law and the Pharisees thought to themselves, "Who is this man who is speaking as if he were God? Only God can forgive sins."

²²But Jesus knew what they were thinking and said, "Why are you thinking these things? ²³Which is easier: to say, 'Your sins are forgiven,' or to say, 'Stand up and walk'? ²⁴But I will prove to you that the Son of Man has authority on earth to forgive sins." So Jesus said to the paralyzed man, "I tell you, stand up, take your mat, and go home."

²⁵At once the man stood up before them, picked up his mat, and went home, praising God. ²⁶All the people were fully amazed and began to praise God. They were filled with much respect and said, "Today we have seen amazing things!"

LEVI FOLLOWS JESUS

²⁷After this, Jesus went out and saw a tax collector named Levi sitting in the tax collector's booth. Jesus said to him, "Follow me!" ²⁸So Levi got up, left everything, and followed him.

²⁹Then Levi gave a big dinner for Jesus at his house. Many tax collectors and other people were eating there, too. ³⁰But the Pharisees and the men who taught the law for the Pharisees began to complain to Jesus' followers, "Why do you eat and drink with tax collectors and sinners?"

³¹Jesus answered them, "It is not the healthy people who need a doctor, but the sick. ³²I have not come to invite good people but sinners to change their hearts and lives."

JESUS ANSWERS A QUESTION

³³They said to Jesus, "John's followers often fast* for a certain time and pray, just as the Pharisees do. But your followers eat and drink all the time."

³⁴Jesus said to them, "You cannot make the friends of the bridegroom fast while he is still with them. ³⁵But the time will come when the bridegroom will be taken away from them, and then they will fast."

³⁶Jesus told them this story: "No one takes cloth off a new coat to cover a hole in an old coat. Otherwise, he ruins the new coat, and the cloth from the new coat will not be the same as the old cloth. ³⁷Also, no one ever pours new wine into old leather bags. Otherwise, the new wine will break the bags, the wine will spill out, and the leather bags will be ruined. ³⁸New wine must be put into new leather bags. ³⁹No one after drinking old wine wants new wine, because he says, 'The old wine is better.' "

JESUS IS LORD OVER THE SABBATH

6 One Sabbath day Jesus was walking through some fields of grain. His followers picked the heads of grain, rubbed them in their hands, and ate them. ²Some Pharisees said, "Why do you do what is not lawful on the Sabbath day?"

Q: I heard somebody say that God doesn't want us to act religious. Is that right?

A: God doesn't want us to fool people into thinking we're walking with him. He wants us to actually walk with him. And that means admitting our mistakes. One of the words Jesus used to describe the religious leaders of his day was "hypocrite" (Mark 7:6). *Hypocrite* means being a fake or posing as one thing while really being something else. You'll notice that the most mature Christians are also the most humble, because they're honest about their shortcomings.

Q: Sometimes I lie when I'm embarrassed to tell the truth. What should I do?

A: It's easy to tell a lie when it gets you out of trouble in the short term. Yet God said "Do not lie" in the Ten Commandments (Exodus 20:7–17). Telling the truth will save you from getting into a lot of trouble later on. Abraham Lincoln, who faced many difficult decisions as president, said it well: "Honesty is the best policy."

Q: Was any part of the Bible written to be entertaining or is it all serious?

A: The Bible was written to deal with a very serious problem: human rebellion against God and its consequences. So it's not what you'd call "light reading." The Bible was written to instruct and not entertain, yet many stories that Jesus told are ironic (meaning that you expect one thing but another thing actually happens)—and that can be entertaining. There are also many stories of adventures and heroic deeds in the Bible, which generations of readers have found exciting and inspiring.

⭐ **5:33 fast** The people would give up eating for a special time of prayer and worship to God. It was also done to show sadness and disappointment.

ROCK SOLID

Luke 5:8-10

We've all done some things we wish we hadn't done. Do you ever wish you could start over, that you could erase everything in your past that you're not happy about and become a totally different person?

God says it's possible! When Peter the fisherman saw Jesus perform a miracle right next to his boat, he said, "Go away from me, Lord. I am a sinful man!" But Jesus said, "Don't be afraid. From now on you will fish for people" (Luke 5:8–10).

Beginning a relationship with Jesus Christ isn't like starting a new hobby; it's becoming a totally different person—a new you. Everything—not just a few things—is brand-new!

Has your life been one big mess to this point? You don't have to live that way. It doesn't have to be like that. Jesus is ready to give you a whole new life. It's even better than getting a new house, a new video game, a new bike, or a whole new wardrobe. It's like getting a whole new you! Isn't it time to have everything made new?

[3]Jesus answered, "Have you not read what David did when he and those with him were hungry? [4]He went into God's house and took and ate the holy bread, which is lawful only for priests to eat. And he gave some to the people who were with him." [5]Then Jesus said to the Pharisees, "The Son of Man is Lord of the Sabbath day."

JESUS HEALS A MAN'S HAND

[6]On another Sabbath day Jesus went into the synagogue and was teaching, and a man with a crippled right hand was there. [7]The teachers of the law and the Pharisees were watching closely to see if Jesus would heal on the Sabbath day so they could accuse him. [8]But he knew what they were thinking, and he said to the man with the crippled hand, "Stand up here in the middle of everyone." The man got up and stood there. [9]Then Jesus said to them, "I ask you, which is lawful on the Sabbath day: to do good or to do evil, to save a life or to destroy it?" [10]Jesus looked around at all of them and said to the man, "Hold out your hand." The man held out his hand, and it was healed.

[11]But the Pharisees and the teachers of the law were very angry and discussed with each other what they could do to Jesus.

JESUS CHOOSES HIS APOSTLES

[12]At that time Jesus went off to a mountain to pray, and he spent the night praying to God. [13]The next morning, Jesus called his followers to him and chose twelve of them, whom he named apostles: [14]Simon (Jesus named him Peter), his brother Andrew, James, John, Philip, Bartholomew, [15]Matthew, Thomas, James son of Alphaeus, Simon (called the Zealot), [16]Judas son of James, and Judas Iscariot, who later turned Jesus over to his enemies.

JESUS TEACHES AND HEALS

[17]Jesus and the apostles came down from the mountain, and he stood on level ground. A large group of his followers was there, as well as many people from all around Judea, Jerusalem, and the seacoast cities of Tyre and Sidon. [18]They all came to hear Jesus teach and to be healed of their sicknesses, and he healed those who were troubled by evil spirits. [19]All the people were trying to touch Jesus, because power was coming from him and healing them all.

[20]Jesus looked at his followers and said,
"You people who are poor are blessed,
    because the kingdom of God belongs
        to you.

[21]You people who are now hungry are
        blessed,
    because you will be satisfied.
You people who are now crying are
        blessed,
    because you will laugh with joy.

[22]"People will hate you, shut you out, insult you, and say you are evil because you follow the Son of Man. But when they do, you will be blessed. [23]Be full of joy at that time, because you have a great reward in heaven. Their ancestors did the same things to the prophets.

[24]"But how terrible it will be for you who are
        rich,
    because you have had your easy life.
[25]How terrible it will be for you who are full
        now,
    because you will be hungry.
How terrible it will be for you who are
        laughing now,
    because you will be sad and cry.

[26]"How terrible when everyone says only good things about you, because their ancestors said the same things about the false prophets.

LOVE YOUR ENEMIES

[27]"But I say to you who are listening, love your enemies. Do good to those who hate you, [28]bless those who curse you, pray for those who are cruel to you. [29]If anyone slaps you on one cheek, offer him the other cheek, too. If someone takes your coat, do not stop him from taking your shirt. [30]Give to everyone who asks you, and when someone takes something that is yours, don't ask for it back. [31]Do to others what you would want them to do to you. [32]If you love only the people who love you, what praise should you get? Even sinners love the people who love them. [33]If you do good only to those who do good to you, what praise should you get? Even sinners do that! [34]If you lend things to people, always hoping to get something back, what praise should you get? Even sinners lend to other sinners so that they can get back the same amount! [35]But love your enemies, do good to them, and lend to them without hoping to get anything back. Then you will have a great reward, and you will be children of the Most High God, because he is kind even to people who are ungrateful and full of sin. [36]Show mercy, just as your Father shows mercy.

LOOK AT YOURSELVES

[37]"Don't judge others, and you will not be judged. Don't accuse others of being guilty, and you will not be accused of being guilty.

Forgive, and you will be forgiven. ³⁸Give, and you will receive. You will be given much. Pressed down, shaken together, and running over, it will spill into your lap. The way you give to others is the way God will give to you."

³⁹Jesus told them this story: "Can a blind person lead another blind person? No! Both of them will fall into a ditch. ⁴⁰A student is not better than the teacher, but the student who has been fully trained will be like the teacher.

⁴¹"Why do you notice the little piece of dust in your friend's eye, but you don't notice the big piece of wood in your own eye? ⁴²How can you say to your friend, 'Friend, let me take that little piece of dust out of your eye' when you cannot see that big piece of wood in your own eye! You hypocrite! First, take the wood out of your own eye. Then you will see clearly to take the dust out of your friend's eye.

TWO KINDS OF FRUIT

⁴³"A good tree does not produce bad fruit, nor does a bad tree produce good fruit. ⁴⁴Each tree is known by its own fruit. People don't gather figs from thornbushes, and they don't get grapes from bushes. ⁴⁵Good people bring good things out of the good they stored in their hearts. But evil people bring evil things out of the evil they stored in their hearts. People speak the things that are in their hearts.

TWO KINDS OF PEOPLE

⁴⁶"Why do you call me, 'Lord, Lord,' but do not do what I say? ⁴⁷I will show you what everyone is like who comes to me and hears my words and obeys. ⁴⁸That person is like a man building a house who dug deep and laid the foundation on rock. When the floods came, the water tried to wash the house away, but it could not shake it, because the house was built well. ⁴⁹But the one who hears my words and does not obey is like a man who built his house on the ground without a foundation. When the floods came, the house quickly fell and was completely destroyed."

JESUS HEALS A SOLDIER'S SERVANT

7 When Jesus finished saying all these things to the people, he went to Capernaum. ²There was an army officer who had a servant who was very important to him. The servant was so sick he was nearly dead. ³When the officer heard about Jesus, he sent some Jewish elders to him to ask Jesus to come and heal his servant. ⁴The men went to Jesus and begged him, saying, "This officer is worthy of your help. ⁵He loves our people, and he built us a synagogue."

⁶So Jesus went with the men. He was getting near the officer's house when the officer sent friends to say, "Lord, don't trouble yourself, because I am not worthy to have you come into my house. ⁷That is why I did not come to you myself. But you only need to command it, and my servant will be healed. ⁸I, too, am a man under the authority of others, and I have soldiers under my command. I tell one soldier, 'Go,' and he goes. I tell another soldier, 'Come,' and he comes. I say to my servant, 'Do this,' and my servant does it."

⁹When Jesus heard this, he was amazed. Turning to the crowd that was following him, he said, "I tell you, this is the greatest faith I have found anywhere, even in Israel."

¹⁰Those who had been sent to Jesus went back to the house where they found the servant in good health.

JESUS BRINGS A MAN BACK TO LIFE

¹¹Soon afterwards Jesus went to a town called Nain, and his followers and a large crowd traveled with him. ¹²When he came near the town gate, he saw a funeral. A mother, who was a widow, had lost her only son. A large crowd from the town was with the mother while her son was being carried out. ¹³When the Lord saw her, he felt very sorry for her and said, "Don't cry." ¹⁴He went up and touched the coffin, and the people who were carrying it stopped. Jesus said, "Young man, I tell you, get up!" ¹⁵And the son sat up and began to talk. Then Jesus gave him back to his mother.

trustables

Luke 6:38

Are you familiar with the phrase "You can't have your cake and eat it, too"? It's a logical impossibility. Once you gobble down that moist, delicious cake and lick the frosting off the plate, it's gone. As much as we might still want that piece of cake, we can no longer have it.

Something else that seems illogical (but is true) is this: if you want to get something, you should give it away. Actually, this is a promise in the Bible! Luke 6:38 tells us, "Give, and you will be given much.…It will spill into your lap." In other words, when we are willing to give something away, it comes back to us even bigger. It could be money. It could be friendship. It could be time.

The logical thing would be to hang on to something so we don't risk losing what we already have. But God isn't always logical to humans! He wants to see that we trust him with our stuff. If we are willing to give it away, he can see that we trust him. Then he is delighted to give us more than we ever had in the first place. It's amazing but true. Try it out. Give something away and then sit back and watch as God makes it "spill into your lap."

"MAKE A DIFFERENCE"

"What are you thinking about, Jared?" Grandpa Vernon's voice interrupted.

"What the pastor said about making a difference. I mean, I can't preach yet, and I don't think Mom would let me be a missionary in Africa."

"Hmm, I see what you mean." Grandpa Vernon smiled. "Want a surefire idea?"

"Yeah!" Jared answered.

"Well, since Pastor was talking about loving our neighbors, let's start there. One way I feel loved is when someone listens to me—listens really carefully."

"Yeah, I like that, too!" Jared said. "But how can I do that?"

"Well, seems to me you're doing a good job right now. You're looking right at me, you're smiling, and you're paying attention to what I say. There are a lot of folks who'd understand a whole lot more about God's love if someone would listen the way you are. Why don't you give it a try?"

Jared turned to leave.

"Well, now what about listening to me?" Grandpa Vernon teased. "Just kidding, Jared. You go ahead. You got a lot of people to love."

If you look at the person you're listening to, smile, and pay attention to what's being said, you can make a difference, too!

[16]All the people were amazed and began praising God, saying, "A great prophet has come to us! God has come to help his people."

[17]This news about Jesus spread through all Judea and into all the places around there.

JOHN ASKS A QUESTION

[18]John's followers told him about all these things. He called for two of his followers [19]and sent them to the Lord to ask, "Are you the One who is to come, or should we wait for someone else?"

[20]When the men came to Jesus, they said, "John the Baptist sent us to you with this question: 'Are you the One who is to come, or should we wait for someone else?' "

[21]At that time, Jesus healed many people of their sicknesses, diseases, and evil spirits, and he gave sight to many blind people. [22]Then Jesus answered John's followers, "Go tell John what you saw and heard here. The blind can see, the crippled can walk, and people with skin diseases are healed. The deaf can hear, the dead are raised to life, and the Good News is preached to the poor. [23]Those who do not stumble in their faith because of me are blessed!"

[24]When John's followers left, Jesus began talking to the people about John: "What did you go out into the desert to see? A reed[n] blown by the wind? [25]What did you go out to see? A man dressed in fine clothes? No, people who have fine clothes and much wealth live in kings' palaces. [26]But what did you go out to see? A prophet? Yes, and I tell you, John is more than a prophet. [27]This was written about him:

'I will send my messenger ahead of you,
who will prepare the way for you.'

Malachi 3:1

[28]I tell you, John is greater than any other person ever born, but even the least important person in the kingdom of God is greater than John."

[29](When the people, including the tax collectors, heard this, they all agreed that God's teaching was good, because they had been baptized by John. [30]But the Pharisees and experts on the law refused to accept God's plan for themselves; they did not let John baptize them.)

[31]Then Jesus said, "What shall I say about the people of this time? What are they like? [32]They are like children sitting in the marketplace, calling to one another and saying,

'We played music for you, but you did not dance;
we sang a sad song, but you did not cry.'

[33]John the Baptist came and did not eat bread or drink wine, and you say, 'He has a demon in him.' [34]The Son of Man came eating and drinking, and you say, 'Look at him! He eats too much and drinks too much wine, and he is a friend of tax collectors and sinners!' [35]But wisdom is proved to be right by what it does."

A WOMAN WASHES JESUS' FEET

[36]One of the Pharisees asked Jesus to eat with him, so Jesus went into the Pharisee's house and sat at the table. [37]A sinful woman in the town learned that Jesus was eating at the Pharisee's house. So she brought an alabaster jar of perfume [38]and stood behind Jesus at his feet, crying. She began to wash his feet with her tears, and she dried them with her hair, kissing them many times and rubbing them with the perfume. [39]When the Pharisee who asked Jesus to come to his house saw this, he thought to himself, "If Jesus were a prophet, he would know that the woman touching him is a sinner!"

[40]Jesus said to the Pharisee, "Simon, I have something to say to you."

Simon said, "Teacher, tell me."

[41]Jesus said, "Two people owed money to the same banker. One owed five hundred coins[n] and the other owed fifty. [42]They had no money to pay what they owed, but the banker told both of them they did not have to pay him. Which person will love the banker more?"

[43]Simon, the Pharisee, answered, "I think it would be the one who owed him the most money."

Jesus said to Simon, "You are right." [44]Then Jesus turned toward the woman and

---

⭐ **7:24 reed** It means that John was not ordinary or weak like grass blown by the wind.   **7:41 coins** Roman denarii. One coin was the average pay for one day's work.

said to Simon, "Do you see this woman? When I came into your house, you gave me no water for my feet, but she washed my feet with her tears and dried them with her hair. ⁴⁵You gave me no kiss of greeting, but she has been kissing my feet since I came in. ⁴⁶You did not put oil on my head, but she poured perfume on my feet. ⁴⁷I tell you that her many sins are forgiven, so she showed great love. But the person who is forgiven only a little will love only a little."

⁴⁸Then Jesus said to her, "Your sins are forgiven."

⁴⁹The people sitting at the table began to say among themselves, "Who is this who even forgives sins?"

⁵⁰Jesus said to the woman, "Because you believed, you are saved from your sins. Go in peace."

THE GROUP WITH JESUS

8 After this, while Jesus was traveling through some cities and small towns, he preached and told the Good News about God's kingdom. The twelve apostles were with him, ²and also some women who had been healed of sicknesses and evil spirits: Mary, called Magdalene, from whom seven demons had gone out; ³Joanna, the wife of Cuza (the manager of Herod's house); Susanna; and many others. These women used their own money to help Jesus and his apostles.

A STORY ABOUT PLANTING SEED

⁴When a great crowd was gathered, and people were coming to Jesus from every town, he told them this story:

⁵"A farmer went out to plant his seed. While he was planting, some seed fell by the road. People walked on the seed, and the birds ate it up. ⁶Some seed fell on rock, and when it began to grow, it died because it had no water. ⁷Some seed fell among thorny weeds, but the weeds grew up with it and choked the good plants. ⁸And some seed fell on good ground and grew and made a hundred times more."

As Jesus finished the story, he called out, "Let those with ears use them and listen!"

⁹Jesus' followers asked him what this story meant.

¹⁰Jesus said, "You have been chosen to know the secrets about the kingdom of God. But I use stories to speak to other people so that:

'They will look, but they may not see.
They will listen, but they may not
    understand.'   *Isaiah 6:9*

¹¹"This is what the story means: The seed is God's message. ¹²The seed that fell beside the road is like the people who hear God's teaching, but the devil comes and takes it away from them so they cannot believe it and be saved. ¹³The seed that fell on rock is like those who hear God's teaching and accept it gladly, but they don't allow the teaching to go deep into their lives. They believe for a while, but when trouble comes, they give up. ¹⁴The seed that

fell among the thorny weeds is like those who hear God's teaching, but they let the worries, riches, and pleasures of this life keep them from growing and producing good fruit. ¹⁵And the seed that fell on the good ground is like those who hear God's teaching with good, honest hearts and obey it and patiently produce good fruit.

USE WHAT YOU HAVE

¹⁶"No one after lighting a lamp covers it with a bowl or hides it under a bed. Instead, the person puts it on a lampstand so those who come in will see the light. ¹⁷Everything that is hidden will become clear, and every secret thing will be made known. ¹⁸So be careful how you listen. Those who have understanding will be given more. But those who do not have understanding, even what they think they have will be taken away from them."

JESUS' TRUE FAMILY

¹⁹Jesus' mother and brothers came to see him, but there was such a crowd they could not get to him. ²⁰Someone said to Jesus, "Your mother and your brothers are standing outside, wanting to see you."

²¹Jesus answered them, "My mother and my brothers are those who listen to God's teaching and obey it!"

SMART TIPS!

Keep Your Promises

How do you feel when someone breaks a promise to you? Probably lousy! It's hard to trust people who break promises. God never breaks his promises; neither should we. That means doing what we say we will do. No excuses!

---

dare to do

Matthew 9:11
Read It: Jesus spent time with the rejects of society.
Do It: Ask your parents about how you can help a homeless person. Jesus loves the homeless just as much as he loves you.

Matthew 9:12
Read It: Jesus didn't come for people who have it all together.
Do It: Don't just witness to the people you think would make good Christians. Go to the people no one else likes: the bully, the nerd, or the poor kid.

Matthew 9:13
Read It: God wants kindness more than sacrifice.
Do It: Worship is important, but so is living out your faith. Offer a helping hand to someone who needs it.

dare to do

Matthew 10:34
Read It: Sometimes the name of Jesus will divide people.
Do It: Don't be surprised if you stand up for Jesus and people get mad. Remember, they don't like *you* because they don't like him.

Matthew 10:35
Read It: If you follow Jesus, people in your own family may even hate you.
Do It: If your family is against your following Jesus, then look to your church and other Christians for support; they are your new "family."

Matthew 10:37
Read It: Following Jesus means you love him more than any other person in your life.
Do It: Who do you love the most? If it's not Jesus, ask God to give you more love for him.

JESUS CALMS A STORM

[22] One day Jesus and his followers got into a boat, and he said to them, "Let's go across the lake." And so they started across. [23] While they were sailing, Jesus fell asleep. A very strong wind blew up on the lake, causing the boat to fill with water, and they were in danger. [24] The followers went to Jesus and woke him, saying, "Master! Master! We will drown!"

Jesus got up and gave a command to the wind and the waves. They stopped, and it became calm. [25] Jesus said to his followers, "Where is your faith?"

The followers were afraid and amazed and said to each other, "Who is this that commands even the wind and the water, and they obey him?"

A MAN WITH DEMONS INSIDE HIM

[26] Jesus and his followers sailed across the lake from Galilee to the area of the Gerasene[n] people. [27] When Jesus got out on the land, a man from the town who had demons inside him came to Jesus. For a long time he had worn no clothes and had lived in the burial caves, not in a house. [28] When he saw Jesus, he cried out and fell down before him. He said with a loud voice, "What do you want with me, Jesus, Son of the Most High God? I beg you, don't torture me!" [29] He said this because Jesus was commanding the evil spirit to come out of the man. Many times it had taken hold of him. Though he had been kept under guard and chained hand and foot, he had broken his chains and had been forced by the demon out into a lonely place.

[30] Jesus asked him, "What is your name?"

He answered, "Legion,"[n] because many demons were in him. [31] The demons begged Jesus not to send them into eternal darkness.[n] [32] A large herd of pigs was feeding on a hill, and the demons begged Jesus to allow them to go into the pigs. So Jesus allowed them to do this. [33] When the demons came out of the man, they went into the pigs, and the herd ran down the hill into the lake and was drowned.

[34] When the herdsmen saw what had happened, they ran away and told about this in the town and the countryside. [35] And people went to see what had happened. When they came to Jesus, they found the man sitting at Jesus' feet, clothed and in his right mind, because the demons were gone. But the people were frightened. [36] The people who saw this happen told the others how Jesus had made the man well. [37] All the people of the Gerasene country asked Jesus to leave, because they were all very afraid. So Jesus got into the boat and went back to Galilee.

[38] The man whom Jesus had healed begged to go with him, but Jesus sent him away, saying, [39] "Go back home and tell people how much God has done for you." So the man went all over town telling how much Jesus had done for him.

JESUS GIVES LIFE TO A DEAD GIRL AND HEALS A SICK WOMAN

[40] When Jesus got back to Galilee, a crowd welcomed him, because everyone was waiting for him. [41] A man named Jairus, a leader of the synagogue, came to Jesus and fell at his feet, begging him to come to his house. [42] Jairus' only daughter, about twelve years old, was dying.

While Jesus was on his way to Jairus' house, the people were crowding all around him. [43] A woman was in the crowd who had been bleeding for twelve years,[n] but no one was able to heal her. [44] She came up behind Jesus and touched the edge of his coat, and instantly her bleeding stopped. [45] Then Jesus said, "Who touched me?"

When all the people said they had not touched him, Peter said, "Master, the people are all around you and are pushing against you."

[46] But Jesus said, "Someone did touch me, because I felt power go out from me." [47] When the woman saw she could not hide, she came forward, shaking, and fell down before Jesus. While all the people listened, she told why she had touched him and how she had been instantly healed. [48] Jesus said to her, "Dear woman, you are made well because you believed. Go in peace."

[49] While Jesus was still speaking, someone came from the house of the synagogue leader and said to him, "Your daughter is dead. Don't bother the teacher anymore."

[50] When Jesus heard this, he said to Jairus, "Don't be afraid. Just believe, and your daughter will be well."

[51] When Jesus went to the house, he let only Peter, John, James, and the girl's father and mother go inside with him. [52] All the people were crying and feeling sad because the girl was dead, but Jesus said, "Stop crying. She is not dead, only asleep."

[53] The people laughed at Jesus because they knew the girl was dead. [54] But Jesus took hold of her hand and called to her, "My child, stand up!" [55] Her spirit came back into her, and she stood up at once. Then Jesus ordered that she be given something to eat. [56] The girl's parents were amazed, but Jesus told them not to tell anyone what had happened.

JESUS SENDS OUT THE APOSTLES

9 Jesus called the twelve apostles together and gave them power and authority over all demons and the ability to heal sicknesses. [2] He sent the apostles out to tell about God's kingdom and to heal the sick. [3] He said to them, "Take nothing for your trip, neither a walking stick, bag, bread, money, or extra clothes. [4] When you enter a house, stay there until it is time to leave. [5] If people do not

---

8:26 Gerasene From Gerasa, an area southeast of Lake Galilee. The exact location is uncertain and some Greek copies read "Gadarene"; others read "Gergesene." **8:30 Legion** Means very many. A legion was about five thousand men in the Roman army. **8:31 eternal darkness** Literally, "the abyss," something like a pit or a hole that has no end. **8:43 years** Some Greek copies continue, "and she had spent all the money she had on doctors."

welcome you, shake the dust off of your feet" as you leave the town, as a warning to them."

[6]So the apostles went out and traveled through all the towns, preaching the Good News and healing people everywhere.

HEROD IS CONFUSED ABOUT JESUS

[7]Herod, the governor, heard about all the things that were happening and was confused, because some people said, "John the Baptist has risen from the dead." [8]Others said, "Elijah has come to us." And still others said, "One of the prophets who lived long ago has risen from the dead." [9]Herod said, "I cut off John's head, so who is this man I hear such things about?" And Herod kept trying to see Jesus.

MORE THAN FIVE THOUSAND FED

[10]When the apostles returned, they told Jesus everything they had done. Then Jesus took them with him to a town called Bethsaida where they could be alone together. [11]But the people learned where Jesus went and followed him. He welcomed them and talked with them about God's kingdom and healed those who needed to be healed.

[12]Late in the afternoon, the twelve apostles came to Jesus and said, "Send the people away. They need to go to the towns and countryside around here and find places to sleep and something to eat, because no one lives in this place."

[13]But Jesus said to them, "You give them something to eat."

They said, "We have only five loaves of bread and two fish, unless we go buy food for all these people." [14](There were about five thousand men there.)

Jesus said to his followers, "Tell the people to sit in groups of about fifty people."

[15]So the followers did this, and all the people sat down. [16]Then Jesus took the five loaves of bread and two fish, and looking up to heaven, he thanked God for the food. Then he divided the food and gave it to the followers to give to the people. [17]They all ate and were satisfied, and what was left over was gathered up, filling twelve baskets.

JESUS IS THE CHRIST

[18]One time when Jesus was praying alone, his followers were with him, and he asked them, "Who do the people say I am?"

[19]They answered, "Some say you are John the Baptist. Others say you are Elijah." And others say you are one of the prophets from long ago who has come back to life."

[20]Then Jesus asked, "But who do you say I am?"

Peter answered, "You are the Christ from God."

[21]Jesus warned them not to tell anyone, saying, [22]"The Son of Man must suffer many things. He will be rejected by the Jewish elders, the leading priests, and the teachers of the law. He will be killed and after three days will be raised from the dead."

[23]Jesus said to all of them, "If people want to follow me, they must give up the things they want. They must be willing to give up their lives daily to follow me. [24]Those who want to save their lives will give up true life. But those who give up their lives for me will have true life. [25]It is worthless to have the whole world if they themselves are destroyed or lost. [26]If people are ashamed of me and my teaching, then the Son of Man will be ashamed of them when he comes in his glory and with the glory of the Father and the holy angels. [27]I tell you the truth, some people standing here will see the kingdom of God before they die."

Q: Are all other religions besides Christianity wrong?

A: Other religions have some truth in them. But only Christianity is 100 percent true. Followers of Judaism believe in the same Old Testament as Christians do, but they don't accept Jesus as the Messiah. Buddhism has some excellent teaching on self-control but no way to pay for our sin and no belief in God. Some people say it doesn't matter which religion you follow. But it does! Christianity is very different from other religions, and if you follow something else you will not receive eternal life (John 14:6).

Q: Does God get angry?

A: Yes, God does get angry. But it's not the kind of anger we experience. God doesn't have an angry emotion that causes him to do something on the spur of the moment. He has godly anger, which means that he gets angry at sin and people who do evil. He desires for people to get what they really deserve. God's *mercy* is when he does not give us what we deserve, and instead pays the price for our sins himself.

Q: Why does every country speak its own language?

A: When people live together in a community, they tend to develop their own way of talking. Over generations, they end up with their own language. The country of India has many people groups who live in areas that are difficult to travel in and out of, so each group has their own language. Because it's easy to travel across the U.S., there is only one official language. The Bible tells us that humans originally spoke one language (Genesis 11:1-9)—but now there are thousands.

9:5 shake . . . feet A warning. It showed that they had rejected these people.   **9:19 Elijah** A man who spoke for God and who lived hundreds of years before Christ. See 1 Kings 17.

JESUS TALKS WITH MOSES AND ELIJAH

²⁸About eight days after Jesus said these things, he took Peter, John, and James and went up on a mountain to pray. ²⁹While Jesus was praying, the appearance of his face changed, and his clothes became shining white. ³⁰Then two men, Moses and Elijah,ⁿ were talking with Jesus. ³¹They appeared in heavenly glory, talking about his departure which he would soon bring about in Jerusalem. ³²Peter and the others were very sleepy, but when they awoke fully, they saw the glory of Jesus and the two men standing with him. ³³When Moses and Elijah were about to leave, Peter said to Jesus, "Master, it is good that we are here. Let us make three tents—one for you, one for Moses, and one for Elijah." (Peter did not know what he was talking about.)

³⁴While he was saying these things, a cloud came and covered them, and they became afraid as the cloud covered them. ³⁵A voice came from the cloud, saying, "This is my Son, whom I have chosen. Listen to him!"

³⁶When the voice finished speaking, only Jesus was there. Peter, John, and James said nothing and told no one at that time what they had seen.

JESUS HEALS A SICK BOY

³⁷The next day, when they came down from the mountain, a large crowd met Jesus. ³⁸A man in the crowd shouted to him, "Teacher, please come and look at my son, because he is my only child. ³⁹An evil spirit seizes my son, and suddenly he screams. It causes him to lose control of himself and foam at the mouth. The evil spirit keeps on hurting him and almost never leaves him. ⁴⁰I begged your followers to force the evil spirit out, but they could not do it."

⁴¹Jesus answered, "You people have no faith, and your lives are all wrong. How long must I stay with you and put up with you? Bring your son here."

⁴²While the boy was coming, the demon threw him on the ground and made him lose control of himself. But Jesus gave a strong command to the evil spirit and healed the boy and gave him back to his father. ⁴³All the people were amazed at the great power of God.

85% of kids call their grandparents at least once a month.

Trends & Tudes. Harris Interactive. July 2005.

JESUS TALKS ABOUT HIS DEATH

While everyone was wondering about all that Jesus did, he said to his followers, ⁴⁴"Don't forget what I tell you now: The Son of Man will be handed over to people." ⁴⁵But the followers did not understand what this meant; the meaning was hidden from them so they could not understand. But they were afraid to ask Jesus about it.

WHO IS THE GREATEST?

⁴⁶Jesus' followers began to have an argument about which one of them was the greatest. ⁴⁷Jesus knew what they were thinking, so he took a little child and stood the child beside him. ⁴⁸Then Jesus said, "Whoever accepts this little child in my name accepts me. And whoever accepts me accepts the One who sent me, because whoever is least among you all is really the greatest."

ANYONE NOT AGAINST US IS FOR US

⁴⁹John answered, "Master, we saw someone using your name to force demons out of people. We told him to stop, because he does not belong to our group."

⁵⁰But Jesus said to him, "Don't stop him, because whoever is not against you is for you."

A TOWN REJECTS JESUS

⁵¹When the time was coming near for Jesus to depart, he was determined to go to Jerusalem. ⁵²He sent some messengers ahead of him, who went into a town in Samaria to make everything ready for him. ⁵³But the people there would not welcome him, because he was set on going to Jerusalem. ⁵⁴When James and John, followers of Jesus, saw this, they said, "Lord, do you want us to call fire down from heaven and destroy those people?"ⁿ

⁵⁵But Jesus turned and scolded them. [And Jesus said, "You don't know what kind of spirit you belong to. ⁵⁶The Son of Man did not come to destroy the souls of people but to save them."]ⁿ Then they went to another town.

FOLLOWING JESUS

⁵⁷As they were going along the road, someone said to Jesus, "I will follow you any place you go."

⁵⁸Jesus said to them, "The foxes have holes to live in, and the birds have nests, but the Son of Man has no place to rest his head."

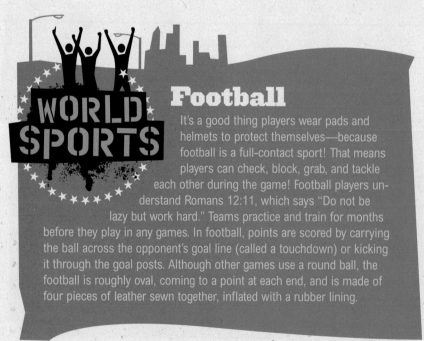

WORLD SPORTS

Football

It's a good thing players wear pads and helmets to protect themselves—because football is a full-contact sport! That means players can check, block, grab, and tackle each other during the game! Football players understand Romans 12:11, which says "Do not be lazy but work hard." Teams practice and train for months before they play in any games. In football, points are scored by carrying the ball across the opponent's goal line (called a touchdown) or kicking it through the goal posts. Although other games use a round ball, the football is roughly oval, coming to a point at each end, and is made of four pieces of leather sewn together, inflated with a rubber lining.

9:30 Moses and Elijah Two of the most important Jewish leaders in the past. God had given Moses the Law, and Elijah was an important prophet. **9:54 people** Some Greek copies continue " as Elijah did." **9:55–56 And . . . them."** Some Greek copies do not contain the bracketed text.

⁵⁹Jesus said to another man, "Follow me!"

But he said, "Lord, first let me go and bury my father."

⁶⁰But Jesus said to him, "Let the people who are dead bury their own dead. You must go and tell about the kingdom of God."

⁶¹Another man said, "I will follow you, Lord, but first let me go and say good-bye to my family."

⁶²Jesus said, "Anyone who begins to plow a field but keeps looking back is of no use in the kingdom of God."

JESUS SENDS OUT THE SEVENTY-TWO

10 After this, the Lord chose seventy-two" others and sent them out in pairs ahead of him into every town and place where he planned to go. ²He said to them, "There are a great many people to harvest, but there are only a few workers. So pray to God, who owns the harvest, that he will send more workers to help gather his harvest. ³Go now, but listen! I am sending you out like sheep among wolves. ⁴Don't carry a purse, a bag, or sandals, and don't waste time talking with people on the road. ⁵Before you go into a house, say, 'Peace be with this house.' ⁶If peace-loving people live there, your blessing of peace will stay with them, but if not, then your blessing will come back to you. ⁷Stay in the same house, eating and drinking what the people there give you. A worker should be given his pay. Don't move from house to house. ⁸If you go into a town and the people welcome you, eat what they give you. ⁹Heal the sick who live there, and tell them, 'The kingdom

of God is near you.' ¹⁰But if you go into a town, and the people don't welcome you, then go into the streets and say, ¹¹"Even the dirt from your town that sticks to our feet we wipe off against you." But remember that the kingdom of God is near.' ¹²I tell you, on the Judgment Day it will be better for the people of Sodom" than for the people of that town.

JESUS WARNS UNBELIEVERS

¹³"How terrible for you, Korazin! How terrible for you, Bethsaida! If the miracles I did in you had happened in Tyre and Sidon," those people would have changed their lives long ago. They would have worn rough cloth and put ashes on themselves to show they had changed. ¹⁴But on the Judgment Day it will be better for Tyre and Sidon than for you. ¹⁵And you, Capernaum," will you be lifted up to heaven? No! You will be thrown down to the depths!

¹⁶"Whoever listens to you listens to me, and whoever refuses to accept you refuses to accept me. And whoever refuses to accept me refuses to accept the One who sent me."

SATAN FALLS

¹⁷When the seventy-two" came back, they were very happy and said, "Lord, even the demons obeyed us when we used your name!"

¹⁸Jesus said, "I saw Satan fall like lightning from heaven. ¹⁹Listen, I have given you power to walk on snakes and scorpions, power that is greater than the enemy has. So nothing will hurt you. ²⁰But you should not be happy because the spirits obey you but because your names are written in heaven."

JESUS PRAYS TO THE FATHER

²¹Then Jesus rejoiced in the Holy Spirit and said, "I praise you, Father, Lord of heaven and earth, because you have hidden these things from the people who are wise and smart. But you have shown them to those who are like little children. Yes, Father, this is what you really wanted.

²²"My Father has given me all things. No one knows who the Son is, except the Father.

World's Greatest Detective

Sherlock Holmes is the most famous detective of all time. He starred in fifty-six stories and four novels. He had an IQ of 190, played the violin, and was an expert boxer and swordsman.

Created by Sir Arthur Conan Doyle, Holmes was based on a real man, a surgeon and teacher named Joseph Bell. Bell was known for his keen powers of observation. He could tell a lot about people just by looking at them.

Jesus was also a shrewd judge of people. He could read the people he met like open books.

He still can.

COOL!

BIBLE SUPERHEROES

Timothy

See Acts 16:1–5; 1 and 2 Timothy.

Timothy was a rising star in the early church. He was the apostle Paul's right-hand man. He grew up in the city of Lystra and had a pagan dad and a Jewish mom. She taught him the Old Testament. When he heard Paul preach, Timothy became a Christian!

Timothy went with the apostle Paul on his travels. Paul trusted him to do some tough jobs in faraway cities. Timothy was very successful, but he was no spiritual giant: he was young (1 Timothy 4:12), he was shy (1 Corinthians 16:10), and he was often sick (1 Timothy 5:23).

Timothy didn't let these things stop him from serving Jesus. Neither should we. His example shows us that God can use even weak and shy people if they have willing hearts.

And no one knows who the Father is, except the Son and those whom the Son chooses to tell."

[23] Then Jesus turned to his followers and said privately, "You are blessed to see what you now see. [24] I tell you, many prophets and kings wanted to see what you now see, but they did not, and they wanted to hear what you now hear, but they did not."

THE GOOD SAMARITAN

[25] Then an expert on the law stood up to test Jesus, saying, "Teacher, what must I do to get life forever?"

[26] Jesus said, "What is written in the law? What do you read there?"

[27] The man answered, "Love the Lord your God with all your heart, all your soul, all your strength, and all your mind."[n] Also, "Love your neighbor as you love yourself."[n]

[28] Jesus said to him, "Your answer is right. Do this and you will live."

[29] But the man, wanting to show the importance of his question, said to Jesus, "And who is my neighbor?"

[30] Jesus answered, "As a man was going down from Jerusalem to Jericho, some robbers attacked him. They tore off his clothes, beat him, and left him lying there, almost dead. [31] It happened that a priest was going down that road. When he saw the man, he walked by on the other side. [32] Next, a Levite[n] came there, and after he went over and looked at the man, he walked by on the other side of the road. [33] Then a Samaritan[n] traveling down the road came to where the hurt man was. When he saw the man, he felt very sorry for him. [34] The Samaritan went to him, poured olive oil and wine[n] on his wounds, and bandaged them. Then he put the hurt man on his own donkey and took him to an inn where he cared for him. [35] The next day, the Samaritan brought out two coins,[n] gave them to the innkeeper, and said, 'Take care of this man. If you spend more money on him, I will pay it back to you when I come again.' "

[36] Then Jesus said, "Which one of these three men do you think was a neighbor to the man who was attacked by the robbers?"

[37] The expert on the law answered, "The one who showed him mercy."

Jesus said to him, "Then go and do what he did."

MARY AND MARTHA

[38] While Jesus and his followers were traveling, Jesus went into a town. A woman named Martha let Jesus stay at her house. [39] Martha had a sister named Mary, who was sitting at Jesus' feet and listening to him teach. [40] But Martha was busy with all the work to be done. She went in and said, "Lord, don't you care that my sister has left me alone to do all the work? Tell her to help me."

[41] But the Lord answered her, "Martha, Martha, you are worried and upset about many things. [42] Only one thing is important. Mary has chosen the better thing, and it will never be taken away from her."

JESUS TEACHES ABOUT PRAYER

11 One time Jesus was praying in a certain place. When he finished, one of his followers said to him, "Lord, teach us to pray as John taught his followers."

[2] Jesus said to them, "When you pray, say:
'Father, may your name always be kept holy.
May your kingdom come.
[3] Give us the food we need for each day.
[4] Forgive us for our sins,
because we forgive everyone who has done wrong to us.
And do not cause us to be tempted.' "[n]

CONTINUE TO ASK

[5] Then Jesus said to them, "Suppose one of you went to your friend's house at midnight and said to him, 'Friend, loan me three loaves of bread. [6] A friend of mine has come into town to visit me, but I have nothing for him to eat.' [7] Your friend inside the house answers, 'Don't bother me! The door is already locked, and my children and I are in bed. I cannot get up and give you anything.' [8] I tell you, if friendship is not enough to make him get up to give you the bread, your boldness will make him get up and give you whatever you need. [9] So I tell you, ask, and God will give to you. Search, and you will find. Knock, and the door will open for you. [10] Yes, everyone who asks will receive. The one who searches will find. And everyone who knocks will have the door opened. [11] If your children ask for[n] a fish, which of you would give them a snake instead? [12] Or, if your children ask for an egg, would you give them a scorpion? [13] Even though you are bad, you know how to give good things to your children. How much more your heavenly Father will give the Holy Spirit to those who ask him!"

10:27 "Love . . . mind." Quotation from Deuteronomy 6:5.   **10:27 "Love . . . yourself."** Quotation from Leviticus 19:18.   **10:32 Levite** Levites were members of the tribe of Levi who helped the Jewish priests with their work in the Temple. Read 1 Chronicles 23:24–32.   **10:33 Samaritan** Samaritans were people from Samaria. These people were part Jewish, but the Jews did not accept them as true Jews. Samaritans and Jews disliked each other.   **10:34 olive oil and wine** Oil and wine were used like medicine to soften and clean wounds.   **10:35 coins** Roman denarii. One coin was the average pay for one day's work.   **11:2–4 'Father . . . tempted.'** Some Greek copies include phrases from Matthew's version of this prayer (Matthew 6:9–13).   **11:11 for** Some Greek copies include the phrase "for bread, which of you would give them a stone, or if they ask for . . . "

JESUS' POWER IS FROM GOD

[14]One time Jesus was sending out a demon who could not talk. When the demon came out, the man who had been unable to speak, then spoke. The people were amazed. [15]But some of them said, "Jesus uses the power of Beelzebul, the ruler of demons, to force demons out of people."

[16]Other people, wanting to test Jesus, asked him to give them a sign from heaven. [17]But knowing their thoughts, he said to them, "Every kingdom that is divided against itself will be destroyed. And a family that is divided against itself will not continue. [18]So if Satan is divided against himself, his kingdom will not continue. You say that I use the power of Beelzebul to force out demons. [19]But if I use the power of Beelzebul to force out demons, what power do your people use to force demons out? So they will be your judges. [20]But if I use the power of God to force out demons, then the kingdom of God has come to you.

[21]"When a strong person with many weapons guards his own house, his possessions are safe. [22]But when someone stronger comes and defeats him, the stronger one will take away the weapons the first man trusted and will give away the possessions.

[23]"Anyone who is not with me is against me, and anyone who does not work with me is working against me.

THE EMPTY PERSON

[24]"When an evil spirit comes out of a person, it travels through dry places, looking for a place to rest. But when it finds no place, it says, 'I will go back to the house I left.' [25]And when it comes back, it finds that house swept clean and made neat. [26]Then the evil spirit goes out and brings seven other spirits more evil than it is, and they go in and live there. So the person has even more trouble than before."

PEOPLE WHO ARE TRULY BLESSED

[27]As Jesus was saying these things, a woman in the crowd called out to Jesus, "Blessed is the mother who gave birth to you and nursed you."

[28]But Jesus said, "No, blessed are those who hear the teaching of God and obey it."

THE PEOPLE WANT A MIRACLE

[29]As the crowd grew larger, Jesus said, "The people who live today are evil. They want to see a miracle for a sign, but no sign will be given them, except the sign of Jonah." [30]As Jonah was a sign for those people who lived in Nineveh, the Son of Man will be a sign for the people of this time. [31]On the Judgment Day the Queen of the South" will stand up with the people who live now. She will show they are guilty, because she came from far away to listen to Solomon's wise teaching. And I tell you that someone greater than Solomon is here.

[32]On the Judgment Day the people of Nineveh will stand up with the people who live now, and they will show that you are guilty. When Jonah preached to them, they were sorry and changed their lives. And I tell you that someone greater than Jonah is here.

BE A LIGHT FOR THE WORLD

[33]"No one lights a lamp and puts it in a secret place or under a bowl, but on a lampstand so the people who come in can see. [34]Your eye is a light for the body. When your eyes are good, your whole body will be full of light. But when your eyes are evil, your whole body will be full of darkness. [35]So be careful not to let the light in you become darkness. [36]If your whole body is full of light, and none of it is dark, then you will shine bright, as when a lamp shines on you."

JESUS ACCUSES THE PHARISEES

[37]After Jesus had finished speaking, a Pharisee asked Jesus to eat with him. So Jesus went in and sat at the table. [38]But the Pharisee was surprised when he saw that Jesus did not wash his hands" before the meal. [39]The Lord said to him, "You Pharisees clean the outside of the cup and the dish, but inside you are full of greed and evil. [40]You foolish people! The same one who made what is outside also made what is inside. [41]So give what is in your dishes to the poor, and

---

Luke 11:34

Did you know that it's possible to make yourself glow? The first way is by eating radioactive material—but that kills you pretty soon, so don't try that. There's a second way, but it's a secret so not very many people know about it. Jesus knew all about it and told us how to glow.

Jesus said, "Your eye is a light for the body. When your eyes are good, your whole body will be full of light. But when your eyes are evil, your whole body will be full of darkness" (Luke 11:34).

If you have good eyes, your body will glow. What does that mean? Jesus meant that if you look at good things, your body will be "good" (full of light), but if you look at bad things, your body will be "bad" (full of darkness).

Here's the deal: if you're watching movies, reading books, looking at magazines, playing games that aren't good, it hurts your body. It actually brings sin and darkness into your body.

Take some of your movies, books, and videogames, to an older Christian you trust. Ask him if your things are good or bad. Get rid of stuff that hurts you and replace it with good stuff like the Bible. Guess what? You'll glow!

11:29 sign of Jonah Jonah's three days in the fish are like Jesus' three days in the tomb. See Matthew 12:40. **11:31 Queen of the South** The Queen of Sheba. She traveled a thousand miles to learn God's wisdom from Solomon. Read 1 Kings 10:1–3. **11:38 wash his hands** This was a Jewish religious custom that the Pharisees thought was very important.

then you will be fully clean. [42]How terrible for you Pharisees! You give God one-tenth of even your mint, your rue, and every other plant in your garden. But you fail to be fair to others and to love God. These are the things you should do while continuing to do those other things. [43]How terrible for you Pharisees, because you love to have the most important seats in the synagogues, and you love to be greeted with respect in the marketplaces. [44]How terrible for you, because you are like hidden graves, which people walk on without knowing."

JESUS TALKS TO EXPERTS ON THE LAW

[45]One of the experts on the law said to Jesus, "Teacher, when you say these things, you are insulting us, too."

[46]Jesus answered, "How terrible for you, you experts on the law! You make strict rules that are very hard for people to obey, but you yourselves don't even try to follow those rules. [47]How terrible for you, because you build tombs for the prophets whom your ancestors killed! [48]And now you show that you approve of what your ancestors did. They killed the prophets, and you build tombs for them! [49]This is why in his wisdom God said, 'I will send prophets and apostles to them. They will kill some, and they will treat others cruelly.' [50]So you who live now will be punished for the deaths of all the prophets who were killed

since the beginning of the world— [51]from the killing of Abel to the killing of Zechariah," who died between the altar and the Temple. Yes, I tell you that you who are alive now will be punished for them all.

[52]"How terrible for you, you experts on the law. You have taken away the key to learning about God. You yourselves would not learn, and you stopped others from learning, too."

[53]When Jesus left, the teachers of the law and the Pharisees began to give him trouble, asking him questions about many things, [54]trying to catch him saying something wrong.

DON'T BE LIKE THE PHARISEES

12 So many thousands of people had gathered that they were stepping on each other. Jesus spoke first to his followers, saying, "Beware of the yeast of the Pharisees, because they are hypocrites. [2]Everything that is hidden will be shown, and everything that is secret will be made known. [3]What you have said in the dark will be heard in the light, and what you have whispered in an inner room will be shouted from the housetops.

[4]"I tell you, my friends, don't be afraid of people who can kill the body but after that can do nothing more to hurt you. [5]I will show you the one to fear. Fear the one who has the power to kill you and also to throw you into hell. Yes, this is the one you should fear.

[6]"Five sparrows are sold for only two pennies, and God does not forget any of them. [7]But God even knows how many hairs you have on your head. Don't be afraid. You are worth much more than many sparrows.

DON'T BE ASHAMED OF JESUS

[8]"I tell you, all those who stand before others and say they believe in me, I, the Son of Man, will say before the angels of God that they belong to me. [9]But all who stand before others and say they do not believe in me, I will say before the angels of God that they do not belong to me.

[10]"Anyone who speaks against the Son of Man can be forgiven, but anyone who speaks against the Holy Spirit will not be forgiven.

[11]"When you are brought into the synagogues before the leaders and other powerful people, don't worry about how to defend yourself or what to say. [12]At that time the Holy Spirit will teach you what you must say."

JESUS WARNS AGAINST SELFISHNESS

[13]Someone in the crowd said to Jesus, "Teacher, tell my brother to divide with me the property our father left us."

[14]But Jesus said to him, "Who said I should judge or decide between you?" [15]Then Jesus said to them, "Be careful and guard against all

Luke 12:31

It's amazing how much cool stuff can be bought. There are video games, sporting goods, and new CDs. Would you be happy if you could have it all? The reality is, you'd be more dissatisfied than ever. Why? Because those are things you want. They're not what you need.

The great news is, God knows what you need...and he's promised you can have it. How? Listen to what Jesus says: "But seek God's kingdom, and all your other needs will be met as well" (Luke 12:31).

Desiring *things* isn't necessarily wrong. After all, we all need food, clothes, and a home. But *people* are even more important—your family and friends at school, at church, on your team, and in your neighborhood.

Our first and greatest need, though, is for God himself! Have you invited him into your life? If so, God has given you a new heart—and new desires. When your desires line up with what God wants, great things happen—you get everything else you need.

What do you need? Tell God and be sure to ask him to help you love him more. While you're at it, ask God to help you love others in a deeper way. Then watch out—God is going to take care of everything else you need!

11:51 Abel . . . Zechariah In the Hebrew Old Testament, the first and last men to be murdered.

driving

Soon you won't have to say, "Thanks for the ride, Mom!" every day before school. Your own driver's license is the key to total freedom on the road (as much freedom as the law allows, anyway!). You might dream of racing at Daytona Beach, but don't be tempted to disobey the rules of the road. There are a few things you should know about driving before you take off. When you're ready to get your license, you'll want to be prepared.

Each state and province has individual rules and requirements for getting a permit or license. Ask your parents or older brother or sister to tell you what the laws in your area are (check out www.dmv.org for more information). In many places, you must be fifteen to begin driving with a "permit," which means you have to have an adult with a license in the car with you. Around sixteen years old, you can get your own license, although some states impose curfews or other restrictions for brand-new drivers.

There is usually a written test and a driving test. The written part checks to make sure you understand important driving laws, safety tips, and parts of the car (for example, do you know how to turn on the left signal light?). Before attempting the written exam, make sure to pick up (and study!) a driver's manual. Inside the manual, you'll find all the information you need to pass your test the first time.

The driving, or behind-the-wheel, test will probably involve you and a government employee who will ride along in your car to see how you drive. If you pass both of these tests, you'll be on the road!

Guys generally have higher insurance rates than girls—and you have to have insurance to drive, no matter where you live. Unless your parents are going to pay for all of your insurance, you'll need a job when you get your license.

Having your own sports car may be your dream, but in reality, many teenagers drive whatever they can get. Don't be embarrassed to drive your grandpa's old beater; at least you have a way to get around on your own!

Driving takes responsibility and common sense. And God has a say in your driving, too. First Peter 2:13 says, "For the Lord's sake, yield to the people who have authority in this world." While you're on the road, the driving laws are your authority. For the Lord's sake, "yield" to the rules!

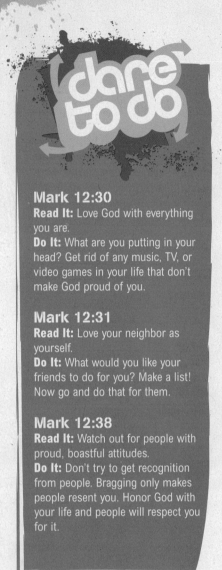

Mark 12:30

Read It: Love God with everything you are.

Do It: What are you putting in your head? Get rid of any music, TV, or video games in your life that don't make God proud of you.

Mark 12:31

Read It: Love your neighbor as yourself.

Do It: What would you like your friends to do for you? Make a list! Now go and do that for them.

Mark 12:38

Read It: Watch out for people with proud, boastful attitudes.

Do It: Don't try to get recognition from people. Bragging only makes people resent you. Honor God with your life and people will respect you for it.

kinds of greed. Life is not measured by how much one owns."

¹⁶Then Jesus told this story: "There was a rich man who had some land, which grew a good crop. ¹⁷He thought to himself, 'What will I do? I have no place to keep all my crops.' ¹⁸Then he said, 'This is what I will do: I will tear down my barns and build bigger ones, and there I will store all my grain and other goods. ¹⁹Then I can say to myself, "I have enough good things stored to last for many years. Rest, eat, drink, and enjoy life!" '

²⁰"But God said to him, 'Foolish man! Tonight your life will be taken from you. So who will get those things you have prepared for yourself?'

²¹"This is how it will be for those who store up things for themselves and are not rich toward God."

DON'T WORRY

²²Jesus said to his followers, "So I tell you, don't worry about the food you need to live, or about the clothes you need for your body. ²³Life is more than food, and the body is more than clothes. ²⁴Look at the birds. They don't plant or harvest, they don't have storerooms or barns, but God feeds them. And you are worth much more than birds. ²⁵You cannot add any time to your life by worrying about it. ²⁶If you cannot do even the little things, then why worry about the big things? ²⁷Consider how the lilies grow; they don't work or make clothes for themselves. But I tell you that even Solomon with his riches was not dressed as beautifully as one of these flowers. ²⁸God clothes the grass in the field, which is alive today but tomorrow is thrown into the fire. So how much more will God clothe you? Don't have so little faith! ²⁹Don't always think about what you will eat or what you will drink, and don't keep worrying. ³⁰All the people in the world are trying to get these things, and your Father knows you need them. ³¹But seek God's kingdom, and all your other needs will be met as well.

DON'T TRUST IN MONEY

³²"Don't fear, little flock, because your Father wants to give you the kingdom. ³³Sell your possessions and give to the poor. Get for yourselves purses that will not wear out, the treasure in heaven that never runs out, where thieves can't steal and moths can't destroy. ³⁴Your heart will be where your treasure is.

ALWAYS BE READY

³⁵"Be dressed, ready for service, and have your lamps shining. ³⁶Be like servants who are waiting for their master to come home from a wedding party. When he comes and knocks, the servants immediately open the door for him. ³⁷They will be blessed when their master comes home, because he sees that they were watching for him. I tell you the truth, the master will dress himself to serve and tell the servants to sit at the table, and he will serve them. ³⁸Those servants will be blessed when he comes in and finds them still waiting, even if it is midnight or later. ³⁹"Remember this: If the owner of the house knew what time a thief was coming, he would not allow the thief to enter his house. ⁴⁰So you also must be ready, because the Son of Man will come at a time when you don't expect him!"

WHO IS THE TRUSTED SERVANT?

⁴¹Peter said, "Lord, did you tell this story to us or to all people?"

⁴²The Lord said, "Who is the wise and trusted servant that the master trusts to give the other servants their food at the right time? ⁴³When the master comes and finds the servant doing his work, the servant will be blessed. ⁴⁴I tell you the truth, the master will choose that servant to take care of everything he owns. ⁴⁵But suppose the servant thinks to himself, 'My master will not come back soon,' and he begins to beat the other servants, men and women, and to eat and drink and get drunk. ⁴⁶The master will come when that servant is not ready and is not expecting him. Then the master will cut him in pieces and send him away to be with the others who don't obey.

⁴⁷"The servant who knows what his master wants but is not ready, or who does not do what the master wants, will be beaten with many blows! ⁴⁸But the servant who does not know what his master wants and does things that should be punished will be beaten with few blows. From everyone who has been given much, much will be demanded. And from the one trusted with much, much more will be expected.

JESUS CAUSES DIVISION

⁴⁹"I came to set fire to the world, and I wish it were already burning! ⁵⁰I have a baptism* to suffer through, and I feel very troubled until it is over. ⁵¹Do you think I came to give peace to

DID YOU KNOW?

13% of middle and high schoolers have a grandparent living in their home.

Trends & Tudes. Harris Interactive, July 2005.

the earth? No, I tell you, I came to divide it. [52]From now on, a family with five people will be divided, three against two, and two against three. [53]They will be divided: father against son and son against father, mother against daughter and daughter against mother, mother-in-law against daughter-in-law and daughter-in-law against mother-in-law."

UNDERSTANDING THE TIMES

[54]Then Jesus said to the people, "When you see clouds coming up in the west, you say, 'It's going to rain,' and it happens. [55]When you feel the wind begin to blow from the south, you say, 'It will be a hot day,' and it happens. [56]Hypocrites! You know how to understand the appearance of the earth and sky. Why don't you understand what is happening now?

SETTLE YOUR PROBLEMS

[57]"Why can't you decide for yourselves what is right? [58]If your enemy is taking you to court, try hard to settle it on the way. If you don't, your enemy might take you to the judge, and the judge might turn you over to the officer, and the officer might throw you into jail. [59]I tell you, you will not get out of there until you have paid everything you owe."

CHANGE YOUR HEARTS

13 At that time some people were there who told Jesus that Pilate[n] had killed some people from Galilee while they were worshiping. He mixed their blood with the blood of the animals they were sacrificing to God. [2]Jesus answered, "Do you think this happened to them because they were more sinful than all others from Galilee? [3]No, I tell you. But unless you change your hearts and lives, you will be destroyed as they were! [4]What about those eighteen people who died when the tower of Siloam fell on them? Do you think they were more sinful than all the others who live in Jerusalem? [5]No, I tell you. But unless you change your hearts and lives, you will all be destroyed too!"

THE USELESS TREE

[6]Jesus told this story: "A man had a fig tree planted in his vineyard. He came looking for some fruit on the tree, but he found none. [7]So the man said to his gardener, 'I have been looking for fruit on this tree for three years, but I never find any. Cut it down. Why should it waste the ground?' [8]But the servant answered, 'Master, let the tree have one more year to produce fruit. Let me dig up the dirt around it

TOP 10 X

People to Pray For

1. **Parents**
2. **Siblings**
3. **Pastor**
4. **Your teachers**
5. **Classmates**
6. **The leader of your country**
7. **Friends**
8. **Grandparents and other relatives**
9. **Neighbors**
10. **Your enemies**

and put on some fertilizer. [9]If the tree produces fruit next year, good. But if not, you can cut it down.' "

JESUS HEALS ON THE SABBATH

[10]Jesus was teaching in one of the synagogues on the Sabbath day. [11]A woman was there who, for eighteen years, had an evil spirit in her that made her crippled. Her back was always bent; she could not stand up straight. [12]When Jesus saw her, he called her over and said, "Woman, you are free from your sickness." [13]Jesus put his hands on her, and immediately she was able to stand up straight and began praising God.

[14]The synagogue leader was angry because Jesus healed on the Sabbath day. He said to the people, "There are six days when one has to work. So come to be healed on one of those days, and not on the Sabbath day."

[15]The Lord answered, "You hypocrites! Doesn't each of you untie your work animals and lead them to drink water every day—even on the Sabbath day? [16]This woman that I healed, a daughter of Abraham, has been held by Satan for eighteen years. Surely it is not wrong for her to be freed from her sickness on a Sabbath day!" [17]When Jesus said this, all of those who were criticizing him were ashamed, but the entire crowd rejoiced at all the wonderful things Jesus was doing.

STORIES OF MUSTARD SEED AND YEAST

[18]Then Jesus said, "What is God's kingdom like? What can I compare it with? [19]It is like a

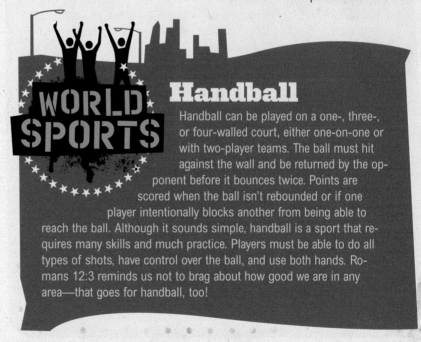

WORLD SPORTS

Handball

Handball can be played on a one-, three-, or four-walled court, either one-on-one or with two-player teams. The ball must hit against the wall and be returned by the opponent before it bounces twice. Points are scored when the ball isn't rebounded or if one player intentionally blocks another from being able to reach the ball. Although it sounds simple, handball is a sport that requires many skills and much practice. Players must be able to do all types of shots, have control over the ball, and use both hands. Romans 12:3 reminds us not to brag about how good we are in any area—that goes for handball, too!

13:1 **Pilate** Pontius Pilate was the Roman governor of Judea from A.D. 26 to A.D. 36.

mustard seed that a man plants in his garden. The seed grows and becomes a tree, and the wild birds build nests in its branches."

[20]Jesus said again, "What can I compare God's kingdom with? [21]It is like yeast that a woman took and hid in a large tub of flour until it made all the dough rise."

THE NARROW DOOR

[22]Jesus was teaching in every town and village as he traveled toward Jerusalem. [23]Someone said to Jesus, "Lord, will only a few people be saved?"

Jesus said, [24]"Try hard to enter through the narrow door, because many people will try to enter there, but they will not be able. [25]When the owner of the house gets up and closes the door, you can stand outside and knock on the door and say, 'Sir, open the door for us.' But he will answer, 'I don't know you or where you come from.' [26]Then you will say, 'We ate and drank with you, and you taught in the streets of our town.' [27]But he will say to you, 'I don't know you or where you come from. Go away from me, all you who do evil!' [28]You will cry

and grind your teeth with pain when you see Abraham, Isaac, Jacob, and all the prophets in God's kingdom, but you yourselves thrown outside. [29]People will come from the east, west, north, and south and will sit down at the table in the kingdom of God. [30]There are those who are last now who will be first in the future. And there are those who are first now who will be last in the future."

JESUS WILL DIE IN JERUSALEM

[31]At that time some Pharisees came to Jesus and said, "Go away from here! Herod wants to kill you!"

[32]Jesus said to them, "Go tell that fox Herod, 'Today and tomorrow I am forcing demons out and healing people. Then, on the third day, I will reach my goal.' [33]Yet I must be on my way today and tomorrow and the next day. Surely it cannot be right for a prophet to be killed anywhere except in Jerusalem.

[34]"Jerusalem, Jerusalem! You kill the prophets and stone to death those who are sent to you. Many times I wanted to gather your people as a hen gathers her chicks under her wings, but you would not let me.

[35]Now your house is left completely empty. I tell you, you will not see me until that time when you will say, 'God bless the One who comes in the name of the Lord.' "[n]

HEALING ON THE SABBATH

14 On a Sabbath day, when Jesus went to eat at the home of a leading Pharisee, the people were watching Jesus very closely. [2]And in front of him was a man with dropsy.[n] [3]Jesus said to the Pharisees and experts on the law, "Is it right or wrong to heal on the Sabbath day?" [4]But they would not answer his question. So Jesus took the man, healed him, and sent him away. [5]Jesus said to the Pharisees and teachers of the law, "If your child[n] or ox falls into a well on the Sabbath day, will you not pull him out quickly?" [6]And they could not answer him.

DON'T MAKE YOURSELF IMPORTANT

[7]When Jesus noticed that some of the guests were choosing the best places to sit, he told this story: [8]"When someone invites you to a wedding feast, don't take the most important seat, because someone more important than you may have been invited. [9]The host, who invited both of you, will come to you and say, 'Give this person your seat.' Then you will be embarrassed and will have to move to the last place. [10]So when you are invited, go sit in a seat that is not important. When the host comes to you, he may say, 'Friend, move up here to a more important place.' Then all the other guests will respect you. [11]All who make themselves great will be made humble, but those who make themselves humble will be made great."

YOU WILL BE REWARDED

[12]Then Jesus said to the man who had invited him, "When you give a lunch or a dinner, don't invite only your friends, your family, your other relatives, and your rich neighbors. At another time they will invite you to eat with them, and you will be repaid. [13]Instead, when you give a feast, invite the poor, the crippled, the lame, and the blind. [14]Then you will be blessed, because they have nothing and cannot pay you back. But you will be repaid when the good people rise from the dead."

A STORY ABOUT A BIG BANQUET

[15]One of those at the table with Jesus heard these things and said to him, "Blessed

Luke 14:28

A guy wanted to build a skate park, so he leveled out the ground and laid a big, fat cement slab in the middle of town. It was going to be the sweetest park ever built, with two big half-pipes, miniramps, massive fun boxes, and tons of great rails. He started building the metal frames for the ramps, but while he was building, he ran out of money! All that was in the "park" were metal frames; the park was totally useless and everyone made fun of him.

Jesus warns us not to be like that guy. "If you want to build a tower, you first sit down and decide how much it will cost, to see if you have enough money to finish the job." Whether it's a tower or a skate park, the point is the same: don't start something you can't finish.

Jesus wasn't just talking about towers; he was talking about being a Christian. His message is this: don't start following me if you're not going to finish.

Following Jesus is a 100 percent deal. You can't do it part-time and you can't quit in the middle.

If you're thinking about following Jesus, then it's important to realize that it takes everything you've got. You have to be willing to go all the way.

are the people who will share in the meal in God's kingdom."

16 Jesus said to him, "A man gave a big banquet and invited many people. 17 When it was time to eat, the man sent his servant to tell the guests, 'Come. Everything is ready.'

18 "But all the guests made excuses. The first one said, 'I have just bought a field, and I must go look at it. Please excuse me.' 19 Another said, 'I have just bought five pairs of oxen; I must go and try them. Please excuse me.' 20 A third person said, 'I just got married; I can't come.' 21 So the servant returned and told his master what had happened. Then the master became angry and said, 'Go at once into the streets and alleys of the town, and bring in the poor, the crippled, the blind, and the lame.' 22 Later the servant said to him, 'Master, I did what you commanded, but we still have room.' 23 The master said to the servant, 'Go out to the roads and country lanes, and urge the people there to come so my house will be full. 24 I tell you, none of those whom I invited first will eat with me.' "

THE COST OF BEING JESUS' FOLLOWER

25 Large crowds were traveling with Jesus, and he turned and said to them, 26 "If anyone comes to me but loves his father, mother, wife, children, brothers, or sisters—or even life—more than me, he cannot be my follower. 27 Whoever is not willing to carry his cross and follow me cannot be my follower. 28 If you want to build a tower, you first sit down and decide how much it will cost, to see if you have enough money to finish the job. 29 If you don't, you might lay the foundation, but you would not be able to finish. Then all who would see it would make fun of you, 30 saying, 'This person began to build but was not able to finish.'

31 "If a king is going to fight another king, first he will sit down and plan. He will decide if he and his ten thousand soldiers can defeat the other king who has twenty thousand soldiers. 32 If he can't, then while the other king is still far away, he will send some people to speak to him and ask for peace. 33 In the same way, you must give up everything you have to be my follower.

DON'T LOSE YOUR INFLUENCE

34 "Salt is good, but if it loses its salty taste, you cannot make it salty again. 35 It is no good for the soil or for manure; it is thrown away.

"Let those with ears use them and listen."

A LOST SHEEP, A LOST COIN

15 The tax collectors and sinners all came to listen to Jesus. 2 But the Pharisees and the teachers of the law began to complain: "Look, this man welcomes sinners and even eats with them."

3 Then Jesus told them this story: 4 "Suppose one of you has a hundred sheep but loses one of them. Then he will leave the other ninety-nine sheep in the open field and go out and look for the lost sheep until he finds it. 5 And when he finds it, he happily puts it on his shoulders 6 and goes home. He calls to his friends and neighbors and says, 'Be happy with me because I found my lost sheep.' 7 In the same way, I tell you there is more joy in heaven over one sinner who changes his heart and life, than over ninety-nine good people who don't need to change.

8 "Suppose a woman has ten silver coins," but loses one. She will light a lamp, sweep the house, and look carefully for the coin until she finds it. 9 And when she finds it, she will call her friends and neighbors and say, 'Be happy with

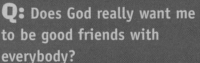

Q: Does God really want me to be good friends with everybody?

A: It's impossible to be *close* friends with everybody. Some people try this because it makes them feel popular. But you will never have more than a few people you share a special connection with. Jesus is your best example. He was ready to help anybody he met, but he had a close group of friends that he spent most of his time with.

Q: I love buying stuff all the time. Is there anything wrong with that?

A: Buying things gives most people a good feeling—even if it's something they don't need. It's fun to see something you want, take it to the cash register, and make it yours. But there's a danger in this. First of all, if you always want to get the "next thing," you learn to be unthankful and discontented with what you have. This is not pleasing to God. Rather than using all of your money on the things you want now, try saving part of your money to use in the future.

Q: I like to watch movies all day, but my mom says this will rot my brain. Is she exaggerating?

A: Doctors say that after four movies in a row, a small part of your brain will ooze out of your ears. Just kidding! The real problem with movies is that you don't have to imagine anything, so you don't use much of your brain. Books make you build the scenes in your mind, which exercises your imagination. A few good movies here and there are okay. But God doesn't want you to be a mental slug.

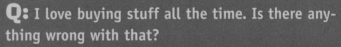

15:8 **silver coins** Roman denarii. One coin was the average pay for one day's work.

COOL!

Jesus and Money

Money. They print more of it every day, but does anyone have enough?

Jesus never had much money, yet he had a lot to say about it. Almost half of his stories have something to do with money or possessions. Amazingly, one out of every ten verses in the Gospels (Matthew through John)—288 in all—deal with money.

The Bible has less than 500 verses on faith, about 500 verses dealing with prayer, and more than 2,350 verses about money and possessions. Jesus obviously thinks that it's very important to treat money correctly!

me because I have found the coin that I lost.' [10]In the same way, there is joy in the presence of the angels of God when one sinner changes his heart and life."

THE SON WHO LEFT HOME

[11]Then Jesus said, "A man had two sons. [12]The younger son said to his father, 'Give me my share of the property.' So the father divided the property between his two sons. [13]Then the younger son gathered up all that was his and traveled far away to another country. There he wasted his money in foolish living. [14]After he had spent everything, a time came when there was no food anywhere in the country, and the son was poor and hungry. [15]So he got a job with one of the citizens there who sent the son into the fields to feed pigs. [16]The son was so hungry that he wanted to eat the pods the pigs were eating, but no one gave him anything. [17]When he realized what he was doing, he thought, 'All of my father's servants have plenty of food. But I am here, almost dying with hunger. [18]I will leave and return to my father and say to him, "Father, I have sinned against God and against you. [19]I am no longer worthy to be called your son, but let me be like one of your servants."' [20]So the son left and went to his father.

"While the son was still a long way off, his father saw him and felt sorry for his son. So the father ran to him and hugged and kissed him. [21]The son said, 'Father, I have sinned against God and against you. I am no longer worthy to be called your son.'[n] [22]But the father said to his servants, 'Hurry! Bring the best clothes and put them on him. Also, put a ring on his finger

and sandals on his feet. [23]And get our fat calf and kill it so we can have a feast and celebrate. [24]My son was dead, but now he is alive again! He was lost, but now he is found!' So they began to celebrate.

[25]"The older son was in the field, and as he came closer to the house, he heard the sound of music and dancing. [26]So he called to one of the servants and asked what all this meant. [27]The servant said, 'Your brother has come back, and your father killed the fat calf, because your brother came home safely.' [28]The older son was angry and would not go in to the feast. So his father went out and begged him to come in. [29]But the older son said to his father, 'I have served you like a slave for many years and have always obeyed your commands. But you never gave me even a young goat to have at a feast with my friends. [30]But your other son, who wasted all your money on prostitutes, comes home, and you kill the fat calf for him!' [31]The father said to him, 'Son, you are always with me, and all that I have is yours. [32]We had to celebrate and be happy because your brother was dead, but now he is alive. He was lost, but now he is found.' "

TRUE WEALTH

16 Jesus also said to his followers, "Once there was a rich man who had a manager to take care of his business. This manager was accused of cheating him. [2]So he called the manager in and said to him, 'What is this I hear about you? Give me a report of what you have done with my money, because you can't be my manager any longer.' [3]The

manager thought to himself, 'What will I do since my master is taking my job away from me? I am not strong enough to dig ditches, and I am ashamed to beg. [4]I know what I'll do so that when I lose my job people will welcome me into their homes.'

[5]"So the manager called in everyone who owed the master any money. He asked the first one, 'How much do you owe?' [6]He answered, 'Eight hundred gallons of olive oil.' The manager said to him, 'Take your bill, sit down quickly, and write four hundred gallons.' [7]Then the manager asked another one, 'How much do you owe?' He answered, 'One thousand bushels of wheat.' Then the manager said to him, 'Take your bill and write eight hundred bushels.' [8]So, the master praised the dishonest manager for being clever. Yes, worldly people are more clever with their own kind than spiritual people are.

[9]"I tell you, make friends for yourselves using worldly riches so that when those riches are gone, you will be welcomed in those homes that continue forever. [10]Whoever can be trusted with a little can also be trusted with a lot, and whoever is dishonest with a little is dishonest with a lot. [11]If you cannot be trusted with worldly riches, then who will trust you with true riches? [12]And if you cannot be trusted with things that belong to someone else, who will give you things of your own?

[13]"No servant can serve two masters. The servant will hate one master and love the other, or will follow one master and refuse to follow the other. You cannot serve both God and worldly riches."

⭐ **15:21 son** Some Greek copies continue, "but let me be like one of your servants" (see verse 19).

GOD'S LAW CANNOT BE CHANGED

[14] The Pharisees, who loved money, were listening to all these things and made fun of Jesus. [15] He said to them, "You make yourselves look good in front of people, but God knows what is really in your hearts. What is important to people is hateful in God's sight.

[16] "The law of Moses and the writings of the prophets were preached until John[n] came. Since then the Good News about the kingdom of God is being told, and everyone tries to enter it by force. [17] It would be easier for heaven and earth to pass away than for the smallest part of a letter in the law to be changed.

DIVORCE AND REMARRIAGE

[18] "If a man divorces his wife and marries another woman, he is guilty of adultery, and the man who marries a divorced woman is also guilty of adultery."

THE RICH MAN AND LAZARUS

[19] Jesus said, "There was a rich man who always dressed in the finest clothes and lived in luxury every day. [20] And a very poor man named Lazarus, whose body was covered with sores, was laid at the rich man's gate. [21] He wanted to eat only the small pieces of food that fell from the rich man's table. And the dogs would come and lick his sores. [22] Later, Lazarus died, and the angels carried him to the arms of Abraham. The rich man died, too, and was buried. [23] In the place of the dead, he was in much pain. The rich man saw Abraham far away with Lazarus at his side. [24] He called, 'Father Abraham, have mercy on me! Send Lazarus to dip his finger in water and cool my tongue, because I am suffering in this fire!' [25] But Abraham said, 'Child, remember when you were alive you had the good things in life, but bad things happened to Lazarus. Now he is comforted here, and you are suffering. [26] Besides, there is a big pit between you and us, so no one can cross over to you, and no one can leave there and come here.' [27] The rich man said, 'Father, then please send Lazarus to my father's house. [28] I have five brothers, and Lazarus could warn them so that they will not come to this place of pain.' [29] But Abraham said, 'They have the law of Moses and the writings of the prophets; let them learn from them.' [30] The rich man said, 'No, father Abraham! If someone goes to them from the dead, they would believe and change their hearts and lives.' [31] But Abraham said to him, 'If they will not listen to Moses and the prophets, they will not listen to someone who comes back from the dead.' "

SIN AND FORGIVENESS

17 Jesus said to his followers, "Things that cause people to sin will happen, but how terrible for the person who causes them to happen! [2] It would be better for you to be thrown into the sea with a large stone around your neck than to cause one of these little ones to sin. [3] So be careful!

"If another follower sins, warn him, and if he is sorry and stops sinning, forgive him. [4] If he sins against you seven times in one day and says that he is sorry each time, forgive him."

HOW BIG IS YOUR FAITH?

[5] The apostles said to the Lord, "Give us more faith!"

[6] The Lord said, "If your faith were the size of a mustard seed, you could say to this mulberry tree, 'Dig yourself up and plant yourself in the sea,' and it would obey you.

BE GOOD SERVANTS

[7] "Suppose one of you has a servant who has been plowing the ground or caring for the sheep. When the servant comes in from working in the field, would you say, 'Come in and sit down to eat'? [8] No, you would say to him, 'Prepare something for me to eat. Then get yourself ready and serve me. After I finish eating and

trustables

Luke 17:6

If you've seen any of the *Star Wars* movies, you may have tried to move something with your mind. You focused really hard on a pencil or a book just to see if you could get it to slide across the table. Don't be embarrassed—lots of people have tried! It usually doesn't work, but you never know…

Although, if you've ever read the Book of Luke, you might start to get your hopes up! In Luke 17:6, Jesus says, "If your faith were the size of a mustard seed, you could say to this mulberry tree, 'Dig yourself up and plant yourself in the sea,' and it would obey you." Wow! First question: how big is a mustard seed? Much smaller than a sunflower seed. And with only that much faith you could move a tree? Just think how easy yard work would be!

Since we don't see a lot of plant life in midflight, it must mean that, as humans, our faith is pretty small. But it also means that God is all-powerful! If we trust him just a little bit, he can help us do great things! He can help us pass a test, find good friends, and change people's lives for the better. After all, he has the power to do *anything*.

16:16 John John the Baptist, who preached to people about Christ's coming (Matthew 3, Luke 3).

YOU SPEAK OUT!

Q: What do you like to do after school?
A: "I like to play on the computer or play LEGOs. I like to read, too." (Ben, 12)

Q: What is your favorite thing to do?
A: "My favorite thing to do is to play pretend." (Karl, 10)

Q: Where is your favorite place to be?
A: "My bedroom is my favorite place to be." (Ben, 12)

Samaritan the only one who came back to thank God?" [19] Then Jesus said to him, "Stand up and go on your way. You were healed because you believed."

GOD'S KINGDOM IS WITHIN YOU

[20] Some of the Pharisees asked Jesus, "When will the kingdom of God come?"

Jesus answered, "God's kingdom is coming, but not in a way that you will be able to see with your eyes. [21] People will not say, 'Look, here it is!' or, 'There it is!' because God's kingdom is within[n] you."

[22] Then Jesus said to his followers, "The time will come when you will want very much to see one of the days of the Son of Man. But you will not see it. [23] People will say to you, 'Look, there he is!' or, 'Look, here he is!' Stay where you are; don't go away and search.

WHEN JESUS COMES AGAIN

[24] "When the Son of Man comes again, he will shine like lightning, which flashes across the sky and lights it up from one side to the other. [25] But first he must suffer many things and be rejected by the people of this time. [26] When the Son of Man comes again, it will be as it was when Noah lived. [27] People were eating, drinking, marrying, and giving their children to be married until the day Noah entered the boat. Then the flood came and killed them all. [28] It will be the same as during the time of Lot. People were eating, drinking, buying, selling, planting, and building. [29] But the day Lot

drinking, you can eat.' [9] The servant does not get any special thanks for doing what his master commanded. [10] It is the same with you. When you have done everything you are told to do, you should say, 'We are unworthy servants; we have only done the work we should do.'"

BE THANKFUL

[11] While Jesus was on his way to Jerusalem, he was going through the area between Samaria and Galilee. [12] As he came into a small town, ten men who had a skin disease met him there. They did not come close to Jesus [13] but called to him, "Jesus! Master! Have mercy on us!"

[14] When Jesus saw the men, he said, "Go and show yourselves to the priests."[n]

As the ten men were going, they were healed. [15] When one of them saw that he was healed, he went back to Jesus, praising God in a loud voice. [16] Then he bowed down at Jesus' feet and thanked him. (And this man was a Samaritan.) [17] Jesus said, "Weren't ten men healed? Where are the other nine? [18] Is this

BIBLE SUPERHEROES

Luke

See Acts 16:10–17; 20:5–15.

The man who wrote the Gospel of Luke and the Book of Acts was a Gentile (non-Jew) and a doctor. Rather than staying home and making lots of money, Luke became a missionary. He was the apostle Paul's physician and often traveled with him (Acts 16:10–17; 20:5–15).

Luke was also a careful historian. He wrote down what happened in the early church. He took a special interest in the poor and in women. These two groups were not well treated back then. Luke shows how Christians reached out and included them in God's new kingdom.

Not only was Luke a doctor, a writer, and a missionary, he probably wound up a martyr (someone who dies for his faith).

What's more impressive than dying for your faith? Living it every day.

March

1 Mmmmm . . . today is *"Peanut Butter Lover's Day."* Put peanut butter on everything you eat!

2 Pray for a person of influence: it's surfer Laird Hamilton's birthday.

3 Ponder this . . . it's *"If Pets Had Thumbs Day."*

4

5 It's *"Say Hi to Mom Day"*— Give your mom a quick "what's up" on your way out.

6

7

8 Pray for a person of influence: it's actor Freddie Prinze Jr.'s birthday.

9 Pray for a person of influence: rapper Bow Wow has another birthday today.

10 Brainstorm activities for your youth group. E-mail them to your youth leader.

11

12

13

14

15 Pray for a person of influence: it's actress Eva Longoria's birthday.

16 *St. Patrick's Day*— Don't forget to wear green!

17 Celebrate *you!* It's *"Absolutely Incredible Kid Day"!*

18

19

20 Actually listen to your pastor's sermon on Sunday. Talk about it with your friends after church.

21

22 Are you a Trekkie? William Shatner (*Star Trek* captain James T. Kirk) is having a birthday.

23

24 Pray for a person of influence: rapper Mase has a birthday today.

25

26 It's *"Make Up Your Own Holiday Day"* . . . an excuse to celebrate your favorite things!

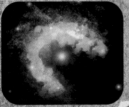

29 Read Luke 14:26. Do you love God more than anybody in your life?

30

28 Pray for a person of influence: actor Ewan McGregor celebrates his birthday today.

left Sodom," fire and sulfur rained down from the sky and killed them all. ³⁰This is how it will be when the Son of Man comes again.

³¹"On that day, a person who is on the roof and whose belongings are in the house should not go inside to get them. A person who is in the field should not go back home. ³²Remember Lot's wife." ³³Those who try to keep their lives will lose them. But those who give up their lives will save them. ³⁴I tell you, on that night two people will be sleeping in one bed; one will be taken and the other will be left. ³⁵There will be two women grinding grain together; one will be taken, and the other will be left. [³⁶Two people will be in the field. One will be taken, and the other will be left.]"

³⁷The followers asked Jesus, "Where will this be, Lord?"

Jesus answered, "Where there is a dead body, there the vultures will gather."

GOD WILL ANSWER HIS PEOPLE

18 Then Jesus used this story to teach his followers that they should always pray and never lose hope. ²"In a certain town there was a judge who did not respect God or care about people. ³In that same town there was a widow who kept coming to this judge, saying, 'Give me my rights against my enemy.' ⁴For a while the judge refused to help her. But afterwards, he thought to himself, 'Even though I don't respect God or care about people, ⁵I will see that she gets her rights. Otherwise she will continue to bother me until I am worn out.' "

⁶The Lord said, "Listen to what the unfair judge said. ⁷God will always give what is right to his people who cry to him night and day, and he will not be slow to answer them. ⁸I tell you, God will help his people quickly. But when the Son of Man comes again, will he find those on earth who believe in him?"

BEING RIGHT WITH GOD

⁹Jesus told this story to some people who thought they were very good and looked down on everyone else: ¹⁰"A Pharisee and a tax collector both went to the Temple to pray. ¹¹The Pharisee stood alone and prayed, 'God, I thank you that I am not like other people who steal, cheat, or take part in adultery, or even like this tax collector. ¹²I fast" twice a week, and I give one-tenth of everything I get!'

¹³"The tax collector, standing at a distance, would not even look up to heaven. But he beat on his chest because he was so sad. He said, 'God, have mercy on me, a sinner.' ¹⁴I tell you, when this man went home, he was right with God, but the Pharisee was not. All who make themselves great will be made humble, but all who make themselves humble will be made great."

WHO WILL ENTER GOD'S KINGDOM?

¹⁵Some people brought even their babies to Jesus so he could touch them. When the followers saw this, they told them to stop. ¹⁶But Jesus called for the children, saying, "Let the little children come to me. Don't stop them, because the kingdom of God belongs to people who are like these children. ¹⁷I tell you the truth, you must accept the kingdom of God as if you were a child, or you will never enter it."

A RICH MAN'S QUESTION

¹⁸A certain leader asked Jesus, "Good Teacher, what must I do to have life forever?"

¹⁹Jesus said to him, "Why do you call me good? Only God is good. ²⁰You know the commands: 'You must not be guilty of adultery. You must not murder anyone. You must not steal. You must not tell lies about your neighbor. Honor your father and mother.' "

²¹But the leader said, "I have obeyed all these commands since I was a boy."

²²When Jesus heard this, he said to him, "There is still one more thing you need to do. Sell everything you have and give it to the poor, and you will have treasure in heaven. Then come and follow me." ²³But when the man heard this, he became very sad, because he was very rich.

²⁴Jesus looked at him and said, "It is very hard for rich people to enter the kingdom of God. ²⁵It is easier for a camel to go through the

ROCK SOLID

Luke 19:9–10

When does eternal life start? If you have a relationship with Jesus, you have eternal life right now. God gave you eternal life the moment you invited Jesus into your life. You are already living in eternity!

No, this isn't heaven, but eternal life is good for life here on earth, too.

During his time on earth, Jesus loved to enjoy a good meal with people—important, religious, common, or sinful—it didn't matter to him. On one occasion, Jesus had dinner with a notorious tax collector. The tax collector had sometimes cheated people and kept the profits for himself. When the man publicly said he was changing his ways, Jesus told the other dinner guests: "Salvation has come to this house today" (Luke 19:9).

Believing in Jesus does a lot of earthly good!

If you make a hard-core commitment to treating people right, obeying your parents, and living by God's instructions in the Bible, your life on earth will begin to look more and more like what your life in heaven will be someday.

Don't wait for heaven! Begin enjoying eternal life here and now.

17:29 **Sodom** City that God destroyed because the people were so evil.   17:32 **Lot's wife** A story about what happened to Lot's wife is found in Genesis 19:15–17, 26.   17:36 **Two . . . left.** Some Greek copies do not contain the bracketed text.   18:12 **fast** The people would give up eating for a special time of prayer and worship to God. It was also done to show sadness and disappointment.   18:20 **'You . . . mother.'** Quotation from Exodus 20:12–16; Deuteronomy 5:16–20.

eye of a needle than for a rich person to enter the kingdom of God."

WHO CAN BE SAVED?

[26]When the people heard this, they asked, "Then who can be saved?"

[27]Jesus answered, "The things impossible for people are possible for God."

[28]Peter said, "Look, we have left everything and followed you."

[29]Jesus said, "I tell you the truth, all those who have left houses, wives, brothers, parents, or children for the kingdom of God [30]will get much more in this life. And in the age that is coming, they will have life forever."

JESUS WILL RISE FROM THE DEAD

[31]Then Jesus took the twelve apostles aside and said to them, "We are going to Jerusalem. Everything the prophets wrote about the Son of Man will happen. [32]He will be turned over to those who are evil. They will laugh at him, insult him, spit on him, [33]beat him with whips, and kill him. But on the third day, he will rise to life again." [34]The apostles did not understand this; the meaning was hidden from them, and they did not realize what was said.

JESUS HEALS A BLIND MAN

[35]As Jesus came near the city of Jericho, a blind man was sitting beside the road, begging. [36]When he heard the people coming down the road, he asked, "What is happening?"

[37]They told him, "Jesus, from Nazareth, is going by."

[38]The blind man cried out, "Jesus, Son of David, have mercy on me!"

[39]The people leading the group warned the blind man to be quiet. But the blind man shouted even more, "Son of David, have mercy on me!"

[40]Jesus stopped and ordered the blind man to be brought to him. When he came near, Jesus asked him, [41]"What do you want me to do for you?"

He said, "Lord, I want to see."

[42]Jesus said to him, "Then see. You are healed because you believed."

[43]At once the man was able to see, and he followed Jesus, thanking God. All the people who saw this praised God.

ZACCHAEUS MEETS JESUS

19 Jesus was going through the city of Jericho. [2]A man was there named Zacchaeus, who was a very important tax collector, and he was wealthy. [3]He wanted to see who Jesus was, but he was not able because he was too short to see above the crowd. [4]He ran ahead to a place where Jesus would come, and he climbed a sycamore tree so he could see him. [5]When Jesus came to that place, he looked up and said to him, "Zacchaeus, hurry and come down! I must stay at your house today."

[6]Zacchaeus came down quickly and welcomed him gladly. [7]All the people saw this and began to complain, "Jesus is staying with a sinner!"

[8]But Zacchaeus stood and said to the Lord, "I will give half of my possessions to the poor. And if I have cheated anyone, I will pay back four times more."

[9]Jesus said to him, "Salvation has come to this house today, because this man also belongs to the family of Abraham. [10]The Son of Man came to find lost people and save them."

A STORY ABOUT THREE SERVANTS

[11]As the people were listening to this, Jesus told them a story because he was near Jerusalem and they thought God's kingdom would appear immediately. [12]He said: "A very important man went to a country far away to be made a king and then to return home. [13]So he called ten of his servants and gave a coin[*] to each servant. He said, 'Do business with this money until I get back.' [14]But the people in the kingdom hated the man. So they sent a group to follow him and say, 'We don't want this man to be our king.'

[15]"But the man became king. When he returned home, he said, 'Call those servants who have my money so I can know how much they earned with it.'

[16]"The first servant came and said, 'Sir, I earned ten coins with the one you gave me.' [17]The king said to the servant, 'Excellent! You are a good servant. Since I can trust you with small things, I will let you rule over ten of my cities.'

[18]"The second servant said, 'Sir, I earned five coins with your one.' [19]The king said to this servant, 'You can rule over five cities.'

[20]"Then another servant came in and said to the king, 'Sir, here is your coin which I wrapped in a piece of cloth and hid. [21]I was afraid of you, because you are a hard man. You even take money that you didn't earn and gather food that you didn't plant.' [22]Then the king said to the servant, 'I will condemn you by your own words, you evil servant. You knew that I am a hard man, taking money that I didn't earn and gathering food that I didn't plant. [23]Why then didn't you put my money in the bank? Then when I came back, my money would have earned some interest.'

[24]"The king said to the men who were standing by, 'Take the coin away from this servant and give it to the servant who earned ten coins.' [25]They said, 'But sir, that servant already has ten coins.' [26]The king said, 'Those who have will be given more, but those who do not have anything will have everything taken away from them. [27]Now where are my enemies who

---

⭐ **19:13 coin** A Greek "mina." One mina was enough money to pay a person for working three months.

didn't want me to be king? Bring them here and kill them before me.' "

JESUS ENTERS JERUSALEM AS A KING

[28]After Jesus said this, he went on toward Jerusalem. [29]As Jesus came near Bethphage and Bethany, towns near the hill called the Mount of Olives, he sent out two of his followers. [30]He said, "Go to the town you can see there. When you enter it, you will find a colt tied there, which no one has ever ridden. Untie it and bring it here to me. [31]If anyone asks you why you are untying it, say that the Master needs it."

[32]The two followers went into town and found the colt just as Jesus had told them. [33]As they were untying it, its owners came out and asked the followers, "Why are you untying our colt?"

[34]The followers answered, "The Master needs it." [35]So they brought it to Jesus, threw their coats on the colt's back, and put Jesus on it. [36]As Jesus rode toward Jerusalem, others spread their coats on the road before him.

[37]As he was coming close to Jerusalem, on the way down the Mount of Olives, the whole crowd of followers began joyfully shouting praise to God for all the miracles they had seen. [38]They said,

"God bless the king who comes in the
name of the Lord!   *Psalm 118:26*
There is peace in heaven and glory to
God!"

[39]Some of the Pharisees in the crowd said to Jesus, "Teacher, tell your followers not to say these things."

[40]But Jesus answered, "I tell you, if my followers didn't

say these things, then the stones would cry out."

JESUS CRIES FOR JERUSALEM

[41]As Jesus came near Jerusalem, he saw the city and cried for it, [42]saying, "I wish you knew today what would bring you peace. But now it is hidden from you. [43]The time is coming when your enemies will build a wall around you and will hold you in on all sides. [44]They will destroy you and all your people, and not one stone will be left on another. All this will happen because you did not recognize the time when God came to save you."

JESUS GOES TO THE TEMPLE

[45]Jesus went into the Temple and began to throw out the people who were selling things there. [46]He said, "It is written in the Scriptures, 'My Temple will be a house for prayer.'" But you have changed it into a 'hideout for robbers'!"

[47]Jesus taught in the Temple every day. The leading priests, the experts on the law, and some of the leaders of the people wanted to kill Jesus. [48]But they did not know how they could do it, because all the people were listening closely to him.

JEWISH LEADERS QUESTION JESUS

20 One day Jesus was in the Temple, teaching the people and telling them the Good News. The leading priests, teachers of the law, and elders came up to talk with him, [2]saying, "Tell us what authority you have to do these things? Who gave you this authority?"

[3]Jesus answered, "I will also ask you a question. Tell me: [4]When John baptized people, was that authority from God or just from other people?"

[5]They argued about this, saying, "If we answer, 'John's baptism was from God,' Jesus will say, 'Then why did you not believe him?' [6]But if we say, 'It was from other people,' all the people will stone us to death, because they believe John was a prophet." [7]So they answered that they didn't know where it came from.

[8]Jesus said to them, "Then I won't tell you what authority I have to do these things."

A STORY ABOUT GOD'S SON

[9]Then Jesus told the people this story: "A man planted a vineyard and leased it to some farmers. Then he went away for a long time. [10]When it was time for the grapes to be picked, he sent a servant to the farmers to get some of the grapes. But they beat the servant and sent him away empty-handed. [11]Then he sent another servant. They beat this servant also, and showed no respect for him, and sent him away empty-handed. [12]So the man sent a third servant. The farmers wounded him and threw him out. [13]The owner of the vineyard said, 'What will I do now? I will send my son whom I love. Maybe they will respect him.' [14]But when the farmers saw the son, they said to each other, 'This son will inherit the vineyard. If we kill him, it will be ours.' [15]So the farmers threw the son out of the vineyard and killed him.

"What will the owner of this vineyard do to them? [16]He will come and kill those farmers and will give the vineyard to other farmers."

When the people heard this story, they said, "Let this never happen!"

[17]But Jesus looked at them and said, "Then what does this verse mean:

'The stone that the builders rejected
became the cornerstone'?   *Psalm 118:22*
[18]Everyone who falls on that stone will be broken, and the person on whom it falls, that person will be crushed!"

[19]The teachers of the law and the leading priests wanted to arrest Jesus at once, because they knew the story was about them. But they were afraid of what the people would do.

IS IT RIGHT TO PAY TAXES OR NOT?

[20]So they watched Jesus and sent some spies who acted as if they were sincere. They wanted to trap Jesus in saying something

KNOW THE WORD!

HEAVEN

Some people imagine that heaven is about angels floating on clouds, strumming little harps. Others think that heaven will be a boring, never-ending time of singing. Some think that it will be a "new and improved" earth.

We don't know everything about what heaven is like. The apostle John saw a vision of heaven (check out the Book of Revelation), and he could barely find words to describe it! *Heaven* is the place where Christians live after their bodies die. It's also the place where God has his throne and angels and other creatures worship him day and night.

Heaven is anything but boring! It is better than anything you can imagine. If Jesus is your Savior, then you'll get to live there forever.

wrong so they could hand him over to the authority and power of the governor. [21]So the spies asked Jesus, "Teacher, we know that what you say and teach is true. You pay no attention to who people are, and you always teach the truth about God's way. [22]Tell us, is it right for us to pay taxes to Caesar or not?"

[23]But Jesus, knowing they were trying to trick him, said, [24]"Show me a coin. Whose image and name are on it?"

They said, "Caesar's."

[25]Jesus said to them, "Then give to Caesar the things that are Caesar's, and give to God the things that are God's."

[26]So they were not able to trap Jesus in anything he said in the presence of the people. And being amazed at his answer, they became silent.

SOME SADDUCEES TRY TO TRICK JESUS

[27]Some Sadducees, who believed people would not rise from the dead, came to Jesus. [28]They asked, "Teacher, Moses wrote that if a man's brother dies and leaves a wife but no children, then that man must marry the widow and have children for his brother. [29]Once there were seven brothers. The first brother married and died, but had no children. [30]Then the second brother married the widow, and he died. [31]And the third brother married the widow, and he died. The same thing happened with all seven brothers; they died and had no children. [32]Finally, the woman died also. [33]Since all seven brothers had married her, whose wife will she be when people rise from the dead?"

[34]Jesus said to them, "On earth, people marry and are given to someone to marry. [35]But those who will be worthy to be raised from the dead and live again will not marry, nor will they be given to someone to marry. [36]In that life they are like angels and cannot die. They are children of God, because they have been raised from the dead. [37]Even Moses clearly showed that the dead are raised to life. When he wrote about the burning bush," he said that the Lord is 'the God of Abraham, the God of Isaac, and the God of Jacob.'" [38]God is the God of the living, not the dead, because all people are alive to him."

[39]Some of the teachers of the law said, "Teacher, your answer was good." [40]No one was brave enough to ask him another question.

IS THE CHRIST THE SON OF DAVID?

[41]Then Jesus said, "Why do people say that the Christ is the Son of David? [42]In the book of Psalms, David himself says:

'The Lord said to my Lord,

"Sit by me at my right side,

[43]   until I put your enemies under your

control." '[n]   *Psalm 110:1*

[44]David calls the Christ 'Lord,' so how can the Christ be his son?"

JESUS ACCUSES SOME LEADERS

[45]While all the people were listening, Jesus said to his followers, [46]"Beware of the teachers of the law. They like to walk around wearing fancy clothes, and they love for people to greet them with respect in the marketplaces. They love to have the most important seats in the synagogues and at feasts. [47]But they cheat widows and steal their houses and then try to make themselves look good by saying long prayers. They will receive a greater punishment."

TRUE GIVING

21 As Jesus looked up, he saw some rich people putting their gifts into the Temple money box." [2]Then he saw a poor widow putting two small copper coins into the box. [3]He said, "I tell you the truth, this poor widow gave more than all those rich people. [4]They gave only what they did not need. This woman is very poor, but she gave all she had to live on."

THE TEMPLE WILL BE DESTROYED

[5]Some people were talking about the Temple and how it was decorated with beautiful stones and gifts offered to God.

But Jesus said, [6]"As for these things you are looking at, the time will come when not one stone will be left on another. Every stone will be thrown down."

[7]They asked Jesus, "Teacher, when will these things happen? What will be the sign that they are about to take place?"

[8]Jesus said, "Be careful so you are not fooled. Many people will come in my name, saying, 'I am the One' and, 'The time has come!' But don't follow them. [9]When you hear about wars and riots, don't be afraid, because these things must happen first, but the end will come later."

[10]Then he said to them, "Nations will fight against other nations, and kingdoms against other kingdoms. [11]In various places there will be great earthquakes, sicknesses, and a lack of food. Fearful events and great signs will come from heaven.

[12]"But before all these things happen, people will arrest you and treat you cruelly. They will judge you in their synagogues and put you

ROCK SOLID

Luke 21:1–4

What's the secret to being happy? Is it being popular? Is it having the world's coolest house with a swimming pool and a diving board off your balcony? Is it being a great athlete or traveling all over the world?

Way off. We think we would be happy if only…and we name something we have to own or a circumstance that needs to be just right. But in reality the secret to being happy is the opposite of having the right circumstance. It's being content right where you are no matter the circumstance! It's turning your focus to what really matters to God.

The Bible says, "As Jesus looked up, he saw some rich people putting their gifts into the Temple money box. Then he saw a poor widow putting two small copper coins into the box. He said, 'I tell you the truth, this poor widow gave more than all those rich people. They gave only what they did not need. This woman is very poor, but she gave all she had to live on'" (Luke 21:1–4).

You can be sure that God satisfied the needs of that poor woman, perhaps even a few minutes later thanks to the generosity of Jesus and his followers.

Whatever your circumstances are today, choose to be happy in Jesus.

in jail and force you to stand before kings and governors, because you follow me. [13]But this will give you an opportunity to tell about me. [14]Make up your minds not to worry ahead of time about what you will say. [15]I will give you the wisdom to say things that none of your enemies will be able to stand against or prove wrong. [16]Even your parents, brothers, relatives, and friends will turn against you, and they will kill some of you. [17]All people will hate you because you follow me. [18]But none of these things can really harm you. [19]By continuing to have faith you will save your lives.

JERUSALEM WILL BE DESTROYED

[20]"When you see armies all around Jerusalem, you will know it will soon be destroyed. [21]At that time, the people in Judea should run away to the mountains. The people in Jerusalem must get out, and those who are near the city should not go in. [22]These are the days of punishment to bring about all that is written in the Scriptures. [23]How terrible it will be for women who are pregnant or have nursing babies! Great trouble will come upon this land, and God will be angry with these people. [24]They will be killed by the sword and taken as prisoners to all nations. Jerusalem will be crushed by non-Jewish people until their time is over.

DON'T FEAR

[25]"There will be signs in the sun, moon, and stars. On earth, nations will be afraid and confused because of the roar and fury of the sea. [26]People will be so afraid they will faint, wondering what is happening to the world, because the powers of the heavens will be shaken. [27]Then people will see the Son of Man coming in a cloud with power and great glory. [28]When these things begin to happen, look up and hold your heads high, because the time when God will free you is near!"

JESUS' WORDS WILL LIVE FOREVER

[29]Then Jesus told this story: "Look at the fig tree and all the other trees. [30]When their leaves appear, you know that summer is near. [31]In the same way, when you see these things happening, you will know that God's kingdom is near.

[32]"I tell you the truth, all these things will happen while the people of this time are still living. [33]Earth and sky will be destroyed, but the words I have spoken will never be destroyed.

BE READY ALL THE TIME

[34]"Be careful not to spend your time feasting, drinking, or worrying about worldly things. If you do, that day might come on you suddenly, [35]like a trap on all people on earth. [36]So be ready all the time. Pray that you will be strong enough to escape all these things that will happen and that you will be able to stand before the Son of Man."

[37]During the day, Jesus taught the people in the Temple, and at night he went out of the city and stayed on the Mount of Olives. [38]Every morning all the people got up early to go to the Temple to listen to him.

JUDAS BECOMES AN ENEMY OF JESUS

22 It was almost time for the Feast of Unleavened Bread, called the Passover Feast. [2]The leading priests and teachers of the law were trying to find a way to kill Jesus, because they were afraid of the people.

[3]Satan entered Judas Iscariot, one of Jesus' twelve apostles. [4]Judas went to the leading priests and some of the soldiers who guarded the Temple and talked to them about a way to hand Jesus over to them. [5]They were pleased and agreed to give Judas money. [6]He agreed and watched for the best time to hand Jesus

"Make a Difference"

"Mr. Rawlings, our choir teacher, just asked us to pray for him!" Gil and Chuck beamed as they shared the news at their lunchtime prayer meeting.

"Yeah, we were standing near the office door talking about next year and Gil mentioned praying for each other. We didn't know Mr. Rawlings was in there, but he stepped out and asked us to pray for him, too," Gil added.

Many guys and girls like you around the world make a difference for Jesus Christ in their public school classrooms—often they even impact the lives of their teachers. Gil and Chuck met at lunch with several other Christian students in their middle school cafeteria. They prayed for fellow students and for their teachers.

Sometimes God answered their prayers in hidden ways, sometimes out in the open—like in the case of Mr. Rawlings. Either way, they were able to make a difference, even in the lives of their teachers. Starting a prayer group at school or in a neighborhood is one way you can make a difference for Jesus Christ.

Top 10 Ways to Be Beyond "Cool"

1. Clean a yard for someone.
2. Start a Christian garage band.
3. Take pictures of your friends and make a collage.
4. At your birthday party, give your friends gifts instead.
5. Sit with someone at lunch who is alone.
6. Wash the church staff's cars while they're in their offices.
7. Have a driveway-sweeping party.
8. Pick up trash at school.
9. Help an elderly person with his computer.
10. Hug your mom.

over to them when he was away from the crowd.

JESUS EATS THE PASSOVER MEAL

[7] The Day of Unleavened Bread came when the Passover lambs had to be sacrificed. [8] Jesus said to Peter and John, "Go and prepare the Passover meal for us to eat."

[9] They asked, "Where do you want us to prepare it?" [10] Jesus said to them, "After you go into the city, a man carrying a jar of water will meet you. Follow him into the house that he enters, [11] and tell the owner of the house, 'The Teacher says: "Where is the guest room in which I may eat the Passover meal with my followers?"' [12] Then he will show you a large, furnished room upstairs. Prepare the Passover meal there."

[13] So Peter and John left and found everything as Jesus had said. And they prepared the Passover meal.

THE LORD'S SUPPER

[14] When the time came, Jesus and the apostles were sitting at the table. [15] He said to them, "I wanted very much to eat this Passover meal with you before I suffer. [16] I will not eat another Passover meal until it is given its true meaning in the kingdom of God."

[17] Then Jesus took a cup, gave thanks, and said, "Take this cup and share it among yourselves. [18] I will not drink again from the fruit of the vine[n] until God's kingdom comes."

[19] Then Jesus took some bread, gave thanks, broke it, and gave it to the apostles, saying, "This is my body,"[n] which I am giving for you. Do this to remember me." [20] In the same way, after supper, Jesus took the cup and said, "This cup is the new agreement that God makes with his people. This new agreement begins with my blood which is poured out for you.

WHO WILL TURN AGAINST JESUS?

[21] "But one of you will turn against me, and his hand is with mine on the table. [22] What God has planned for the Son of Man will happen, but how terrible it will be for that one who turns against the Son of Man."

[23] Then the apostles asked each other which one of them would do that.

BE LIKE A SERVANT

[24] The apostles also began to argue about which one of them was the most important. [25] But Jesus said to them, "The kings of the non-Jewish people rule over them, and those who have authority over others like to be called 'friends of the people.' [26] But you must not be like that. Instead, the greatest among you should be like the youngest, and the leader should be like the servant. [27] Who is more important: the one sitting at the table or the one serving? You think the one at the table is more important, but I am like a servant among you.

[28] "You have stayed with me through my struggles. [29] Just as my Father has given me a kingdom, I also give you a kingdom [30] so you may eat and drink at my table in my kingdom. And you will sit on thrones, judging the twelve tribes of Israel.

DON'T LOSE YOUR FAITH!

[31] "Simon, Simon, Satan has asked to test all of you as a farmer sifts his wheat. [32] I have prayed that you will not lose your faith! Help your brothers be stronger when you come back to me."

[33] But Peter said to Jesus, "Lord, I am ready to go with you to prison and even to die with you!"

[34] But Jesus said, "Peter, before the rooster crows this day, you will say three times that you don't know me."

BE READY FOR TROUBLE

[35] Then Jesus said to the apostles, "When I sent you out without a purse, a bag, or sandals, did you need anything?"

They said, "No."

[36] He said to them, "But now if you have a purse or a bag, carry that with you. If you don't have a sword, sell your coat and buy one. [37] The Scripture says, 'He was treated like a criminal,'[n] and I tell you this scripture must have its full meaning. It was written about me, and it is happening now."

[38] His followers said, "Look, Lord, here are two swords."

He said to them, "That is enough."

JESUS PRAYS ALONE

[39] Jesus left the city and went to the Mount of Olives, as he often did, and his followers went with him. [40] When he reached the place, he said to them, "Pray for strength against temptation."

[41] Then Jesus went about a stone's throw away from them. He kneeled down and prayed, [42] "Father, if you are willing, take away this cup[n] of suffering. But do what you want, not what I want." [43] Then an angel from heaven appeared to him to strengthen him. [44] Being full of pain, Jesus prayed even harder. His sweat was like drops of blood falling to the ground. [45] When he finished praying, he went to his followers and found them asleep because of their sadness. [46] Jesus said to them, "Why are you sleeping? Get up and pray for strength against temptation."

GET CONNECTED

LOSING A FRIEND

If you've ever had a friend walk out of your life (maybe because he wanted to hang with "the cool crowd"), you know what the ache feels like. What can you do when you feel like you've lost your best friend?

Send him a fun card that shares one of your favorite memories with him. Even if he doesn't want to be friends again right away, you'll feel better. Why? Because you'll know that he knows he can always depend on at least two true friends—you and God.

22:18 fruit of the vine Product of the grapevine; this may also be translated "wine." **22:19b–20 body** Some Greek copies do not have the rest of verse 19 or verse 20. **22:37 'He . . . criminal.'** Quotation from Isaiah 53:12. **22:42 cup** Jesus is talking about the painful things that will happen to him. Accepting these things will be hard, like drinking a cup of something bitter.

JESUS IS ARRESTED

⁴⁷While Jesus was speaking, a crowd came up, and Judas, one of the twelve apostles, was leading them. He came close to Jesus so he could kiss him.

⁴⁸But Jesus said to him, "Judas, are you using the kiss to give the Son of Man to his enemies?"

⁴⁹When those who were standing around him saw what was happening, they said, "Lord, should we strike them with our swords?" ⁵⁰And one of them struck the servant of the high priest and cut off his right ear.

⁵¹Jesus said, "Stop! No more of this." Then he touched the servant's ear and healed him.

⁵²Those who came to arrest Jesus were the leading priests, the soldiers who guarded the Temple, and the elders. Jesus said to them, "You came out here with swords and clubs as though I were a criminal. ⁵³I was with you every day in the Temple, and you didn't arrest me there. But this is your time—the time when darkness rules."

PETER SAYS HE DOESN'T KNOW JESUS

⁵⁴They arrested Jesus, and led him away, and brought him into the house of the high priest. Peter followed far behind them. ⁵⁵After the soldiers started a fire in the middle of the courtyard and sat together, Peter sat with them. ⁵⁶A servant girl saw Peter sitting there in the firelight, and looking closely at him, she said, "This man was also with him."

⁵⁷But Peter said this was not true; he said, "Woman, I don't know him."

⁵⁸A short time later, another person saw Peter and said, "You are also one of them."

But Peter said, "Man, I am not!"

⁵⁹About an hour later, another man insisted, "Certainly this man was with him, because he is from Galilee, too."

⁶⁰But Peter said, "Man, I don't know what you are talking about!"

At once, while Peter was still speaking, a rooster crowed. ⁶¹Then the Lord turned and looked straight at Peter. And Peter remembered what the Lord had said: "Before the rooster crows this day, you will say three times that you don't know me." ⁶²Then Peter went outside and cried painfully.

THE PEOPLE MAKE FUN OF JESUS

⁶³The men who were guarding Jesus began making fun of him and beating him. ⁶⁴They blindfolded him and said, "Prove that you are a prophet, and tell us who hit you." ⁶⁵They said many cruel things to Jesus.

JESUS BEFORE THE LEADERS

⁶⁶When day came, the council of the elders of the people, both the leading priests and the teachers of the law, came together and led Jesus to their highest court. ⁶⁷They said, "If you are the Christ, tell us."

Jesus said to them, "If I tell you, you will not believe me. ⁶⁸And if I ask you, you will not answer. ⁶⁹But from now on, the Son of Man will sit at the right hand of the powerful God."

⁷⁰They all said, "Then are you the Son of God?"

Jesus said to them, "You say that I am."

⁷¹They said, "Why do we need witnesses now? We ourselves heard him say this."

PILATE QUESTIONS JESUS

23 Then the whole group stood up and led Jesus to Pilate." ²They began to accuse Jesus, saying, "We caught this man telling things that mislead our people. He says that we should not pay taxes to Caesar, and he calls himself the Christ, a king."

³Pilate asked Jesus, "Are you the king of the Jews?"

Jesus answered, "Those are your words."

⁴Pilate said to the leading priests and the people, "I find nothing against this man."

⁵They were insisting, saying, "But Jesus makes trouble with the people, teaching all around Judea. He began in Galilee, and now he is here."

PILATE SENDS JESUS TO HEROD

⁶Pilate heard this and asked if Jesus was from Galilee. ⁷Since Jesus was under Herod's authority, Pilate sent Jesus to Herod, who was in Jerusalem at that time. ⁸When Herod saw Jesus, he was very glad, because he had heard about Jesus and had wanted to meet him for a long time. He was hoping to see Jesus work a miracle. ⁹Herod asked Jesus many questions, but Jesus said nothing. ¹⁰The leading priests and teachers of the law were standing there, strongly accusing Jesus. ¹¹After Herod and his soldiers had made fun of Jesus, they dressed him in a kingly robe and sent him back to Pilate. ¹²In the past, Pilate and Herod had always been enemies, but on that day they became friends.

JESUS MUST DIE

¹³Pilate called the people together with the leading priests and the rulers. ¹⁴He said to them, "You brought this man to me, saying he makes trouble among the people. But I have questioned him before you all, and I have not found him guilty of what you say. ¹⁵Also, Herod found nothing wrong with him; he sent him back to us. Look, he has done nothing for which he should die. ¹⁶So, after I punish him, I will let him go free." [¹⁷Every year at the Passover Feast, Pilate had to release one prisoner to the people.]"

23:1 Pilate Pontius Pilate was the Roman governor of Judea from A.D. 26 to A.D. 36.   **23:17 Every . . . people.** Some Greek copies do not contain the bracketed text.

[18]But the people shouted together, "Take this man away! Let Barabbas go free!" [19](Barabbas was a man who was in prison for his part in a riot in the city and for murder.)

[20]Pilate wanted to let Jesus go free and told this to the crowd. [21]But they shouted again, "Crucify him! Crucify him!"

[22]A third time Pilate said to them, "Why? What wrong has he done? I can find no reason to kill him. So I will have him punished and set him free."

[23]But they continued to shout, demanding that Jesus be crucified. Their yelling became so loud that [24]Pilate decided to give them what they wanted. [25]He set free the man who was in jail for rioting and murder, and he handed Jesus over to them to do with him as they wished.

JESUS IS CRUCIFIED

[26]As they led Jesus away, Simon, a man from Cyrene, was coming in from the fields. They forced him to carry Jesus' cross and to walk behind him.

[27]A large crowd of people was following Jesus, including some women who were sad and crying for him. [28]But Jesus turned and said to them, "Women of Jerusalem, don't cry for me. Cry for yourselves and for your children. [29]The time is coming when people will say, 'Blessed are the women who cannot have children and who have no babies to nurse.' [30]Then people will say to the mountains, 'Fall on us!' And they will say to the hills, 'Cover us!' [31]If they act like this now when life is good, what will happen when bad times come?"[n]

[32]There were also two criminals led out with Jesus to be put to death. [33]When they came to a place called the Skull, the soldiers crucified Jesus and the criminals—one on his right and the other on his left. [34]Jesus said, "Father, forgive them, because they don't know what they are doing."[n]

The soldiers threw lots to decide who would get his clothes. [35]The people stood there watching. And the leaders made fun of Jesus, saying, "He saved others. Let him save himself if he is God's Chosen One, the Christ."

[36]The soldiers also made fun of him, coming to Jesus and offering him some vinegar. [37]They said, "If you are the king of the Jews, save yourself!" [38]At the top of the cross these words were written: THIS IS THE KING OF THE JEWS.

[39]One of the criminals on a cross began to shout insults at Jesus: "Aren't you the Christ? Then save yourself and us."

[40]But the other criminal stopped him and said, "You should fear God! You are getting the same punishment he is. [41]We are punished justly, getting what we deserve for what we did. But this man has done nothing wrong." [42]Then he said, "Jesus, remember me when you come into your kingdom."

[43]Jesus said to him, "I tell you the truth, today you will be with me in paradise."[n]

JESUS DIES

[44]It was about noon, and the whole land became dark until three o'clock in the afternoon, [45]because the sun did not shine. The curtain in the Temple[n] was torn in two. [46]Jesus cried out in a loud voice, "Father, I give you my life." After Jesus said this, he died.

[47]When the army officer there saw what happened, he praised God, saying, "Surely this was a good man!"

[48]When all the people who had gathered there to watch saw what happened, they returned home, beating their chests because they were so sad. [49]But those who were close friends of Jesus, including the women who had followed him from Galilee, stood at a distance and watched.

JOSEPH TAKES JESUS' BODY

[50]There was a good and religious man named Joseph who was a member of the council. [51]But he had not agreed to the other leaders' plans and actions against Jesus. He was from the town of Arimathea and was waiting for the kingdom of God to come. [52]Joseph went to Pilate to ask for the body of Jesus. [53]He took the body down from the cross, wrapped it in cloth, and put it in a tomb that was cut out of a wall of rock. This tomb had never been used before. [54]This was late on Preparation Day, and when the sun went down, the Sabbath day would begin.

[55]The women who had come from Galilee with Jesus followed Joseph and saw the tomb and how Jesus' body was laid. [56]Then the women left to prepare spices and perfumes.

On the Sabbath day they rested, as the law of Moses commanded.

JESUS RISES FROM THE DEAD

24 Very early on the first day of the week, at dawn, the women came to the tomb, bringing the spices they had prepared. [2]They found the stone rolled away from the entrance of the tomb, [3]but when they went in, they did not find the body of the Lord Jesus. [4]While they were wondering about this, two men in shining clothes suddenly stood beside them. [5]The women were very afraid and bowed their heads to the ground. The men said to them, "Why are you looking for a living person in this place for the dead? [6]He is not here; he has risen from the dead. Do you remember what he told you in Galilee? [7]He said the Son of Man must be handed over to sinful people, be crucified, and rise from the dead on the third day." [8]Then the women remembered what Jesus had said.

[9]The women left the tomb and told all these things to the eleven apostles and the other followers. [10]It was Mary Magdalene, Joanna, Mary the mother of James, and some other women who told the apostles everything that had happened at the tomb. [11]But they did not believe the women, because it sounded like nonsense. [12]But Peter got up and ran to the tomb. Bending down and looking in, he saw only the cloth that Jesus' body had been wrapped in. Peter went away to his home, wondering about what had happened.

JESUS ON THE ROAD TO EMMAUS

[13]That same day two of Jesus' followers were going to a town named Emmaus, about seven miles from Jerusalem. [14]They were talking about everything that had happened. [15]While they were talking and discussing, Jesus himself came near and began walking with them, [16]but they were kept from recognizing

Careful What You Watch

What you spend your time on will shape how you think. If you watch a lot of TV, it will influence the choices you make. The Bible gives a radically different way of thinking from what you'll find on TV. Do you want your thinking to be shaped by television or by God?

23:31 If . . . come? Literally, "If they do these things in the green tree, what will happen in the dry?" **23:34 Jesus . . . doing."** Some Greek copies do not have this first part of verse 34. **23:43 paradise** Another word for heaven. **23:45 curtain in the Temple** A curtain divided the Most Holy Place from the other part of the Temple, the special building in Jerusalem where God commanded the Jewish people to worship him.

him. [17]Then he said, "What are these things you are talking about while you walk?"

The two followers stopped, looking very sad. [18]The one named Cleopas answered, "Are you the only visitor in Jerusalem who does not know what just happened there?"

[19]Jesus said to them, "What are you talking about?"

They said, "About Jesus of Nazareth. He was a prophet who said and did many powerful things before God and all the people. [20]Our leaders and the leading priests handed him over to be sentenced to death, and they crucified him. [21]But we were hoping that he would free Israel. Besides this, it is now the third day since this happened. [22]And today some women among us amazed us. Early this morning they went to the tomb, [23]but they did not find his body there. They came and told us that they had seen a vision of angels who said that Jesus was alive! [24]So some of our group went to the tomb, too. They found it just as the women said, but they did not see Jesus."

[25]Then Jesus said to them, "You are foolish and slow to believe everything the prophets said. [26]They said that the Christ must suffer these things before he enters his glory." [27]Then starting with what Moses and all the prophets had said about him, Jesus began to explain everything that had been written about himself in the Scriptures.

[28]They came near the town of Emmaus, and Jesus acted as if he were going farther. [29]But they begged him, "Stay with us, because it is late; it is almost night." So he went in to stay with them.

[30]When Jesus was at the table with them, he took some bread, gave thanks, divided it, and gave it to them. [31]And then, they were allowed to recognize Jesus. But when they saw who he was, he disappeared. [32]They said to each other, "It felt like a fire burning in us when Jesus talked to us on the road and explained the Scriptures to us."

[33]So the two followers got up at once and went back to Jerusalem. There they found the eleven apostles and others gathered. [34]They were saying, "The Lord really has risen from the dead! He showed himself to Simon."

[35]Then the two followers told what had happened on the road and how they recognized Jesus when he divided the bread.

JESUS APPEARS TO HIS FOLLOWERS

[36]While the two followers were telling this, Jesus himself stood right in the middle of them and said, "Peace be with you."

[37]They were fearful and terrified and thought they were seeing a ghost. [38]But Jesus said, "Why are you troubled? Why do you doubt what you see? [39]Look at my hands and my feet. It is I myself! Touch me and see, because a ghost does not have a living body as you see I have."

[40]After Jesus said this, he showed them his hands and feet. [41]While they still could not believe it because they were amazed and happy, Jesus said to them, "Do you have any food here?" [42]They gave him a piece of broiled fish. [43]While the followers watched, Jesus took the fish and ate it.

[44]He said to them, "Remember when I was with you before? I said that everything written about me must happen—everything in the law of Moses, the books of the prophets, and the Psalms."

[45]Then Jesus opened their minds so they could understand the Scriptures. [46]He said to them, "It is written that the Christ would suffer and rise from the dead on the third day [47]and that a change of hearts and lives and forgiveness of sins would be preached in his name to all nations, starting at Jerusalem. [48]You are witnesses of these things. [49]I will send you what my Father has promised, but you must stay in Jerusalem until you have received that power from heaven."

JESUS GOES BACK TO HEAVEN

[50]Jesus led his followers as far as Bethany, and he raised his hands and blessed them. [51]While he was blessing them, he was separated from them and carried into heaven. [52]They worshiped him and returned to Jerusalem very happy. [53]They stayed in the Temple all the time, praising God.

COOL!

Best-seller of All Time

The best-selling book in the world never appears on the best-seller lists, even though it blows away the competition—even Harry Potter—week after week.

★ 168,000 Bibles are sold or given away in the U.S. every *day*.
★ At least 20 million Bibles are sold each *year* in the U.S.
★ The American Bible Society has given away over 7 billion Bibles since 1816.
★ The Gideons have given away almost 2 billion Bibles since they began in 1899.
★ About 92 percent of Americans own a Bible; the average Bible reader owns nine copies.

Have you ever wondered what God would look like with skin on?

This book tells you.

John's was the last Gospel written, and it doesn't repeat a lot of stuff from Matthew, Mark, and Luke. John doesn't start with the birth of the baby Jesus, either. He goes much further back: "In the beginning there was the Word. The Word was with God, and the Word was God" (1:1).

John says this eternal God-Word "became a human and lived among us" (1:14). Imagine that! God became a man in Jesus Christ and visited the world he created!

In a very orderly way, John tells us some of what Jesus did and said while he was here. He reports seven of Jesus' miracles, like turning water into wine and raising his friend Lazarus from the dead. He also carefully records seven amazing claims Jesus made about himself. See how many you can find as you read this book:

- I AM the Bread of Life;
- I AM the Light of the World;
- I AM the Gate for the Sheep;
- I AM the Good Shepherd;
- I AM the Resurrection and the Life;
- I AM the Way, the Truth, and the Life;
- I AM the True Vine.

John has a clear purpose in writing. He hopes to convince you "that Jesus is the Christ, the Son of God. Then, by believing, you may have life through his name" (20:31).

Read on with an open mind and an open heart!

JOHN

CHRIST COMES TO THE WORLD

1 In the beginning there was the Word." The Word was with God, and the Word was God. ²He was with God in the beginning. ³All things were made by him, and nothing was made without him. ⁴In him there was life, and that life was the light of all people. ⁵The Light shines in the darkness, and the darkness has not overpowered" it.

⁶There was a man named John" who was sent by God. ⁷He came to tell people the truth about the Light so that through him all people could hear about the Light and believe. ⁸John was not the Light, but he came to tell people the truth about the Light. ⁹The true Light that gives light to all was coming into the world!

¹⁰The Word was in the world, and the world was made by him, but the world did not know him. ¹¹He came to the world that was his own, but his own people did not accept him. ¹²But to all who did accept him and believe in him he gave the right to become children of God. ¹³They did not become his children in any human way—by any human parents or human desire. They were born of God.

¹⁴The Word became a human and lived among us. We saw his glory—the glory that belongs to the only Son of the Father—and he was full of grace and truth. ¹⁵John tells the truth about him and cries out, saying, "This is

DID YOU KNOW?

88% of kids collect something, like coins, rocks, stamps, or sports cards.

KidScreen Magazine. "KidThink: What Today's Kids are Thinking: Most kids are avid collectors."

the One I told you about: 'The One who comes after me is greater than I am, because he was living before me.' "

¹⁶Because he was full of grace and truth, from him we all received one gift after another. ¹⁷The law was given through Moses, but grace and truth came through Jesus Christ. ¹⁸No one has ever seen God. But God the only Son is very close to the Father," and he has shown us what God is like.

JOHN TELLS PEOPLE ABOUT JESUS

¹⁹Here is the truth John" told when the leaders in Jerusalem sent priests and Levites to ask him, "Who are you?"

²⁰John spoke freely and did not refuse to answer. He said, "I am not the Christ."

²¹So they asked him, "Then who are you? Are you Elijah?""

He answered, "No, I am not."

"Are you the Prophet?"" they asked.

He answered, "No."

²²Then they said, "Who are you? Give us an answer to tell those who sent us. What do you say about yourself?"

²³John told them in the words of the prophet Isaiah:

"I am the voice of one
    calling out in the desert:
'Make the road straight for the Lord.' "

Isaiah 40:3

²⁴Some Pharisees who had been sent asked John: ²⁵"If you are not the Christ or Elijah or the Prophet, why do you baptize people?"

²⁶John answered, "I baptize with water, but there is one here with you that you don't know about. ²⁷He is the One who comes after

trustables

John 1:12

Do you know your rights? When you turn eighteen, you have the right to vote. Americans have the right to free speech and to bear arms. If you get arrested (and let's hope you don't!), you have the right to remain silent.

Have you ever felt like you had the *right* to become a child of God? You know, a full-fledged member of the family? You can make yourself at home, help yourself to anything in the fridge, and play with all the cool toys. Sometimes it's hard to imagine having that kind of freedom with God.

But the Bible says that we do have this right!

There's just one condition: accept Jesus as God's Son. If you do that, then you're in! John 1:12 says, "To all who did accept him and believe in him he gave the *right* to become children of God."

Having a "right" is a lot bigger than having a "privilege." A privilege is something that can be taken away. Rights can't. They're yours forever. This is the best deal you'll ever find in your entire life: the right to be God's child for the simple act of believing in his Son. It's a no-brainer!

Are you in the family yet?

1:1 Word The Greek word is "logos," meaning any kind of communication; it could be translated "message." Here, it means Christ, because Christ was the way God told people about himself. **1:5 overpowered** This can also be translated, "understood." **1:6, 19 John** John the Baptist, who preached to people about Christ's coming (Matthew 3, Luke 3). **1:18 But . . . Father** This could be translated, "But the only God is very close to the Father." Also, some Greek copies read "But the only Son is very close to the Father." **1:21 Elijah** A prophet who spoke for God. He lived hundreds of years before Christ and was expected to return before Christ (Malachi 4:5–6). **1:21 Prophet** They probably meant the prophet that God told Moses he would send (Deuteronomy 18:15–19).

me. I am not good enough to untie the strings of his sandals."

[28] This all happened at Bethany on the other side of the Jordan River, where John was baptizing people.

[29] The next day John saw Jesus coming toward him. John said, "Look, the Lamb of God,[n] who takes away the sin of the world! [30] This is the One I was talking about when I said, 'A man will come after me, but he is greater than I am, because he was living before me.' [31] Even I did not know who he was, although I came baptizing with water so that the people of Israel would know who he is."

[32-33] Then John said, "I saw the Spirit come down from heaven in the form of a dove and rest on him. Until then I did not know who the Christ was. But the God who sent me to baptize with water told me, 'You will see the Spirit come down and rest on a man; he is the One who will baptize with the Holy Spirit.' [34] I have seen this happen, and I tell you the truth: This man is the Son of God."[n]

THE FIRST FOLLOWERS OF JESUS

[35] The next day John[n] was there again with two of his followers. [36] When he saw Jesus walking by, he said, "Look, the Lamb of God!"[n]

[37] The two followers heard John say this, so they followed Jesus. [38] When Jesus turned and saw them following him, he asked, "What are you looking for?"

They said, "Rabbi, where are you staying?" ("Rabbi" means "Teacher.")

[39] He answered, "Come and see." So the two men went with Jesus and saw where he was staying and stayed there with him that day. It was about four o'clock in the afternoon.

[40] One of the two men who followed Jesus after they heard John speak about him was Andrew, Simon Peter's brother. [41] The first thing Andrew did was to find his brother Simon and say to him, "We have found the Messiah." ("Messiah" means "Christ.")

[42] Then Andrew took Simon to Jesus. Jesus looked at him and said, "You are Simon son of John. You will be called Cephas." ("Cephas" means "Peter."[n])

[43] The next day Jesus decided to go to Galilee. He found Philip and said to him, "Follow me."

[44] Philip was from the town of Bethsaida, where Andrew and Peter lived. [45] Philip found Nathanael and told him, "We have found the man that Moses wrote about in the law, and the prophets also wrote about him. He is Jesus, the son of Joseph, from Nazareth."

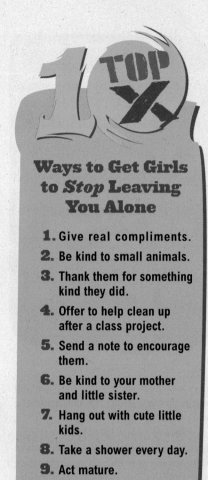

TOP 10

Ways to Get Girls to *Stop* Leaving You Alone

1. **Give real compliments.**
2. **Be kind to small animals.**
3. **Thank them for something kind they did.**
4. **Offer to help clean up after a class project.**
5. **Send a note to encourage them.**
6. **Be kind to your mother and little sister.**
7. **Hang out with cute little kids.**
8. **Take a shower every day.**
9. **Act mature.**
10. **Be yourself.**

[46] But Nathanael said to Philip, "Can anything good come from Nazareth?"

Philip answered, "Come and see."

[47] As Jesus saw Nathanael coming toward him, he said, "Here is truly an Israelite. There is nothing false in him."

[48] Nathanael asked, "How do you know me?"

Jesus answered, "I saw you when you were under the fig tree, before Philip told you about me."

[49] Then Nathanael said to Jesus, "Teacher, you are the Son of God; you are the King of Israel."

[50] Jesus said to Nathanael, "Do you believe simply because I told you I saw you under the fig tree? You will see greater things than that." [51] And Jesus said to them, "I tell you the truth, you will all see heaven open and 'angels of God going up and coming down'[n] on the Son of Man."

THE WEDDING AT CANA

2 Two days later there was a wedding in the town of Cana in Galilee. Jesus' mother was there, [2] and Jesus and his followers were also invited to the wedding. [3] When all the wine was gone, Jesus' mother said to him, "They have no more wine."

[4] Jesus answered, "Dear woman, why come to me? My time has not yet come."

[5] His mother said to the servants, "Do whatever he tells you to do."

[6] In that place there were six stone water jars that the Jews used in their washing ceremony.[n] Each jar held about twenty or thirty gallons.

[7] Jesus said to the servants, "Fill the jars with water." So they filled the jars to the top.

[8] Then he said to them, "Now take some out and give it to the master of the feast."

So they took the water to the master. [9] When he tasted it, the water had become wine. He did not know where the wine came from, but the servants who had brought the water knew. The master of the wedding called the bridegroom [10] and said to him, "People always serve the best wine first. Later, after the guests have been drinking awhile, they serve the cheaper wine. But you have saved the best wine till now."

[11] So in Cana of Galilee Jesus did his first miracle. There he showed his glory, and his followers believed in him.

JESUS IN THE TEMPLE

[12] After this, Jesus went to the town of Capernaum with his mother, brothers, and followers. They stayed there for just a few days. [13] When it was almost time for the Jewish Passover Feast, Jesus went to Jerusalem. [14] In the Temple he found people selling cattle, sheep, and doves. He saw others sitting at tables, exchanging different kinds of money. [15] Jesus made a whip out of cords and forced all of them, both the sheep and cattle, to leave the Temple. He turned over the tables and scattered the money of those who were exchanging it. [16] Then he said to those who were selling pigeons, "Take these things out of here! Don't make my Father's house a place for buying and selling!"

[17] When this happened, the followers remembered what was written in the Scriptures: "My strong love for your Temple completely controls me."[n]

[18] Some of his people said to Jesus, "Show us a miracle to prove you have the right to do these things."

1:29, 36 **Lamb of God** Name for Jesus. Jesus is like the lambs that were offered for a sacrifice to God.   1:34 **the Son of God** Some Greek copies read "God's Chosen One."   1:35 **John** John the Baptist, who preached to people about Christ's coming (Matthew 3, Luke 3).   1:42 **Peter** The Greek name "Peter," like the Aramaic name "Cephas," means "rock."   1:51 **'angels . . . down'** These words are from Genesis 28:12.   2:6 **washing ceremony** The Jewish people washed themselves in special ways before eating, before worshiping in the Temple, and at other special times.   2:17 **"My . . . me."** Quotation from Psalm 69:9.

[19]Jesus answered them, "Destroy this temple, and I will build it again in three days."

[20]They answered, "It took forty-six years to build this Temple! Do you really believe you can build it again in three days?"

[21](But the temple Jesus meant was his own body. [22]After Jesus was raised from the dead, his followers remembered that Jesus had said this. Then they believed the Scripture and the words Jesus had said.)

[23]When Jesus was in Jerusalem for the Passover Feast, many people believed in him because they saw the miracles he did. [24]But Jesus did not believe in them because he knew them all. [25]He did not need anyone to tell him about people, because he knew what was in people's minds.

NICODEMUS COMES TO JESUS

3 There was a man named Nicodemus who was one of the Pharisees and an important Jewish leader. [2]One night Nicodemus came to Jesus and said, "Teacher, we know you are a teacher sent from God, because no one can do the miracles you do unless God is with him."

[3]Jesus answered, "I tell you the truth, unless you are born again, you cannot be in God's kingdom."

[4]Nicodemus said, "But if a person is already old, how can he be born again? He cannot enter his mother's womb again. So how can a person be born a second time?"

[5]But Jesus answered, "I tell you the truth, unless you are born from water and the Spirit, you cannot enter God's kingdom. [6]Human life comes from human parents, but spiritual life comes from the Spirit. [7]Don't be surprised when I tell you, 'You must all be born again.' [8]The wind blows where it wants to and you hear the sound of it, but you don't know where the wind comes from or where it is going. It is the same with every person who is born from the Spirit."

[9]Nicodemus asked, "How can this happen?"

[10]Jesus said, "You are an important teacher in Israel, and you don't understand these things? [11]I tell you the truth, we talk about what we know, and we tell about what we have seen, but you don't accept what we tell you. [12]I have told you about things here on earth, and you do not believe me. So you will not believe me if I tell you about things of heaven. [13]The only one who has ever gone up to heaven is the One who came down from heaven—the Son of Man."

[14]"Just as Moses lifted up the snake in the desert," the Son of Man must also be lifted up. [15]So that everyone who believes can have eternal life in him.

[16]"God loved the world so much that he gave his one and only Son so that whoever believes in him may not be lost, but have eternal life. [17]God did not send his Son into the world to judge the world guilty, but to save the world through him. [18]People who believe in God's Son are not judged guilty. Those who do not believe have already been judged guilty, because they have not believed in God's one and only Son. [19]They are judged by this fact: The Light has come into the world, but they did not want light. They wanted darkness, because they were doing evil things. [20]All who do evil hate the light and will not come to the light, because it will show all the evil things they do. [21]But those who follow the true way come to the light, and it shows that the things they do were done through God."

JESUS AND JOHN THE BAPTIST

[22]After this, Jesus and his followers went into the area of Judea, where he stayed with his followers and baptized people. [23]John was also baptizing in Aenon, near Salim, because there was plenty of water there. People were going there to be baptized. [24](This was before John was put into prison.)

[25]Some of John's followers had an argument with a Jew about religious washing." [26]So they came to John and said, "Teacher, remember the man who was with you on the other

Q&A

Q: My friends get to see any movie that comes out, but I don't even get to see some PG movies. It's embarrassing! How can I make my parents let me watch the movies I want to see?

A: The Bible says that you will become the things you think about: "Be careful what you think, because your thoughts run your life" (Proverbs 4:23). Every adult has seen things they wish they could forget. That's probably why your parents will be pretty strict about what movies they let you see. Remember, they love you and want the best for you!

Q: Does God want us to be joyful?

A: The answer is a big YES—God wants us to be filled with joy! Being *joyful* means being glad even when things are not going our way. God wants us to have a joyful heart no matter what is going on in our lives. We know that he's with us through both fun and tough times and that he's going to use even the bad things for our good. That's a great reason to have joy!

Q: If we can just solve problems like growing enough food and curing diseases, then will everybody live in peace?

A: Sadly, no. The Bible tells us that each of us is born with a selfish desire to do wrong. Jeremiah 17:9 says, "More than anything else, a person's mind is evil and cannot be healed." We can never change that by improving outside conditions. That's why God really cares about changing people from the inside.

3:13 the Son of Man Some Greek copies continue, "who is in heaven." **3:14 Moses . . . desert** When the Israelites were dying from snakebites, God told Moses to put a bronze snake on a pole. The people who looked at the snake were healed (Numbers 21:4–9). **3:25 religious washing** The Jewish people washed themselves in special ways before eating, before worshiping in the Temple, and at other special times.

side of the Jordan River, the one you spoke about so much? He is baptizing, and everyone is going to him."

[27]John answered, "A man can get only what God gives him. [28]You yourselves heard me say, 'I am not the Christ, but I am the one sent to prepare the way for him.' [29]The bride belongs only to the bridegroom. But the friend who helps the bridegroom stands by and listens to him. He is thrilled that he gets to hear the bridegroom's voice. In the same way, I am really happy. [30]He must become greater, and I must become less important.

THE ONE WHO COMES FROM HEAVEN

[31]"The One who comes from above is greater than all. The one who is from the earth belongs to the earth and talks about things on the earth. But the One who comes from heaven is greater than all. [32]He tells what he has seen and heard, but no one accepts what he says. [33]Whoever accepts what he says has proven that God is true. [34]The One whom God sent speaks the words of God, because God gives him the Spirit fully. [35]The Father loves the Son and has given him power over everything. [36]Those who believe in the Son have eternal life, but those who do not obey the Son will never have life. God's anger stays on them."

JESUS AND A SAMARITAN WOMAN

4 The Pharisees heard that Jesus was making and baptizing more followers than John, [2]although Jesus himself did not baptize people, but his followers did. [3]Jesus knew that the Pharisees had heard about him, so he left Judea and went back to Galilee. [4]But on the way he had to go through the country of Samaria.

[5]In Samaria Jesus came to the town called Sychar, which is near the field Jacob gave to his son Joseph. [6]Jacob's well was there. Jesus was tired from his long trip, so he sat down beside the well. It was about twelve o'clock noon. [7]When a Samaritan woman came to the well to get some water, Jesus said to her, "Please give me a drink." [8](This happened while Jesus' followers were in town buying some food.)

[9]The woman said, "I am surprised that you ask me for a drink, since you are a Jewish man and I am a Samaritan woman." (Jewish people are not friends with Samaritans.")

[10]Jesus said, "If you only knew the free gift of God and who it is that is asking you for water, you would have asked him, and he would have given you living water."

[11]The woman said, "Sir, where will you get this living water? The well is very deep, and you have nothing to get water with. [12]Are you greater than Jacob, our father, who gave us this well and drank from it himself along with his sons and flocks?"

[13]Jesus answered, "Everyone who drinks this water will be thirsty again, [14]but whoever drinks the water I give will never be thirsty. The water I give will become a spring of water gushing up inside that person, giving eternal life."

[15]The woman said to him, "Sir, give me this water so I will never be thirsty again and will not have to come back here to get more water."

[16]Jesus told her, "Go get your husband and come back here."

[17]The woman answered, "I have no husband."

Jesus said to her, "You are right to say you have no husband. [18]Really you have had five husbands, and the man you live with now is not your husband. You told the truth."

[19]The woman said, "Sir, I can see that you are a prophet. [20]Our ancestors worshiped on this mountain, but you say that Jerusalem is the place where people must worship."

[21]Jesus said, "Believe me, woman. The time is coming when neither in Jerusalem nor on this mountain will you actually worship the Father. [22]You Samaritans worship something you don't understand. We understand what we worship, because salvation comes from the Jews. [23]The time is coming when the true worshipers will worship the Father in spirit and truth, and that time is here already. You see, the Father too is actively seeking such people to worship him. [24]God is spirit, and those who worship him must worship in spirit and truth."

[25]The woman said, "I know that the Messiah is coming." (Messiah is the One called Christ.) "When the Messiah comes, he will explain everything to us."

[26]Then Jesus said, "I am he—I, the one talking to you."

[27]Just then his followers came back from town and were surprised to see him talking with a woman. But none of them asked, "What do you want?" or "Why are you talking with her?"

[28]Then the woman left her water jar and went back to town. She said to the people, [29]"Come and see a man who told me every-

ROCK SOLID

John 3:16

A king who rules over a kingdom of any size, when all is said and done, probably won't know that many of his subjects. Of course, he'll know which ones he considers the best and most important, but the rest are just the masses.

Is that how it is with God? He has millions of children all over the world. How could he keep track of any except the most outstanding? The rest of us ordinary Christians, we're just part of the crowd, right?

Wrong! The Bible says, "God loved the world so much that he gave his one and only Son so that *whoever* believes in him may not be lost, but have eternal life" (John 3:16). That means that before God spoke the Milky Way galaxy into existence, before he formed the sun and the earth, and before he created the first human being, he had already chosen to love *you*.

If one of your Christian friends is struggling with feeling unimportant, remind him of how important he is to God. And remind yourself of this truth: You're not just one of the crowd. God directed history so that you would be born; he chose you for a special purpose.

God isn't just any old king. God is the King of kings, and he loves you!

4:9 **Jewish people . . . Samaritans.** This can also be translated "Jewish people don't use things that Samaritans have used."

Track and Field

Taking part in track and field can mean a lot of different things! Track and field is a group of running, hurdling, jumping, and throwing events. The running events are sprints, middle distances, long distances, relay races, hurdles, steeplechase, and racewalking. The jumping events are the high jump, pole vault, long jump, and triple jump. The throwing events include shot put, discus, hammer, and javelin. Individuals and teams from all over the world train long and hard to compete in the Olympic track and field events. Your life also takes hard work and training. Philippians 3:13b–14 tells us to strain toward what is ahead to reach the goal!

thing I ever did. Do you think he might be the Christ?" [30]So the people left the town and went to see Jesus.

[31]Meanwhile, his followers were begging him, "Teacher, eat something."

[32]But Jesus answered, "I have food to eat that you know nothing about."

[33]So the followers asked themselves, "Did somebody already bring him food?"

[34]Jesus said, "My food is to do what the One who sent me wants me to do and to finish his work. [35]You have a saying, 'Four more months till harvest.' But I tell you, open your eyes and look at the fields ready for harvest now. [36]Already, the one who harvests is being paid and is gathering crops for eternal life. So the one who plants and the one who harvests celebrate at the same time. [37]Here the saying is true, 'One person plants, and another harvests.' [38]I sent you to harvest a crop that you did not work on. Others did the work, and you get to finish up their work."[n]

[39]Many of the Samaritans in that town believed in Jesus because of what the woman said: "He told me everything I ever did."

[40]When the Samaritans came to Jesus, they begged him to stay with them, so he stayed there two more days. [41]And many more believed because of the things he said.

[42]They said to the woman, "First we believed in Jesus because of what you said, but now we believe because we heard him ourselves. We know that this man really is the Savior of the world."

JESUS HEALS AN OFFICER'S SON

[43]Two days later, Jesus left and went to Galilee. [44](Jesus had said before that a prophet is not respected in his own country.) [45]When Jesus arrived in Galilee, the people there welcomed him. They had seen all the things he did at the Passover Feast in Jerusalem, because they had been there, too.

[46]Jesus went again to visit Cana in Galilee where he had changed the water into wine. One of the king's important officers lived in the city of Capernaum, and his son was sick. [47]When he heard that Jesus had come from Judea to Galilee, he went to Jesus and begged him to come to Capernaum and heal his son, because his son was almost dead. [48]Jesus said to him, "You people must see signs and miracles before you will believe in me."

[49]The officer said, "Sir, come before my child dies."

[50]Jesus answered, "Go. Your son will live."

The man believed what Jesus told him and went home. [51]On the way the man's servants came and met him and told him, "Your son is alive."

COOL!

Little Campers

Snails are mollusks of the class *Gastropoda*, which means "belly-footed." There are more than 50,000 kinds of snails living on land or in the water. Many snails have eyes on the end of their tentacles, making it easier to move them around. They also carry their own sturdy houses on their backs. They are "at home" no matter what! God designed snails to be self-contained little campers.

Just like the snail, no matter where you are, you can be "at home" when you keep God close to you. He will always protect you and provide for you.

4:38 I . . . their work. As a farmer sends workers to harvest grain, Jesus sends his followers out to bring people to God.

[52] The man asked, "What time did my son begin to get well?"

They answered, "Yesterday at one o'clock the fever left him."

[53] The father knew that one o'clock was the exact time that Jesus had said, "Your son will live." So the man and all the people who lived in his house believed in Jesus.

[54] That was the second miracle Jesus did after coming from Judea to Galilee.

JESUS HEALS A MAN AT A POOL

5 Later Jesus went to Jerusalem for a special feast. [2] In Jerusalem there is a pool with five covered porches, which is called Bethesda[a] in the Hebrew language.[b] This pool is near the Sheep Gate. [3] Many sick people were lying on the porches beside the pool. Some were blind, some were crippled, and some were paralyzed [, and they waited for the water to move. [4] Sometimes an angel of the Lord came down to the pool and stirred up the water. After the angel did this, the first person to go into the pool was healed from any sickness he had]. [5] A man was lying there who had been sick for thirty-eight years. [6] When Jesus saw the man and knew that he had been sick for such a long time, Jesus asked him, "Do you want to be well?"

[7] The sick man answered, "Sir, there is no one to help me get into the pool when the water starts moving. While I am coming to the water, someone else always gets in before me."

[8] Then Jesus said, "Stand up. Pick up your mat and walk." [9] And immediately the man was well; he picked up his mat and began to walk.

The day this happened was a Sabbath day. [10] So the Jews said to the man who had been healed, "Today is the Sabbath. It is against our law for you to carry your mat on the Sabbath day."

[11] But he answered, "The man who made me well told me, 'Pick up your mat and walk.' "

[12] Then they asked him, "Who is the man who told you to pick up your mat and walk?"

[13] But the man who had been healed did not know who it was, because there were many people in that place, and Jesus had left.

[14] Later, Jesus found the man at the Temple and said to him, "See, you are well now. Stop sinning so that something worse does not happen to you."

[15] Then the man left and told his people that Jesus was the one who had made him well.

[16] Because Jesus was doing this on the Sabbath day, some evil people began to persecute him. [17] But Jesus said to them, "My Father never stops working, and so I keep working, too."

[18] This made them try still harder to kill him. They said, "First Jesus was breaking the law about the Sabbath day. Now he says that God is his own Father, making himself equal with God!"

JESUS HAS GOD'S AUTHORITY

[19] But Jesus said, "I tell you the truth, the Son can do nothing alone. The Son does only what he sees the Father doing, because the Son does whatever the Father does. [20] The Father loves the Son and shows the Son all the things he himself does. But the Father will show the Son even greater things than this so that you can all be amazed. [21] Just as the Father raises the dead and gives them life, so also the Son gives life to those he wants to. [22] In fact, the Father judges no one, but he has given the Son power to do all the judging [23] so that all people will honor the Son as much as they honor the Father. Anyone who does not honor the Son does not honor the Father who sent him.

[24] "I tell you the truth, whoever hears what I say and believes in the One who sent me has eternal life. That person will not be judged guilty but has already left death and entered life. [25] I tell you the truth, the time is coming and is already here when the dead will hear the voice of the Son of God, and those who hear will have life. [26] Life comes from the Father himself, and he has allowed the Son to have life in himself as well. [27] And the Father has given the Son the approval to judge, because he is the Son of Man. [28] Don't be surprised at this: A time is coming when all who are dead and in

ROCK SOLID

John 4:23

When you go to church on Sunday, you hear people talk about *worship* in many different ways: "the worship service," "worship songs," "praise and worship," "we're here to worship God." What exactly is worship and how do you do it?

Jesus says worship involves both your heart and your head. "The time is coming when the true worshipers will worship the Father in spirit and truth, and that time is here already" (John 4:23). He wants you to worship him in spirit, which involves your heart—*and* in truth, which involves your head.

So you find a balance between the two, right? No, you've got to get extreme about both. Study the Bible hard; think and discuss difficult topics with friends, like "What is God like?" and "What does it mean to be created in his image?" Also, be open to experiencing God; ask him to speak to you, to let you feel his love, grace, and mercy.

That's all a part of worship—to put the full attention of your head and your heart on God. When you do, God will begin doing amazing things in your life. The rest of John 4:23 says, "You see, the Father too is actively seeking such people to worship him." God is on the lookout. Will he find what he's looking for in you?

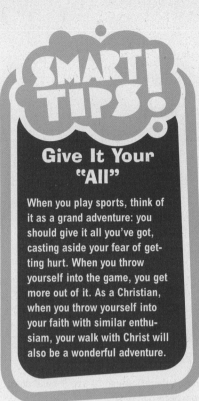

SMART TIPS!

Give It Your "All"

When you play sports, think of it as a grand adventure: you should give it all you've got, casting aside your fear of getting hurt. When you throw yourself into the game, you get more out of it. As a Christian, when you throw yourself into your faith with similar enthusiam, your walk with Christ will also be a wonderful adventure.

their graves will hear his voice. [29] Then they will come out of their graves. Those who did good will rise and have life forever, but those who did evil will rise to be judged guilty.

JESUS IS GOD'S SON

[30]"I can do nothing alone. I judge only the way I am told, so my judgment is fair. I don't try to please myself, but I try to please the One who sent me.

[31]"If only I tell people about myself, what I say is not true. [32]But there is another who tells about me, and I know that the things he says about me are true.

[33]"You have sent people to John, and he has told you the truth. [34]It is not that I need what humans say; I tell you this so you can be saved. [35]John was like a burning and shining lamp, and you were happy to enjoy his light for a while.

[36]"But I have a proof about myself that is greater than that of John. The things I do, which are the things my Father gave me to do, prove that the Father sent me. [37]And the Father himself who sent me has given proof about me. You have never heard his voice or seen what he looks like. [38]His teaching does not live in you, because you don't believe in the One the Father sent. [39]You carefully study the Scriptures because you think they give you eternal life. They do in fact tell about me, [40]but you refuse to come to me to have that life.

[41]"I don't need praise from people. [42]But I know you—I know that you don't have God's love in you. [43]I have come from my Father and speak for him, but you don't accept me. But when another person comes, speaking only for himself, you will accept him. [44]You try to get praise from each other, but you do not try to get the praise that comes from the only God. So how can you believe? [45]Don't think that I will stand before the Father and say you are wrong. The one who says you are wrong is Moses, the one you hoped would save you. [46]If you really believed Moses, you would believe me, because Moses wrote about me. [47]But if you don't believe what Moses wrote, how can you believe what I say?"

MORE THAN FIVE THOUSAND FED

6 After this, Jesus went across Lake Galilee (or, Lake Tiberias). [2]Many people followed him because they saw the miracles he did to heal the sick. [3]Jesus went up on a hill and sat down there with his followers. [4]It was almost the time for the Jewish Passover Feast.

[5]When Jesus looked up and saw a large crowd coming toward him, he said to Philip, "Where can we buy enough bread for all these people to eat?" [6](Jesus asked Philip this question to test him, because Jesus already knew what he planned to do.)

[7]Philip answered, "Someone would have to work almost a year to buy enough bread for each person to have only a little piece."

[8]Another one of his followers, Andrew, Simon Peter's brother, said, [9]"Here is a boy with five loaves of barley bread and two little fish, but that is not enough for so many people."

[10]Jesus said, "Tell the people to sit down." There was plenty of grass there, and about five thousand men sat down there. [11]Then Jesus took the loaves of bread, thanked God for them, and gave them to the people who were sitting there. He did the same with the fish, giving as much as the people wanted.

[12]When they had all had enough to eat, Jesus said to his followers, "Gather the leftover pieces of fish and bread so that nothing is wasted." [13]So they gathered up the pieces and filled twelve baskets with the pieces left from the five barley loaves.

[14]When the people saw this miracle that Jesus did, they said, "He must truly be the Prophet* who is coming into the world."

[15]Jesus knew that the people planned to come and take him by force and make him their king, so he left and went into the hills alone.

JESUS WALKS ON THE WATER

[16]That evening Jesus' followers went down to Lake Galilee. [17]It was dark now, and Jesus had not yet come to them. The followers got into a boat and started across the lake to Capernaum. [18]By now a strong wind was blowing, and the waves on the lake were getting bigger.

dare to do

Luke 5:4
Read It: Sometimes Jesus will ask you to do things that don't make sense to you.
Do It: If you have to move to a new city or start a new school, don't be afraid—it's all according to God's plan.

Luke 5:5
Read It: Peter said, "If you say so, Jesus, then I will."
Do It: When you feel like God is asking you to do something, say, "Yes, Lord! You can count on me."

Luke 5:6
Read It: When you obey Jesus, the blessing is way beyond anything you can imagine.
Do It: Obey God's Word even if it seems crazy (like "love your enemies"), and the blessing will blow you away.

6:14 Prophet They probably meant the prophet that God told Moses he would send (Deuteronomy 18:15–19).

COOL!

Hotter Than the Sun

"Do you know how God controls the clouds and makes his lightning flash?" one of Job's (a character in the Old Testament) friends asked him (Job 37:15). Modern scientists know.

A lightning strike is the sudden, massive flow of electrons from a cloud to the ground.

A LOT of electrons! A single bolt can pack a billion volts of electricity and get hotter than the surface of the sun! The air around a strike gets so hot it actually explodes.

Lightning is the most powerful force on earth, but it's no sweat for God to make.

[19]When they had rowed the boat about three or four miles, they saw Jesus walking on the water, coming toward the boat. The followers were afraid, [20]but Jesus said to them, "It is I. Do not be afraid." [21]Then they were glad to take him into the boat. At once the boat came to land at the place where they wanted to go.

THE PEOPLE SEEK JESUS

[22]The next day the people who had stayed on the other side of the lake knew that Jesus had not gone in the boat with his followers but that they had left without him. And they knew that only one boat had been there. [23]But then some boats came from Tiberias and landed near the place where the people had eaten the bread after the Lord had given thanks. [24]When the people saw that Jesus and his followers were not there now, they got into boats and went to Capernaum to find Jesus.

JESUS, THE BREAD OF LIFE

[25]When the people found Jesus on the other side of the lake, they asked him, "Teacher, when did you come here?"

[26]Jesus answered, "I tell you the truth, you aren't looking for me because you saw me do miracles. You are looking for me because you ate the bread and were satisfied. [27]Don't work for the food that spoils. Work for the food that stays good always and gives eternal life. The Son of Man will give you this food, because on him God the Father has put his power."

[28]The people asked Jesus, "What are the things God wants us to do?"

[29]Jesus answered, "The work God wants you to do is this: Believe the One he sent."

[30]So the people asked, "What miracle will you do? If we see a miracle, we will believe you. What will you do? [31]Our ancestors ate the manna in the desert. This is written in the Scriptures: 'He gave them bread from heaven to eat.' "[n]

[32]Jesus said, "I tell you the truth, it was not Moses who gave you bread from heaven; it is my Father who is giving you the true bread from heaven. [33]God's bread is the One who comes down from heaven and gives life to the world."

[34]The people said, "Sir, give us this bread always."

[35]Then Jesus said, "I am the bread that gives life. Whoever comes to me will never be hungry, and whoever believes in me will never be thirsty. [36]But as I told you before, you have seen me and still don't believe. [37]The Father gives me the people who are mine. Every one of them will come to me, and I will always accept them. [38]I came down from heaven to do what God wants me to do, not what I want to do. [39]Here is what the One who sent me wants me to do: I must not lose even one whom God gave me, but I must raise them all on the last day. [40]Those who see the Son and believe in him have eternal life, and I will raise them on the last day. This is what my Father wants."

[41]Some people began to complain about Jesus because he said, "I am the bread that comes down from heaven." [42]They said, "This is Jesus, the son of Joseph. We know his father

and mother. How can he say, 'I came down from heaven'?"

[43]But Jesus answered, "Stop complaining to each other. [44]The Father is the One who sent me. No one can come to me unless the Father draws him to me, and I will raise that person up on the last day. [45]It is written in the prophets, 'They will all be taught by God.'[n] Everyone who listens to the Father and learns from him comes to me. [46]No one has seen the Father except the One who is from God; only he has seen the Father. [47]I tell you the truth, whoever believes has eternal life. [48]I am the bread that gives life. [49]Your ancestors ate the manna in the desert, but still they died. [50]Here is the bread that comes down from heaven. Anyone who eats this bread will never die. [51]I am the living bread that came down from heaven. Anyone who eats this bread will live forever. This bread is my flesh, which I will give up so that the world may have life."

[52]Then the evil people began to argue among themselves, saying, "How can this man give us his flesh to eat?"

[53]Jesus said, "I tell you the truth, you must eat the flesh of the Son of Man and drink his blood. Otherwise, you won't have real life in you. [54]Those who eat my flesh and drink my blood have eternal life, and I will raise them up on the last day. [55]My flesh is true food, and my blood is true drink. [56]Those who eat my flesh and drink my blood live in me, and I live in them. [57]The living Father sent me, and I live because of the Father. So whoever eats me will live because of me. [58]I am not like the bread

6:31 'He gave . . . eat.' Quotation from Psalm 78:24.   **6:45** 'They . . . God.' Quotation from Isaiah 54:13.

your ancestors ate. They ate that bread and still died. I am the bread that came down from heaven, and whoever eats this bread will live forever." [59]Jesus said all these things while he was teaching in the synagogue in Capernaum.

THE WORDS OF ETERNAL LIFE

[60]When the followers of Jesus heard this, many of them said, "This teaching is hard. Who can accept it?"

[61]Knowing that his followers were complaining about this, Jesus said, "Does this teaching bother you? [62]Then will it also bother you to see the Son of Man going back to the place where he came from? [63]It is the Spirit that gives life. The flesh doesn't give life. The words I told you are spirit, and they give life. [64]But some of you don't believe." (Jesus knew from the beginning who did not believe and who would turn against him.) [65]Jesus said, "That is the reason I said, 'If the Father does not bring a person to me, that one cannot come.' "

[66]After Jesus said this, many of his followers left him and stopped following him.

[67]Jesus asked the twelve followers, "Do you want to leave, too?"

[68]Simon Peter answered him, "Lord, who would we go to? You have the words that give eternal life. [69]We believe and know that you are the Holy One from God."

[70]Then Jesus answered, "I chose all twelve of you, but one of you is a devil."

[71]Jesus was talking about Judas, the son of Simon Iscariot. Judas was one of the twelve, but later he was going to turn against Jesus.

JESUS' BROTHERS DON'T BELIEVE

7 After this, Jesus traveled around Galilee. He did not want to travel in Judea, because some evil people there wanted to kill him. [2]It was time for the Feast of Shelters. [3]So Jesus' brothers said to him, "You should leave here and go to Judea so your followers there can see the miracles you do. [4]Anyone who wants to be well known does not hide what he does. If you are doing these things, show yourself to the world." [5](Even Jesus' brothers did not believe in him.)

[6]Jesus said to his brothers, "The right time for me has not yet come, but any time is right for you. [7]The world cannot hate you, but it hates me, because I tell it the evil things it does. [8]So you go to the feast. I will not go yet* to this feast, because the right time for me has not yet come." [9]After saying this, Jesus stayed in Galilee.

[10]But after Jesus' brothers had gone to the feast, Jesus went also. But he did not let people see him. [11]At the feast some people were looking for him and saying, "Where is that man?"

[12]Within the large crowd there, many people were whispering to each other about Jesus. Some said, "He is a good man."

Others said, "No, he fools the people." [13]But no one was brave enough to talk about Jesus openly, because they were afraid of the elders.

JESUS TEACHES AT THE FEAST

[14]When the feast was about half over, Jesus went to the Temple and began to teach. [15]The people were amazed and said, "This man has never studied in school. How did he learn so much?"

[16]Jesus answered, "The things I teach are not my own, but they come from him who sent me. [17]If people choose to do what God wants, they will know that my teaching comes from God and not from me. [18]Those who teach their own ideas are trying to get honor for themselves. But those who try to bring honor to the

---

Q: There's this kid at school that nobody likes because he's a jerk. Does God expect me to be his friend?

A: The short answer is yes. When we're friendly to the people who deserve it, it's not all that hard. But when we show friendship to someone who we really want to dislike, that's showing God's special love. It's the same love he shows all of us when he forgives us for being selfish, lying, and ignoring him. Even if you're not best friends, you can show God's love by being kind when you see him.

Q: I have a friend who wants to play games all the time, but he's a really poor sport. If he doesn't win, he acts like a baby. What can I do?

A: Next time he wants to play a game with you, gently explain to him that his attitude in the game makes you not want to play. If he agrees he needs to change, be patient with him. His bad attitude might show up again. Pray that God will help him make a real change.

Q: Why are there homeless people?

A: There are dozens of reasons people become homeless. The two most common are addiction to drugs or alcohol and mental illness. In both of those cases, the person's problems left him or her unable to keep a job and pay for a place to live. Jesus always had special love for the poor and weak. We should follow his example by loving homeless people.

7:8 yet Some Greek copies do not have this word.

one who sent them speak the truth, and there is nothing false in them. [19]Moses gave you the law," but none of you obeys that law. Why are you trying to kill me?"

[20]The people answered, "A demon has come into you. We are not trying to kill you."

[21]Jesus said to them, "I did one miracle, and you are all amazed. [22]Moses gave you the law about circumcision. (But really Moses did not give you circumcision; it came from our ancestors.) And yet you circumcise a baby boy on a Sabbath day. [23]If a baby boy can be circumcised on a Sabbath day to obey the law of Moses, why are you angry at me for healing a person's whole body on the Sabbath day? [24]Stop judging by the way things look, but judge by what is really right."

IS JESUS THE CHRIST?

[25]Then some of the people who lived in Jerusalem said, "This is the man they are trying to kill. [26]But he is teaching where everyone can see and hear him, and no one is trying to stop him. Maybe the leaders have decided he really is the Christ. [27]But we know where this man is from. Yet when the real Christ comes, no one will know where he comes from."

[28]Jesus, teaching in the Temple, cried out, "Yes, you know me, and you know where I am from. But I have not come by my own authority. I was sent by the One who is true, whom you don't know. [29]But I know him, because I am from him, and he sent me."

[30]When Jesus said this, they tried to seize him. But no one was able to touch him, because it was not yet the right time. [31]But many of the people believed in Jesus. They said, "When the Christ comes, will he do more miracles than this man has done?"

THE LEADERS TRY TO ARREST JESUS

[32]The Pharisees heard the crowd whispering these things about Jesus. So the leading priests and the Pharisees sent some Temple guards to arrest him. [33]Jesus said, "I will be with you a little while longer. Then I will go back to the One who sent me. [34]You will look for me, but you will not find me. And you cannot come where I am."

[35]Some people said to each other, "Where will this man go so we cannot find him? Will he go to the Greek cities where our people live and teach the Greek people there? [36]What did he mean when he said, 'You will look for me, but you will not find me,' and 'You cannot come where I am'?"

JESUS TALKS ABOUT THE SPIRIT

[37]On the last and most important day of the feast Jesus stood up and said in a loud voice, "Let anyone who is thirsty come to me and drink. [38]If anyone believes in me, rivers of living water will flow out from that person's heart, as the Scripture says." [39]Jesus was talking about the Holy Spirit. The Spirit had not yet been given, because Jesus had not yet been raised to glory. But later, those who believed in Jesus would receive the Spirit.

THE PEOPLE ARGUE ABOUT JESUS

[40]When the people heard Jesus' words, some of them said, "This man really is the Prophet."[n]

[41]Others said, "He is the Christ."

Still others said, "The Christ will not come from Galilee. [42]The Scripture says that the Christ will come from David's family and from Bethlehem, the town where David lived." [43]So the people did not agree with each other about Jesus. [44]Some of them wanted to arrest him, but no one was able to touch him.

SOME LEADERS WON'T BELIEVE

[45]The Temple guards went back to the leading priests and the Pharisees, who asked, "Why didn't you bring Jesus?"

[46]The guards answered, "The words he says are greater than the words of any other person who has ever spoken!"

[47]The Pharisees answered, "So Jesus has

trustables

John 6:35

Have you noticed that convenience store drink sizes just keep getting bigger? First there was "large." Then came "jumbo." Then "super-quencher." Pretty soon they'll be up to "bucket." But despite this super-sizing trend, people can't seem to fully quench their thirst! It still comes back an hour or so later. If it didn't, convenience stores might go out of business!

Jesus made a very interesting promise when he was here on earth. He called himself "the bread that gives life." And he said that if we come to him, we never will be hungry or thirsty again. Could this mean the end of burger places and soda machines? Actually, no.

Just like with physical hunger and thirst, all people have a deep spiritual hunger and thirst. We crave nourishment from God. His love and purpose in our lives is like an all-you-can-eat buffet!

We sometimes try and fill ourselves with spiritual "junk food" that doesn't satisfy. But Jesus is the only real way to bring satisfaction to our spiritual hunger and thirst. If we will only get our fill of what he has to offer, our lives will be full and quenched.

7:19 law Moses gave God's people the Law that God gave him on Mount Sinai (Exodus 34:29–32).　**7:40 Prophet** They probably meant the prophet God told Moses he would send (Deuteronomy 18:15–19).

April

1 — April Fool's Day— Instead of playing a joke on someone, do something nice!

2

3 — Pray for a person of influence: it's actress Amanda Bynes's birthday.

4 — Serve up a big glass of OJ for breakfast: it's "Vitamin C Day."

6

8 — If life's been tough lately, read James 1:2 for encouragement.

9

10 — In honor of "Siblings Day," do something nice for your brother or sister.

11 — Family planning a trip? Find websites with info about your destination. Suggest things to do.

12

13 — Pray for your parents. Ask God to guide their decisions for your life.

14

15 — Pray for a person of influence: skateboarder Danny Way celebrates a birthday today.

16 — Take silly pictures of your friends today.

17

18 — Read Galatians 5:22-23. Pray that God will strengthen your weak fruits.

19 — Pray for a person of influence: it's actress Kate Hudson's birthday.

20

21 — Invent a new sport. Read the *World Sports* articles for inspiration.

22 — It's "Earth Day"! Pick up litter, walk to school, or plant a tree.

24 — Pray for a person of influence: singer Kelly Clarkson has a birthday today.

25 — Try to not complain all day long!

27 — Ask if you can pray at dinner tonight. Thank God for your food and family.

28 — Pray for a person of influence: wish comedian Jay Leno a happy birthday.

29 — Pray for a person of influence: it's comedian Jerry Seinfeld's birthday.

30 — Something you're embarrassed to talk to God about? Pray! He already knows, and you'll grow closer to him.

Chores like shoveling snow or mowing the lawn can be a drag. But it's a little easier when you're doing it with friends—and for a good purpose!

Two brothers, Matt and Andy, along with a few of their friends, have spent many Saturdays volunteering at their church—helping with yard work, mowing the grass, or doing repairs. They enjoy it because they know that they are not only helping the church's groundskeeper; they are also serving God!

Of course, the church property is much larger than just someone's backyard, so they have been able to do some cool things, like work on an underground sprinkler system and collect debris for a huge burn pile. Even shoveling snow in the winter is fun when you can have a giant snowball fight at the end!

"It wasn't that hard when we worked together," Matt says, "and we knew we were doing a good thing."

See if there's something you can do at your church. Whether it's raking leaves, shoveling snow, or planting flowers, God loves it when we take care of his church!

fooled you also! [48]Have any of the leaders or the Pharisees believed in him? No! [49]But these people, who know nothing about the law, are under God's curse."

[50]Nicodemus, who had gone to see Jesus before, was in that group." He said, [51]"Our law does not judge a person without hearing him and knowing what he has done."

[52]They answered, "Are you from Galilee, too? Study the Scriptures, and you will learn that no prophet comes from Galilee."

———

Some of the earliest surviving Greek copies do not contain 7:53—8:11.

[[53]And everyone left and went home.

THE WOMAN CAUGHT IN ADULTERY

8 Jesus went to the Mount of Olives. [2]But early in the morning he went back to the Temple, and all the people came to him, and he sat and taught them. [3]The teachers of the law and the Pharisees brought a woman who had been caught in adultery. They forced her to stand before the people. [4]They said to Jesus, "Teacher, this woman was caught having sexual relations with a man who is not her husband. [5]The law of Moses commands that we stone to death every woman who does this. What do you say we should do?" [6]They were asking this to trick Jesus so that they could have some charge against him.

But Jesus bent over and started writing on the ground with his finger. [7]When they continued to ask Jesus their question, he raised up and said, "Anyone here who has never sinned can throw the first stone at her." [8]Then Jesus bent over again and wrote on the ground.

[9]Those who heard Jesus began to leave one by one, first the older men and then the others. Jesus was left there alone with the woman standing before him. [10]Jesus raised up again and asked her, "Woman, where are they? Has no one judged you guilty?"

[11]She answered, "No one, sir."

Then Jesus said, "I also don't judge you guilty. You may go now, but don't sin anymore."]

———

JESUS IS THE LIGHT OF THE WORLD

[12]Later, Jesus talked to the people again, saying, "I am the light of the world. The person who follows me will never live in darkness but will have the light that gives life."

[13]The Pharisees said to Jesus, "When you talk about yourself, you are the only one to say

these things are true. We cannot accept what you say."

[14]Jesus answered, "Yes, I am saying these things about myself, but they are true. I know where I came from and where I am going. But you don't know where I came from or where I am going. [15]You judge by human standards. I am not judging anyone. [16]But when I do judge, I judge truthfully, because I am not alone. The Father who sent me is with me. [17]Your own law says that when two witnesses say the same thing, you must accept what they say. [18]I am one of the witnesses who speaks about myself, and the Father who sent me is the other witness."

[19]They asked, "Where is your father?"

Jesus answered, "You don't know me or my Father. If you knew me, you would know my Father, too." [20]Jesus said these things while he was teaching in the Temple, near where the money is kept. But no one arrested him, because the right time for him had not yet come.

THE PEOPLE MISUNDERSTAND JESUS

[21]Again, Jesus said to the people, "I will leave you, and you will look for me, but you will die in your sins. You cannot come where I am going."

[22]So the Jews asked, "Will he kill himself? Is that why he said, 'You cannot come where I am going'?"

[23]Jesus said, "You people are from here below, but I am from above. You belong to this world, but I don't belong to this world. [24]So I told you that you would die in your sins. Yes, you will die in your sins if you don't believe that I am he."

[25]They asked, "Then who are you?"

Jesus answered, "I am what I have told you from the beginning. [26]I have many things to say and decide about you. But I tell people only the things I have heard from the One who sent me, and he speaks the truth."

[27]The people did not understand that he was talking to them about the Father. [28]So Jesus said to them, "When you lift up the Son of Man, you will know that I am he. You will know that these things I do are not by my own authority but that I say only what the Father has taught me. [29]The One who sent me is with me. I always do what is pleasing to him, so he has not left me alone." [30]While Jesus was saying these things, many people believed in him.

FREEDOM FROM SIN

[31]So Jesus said to the Jews who believed in him, "If you continue to obey my teaching, you are truly my followers. [32]Then you will

know the truth, and the truth will make you free."

³³They answered, "We are Abraham's children, and we have never been anyone's slaves. So why do you say we will be free?"

³⁴Jesus answered, "I tell you the truth, everyone who lives in sin is a slave to sin. ³⁵A slave does not stay with a family forever, but a son belongs to the family forever. ³⁶So if the Son makes you free, you will be truly free. ³⁷I know you are Abraham's children, but you want to kill me because you don't accept my teaching. ³⁸I am telling you what my Father has shown me, but you do what your father has told you."

³⁹They answered, "Our father is Abraham."

Jesus said, "If you were really Abraham's children, you would do* the things Abraham did. ⁴⁰I am a man who has told you the truth which I heard from God, but you are trying to kill me. Abraham did nothing like that. ⁴¹So you are doing the things your own father did."

But they said, "We are not like children who never knew who their father was. God is our Father; he is the only Father we have."

⁴²Jesus said to them, "If God were really your Father, you would love me, because I came from God and now I am here. I did not come by my own authority; God sent me. ⁴³You don't understand what I say, because you cannot accept my teaching. ⁴⁴You belong to your father the devil, and you want to do what he wants. He was a murderer from the beginning and was against the truth, because there is no truth in him. When he tells a lie, he shows what he is really like, because he is a liar and the father of lies. ⁴⁵But because I speak the truth, you don't believe me. ⁴⁶Can any of you prove that I am guilty of sin? If I am telling the truth, why don't you believe me? ⁴⁷The person who belongs to God accepts what God says. But you don't accept what God says, because you don't belong to God."

JESUS IS GREATER THAN ABRAHAM

⁴⁸They answered, "We say you are a Samaritan and have a demon in you. Are we not right?"

⁴⁹Jesus answered, "I have no demon in me. I give honor to my Father, but you dishonor me. ⁵⁰I am not trying to get honor for myself. There is One who wants this honor for me, and he is the judge. ⁵¹I tell you the truth, whoever obeys my teaching will never die."

⁵²They said to Jesus, "Now we know that you have a demon in you! Even Abraham and the prophets died. But you say, 'Whoever obeys my teaching will never die.' ⁵³Do you think you are greater than our father Abraham, who died? And the prophets died, too. Who do you think you are?"

⁵⁴Jesus answered, "If I give honor to myself, that honor is worth nothing. The One who gives me honor is my Father, and you say he is your God. ⁵⁵You don't really know him, but I

dare to do

Luke 5:8
Read It: People turn away from sinning when they see how good Jesus is.
Do It: Live so that people see how Jesus has made your life better, and they will want to know him personally.

Luke 5:10
Read It: Jesus wants you to "fish for people" by helping others accept him as Savior.
Do It: Pick one person to pray for until he trusts Jesus. Note: It may take anywhere from one day to a whole lifetime.

Luke 5:11
Read It: Jesus' followers left everything and went with him.
Do It: If there is anything in your life keeping you from following Jesus, get rid of it! Ask God to help you follow him with your whole heart.

ROCK SOLID

John 7:37-39

Have you ever gone to the ocean to watch for whales? It's not hard to know once you've spotted one. No one mixes up a flounder or a salmon with a whale. Whales are distinct from all other creatures in the sea.

What about Christians? If you were watching for Christians, what would you look for? How could you be sure that you had found one? Are they easy to mix up with other kinds of people? They shouldn't be.

Jesus told his followers, "If anyone believes in me, rivers of living water will flow out from that person's heart" (John 7:38). Jesus was talking about the fact that every real Christian would have the Holy Spirit living in him. The evidence is the kind of "water" that flows out of that person's life.

The Holy Spirit makes a Christian look more and more like Jesus—loving and patient and kind.

Unfortunately, a lot of people say they are Christians but really aren't. How will you know? Well, could a trout trick you into thinking it's a whale? People pretending to be Christians can't hide long.

8:39 **If . . . do** Some Greek copies read "If you are really Abraham's children, you will do."

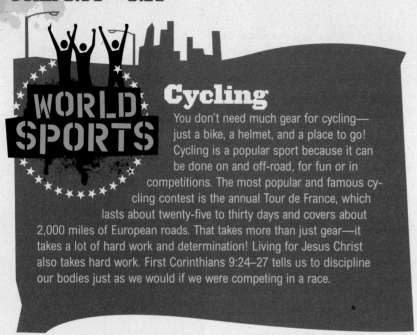

Cycling

You don't need much gear for cycling—just a bike, a helmet, and a place to go! Cycling is a popular sport because it can be done on and off-road, for fun or in competitions. The most popular and famous cycling contest is the annual Tour de France, which lasts about twenty-five to thirty days and covers about 2,000 miles of European roads. That takes more than just gear—it takes a lot of hard work and determination! Living for Jesus Christ also takes hard work. First Corinthians 9:24–27 tells us to discipline our bodies just as we would if we were competing in a race.

know him. If I said I did not know him, I would be a liar like you. But I do know him, and I obey what he says. [56]Your father Abraham was very happy that he would see my day. He saw that day and was glad."

[57]They said to him, "You have never seen Abraham! You are not even fifty years old."

[58]Jesus answered, "I tell you the truth, before Abraham was even born, I am!" [59]When Jesus said this, the people picked up stones to throw at him. But Jesus hid himself, and then he left the Temple.

JESUS HEALS A MAN BORN BLIND

9 As Jesus was walking along, he saw a man who had been born blind. [2]His followers asked him, "Teacher, whose sin caused this man to be born blind—his own sin or his parents' sin?"

[3]Jesus answered, "It is not this man's sin or his parents' sin that made him blind. This man was born blind so that God's power could be shown in him. [4]While it is daytime, we must continue doing the work of the One who sent me.

Night is coming, when no one can work. [5]While I am in the world, I am the light of the world."

[6]After Jesus said this, he spit on the ground and made some mud with it and put the mud on the man's eyes. [7]Then he told the man, "Go and wash in the Pool of Siloam." (Siloam means Sent.) So the man went, washed, and came back seeing.

[8]The neighbors and some people who had earlier seen this man begging said, "Isn't this the same man who used to sit and beg?"

[9]Some said, "He is the one," but others said, "No, he only looks like him."

The man himself said, "I am the man."

[10]They asked, "How did you get your sight?"

[11]He answered, "The man named Jesus made some mud and put it on my eyes. Then he told me to go to Siloam and wash. So I went and washed, and then I could see."

[12]They asked him, "Where is this man?"

"I don't know," he answered.

PHARISEES QUESTION THE HEALING

[13]Then the people took to the Pharisees the man who had been blind. [14]The day Jesus had made mud and healed his eyes was a Sabbath day. [15]So now the Pharisees asked the man, "How did you get your sight?"

He answered, "He put mud on my eyes, I washed, and now I see."

[16]So some of the Pharisees were saying, "This man does not keep the Sabbath day, so he is not from God."

Cornelius
See Acts 10.

Cornelius was an army officer; a centurion of the Roman Regiment (he was in charge of one hundred troops). He was a tough, hard man, but he also feared God. When an angel appeared and told him to send for the apostle Peter, he did so right away. Wouldn't you?

At first, Peter didn't want to go because Cornelius was a Gentile (non-Jew) and Peter was a Jew. The two groups didn't mix. But God gave Peter a vision of his own, so he went and preached.

Cornelius and his family believed Peter's message and were baptized. Cornelius became a new man in Christ, but he didn't quit the army. Christians can honor God in the military. They can be even better soldiers and officers because they serve a Higher Power.

But others said, "A man who is a sinner can't do miracles like these." So they could not agree with each other.

[17] They asked the man again, "What do you say about him since it was your eyes he opened?"

The man answered, "He is a prophet."

[18] These leaders did not believe that he had been blind and could now see again. So they sent for the man's parents [19] and asked them, "Is this your son who you say was born blind? Then how does he now see?"

[20] His parents answered, "We know that this is our son and that he was born blind. [21] But we don't know how he can now see. We don't know who opened his eyes. Ask him. He is old enough to speak for himself." [22] His parents said this because they were afraid of the elders, who had already decided that anyone who said Jesus was the Christ would be avoided. [23] That is why his parents said, "He is old enough. Ask him."

[24] So for the second time, they called the man who had been blind. They said, "You should give God the glory by telling the truth. We know that this man is a sinner."

[25] He answered, "I don't know if he is a sinner. One thing I do know: I was blind, and now I see."

[26] They asked, "What did he do to you? How did he make you see again?"

[27] He answered, "I already told you, and you didn't listen. Why do you want to hear it again? Do you want to become his followers, too?"

[28] Then they insulted him and said, "You are his follower, but we are followers of Moses. [29] We know that God spoke to Moses, but we don't even know where this man comes from."

[30] The man answered, "This is a very strange thing. You don't know where he comes from, and yet he opened my eyes. [31] We all know that God does not listen to sinners, but he listens to anyone who worships and obeys him. [32] Nobody has ever heard of anyone giving sight to a man born blind. [33] If this man were not from God, he could do nothing."

[34] They answered, "You were born full of sin! Are you trying to teach us?" And they threw him out.

SPIRITUAL BLINDNESS

[35] When Jesus heard that they had thrown him out, Jesus found him and said, "Do you believe in the Son of Man?"

[36] He asked, "Who is the Son of Man, sir, so that I can believe in him?"

[37] Jesus said to him, "You have seen him. The Son of Man is the one talking with you."

[38] He said, "Lord, I believe!" Then the man worshiped Jesus.

[39] Jesus said, "I came into this world so that the world could be judged. I came so that the blind" would see and so that those who see will become blind."

[40] Some of the Pharisees who were nearby heard Jesus say this and asked, "Are you saying we are blind, too?"

[41] Jesus said, "If you were blind, you would not be guilty of sin. But since you keep saying you see, your guilt remains."

THE SHEPHERD AND HIS SHEEP

10 Jesus said, "I tell you the truth, the person who does not enter the sheepfold by the door, but climbs in some other way, is a thief and a robber. [2] The one who enters by the door is the shepherd of the sheep. [3] The one who guards the door opens it for him. And the sheep listen to the voice of the shepherd. He calls his own sheep by name and leads them out. [4] When he brings all his

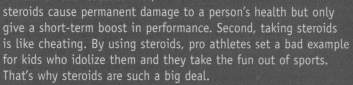

Q: Why do professional athletes get in trouble for using steroids?

A: Using steroids to "bulk up" is very hard on your body. That's why they've been banned from professional sports. Athletes who use them anyway are making a foolish choice for two reasons. First, steroids cause permanent damage to a person's health but only give a short-term boost in performance. Second, taking steroids is like cheating. By using steroids, pro athletes set a bad example for kids who idolize them and they take the fun out of sports. That's why steroids are such a big deal.

Q: Why do I have to wear a bike helmet? They're annoying, and they don't look very cool.

A: For one thing, in most places, it's the law! At your age, you have to wear a helmet whenever you're riding in the street because a car can come up suddenly and the driver may not even see you. It's also important to make sure you wear your helmet properly. Helmets have protected lots of people from dying in bike crashes. They may be annoying, but you can't be cool if you're dead!

Q: What were the big sports during the time of Jesus?

A: Jesus lived during the height of the Roman Empire. They didn't have any of our big sports like football, basketball, baseball, or hockey. But they did have some you'd recognize, like wrestling, track and field events, and horse races. They also had extremely violent fights between armed men who were called gladiators. In many cases, the fight wasn't over until one of them was dead.

⭐ **9:39 blind** Jesus is talking about people who are spiritually blind, not physically blind.

sheep out, he goes ahead of them, and they follow him because they know his voice. [5]But they will never follow a stranger. They will run away from him because they don't know his voice." [6]Jesus told the people this story, but they did not understand what it meant.

JESUS IS THE GOOD SHEPHERD

[7]So Jesus said again, "I tell you the truth, I am the door for the sheep. [8]All the people who came before me were thieves and robbers. The sheep did not listen to them. [9]I am the door, and the person who enters through me will be saved and will be able to come in and go out and find pasture. [10]A thief comes to steal and kill and destroy, but I came to give life—life in all its fullness.

[11]"I am the good shepherd. The good shepherd gives his life for the sheep. [12]The worker who is paid to keep the sheep is different from the shepherd who owns them. When the worker sees a wolf coming, he runs away and leaves the sheep alone. Then the wolf attacks the sheep and scatters them. [13]The man runs away because he is only a paid worker and does not really care about the sheep.

[14]"I am the good shepherd. I know my sheep, and my sheep know me, [15]just as the Father knows me, and I know the Father. I give my life for the sheep. [16]I have other sheep that are not in this flock, and I must bring them also. They will listen to my voice, and there will be one flock and one shepherd. [17]The Father loves me because I give my life so that I can take it back again. [18]No one takes it away from me; I give my own life freely. I have the right to give my life, and I have the right to take it back. This is what my Father commanded me to do."

[19]Again the leaders did not agree with each other because of these words of Jesus. [20]Many of them said, "A demon has come into him and made him crazy. Why listen to him?"

[21]But others said, "A man who is crazy with a demon does not say things like this. Can a demon open the eyes of the blind?"

JESUS IS REJECTED

[22]The time came for the Feast of Dedication at Jerusalem. It was winter, [23]and Jesus was walking in the Temple in Solomon's Porch. [24]Some people gathered around him and said, "How long will you make us wonder about you? If you are the Christ, tell us plainly."

[25]Jesus answered, "I told you already, but you did not believe. The miracles I do in my Father's name show who I am. [26]But you don't

BIBLE SUPERHEROES

Lydia
See Acts 16:11-15.

Paul's first convert in Europe was a rich lady. Her name was Lydia and she was a famous cloth merchant in the city of Philippi. That's like being a top fashion designer in New York City today. She had servants and a big home.

Lydia was down by the river one day when some strangers started preaching. She believed what the apostle Paul said about Jesus Christ and was baptized.

Right away, she opened her home to other believers in spite of the public anger against Christians. Her house became the first church in Philippi. At a time when women were treated like second-class citizens, the church treated them with respect. Some, like Lydia, even became leaders.

Lydia was not ashamed of her new faith. She was as bold as her purple cloth.

drugs & alcohol

You might dream about the day you get to make all your own decisions without your parents' supervision. But growing up involves making decisions about serious issues, too. If you know what you're going to choose before you're faced with the choice, it will make your life a lot easier!

One important decision each person has to make in life is whether or not to use street (illegal) drugs or alcohol. Trying these substances often seems like a good idea to teenagers because they do not understand the consequences of using them. In movies and on TV, the use of drugs and alcohol looks like the normal thing to do. But in reality, street drugs are against the law, as is underage drinking, and both can be very harmful to your body.

Have you ever been around someone who thinks that being or seeing others drunk is funny? They might tell a story about silly things someone did while drinking, but there are deeper issues beneath the story. Alcohol is a drug that affects how your body and mind work—and can be dangerous, especially to young people and in large amounts. The reason that youth are not supposed to drink alcohol until they reach a certain age is because the government wants to protect you from making unwise decisions.

Drugs that are illegal are against the law for good reasons; they can cause you harm or even death. The consequences for using street drugs are very serious—besides becoming addicted, you can go to jail!

If your peers offer you drugs or alcohol, make sure that your "no" is firm. It's important for them to know how seriously you take this decision. If you are in a situation where others are using drugs or alcohol, keep yourself safe by getting away as fast as you can! You can always call your parents to pick you up—and they'll be glad you did!

You can hope your friends will make wise choices and steer clear of drugs and alcohol. Surrounding yourself with others who share your view on drugs and alcohol will help you make good decisions, too. As you get older, some of your peers will probably begin trying out things that you know are wrong, and you can learn from their mistakes without making them yourself. The important thing to remember is that you are in charge of yourself and your decisions. And remember what Ephesians 5:18 says—"Do not be drunk with wine, which will ruin you, but be filled with the Spirit."

believe, because you are not my sheep. ²⁷My sheep listen to my voice; I know them, and they follow me. ²⁸I give them eternal life, and they will never die, and no one can steal them out of my hand. ²⁹My Father gave my sheep to me. He is greater than all, and no person can steal my sheep out of my Father's hand. ³⁰The Father and I are one."

³¹Again some of the people picked up stones to kill Jesus. ³²But he said to them, "I have done many good works from the Father. Which of these good works are you killing me for?"

³³They answered, "We are not killing you because of any good work you did, but because you speak against God. You are only a human, but you say you are the same as God!"

³⁴Jesus answered, "It is written in your law that God said, 'I said, you are gods.'ⁿ ³⁵This Scripture called those people gods who received God's message, and Scripture is always true. ³⁶So why do you say that I speak against God because I said, 'I am God's Son'? I am the one God chose and sent into the world. ³⁷If I don't do what my Father does, then don't believe me. ³⁸But if I do what my Father does, even though you don't believe in me, believe what I do. Then you will know and understand that the Father is in me and I am in the Father."

³⁹They tried to take Jesus again, but he escaped from them.

⁴⁰Then he went back across the Jordan River to the place where John had first baptized. Jesus stayed there, ⁴¹and many people came to him and said, "John never did a miracle, but everything John said about this man is true." ⁴²And in that place many believed in Jesus.

THE DEATH OF LAZARUS

11 A man named Lazarus was sick. He lived in the town of Bethany, where Mary and her sister Martha lived. ²Mary was the woman who later put perfume on the Lord and wiped his feet with her hair. Mary's brother was Lazarus, the man who was now sick. ³So Mary and Martha sent someone to tell Jesus, "Lord, the one you love is sick."

⁴When Jesus heard this, he said, "This sickness will not end in death. It is for the glory of God, to bring glory to the Son of God." ⁵Jesus loved Martha and her sister and Lazarus. ⁶But when he heard that Lazarus was sick, he stayed where he was for two more days. ⁷Then Jesus said to his followers, "Let's go back to Judea."

⁸The followers said, "But Teacher, some people there tried to stone you to death only a short time ago. Now you want to go back there?"

⁹Jesus answered, "Are there not twelve hours in the day? If anyone walks in the daylight, he will not stumble, because he can see by this world's light. ¹⁰But if anyone walks at night, he stumbles because there is no light to help him see."

¹¹After Jesus said this, he added, "Our friend Lazarus has fallen asleep, but I am going there to wake him."

¹²The followers said, "But Lord, if he is only asleep, he will be all right."

¹³Jesus meant that Lazarus was dead, but his followers thought he meant Lazarus was really sleeping. ¹⁴So then Jesus said plainly, "Lazarus is dead. ¹⁵And I am glad for your sakes I was not there so that you may believe. But let's go to him now."

¹⁶Then Thomas (the one called Didymus) said to the other followers, "Let us also go so that we can die with him."

JESUS IN BETHANY

¹⁷When Jesus arrived, he learned that Lazarus had already been dead and in the tomb for four days. ¹⁸Bethany was about two miles from Jerusalem. ¹⁹Many of the Jews had come there to comfort Martha and Mary about their brother.

²⁰When Martha heard that Jesus was coming, she went out to meet him, but Mary stayed home. ²¹Martha said to Jesus, "Lord, if you had been here, my brother would not have died. ²²But I know that even now God will give you anything you ask."

ROCK SOLID

John 11:33

Do you ever have trouble relating to Jesus? Remember that Jesus isn't just God—he's also 100 percent human. As a human being, he wants to be your friend.

When Jesus lived on earth, he had close friendships and responded to his friends just as any human would. For example, John wrote, "When Jesus saw Mary crying and the Jews who came with her also crying, he was upset and was deeply troubled" (John 11:33).

Jesus was friends with Mary, Martha, and Lazarus—two sisters and a brother. Lazarus got sick and died. Jesus had already told his followers that he was going to raise Lazarus from the dead, but Mary and Martha didn't know this. Naturally, the sisters felt deep sadness and grief over the loss of their brother.

But why was Jesus so troubled when he knew he was going to bring Lazarus back to life?

This is where it gets personal. Jesus wasn't worried about Lazarus. Instead, he was hurting for Mary and Martha, his friends. He was sad that they had to go through such a tough experience.

Jesus is just as sad when you go through hard times—when you lose a friend, when a grandparent dies, when someone you trust lets you down. When you're hurting, Jesus hurts with you...deeply. He's there to help you through every tough time.

[23] Jesus said, "Your brother will rise and live again."

[24] Martha answered, "I know that he will rise and live again in the resurrection" on the last day."

[25] Jesus said to her, "I am the resurrection and the life. Those who believe in me will have life even if they die. [26] And everyone who lives and believes in me will never die. Martha, do you believe this?"

[27] Martha answered, "Yes, Lord. I believe that you are the Christ, the Son of God, the One coming to the world."

JESUS CRIES

[28] After Martha said this, she went back and talked to her sister Mary alone. Martha said, "The Teacher is here and he is asking for you." [29] When Mary heard this, she got up quickly and went to Jesus. [30] Jesus had not yet come into the town but was still at the place where Martha had met him. [31] The Jews were with Mary in the house, comforting her. When they saw her stand and leave quickly, they followed her, thinking she was going to the tomb to cry there.

[32] But Mary went to the place where Jesus was. When she saw him, she fell at his feet and said, "Lord, if you had been here, my brother would not have died."

[33] When Jesus saw Mary crying and the Jews who came with her also crying, he was upset and was deeply troubled. [34] He asked, "Where did you bury him?"

"Come and see, Lord," they said.

[35] Jesus cried.

[36] So the Jews said, "See how much he loved him."

[37] But some of them said, "If Jesus opened the eyes of the blind man, why couldn't he keep Lazarus from dying?"

JESUS RAISES LAZARUS

[38] Again feeling very upset, Jesus came to the tomb. It was a cave with a large stone covering the entrance. [39] Jesus said, "Move the stone away."

Martha, the sister of the dead man, said, "But, Lord, it has been four days since he died. There will be a bad smell."

[40] Then Jesus said to her, "Didn't I tell you that if you believed you would see the glory of God?"

[41] So they moved the stone away from the entrance. Then Jesus looked up and said, "Father, I thank you that you heard me. [42] I know that you always hear me, but I said these things because of the people here around me. I want them to believe that you sent me." [43] After Jesus said this, he cried out in a loud voice, "Lazarus, come out!" [44] The dead man came out, his hands and feet wrapped with pieces of cloth, and a cloth around his face.

Jesus said to them, "Take the cloth off of him and let him go."

THE PLAN TO KILL JESUS

[45] Many of the people, who had come to visit Mary and saw what Jesus did, believed in him. [46] But some of them went to the Pharisees and told them what Jesus had done. [47] Then the leading priests and Pharisees called a meeting of the council. They asked, "What should we do? This man is doing many miracles. [48] If we let him continue doing these things, everyone will believe in him. Then the Romans will come and take away our Temple and our nation."

[49] One of the men there was Caiaphas, the high priest that year. He said, "You people know nothing! [50] You don't realize that it is better for one man to die for the people than for the whole nation to be destroyed."

[51] Caiaphas did not think of this himself. As high priest that year, he was really prophesying that Jesus would die for their nation [52] and for God's scattered children to bring them all together and make them one.

[53] That day they started planning to kill Jesus. [54] So Jesus no longer traveled openly among the people. He left there and went to a place near the desert, to a town called Ephraim and stayed there with his followers.

[55] It was almost time for the Passover Feast. Many from the country went up to Jerusalem before the Passover to do the special things to make themselves pure. [56] The people looked for Jesus and stood in the Temple asking each other, "Is he coming to the Feast? What do you think?" [57] But the leading priests and the Pharisees had given orders that if anyone knew where Jesus was, he must tell them. Then they could arrest him.

dare to do

Luke 6:12
Read It: Jesus spent an entire night praying before he selected the apostles, his twelve closest followers.
Do It: Have a tough decision to make? Take it to God in prayer.

Luke 6:24
Read It: People who are rich have their happiness in this life.
Do It: None of the money or stuff you have will matter after you die. Prepare for heaven by spending your time and money on things for God, not stuff.

Luke 6:30
Read It: If someone steals something from you, don't try to get it back.
Do It: If someone at school takes something from you, don't yell or fight back. Let him have it—he will be so amazed that it might give you the chance to tell him why Jesus has made you different!

 11:24 resurrection Being raised from the dead to live again.

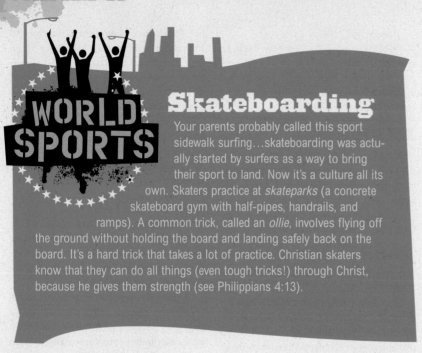

Skateboarding

Your parents probably called this sport sidewalk surfing…skateboarding was actually started by surfers as a way to bring their sport to land. Now it's a culture all its own. Skaters practice at *skateparks* (a concrete skateboard gym with half-pipes, handrails, and ramps). A common trick, called an *ollie*, involves flying off the ground without holding the board and landing safely back on the board. It's a hard trick that takes a lot of practice. Christian skaters know that they can do all things (even tough tricks!) through Christ, because he gives them strength (see Philippians 4:13).

JESUS WITH FRIENDS IN BETHANY

12 Six days before the Passover Feast, Jesus went to Bethany, where Lazarus lived. (Lazarus is the man Jesus raised from the dead.) [2]There they had a dinner for Jesus. Martha served the food, and Lazarus was one of the people eating with Jesus. [3]Mary brought in a pint of very expensive perfume made from pure nard. She poured the perfume on Jesus' feet, and then she wiped his feet with her hair. And the sweet smell from the perfume filled the whole house.

[4]Judas Iscariot, one of Jesus' followers who would later turn against him, was there. Judas said, [5]"This perfume was worth an entire year's wages. Why wasn't it sold and the money given to the poor?" [6]But Judas did not really care about the poor; he said this because he was a thief. He was the one who kept the money box, and he often stole from it.

[7]Jesus answered, "Leave her alone. It was right for her to save this perfume for today, the day for me to be prepared for burial. [8]You will always have the poor with you, but you will not always have me."

THE PLOT AGAINST LAZARUS

[9]A large crowd of people heard that Jesus was in Bethany. So they went there to see not only Jesus but Lazarus, whom Jesus raised from the dead. [10]So the leading priests made plans to kill Lazarus, too. [11]Because of Lazarus many of the Jews were leaving them and believing in Jesus.

JESUS ENTERS JERUSALEM

[12]The next day a great crowd who had come to Jerusalem for the Passover Feast heard that Jesus was coming there. [13]So they took branches of palm trees and went out to meet Jesus, shouting,

"Praise" God!
God bless the One who comes in the name of the Lord!

trustables

John 14:12

You've probably heard the saying "You can do anything you put your mind to." It sounds good, but doesn't really work for things like shooting laser beams out of your eyes or getting a good grade without studying.

It is true, however, that every human being has amazing potential to impact the world. The trick isn't "putting your mind to it," but believing in Jesus. In John 14:12, Jesus says, "Whoever believes in me will do the same things that I do. Those who believe will do even greater things than these…"

We can do the same things that Jesus did? Really? Jesus healed people. He gave sight to the blind. He helped crippled people walk again. It's hard to imagine that you could do these things, isn't it? But when was the last time you tried?

Jesus wants to work miracles through us. He is in control of the entire universe. If you pray for a blind person to see again, if Jesus wants to, he can grant that request. The important thing is to realize that he *wants* you to ask. He wants us to see that the world is a place that needs people who care enough to ask for God's help. So get out there and pray for a miracle!

⭐ **12:13 Praise** Literally, "Hosanna," a Hebrew word used at first in praying to God for help, but at this time it was probably a shout of joy used in praising God or his Messiah.

God bless the King of Israel!"

Psalm 118:25–26

[14]Jesus found a colt and sat on it. This was as the Scripture says,

[15]"Don't be afraid, people of Jerusalem!
Your king is coming,
sitting on the colt of a donkey."

Zechariah 9:9

[16]The followers of Jesus did not understand this at first. But after Jesus was raised to glory, they remembered that this had been written about him and that they had done these things to him.

PEOPLE TELL ABOUT JESUS

[17]There had been many people with Jesus when he raised Lazarus from the dead and told him to come out of the tomb. Now they were telling others about what Jesus did. [18]Many people went out to meet Jesus, because they had heard about this miracle. [19]So the Pharisees said to each other, "You can see that nothing is going right for us. Look! The whole world is following him."

JESUS TALKS ABOUT HIS DEATH

[20]There were some Greek people, too, who came to Jerusalem to worship at the Passover Feast. [21]They went to Philip, who was from Bethsaida in Galilee, and said, "Sir, we would like to see Jesus." [22]Philip told Andrew, and then Andrew and Philip told Jesus.

[23]Jesus said to them, "The time has come for the Son of Man to receive his glory. [24]I tell you the truth, a grain of wheat must fall to the ground and die to make many seeds. But if it never dies, it remains only a single seed. [25]Those who love their lives will lose them, but those who hate their lives in this world will keep true life forever. [26]Whoever serves me must follow me. Then my servant will be with me everywhere I am. My Father will honor anyone who serves me.

SMART TIPS!

Start Small

Is your schoolwork starting to pile up? An easy way to keep from stressing out is to write down everything you have to do and then start with the most important. There will be a lot of things in your spiritual life that need work, but take them one at a time.

[27]"Now I am very troubled. Should I say, 'Father, save me from this time'? No, I came to this time so I could suffer. [28]Father, bring glory to your name!"

Then a voice came from heaven, "I have brought glory to it, and I will do it again."

[29]The crowd standing there, who heard the voice, said it was thunder.

But others said, "An angel has spoken to him."

[30]Jesus said, "That voice was for your sake, not mine. [31]Now is the time for the world to be judged; now the ruler of this world will be thrown down. [32]If I am lifted up from the earth, I will draw all people toward me." [33]Jesus said this to show how he would die.

[34]The crowd said, "We have heard from the law that the Christ will live forever. So why do you say, 'The Son of Man must be lifted up'? Who is this 'Son of Man'?"

[35]Then Jesus said, "The light will be with you for a little longer, so walk while you have the light. Then the darkness will not catch you. If you walk in the darkness, you will not know where you are going. [36]Believe in the light while you still have it so that you will become children of light." When Jesus had said this, he left and hid himself from them.

SOME PEOPLE WON'T BELIEVE IN JESUS

[37]Though Jesus had done many miracles in front of the people, they still did not believe in him. [38]This was to bring about what Isaiah the prophet had said:

"Lord, who believed what we told them?

COOL! Jesus Never Went to Church

There were no churches in Jesus' day. Since he was Jewish, Jesus went to synagogue (a Jewish place of worship) on the Sabbath, or Saturday. The men and women sat separately and learned the Old Testament scriptures.

Any man could speak in the synagogue, and Jesus often did! He preached God's Word and healed sick people, which got him into trouble.

Later, Paul and other missionaries preached in the synagogues until they were kicked out. But Christians had already started their own meetings on a different day—Sunday, the day of the week on which Jesus came back to life!

Who saw the Lord's power in this?"

Isaiah 53:1

[39]This is why the people could not believe: Isaiah also had said,

[40]"He has blinded their eyes,
and he has closed their minds.
Otherwise they would see with their eyes
and understand in their minds
and come back to me and be healed."

Isaiah 6:10

[41]Isaiah said this because he saw Jesus' glory and spoke about him.

[42]But many believed in Jesus, even many of the leaders. But because of the Pharisees, they did not say they believed in him for fear they would be put out of the synagogue. [43]They loved praise from people more than praise from God.

[44]Then Jesus cried out, "Whoever believes in me is really believing in the One who sent me. [45]Whoever sees me sees the One who sent me. [46]I have come as light into the world so that whoever believes in me would not stay in darkness.

[47]"Anyone who hears my words and does not obey them, I do not judge, because I did not come to judge the world, but to save the world. [48]There is a judge for those who refuse to believe in me and do not accept my words.

The word I have taught will be their judge on the last day. [49]The things I taught were not from myself. The Father who sent me told me what to say and what to teach. [50]And I know that eternal life comes from what the Father commands. So whatever I say is what the Father told me to say."

JESUS WASHES HIS FOLLOWERS' FEET

13 It was almost time for the Passover Feast. Jesus knew that it was time for him to leave this world and go back to the Father. He had always loved those who were his own in the world, and he loved them all the way to the end.

[2]Jesus and his followers were at the evening meal. The devil had already persuaded Judas Iscariot, the son of Simon, to turn against Jesus. [3]Jesus knew that the Father had given him power over everything and that he had come from God and was going back to God. [4]So during the meal Jesus stood up and took off his outer clothing. Taking a towel, he wrapped it around his waist. [5]Then he poured water into a bowl and began to wash the followers' feet, drying them with the towel that was wrapped around him.

[6]Jesus came to Simon Peter, who said to him, "Lord, are you going to wash my feet?"

[7]Jesus answered, "You don't understand now what I am doing, but you will understand later."

[8]Peter said, "No, you will never wash my feet."

Jesus answered, "If I don't wash your feet, you are not one of my people."

[9]Simon Peter answered, "Lord, then wash not only my feet, but wash my hands and my head, too!"

[10]Jesus said, "After a person has had a bath, his whole body is clean. He needs only to wash his feet. And you men are clean, but not all of you." [11]Jesus knew who would turn against him, and that is why he said, "Not all of you are clean."

[12]When he had finished washing their feet, he put on his clothes and sat down again. He asked, "Do you understand what I have just done for you? [13]You call me 'Teacher' and 'Lord,' and you are right, because that is what I am. [14]If I, your Lord and Teacher, have washed your feet, you also should wash each other's feet. [15]I did this as an example so that you should do as I have done for you. [16]I tell you

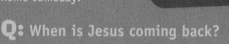

Q: One of my friends at school told me he did something that will get him in trouble. Does God want me to tell on him?

A: Keeping secrets is important. But there are times when keeping a secret like this can make a lot of bad things happen. Encourage your friend to tell his parents and/or the principal. He'll feel a lot better when he gets it off his chest. If he won't, and someone has been hurt or property has been damaged, then tell your parents and let them decide what you should do. If your friend gets away with it this time, he will probably try something worse next time.

Q: My parents don't want me to have a dog. How can I convince them that I'm responsible enough?

A: Ask your parents what you can do to show that you can take care of a pet. They might have

you take on some additional responsibilities at home. Be prepared to put in some extra work if you want to be able to get a dog. If your parents just don't want an animal around the house, respect their decision and have fun playing with your friends' dogs until you have your own home someday!

Q: When is Jesus coming back?

A: It could be in a hundred years, or before you finish reading this page. Jesus said that nobody knows the day or time he'll come back (Mark 13:32). Since we don't know, the smart thing to do is to live every day prepared for his return. You can prepare by getting to know Jesus better through praying and reading the Bible.

the truth, a servant is not greater than his master. A messenger is not greater than the one who sent him. [17]If you know these things, you will be blessed if you do them.

[18]"I am not talking about all of you. I know those I have chosen. But this is to bring about what the Scripture said: 'The man who ate at my table has turned against me.'[n] [19]I am telling you this now before it happens so that when it happens, you will believe that I am he. [20]I tell you the truth, whoever accepts anyone I send also accepts me. And whoever accepts me also accepts the One who sent me."

JESUS TALKS ABOUT HIS DEATH

[21]After Jesus said this, he was very troubled. He said openly, "I tell you the truth, one of you will turn against me."

[22]The followers all looked at each other, because they did not know whom Jesus was talking about. [23]One of the followers sitting[n] next to Jesus was the follower Jesus loved. [24]Simon Peter motioned to him to ask Jesus whom he was talking about.

[25]That follower leaned closer to Jesus and asked, "Lord, who is it?"

[26]Jesus answered, "I will dip this bread into the dish. The man I give it to is the man who will turn against me." So Jesus took a piece of bread, dipped it, and gave it to Judas Iscariot, the son of Simon. [27]As soon as Judas took the bread, Satan entered him. Jesus said to him, "The thing that you will do—do it quickly." [28]No one at the table understood why Jesus said this to Judas. [29]Since he was the one who kept the money box, some of the followers thought Jesus was telling him to buy what was needed for the feast or to give something to the poor.

[30]Judas took the bread Jesus gave him and immediately went out. It was night.

[31]When Judas was gone, Jesus said, "Now the Son of Man receives his glory, and God receives glory through him. [32]If God receives glory through him,[n] then God will give glory to the Son through himself. And God will give him glory quickly."

[33]Jesus said, "My children, I will be with you only a little longer. You will look for me, and what I told the Jews, I tell you now: Where I am going you cannot come.

[34]"I give you a new command: Love each other. You must love each other as I have loved you. [35]All people will know that you are my followers if you love each other."

PETER WILL SAY HE DOESN'T KNOW JESUS

[36]Simon Peter asked Jesus, "Lord, where are you going?"

Jesus answered, "Where I am going you cannot follow now, but you will follow later."

[37]Peter asked, "Lord, why can't I follow you now? I am ready to die for you!"

[38]Jesus answered, "Are you ready to die for me? I tell you the truth, before the rooster crows, you will say three times that you don't know me."

JESUS COMFORTS HIS FOLLOWERS

14 Jesus said, "Don't let your hearts be troubled. Trust in God, and trust in me. [2]There are many rooms in my Father's house; I would not tell you this if it were not true. I am going there to prepare a place for you. [3]After I go and prepare a place for you, I will come back and take you to be with me so that you may be where I am. [4]You know the way to the place where I am going."[n]

[5]Thomas said to Jesus, "Lord, we don't know where you are going. So how can we know the way?"

[6]Jesus answered, "I am the way, and the truth, and the life. The only way to the Father is through me. [7]If you really knew me, you would know my Father, too. But now you do know him, and you have seen him."

[8]Philip said to him, "Lord, show us the Father. That is all we need."

[9]Jesus answered, "I have been with you a long time now. Do you still not know me, Philip? Whoever has seen me has seen the Father. So why do you say, 'Show us the Father'? [10]Don't you believe that I am in the Father and the Father is in me? The words I say to you don't come from me, but the Father lives in me and does his own work. [11]Believe me when I say that I am in the Father and the Father is in me. Or believe because of the miracles I have done. [12]I tell you the truth, whoever believes in me will do the same things that I do. Those who believe will do even greater things than these, because I am going to the Father. [13]And if you ask for anything in my name, I will do it for you so that the Father's glory will be shown through the Son. [14]If you ask me for anything in my name, I will do it.

THE PROMISE OF THE HOLY SPIRIT

[15]"If you love me, you will obey my commands. [16]I will ask the Father, and he will give you another Helper[n] to be with you forever— [17]the Spirit of truth. The world cannot accept him, because it does not see him or know him. But you know him, because he lives with you and he will be in you.

[18]"I will not leave you all alone like orphans; I will come back to you. [19]In a little while the

KNOW THE WORD!

HELL

Some people think that hell is a funny thing to joke about. But when the Bible talks about hell, it's dead serious. Hell wasn't originally made for humans; it was made for Satan and his demons. But people turned away from God and decided to go their own way.

God can't allow evil or sin in his perfect heaven. If people don't want to follow God, he doesn't make them. But he also can't just forget about their sin.

Hell is a lonely place of never-ending suffering. The worst thing about hell is that it's the one place where God cannot be.

If you trust in Jesus to save you, you don't have to worry about going to hell...but it's still no joking matter.

22 Then Judas (not Judas Iscariot) said, "But, Lord, why do you plan to show yourself to us and not to the rest of the world?"

23 Jesus answered, "If people love me, they will obey my teaching. My Father will love them, and we will come to them and make our home with them. 24 Those who do not love me do not obey my teaching. This teaching that you hear is not really mine; it is from my Father, who sent me.

25 "I have told you all these things while I am with you. 26 But the Helper will teach you everything and will cause you to remember all that I told you. This Helper is the Holy Spirit whom the Father will send in my name.

27 "I leave you peace; my peace I give you. I do not give it to you as the world does. So don't let your hearts be troubled or afraid. 28 You heard me say to you, 'I am going, but I am coming back to you.' If you loved me, you should be happy that I am going back to the Father, because he is greater than I am. 29 I have told you this now, before it happens, so that when it happens, you will believe. 30 I will not talk with you much longer, because the ruler of this world is coming. He has no power over me, 31 but the world must know that I love the Father, so I do exactly what the Father told me to do.

"Come now, let us go."

JESUS IS LIKE A VINE

15 "I am the true vine; my Father is the gardener. 2 He cuts off every branch of mine that does not produce fruit. And he trims and cleans every branch that produces fruit so that it will produce even more fruit. 3 You are already clean because of the words I have spoken to you. 4 Remain in me, and I will remain in you. A branch cannot produce fruit alone but must remain in the vine. In the same way, you cannot produce fruit alone but must remain in me.

5 "I am the vine, and you are the branches. If any remain in me and I remain in them, they produce much fruit. But without me they can do nothing. 6 If any do not remain in me, they are like a branch that is thrown away and then dies. People pick up dead branches, throw them into the fire, and burn them. 7 If you remain in me and follow my teachings, you can ask anything you want, and it will be given to you. 8 You should produce much fruit and show that you are my followers, which brings glory to my Father. 9 I loved you as the Father loved me. Now remain in my love. 10 I have obeyed my Father's commands, and I remain in his love. In the same way, if you obey my commands, you will remain in my love. 11 I have told you these things so that you can have the same joy I have and so that your joy will be the fullest possible joy.

12 "This is my command: Love each other as I have loved you. 13 The greatest love a person can show is to die for his friends. 14 You are my friends if you do what I command you. 15 I no longer call you servants, because a servant does not know what his master is doing. But I call you friends, because I have made known to you everything I heard from my Father. 16 You did not choose me; I chose you. And I gave you this work: to go and produce fruit, fruit that will last. Then the Father will give you anything you ask for in my name. 17 This is my command: Love each other.

JESUS WARNS HIS FOLLOWERS

18 "If the world hates you, remember that it hated me first. 19 If you belonged to the world, it would love you as it loves its own. But I have chosen you out of the world, so you don't be-

world will not see me anymore, but you will see me. Because I live, you will live, too. 20 On that day you will know that I am in my Father, and that you are in me and I am in you. 21 Those who know my commands and obey them are the ones who love me, and my Father will love those who love me. I will love them and will show myself to them."

GET CONNECTED

BUT MY CHRISTIAN FRIENDS ARE BORING!

When John first became a Christian, every day seemed exciting—like a twenty-four-hour extreme sport. Later, though, he complained more and more that his friends at church were boring. What had changed?

It wasn't his friends. John simply lost enthusiasm. Everyone does from time to time. No spiritual high lasts forever—not until heaven.

That's the way it is with your boredom, too. John found excitement by thinking less about his feelings and more about others (see Philippians 2:4). So can you.

long to it. That is why the world hates you. [20]Remember what I told you: A servant is not greater than his master. If people did wrong to me, they will do wrong to you, too. And if they obeyed my teaching, they will obey yours, too. [21]They will do all this to you on account of me, because they do not know the One who sent me. [22]If I had not come and spoken to them, they would not be guilty of sin, but now they have no excuse for their sin. [23]Whoever hates me also hates my Father. [24]I did works among them that no one else has ever done. If I had not done these works, they would not be guilty of sin. But now they have seen what I have done, and yet they have hated both me and my Father. [25]But this happened so that what is written in their law would be true: 'They hated me for no reason.'"

[26]"I will send you the Helper* from the Father; he is the Spirit of truth who comes from the Father. When he comes, he will tell about me, [27]and you also must tell people about me, because you have been with me from the beginning.

16 "I have told you these things to keep you from giving up. [2]People will put you out of their synagogues. Yes, the time is coming when those who kill you will think they are offering service to God. [3]They will do this because they have not known the Father and they have not known me. [4]I have told you these things now so that when the time comes you will remember that I warned you.

dare to do

Luke 6:33
Read It: What's special about being nice to people who are nice to you? Everyone does that.
Do It: Be nice to someone who's a jerk to you; then they'll know you're a Christian.

Luke 6:34
Read It: If you lend stuff only because you expect something in return, what makes you different from anyone else?
Do It: Living for Christ is radical: when you let a friend borrow something, don't immediately ask to borrow something of his. Be generous with your stuff.

Luke 6:41
Read It: Do you notice the little faults others have before you notice the huge ones you have?
Do It: Do a self-check before you criticize a friend or family member.

THE WORK OF THE HOLY SPIRIT

"I did not tell you these things at the beginning, because I was with you then. [5]Now I am going back to the One who sent me. But none of you asks me, 'Where are you going?' [6]Your hearts are filled with sadness because I have told you these things. [7]But I tell you the truth, it is better for you that I go away. When I go away, I will send the Helper* to you. If I do not go away, the Helper will not come. [8]When the Helper comes, he will prove to the people of the world the truth about sin, about being right with God, and about judgment. [9]He will prove to them that sin is not believing in me. [10]He will prove to them that being right with God comes from my going to the Father and not being seen anymore. [11]And the Helper will

COOL!

Fun and Games

The Isthmian Games were the ancient version of the Olympics, only smaller. They were held every two years at Corinth. The winners got crowns of wild celery, and later, crowns of pine branches.

Paul had these games in mind when he wrote, "All those who compete in the games use self-control so they can win a crown. That crown is an earthly thing that lasts only a short time, but our crown will never be destroyed" (1 Corinthians 9:25).

By living for God, we can win crowns that will last forever. Sure beats celery!

15:25 'They . . . reason.' These words could be from Psalm 35:19 or Psalm 69:4.   15:26; 16:7 Helper "Counselor" or "Comforter." Jesus is talking about the Holy Spirit.

prove to them that judgment happened when the ruler of this world was judged.

[12]"I have many more things to say to you, but they are too much for you now. [13]But when the Spirit of truth comes, he will lead you into all truth. He will not speak his own words, but he will speak only what he hears, and he will tell you what is to come. [14]The Spirit of truth will bring glory to me, because he will take what I have to say and tell it to you. [15]All that the Father has is mine. That is why I said that the Spirit will take what I have to say and tell it to you.

SADNESS WILL BECOME HAPPINESS

[16]"After a little while you will not see me, and then after a little while you will see me again."

[17]Some of the followers said to each other, "What does Jesus mean when he says, 'After a little while you will not see me, and then after a little while you will see me again'? And what does he mean when he says, 'Because I am going to the Father'?" [18]They also asked, "What does he mean by 'a little while'? We don't understand what he is saying."

[19]Jesus saw that the followers wanted to ask him about this, so he said to them, "Are you asking each other what I meant when I said, 'After a little while you will not see me, and then after a little while you will see me again'? [20]I tell you the truth, you will cry and be sad, but the world will be happy. You will be sad, but your sadness will become joy. [21]When a woman gives birth to a baby, she has pain, because her time has come. But when her baby is born, she forgets the pain, because she is so happy that a child has been born into the world. [22]It is the same with you. Now you are sad, but I will see you again and you will be happy, and no one will take away your joy. [23]In that day you will not ask me for anything. I tell you the truth, my Father will give you anything you ask for in my name. [24]Until now you have not asked for anything in my name. Ask and you will receive, so that your joy will be the fullest possible joy.

VICTORY OVER THE WORLD

[25]"I have told you these things indirectly in stories. But the time will come when I will not use stories like that to tell you things; I will speak to you in plain words about the Father. [26]In that day you will ask the Father for things in my name. I mean, I will not need to ask the Father for you. [27]The Father himself loves you. He loves you because you loved me and believed that I came from God. [28]I came from the Father into the world. Now I am leaving the world and going back to the Father."

[29]Then the followers of Jesus said, "You are speaking clearly to us now and are not using stories that are hard to understand. [30]We can see now that you know all things. You can answer a person's question even before it is asked. This makes us believe you came from God."

[31]Jesus answered, "So now you believe? [32]Listen to me; a time is coming when you will be scattered, each to your own home. That time is now here. You will leave me alone, but I am never really alone, because the Father is with me.

[33]"I told you these things so that you can have peace in me. In this world you will have trouble, but be brave! I have defeated the world."

TOP 10

Cool Things to Do at a Sleepover

1. Have a pillow fight in your sleeping bags.
2. Project your game system onto the wall.
3. Play flashlight tag.
4. Watch your favorite cartoon collection on DVD.
5. Make homemade milkshakes.
6. Have a water balloon toss (outside!).
7. Start a story circle.
8. Make s'mores in the microwave.
9. Have a scavenger hunt around the neighborhood.
10. Watch the entire *Star Wars* series straight through.

Bible Villains

Herod Antipas
See Mark 6:14–29; Luke 23:7–12.

Herod Antipas was a good politician and a bad man. He was the Roman puppet-ruler of Galilee during the time of Jesus. Jesus called Herod a "fox" because he was sly, cunning, and ruthless.

Like many politicians, Herod had a big ego. His wife used his pride to trick him into killing John the Baptist, whom he had locked in his dungeon.

After cutting off John's head, Herod heard about a miracle-worker who was even more popular. He tried to see this man—Jesus—but never got the chance until after Jesus was arrested.

Jesus didn't speak to the Fox when they met. He knew that one day the roles would be switched, and Herod would stand before him and pay for all the evil he had done.

JESUS PRAYS FOR HIS FOLLOWERS

17 After Jesus said these things, he looked toward heaven and prayed, "Father, the time has come. Give glory to your Son so that the Son can give glory to you. [2]You gave the Son power over all people so that the Son could give eternal life to all those you gave him. [3]And this is eternal life: that people know you, the only true God, and that they know Jesus Christ, the One you sent. [4]Having finished the work you gave me to do, I brought you glory on earth. [5]And now, Father, give me glory with you; give me the glory I had with you before the world was made.

[6]"I showed what you are like to those you gave me from the world. They belonged to you, and you gave them to me, and they have obeyed your teaching. [7]Now they know that everything you gave me comes from you. [8]I gave them the teachings you gave me, and they accepted them. They knew that I truly came from you, and they believed that you sent me. [9]I am praying for them. I am not praying for people in the world but for those you gave me, because they are yours. [10]All I have is yours, and all you have is mine. And my glory is shown through them. [11]I am coming to you; I will not stay in the world any longer. But they are still in the world. Holy Father, keep them safe by the power of your name, the name you gave me, so that they will be one, just as you and I are one. [12]While I was with them, I kept them safe by the power of your name, the name you gave me. I protected them, and only one of them, the one worthy of destruction, was lost so that the Scripture would come true.

[13]"I am coming to you now. But I pray these things while I am still in the world so that these followers can have all of my joy in them. [14]I have given them your teaching. And the world has hated them, because they don't belong to the world, just as I don't belong to the world. [15]I am not asking you to take them out of the world but to keep them safe from the Evil One. [16]They don't belong to the world, just as I don't belong to the world. [17]Make them ready for your service through your truth; your teaching is truth. [18]I have sent them into the world, just as you sent me into the world. [19]For their sake, I am making myself ready to serve so that they can be ready for their service of the truth.

[20]"I pray for these followers, but I am also praying for all those who will believe in me because of their teaching. [21]Father, I pray that they can be one. As you are in me and I am in you, I pray that they can also be one in us. Then the world will believe that you sent me. [22]I have given these people the glory that you gave me so that they can be one, just as you and I are one. [23]I will be in them and you will be in me so that they will be completely one. Then the world will know that you sent me and that you loved them just as much as you loved me.

[24]"Father, I want these people that you gave me to be with me where I am. I want them to see my glory, which you gave me because you loved me before the world was made. [25]Father, you are the One who is good. The world does not know you, but I know you, and these people know you sent me. [26]I showed them what you are like, and I will show them again. Then they will have the same love that you have for me, and I will live in them."

JESUS IS ARRESTED

18 When Jesus finished praying, he went with his followers across the Kidron Valley. On the other side there was a garden, and Jesus and his followers went into it.

[2]Judas knew where this place was, because Jesus met there often with his followers. Judas was the one who turned against Jesus. [3]So Judas came there with a group of soldiers and some guards from the leading priests and the Pharisees. They were carrying torches, lanterns, and weapons.

[4]Knowing everything that would happen to him, Jesus went out and asked, "Who is it you are looking for?"

[5]They answered, "Jesus from Nazareth."

"I am he," Jesus said. (Judas, the one who turned against Jesus, was standing there with

ROCK SOLID

John 19:10–11

When you close your eyes and think of Jesus, what do you imagine him like? Gentle? Kind? How about when you imagine him being tried, sentenced, beaten, and crucified? Would you call him a victim? Was he simply unable to fight back when they captured and tortured him? That's not the picture of Jesus the Bible describes.

Jesus was tough and strong. There wasn't anything Jesus couldn't handle. At one point during his trial, Pontius Pilate looked at Jesus and said, "Don't you know I have power to set you free and power to have you crucified?" (John 19:10). Jesus flatly replied, "The only power you have over me is the power given to you by God" (verse 11).

In other words, Jesus wasn't there by accident or because anyone was forcing him to be. He was there by choice, allowing these things to happen.

When we have a true understanding of what Jesus was like, it helps us understand how big a sacrifice it was to undergo that brutal death for us. He could have escaped. With a word he could have called fire down from heaven to consume his enemies. But his love for us is so great that he was willing to go through it for us. That's tough. That's power. That's the real Jesus.

them.) [6]When Jesus said, "I am he," they moved back and fell to the ground.

[7]Jesus asked them again, "Who is it you are looking for?"

They said, "Jesus of Nazareth."

[8]"I told you that I am he," Jesus said. "So if you are looking for me, let the others go." [9]This happened so that the words Jesus said before would come true: "I have not lost any of the ones you gave me."

[10]Simon Peter, who had a sword, pulled it out and struck the servant of the high priest, cutting off his right ear. (The servant's name was Malchus.) [11]Jesus said to Peter, "Put your sword back. Shouldn't I drink the cup" the Father gave me?"

JESUS IS BROUGHT BEFORE ANNAS

[12]Then the soldiers with their commander and the guards arrested Jesus. They tied him [13]and led him first to Annas, the father-in-law of Caiaphas, the high priest that year. [14]Caiaphas was the one who told the Jews that it would be better if one man died for all the people.

PETER SAYS HE DOESN'T KNOW JESUS

[15]Simon Peter and another one of Jesus' followers went along after Jesus. This follower knew the high priest, so he went with Jesus into the high priest's courtyard. [16]But Peter waited outside near the door. The follower who knew the high priest came back outside, spoke to the girl at the door, and brought Peter inside. [17]The girl at the door said to Peter, "Aren't you also one of that man's followers?"

Peter answered, "No, I am not!"

[18]It was cold, so the servants and guards had built a fire and were standing around it, warming themselves. Peter also was standing with them, warming himself.

THE HIGH PRIEST QUESTIONS JESUS

[19]The high priest asked Jesus questions about his followers and his teaching. [20]Jesus answered, "I have spoken openly to everyone. I have always taught in synagogues and in the Temple, where all the Jews come together. I never said anything in secret. [21]So why do you question me? Ask the people who heard my teaching. They know what I said."

[22]When Jesus said this, one of the guards standing there hit him. The guard said, "Is that the way you answer the high priest?"

[23]Jesus answered him, "If I said something wrong, then show what it was. But if what I said is true, why do you hit me?"

[24]Then Annas sent Jesus, who was still tied, to Caiaphas the high priest.

PETER SAYS AGAIN HE DOESN'T KNOW JESUS

[25]As Simon Peter was standing and warming himself, they said to him, "Aren't you one of that man's followers?"

Peter said it was not true; he said, "No, I am not."

[26]One of the servants of the high priest was there. This servant was a relative of the man whose ear Peter had cut off. The servant said, "Didn't I see you with him in the garden?"

[27]Again Peter said it wasn't true. At once a rooster crowed.

JESUS IS BROUGHT BEFORE PILATE

[28]Early in the morning they led Jesus from Caiaphas's house to the Roman governor's palace. They would not go inside the palace, because they did not want to make themselves unclean;" they wanted to eat the Passover meal. [29]So Pilate went outside to them and asked, "What charges do you bring against this man?"

[30]They answered, "If he were not a criminal, we wouldn't have brought him to you."

[31]Pilate said to them, "Take him yourselves and judge him by your own law."

"But we are not allowed to put anyone to death," the Jews answered. [32](This happened

trustables

John 20:19-20

Death. It's hard to imagine a more difficult experience than facing the death of a friend or loved one. But when a Christian friend or loved one dies, everything is different. Yes, it still hurts something fierce. But there's hope!

Imagine how you would have felt the weekend after Jesus was crucified. You've spent the best three years of your life with Jesus. Suddenly, all your hopes and dreams lie smashed on the ground. Your best friend has been murdered. Now the same men want to kill you.

John 20:19 tells us: "When it was evening on the first day of the week, Jesus' followers were together.

The doors were locked, because they were afraid... Then Jesus came and stood right in the middle of them and said, 'Peace be with you.'"

The next verse says: "After he said this, he showed them his hands and his side. His followers were thrilled when they saw the Lord." They couldn't believe it: *Jesus is alive!*

Because Jesus lives, we can experience incredible peace after someone we loves dies. It's a peace only God can give. It's okay to cry and miss that person, but never lose hope. Just make sure you're ready for heaven. If you are, you will be with your Christian friends and loved ones forever.

18:11 cup Jesus is talking about the painful things that will happen to him. Accepting these things will be very hard, like drinking a cup of something bitter.   **18:28 unclean** Going into the Roman palace would make them unfit to eat the Passover Feast, according to their Law.

so that what Jesus said about how he would die would come true.)

[33]Then Pilate went back inside the palace and called Jesus to him and asked, "Are you the king of the Jews?"

[34]Jesus said, "Is that your own question, or did others tell you about me?"

[35]Pilate answered, "I am not one of you. It was your own people and their leading priests who handed you over to me. What have you done wrong?"

[36]Jesus answered, "My kingdom does not belong to this world. If it belonged to this world, my servants would have fought to keep me from being given over to the Jewish leaders. But my kingdom is from another place."

[37]Pilate said, "So you are a king!"

Jesus answered, "You are the one saying I am a king. This is why I was born and came into the world: to tell people the truth. And everyone who belongs to the truth listens to me."

[38]Pilate said, "What is truth?" After he said this, he went out to the crowd again and said to them, "I find nothing against this man. [39]But it is your custom that I free one prisoner to you at Passover time. Do you want me to free the 'king of the Jews'?"

[40]They shouted back, "No, not him! Let Barabbas go free!" (Barabbas was a robber.)

19 Then Pilate ordered that Jesus be taken away and whipped. [2]The soldiers made a crown from some thorny branches and put it on Jesus' head and put a purple robe around him. [3]Then they came to him many times and said, "Hail, King of the Jews!" and hit him in the face.

[4]Again Pilate came out and said to them, "Look, I am bringing Jesus out to you. I want you to know that I find nothing against him." [5]So Jesus came out, wearing the crown of thorns and the purple robe. Pilate said to them, "Here is the man!"

[6]When the leading priests and the guards saw Jesus, they shouted, "Crucify him! Crucify him!"

But Pilate answered, "Crucify him yourselves, because I find nothing against him."

[7]The leaders answered, "We have a law that says he should die, because he said he is the Son of God."

[8]When Pilate heard this, he was even more afraid. [9]He went back inside the palace and asked Jesus, "Where do you come from?" But Jesus did not answer him. [10]Pilate said, "You refuse to speak to me? Don't you know I have power to set you free and power to have you crucified?"

[11]Jesus answered, "The only power you

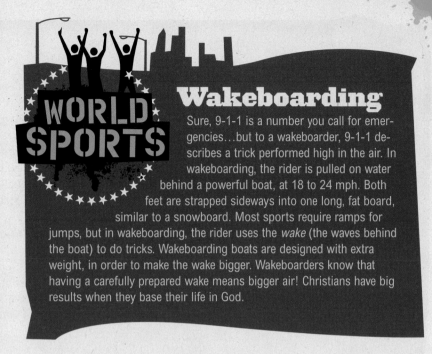

WORLD SPORTS

Wakeboarding

Sure, 9-1-1 is a number you call for emergencies…but to a wakeboarder, 9-1-1 describes a trick performed high in the air. In wakeboarding, the rider is pulled on water behind a powerful boat, at 18 to 24 mph. Both feet are strapped sideways into one long, fat board, similar to a snowboard. Most sports require ramps for jumps, but in wakeboarding, the rider uses the *wake* (the waves behind the boat) to do tricks. Wakeboarding boats are designed with extra weight, in order to make the wake bigger. Wakeboarders know that having a carefully prepared wake means bigger air! Christians have big results when they base their life in God.

have over me is the power given to you by God. The man who turned me in to you is guilty of a greater sin."

[12]After this, Pilate tried to let Jesus go. But some in the crowd cried out, "Anyone who makes himself king is against Caesar. If you let this man go, you are no friend of Caesar."

[13]When Pilate heard what they were saying, he brought Jesus out and sat down on the judge's seat at the place called The Stone Pavement. (In the Hebrew language[n] the name is Gabbatha.) [14]It was about noon on Preparation Day of Passover week. Pilate said to the crowd, "Here is your king!"

[15]They shouted, "Take him away! Take him away! Crucify him!"

Pilate asked them, "Do you want me to crucify your king?"

The leading priests answered, "The only king we have is Caesar."

[16]So Pilate handed Jesus over to them to be crucified.

JESUS IS CRUCIFIED

The soldiers took charge of Jesus. [17]Carrying his own cross, Jesus went out to a place called The Place of the Skull, which in the Hebrew language[n] is called Golgotha. [18]There they crucified Jesus. They also crucified two other men, one on each side, with Jesus in the middle. [19]Pilate wrote a sign and put it on the cross. It read: JESUS OF NAZARETH, THE KING OF THE JEWS. [20]The sign was written in Hebrew, in Latin, and in Greek. Many of the people read the sign, because the place where Jesus was

crucified was near the city. [21]The leading priests said to Pilate, "Don't write, 'The King of the Jews.' But write, 'This man said, "I am the King of the Jews." ' "

[22]Pilate answered, "What I have written, I have written."

[23]After the soldiers crucified Jesus, they took his clothes and divided them into four parts, with each soldier getting one part. They also took his long shirt, which was all one piece of cloth, woven from top to bottom. [24]So the soldiers said to each other, "We should not tear this into parts. Let's throw lots to see who will get it." This happened so that this Scripture would come true:

"They divided my clothes among them,
    and they threw lots for my clothing."
    Psalm 22:18

So the soldiers did this.

[25]Standing near his cross were Jesus' mother, his mother's sister, Mary the wife of Clopas, and Mary Magdalene. [26]When Jesus saw his mother and the follower he loved standing nearby, he said to his mother, "Dear woman, here is your son." [27]Then he said to the follower, "Here is your mother." From that time on, the follower took her to live in his home.

JESUS DIES

[28]After this, Jesus knew that everything had been done. So that the Scripture would come true, he said, "I am thirsty."[n] [29]There was a jar full of vinegar there, so the soldiers soaked a sponge in it, put the sponge on a branch of a

ROCK SOLID

John 20:24-29

Ever heard someone called a "doubting Thomas" because he wouldn't believe in something? This expression comes from one of Jesus' followers. It's true! He was a big doubter. Even though he spent almost every day hanging out with Jesus, he still struggled with doubt.

Right after Jesus was crucified and buried, all the followers were in a room together. There were rumors that Jesus had come back to life. But even though Thomas had seen Jesus perform dozens of miracles, he just couldn't believe in this one. He said, "I will not believe it until I see the nail marks in his hands and put my finger where the nails were and put my hand into his side" (John 20:25). He wanted proof!

A week later, Jesus gave Thomas exactly that. He appeared to Thomas and showed him his scarred hands, feet, and side. Thomas was amazed. But Jesus said that anyone who believes *without* this kind of proof will be truly blessed!

Do you struggle with doubt? You're not alone. Jesus wants to prove himself to you. Pray to him and ask him to reveal himself to you. He probably won't appear as he did with Thomas. But in a way unique to you, he will take away your doubt and give you confidence to believe and follow him.

---

hyssop plant, and lifted it to Jesus' mouth. [30]When Jesus tasted the vinegar, he said, "It is finished." Then he bowed his head and died.

[31]This day was Preparation Day, and the next day was a special Sabbath day. Since the religious leaders did not want the bodies to stay on the cross on the Sabbath day, they asked Pilate to order that the legs of the men be broken[n] and the bodies be taken away. [32]So the soldiers came and broke the legs of the first man on the cross beside Jesus. Then they broke the legs of the man on the other cross beside Jesus. [33]But when the soldiers came to Jesus and saw that he was already dead, they did not break his legs. [34]But one of the soldiers stuck his spear into Jesus' side, and at once blood and water came out. [35](The one who saw this happen is the one who told us this, and whatever he says is true. And he knows that he tells the truth, and he tells it so that you might believe.) [36]These things happened to make the Scripture come true: "Not one of his bones will be broken."[n] [37]And another Scripture says, "They will look at the one they stabbed."[n]

JESUS IS BURIED

[38]Later, Joseph from Arimathea asked Pilate if he could take the body of Jesus. (Joseph was a secret follower of Jesus, because he was afraid of some of the leaders.) Pilate gave his permission, so Joseph came and took Jesus' body away. [39]Nicodemus, who earlier had come to Jesus at night, went with Joseph. He brought about seventy-five pounds of myrrh and aloes. [40]These two men took Jesus' body and wrapped it with the spices in pieces of linen cloth, which is how they bury the dead. [41]In the place where Jesus was crucified, there was a garden. In the garden was a new tomb that had never been used before. [42]The men laid Jesus in that tomb because it was nearby, and they were preparing to start their Sabbath day.

JESUS' TOMB IS EMPTY

20 Early on the first day of the week, Mary Magdalene went to the tomb while it was still dark. When she saw that the large stone had been moved away from the tomb, [2]she ran to Simon Peter and the follower whom Jesus loved. Mary said, "They have taken the Lord out of the tomb, and we don't know where they have put him."

[3]So Peter and the other follower started for the tomb. [4]They were both running, but the other follower ran faster than Peter and reached the tomb first. [5]He bent down and looked in and saw the strips of linen cloth lying there, but he did not go in. [6]Then following him, Simon Peter arrived and went into the tomb and saw the strips of linen lying there. [7]He also saw the cloth that had been around Jesus' head, which was folded up and laid in a different place from the strips of linen. [8]Then the other follower, who had reached the tomb first, also went in. He saw and believed. [9](They did not yet understand from the Scriptures that Jesus must rise from the dead.)

JESUS APPEARS TO MARY MAGDALENE

[10]Then the followers went back home. [11]But Mary stood outside the tomb, crying. As she was crying, she bent down and looked inside the tomb. [12]She saw two angels dressed in white, sitting where Jesus' body had been, one at the head and one at the feet.

[13]They asked her, "Woman, why are you crying?"

She answered, "They have taken away my Lord, and I don't know where they have put him." [14]When Mary said this, she turned around and saw Jesus standing there, but she did not know it was Jesus.

[15]Jesus asked her, "Woman, why are you crying? Whom are you looking for?"

Thinking he was the gardener, she said to him, "Did you take him away, sir? Tell me where you put him, and I will get him."

[16]Jesus said to her, "Mary."

Mary turned toward Jesus and said in the Hebrew language,[n] "Rabboni."[n] (This means "Teacher.")

[17]Jesus said to her, "Don't hold on to me, because I have not yet gone up to the Father. But go to my brothers and tell them, 'I am going back to my Father and your Father, to my God and your God.'"

 19:31 broken The breaking of their bones would make them die sooner.   **19:36 "Not one . . . broken."** Quotation from Psalm 34:20. The idea is from Exodus 12:46; Numbers 9:12.   **19:37 "They . . . stabbed."** Quotation from Zechariah 12:10.   **20:16 Hebrew language** Or Aramaic, the languages of many people in this region in the first century.

[18]Mary Magdalene went and said to the followers, "I saw the Lord!" And she told them what Jesus had said to her.

JESUS APPEARS TO HIS FOLLOWERS

[19]When it was evening on the first day of the week, Jesus' followers were together. The doors were locked, because they were afraid of the elders. Then Jesus came and stood right in the middle of them and said, "Peace be with you." [20]After he said this, he showed them his hands and his side. His followers were thrilled when they saw the Lord.

[21]Then Jesus said again, "Peace be with you. As the Father sent me, I now send you." [22]After he said this, he breathed on them and said, "Receive the Holy Spirit. [23]If you forgive anyone his sins, they are forgiven. If you don't forgive them, they are not forgiven."

JESUS APPEARS TO THOMAS

[24]Thomas (called Didymus), who was one of the twelve, was not with them when Jesus came. [25]The other followers kept telling Thomas, "We saw the Lord."

But Thomas said, "I will not believe it until I see the nail marks in his hands and put my finger where the nails were and put my hand into his side."

[26]A week later the followers were in the house again, and Thomas was with them. The doors were locked, but Jesus came in and stood right in the middle of them. He said, "Peace be with you." [27]Then he said to Thomas, "Put your finger here, and look at my hands. Put your hand here in my side. Stop being an unbeliever and believe."

[28]Thomas said to him, "My Lord and my God!"

[29]Then Jesus told him, "You believe because you see me. Those who believe without seeing me will be truly blessed."

WHY JOHN WROTE THIS BOOK

[30]Jesus did many other miracles in the presence of his followers that are not written in this book. [31]But these are written so that you may believe that Jesus is the Christ, the Son of God. Then, by believing, you may have life through his name.

JESUS APPEARS TO SEVEN FOLLOWERS

21 Later, Jesus showed himself to his followers again—this time at Lake Galilee." This is how he showed himself: [2]Some of the followers were together: Simon Peter, Thomas (called Didymus), Nathanael from Cana in Galilee, the two sons of Zebedee, and two other followers. [3]Simon Peter said, "I am going out to fish."

The others said, "We will go with you." So they went out and got into the boat. They fished that night but caught nothing.

[4]Early the next morning Jesus stood on the shore, but the followers did not know it was Jesus. [5]Then he said to them, "Friends, did you catch any fish?"

They answered, "No."

[6]He said, "Throw your net on the right side of the boat, and you will find some." So they did, and they caught so many fish they could not pull the net back into the boat.

[7]The follower whom Jesus loved said to Peter, "It is the Lord!" When Peter heard him say this, he wrapped his coat around himself. (Peter had taken his clothes off.) Then he jumped into the water. [8]The other followers went to shore in the boat, dragging the net full of fish. They were not very far from shore, only about a hundred yards. [9]When the followers

Q: What do I do if my parents don't believe in God?

A: Talk to God about it every day. You may have already told your parents that you believe God has forgiven your sins because of Jesus. That's great. They should know what you believe. But you may wonder what to say to your parents to get them to believe, too. There is no way you can argue them into believing in God. Don't give up if you don't see a change right away. Remember: it's God's job to bring people to himself; we are only expected to share the Good News and live in a way that makes God happy.

Q: If I had all the money my dad makes, I'd go to the videogame store every day. Why doesn't he?

A: All the money your dad makes has to go for the house payment, food, car insurance, and about a hundred other things (just ask him). He probably doesn't have all the spending money you think he has. The other reason is that video games get a little less exciting as you get older.

Q: I've heard adults say that playing sports builds character. What do they mean?

A: Playing sports puts you in situations where you have to dig down and really try hard, and learn to be part of a team. In the middle of a basketball game, you don't quit just because you're tired; and you don't stop playing as a team just because you and the point guard don't get along. Aside from being good exercise, sports are good practice for situations you'll face in other areas of your life.

21:1 Lake Galilee Literally, "Sea of Tiberias."

stepped out of the boat and onto the shore, they saw a fire of hot coals. There were fish on the fire, and there was bread.

[10]Then Jesus said, "Bring some of the fish you just caught."

[11]Simon Peter went into the boat and pulled the net to the shore. It was full of big fish, one hundred fifty-three in all, but even though there were so many, the net did not tear. [12]Jesus said to them, "Come and eat." None of the followers dared ask him, "Who are you?" because they knew it was the Lord. [13]Jesus came and took the bread and gave it to them, along with the fish.

[14]This was now the third time Jesus showed himself to his followers after he was raised from the dead.

JESUS TALKS TO PETER

[15]When they finished eating, Jesus said to Simon Peter, "Simon son of John, do you love me more than these?"

He answered, "Yes, Lord, you know that I love you."

Jesus said, "Feed my lambs."

[16]Again Jesus said, "Simon son of John, do you love me?"

He answered, "Yes, Lord, you know that I love you."

Jesus said, "Take care of my sheep."

78% of middle and high schoolers believe they are creative.

"Life Would Be Boring Without It": What Do Kids Really Think About the Arts?" Harris Interactive. December 2003.

[17]A third time he said, "Simon son of John, do you love me?"

Peter was hurt because Jesus asked him the third time, "Do you love me?" Peter said, "Lord, you know everything; you know that I love you!"

He said to him, "Feed my sheep. [18]I tell you the truth, when you were younger, you tied your own belt and went where you wanted. But when you are old, you will put out your hands and someone else will tie you and take you where you don't want to go." [19](Jesus said this to show how Peter would die to give glory to God.) Then Jesus said to Peter, "Follow me!"

[20]Peter turned and saw that the follower Jesus loved was walking behind them. (This was the follower who had leaned against Jesus at the supper and had said, "Lord, who will turn against you?") [21]When Peter saw him behind them, he asked Jesus, "Lord, what about him?"

[22]Jesus answered, "If I want him to live until I come back, that is not your business. You follow me."

[23]So a story spread among the followers that this one would not die. But Jesus did not say he would not die. He only said, "If I want him to live until I come back, that is not your business."

[24]That follower is the one who is telling these things and who has now written them down. We know that what he says is true.

[25]There are many other things Jesus did. If every one of them were written down, I suppose the whole world would not be big enough for all the books that would be written.

Before returning to heaven after he rose from the dead, Jesus gave a final order to his followers.

He told them to "go and make followers of all people in the world" (Matthew 28:19). The Book of Acts tells how they did this. It continues the story Doctor Luke started in his Gospel.

A few days after Jesus left, he sent the Holy Spirit (one of the three persons of God; the other two are the Father and the Son) to start the work of building the church. The church is made up of everyone who believes in Jesus Christ.

There was some powerful preaching in those days, and soon the Good News about Jesus spread to the nearby towns. Then one of the most important events in history happened—Saul of Tarsus became a Christian (9:1–30).

ACTS

Saul went on to become Paul the apostle (an "apostle" is a special messenger). The rest of Acts is mostly about his preaching trips around the Roman Empire:

- First journey (chapters 12–14)
- Second journey (chapters 15–18)
- Third journey (chapters 18–21)
- The final chapters tell of Paul's arrest and trip to Rome to stand trial (chapters 21–28).

This book is only the beginning of church history. In every generation, the Holy Spirit brings people to faith in Jesus. Only when this task is finished will Jesus come back to take his church to be with him in heaven.

Will this happen in our lifetime? Maybe. One thing's for sure: his return is closer than ever before!

Are you ready?

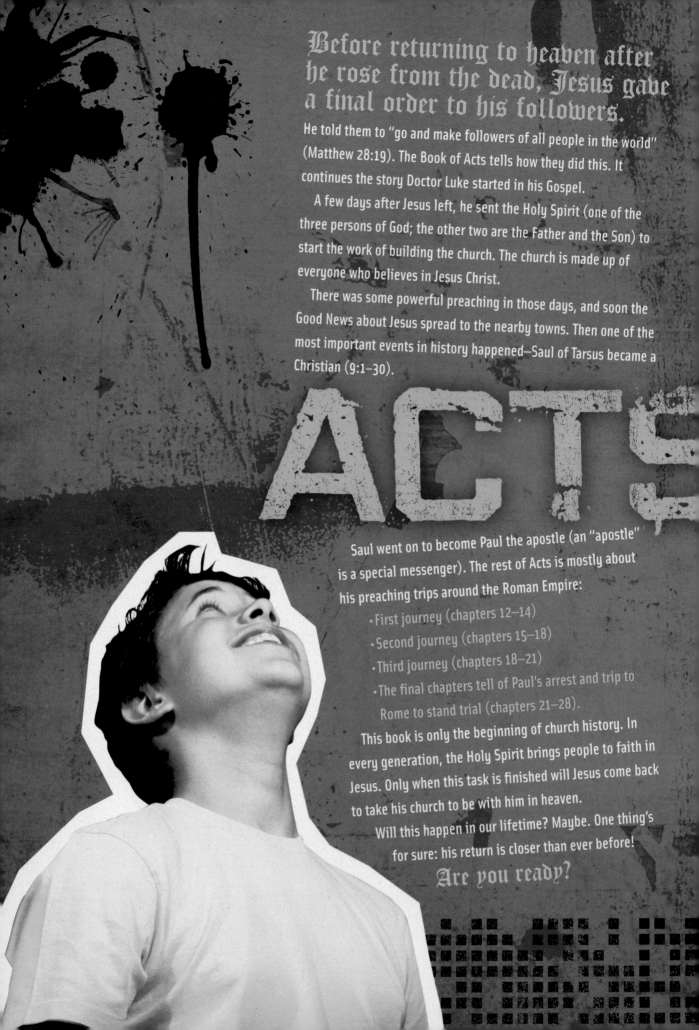

LUKE WRITES ANOTHER BOOK

1 To Theophilus.

The first book I wrote was about everything Jesus began to do and teach [2]until the day he was taken up into heaven. Before this, with the help of the Holy Spirit, Jesus told the apostles he had chosen what they should do. [3]After his death, he showed himself to them and proved in many ways that he was alive. The apostles saw Jesus during the forty days after he was raised from the dead, and he spoke to them about the kingdom of God.

[4]Once when he was eating with them, he told them not to leave Jerusalem. He said, "'Wait here to receive the promise from the Father which I told you about. [5]John baptized people with water, but in a few days you will be baptized with the Holy Spirit."

JESUS IS TAKEN UP INTO HEAVEN

[6]When the apostles were all together, they asked Jesus, "Lord, are you now going to give the kingdom back to Israel?"

[7]Jesus said to them, "The Father is the only One who has the authority to decide dates and times. These things are not for you to know. [8]But when the Holy Spirit comes to you, you will receive power. You will be my witnesses—in Jerusalem, in all of Judea, in Samaria, and in every part of the world."

[9]After he said this, as they were watching, he was lifted up, and a cloud hid him from their sight. [10]As he was going, they were looking into the sky. Suddenly, two men wearing white clothes stood beside them. [11]They said, "Men of Galilee, why are you standing here looking into the sky? Jesus, whom you saw taken up from you into heaven, will come back in the same way you saw him go."

A NEW APOSTLE IS CHOSEN

[12]Then they went back to Jerusalem from the Mount of Olives. (This mountain is about half a mile from Jerusalem.) [13]When they entered the city, they went to the upstairs room where they were staying. Peter, John, James, Andrew, Philip, Thomas, Bartholomew, Matthew, James son of Alphaeus, Simon (known as the Zealot), and Judas son of James were there. [14]They all continued praying together with some women, including Mary the mother of Jesus, and Jesus' brothers.

[15]During this time there was a meeting of the believers (about one hundred twenty of them). Peter stood up and said, [16-17]"Brothers and sisters, in the Scriptures the Holy Spirit said through David something that must happen involving Judas. He was one of our own group and served together with us. He led those who arrested Jesus." [18](Judas bought a field with the money he got for his evil act. But he fell to his death, his body burst open, and all his intestines poured out. [19]Everyone in Jerusalem learned about this so they named this place Akeldama. In their language Akeldama means "Field of Blood.") [20]"In the Book of Psalms," Peter said, "this is written:

'May his place be empty;
     leave no one to live in it.'   *Psalm 69:25*

And it is also written:

'Let another man replace him as leader.'
                                   Psalm 109:8

[21-22]"So now a man must become a witness with us of Jesus' being raised from the dead. He must be one of the men who were part of our group during all the time the Lord Jesus was among us—from the time John was baptizing people until the day Jesus was taken up from us to heaven."

[23]They put the names of two men before the group. One was Joseph Barsabbas, who was also called Justus. The other was Matthias. [24-25]The apostles prayed, "Lord, you know the thoughts of everyone. Show us which one of these two you have chosen to do this work. Show us who should be an apostle in place of Judas, who turned away and went where he belongs." [26]Then they used lots to choose between them, and the lots showed that

dare to do

Luke 11:2

Read It: Pray with God's holiness in mind.

Do It: When you pray, you should bow your head, close your eyes, and remember that you are talking with the Creator of the universe. He is listening closely to what you are saying.

Luke 11:3

Read It: Pray with God's power in mind.

Do It: Remember it is God who provides for all your needs and who has a great plan for your life.

Luke 11:4

Read It: Pray with God's grace in mind.

Do It: No matter what you've done wrong in the past, God wants to forgive you and help you live a good life.

TOP 10

Secrets to Making New Friends

1. Ask questions.
2. Say something nice to him.
3. Look for someone who sits alone at lunch, and go sit with him.
4. Be interested in what others are talking about!
5. Play sports.
6. Join a club.
7. Offer to help him with homework.
8. Share your stuff.
9. Exchange phone numbers (if it's okay with your parents).
10. Get to know your friends' other friends.

KNOW THE WORD!

PROPHECY

Prophecy means that God uses people to say what will happen in the future. It's real prophecy if it's really God's message and if it comes true! The Old Testament is full of prophecies (spoken by prophets) about the things that were to come for the Jews and for the world.

The most important prophecies were the ones that predicted long ago that God would send his Son to save the world. Jesus fulfilled all of the prophecies about him from the Old Testament! The only book of prophecy in the New Testament is Revelation, which tells us what will happen at the end of time. Read Revelation to find out what prophecy is all about!

Matthias was the one. So he became an apostle with the other eleven.

THE COMING OF THE HOLY SPIRIT

2 When the day of Pentecost came, they were all together in one place. ²Suddenly a noise like a strong, blowing wind came from heaven and filled the whole house where they were sitting. ³They saw something like flames of fire that were separated and stood over each person there. ⁴They were all filled with the Holy Spirit, and they began to speak different languages" by the power the Holy Spirit was giving them.

⁵There were some religious Jews staying in Jerusalem who were from every country in the world. ⁶When they heard this noise, a crowd came together. They were all surprised, because each one heard them speaking in his own language. ⁷They were completely amazed at this. They said, "Look! Aren't all these people that we hear speaking from Galilee? ⁸Then how is it possible that we each hear them in our own languages? We are from different places: ⁹Parthia, Media, Elam, Mesopotamia, Judea, Cappadocia, Pontus, Asia, ¹⁰Phrygia, Pamphylia, Egypt, the areas of Libya near Cyrene, Rome ¹¹(both Jews and those who had become Jews), Crete, and Arabia. But we hear them telling in our own languages about the great things God has done!" ¹²They were all amazed and confused, asking each other, "What does this mean?"

¹³But others were making fun of them, saying, "They have had too much wine."

PETER SPEAKS TO THE PEOPLE

¹⁴But Peter stood up with the eleven apostles, and in a loud voice he spoke to the crowd: "My fellow Jews, and all of you who are in Jerusalem, listen to me. Pay attention to what I have to say. ¹⁵These people are not drunk, as you think; it is only nine o'clock in the morning! ¹⁶But Joel the prophet wrote about what is happening here today:

¹⁷'God says: In the last days
   I will pour out my Spirit on all kinds of
      people.
   Your sons and daughters will prophesy.
      Your young men will see visions,
      and your old men will dream dreams.
¹⁸At that time I will pour out my Spirit
      also on my male slaves and female
         slaves,
      and they will prophesy.
¹⁹I will show miracles
      in the sky and on the earth:
      blood, fire, and thick smoke.
²⁰The sun will become dark,
      the moon red as blood,
      before the overwhelming and glorious
         day of the Lord will come.
²¹Then anyone who calls on the Lord will be
         saved.'
                              Joel 2:28–32

²²"People of Israel, listen to these words: Jesus from Nazareth was a very special man. God clearly showed this to you by the miracles, wonders, and signs he did through Jesus. You all know this, because it happened right here

COOL!

He's Got the Whole World in His Hands

God loves the whole world, and that's a lot of people! According to the Population Resource Center:

★ The world's population will reach 9.3 billion by 2050.
★ The percentage of children aged 0–14 will drop from 30 percent in 2000 to 21 percent in 2050.
★ The number of teens will reach 1.13 billion by 2025.
★ Over 60 percent of the world's population lives in Asia, 13 percent live in Africa, 12 percent live in Europe, and 14 percent live in the Americas and Oceania.

God knows all these people by name and every one of them. Including *you*!

⭐ **2:4 languages** This can also be translated "tongues."

SMART TIPS!

Don't Pursue Possessions

Don't go after stuff. The richest people in the world are not always the happiest. Strangely enough, you'll find some of the happiest people in countries that are a lot poorer than yours. Think of the best possible thing you could ever have…if it isn't God, then you're settling for second best.

among you. ²³Jesus was given to you, and with the help of those who don't know the law, you put him to death by nailing him to a cross. But this was God's plan which he had made long ago; he knew all this would happen. ²⁴God raised Jesus from the dead and set him free from the pain of death, because death could not hold him. ²⁵For David said this about him:

'I keep the Lord before me always.
  Because he is close by my side,
  I will not be hurt.
²⁶So I am glad, and I rejoice.
  Even my body has hope,
²⁷because you will not leave me in the grave.
  You will not let your Holy One rot.
²⁸You will teach me how to live a holy life.
  Being with you will fill me with joy.'

Psalm 16:8–11

²⁹"Brothers and sisters, I can tell you truly that David, our ancestor, died and was buried. His grave is still here with us today. ³⁰He was a prophet and knew God had promised him that he would make a person from David's family a king just as he was." ³¹Knowing this before it happened, David talked about the Christ rising from the dead. He said:

'He was not left in the grave.
  His body did not rot.'
³²So Jesus is the One whom God raised from the dead. And we are all witnesses to this. ³³Jesus was lifted up to heaven and is now at

God's right side. The Father has given the Holy Spirit to Jesus as he promised. So Jesus has poured out that Spirit, and this is what you now see and hear. ³⁴David was not the one who was lifted up to heaven, but he said:

'The Lord said to my Lord,
  "Sit by me at my right side,
³⁵ until I put your enemies under your
    control." 'ⁿ *Psalm 110:1*
³⁶"So, all the people of Israel should know this truly: God has made Jesus—the man you nailed to the cross—both Lord and Christ."

³⁷When the people heard this, they felt guilty and asked Peter and the other apostles, "What shall we do?"

³⁸Peter said to them, "Change your hearts and lives and be baptized, each one of you, in the name of Jesus Christ for the forgiveness of your sins. And you will receive the gift of the Holy Spirit. ³⁹This promise is for you, for your children, and for all who are far away. It is for everyone the Lord our God calls to himself."

⁴⁰Peter warned them with many other words. He begged them, "Save yourselves from the evil of today's people!" ⁴¹Then those people who accepted what Peter said were baptized. About three thousand people were added to the number of believers that day. ⁴²They spent their time learning the apostles' teaching, sharing, breaking bread,ⁿ and praying together.

THE BELIEVERS SHARE

⁴³The apostles were doing many miracles and signs, and everyone felt great respect for

God. ⁴⁴All the believers were together and shared everything. ⁴⁵They would sell their land and the things they owned and then divide the money and give it to anyone who needed it. ⁴⁶The believers met together in the Temple every day. They ate together in their homes, happy to share their food with joyful hearts. ⁴⁷They praised God and were liked by all the people. Every day the Lord added those who were being saved to the group of believers.

PETER HEALS A CRIPPLED MAN

3 One day Peter and John went to the Temple at three o'clock, the time set each day for the afternoon prayer service. ²There, at the Temple gate called Beautiful Gate, was a man who had been crippled all his life. Every day he was carried to this gate to beg for money from the people going into the Temple. ³The man saw Peter and John going into the Temple and asked them for money. ⁴Peter and John looked straight at him and said, "Look at us!" ⁵The man looked at them, thinking they were going to give him some money. ⁶But Peter said, "I don't have any silver or gold, but I do have something else I can give you. By the power of Jesus Christ from Nazareth, stand up and walk!" ⁷Then Peter took the man's right hand and lifted him up. Immediately the man's feet and ankles became strong. ⁸He jumped up, stood on his feet, and began to walk. He went into the Temple with them, walking and jumping and praising God.

dare to do

Luke 11:28
Read It: You'll be blessed if you hear God's Word and obey it.
Do It: Open your Bible and read it. Go to church, Sunday school, and youth group to get as much of God's Word in your heart as you possibly can.

Luke 11:39
Read It: Some people look spiritual on the outside, but are full of sin on the inside.
Do It: Do a heart check: confess your sin that no one else knows about.

Luke 11:43
Read It: Your main goal in life should not be for people to like you.
Do It: Don't worry what people at school think about you. Instead, try to "impress" God!

 2:30 God . . . was See 2 Samuel 7:13; Psalm 132:11. **2:35 until . . . control** Literally, "until I make your enemies a footstool for your feet." **2:42 breaking bread** This may mean a meal as in verse 46, or the Lord's Supper, the special meal Jesus told his followers to eat to remember him (Luke 22:14–20).

9-10All the people recognized him as the crippled man who always sat by the Beautiful Gate begging for money. Now they saw this same man walking and praising God, and they were amazed. They wondered how this could happen.

PETER SPEAKS TO THE PEOPLE

11While the man was holding on to Peter and John, all the people were amazed and ran to them at Solomon's Porch. 12When Peter saw this, he said to them, "People of Israel, why are you surprised? You are looking at us as if it were our own power or goodness that made this man walk. 13The God of Abraham, Isaac, and Jacob, the God of our ancestors, gave glory to Jesus, his servant. But you handed him over to be killed. Pilate decided to let him go free, but you told Pilate you did not want Jesus. 14You did not want the One who is holy and good but asked Pilate to give you a murderer[n] instead. 15And so you killed the One who gives life, but God raised him from the dead. We are witnesses to this. 16It was faith in Jesus that made this crippled man well. You can see this man, and you know him. He was made completely well because of trust in Jesus, and you all saw it happen!

17"Brothers and sisters, I know you did those things to Jesus because neither you nor your leaders understood what you were doing. 18God said through the prophets that his Christ would suffer and die. And now God has made these things come true in this way. 19So you must change your hearts and lives! Come back to God, and he will forgive your

sins. Then the Lord will send the time of rest. 20And he will send Jesus, the One he chose to be the Christ. 21But Jesus must stay in heaven until the time comes when all things will be made right again. God told about this time long ago when he spoke through his holy prophets. 22Moses said, 'The Lord your God will give you a prophet like me, who is one of your own people. You must listen to everything he tells you. 23Anyone who does not listen to that prophet will die, cut off from God's

people.'[n] 24Samuel, and all the other prophets who spoke for God after Samuel, told about this time now. 25You are descendants of the prophets. You have received the agreement God made with your ancestors. He said to your father Abraham, 'Through your descendants all the nations on the earth will be blessed.'[n] 26God has raised up his servant Jesus and sent him to you first to bless you by turning each of you away from doing evil."

PETER AND JOHN AT THE COUNCIL

4 While Peter and John were speaking to the people, priests, the captain of the soldiers that guarded the Temple, and Sadducees came up to them. 2They were upset because the two apostles were teaching the people and were preaching that people will rise from the dead through the power of Jesus. 3The older leaders grabbed Peter and John and put them in jail. Since it was already night, they kept them in jail until the next day. 4But many of those who had heard Peter and John preach believed the things they said. There were now about five thousand in the group of believers.

5The next day the rulers, the elders, and the teachers of the law met in Jerusalem. 6Annas the high priest, Caiaphas, John, and Alexander were there, as well as everyone from the high priest's family. 7They made Peter and John stand before them and then asked them, "By what power or authority did you do this?"

8Then Peter, filled with the Holy Spirit, said to them, "Rulers of the people and you elders,

DID YOU KNOW?

Playing a musical instrument is a favorite activity for 19% of kids.

"Life Would Be Boring Without It": What Do Kids Really Think About the Arts?" Harris Interactive. December 2003.

COOL!

World Wide Web

The World Wide Web is a growing system of computers and files linked together through the Internet. There were more than 600,000,000,000 pages on the Web in 2005. That's about 100 pages for every person alive. This is even more amazing when you realize the Web has only been around for ten years!

The Web is available to more than a billion people. It is becoming the storehouse of all human knowledge, but there's nothing in its vast collection of truth and trivia that God doesn't already know.

[9]are you questioning us about a good thing that was done to a crippled man? Are you asking us who made him well? [10]We want all of you and all the people to know that this man was made well by the power of Jesus Christ from Nazareth. You crucified him, but God raised him from the dead. This man was crippled, but he is now well and able to stand here before you because of the power of Jesus. [11]Jesus is

'the stone" that you builders rejected,
which has become the cornerstone.'

Psalm 118:22

[12]Jesus is the only One who can save people. No one else in the world is able to save us."

[13]The leaders saw that Peter and John were not afraid to speak, and they understood that these men had no special training or education. So they were amazed. Then they realized that Peter and John had been with Jesus. [14]Because they saw the healed man standing there beside the two apostles, they could say nothing against them. [15]After the leaders ordered them to leave the meeting, they began to talk to each other. [16]They said, "What shall we do with these men? Everyone in Jerusalem knows they have done a great miracle, and we cannot say it is not true. [17]But to keep it from spreading among the people, we must warn them not to talk to people anymore using that name."

[18]So they called Peter and John in again and told them not to speak or to teach at all in the name of Jesus. [19]But Peter and John answered them, "You decide what God would want. Should we obey you or God? [20]We cannot keep quiet. We must speak about what we have seen and heard." [21]The leaders warned the apostles again and let them go free. They could not find a way to punish them, because all the people were praising God for what had been done. [22]The man who received the miracle of healing was more than forty years old.

THE BELIEVERS PRAY

[23]After Peter and John left the meeting of leaders, they went to their own group and told them everything the leading priests and the elders had said to them. [24]When the believers heard this, they prayed to God together, "Lord, you are the One who made the sky, the earth, the sea, and everything in them. [25]By the Holy Spirit, through our father David your servant, you said:

'Why are the nations so angry?
Why are the people making useless plans?
[26]The kings of the earth prepare to fight,

and their leaders make plans together against the Lord
and his Christ.'

Psalm 2:1-2

[27]These things really happened when Herod, Pontius Pilate, and some Jews and non-Jews all came together against Jesus here in Jerusalem. Jesus is your holy servant, the One you made to be the Christ. [28]These people made your plan happen because of your power and your will. [29]And now, Lord, listen to their threats. Lord, help us, your servants, to speak your word without fear. [30]Show us your power to heal. Give proofs and make miracles happen by the power of Jesus, your holy servant."

[31]After they had prayed, the place where they were meeting was shaken. They were all filled with the Holy Spirit, and they spoke God's word without fear.

THE BELIEVERS SHARE

[32]The group of believers were united in their hearts and spirit. All those in the group acted as though their private property belonged to everyone in the group. In fact, they shared everything. [33]With great power the apostles

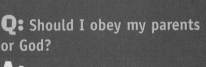

Q: Should I obey my parents or God?

A: Most of the time, parents want you to do the same things God wants you to do: obey the rules and think of others. The only times your parents might ask you to do something that would not please God would be if they told you to steal, tell a lie for them, or be unkind to somebody they don't like. If this happens to you, say respectfully that you don't want to do what's wrong. If this continues, talk about it to your grandparents, an aunt or uncle, or another adult you trust.

Q: How come girls are so worried about being skinny?

A: Right now the fashion world, TV shows, magazines, and Hollywood say that skinny is in. So girls will try to do whatever they can to look thin...even if it's unhealthy. Throughout history, the "ideal shape" for a woman's body has changed lots of times. It's sad, because God has made girls in many shapes—and he thinks they're beautiful just the way they are. Encourage girls you know by telling them that God says they are beautiful exactly how he made them.

Q: Is it OK for Christians to read or watch fiction since it isn't true?

A: Reading or watching fiction is fine as long as you remember that it didn't actually happen. Jesus told fictional stories (called *parables*) to help people understand his teachings. When he told the story of the Good Samaritan (Luke 10:25–37), everybody listening knew that it never actually happened. But it explained who our neighbors are better than any true story could!

 4:11 stone A symbol meaning Jesus.

were telling people that the Lord Jesus was truly raised from the dead. And God blessed all the believers very much. [34]There were no needy people among them. From time to time those who owned fields or houses sold them, brought the money, [35]and gave it to the apostles. Then the money was given to anyone who needed it.

[36]One of the believers was named Joseph, a Levite born in Cyprus. The apostles called him Barnabas (which means "one who encourages"). [37]Joseph owned a field, sold it, brought the money, and gave it to the apostles.

ANANIAS AND SAPPHIRA DIE

5 But a man named Ananias and his wife Sapphira sold some land. [2]He kept back part of the money for himself; his wife knew about this and agreed to it. But he brought the rest of the money and gave it to the apostles. [3]Peter said, "Ananias, why did you let Satan rule your thoughts to lie to the Holy Spirit and to keep for yourself part of the money you received for the land? [4]Before you sold the land, it belonged to you. And even after you sold it, you could have used the money any way you wanted. Why did you think of doing this? You lied to God, not to us!" [5-6]When Ananias heard this, he fell down and died. Some young men came in, wrapped up his body, carried it out, and buried it. And everyone who heard about this was filled with fear.

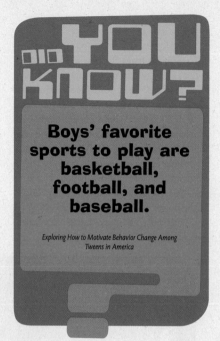

Boys' favorite sports to play are basketball, football, and baseball.

Exploring How to Motivate Behavior Change Among Tweens in America

[7]About three hours later his wife came in, but she did not know what had happened. [8]Peter said to her, "Tell me, was the money you got for your field this much?"

Sapphira answered, "Yes, that was the price."

[9]Peter said to her, "Why did you and your husband agree to test the Spirit of the Lord? Look! The men who buried your husband are at the door, and they will carry you out." [10]At that moment Sapphira fell down by his feet and died. When the young men came in and saw that she was dead, they carried her out and buried her beside her husband. [11]The whole church and all the others who heard about these things were filled with fear.

THE APOSTLES HEAL MANY

[12]The apostles did many signs and miracles among the people. And they would all meet together on Solomon's Porch. [13]None of the others dared to join them, but all the people respected them. [14]More and more men and women believed in the Lord and were added to the group of believers. [15]The people placed their sick on beds and mats in the streets, hoping that when Peter passed by at least his shadow might fall on them. [16]Crowds came from all the towns around Jerusalem, bringing their sick and those who were bothered by evil spirits, and all of them were healed.

LEADERS TRY TO STOP THE APOSTLES

[17]The high priest and all his friends (a group called the Sadducees) became very jealous. [18]They took the apostles and put them in jail. [19]But during the night, an angel of the Lord opened the doors of the jail and led the apostles outside. The angel said, [20]"Go stand in the Temple and tell the people everything about this new life." [21]When the apostles heard this,

Acts 5:1-11

Have you ever gotten in trouble for something and felt like the punishment was a little too severe—like getting grounded for a week for walking on the carpet with muddy shoes? Adults explain this behavior as "making an example" out of you.

Can you imagine being killed by God for telling a lie? Sound excessive? Well, it happened. It was when the church first began after Jesus left the earth.

Many believers were selling their possessions and giving the money to the church. One couple decided they would do the same. When they gave the money, they claimed they had donated all of it. But really they had kept some of it for themselves. They didn't have to give all the money. Lying about what they had done was the real problem. When they were confronted with their lie, they both fell down dead! The Bible says that "everyone who heard about this was filled with fear" (Acts 5:6).

It might sound like a really harsh punishment, but God was trying to make an example of them. Sometimes we act like we're better than we really are. God wants his followers to be genuinely kind and giving, not just pretending to be. Don't be a phony! You might be able to fool people, but you'll never fool God.

May

It's *"Save the Rhino Day"*—watch the movie *The Gods Must Be Crazy.* **1**

Give your mom an extra hug for Mother's Day this month! **2**

3

4

Don't forget to pray today—it's the *"Day of Prayer."* **5**

Highlight Bible verses with special meaning to you. **7**

Pray for a person of influence: it's singer Enrique Iglesias's birthday. **8**

Today is *"Lost Sock Memorial Day."* **9**

Pray for a person of influence: skateboarder Tony Hawk has a birthday today. **11**

13

If you're adopted, take a minute to thank God for your adoptive parents! **14**

May is *"Better Sleep Month,"* and today is *"Flip Your Mattress Day."* Rest well! **15**

Make an effort to listen to your friends today. Read James 1:19 for encouragement. **16**

17

Pray for a person of influence: it's actress Tina Fey's birthday. **18**

19

Pray for a person of influence: rapper Busta Rhymes celebrates another birthday today. **20**

21

Read Romans 15:1–3. Are you pleasing others? **22**

24

Today is *"Missing Children Day."* Pray that kidnapped children will return safely to their families. **25**

While you're in the car, tune the radio to the Christian music station in your town. **26**

27

In case you wanted to know. . . Darwin, Minnesota, is home to the World's Largest Ball of Twine. **29**

30

31

they obeyed and went into the Temple early in the morning and continued teaching.

When the high priest and his friends arrived, they called a meeting of the leaders and all the important elders. They sent some men to the jail to bring the apostles to them. [22]But, upon arriving, the officers could not find the apostles. So they went back and reported to the leaders. [23]They said, "The jail was closed and locked, and the guards were standing at the doors. But when we opened the doors, the jail was empty!" [24]Hearing this, the captain of the Temple guards and the leading priests were confused and wondered what was happening.

[25]Then someone came and told them, "Listen! The men you put in jail are standing in the Temple teaching the people." [26]Then the captain and his men went out and brought the apostles back. But the soldiers did not use force, because they were afraid the people would stone them to death.

[27]The soldiers brought the apostles to the meeting and made them stand before the leaders. The high priest questioned them, [28]saying, "We gave you strict orders not to continue teaching in that name. But look, you have filled Jerusalem with your teaching and are trying to make us responsible for this man's death."

[29]Peter and the other apostles answered, "We must obey God, not human authority! [30]You killed Jesus by hanging him on a cross. But God, the God of our ancestors, raised Jesus up from the dead! [31]Jesus is the One whom God raised to be on his right side, as Leader and Savior. Through him, all people could change their hearts and lives and have their sins forgiven. [32]We saw all these things happen. The Holy Spirit, whom God has given to all who obey him, also proves these things are true."

[33]When the leaders heard this, they became angry and wanted to kill them. [34]But a Pharisee named Gamaliel stood up in the meeting. He was a teacher of the law, and all the people respected him. He ordered the apostles to leave the meeting for a little while. [35]Then he said, "People of Israel, be careful what you are planning to do to these men. [36]Remember when Theudas appeared? He said he was a great man, and about four hundred men joined him. But he was killed, and all his followers were scattered; they were able to do nothing. [37]Later, a man named Judas came from Galilee at the time of the registration." He also led a group of followers and was killed, and all his followers were scattered. [38]And so now I tell you: Stay away from these men, and leave them alone. If their plan comes from human authority, it will fail. [39]But if it is from God, you will not be able to stop them. You might even be fighting against God himself!"

The leaders agreed with what Gamaliel said. [40]They called the apostles in, beat them, and told them not to speak in the name of Jesus again. Then they let them go free. [41]The apostles left the meeting full of joy because they were given the honor of suffering disgrace for Jesus. [42]Every day in the Temple and in people's homes they continued teaching the people and telling the Good News—that Jesus is the Christ.

SEVEN LEADERS ARE CHOSEN

6 The number of followers was growing. But during this same time, the Greek-speaking followers had an argument with the other followers. The Greek-speaking widows were not getting their share of the food that was given out every day. [2]The twelve apostles called the whole group of followers together and said, "It is not right for us to stop our work of teaching God's word in order to serve tables. [3]So, brothers and sisters, choose seven of your own men who are good, full of the Spirit and full of wisdom. We will put them in charge of this work. [4]Then we can continue to pray and to teach the word of God."

[5]The whole group liked the idea, so they chose these seven men: Stephen (a man with

Acts 5:31

Hip, cool, and off the hook—these are ways of talking about things that are "in." If you are a member of the cool crowd, you may feel "in." But when it comes to God, anyone who is not in Jesus Christ is "out." The Bible says, "Jesus is the One whom God raised to be on his right side, as Leader and Savior. Through him, all people could change their hearts and lives and have their sins forgiven" (Acts 5:31).

We know that everyone breaks God's rules and sins. Because of our sin, we couldn't get close to God. We were doomed—without hope—unless God did something! Here's what God did: he says those who believe in Jesus Christ are definitely in! There is no special treatment for certain kinds of people. Everyone can be close to God.

The only way to get in with God? Believe that Jesus, the Son of God, died for your sins and was raised to life again. Accept him as the Leader and Savior of your life and follow him.

It's not hard to get in with God, but it is a limited time offer. If you haven't chosen Jesus to be Lord of your life before your time runs out, then you're out—forever. So get in with God now!

⭐ **5:37 registration** Census. A counting of all the people and the things they own.

WORLD SPORTS

Snowboarding

You've probably heard of snowboarding, but did you know that there are four types? *Freeriding* is all about boarding down the mountain for fun. *Freestyle* uses ramps and half-pipes to score massive air (make jumps). *Alpine* snowboarders carve to the extreme; they lean so far to the side that their whole body touches the snow. Finally, riders who blaze their own trails (outside of established ski slopes) are doing *backcountry* snowboarding. Snowboarding is a fun sport to do with buddies—people who can spot your jumps and push you to try new things. Same goes for walking with God—it's important to have other Christian friends to support your faith.

great faith and full of the Holy Spirit), Philip,[n] Procorus, Nicanor, Timon, Parmenas, and Nicolas (a man from Antioch who had become a follower of the Jewish religion). [6]Then they put these men before the apostles, who prayed and laid their hands[n] on them.

[7]The word of God was continuing to spread. The group of followers in Jerusalem increased, and a great number of the Jewish priests believed and obeyed.

STEPHEN IS ACCUSED

[8]Stephen was richly blessed by God who gave him the power to do great miracles and signs among the people. [9]But some people were against him. They belonged to the synagogue of Free Men[n] (as it was called), which included people from Cyrene, Alexandria, Cilicia, and Asia. They all came and argued with Stephen.

[10]But the Spirit was helping him to speak with wisdom, and his words were so strong that they could not argue with him. [11]So they secretly urged some men to say, "We heard Stephen speak against Moses and against God."

[12]This upset the people, the elders, and the teachers of the law. They came and grabbed Stephen and brought him to a meeting of the leaders. [13]They brought in some people to tell lies about Stephen, saying, "This man is always speaking against this holy place and the law of Moses. [14]We heard him say that Jesus from Nazareth will destroy this place and that Jesus will change the customs Moses gave us." [15]All the people in the meeting were watching Stephen closely and saw that his face looked like the face of an angel.

STEPHEN'S SPEECH

7 The high priest said to Stephen, "Are these things true?"

[2]Stephen answered, "Brothers and fathers, listen to me. Our glorious God appeared to Abraham, our ancestor, in Mesopotamia before he lived in Haran. [3]God said to Abraham, 'Leave your country and your relatives, and go to the land I will show you.'[n] [4]So Abraham left the country of Chaldea and went to live in Haran. After Abraham's father died, God sent him to this place where you now live. [5]God did not give Abraham any of this land, not even a foot of it. But God promised that he would give this land to him and his descendants, even before Abraham had a child. [6]This is what God said to him: 'Your descendants will be strangers in a land they don't own. The people there will make them slaves and will mistreat them for four hundred years. [7]But I will punish the nation where they are slaves. Then your descendants will leave that land and will worship me in this place.'[n] [8]God made an agreement with Abraham, the sign of which was circumcision. And so when Abraham had his son Isaac, Abraham circumcised him when he was eight days old. Isaac also circumcised his son Jacob, and Jacob did the same for his sons, the twelve ancestors[n] of our people.

[9]"Jacob's sons became jealous of Joseph and sold him to be a slave in Egypt. But God was with him [10]and saved him from all his troubles. The king of Egypt liked Joseph and respected him because of the wisdom God gave him. The king made him governor of Egypt and put him in charge of all the people in his palace.

[11]"Then all the land of Egypt and Canaan became so dry that nothing would grow, and the people suffered very much. Jacob's sons,

dare to do

Luke 12:2
Read It: One day all your secrets will be shown for the world to see.
Do It: The next time you are by yourself, ask, "Would I want the whole world to see me doing this?"

Luke 12:8
Read It: If you tell other people you belong to Jesus, he will tell God that you belong to him.
Do It: Show people you belong to Jesus. You can start by getting baptized.

Luke 12:12
Read It: The Holy Spirit will help you to share about Jesus.
Do It: Before you start to speak, pause for a second and ask the Holy Spirit to help you know what to say.

6:5 Philip Not the apostle named Philip. **6:6 laid their hands** The laying on of hands had many purposes, including the giving of a blessing, power, or authority. **6:9 Free Men** Jewish people who had been slaves or whose fathers had been slaves, but were now free. **7:3 'Leave . . . you.'** Quotation from Genesis 12:1. **7:6–7 'Your descendants . . . place.'** Quotation from Genesis 15:13–14 and Exodus 3:12. **7:8 twelve ancestors** Important ancestors of the people of Israel; the leaders of the twelve tribes of Israel.

dare to do

Luke 12:20

Read It: If you died tonight, someone else would get all your stuff. You can't take it with you.

Do It: Give your money to God. You could put it in the offering at church or send it to missionaries. Besides, it's his money anyway!

Luke 12:23

Read It: Life is a lot more than food and clothes.

Do It: Ask your parents if you can try fasting (going without food to concentrate on God) for one meal. Spend the extra time praying.

Luke 12:31

Read It: When your focus in life is to get near to God, he takes care of everything else.

Do It: Start right now! Open your Bible and pray, "God, I want to know you!"

our ancestors, could not find anything to eat. [12]But when Jacob heard there was grain in Egypt, he sent his sons there. This was their first trip to Egypt. [13]When they went there a second time, Joseph told his brothers who he was, and the king learned about Joseph's family. [14]Then Joseph sent messengers to invite Jacob, his father, to come to Egypt along with all his relatives (seventy-five persons altogether), [15]So Jacob went down to Egypt, where he and his sons died. [16]Later their bod-

ies were moved to Shechem and put in a grave there. (It was the same grave Abraham had bought for a sum of money from the sons of Hamor in Shechem.)

[17]"The promise God made to Abraham was soon to come true, and the number of people in Egypt grew large. [18]Then a new king, who did not know who Joseph was, began to rule Egypt. [19]This king tricked our people and was cruel to our ancestors, forcing them to leave their babies outside to die. [20]At this time Moses was born, and he was very beautiful. For three months Moses was cared for in his father's house. [21]When they put Moses outside, the king's daughter adopted him and raised him as if he were her own son. [22]The Egyptians taught Moses everything they knew, and he was a powerful man in what he said and did.

[23]"When Moses was about forty years old, he thought it would be good to visit his own people, the people of Israel. [24]Moses saw an Egyptian mistreating one of his people, so he defended the Israelite and punished the Egyptian by killing him. [25]Moses thought his own people would understand that God was using him to save them, but they did not. [26]The next day when Moses saw two men of Israel fighting, he tried to make peace between them. He said, 'Men, you are brothers. Why are you hurting each other?' [27]The man who was hurting the other pushed Moses away and said, 'Who made you our ruler and judge? [28]Are you going to kill me as you killed the Egyptian yesterday?'[n] [29]When Moses heard him say this, he left Egypt and went to live in the land of Midian where he was a stranger. While Moses lived in Midian, he had two sons.

[30]"Forty years later an angel appeared to Moses in the flames of a burning bush as he was in the desert near Mount Sinai. [31]When Moses saw this, he was amazed and went near to look closer. Moses heard the Lord's voice say, [32]'I am the God of your ancestors, the God of Abraham, Isaac, and Jacob.'[n] Moses began to shake with fear and was afraid to look. [33]The Lord said to him, 'Take off your sandals, because you are standing on holy ground. [34]I have seen the troubles my people have suffered in Egypt. I have heard their cries and have come down to save them. And now, Moses, I am sending you back to Egypt.'[n]

[35]"This Moses was the same man the two men of Israel rejected, saying, 'Who made you a ruler and judge?'[n] Moses is the same man God sent to be a ruler and savior, with the help of the angel that Moses saw in the burning bush. [36]So Moses led the people out of Egypt. He worked miracles and signs in Egypt, at the

Red Sea, and then in the desert for forty years. [37]This is the same Moses that said to the people of Israel, 'God will give you a prophet like me, who is one of your own people.'[n] [38]This is the Moses who was with the gathering of the Israelites in the desert. He was with the angel that spoke to him at Mount Sinai, and he was with our ancestors. He received commands from God that give life, and he gave those commands to us.

[39]"But our ancestors did not want to obey Moses. They rejected him and wanted to go back to Egypt. [40]They said to Aaron, 'Make us gods who will lead us. Moses led us out of Egypt, but we don't know what has happened to him.'[n] [41]So the people made an idol that looked like a calf. Then they brought sacrifices to it and were proud of what they had made with their own hands. [42]But God turned against them and did not try to stop them from worshiping the sun, moon, and stars. This is what is written in the book of the prophets: God says,

'People of Israel, you did not bring me
      sacrifices and offerings
   while you traveled in the desert for forty
      years.
[43]You have carried with you
   the tent to worship Molech
   and the idols of the star god Rephan
      that you made to worship.
So I will send you away beyond Babylon.'

Amos 5:25–27

[44]"The Holy Tent where God spoke to our ancestors was with them in the desert. God told Moses how to make this Tent, and he made it like the plan God showed him. [45]Later, Joshua led our ancestors to capture the lands

DID YOU KNOW?

20% of middle and high schoolers consider their grandparents role models.

Trends & Tudes. Harris Interactive. July 2005.

YOU SPEAK OUT!

Q: Why should Christians tell other people about Jesus?
A: "So there will be more Christians in the world." (C.J., 11)

Q: What do you worry about?
A: "I worry about encountering spiders." (Jason, 9)

Q: What is the coolest part of being your age?
A: "Having more freedom to do things that I did not have when I was younger or smaller." (Jason, 9)

of the other nations. Our people went in, and God forced the other people out. When our people went into this new land, they took with them this same Tent they had received from their ancestors. They kept it until the time of David, 46who pleased God and asked God to let him build a house for him, the God of Jacob." 47But Solomon was the one who built the Temple.

48"But the Most High does not live in houses that people build with their hands. As the prophet says:

49'Heaven is my throne,
and the earth is my footstool.

So do you think you can build a house for
me? says the Lord.
Do I need a place to rest?
50Remember, my hand made all these things!'"

Isaiah 66:1–2

51Stephen continued speaking: "You stubborn people! You have not given your hearts to God, nor will you listen to him! You are always against what the Holy Spirit is trying to tell you, just as your ancestors were. 52Your ancestors tried to hurt every prophet who ever lived. Those prophets said long ago that the One who is good would come, but your ances-tors killed them. And now you have turned against and killed the One who is good. 53You received the law of Moses, which God gave you through his angels, but you haven't obeyed it."

STEPHEN IS KILLED

54When the leaders heard this, they became furious. They were so mad they were grinding their teeth at Stephen. 55But Stephen was full of the Holy Spirit. He looked up to heaven and saw the glory of God and Jesus standing at God's right side. 56He said, "Look! I see heaven open and the Son of Man standing at God's right side."

57Then they shouted loudly and covered their ears and all ran at Stephen. 58They took him out of the city and began to throw stones at him to kill him. And those who told lies against Stephen left their coats with a young man named Saul. 59While they were throwing stones, Stephen prayed, "Lord Jesus, receive my spirit." 60He fell on his knees and cried in a loud voice, "Lord, do not hold this sin against them." After Stephen said this, he died.

8 Saul agreed that the killing of Stephen was good.

TROUBLES FOR THE BELIEVERS

On that day the church of Jerusalem began to be persecuted, and all the believers, except the apostles, were scattered throughout Judea and Samaria.

2And some religious people buried Stephen and cried loudly for him. 3Saul was also trying

COOL!

The Toughest Shield

If you put a piece of tough, see-through plastic (the technical name is polycarbonate laminate) between two layers of glass, it will stop a bullet! The special plastic causes the force of the bullet to be spread throughout the material, so the bullet can't get through.

You would feel pretty safe hanging out behind that bullet-proof shield, wouldn't you? You can also feel safe spiritually when you stay behind the "shield of faith" (see Ephesians 6:16). This shield will protect you from the devil's temptation "bullets"!

7:46 Jacob Some Greek copies read "the house of Jacob." This means the people of Israel.

BIBLE SUPERHEROES

Silas

See Acts 15:22–17:15.

Silas was a prophet and a leader in the Jerusalem church. He went with the apostle Paul and Barnabas on their preaching trips. He was with Paul in the city of Philippi where they were beaten and thrown in jail.

Silas didn't quit after such bad treatment. He followed Paul to cities like Berea and Corinth and Athens. They started the church in Thessalonica, then had to sneak out of town to keep from being killed.

This may be the same guy Peter referred to when he said, "I wrote this short letter with the help of Silas, who I know is a faithful brother in Christ" (1 Peter 5:12).

This faithful brother didn't mind serving in the shadow of others as long as Jesus Christ got the glory.

to destroy the church, going from house to house, dragging out men and women and putting them in jail. [4]And wherever they were scattered, they told people the Good News.

PHILIP PREACHES IN SAMARIA

[5]Philip went to the city of Samaria and preached about the Christ. [6]When the people there heard Philip and saw the miracles he was doing, they all listened carefully to what he said. [7]Many of these people had evil spirits in them, but Philip made the evil spirits leave. The spirits made a loud noise when they came out. Philip also healed many weak and crippled people there. [8]So the people in that city were very happy.

[9]But there was a man named Simon in that city. Before Philip came there, Simon had practiced magic and amazed all the people of Samaria. He bragged and called himself a great man. [10]All the people—the least important and the most important—paid attention to Simon, saying, "This man has the power of God, called 'the Great Power'!" [11]Simon had amazed them with his magic so long that the people became his followers. [12]But when Philip told them the Good News about the kingdom of God and the power of Jesus Christ, men and women believed Philip and were baptized. [13]Simon himself believed, and after he was baptized, he stayed very close to Philip. When he saw the miracles and the powerful things Philip did, Simon was amazed.

[14]When the apostles who were still in Jerusalem heard that the people of Samaria had accepted the word of God, they sent Peter and John to them. [15]When Peter and John arrived, they prayed that the Samaritan believers might receive the Holy Spirit. [16]These people had been baptized in the name of the Lord Jesus, but the Holy Spirit had not yet come upon any of them. [17]Then, when the two apostles began laying their hands on the people, they received the Holy Spirit.

[18]Simon saw that the Spirit was given to people when the apostles laid their hands on them. So he offered the apostles money, [19]saying, "Give me also this power so that anyone on whom I lay my hands will receive the Holy Spirit."

[20]Peter said to him, "You and your money should both be destroyed, because you thought you could buy God's gift with money. [21]You cannot share with us in this work since your heart is not right before God. [22]Change your heart! Turn away from this evil thing you have done, and pray to the Lord. Maybe he will forgive you for thinking this. [23]I see that you are full of bitter jealousy and ruled by sin."

[24]Simon answered, "Both of you pray for

GET CONNECTED

ARGUING

Have you ever lost an argument when you knew you were right? Have you ever thought, *He's just better at arguing than I am*? Well, you're not alone. Still, no guy wants to lose. So what's the secret to winning an argument?

Ephesians 4:29 says, "Say what people need—words that will help others become stronger." That may not sound like a way to win an argument, but it is. When the person you're arguing with becomes *more important* to you than winning the argument, everyone wins.

me to the Lord so the things you have said will not happen to me."

[25] After Peter and John told the people what they had seen Jesus do and after they had spoken the message of the Lord, they went back to Jerusalem. On the way, they went through many Samaritan towns and preached the Good News to the people.

PHILIP TEACHES AN ETHIOPIAN

[26] An angel of the Lord said to Philip, "Get ready and go south to the road that leads down to Gaza from Jerusalem—the desert road." [27] So Philip got ready and went. On the road he saw a man from Ethiopia, a eunuch. He was an important officer in the service of Candace, the queen of the Ethiopians; he was responsible for taking care of all her money. He had gone to Jerusalem to worship. [28] Now, as he was on his way home, he was sitting in his chariot reading from the Book of Isaiah, the prophet. [29] The Spirit said to Philip, "Go to that chariot and stay near it."

[30] So when Philip ran toward the chariot, he heard the man reading from Isaiah the prophet. Philip asked, "Do you understand what you are reading?"

[31] He answered, "How can I understand unless someone explains it to me?" Then he invited Philip to climb in and sit with him. [32] The portion of Scripture he was reading was this:

"He was like a sheep being led to be killed.
    He was quiet, as a lamb is quiet while its
        wool is being cut;
he never opened his mouth.
[33]   He was shamed and was treated unfairly.
    He died without children to continue his
        family.
    His life on earth has ended."

Isaiah 53:7–8

[34] The officer said to Philip, "Please tell me, who is the prophet talking about—himself or someone else?" [35] Philip began to speak, and starting with this same Scripture, he told the man the Good News about Jesus.

[36] While they were traveling down the road, they came to some water. The officer said, "Look, here is water. What is stopping me from being baptized?" [[37] Philip answered, "If you believe with all your heart, you can." The officer said, "I believe that Jesus Christ is the Son of God."] [38] Then the officer commanded the chariot to stop. Both Philip and the officer went down into the water, and Philip baptized him. [39] When they came up out of the water, the Spirit of the Lord took Philip away; the officer never saw him again. And the officer continued on his way home, full of joy. [40] But Philip

appeared in a city called Azotus and preached the Good News in all the towns on the way from Azotus to Caesarea.

SAUL IS CONVERTED

9 In Jerusalem Saul was still threatening the followers of the Lord by saying he would kill them. So he went to the high priest [2] and asked him to write letters to the synagogues in the city of Damascus. Then if Saul found any followers of Christ's Way, men or women, he would arrest them and bring them back to Jerusalem.

[3] So Saul headed toward Damascus. As he came near the city, a bright light from heaven suddenly flashed around him. [4] Saul fell to the ground and heard a voice saying to him, "Saul, Saul! Why are you persecuting me?"

[5] Saul said, "Who are you, Lord?"

The voice answered, "I am Jesus, whom you are persecuting. [6] Get up now and go into the city. Someone there will tell you what you must do."

[7] The people traveling with Saul stood there but said nothing. They heard the voice, but they saw no one. [8] Saul got up from the ground and opened his eyes, but he could not see. So those with Saul took his hand and led him into Damascus. [9] For three days Saul could not see and did not eat or drink.

[10] There was a follower of Jesus in Damascus named Ananias. The Lord spoke to Ananias in a vision, "Ananias!"

Ananias answered, "Here I am, Lord."

[11] The Lord said to him, "Get up and go to Straight Street. Find the house of Judas," and ask for a man named Saul from the city of Tarsus. He is there now, praying. [12] Saul has seen a vision in which a man named Ananias comes

ROCK SOLID

Acts 9:40

If you play video games, you know that eventually you will get shot, stung, zapped, or vaporized enough times that you will get a "Game over" message. That's no big deal, of course. Just press "Restart" and you're back in business! But in real life, there is no restart button.

Have you ever experienced real death? Perhaps the death of a grandparent or family friend? It's a pretty bizarre and confusing thing. We aren't used to saying a last goodbye. If you've ever known someone who died, you realize how final it seems. That person is just not coming back.

That's what makes Peter's words in Acts 9:40 so amazing. Because of the resurrection power and life of Jesus, he could walk into the room of a dead woman, say, "Tabitha, stand up," and see her instantly come back to life! True, after a while, she died again. But imagine the joy of the extra time she lived.

Still, no matter how great life is here on earth, or how old we are when we die, nothing beats believing in Jesus and living forever in heaven. Physical death is not the end.

Eternal life means never hearing the words "Game over." Now that you know, don't keep it to yourself. Go out and share it with the world!

8:37 **Philip . . . God."** Some Greek copies do not contain the bracketed text.   9:11 **Judas** This is not either of the apostles named Judas.

to him and lays his hands on him. Then he is able to see again."

¹³But Ananias answered, "Lord, many people have told me about this man and the terrible things he did to your holy people in Jerusalem. ¹⁴Now he has come here to Damascus, and the leading priests have given him the power to arrest everyone who worships you."

¹⁵But the Lord said to Ananias, "Go! I have chosen Saul for an important work. He must tell about me to those who are not Jews, to kings, and to the people of Israel. ¹⁶I will show him how much he must suffer for my name."

¹⁷So Ananias went to the house of Judas. He laid his hands on Saul and said, "Brother Saul, the Lord Jesus sent me. He is the one you saw on the road on your way here. He sent me so that you can see again and be filled with the Holy Spirit." ¹⁸Immediately, something that looked like fish scales fell from Saul's eyes, and he was able to see again! Then Saul got up and was baptized. ¹⁹After he ate some food, his strength returned.

SAUL PREACHES IN DAMASCUS

Saul stayed with the followers of Jesus in Damascus for a few days. ²⁰Soon he began to preach about Jesus in the synagogues, saying, "Jesus is the Son of God."

²¹All the people who heard him were amazed. They said, "This is the man who was in Jerusalem trying to destroy those who trust in this name! He came here to arrest the followers of Jesus and take them back to the leading priests."

²²But Saul grew more powerful. His proofs that Jesus is the Christ were so strong that his own people in Damascus could not argue with him.

²³After many days, they made plans to kill Saul. ²⁴They were watching the city gates day and night, but Saul learned about their plan. ²⁵One night some followers of Saul helped him leave the city by lowering him in a basket through an opening in the city wall.

SAUL PREACHES IN JERUSALEM

²⁶When Saul went to Jerusalem, he tried to join the group of followers, but they were all afraid of him. They did not believe he was really a follower. ²⁷But Barnabas accepted Saul and took him to the apostles. Barnabas explained to them that Saul had seen the Lord on the road and the Lord had spoken to Saul. Then he told them how boldly Saul had preached in the name of Jesus in Damascus.

²⁸And so Saul stayed with the followers, going everywhere in Jerusalem, preaching boldly in the name of the Lord. ²⁹He would often talk and argue with the Jewish people who spoke Greek, but they were trying to kill him. ³⁰When the followers learned about this, they took Saul to Caesarea and from there sent him to Tarsus.

³¹The church everywhere in Judea, Galilee, and Samaria had a time of peace and became stronger. Respecting the Lord by the way they lived, and being encouraged by the Holy Spirit, the group of believers continued to grow.

PETER HEALS AENEAS

³²As Peter was traveling through all the area, he visited God's people who lived in Lydda. ³³There he met a man named Aeneas, who was paralyzed and had not been able to leave his bed for the past eight years. ³⁴Peter said to him, "Aeneas, Jesus Christ heals you. Stand up and make your bed." Aeneas stood up immediately. ³⁵All the people living in Lydda and on the Plain of Sharon saw him and turned to the Lord.

Q: My dad just moved away; he wasn't very nice to me and my mom. How can God be my "father" when my real dad is so mean?

A: Nobody's father is perfect. Jesus knew this when he talked to crowds of people about God being their Heavenly Father. He explained that our Father in heaven is more powerful and also far more loving than our earthly fathers. If your dad hasn't been so great, pray for him. Read your Bible! Then you will see the true picture of your Heavenly Father.

Q: All of my friends are into snowboarding. But my dad says it's too expensive and my mom says it's too dangerous. How can I get them to change their minds?

A: There's no verse in the Bible that says snowboarding is a sin. But the Bible does say that you are to obey your parents (Ephesians 6:1). Since they've clearly given you their decision on snowboarding, you need to honor them. If this is hard for you to accept, you should pray that God will help change *your* attitude. If you continue to show them respect, they might let you try snowboarding when you are older.

Q: Are there animals to be discovered?

A: Yes. Last year biologists documented dozens of new species in the oceans, jungles, and forests. They'll do it again this year. Just when we think we know everything about God's creation, somebody always discovers a major new animal and scientists say, "How could we have missed it?"

COOL!

Stormy Weather

To become a hurricane, a storm must have steady winds above 74 miles per hour. Besides hurricanes, there are also cyclones and typhoons—two other impressive kinds of storms. Category 5 storms—the most awesome on Earth—can have wind gusts around 200 mph!

In the Bible, storms are sometimes used to picture God's anger. The Old Testament prophet Jeremiah said, "Look, the punishment from the LORD will come like a storm. His anger will be like a hurricane" (Jeremiah 23:19). But those who trust in Jesus and follow him will never have to face God's stormy anger.

PETER HEALS TABITHA

³⁶In the city of Joppa there was a follower named Tabitha (whose Greek name was Dorcas). She was always doing good deeds and kind acts. ³⁷While Peter was in Lydda, Tabitha became sick and died. Her body was washed and put in a room upstairs. ³⁸Since Lydda is near Joppa and the followers in Joppa heard that Peter was in Lydda, they sent two messengers to Peter. They begged him, "Hurry, please come to us!" ³⁹So Peter got ready and went with them. When he arrived, they took him to the upstairs room where all the widows stood around Peter, crying. They showed him the shirts and coats Tabitha had made when she was still alive. ⁴⁰Peter sent everyone out of the room and kneeled and prayed. Then he turned to the body and said, "Tabitha, stand up." She opened her eyes, and when she saw Peter, she sat up. ⁴¹He gave her his hand and helped her up. Then he called the saints and the widows into the room and showed them that Tabitha was alive. ⁴²People everywhere in Joppa learned about this, and many believed in the Lord. ⁴³Peter stayed in Joppa for many days with a man named Simon who was a tanner.

trustables

Acts 13:3

Have you ever prayed for an answer to a test question at school? It's certainly worth a try! Even though writing notes on your hand or your desk is definitely cheating, getting hints from the Almighty is probably all right. Just don't use this as an excuse not to study! God wants you to do your best.

The Bible doesn't say anything about God giving you answers in science, but he did promise to give you wisdom any time you ask for it! The Bible tells us about five very smart, godly Christian leaders. They needed God's wisdom and direction and blessing, so "they fasted and prayed" (Acts 13:3).

So what is wisdom? Wisdom is what helps you make good decisions. It guides you. It protects you from foolish thoughts and helps you see through the lies of the devil. It sheds light on difficult questions. Wisdom from God will help you know how to enjoy God's blessing on your life.

So ask God for wisdom. It's a rare gift, especially in the young. If you ask for it, God has promised he will give it. And if he does, you'll probably know better than to go into a test without studying!

"Hocus Pocus" is a phrase illusionists use when they are about to wow audiences with their "magic." Lots of guys know how to do tricks, but not all of them know how to use "magic" to make a difference for Jesus Christ. Meet a twelve-year-old "magician" named Ryan.

Ryan stood in front of seven friends on his birthday. Since he had a captive audience, he put on his cape and set up one of his favorite tricks. He raised his hand over a jar full of black ink and explained, "Just like this ink shows, our hearts are black with sin. When we believe that Jesus shed his blood for our sins, he makes us clean." Just then he released a drop of red water from a small bottle. It fell into the black ink and immediately turned it clear!

The "magic" made sense to one of Ryan's friends who became a Christian that night. If you like performing tricks, you could use it to make a difference, too!

PETER TEACHES CORNELIUS

10 At Caesarea there was a man named Cornelius, an officer in the Italian group of the Roman army. ²Cornelius was a religious man. He and all the other people who lived in his house worshiped the true God. He gave much of his money to the poor and prayed to God often. ³One afternoon about three o'clock, Cornelius clearly saw a vision. An angel of God came to him and said, "Cornelius!"

⁴Cornelius stared at the angel. He became afraid and said, "What do you want, Lord?"

The angel said, "God has heard your prayers. He has seen that you give to the poor, and he remembers you. ⁵Send some men now to Joppa to bring back a man named Simon who is also called Peter. ⁶He is staying with a man, also named Simon, who is a tanner and has a house beside the sea." ⁷When the angel who spoke to Cornelius left, Cornelius called two of his servants and a soldier, a religious man who worked for him. ⁸Cornelius explained everything to them and sent them to Joppa.

⁹About noon the next day as they came near Joppa, Peter was going up to the roof ⁿ to pray. ¹⁰He was hungry and wanted to eat, but while the food was being prepared, he had a vision. ¹¹He saw heaven opened and something coming down that looked like a big sheet being lowered to earth by its four corners. ¹²In it were all kinds of animals, reptiles, and birds. ¹³Then a voice said to Peter, "Get up, Peter; kill and eat."

¹⁴But Peter said, "No, Lord! I have never eaten food that is unholy or unclean."

¹⁵But the voice said to him again, "God has made these things clean, so don't call them 'unholy'!" ¹⁶This happened three times, and at once the sheet was taken back to heaven.

¹⁷While Peter was wondering what this vision meant, the men Cornelius sent had found Simon's house and were standing at the gate. ¹⁸They asked, "Is Simon Peter staying here?"

¹⁹While Peter was still thinking about the vision, the Spirit said to him, "Listen, three men are looking for you. ²⁰Get up and go downstairs. Go with them without doubting, because I have sent them to you."

²¹So Peter went down to the men and said, "I am the one you are looking for. Why did you come here?"

²²They said, "A holy angel spoke to Cornelius, an army officer and a good man; he worships God. All the people respect him. The angel told Cornelius to ask you to come to his house so that he can hear what you have to say." ²³So Peter asked the men to come in and spend the night.

The next day Peter got ready and went with them, and some of the followers from Joppa joined him. ²⁴On the following day they came to Caesarea. Cornelius was waiting for them and had called together his relatives and close friends. ²⁵When Peter entered, Cornelius met him, fell at his feet, and worshiped him. ²⁶But Peter helped him up, saying, "Stand up. I too am only a human." ²⁷As he talked with Cornelius, Peter went inside where he saw many people gathered. ²⁸He said, "You people

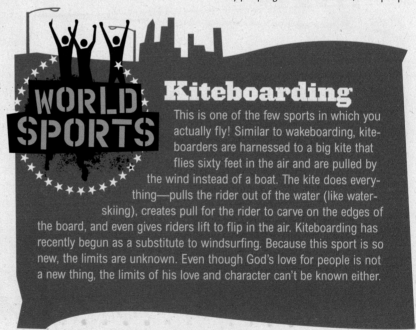

WORLD SPORTS

Kiteboarding

This is one of the few sports in which you actually fly! Similar to wakeboarding, kiteboarders are harnessed to a big kite that flies sixty feet in the air and are pulled by the wind instead of a boat. The kite does everything—pulls the rider out of the water (like waterskiing), creates pull for the rider to carve on the edges of the board, and even gives riders lift to flip in the air. Kiteboarding has recently begun as a substitute to windsurfing. Because this sport is so new, the limits are unknown. Even though God's love for people is not a new thing, the limits of his love and character can't be known either.

10:9 roof In Bible times houses were built with flat roofs. The roof was used for drying things such as flax and fruit. And it was used as an extra room, as a place for worship, and as a cool place to sleep in the summer.

understand that it is against our law for Jewish people to associate with or visit anyone who is not Jewish. But God has shown me that I should not call any person 'unholy' or 'unclean.' [29]That is why I did not argue when I was asked to come here. Now, please tell me why you sent for me."

[30]Cornelius said, "Four days ago, I was praying in my house at this same time—three o'clock in the afternoon. Suddenly, there was a man standing before me wearing shining clothes. [31]He said, 'Cornelius, God has heard your prayer and has seen that you give to the poor and remembers you. [32]So send some men to Joppa and ask Simon Peter to come. Peter is staying in the house of a man, also named Simon, who is a tanner and has a house beside the sea.' [33]So I sent for you immediately, and it was very good of you to come. Now we are all here before God to hear everything the Lord has commanded you to tell us."

[34]Peter began to speak: "I really understand now that to God every person is the same. [35]In every country God accepts anyone who worships him and does what is right. [36]You know the message that God has sent to the people of Israel is the Good News that peace has come through Jesus Christ. Jesus is the Lord of all people! [37]You know what has happened all over Judea, beginning in Galilee after John" preached to the people about baptism. [38]You know about Jesus from Nazareth, that God gave him the Holy Spirit and power. You know how Jesus went everywhere doing good and healing those who were ruled by the devil, because God was with him. [39]We saw what Jesus did in Judea and in Jerusalem, but the Jews in Jerusalem killed him by hanging him on a cross. [40]Yet, on the third day, God raised Jesus to life and caused him to be seen, [41]not by all the people, but only by the witnesses God had already chosen. And we are those witnesses who ate and drank with him after he was raised from the dead. [42]He told us to preach to the people and to tell them that he is the one whom God chose to be the judge of the living and the dead. [43]All the prophets say it is true that all who believe in Jesus will be forgiven of their sins through Jesus' name."

[44]While Peter was still saying this, the Holy Spirit came down on all those who were listening. [45]The Jewish believers who came with Peter were amazed that the gift of the Holy Spirit had been given even to the nations. [46]These believers heard them speaking in different languages" and praising God. Then Peter said, [47]"Can anyone keep these people from being baptized with water? They have received the Holy Spirit just as we did!" [48]So Peter ordered that they be baptized in the name of Jesus Christ. Then they asked Peter to stay with them for a few days.

PETER RETURNS TO JERUSALEM

11 The apostles and the believers in Judea heard that some who were not Jewish had accepted God's teaching too. [2]But when Peter came to Jerusalem, some people argued with him. [3]They said, "You went into the homes of people who are not circumcised and ate with them!"

[4]So Peter explained the whole story to them. [5]He said, "I was in the city of Joppa, and while I was praying, I had a vision. I saw something that looked like a big sheet being lowered from heaven by its four corners. It came very close to me. [6]I looked inside it and saw animals, wild beasts, reptiles, and birds. [7]I heard a voice say to me, 'Get up, Peter. Kill and eat.' [8]But I said, 'No, Lord! I have never eaten anything that is unholy or unclean.' [9]But the voice from heaven spoke again, 'God has made these things clean, so don't call them unholy.' [10]This happened three times. Then the whole thing

Q&A

Q: Why do my parents seem to argue more than anybody else's parents?

A: Your parents don't like to argue in front of other adults. If they have their disagreements when it's just you kids around, it may *seem* like they argue more than other parents. Unfortunately, all parents argue. When your mom and dad raise their voices from time to time, it doesn't mean that they don't love each other. They just don't agree at the moment.

Q: If most people want to live in peace, why are there so many wars going on?

A: As selfish, sinful beings we have so much to fight about. Each one of us has a natural desire to have power over other people. So even when there's plenty of food and land in a country, people will still fight over something, such as who gets to be in charge. True world peace could only come if everyone had God's perfect peace inside their hearts.

Q: My friends get to stay home by themselves, but my parents won't even leave me home alone for an hour. Why are they so unreasonable?

A: God tell us to always honor our parents (see Ephesians 6:1–3), even if we don't like their decisions. Your parents are probably just trying to make sure you stay safe. Talk to your parents respectfully about their rules and ask them when you might be old enough to stay by yourself. In fact, in some places it's against the law to leave a child alone until he is a certain age— your parents might be just obeying the law!

10:37 John John the Baptist, who preached to people about Christ's coming (Luke 3). **10:46 languages** This can also be translated "tongues."

dare to do

Luke 17:1
Read It: Sin is bad enough, but getting someone else to sin is the worst.
Do It: Have you ever gotten a friend to do something wrong? Apologize to him and to God today.

Luke 17:2
Read It: It would be better to have a big rock tied around your neck and be thrown into the ocean than to get a younger person to sin.
Do It: Use your influence for good; get your little brother or sister to pray with you.

Luke 17:3
Read It: If one of your Christian friends sins, warn him.
Do It: If one of your friends is doing something you know is wrong, be a real friend. Go and talk to him about breaking the habit.

was taken back to heaven. ¹¹Right then three men who were sent to me from Caesarea came to the house where I was staying. ¹²The Spirit told me to go with them without doubting. These six believers here also went with me, and we entered the house of Cornelius. ¹³He told us about the angel he saw standing in his house. The angel said to him, 'Send some men to Joppa and invite Simon Peter to come. ¹⁴By the words he will say to you, you and all your family will be saved.' ¹⁵When I began my speech, the Holy Spirit came on them just as he came on us at the beginning. ¹⁶Then I remembered the words of the Lord. He said, 'John baptized with water, but you will be baptized with the Holy Spirit.' ¹⁷Since God gave them the same gift he gave us who believed in the Lord Jesus Christ, how could I stop the work of God?"

¹⁸When the believers heard this, they stopped arguing. They praised God and said, "So God is allowing even other nations to turn to him and live."

THE GOOD NEWS COMES TO ANTIOCH

¹⁹Many of the believers were scattered when they were persecuted after Stephen was killed. Some of them went as far as Phoenicia, Cyprus, and Antioch telling the message to others, but only to Jews. ²⁰Some of these believers were people from Cyprus and Cyrene. When they came to Antioch, they spoke also to Greeks,* telling them the Good News about

the Lord Jesus. ²¹The Lord was helping the believers, and a large group of people believed and turned to the Lord.

²²The church in Jerusalem heard about all of this, so they sent Barnabas to Antioch. ²³⁻²⁴Barnabas was a good man, full of the Holy Spirit and full of faith. When he reached Antioch and saw how God had blessed the people, he was glad. He encouraged all the believers in Antioch always to obey the Lord with all their hearts, and many people became followers of the Lord.

²⁵Then Barnabas went to the city of Tarsus to look for Saul, ²⁶and when he found Saul, he brought him to Antioch. For a whole year Saul and Barnabas met with the church and taught many people there. In Antioch the followers were called Christians for the first time.

²⁷About that time some prophets came from Jerusalem to Antioch. ²⁸One of them, named Agabus, stood up and spoke with the help of the Holy Spirit. He said, "A very hard time is coming to the whole world. There will be no food to eat." (This happened when Claudius ruled.) ²⁹The followers all decided to help the believers who lived in Judea, as much as each one could. ³⁰They gathered the money and gave it to Barnabas and Saul, who brought it to the elders in Judea.

HEROD AGRIPPA HURTS THE CHURCH

12 During that same time King Herod began to mistreat some who be-

longed to the church. ²He ordered James, the brother of John, to be killed by the sword. ³Herod saw that some of the people liked this, so he decided to arrest Peter, too. (This happened during the time of the Feast of Unleavened Bread.)

⁴After Herod arrested Peter, he put him in jail and handed him over to be guarded by sixteen soldiers. Herod planned to bring Peter before the people for trial after the Passover Feast. ⁵So Peter was kept in jail, but the church prayed earnestly to God for him.

PETER LEAVES THE JAIL

⁶The night before Herod was to bring him to trial, Peter was sleeping between two soldiers, bound with two chains. Other soldiers were guarding the door of the jail. ⁷Suddenly, an angel of the Lord stood there, and a light shined in the cell. The angel struck Peter on the side and woke him up. "Hurry! Get up!" the angel said. And the chains fell off Peter's hands. ⁸Then the angel told him, "Get dressed and put on your sandals." And Peter did. Then the angel said, "Put on your coat and follow me." ⁹So Peter followed him out, but he did not know if what the angel was doing was real; he thought he might be seeing a vision. ¹⁰They went past the first and second guards and came to the iron gate that separated them from the city. The gate opened by itself for them, and they went through it. When they had walked down one street, the angel suddenly left him.

¹¹Then Peter realized what had happened. He thought, "Now I know that the Lord really sent his angel to me. He rescued me from Herod and from all the things the people thought would happen."

¹²When he considered this, he went to the home of Mary, the mother of John Mark. Many people were gathered there, praying. ¹³Peter knocked on the outside door, and a servant girl named Rhoda came to answer it. ¹⁴When she recognized Peter's voice, she was so happy she forgot to open the door. Instead, she ran inside and told the group, "Peter is at the door!"

¹⁵They said to her, "You are crazy!" But she kept on saying it was true, so they said, "It must be Peter's angel."

¹⁶Peter continued to knock, and when they opened the door, they saw him and were amazed. ¹⁷Peter made a sign with his hand to tell them to be quiet. He explained how the Lord led him out of the jail, and he said, "Tell James and the other believers what happened." Then he left to go to another place.

11:20 Greeks Some Greek copies read "Hellenists," non-Greeks who spoke Greek.

[18]The next day the soldiers were very upset and wondered what had happened to Peter. [19]Herod looked everywhere for him but could not find him. So he questioned the guards and ordered that they be killed.

THE DEATH OF HEROD AGRIPPA

Later Herod moved from Judea and went to the city of Caesarea, where he stayed. [20]Herod was very angry with the people of Tyre and Sidon, but the people of those cities all came in a group to him. After convincing Blastus, the king's personal servant, to be on their side, they asked Herod for peace, because their country got its food from his country.

[21]On a chosen day Herod put on his royal robes, sat on his throne, and made a speech to the people. [22]They shouted, "This is the voice of a god, not a human!" [23]Because Herod did not give the glory to God, an angel of the Lord immediately caused him to become sick, and he was eaten by worms and died.

[24]God's message continued to spread and reach people.

[25]After Barnabas and Saul finished their task in Jerusalem, they returned to Antioch, taking John Mark with them.

BARNABAS AND SAUL ARE CHOSEN

13 In the church at Antioch there were these prophets and teachers: Barnabas, Simeon (also called Niger), Lucius (from the city of Cyrene), Manaen (who had grown up with Herod, the ruler), and Saul. [2]They were all worshiping the Lord and fasting[n] for a certain time. During this time the Holy Spirit said to them, "Set apart for me Barnabas and Saul to do a special work for which I have chosen them."

[3]So after they fasted and prayed, they laid their hands on[n] Barnabas and Saul and sent them out.

BARNABAS AND SAUL IN CYPRUS

[4]Barnabas and Saul, sent out by the Holy Spirit, went to the city of Seleucia. From there they sailed to the island of Cyprus. [5]When they came to Salamis, they preached the Good News of God in the synagogues. John Mark was with them to help.

[6]They went across the whole island to Paphos where they met a magician named Bar-Jesus. He was a false prophet [7]who always stayed close to Sergius Paulus, the governor and a smart man. He asked Barnabas and Saul to come to him, because he wanted to hear the message of God. [8]But Elymas, the magician, was against them. (Elymas is the name for Bar-Jesus in the Greek language.) He tried to stop the governor from believing in Jesus. [9]But Saul, who was also called Paul, was filled with the Holy Spirit. He looked straight at Elymas [10]and said, "You son of the devil! You are an enemy of everything that is right! You are full of evil tricks and lies, always trying to change the Lord's truths into lies. [11]Now the Lord will touch you, and you will be blind. For a time you will not be able to see anything—not even the light from the sun."

Then everything became dark for Elymas, and he walked around, trying to find someone to lead him by the hand. [12]When the governor saw this, he believed because he was amazed at the teaching about the Lord.

PAUL AND BARNABAS LEAVE CYPRUS

[13]Paul and those with him sailed from Paphos and came to Perga, in Pamphylia. There John Mark left them to return to Jerusalem. [14]They continued their trip from Perga and went to Antioch, a city in Pisidia. On the Sabbath day they went into the synagogue and sat down. [15]After the law of Moses and the writings of the prophets were read, the leaders of the synagogue sent a message to Paul and Barnabas: "Brothers, if you have any message that will encourage the people, please speak."

[16]Paul stood up, raised his hand, and said, "You Israelites and you who worship God, please listen! [17]The God of the Israelites chose our ancestors. He made the people great during the time they lived in Egypt, and he brought them out of that country with great power. [18]And he was patient with them[n] for forty years in the desert. [19]God destroyed seven nations in the land of Canaan and gave

ROCK SOLID

Acts 13:48

Have you heard friends or other kids say things like:

"I don't want to be a Christian and obey all those rules."

"Reading the Bible is boring."

"I want to live my own life. I just want to have fun."

People who say such things have no idea what being a Christian is all about. If they think that being a Christian is just following rules or that it's boring, they got their ideas of Christianity from fakes, or they're just not clued in.

When the non-Jewish people in Antioch, a city in Pisidia, heard the apostle Paul's message about Jesus, "they were *happy* and gave honor to the message of the Lord. And the people who were chosen to have life forever believed the message" (Acts 13:48).

Being a Christian is really about being filled with an unexplainable joy that lasts forever! Does that sound boring? The more we understand who Jesus is and what he has done for us, the greater the joy we have in him.

Read the Book of Acts; and as you do, ask the Holy Spirit to open up your mind to understand and flood your heart with joy. Let your life show people what it's really like to be a Christian—it's awesome!

13:2 fasting The people would give up eating for a special time of prayer and worship to God. It was also done sometimes to show sadness and disappointment.   **13:3 laid their hands on** The laying on of hands had many purposes, including the giving of a blessing, power, or authority.   **13:18 And . . . them** Some Greek copies read "And he cared for them."

the land to his people. [20] All this happened in about four hundred fifty years.

"After this, God gave them judges until the time of Samuel the prophet. [21] Then the people asked for a king, so God gave them Saul son of Kish. Saul was from the tribe of Benjamin and was king for forty years. [22] After God took him away, God made David their king. God said about him: 'I have found in David son of Jesse the kind of man I want. He will do all I want him to do.' [23] So God has brought Jesus, one of David's descendants, to Israel to be its Savior, as he promised. [24] Before Jesus came, John[n] preached to all the people of Israel about a baptism of changed hearts and lives. [25] When he was finishing his work, he said, 'Who do you think I am? I am not the Christ. He is coming later, and I am not worthy to untie his sandals.'

[26] "Brothers, sons of the family of Abraham, and others who worship God, listen! The news about this salvation has been sent to us. [27] Those who live in Jerusalem and their leaders did not realize that Jesus was the Savior. They did not understand the words that the prophets wrote, which are read every Sabbath day. But they made them come true when they said Jesus was guilty. [28] They could not find any real reason for Jesus to be put to death, but they asked Pilate to have him killed. [29] When they had done to him all that the Scriptures had said, they took him down from the cross and laid him in a tomb. [30] But God raised him up from the dead! [31] After this, for many days, those who had gone with Jesus

from Galilee to Jerusalem saw him. They are now his witnesses to the people. [32] We tell you the Good News about the promise God made to our ancestors. [33] God has made this promise come true for us, his children, by raising Jesus from the dead. We read about this also in Psalm 2:

'You are my Son.
   Today I have become your Father.'
Psalm 2:7

[34] God raised Jesus from the dead, and he will never go back to the grave and become dust. So God said:

'I will give you the holy and sure blessings
   that I promised to David.'   *Isaiah 55:3*
[35] But in another place God says:
'You will not let your Holy One rot.'
Psalm 16:10

[36] David did God's will during his lifetime. Then he died and was buried beside his ancestors, and his body did rot in the grave. [37] But the One God raised from the dead did not rot in the grave. [38-39] Brothers, understand what we are telling you: You can have forgiveness of your sins through Jesus. The law of Moses could not free you from your sins. But through Jesus everyone who believes is free from all sins. [40] Be careful! Don't let what the prophets said happen to you:

[41] 'Listen, you people who doubt!
   You can wonder, and then die.
I will do something in your lifetime
   that you won't believe even when you
      are told about it!' "   *Habakkuk 1:5*

[42] While Paul and Barnabas were leaving the synagogue, the people asked them to tell them more about these things on the next Sabbath. [43] When the meeting was over, many people with those who had changed to worship God followed Paul and Barnabas from that place. Paul and Barnabas were persuading them to continue trusting in God's grace.

[44] On the next Sabbath day, almost everyone in the city came to hear the word of the Lord. [45] Seeing the crowd, the Jewish people became very jealous and said insulting things and argued against what Paul said. [46] But Paul and Barnabas spoke very boldly, saying, "We

BIBLE SUPERHEROES

Moses
See Exodus 33:11.

Moses spoke to God face-to-face more than anyone else except Jesus Christ. As a result, he became a powerful man of faith and a great leader.

Moses is a key figure in three world religions: Judaism, Islam, and Christianity. His name shows up more than 750 times in the Old Testament. He is a star in God's "Hall of Faith" in Hebrews 11:24–28. Although he had the chance to be rich and famous, Moses chose to suffer with God's people instead of enjoying sin for a short time. He led God's people, Israel, for many years.

Moses gladly gave up earthly riches because "he was looking for God's reward" (Hebrews 11:26). From his spot in heaven today, do you think he has any regrets?

13:24 John John the Baptist, who preached to people about Christ's coming (Luke 3).

must speak the message of God to you first. But you refuse to listen. You are judging yourselves not worthy of having eternal life! So we will now go to the people of other nations. ⁴⁷This is what the Lord told us to do, saying:

'I have made you a light for the nations;
    you will show people all over the world
        the way to be saved.' ”   *Isaiah 49:6*

⁴⁸When those who were not Jewish heard Paul say this, they were happy and gave honor to the message of the Lord. And the people who were chosen to have life forever believed the message.

⁴⁹So the message of the Lord was spreading through the whole country. ⁵⁰But the Jewish people stirred up some of the important religious women and the leaders of the city. They started trouble against Paul and Barnabas and forced them out of their area. ⁵¹So Paul and Barnabas shook the dust off their feetⁿ and went to Iconium. ⁵²But the followers were filled with joy and the Holy Spirit.

PAUL AND BARNABAS IN ICONIUM

14 In Iconium, Paul and Barnabas went as usual to the synagogue. They spoke so well that a great many Jews and Greeks believed. ²But some people who did not believe excited the others and turned

them against the believers. ³Paul and Barnabas stayed in Iconium a long time and spoke bravely for the Lord. He showed that their message about his grace was true by giving

them the power to work miracles and signs. ⁴But the city was divided. Some of the people agreed with the Jews, and others believed the apostles.

⁵Some who were not Jews, some Jews, and some of their rulers wanted to mistreat Paul and Barnabas and to stone them to death. ⁶When Paul and Barnabas learned about this, they ran away to Lystra and Derbe, cities in Lycaonia, and to the areas around those cities. ⁷They announced the Good News there, too.

PAUL IN LYSTRA AND DERBE

⁸In Lystra there sat a man who had been born crippled; he had never walked. ⁹As this man was listening to Paul speak, Paul looked straight at him and saw that he believed God could heal him. ¹⁰So he cried out, "Stand up on your feet!" The man jumped up and began walking around. ¹¹When the crowds saw what Paul did, they shouted in the Lycaonian language, "The gods have become like humans and have come down to us!" ¹²Then the people began to call Barnabas "Zeus"ⁿ and Paul "Hermes,"ⁿ because he was the main speaker. ¹³The priest in the temple of Zeus, which was near the city, brought some bulls and flowers to the city gates. He and the people wanted to

trustables

Acts 13:49–50

Change is hard. Going to a new school and a new class, moving to a new town, dealing with your parents' divorce, or a death in the family—all these things can be scary. But you can be absolutely confident of this: You are not alone. God is with you.

One of the greatest followers of Jesus, the apostle Paul, proclaimed the life-changing message of Jesus Christ throughout the Roman world (Acts 13:49–50). Every time he saw a crowd of people trust Christ, however, troubles soon followed. He was beaten, whipped, put in prison, and worse.

Later, in the city of Corinth, many people trusted Christ. In the back of his mind, Paul knew he could

be attacked any day. One night, "the Lord told Paul in a vision: 'Don't be afraid. Continue talking to people and don't be quiet. *I am with you*, and no one will hurt you because many of my people are in this city' ” (Acts 18:9–10). And God's promise came true! Paul stayed for eighteen months, safe from harm.

When life gets crazy and complicated and you're not sure you're up to the challenge, remember God's words to Paul—and keep things really simple. Do what God tells you to do in the Bible (remember to read it every day!) and trust God to be with you all the way.

13:51 shook . . . feet A warning. It showed that they had rejected these people.   **14:12 "Zeus"** The Greeks believed in many false gods, of whom Zeus was most important.   **14:12 "Hermes"** The Greeks believed he was a messenger for the other gods.

Ways to Be an Outrageous [Super] Friend

1. **Pay attention when your friend is talking.**
2. **Plan a "New Game Night," and invite everyone over.**
3. **Thank him for something he's done.**
4. **Do things your friend enjoys.**
5. **Pray for your friend.**
6. **Help with his chores.**
7. **Invite him to youth group.**
8. **Call him when he's sick.**
9. **Share your stuff.**
10. **Remember his birthday.**

and dragged him out of town, thinking they had killed him. [20]But the followers gathered around him, and he got up and went back into the town. The next day he and Barnabas left and went to the city of Derbe.

THE RETURN TO ANTIOCH IN SYRIA

[21]Paul and Barnabas told the Good News in Derbe, and many became followers. Paul and Barnabas returned to Lystra, Iconium, and Antioch, [22]making the followers of Jesus stronger and helping them stay in the faith. They said, "We must suffer many things to enter God's kingdom." [23]They chose elders for each church, by praying and fasting[n] for a certain time. These elders had trusted the Lord, so Paul and Barnabas put them in the Lord's care. [24]Then they went through Pisidia and came to Pamphylia. [25]When they had preached the message in Perga, they went down to Attalia. [26]And from there they sailed away to Antioch where the believers had put them into God's care and had sent them out to do this work. Now they had finished.

[27]When they arrived in Antioch, Paul and Barnabas gathered the church together. They told the church all about what God had done with them and how God had made it possible for those who were not Jewish to believe. [28]And they stayed there a long time with the followers.

THE MEETING AT JERUSALEM

15 Then some people came to Antioch from Judea and began teaching the non-Jewish believers: "You cannot be saved if you are not circumcised as Moses taught us." [2]Paul and Barnabas were against this teaching and argued with them about it. So the church decided to send Paul, Barnabas, and some others to Jerusalem where they could talk more about this with the apostles and elders.

[3]The church helped them leave on the trip, and they went through the countries of Phoenicia and Samaria, telling all about how the other nations had turned to God. This made all the believers very happy. [4]When they arrived in Jerusalem, they were welcomed by the apostles, the elders, and the church. Paul, Barnabas, and the others told about everything God had done with them. [5]But some of the believers who belonged to the Pharisee group came forward and said, "The non-Jewish believers must be circumcised. They must be told to obey the law of Moses."

[6]The apostles and the elders gathered to consider this problem. [7]After a long debate, Peter stood up and said to them, "Brothers, you know that in the early days God chose me from among you to preach the Good News to the nations. They heard the Good News from me, and they believed. [8]God, who knows the thoughts of everyone, accepted them. He showed this to us by giving them the Holy Spirit, just as he did to us. [9]To God, those people are not different from us. When they believed, he made their hearts pure. [10]So now why are you testing God by putting a heavy load around the necks of the non-Jewish believers? It is a load that neither we nor our an-

offer a sacrifice to Paul and Barnabas. [14]But when the apostles, Barnabas and Paul, heard about it, they tore their clothes. They ran in among the people, shouting, [15]"Friends, why are you doing these things? We are only human beings like you. We are bringing you the Good News and are telling you to turn away from these worthless things and turn to the living God. He is the One who made the sky, the earth, the sea, and everything in them. [16]In the past, God let all the nations do what they wanted. [17]Yet he proved he is real by showing kindness, by giving you rain from heaven and crops at the right times, by giving you food and filling your hearts with joy." [18]Even with these words, they were barely able to keep the crowd from offering sacrifices to them.

[19]Then some evil people came from Antioch and Iconium and persuaded the people to turn against Paul. So they threw stones at him

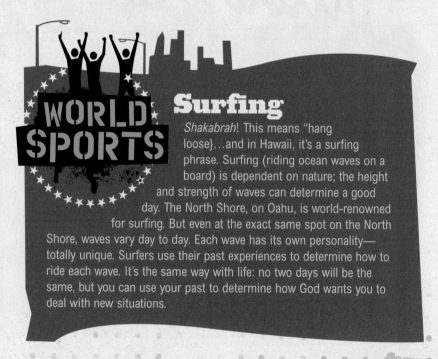

Surfing

Shakabrah! This means "hang loose}…and in Hawaii, it's a surfing phrase. Surfing (riding ocean waves on a board) is dependent on nature; the height and strength of waves can determine a good day. The North Shore, on Oahu, is world-renowned for surfing. But even at the exact same spot on the North Shore, waves vary day to day. Each wave has its own personality—totally unique. Surfers use their past experiences to determine how to ride each wave. It's the same way with life: no two days will be the same, but you can use your past to determine how God wants you to deal with new situations.

⭐ **14:23 fasting** The people would give up eating for a special time of prayer and worship to God. It was also done sometimes to show sadness and disappointment.

cestors were able to carry. [11]But we believe that we and they too will be saved by the grace of the Lord Jesus."

[12]Then the whole group became quiet. They listened to Paul and Barnabas tell about all the miracles and signs that God did through them among the people. [13]After they finished speaking, James said, "Brothers, listen to me. [14]Simon has told us how God showed his love for those people. For the first time he is accepting from among them a people to be his own. [15]The words of the prophets agree with this too:

[16]'After these things I will return.
The kingdom of David is like a fallen tent.
But I will rebuild its ruins,
and I will set it up.
[17]Then those people who are left alive may ask the Lord for help,
and the other nations that belong to me, says the Lord,
who will make it happen.
[18]And these things have been known for a long time.'   *Amos 9:11–12*

[19]"So I think we should not bother the other people who are turning to God. [20]Instead, we should write a letter to them telling them these things: Stay away from food that has been offered to idols (which makes it unclean), any kind of sexual sin, eating animals that have been strangled, and blood. [21]They should do these things, because for a long time in every city the law of Moses has been taught. And it is still read in the synagogue every Sabbath day."

LETTER TO NON-JEWISH BELIEVERS

[22]The apostles, the elders, and the whole church decided to send some of their men with Paul and Barnabas to Antioch. They chose Judas Barsabbas and Silas, who were respected by the believers. [23]They sent the following letter with them:

From the apostles and elders, your brothers.
To all the non-Jewish believers in Antioch, Syria, and Cilicia:
Greetings!
[24]We have heard that some of our group have come to you and said things that trouble and upset you. But we did not tell them to do this. [25]We have all agreed to choose some messengers and send them to you with our dear friends Barnabas and Paul— [26]people who have given their lives to serve our Lord Jesus Christ. [27]So we are sending Judas and Silas, who will tell you the same things. [28]It has pleased the Holy Spirit that you should not have a heavy load to carry, and we agree. You need to do only these things: [29]Stay away from any food that has been offered to idols, eating any animals that have been strangled, and blood, and any kind of sexual sin. If you stay away from these things, you will do well.
Good-bye.

[30]So they left Jerusalem and went to Antioch where they gathered the church and gave them the letter. [31]When they read it, they were very happy because of the encouraging message. [32]Judas and Silas, who were also prophets, said many things to encourage the believers and make them stronger. [33]After some time Judas and Silas were sent off in peace by the believers, and they went back to those who had sent them [, [34]but Silas decided to remain there]."

[35]But Paul and Barnabas stayed in Antioch and, along with many others, preached the Good News and taught the people the message of the Lord.

PAUL AND BARNABAS SEPARATE

[36]After some time, Paul said to Barnabas, "We should go back to all those towns where we preached the message of the Lord. Let's visit the believers and see how they are doing." [37]Barnabas wanted to take John Mark with them, [38]but he had left them at Pamphylia; he did not continue with them in the work. So Paul did not think it was a good idea to take him. [39]Paul and Barnabas had such a serious argument about this that they separated and went different ways. Barnabas took Mark and sailed to Cyprus, [40]but Paul chose Silas and left. The believers in Antioch put Paul into the Lord's care, [41]and he went through Syria and Cilicia, giving strength to the churches.

TIMOTHY GOES WITH PAUL

16 Paul came to Derbe and Lystra, where a follower named Timothy

Luke 18:7
Read It: God quickly answers his children who keep crying out to him.
Do It: Pick one friend of yours who doesn't know Jesus and pray long, loud, and hard for him.

Luke 18:24
Read It: It's hard to give up living for stuff in order to follow Jesus.
Do It: If your Xbox makes you happier than Jesus does, don't be afraid to get rid of it. You can spend your new free time getting to know Jesus.

Luke 18:27
Read It: What people can't do, God can.
Do It: God's the one who saves people, so talk to your friends about Jesus…but pray twice as much as you talk.

15:34 but . . . there Some Greek copies do not contain the bracketed text.

Classrooms provide amazing opportunities to make a difference for Jesus Christ. Eleven-year-old Craig found a way at his school in Colorado Springs, Colorado.

"What are you gonna write your book report about?" Craig's friend, Tony, asked.

"I think I'm going to write about *The Lion, the Witch, and the Wardrobe.*"

"Why?" Tony questioned.

"Because it's about how a lion named Aslan gave his life to save a friend from a deadly spell." Craig shoved his books into his backpack.

"But what about the lion? He dies. What kind of story is that?" Tony asked.

"He doesn't stay dead. Aslan rose again and became the hero of the rest of the story."

"Really? That's a lot like the story of what Jesus did," Tony added.

"Yeah, that's the exciting part! When I give the report, I'll be able to tell the whole class about how Jesus died for us! I wish everyone in our class could have their sins forgiven. Maybe my report will help!"

And it did! That report gave Craig several opportunities to talk about Jesus with his friends. Just like Craig, you can use book reports (and other assignments) to share God's love in the classroom.

lived. Timothy's mother was Jewish and a believer, but his father was a Greek.

[2]The believers in Lystra and Iconium respected Timothy and said good things about him. [3]Paul wanted Timothy to travel with him, but all the people living in that area knew that Timothy's father was Greek. So Paul circumcised Timothy to please his mother's people. [4]Paul and those with him traveled from town to town and gave the decisions made by the apostles and elders in Jerusalem for the people to obey. [5]So the churches became stronger in the faith and grew larger every day.

PAUL IS CALLED OUT OF ASIA

[6]Paul and those with him went through the areas of Phrygia and Galatia since the Holy Spirit did not let them preach the Good News in Asia. [7]When they came near the country of Mysia, they tried to go into Bithynia, but the Spirit of Jesus did not let them. [8]So they passed by Mysia and went to Troas. [9]That night Paul saw in a vision a man from Macedonia. The man stood and begged, "Come over to Macedonia and help us." [10]After Paul had seen the vision, we immediately prepared to leave for Macedonia, understanding that God had called us to tell the Good News to those people.

LYDIA BECOMES A CHRISTIAN

[11]We left Troas and sailed straight to the island of Samothrace. The next day we sailed to Neapolis." [12]Then we went by land to Philippi, a Roman colony" and the leading city in that part of Macedonia. We stayed there for several days.

[13]On the Sabbath day we went outside the city gate to the river where we thought we would find a special place for prayer. Some women had gathered there, so we sat down and talked with them. [14]One of the listeners was a woman named Lydia from the city of Thyatira whose job was selling purple cloth. She worshiped God, and he opened her mind to pay attention to what Paul was saying. [15]She and all the people in her house were baptized. Then she invited us to her home, saying, "If you think I am truly a believer in the Lord, then come stay in my house." And she persuaded us to stay with her.

PAUL AND SILAS IN JAIL

[16]Once, while we were going to the place for prayer, a servant girl met us. She had a special spirit" in her, and she earned a lot of money

for her owners by telling fortunes. [17]This girl followed Paul and us, shouting, "These men are servants of the Most High God. They are telling you how you can be saved."

[18]She kept this up for many days. This bothered Paul, so he turned and said to the spirit, "By the power of Jesus Christ, I command you to come out of her!" Immediately, the spirit came out.

[19]When the owners of the servant girl saw this, they knew that now they could not use her to make money. So they grabbed Paul and Silas and dragged them before the city rulers in the marketplace. [20]They brought Paul and Silas to the Roman rulers and said, "These men are Jews and are making trouble in our city. [21]They are teaching things that are not right for us as Romans to do."

20% of kids wear uniforms at school.

Trends & Tudes. Harris Interactive. September 2003.

[22]The crowd joined the attack against them. The Roman officers tore the clothes of Paul and Silas and had them beaten with rods. [23]Then Paul and Silas were thrown into jail, and the jailer was ordered to guard them carefully. [24]When he heard this order, he put them far inside the jail and pinned their feet down between large blocks of wood.

[25]About midnight Paul and Silas were praying and singing songs to God as the other prisoners listened. [26]Suddenly, there was a strong earthquake that shook the foundation of the jail. Then all the doors of the jail broke open, and all the prisoners were freed from their chains. [27]The jailer woke up and saw that the jail doors were open. Thinking that the prisoners had already escaped, he got his sword and was about to kill himself." [28]But

---

16:11 **Neapolis** City in Macedonia. It was the first city Paul visited on the continent of Europe.   16:12 **Roman colony** A town begun by Romans with Roman laws, customs, and privileges.   16:16 **spirit** This was a spirit from the devil, which caused her to say she had special knowledge.   16:27 **kill himself** He thought the leaders would kill him for letting the prisoners escape.

Paul shouted, "Don't hurt yourself! We are all here."

³⁹The jailer told someone to bring a light. Then he ran inside and, shaking with fear, fell down before Paul and Silas. ³⁰He brought them outside and said, "Men, what must I do to be saved?"

³¹They said to him, "Believe in the Lord Jesus and you will be saved—you and all the people in your house." ³²So Paul and Silas told the message of the Lord to the jailer and all the people in his house. ³³At that hour of the night the jailer took Paul and Silas and washed their wounds. Then he and all his people were baptized immediately. ³⁴After this the jailer took Paul and Silas home and gave them food. He and his family were very happy because they now believed in God.

³⁵The next morning, the Roman officers sent the police to tell the jailer, "Let these men go free."

³⁶The jailer said to Paul, "The officers have sent an order to let you go free. You can leave now. Go in peace."

³⁷But Paul said to the police, "They beat us in public without a trial, even though we are Roman citizens." And they threw us in jail. Now they want to make us go away quietly. No! Let them come themselves and bring us out."

³⁸The police told the Roman officers what Paul said. When the officers heard that Paul and Silas were Roman citizens, they were afraid. ³⁹So they came and told Paul and Silas they were sorry and took them out of jail and asked them to leave the city. ⁴⁰So when they came out of the jail, they went to Lydia's house where they saw some of the believers and encouraged them. Then they left.

PAUL AND SILAS IN THESSALONICA

17 Paul and Silas traveled through Amphipolis and Apollonia and came to Thessalonica where there was a synagogue. ²Paul went into the synagogue as he always did, and on each Sabbath day for three weeks, he talked with his fellow Jews about the Scriptures. ³He explained and proved that the Christ must die and then rise from the dead. He said, "This Jesus I am telling you about is the Christ." ⁴Some of them were convinced and joined Paul and Silas, along with many of the Greeks who worshiped God and many of the important women.

⁵But some others became jealous. So they got some evil men from the marketplace, formed a mob, and started a riot. They ran to Jason's house, looking for Paul and Silas, wanting to bring them out to the people. ⁶But when they did not find them, they dragged Jason and some other believers to the leaders of the city. The people were yelling, "These people have made trouble everywhere in the world, and now they have come here too! ⁷Jason is keeping them in his house. All of them do things against the laws of Caesar, saying there is another king, called Jesus."

⁸When the people and the leaders of the city heard these things, they became very upset. ⁹They made Jason and the others put up a sum of money. Then they let the believers go free.

PAUL AND SILAS GO TO BEREA

¹⁰That same night the believers sent Paul and Silas to Berea where they went to the synagogue. ¹¹These people were more willing to listen than the people in Thessalonica. The Bereans were eager to hear what Paul and Silas said and studied the Scriptures every day to find out if these things were true. ¹²So, many of them believed, as well as many important Greek women and men. ¹³But the people in Thessalonica learned that Paul was preaching the word of God in Berea, too. So they came there, upsetting the people and making trouble. ¹⁴The believers quickly sent Paul away to the coast, but Silas and Timothy stayed in Berea. ¹⁵The people leading Paul went with him to Athens. Then they carried a message from Paul back to Silas and Timothy for them to come to him as soon as they could.

PAUL PREACHES IN ATHENS

¹⁶While Paul was waiting for Silas and Timothy in Athens, he was troubled because he saw that the city was full of idols. ¹⁷In the synagogue, he talked with the Jews and the Greeks who worshiped God. He also talked every day with people in the marketplace. ¹⁸Some of the Epicurean and Stoic philosophers" argued with him, saying, "This man doesn't know what he is talking about. What is he trying to say?" Others said, "He seems to be telling us about some other gods," because Paul was telling them about Jesus and his rising from the dead. ¹⁹They got Paul and took him to a meeting of the Areopagus," where they said, "Please explain to us this new idea you have been teaching. ²⁰The things you are saying are new to us, and we want to know what this teaching means." ²¹(All the people of Athens and those from other countries who lived there always used their time to talk about the newest ideas.)

²²Then Paul stood before the meeting of

ROCK SOLID

Acts 17:25

God doesn't need you. In fact, you don't have anything to give God. God made everything that exists. He's the Creator—everything else is part of his creation. The Bible says, "God is the One who gives life, breath, and everything else to people. He does not need any help from them; he has everything he needs" (Acts 17:25).

Does that make you kind of uncomfortable? We like to think that God wants us, needs us, that we've earned a relationship with him. Almost like we're the center of the universe.

But that's the beauty of it. God doesn't need people at all—*he* is the center of the universe and it's all about him.

So why are we here? What's the meaning of life? We are here so that God can show how great he is and that his love has no limit!

Remember, your life is not about you. Your life is all about God. Ask him to help you focus on living your life for his glory and not your own.

16:37 Roman citizens Roman law said that Roman citizens must not be beaten before they had a trial.   **17:18 Epicurean and Stoic philosophers** Philosophers were those who searched for truth. Epicureans believed that pleasures, especially pleasures of the mind, were the goal of life. Stoics believed that life should be without feelings of joy or grief.   **17:19 Areopagus** A council or group of important leaders in Athens. They were like judges.

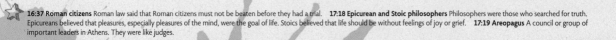

BIBLE SUPERHEROES

Mary Magdalene
See Luke 8:2–3; John 20:1-18.

Mary was from Magdala on the shores of the Sea of Galilee. She became a follower of Jesus after he set her free from seven demons (Mark 16:9).

Mary followed Jesus during his ministry. She was at the cross and watched him die. She went to his tomb on what we now call Easter Sunday to take care of his body. Instead, she met Jesus, who had risen from the dead!

Mary ran to tell Peter and the other followers the good news of the Resurrection. For this reason, she is sometimes called "the apostle to the apostles." She went on to serve Jesus and his church for the rest of her life.

Some people believe that Mary and Jesus got married and had kids. That's pure fiction! What is true is Mary's pure love for her Savior.

the Areopagus and said, "People of Athens, I can see you are very religious in all things. [23]As I was going through your city, I saw the objects you worship. I found an altar that had these words written on it: TO A GOD WHO IS NOT KNOWN. You worship a god that you don't know, and this is the God I am telling you about! [24]The God who made the whole world and everything in it is the Lord of the land and the sky. He does not live in temples built by human hands. [25]This God is the One who gives life, breath, and everything else to people. He does not need any help from them; he has everything he needs. [26]God began by making one person, and from him came all the different people who live every-

where in the world. God decided exactly when and where they must live. [27]God wanted them to look for him and perhaps search all around for him and find him, though he is not far from any of us: [28]'By his power we live and move and exist.' Some of your own poets have said: 'For we are his children.' [29]Since we are God's children, you must not think that God is like something that people imagine or make from gold, silver, or rock. [30]In the past, people did not understand God, and he ignored this. But now, God tells all people in the world to change their hearts and lives. [31]God has set a day that he will judge all the world

with fairness, by the man he chose long ago. And God has proved this to everyone by raising that man from the dead!"

[32]When the people heard about Jesus being raised from the dead, some of them laughed. But others said, "We will hear more about this from you later." [33]So Paul went away from them. [34]But some of the people believed Paul and joined him. Among those who believed was Dionysius, a member of the Areopagus, a woman named Damaris, and some others.

PAUL IN CORINTH

18 Later Paul left Athens and went to Corinth. [2]Here he met a Jew

COOL!

Mission Impossible

Camels can weigh 1,500 pounds and measure twelve feet long. They are famous for going without water for long periods—up to ten days. When they do drink, they can gulp twenty gallons in ten minutes!

Jesus mentioned camels in one of his teachings when he said, "It is easier for a camel to go through the eye of a needle than for a rich person to enter the kingdom of God" (Mark 10:25).

What Jesus meant by this saying is that it is impossible for people who focus on riches to find God. But anyone who wants to come to God can; nothing's impossible with God!

named Aquila who had been born in the country of Pontus. But Aquila and his wife, Priscilla, had recently moved to Corinth from Italy, because Claudius[n] commanded that all Jews must leave Rome. Paul went to visit Aquila and Priscilla. [3]Because they were tentmakers, just as he was, he stayed with them and worked with them. [4]Every Sabbath day he talked with the Jews and Greeks in the synagogue, trying to persuade them to believe in Jesus.

[5]Silas and Timothy came from Macedonia and joined Paul in Corinth. After this, Paul spent all his time telling people the Good News, showing them that Jesus is the Christ. [6]But they would not accept Paul's teaching and said some evil things. So he shook off the dust from his clothes[n] and said to them, "If you are not saved, it will be your own fault! I have done all I can do! After this, I will go to other nations." [7]Paul left the synagogue and moved into the home of Titius Justus, next to the synagogue. This man worshiped God. [8]Crispus was the leader of that synagogue, and he and all the people living in his house believed in the Lord. Many others in Corinth also listened to Paul and believed and were baptized.

[9]During the night, the Lord told Paul in a vision: "Don't be afraid. Continue talking to people and don't be quiet. [10]I am with you, and no one will hurt you because many of my people are in this city." [11]Paul stayed there for a year and a half, teaching God's word to the people.

PAUL IS BROUGHT BEFORE GALLIO

[12]When Gallio was the governor of the country of Southern Greece, some people came together against Paul and took him to the court. [13]They said, "This man is teaching people to worship God in a way that is against our law."

[14]Paul was about to say something, but Gallio spoke, saying, "I would listen to you if you were complaining about a crime or some wrong. [15]But the things you are saying are only questions about words and names—arguments about your own law. So you must solve this problem yourselves. I don't want to be a judge of these things." [16]And Gallio made them leave the court.

[17]Then they all grabbed Sosthenes, the leader of the synagogue, and beat him there before the court. But this did not bother Gallio.

PAUL RETURNS TO ANTIOCH

[18]Paul stayed with the believers for many more days. Then he left and sailed for Syria, with Priscilla and Aquila. At Cenchrea Paul cut off his hair," because he had made a promise to God. [19]Then they went to Ephesus, where Paul left Priscilla and Aquila. While Paul was there, he went into the synagogue and talked with the people. [20]When they asked him to stay with them longer, he refused. [21]But as he left, he said, "I will come back to you again if God wants me to." And so he sailed away from Ephesus.

[22]When Paul landed at Caesarea, he went and gave greetings to the church in Jerusalem. After that, Paul went to Antioch. [23]He stayed there for a while and then left and went through the regions of Galatia and Phrygia. He traveled from town to town in these regions, giving strength to all the followers.

APOLLOS IN EPHESUS AND CORINTH

[24]A Jew named Apollos came to Ephesus. He was born in the city of Alexandria and was a good speaker who knew the Scriptures well. [25]He had been taught about the way of the Lord and was always very excited when he spoke and taught the truth about Jesus. But the only baptism Apollos knew about was the baptism that John[n] taught. [26]Apollos began to speak very boldly in the synagogue, and when Priscilla and Aquila heard him, they took him to their home and helped him better understand the way of God. [27]Now Apollos wanted to go to the country of Southern Greece. So the believers helped him and wrote a letter to the followers there, asking them to accept him. These followers had believed in Jesus because of God's grace, and when Apollos arrived, he helped them very much. [28]He argued very strongly with the Jews before all the people, clearly proving with the Scriptures that Jesus is the Christ.

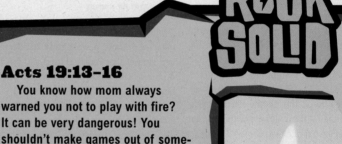

ROCK SOLID

Acts 19:13-16

You know how mom always warned you not to play with fire? It can be very dangerous! You shouldn't make games out of something as powerful as fire. You just might get burned.

The same is true of the spiritual world. It's a powerful force that God has told us about in the Bible. But some people like to make a game of it, toying with witchcraft and fortune-telling.

There's a passage in Acts that shows what can happen when you mess with the spiritual world when you're not prepared to do so. Seven brothers had heard about Jesus through the apostle Paul. They saw him casting out demons, so they decided to have some fun with it.

Once when they approached a demon-possessed man, the demon spoke back to them. "I know Jesus, and I know about Paul, but who are you?" (Acts 19:15). Then the demon got physically violent and beat up all seven brothers, sending them away naked and bleeding.

They were playing with fire when they took on the spirit world without adequate protection. The name of Jesus Christ does guard us from evil, but not when we make a game of it. Be careful about what you do for "fun." You just might get burned.

 18:2 Claudius The emperor (ruler) of Rome, A.D. 41–54.   **18:6 shook . . . clothes** This was a warning to show that Paul was finished talking to the people in that city.   **18:18 cut . . . hair** Jews did this to show that the time of a special promise to God was finished.   **18:25 John** John the Baptist, who preached to people about Christ's coming (Luke 3).

PAUL IN EPHESUS

19 While Apollos was in Corinth, Paul was visiting some places on the way to Ephesus. There he found some followers ²and asked them, "Did you receive the Holy Spirit when you believed?"

They said, "We have never even heard of a Holy Spirit."

³So he asked, "What kind of baptism did you have?"

They said, "It was the baptism that John taught."

⁴Paul said, "John's baptism was a baptism of changed hearts and lives. He told people to believe in the one who would come after him, and that one is Jesus."

⁵When they heard this, they were baptized in the name of the Lord Jesus. ⁶Then Paul laid his hands on them," and the Holy Spirit came upon them. They began speaking different languages" and prophesying. ⁷There were about twelve people in this group.

⁸Paul went into the synagogue and spoke out boldly for three months. He talked with the people and persuaded them to accept the things he said about the kingdom of God. ⁹But some of them became stubborn. They refused to believe and said evil things about the Way of Jesus before all the people. So Paul left them, and taking the followers with him, he went to the school of a man named Tyrannus. There Paul talked with people every day ¹⁰for two years. Because of his work, every Jew and Greek in Asia heard the word of the Lord.

DID YOU KNOW?

49% of kids ask questions in class when they don't understand the teacher.

Trends & Tudes. Harris Interactive. January 2003.

THE SONS OF SCEVA

¹¹God used Paul to do some very special miracles. ¹²Some people took handkerchiefs and clothes that Paul had used and put them on the sick. When they did this, the sick were healed and evil spirits left them.

¹³But some people also were traveling around and making evil spirits go out of people. They tried to use the name of the Lord Jesus to force the evil spirits out. They would say, "By the same Jesus that Paul talks about, I order you to come out!" ¹⁴Seven sons of Sceva, a leading priest, were doing this.

¹⁵But one time an evil spirit said to them, "I know Jesus, and I know about Paul, but who are you?"

¹⁶Then the man who had the evil spirit jumped on them. Because he was so much stronger than all of them, they ran away from the house naked and hurt. ¹⁷All the people in Ephesus—Jews and Greeks—learned about this and were filled with fear and gave great honor to the Lord Jesus. ¹⁸Many of the believers began to confess openly and tell all the evil things they had done. ¹⁹Some of them who had used magic brought their magic books and burned them before everyone. Those books were worth about fifty thousand silver coins."

²⁰So in a powerful way the word of the Lord kept spreading and growing.

²¹After these things, Paul decided to go to Jerusalem, planning to go through the countries of Macedonia and Southern Greece and then on to Jerusalem. He said, "After I have been to Jerusalem, I must also visit Rome." ²²Paul sent Timothy and Erastus, two of his helpers, ahead to Macedonia, but he himself stayed in Asia for a while.

TROUBLE IN EPHESUS

²³And during that time, there was some serious trouble in Ephesus about the Way of Jesus. ²⁴A man named Demetrius, who worked with silver, made little silver models that looked like the temple of the goddess Artemis." Those who did this work made much money. ²⁵Demetrius had a meeting with them and some others who did the same kind of work. He told them, "Men, you know that we make a lot of money from our business. ²⁶But look at what this man Paul is doing. He has convinced and turned away many people in Ephesus and in almost all of Asia! He says the gods made by human hands are not real. ²⁷There is a danger that our business will lose its good name, but there is also another danger: People will begin to think that the temple of the great goddess Artemis is not important. Her greatness will be destroyed, and Artemis is the goddess that everyone in Asia and the whole world worships."

²⁸When the others heard this, they became very angry and shouted, "Artemis, the goddess of Ephesus, is great!" ²⁹The whole city became confused. The people grabbed Gaius and Aristarchus, who were from Macedonia and were traveling with Paul, and ran to the theater. ³⁰Paul wanted to go in and talk to the crowd, but the followers did not let him. ³¹Also, some leaders of Asia who were friends of Paul sent him a message, begging him not to go into the theater. ³²Some people were

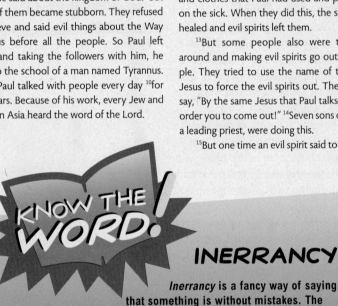

KNOW THE WORD!

INERRANCY

Inerrancy is a fancy way of saying that something is without mistakes. The Bible is inerrant because it is totally true in every way. The Bible wasn't just written by human authors such as the apostle Paul. The ideas that the Bible's authors wrote were from God's mind. The authors used their own words to express the message...but God made sure that everything they said was the truth.

It's important that the Bible is inerrant because that means that we can trust it. If the Bible says it, you can believe it! God made sure that his Word was inerrant so that we can study it to know him personally.

19:6 laid his hands on them The laying on of hands had many purposes, including the giving of a blessing, power, or authority.   **19:6 languages** This can also be translated "tongues."   **19:19 fifty thousand silver coins** Probably drachmas. One coin was enough to pay a worker for one day's labor.   **19:24 Artemis** A Greek goddess that the people of Asia Minor worshiped.

SMART TIPS!

Throw Away Old Socks

Socks are cheap! Why hang on to old, dirty socks that have holes in them? It's a lot like hanging on to little sins in our lives. We should get rid of dirty socks just like we should get rid of sins, because both can make you stink!

shouting one thing, and some were shouting another. The meeting was completely confused; most of them did not know why they had come together. ³³They put a man named Alexander in front of the people, and some of them told him what to do. Alexander waved his hand so he could explain things to the people. ³⁴But when they saw that Alexander was a Jew, they all shouted the same thing for two hours: "Great is Artemis of Ephesus!"

³⁵Then the city clerk made the crowd be quiet. He said, "People of Ephesus, everyone knows that Ephesus is the city that keeps the temple of the great goddess Artemis and her holy stone" that fell from heaven. ³⁶Since no one can say this is not true, you should be quiet. Stop and think before you do anything. ³⁷You brought these men here, but they have not said anything evil against our goddess or stolen anything from her temple. ³⁸If Demetrius and those who work with him have a charge against anyone they should go to the courts and judges where they can argue with each other. ³⁹If there is something else you want to talk about, it can be decided at the regular town meeting of the people. ⁴⁰I say this because some people might see this trouble today and say that we are rioting. We could not explain this, because there is no real reason for this meeting." ⁴¹After the city clerk said these things, he told the people to go home.

PAUL IN MACEDONIA AND GREECE

20 When the trouble stopped, Paul sent for the followers to come to him. After he encouraged them and then told them good-bye, he left and went to the country of Macedonia. ²He said many things to strengthen the followers in the different places on his way through Macedonia. Then he went to Greece, ³where he stayed for three months. He was ready to sail for Syria, but some evil people were planning something against him. So Paul decided to go back through Macedonia to Syria. ⁴The men who went with him were Sopater son of Pyrrhus, from the city of Berea; Aristarchus and Secundus, from the city of Thessalonica; Gaius, from Derbe; Timothy; and Tychicus and Trophimus, two men from Asia. ⁵These men went on ahead and waited for us at Troas. ⁶We sailed from Philippi after the Feast of Unleavened Bread. Five days later we met them in Troas, where we stayed for seven days.

PAUL'S LAST VISIT TO TROAS

⁷On the first day of the week," we all met together to break bread," and Paul spoke to the group. Because he was planning to leave the next day, he kept on talking until midnight. ⁸We were all together in a room upstairs, and there were many lamps in the room. ⁹A young man named Eutychus was sitting in the window. As Paul continued talking, Eutychus was falling into a deep sleep. Finally, he went sound asleep and fell to the ground from the third floor. When they picked him up, he was dead. ¹⁰Paul went down to Eutychus, knelt down, and put his arms around him. He said, "Don't worry. He is alive now." ¹¹Then Paul went upstairs again, broke bread, and ate. He spoke to them a long time, until it was early morning, and then he left. ¹²They took the young man home alive and were greatly comforted.

THE TRIP FROM TROAS TO MILETUS

¹³We went on ahead of Paul and sailed for the city of Assos, where he wanted to join us on the ship. Paul planned it this way because he wanted to go to Assos by land. ¹⁴When he met us there, we took him aboard and went to Mitylene. ¹⁵We sailed from Mitylene and the next day came to a place near Kios. The following day we sailed to Samos, and the next day we reached Miletus. ¹⁶Paul had already decided not to stop at Ephesus, because he did not want to stay too long in Asia. He was hurrying to be in Jerusalem on the day of Pentecost, if that were possible.

THE ELDERS FROM EPHESUS

¹⁷Now from Miletus Paul sent to Ephesus and called for the elders of the church. ¹⁸When they came to him, he said, "You know about my life from the first day I came to Asia. You know the way I lived all the time I was with you. ¹⁹The evil people made plans against me, which troubled me very much. But you know I

dare to do

John 15:4
Read It: It's impossible to make a positive difference in the world without a relationship with God.
Do It: Before you do anything, pray about it and ask God to work through you.

John 15:8
Read It: Good works prove you are a Christian.
Do It: Don't try to blend in. You should stand out as someone who chooses to do what is right.

John 15:12
Read It: Love the people around you like God has loved you.
Do It: Since God loves you despite your flaws, you should show love to people who may not be easy to get along with.

19:35 holy stone Probably a meteorite or stone that the people thought looked like Artemis.   **20:7 first day of the week** Sunday, which for Jews began at sunset on our Saturday. But if in this part of Asia a different system of time was used, then the meeting was on our Sunday night.   **20:7 break bread** Probably the Lord's Supper, the special meal that Jesus told his followers to eat to remember him (Luke 22:14–20).

always served the Lord unselfishly, and I often cried. 20You know I preached to you and did not hold back anything that would help you. You know that I taught you in public and in your homes. 21I warned both Jews and Greeks to change their lives and turn to God and believe in our Lord Jesus. 22But now I must obey the Holy Spirit and go to Jerusalem. I don't know what will happen to me there. 23I know only that in every city the Holy Spirit tells me that troubles and even jail wait for me. 24I don't care about my own life. The most important thing is that I complete my mission, the work that the Lord Jesus gave me—to tell people the Good News about God's grace.

25"And now, I know that none of you among whom I was preaching the kingdom of God will ever see me again. 26So today I tell you that if any of you should be lost, I am not responsible, 27because I have told you everything God wants you to know. 28Be careful for yourselves and for all the people the Holy Spirit has given to you to oversee. You must be like shepherds to the church of God," which he bought with the death of his own son. 29I know that after I leave, some people will come like wild wolves and try to destroy the flock. 30Also, some from your own group will rise up and twist the truth and will lead away followers after them. 31So be careful! Always remember that for three years, day and night, I never stopped warning each of you, and I often cried over you.

32"Now I am putting you in the care of God and the message about his grace. It is able to give you strength, and it will give you the blessings God has for all his holy people. 33When I was with you, I never wanted anyone's money or fine clothes. 34You know I always worked to take care of my own needs and the needs of those who were with me. 35I showed you in all things that you should work as I did and help the weak. I taught you to remember the words Jesus said: 'It is more blessed to give than to receive.' "

36When Paul had said this, he knelt down with all of them and prayed. 37-38And they all cried because Paul had said they would never see him again. They put their arms around him and kissed him. Then they went with him to the ship.

PAUL GOES TO JERUSALEM

21 After we all said good-bye to them, we sailed straight to the island of Cos. The next day we reached Rhodes, and from there we went to Patara. 2There we found a ship going to Phoenicia, so we went aboard and sailed away. 3We sailed near the island of Cyprus, seeing it to the north, but we sailed on to Syria. We stopped at Tyre because the ship needed to unload its cargo there. 4We found some followers in Tyre and stayed with them for seven days. Through the Holy Spirit they warned Paul not to go to Jerusalem. 5When we finished our visit, we left and continued our trip. All the followers, even the women and children, came outside the city with us. After we all knelt on the beach and prayed, 6we said good-bye and got on the ship, and the followers went back home.

7We continued our trip from Tyre and arrived at Ptolemais, where we greeted the believers and stayed with them for a day. 8The next day we left Ptolemais and went to the city of Caesarea. There we went into the home of Philip the preacher, one of the seven helpers," and stayed with him. 9He had four unmarried daughters who had the gift of prophesying. 10After we had been there for some time, a prophet named Agabus arrived from Judea. 11He came to us and borrowed Paul's belt and used it to tie his own hands and feet. He said, "The Holy Spirit says, 'This is how evil people

---

Q: Why do my parents always side with my sister?

A: Your sister might be asking the same question about you! Unfortunately, your parents can only see the fights between you and your sister from the outside. Sometimes it's hard for them to find out what really happened. If you want to know why your parents decide things the way they do, wait until the situation has cooled down and then go and talk to them. They may be showing favoritism, but they are probably not.

Q: Is it a man's job or a woman's job to clean up the house?

A: That's a trick question. Jesus said that you are to treat other people the way you would want to be treated (Matthew 7:12). The real question should be this: if it was *your* job to keep the house clean, would *you* like help? Men and women should work together to get things done—in the house and everywhere else.

Q: Are my dead relatives watching everything I do?

A: Some people believe that our family members who have gone to heaven can see us on earth. The Bible says that when those who believe in Jesus die, they go to be with him (2 Corinthians 5:8). It does not say whether or not they can still observe what's going on down here.

⭐ **20:28 of God** Some Greek copies read "of the Lord."   **21:8 helpers** The seven men chosen for a special work described in Acts 6:1–6. Sometimes they are called "deacons."

GET CONNECTED

TRUE FRIENDS

When Marquis noticed Nathan cheating on a test, he wasn't sure what to do. He remembered that the Bible says we are to help each other with our troubles (Galatians 6:2). He decided to talk with Nathan about the cheating and encourage him to go talk to the teacher and his parents. Nathan did, and they were so glad he told them the truth that they gave him a second chance.

When your friends are in trouble, ask God to help you talk to them and see if you can help. Someday, they will be glad you did!

in Jerusalem will tie up the man who wears this belt. Then they will give him to the older leaders.' "

¹²When we all heard this, we and the people there begged Paul not to go to Jerusalem. ¹³But he said, "Why are you crying and making me so sad? I am not only ready to be tied up in Jerusalem, I am ready to die for the Lord Jesus!"

¹⁴We could not persuade him to stay away from Jerusalem. So we stopped begging him and said, "We pray that what the Lord wants will be done."

¹⁵After this, we got ready and started on our way to Jerusalem. ¹⁶Some of the followers from Caesarea went with us and took us to the home of Mnason, where we would stay. He was from Cyprus and was one of the first followers.

PAUL VISITS JAMES

¹⁷In Jerusalem the believers were glad to see us. ¹⁸The next day Paul went with us to visit James, and all the elders were there. ¹⁹Paul greeted them and told them everything God had done among the other nations through him. ²⁰When they heard this, they praised God. Then they said to Paul, "Brother, you can see that many thousands of our people have become believers. And they think it is very important to obey the law of Moses. ²¹They have heard about your teaching, that you tell our people who live among the nations to leave the law of Moses. They have heard that you tell them not to circumcise their children and not to obey customs. ²²What should we do? They will learn that you have come. ²³So we will tell you what to do: Four of our men have made a promise to

God. ²⁴Take these men with you and share in their cleansing ceremony." Pay their expenses so they can shave their heads." Then it will prove to everyone that what they have heard about you is not true and that you follow the law of Moses in your own life. ²⁵We have already sent a letter to the non-Jewish believers. The letter said: 'Do not eat food that has been offered to idols, or blood, or animals that have been strangled. Do not take part in sexual sin.' "

²⁶The next day Paul took the four men and shared in the cleansing ceremony with them. Then he went to the Temple and announced the time when the days of the cleansing ceremony would be finished. On the last day an offering would be given for each of the men.

²⁷When the seven days were almost over, some of his people from Asia saw Paul at the Temple. They caused all the people to be upset and grabbed Paul. ²⁸They shouted, "People of Israel, help us! This is the man who goes everywhere teaching against the law of Moses, against our people, and against this Temple. Now he has brought some Greeks into the Temple and has made this holy place unclean!" ²⁹(They said this because they had seen Trophimus, a man from Ephesus, with Paul in Jerusalem. They thought that Paul had brought him into the Temple.)

³⁰All the people in Jerusalem became upset. Together they ran, took Paul, and dragged him out of the Temple. The Temple doors were closed immediately. ³¹While they were trying to kill Paul, the commander of the Roman army in Jerusalem learned that there was trouble in the whole city. ³²Immediately he took some officers and soldiers and ran to the place where the crowd was gathered. When

the people saw them, they stopped beating Paul. ³³The commander went to Paul and arrested him. He told his soldiers to tie Paul with two chains. Then he asked who he was and what he had done wrong. ³⁴Some in the crowd were yelling one thing, and some were yelling another. Because of all this confusion and shouting, the commander could not learn what had happened. So he ordered the soldiers to take Paul to the army building. ³⁵When Paul came to the steps, the soldiers had to carry him because the people were ready to hurt him. ³⁶The whole mob was following them, shouting, "Kill him!"

³⁷As the soldiers were about to take Paul into the army building, he spoke to the commander, "May I say something to you?"

The commander said, "Do you speak Greek? ³⁸I thought you were the Egyptian who started some trouble against the government not long ago and led four thousand killers out to the desert."

³⁹Paul said, "No, I am a Jew from Tarsus in the country of Cilicia. I am a citizen of that important city. Please, let me speak to the people."

⁴⁰The commander gave permission, so Paul stood on the steps and waved his hand to quiet the people. When there was silence, he spoke to them in the Hebrew language.

PAUL SPEAKS TO THE PEOPLE

22 Paul said, "Brothers and fathers, listen to my defense to you." ²When they heard him speaking the Hebrew language," they became very quiet. Paul said, ³"I am a Jew, born in Tarsus in the country of Cilicia, but I grew up in this city. I was a student of Gamaliel," who carefully taught me everything

---

21:24 cleansing ceremony The special things Jews did to end the Nazirite promise.   **21:24 shave their heads** Jews did this to show that their promise was finished.   **22:2 Hebrew language** Or Aramaic, the languages of many people in this region in the first century.   **22:3 Gamaliel** A very important teacher of the Pharisees, a Jewish religious group (Acts 5:34).

about the law of our ancestors. I was very serious about serving God, just as are all of you here today. [4]I persecuted the people who followed the Way of Jesus, and some of them were even killed. I arrested men and women and put them in jail. [5]The high priest and the whole council of elders can tell you this is true. They gave me letters to the brothers in Damascus. So I was going there to arrest these people and bring them back to Jerusalem to be punished.

[6]"About noon when I came near Damascus, a bright light from heaven suddenly flashed all around me. [7]I fell to the ground and heard a voice saying, 'Saul, Saul, why are you persecuting me?' [8]I asked, 'Who are you, Lord?' The voice said, 'I am Jesus from Nazareth whom you are persecuting.' [9]Those who were with me did not understand the voice, but they saw the light. [10]I said, 'What shall I do, Lord?' The Lord answered, 'Get up and go to Damascus. There you will be told about all the things I have planned for you to do.' [11]I could not see, because the bright light had made me blind. So my companions led me into Damascus.

[12]"There a man named Ananias came to me. He was a religious man; he obeyed the law of Moses, and all the Jews who lived there respected him. [13]He stood by me and said, 'Brother Saul, see again!' Immediately I was able to see him. [14]He said, 'The God of our ancestors chose you long ago to know his plan, to see the Righteous One, and to hear words from him. [15]You will be his witness to all people, telling them about what you have seen and heard. [16]Now, why wait any longer? Get up, be baptized, and wash your sins away, trusting in him to save you.'

[17]"Later, when I returned to Jerusalem, I was praying in the Temple, and I saw a vision. [18]I saw the Lord saying to me, 'Hurry! Leave Jerusalem now! The people here will not accept the truth about me.' [19]But I said, 'Lord, they know that in every synagogue I put the believers in jail and beat them. [20]They also know I was there when Stephen, your witness, was killed. I stood there agreeing and holding the coats of those who were killing him!' [21]But the Lord said to me, 'Leave now. I will send you far away to the other nations.'"

[22]The crowd listened to Paul until he said this. Then they began shouting, "Get rid of him! He doesn't deserve to live!" [23]They shouted, threw off their coats," and threw dust into the air."

[24]Then the commander ordered the soldiers to take Paul into the army building and beat him. He wanted to make Paul tell why the people were shouting against him like this. [25]But as the soldiers were tying him up, preparing to beat him, Paul said to an officer nearby, "Do you have the right to beat a Roman citizen" who has not been proven guilty?"

[26]When the officer heard this, he went to the commander and reported it. The officer said, "Do you know what you are doing? This man is a Roman citizen."

[27]The commander came to Paul and said, "Tell me, are you really a Roman citizen?"

He answered, "Yes."

[28]The commander said, "I paid a lot of money to become a Roman citizen."

But Paul said, "I was born a citizen."

[29]The men who were preparing to question Paul moved away from him immediately. The commander was frightened because he had already tied Paul, and Paul was a Roman citizen.

PAUL SPEAKS TO LEADERS

[30]The next day the commander decided to learn why the Jews were accusing Paul. So he ordered the leading priests and the council to meet. The commander took Paul's chains off. Then he brought Paul out and stood him before their meeting.

23 Paul looked at the council and said, "Brothers, I have lived my life without guilt feelings before God up to this day." [2]Ananias," the high priest, heard this and told the men who were standing near Paul to hit him on the mouth. [3]Paul said to Ananias, "God will hit you, too! You are like a wall that has been painted white. You sit there and judge me, using the law of Moses, but you are telling them to hit me, and that is against the law."

[4]The men standing near Paul said to him, "You cannot insult God's high priest like that!"

[5]Paul said, "Brothers, I did not know this man was the high priest. It is written in the Scriptures, 'You must not curse a leader of your people.' "[n]

[6]Some of the men in the meeting were Sadducees, and others were Pharisees. Knowing this, Paul shouted to them, "My brothers, I am a Pharisee, and my father was a Pharisee. I am on trial here because I believe that people will rise from the dead."

Acts 23:16–22

If fear is keeping you silent about your faith in Jesus Christ, you're not alone. When Christians are asked why they don't tell others about the Lord, fear is almost always one of the top two or three reasons.

Would it help you to know that the greatest missionary of all time also experienced fear? That fear threatened to keep him from his God-appointed mission! Paul asked his friends to pray for him, especially during the years he was in prison.

On one occasion, God used one of Paul's young nephews to save his life (Acts 23:16–22). Imagine how brave that nephew must have been. You can be sure God was answering a lot of prayers! Later, Paul had the boldness to talk about Jesus with a governor, a king, and Caesar himself.

So what do you do? Do what Paul did; ask people to pray for you. God gives supernatural boldness if we ask him. He'll give you courage like you've never had before. If you're nervous or afraid about sharing your faith, get a group of people praying for you. Ask some of your friends, your youth group, or your family if they'll get behind you on this one and really support you in prayer.

Get ready because God may give you an extra dose of courage today!

---

[7]When Paul said this, there was an argument between the Pharisees and the Sadducees, and the group was divided. [8](The Sadducees do not believe in angels or spirits or that people will rise from the dead. But the Pharisees believe in them all.) [9]So there was a great uproar. Some of the teachers of the law, who were Pharisees, stood up and argued, "We find nothing wrong with this man. Maybe an angel or a spirit did speak to him."

[10]The argument was beginning to turn into such a fight that the commander was afraid some evil people would tear Paul to pieces. So he told the soldiers to go down and take Paul away and put him in the army building.

[11]The next night the Lord came and stood by Paul. He said, "Be brave! You have told people in Jerusalem about me. You must do the same in Rome."

[12]In the morning some evil people made a plan to kill Paul, and they took an oath not to eat or drink anything until they had killed him. [13]There were more than forty men who made this plan. [14]They went to the leading priests and the elders and said, "We have taken an oath not to eat or drink until we have killed Paul. [15]So this is what we want you to do: Send a message to the commander to bring Paul out to you as though you want to ask him more questions. We will be waiting to kill him while he is on the way here."

[16]But Paul's nephew heard about this plan and went to the army building and told Paul. [17]Then Paul called one of the officers and said, "Take this young man to the commander. He has a message for him."

[18]So the officer brought Paul's nephew to the commander and said, "The prisoner, Paul, asked me to bring this young man to you. He wants to tell you something."

[19]The commander took the young man's hand and led him to a place where they could be alone. He asked, "What do you want to tell me?"

[20]The young man said, "The Jews have decided to ask you to bring Paul down to their council meeting tomorrow. They want you to think they are going to ask him more questions. [21]But don't believe them! More than forty men are hiding and waiting to kill Paul. They have all taken an oath not to eat or drink until they have killed him. Now they are waiting for you to agree."

[22]The commander sent the young man away, ordering him, "Don't tell anyone that you have told me about their plan."

Horse Racing

Horse racing is called "the sport of kings." A horse and jockey (rider) work together to run the racecourse. Jockeys often use a *crop* (whip) to communicate with the horse. The top prize in horse racing is the Triple Crown. It's awarded when a horse wins three major races: the Kentucky Derby, the Preakness Stakes, and the Belmont Stakes. A horse must have a lot of endurance to win the Triple Crown. As Christians, if we are faithful to serve God with endurance, we will receive a crown in heaven (2 Timothy 4:8).

PAUL IS SENT TO CAESAREA

[23]Then the commander called two officers and said, "I need some men to go to Caesarea. Get two hundred soldiers, seventy horsemen, and two hundred men with spears ready to leave at nine o'clock tonight. [24]Get some horses for Paul to ride so he can be taken to Governor Felix safely." [25]And he wrote a letter that said:

[26]From Claudius Lysias.

To the Most Excellent Governor Felix: Greetings.

[27]Some of the Jews had taken this man and planned to kill him. But I learned that he is a Roman citizen, so I went with my soldiers and saved him. [28]I wanted to know why they were accusing him, so I brought him before their council meeting. [29]I learned that these people said Paul did some things that were wrong by their own laws, but no charge was worthy of jail or death. [30]When I was told that some of them were planning to kill Paul, I sent him to you at once. I also told them to tell you what they have against him.

[31]So the soldiers did what they were told and took Paul and brought him to the city of Antipatris that night. [32]The next day the horsemen went with Paul to Caesarea, but the other soldiers went back to the army building in Jerusalem. [33]When the horsemen came to Caesarea and gave the letter to the governor, they turned Paul over to him. [34]The governor read the letter and asked Paul, "What area are you from?" When he learned that Paul was from Cilicia, [35]he said, "I will hear your case when those who are against you come here, too." Then the governor gave orders for Paul to be kept under guard in Herod's palace.

PAUL IS ACCUSED

24 Five days later Ananias, the high priest, went to the city of Caesarea with some of the elders and a lawyer named Tertullus. They had come to make charges against Paul before the governor. [2]Paul was called into the meeting, and Tertullus began to accuse him, saying, "Most Excellent Felix! Our people enjoy much peace because of you, and many wrong things in our country are being made right through your wise help. [3]We accept these things always and in every place, and we are thankful for them. [4]But not wanting to take any more of your time, I beg you to be kind and listen to our few words. [5]We have found this man to be a troublemaker, stirring up his people everywhere in the world. He is a leader of the Nazarene group. [6]Also, he was trying to make the Temple unclean, but we stopped him. [And we wanted to judge him by our own law. [7]But the officer Lysias came and used much force to take him from us. [8]And Lysias commanded those who wanted to accuse Paul to come to you.]" By asking him questions yourself, you can decide if all these things are true." [9]The others agreed and said that all of this was true.

[10]When the governor made a sign for Paul

to speak, Paul said, "Governor Felix, I know you have been a judge over this nation for a long time. So I am happy to defend myself before you. [11]You can learn for yourself that I went to worship in Jerusalem only twelve days ago. [12]Those who are accusing me did not find me arguing with anyone in the Temple or stirring up the people in the synagogues or in the city. [13]They cannot prove the things they are saying against me now. [14]But I will tell you this: I worship the God of our ancestors as a follower of the Way of Jesus. The others say that the Way of Jesus is not the right way. But I believe everything that is taught in the law of Moses and that is written in the books of the Prophets. [15]I have the same hope in God that they have—the hope that all people, good and bad, will surely be raised from the dead. [16]This is why I always try to do what I believe is right before God and people.

[17]"After being away from Jerusalem for several years, I went back to bring money to my people and to offer sacrifices. [18]I was doing this when they found me in the Temple. I had finished the cleansing ceremony and had not made any trouble; no people were gathering around me. [19]But there were some people from Asia who should be here, standing before you. If I have really done anything wrong, they are the ones who should accuse me. [20]Or ask these people here if they found any wrong in me when I stood before the council in Jerusalem. [21]But I did shout one thing when I stood before them: 'You are judging me today because I believe that people will rise from the dead!'"

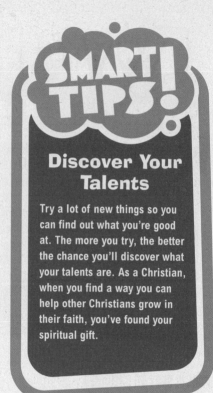

[22]Felix already understood much about the Way of Jesus. He stopped the trial and said, "When commander Lysias comes here, I will decide your case." [23]Felix told the officer to keep Paul guarded but to give him some freedom and to let his friends bring what he needed.

PAUL SPEAKS TO FELIX AND HIS WIFE

[24]After some days Felix came with his wife, Drusilla, who was Jewish, and asked for Paul to be brought to him. He listened to Paul talk about believing in Christ Jesus. [25]But Felix became afraid when Paul spoke about living right, self-control, and the time when God will judge the world. He said, "Go away now. When I have more time, I will call for you." [26]At the same time Felix hoped that Paul would give him some money, so he often sent for Paul and talked with him.

[27]But after two years, Felix was replaced by Porcius Festus as governor. But Felix had left Paul in prison to please the Jews.

PAUL ASKS TO SEE CAESAR

25 Three days after Festus became governor, he went from Caesarea to Jerusalem. [2]There the leading priests and the important leaders made charges against Paul before Festus. [3]They asked Festus to do them a favor. They wanted him to send Paul back to Jerusalem, because they had a plan to kill him on the way. [4]But Festus answered that Paul would be kept in Caesarea and that he himself was returning there soon. [5]He said, "Some of your leaders should go with me. They can accuse the man there in Caesarea, if he has really done something wrong."

[6]Festus stayed in Jerusalem another eight or ten days and then went back to Caesarea. The next day he told the soldiers to bring Paul before him. Festus was seated on the judge's seat [7]when Paul came into the room. The peo-

COOL!

Constellations

Although there are billions of stars, there are only eighty-eight official constellations according to the International Astronomical Union (IAU). The number is limited because the IAU only recognizes one constellation in each part of the sky.

The Big Dipper and Little Dipper aren't official constellations. They are what are known as "asterisms."

Several constellations are mentioned in the Bible: the Bear, Orion, and Pleiades (Job 9:9).

All the stars and constellations were created for one purpose: "The heavens declare the glory of God, and the skies announce what his hands have made" (Psalm 19:1).

ple who had come from Jerusalem stood around him, making serious charges against him, which they could not prove. ⁸This is what Paul said to defend himself: "I have done nothing wrong against the law, against the Temple, or against Caesar."

⁹But Festus wanted to please the people. So he asked Paul, "Do you want to go to Jerusalem for me to judge you there on these charges?"

¹⁰Paul said, "I am standing at Caesar's judgment seat now, where I should be judged. I have done nothing wrong to them; you know this is true. ¹¹If I have done something wrong and the law says I must die, I do not ask to be saved from death. But if these charges are not true, then no one can give me to them. I want Caesar to hear my case!"

¹²Festus talked about this with his advisers. Then he said, "You have asked to see Caesar, so you will go to Caesar!"

PAUL BEFORE KING AGRIPPA

¹³A few days later King Agrippa and Bernice came to Caesarea to visit Festus. ¹⁴They stayed there for some time, and Festus told the king about Paul's case. Festus said, "There is a man that Felix left in prison. ¹⁵When I went to Jerusalem, the leading priests and the elders there made charges against him, asking me to sentence him to death. ¹⁶But I answered, 'When a man is accused of a crime, Romans do not hand him over until he has been allowed to face his accusers and defend himself against their charges.' ¹⁷So when these people came here to Caesarea for the trial, I did not waste time. The next day I sat on the judge's seat and commanded that the man be brought in. ¹⁸They stood up and accused him, but not of any serious crime as I thought they would. ¹⁹The things they said were about their own religion and about a man named Jesus who died. But Paul said that he is still alive. ²⁰Not knowing how to find out about these questions, I asked Paul, 'Do you want to go to Jerusalem and be judged there?' ²¹But he asked to be kept in Caesarea. He wants a decision from the emperor." So I ordered that he be held until I could send him to Caesar."

²²Agrippa said to Festus, "I would also like to hear this man myself."

Festus said, "Tomorrow you will hear him."

²³The next day Agrippa and Bernice appeared with great show, acting like very important people. They went into the judgment room with the army leaders and the important men of Caesarea. Then Festus ordered the soldiers to bring Paul in. ²⁴Festus said, "King

Agrippa and all who are gathered here with us, you see this man. All the people, here and in Jerusalem, have complained to me about him, shouting that he should not live any longer. ²⁵When I judged him, I found no reason to order his death. But since he asked to be judged by Caesar, I decided to send him. ²⁶But I have nothing definite to write the emperor about him. So I have brought him before all of you—especially you, King Agrippa. I hope you can question him and give me something to write. ²⁷I think it is foolish to send a prisoner to Caesar without telling what charges are against him."

PAUL DEFENDS HIMSELF

26 Agrippa said to Paul, "You may now speak to defend yourself."

Then Paul raised his hand and began to speak. ²He said, "King Agrippa, I am very blessed to stand before you and will answer all the charges the evil people make against me. ³You know so much about all the customs and the things they argue about, so please listen to me patiently.

⁴"All my people know about my whole life, how I lived from the beginning in my own country and later in Jerusalem. ⁵They have known me for a long time. If they want to, they can tell you that I was a good Pharisee. And the Pharisees obey the laws of my tradition more carefully than any other group. ⁶Now I am on trial because I hope for the promise that God made to our ancestors. ⁷This is the promise that the twelve tribes of our people hope to receive as they serve God day and night. My king, they have accused me because I hope for this same promise! ⁸Why do any of you people think it is impossible for God to raise people from the dead?

⁹"I, too, thought I ought to do

R⚡CK SOLID

Acts 26:29

What do you value the most in your life? What gives you a sense of security and belonging and fulfillment? Your parents, your friends, school, an iPod?

How about knowing Jesus? In fact, is knowing Jesus so cool that all those other things seem worthless in comparison? The apostle Paul often talked about the supreme importance of knowing Jesus, believing in him, and trusting him for salvation. Paul once told a king and his royal court, "Whether it is a short or a long time, I pray to God that not only you but every person listening to me today would be saved and be like me—except for these chains I have" (Acts 26:29).

How can believing in Jesus and being saved be so amazing? In the Bible, the word "saved" doesn't simply mean "rescued." It means being rescued by God from sin and death and hell and being made holy, given eternal life, and knowing for sure you're going to heaven.

Are you saved? Like the king in Paul's day, you may know facts about Jesus…but do you *know* him? Jesus is so awesome, so beautiful, so loving, so good that—when you know him—he becomes all you can think about…and talk about.

dare to do

Acts 2:44
Read It: Believers in Jesus support one another's needs.
Do It: What do you have that you can share with someone? Don't be stingy with your blessings.

Acts 2:46
Read It: Believers in Jesus spend time with each other.
Do It: Are you part of a Christian club or youth group? If not, ask your parents or pastor about how you can get involved. This is a very important part of your faith.

Acts 2:47
Read It: People are drawn to God when they see his followers gathering together.
Do It: Start a Christian club at school and watch it grow!

many things against Jesus from Nazareth. ¹⁰And that is what I did in Jerusalem. The leading priests gave me the power to put many of God's people in jail, and when they were being killed, I agreed it was a good thing. ¹¹In every synagogue, I often punished them and tried to make them speak against Jesus. I was so angry against them I even went to other cities to find them and punish them.

¹²"One time the leading priests gave me permission and the power to go to Damascus. ¹³On the way there, at noon, I saw a light from heaven. It was brighter than the sun and flashed all around me and those who were traveling with me. ¹⁴We all fell to the ground. Then I heard a voice speaking to me in the Hebrew language," saying, 'Saul, Saul, why are you persecuting me? You are only hurting yourself by fighting me.' ¹⁵I said, 'Who are you, Lord?' The Lord said, 'I am Jesus, the one you are persecuting. ¹⁶Stand up! I have chosen you to be my servant and my witness—you will tell people the things that you have seen and the things that I will show you. This is why I have come to you today. ¹⁷I will keep you safe from your own people and also from the others. I am sending you to them ¹⁸to open their eyes so that they may turn away from darkness to the light, away from the power of Satan and to God. Then their sins can be forgiven, and they can have a place with those people who have been made holy by believing in me.'

¹⁹"King Agrippa, after I had this vision from heaven, I obeyed it. ²⁰I began telling people that they should change their hearts and lives and turn to God and do things to show they really had changed. I told this first to those in Damascus, then in Jerusalem, and in every part of Judea, and also to the other people. ²¹This is why the Jews took me and were trying to kill me in the Temple. ²²But God has helped me, and so I stand here today, telling all people, small and great, what I have seen. But I am saying only what Moses and the prophets said would happen— ²³that the Christ would die, and as the first to rise from the dead, he would bring light to all people."

PAUL TRIES TO PERSUADE AGRIPPA

²⁴While Paul was saying these things to defend himself, Festus said loudly, "Paul, you are out of your mind! Too much study has driven you crazy!"

²⁵Paul said, "Most excellent Festus, I am not crazy. My words are true and sensible. ²⁶King Agrippa knows about these things, and I can speak freely to him. I know he has heard about all of these things, because they did not happen off in a corner. ²⁷King Agrippa, do you believe what the prophets wrote? I know you believe."

²⁸King Agrippa said to Paul, "Do you think you can persuade me to become a Christian in such a short time?"

²⁹Paul said, "Whether it is a short or a long

time, I pray to God that not only you but every person listening to me today would be saved and be like me—except for these chains I have."

³⁰Then King Agrippa, Governor Festus, Bernice, and all the people sitting with them stood up ³¹and left the room. Talking to each other, they said, "There is no reason why this man should die or be put in jail." ³²And Agrippa said to Festus, "We could let this man go free, but he has asked Caesar to hear his case."

PAUL SAILS FOR ROME

27 It was decided that we would sail for Italy. An officer named Julius, who served in the emperor's" army, guarded Paul and some other prisoners. ²We got on a ship that was from the city of Adramyttium and was about to sail to different ports in Asia. Aristarchus, a man from the city of Thessalonica in Macedonia, went with us. ³The next day we came to Sidon. Julius was very good to Paul and gave him freedom to go visit his friends, who took care of his needs. ⁴We left Sidon and sailed close to the island of Cyprus, because the wind was blowing against us. ⁵We went across the sea by Cilicia and Pamphylia and landed at the city of Myra, in Lycia. ⁶There the officer found a ship from Alexandria that was going to Italy, so he put us on it.

⁷We sailed slowly for many days. We had a hard time reaching Cnidus because the wind was blowing against us, and we could not go any farther. So we sailed by the south side of the island of Crete near Salmone. ⁸Sailing past it was hard. Then we came to a place called Fair Havens, near the city of Lasea.

⁹We had lost much time, and it was now dangerous to sail, because it was already after the Day of Cleansing." So Paul warned them, ¹⁰"Men, I can see there will be a lot of trouble on this trip. The ship, the cargo, and even our lives may be lost." ¹¹But the captain and the owner of the ship did not agree with Paul, and the officer believed what the captain and owner of the ship said. ¹²Since that harbor was not a good place for the ship to stay for the winter, most of the men decided that the ship should leave. They hoped we could go to Phoenix and stay there for the winter. Phoenix, a city on the island of Crete, had a harbor which faced southwest and northwest.

THE STORM

¹³When a good wind began to blow from the south, the men on the ship thought, "This

---

 26:14 **Hebrew language** Or Aramaic, the languages of many people in this region in the first century.   27:1 **emperor** The ruler of the Roman Empire, which was almost all the known world.
27:9 **Day of Cleansing** An important Jewish holy day in the fall of the year. This was the time of year that bad storms arose on the sea.

is the wind we wanted, and now we have it." So they pulled up the anchor, and we sailed very close to the island of Crete. [14]But then a very strong wind named the "northeaster" came from the island. [15]The ship was caught in it and could not sail against it. So we stopped trying and let the wind carry us. [16]When we went below a small island named Cauda, we were barely able to bring in the lifeboat. [17]After the men took the lifeboat in, they tied ropes around the ship to hold it together. The men were afraid that the ship would hit the sandbanks of Syrtis," so they lowered the sail and let the wind carry the ship. [18]The next day the storm was blowing us so hard that the men threw out some of the cargo. [19]A day later with their own hands they threw out the ship's equipment. [20]When we could not see the sun or the stars for many days, and the storm was very bad, we lost all hope of being saved.

[21]After the men had gone without food for a long time, Paul stood up before them and said, "Men, you should have listened to me. You should not have sailed from Crete. Then you would not have all this trouble and loss. [22]But now I tell you to cheer up because none of you will die. Only the ship will be lost. [23]Last night an angel came to me from the God I belong to and worship. [24]The angel said, 'Paul, do not be afraid. You must stand before Caesar. And God has promised you that he will save the lives of everyone sailing with you.' [25]So men, have courage. I trust in God that everything will happen as his angel told me. [26]But we will crash on an island."

[27]On the fourteenth night we were still being carried around in the Adriatic Sea." About midnight the sailors thought we were close to land, [28]so they lowered a rope with a weight on the end of it into the water. They found that the water was one hundred twenty feet deep. They went a little farther and lowered the rope again. It was ninety feet deep. [29]The sailors were afraid that we would hit the rocks, so they threw four anchors into the water and prayed for daylight to come. [30]Some of the sailors wanted to leave the ship, and they lowered the lifeboat, pretending they were throwing more anchors from the front of the ship. [31]But Paul told the officer and the other soldiers, "If these men do not stay in the ship, your lives cannot be saved." [32]So the soldiers cut the ropes and let the lifeboat fall into the water.

[33]Just before dawn Paul began persuading all the people to eat something. He said, "For the past fourteen days you have been waiting and watching and not eating. [34]Now I beg you to eat something. You need it to stay alive. None of you will lose even one hair off your heads." [35]After he said this, Paul took some bread and thanked God for it before all of them. He broke off a piece and began eating. [36]They all felt better and started eating, too. [37]There were two hundred seventy-six people on the ship. [38]When they had eaten all they wanted, they began making the ship lighter by throwing the grain into the sea.

THE SHIP IS DESTROYED

[39]When daylight came, the sailors saw land. They did not know what land it was, but they saw a bay with a beach and wanted to sail the ship to the beach if they could. [40]So they cut the ropes to the anchors and left the anchors in the sea. At the same time, they untied the ropes that were holding the rudders. Then they raised the front sail into the wind and sailed toward the beach. [41]But the ship hit a sandbank. The front of the ship stuck there and could not move, but the back of the ship began to break up from the big waves.

[42]The soldiers decided to kill the prisoners so none of them could swim away and escape. [43]But Julius, the officer, wanted to let Paul live and did not allow the soldiers to kill the prisoners. Instead he ordered everyone who could swim to jump into the water first and swim to land. [44]The rest were to follow using wooden boards or pieces of the ship. And this is how all the people made it safely to land.

trustables

Acts 27:35

When you become a teenager, along with all the other changes, you learn how to *stress!* "Stress" means "to be worried or anxious." When you're a kid, it's not a problem. But once you hit the double digits, you start fretting about homework, friends, your parents, your looks, girls, terrorism, and who knows what else? The problem is that stress can ruin your life.

Doctors try and try to cure stress with drugs. But there's a wonderful solution that has amazing results if people would just try it: prayer. Prayer heals stress! Right before a shipwreck, in the midst of a terrible storm, the apostle Paul spoke to his fellow passengers, then "took some bread and thanked God for it" (Acts 27:35). They had been so frightened they hadn't eaten in days. After hearing Paul pray, their fear evaporated and they started eating!

Did you catch that? Prayer brings peace. Peace is the opposite of stress. And this is not just any kind of peace; this is *God's* peace. Peace like that can't be explained. It's the peace that helps people get through disappointment, illness, and fierce storms. So as you get older and feel those feelings of worry start to crop up, don't stress about it. Just pray to God and let his peace fill your heart.

⭐ **27:17 Syrtis** Shallow area in the sea near the Libyan coast.   **27:27 Adriatic Sea** The sea between Greece and Italy, including the central Mediterranean.

PAUL ON THE ISLAND OF MALTA

28 When we were safe on land, we learned that the island was called Malta. [2] The people who lived there were very good to us. Because it was raining and very cold, they made a fire and welcomed all of us. [3] Paul gathered a pile of sticks and was putting them on the fire when a poisonous snake came out because of the heat and bit him on the hand. [4] The people living on the island saw the snake hanging from Paul's hand and said to each other, "This man must be a murderer! He did not die in the sea, but Justice[n] does not want him to live." [5] But Paul shook the snake off into the fire and was not hurt. [6] The people thought that Paul would swell up or fall down dead. They waited and watched him for a long time, but nothing bad happened to him. So they changed their minds and said, "He is a god!"

[7] There were some fields around there owned by Publius, an important man on the island. He welcomed us into his home and was very good to us for three days. [8] Publius' father was sick with a fever and dysentery.[n] Paul went to him, prayed, and put his hands on the man and healed him. [9] After this, all the other sick people on the island came to Paul, and he healed them, too. [10-11] The people on the island gave us many honors. When we were ready to leave, three months later, they gave us the things we needed.

PAUL GOES TO ROME

We got on a ship from Alexandria that had stayed on the island during the winter. On the front of the ship was the sign of the twin gods.[n] [12] We stopped at Syracuse for three days. [13] From there we sailed to Rhegium. The next day a wind began to blow from the south, and a day later we came to Puteoli. [14] We found some believers there who asked us to stay with them for a week. Finally, we came to Rome. [15] The believers in Rome heard that we were

DID YOU KNOW?

Kids have an average income of $15 a week.

License! Magazine. "Who Is Your Customer?" by Lorri Freifeld. June 2005.

there and came out as far as the Market of Appius[n] and the Three Inns[n] to meet us. When Paul saw them, he was encouraged and thanked God.

PAUL IN ROME

[16] When we arrived at Rome, Paul was allowed to live alone, with the soldier who guarded him.

[17] Three days later Paul sent for the leaders there. When they came together, he said, "Brothers, I have done nothing against our people or the customs of our ancestors. But I was arrested in Jerusalem and given to the Romans. [18] After they asked me many questions, they could find no reason why I should be killed. They wanted to let me go free, [19] but the evil people there argued against that. So I had to ask to come to Rome to have my trial before Caesar. But I have no charge to bring against my own people. [20] That is why I wanted to see you and talk with you. I am bound with this chain because I believe in the hope of Israel."

[21] They answered Paul, "We have received

no letters from Judea about you. None of our Jewish brothers who have come from there brought news or told us anything bad about you. [22] But we want to hear your ideas, because we know that people everywhere are speaking against this religious group."

[23] Paul and the people chose a day for a meeting and on that day many more of the Jews met with Paul at the place he was staying. He spoke to them all day long. Using the law of Moses and the prophets' writings, he explained the kingdom of God, and he tried to persuade them to believe these things about Jesus. [24] Some believed what Paul said, but others did not. [25] So they argued and began leaving after Paul said one more thing to them: "The Holy Spirit spoke the truth to your ancestors through Isaiah the prophet, saying,

[26] 'Go to this people and say:
You will listen and listen, but you will not
    understand.
    You will look and look, but you will not
    learn,
[27] because these people have become
    stubborn.
    They don't hear with their ears,
    and they have closed their eyes.
Otherwise, they might really understand
    what they see with their eyes
    and hear with their ears.
They might really understand in their minds
    and come back to me and be healed.'

Isaiah 6:9–10

[28] "I want you to know that God has also sent his salvation to all nations, and they will listen!" [[29] After Paul said this, the Jews left. They were arguing very much with each other.][n]

[30] Paul stayed two full years in his own rented house and welcomed all people who came to visit him. [31] He boldly preached about the kingdom of God and taught about the Lord Jesus Christ, and no one stopped him.

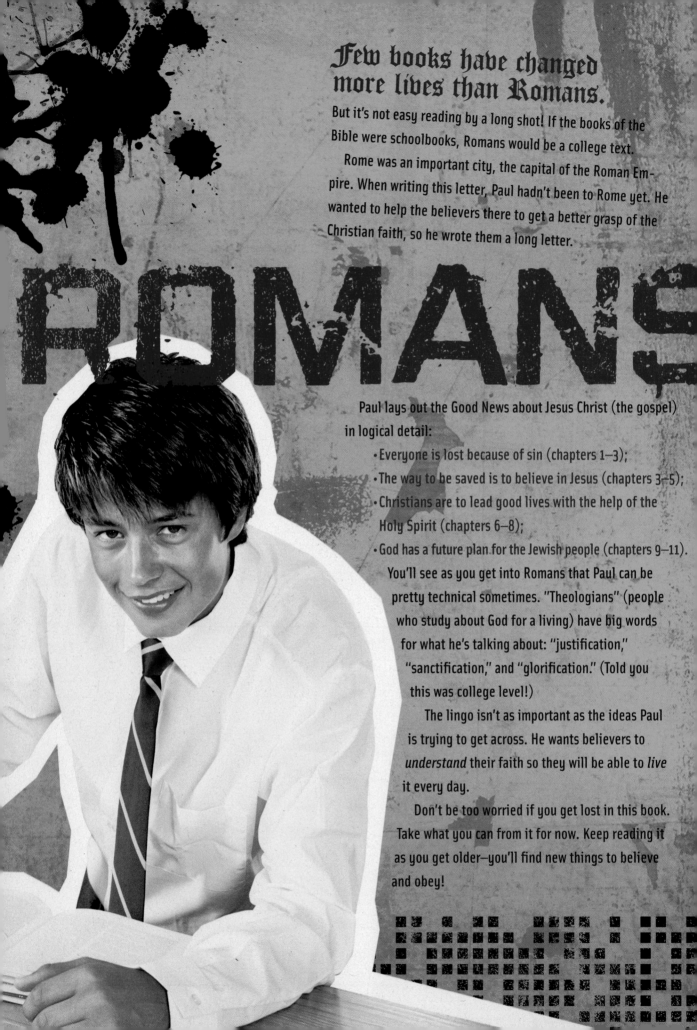

Few books have changed more lives than Romans.

But it's not easy reading by a long shot! If the books of the Bible were schoolbooks, Romans would be a college text.

Rome was an important city, the capital of the Roman Empire. When writing this letter, Paul hadn't been to Rome yet. He wanted to help the believers there to get a better grasp of the Christian faith, so he wrote them a long letter.

ROMANS

Paul lays out the Good News about Jesus Christ (the gospel) in logical detail:

- Everyone is lost because of sin (chapters 1—3);
- The way to be saved is to believe in Jesus (chapters 3—5);
- Christians are to lead good lives with the help of the Holy Spirit (chapters 6—8);
- God has a future plan for the Jewish people (chapters 9—11).

You'll see as you get into Romans that Paul can be pretty technical sometimes. "Theologians" (people who study about God for a living) have big words for what he's talking about: "justification," "sanctification," and "glorification." (Told you this was college level!)

The lingo isn't as important as the ideas Paul is trying to get across. He wants believers to *understand* their faith so they will be able to *live* it every day.

Don't be too worried if you get lost in this book. Take what you can from it for now. Keep reading it as you get older—you'll find new things to believe and obey!

From Paul, a servant of Christ Jesus. God called me to be an apostle and chose me to tell the Good News.

[2]God promised this Good News long ago through his prophets, as it is written in the Holy Scriptures. [3-4]The Good News is about God's Son, Jesus Christ our Lord. As a man, he was born from the family of David. But through the Spirit of holiness he was declared to be God's Son with great power by rising from the dead. [5]Through Christ, God gave me the special work of an apostle, which was to lead people of all nations to believe and obey. I do this work for him. [6]And you who are in Rome are also called to belong to Jesus Christ.

[7]To all of you in Rome whom God loves and has called to be his holy people:

Grace and peace to you from God our Father and the Lord Jesus Christ.

A PRAYER OF THANKS

[8]First I want to say that I thank my God through Jesus Christ for all of you, because people everywhere in the world are talking about your faith. [9]God, whom I serve with my whole heart by telling the Good News about his Son, knows that I always mention you [10]every time I pray. I pray that I will be allowed to come to you, and this will happen if God wants it. [11]I want very much to see you, to give you some spiritual gift to make you strong. [12]I mean that I want us to help each other with the faith we have. Your faith will help me, and my faith will help you. [13]Brothers and sisters, I want you to know that I planned many times to come to you, but this has not been possible. I wanted to come so that I could help you grow spiritually as I have helped the other non-Jewish people.

[14]I have a duty to all people—Greeks and those who are not Greeks, the wise and the foolish. [15]That is why I want so much to preach the Good News to you in Rome.

[16]I am not ashamed of the Good News, because it is the power God uses to save everyone who believes—to save the Jews first, and then to save non-Jews. [17]The Good News shows how God makes people right with himself—that it begins and ends with faith. As the Scripture says, "But those who are right with God will live by faith."[n]

ALL PEOPLE HAVE DONE WRONG

[18]God's anger is shown from heaven against all the evil and wrong things people do. By their own evil lives they hide the truth. [19]God shows his anger because some knowledge of him has been made clear to them. Yes, God has shown himself to them. [20]There are things about him that people cannot see—his eternal power and all the things that make him God. But since the beginning of the world those things have been easy to understand by what God has made. So people have no excuse for the bad things they do. [21]They knew God, but they did not give glory to God or thank him. Their thinking became useless. Their foolish minds were filled with darkness. [22]They said they were wise, but they became fools. [23]They traded the glory of God who lives forever for the worship of idols made to look like earthly people, birds, animals, and snakes.

[24]Because they did these things, God left them and let them go their sinful way, wanting only to do evil. As a result, they became full of sexual sin, using their bodies wrongly with each other. [25]They traded the truth of God for a lie. They worshiped and served what had been created instead of the God who created those things, who should be praised forever. Amen.

[26]Because people did those things, God left them and let them do the shameful things

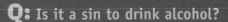

Q: Everybody else's parents seem so cool, but mine only seem to like clothes and music from twenty years ago. What's wrong with them?

A: They're perfectly normal. Most of us like things that are familiar to us. If you grew up when your parents did, you'd probably like the same music and clothes that they like. As a kid, you're always growing out of your clothes, which gives you lots of chances to try new styles.

Q: Is it a sin to drink alcohol?

A: Not necessarily. Jesus drank wine. In fact, he even made some wine out of water (John 2:1–11). But the Bible does say it's wrong to have so much alcohol that you get drunk (Ephesians 5:18). One way to make sure you never get drunk is to stay away from alcohol completely, and some Christians choose to do this. It can also be a sin to drink alcohol if you are breaking the law by drinking.

Q: I have a friend who uses a lot of swear words. Sometimes I find myself saying some of them, too. What should I do?

A: Swearing and cussing, especially when it involves using Jesus Christ's name disrespectfully, does not honor God. Ask your friend not to use those words around you, or stop spending so much time with him. The Bible says that hanging out with the wrong people can make us do wrong things, too (1 Corinthians 15:33). When you are around that friend, try to talk about things that would honor God.

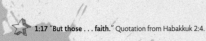

1:17 "But those . . . faith." Quotation from Habakkuk 2:4.

Simple Secrets to Better Grades

1. **Show respect to your teachers.**
2. **Keep a school assignment calendar.**
3. **Review the questions at the end of the chapter first.**
4. **Pay attention to words in bold as you read.**
5. **When your teacher repeats something, pay attention.**
6. **Pretend your homework is due a day early.**
7. **Don't talk in class.**
8. **Practice basic skills.**
9. **Ask your parents or older siblings for help.**
10. **Work on neat handwriting and accurate typing.**

they wanted to do. Women stopped having natural sex and started having sex with other women. [27] In the same way, men stopped having natural sex and began wanting each other. Men did shameful things with other men, and in their bodies they received the punishment for those wrongs.

[28] People did not think it was important to have a true knowledge of God. So God left them and allowed them to have their own worthless thinking and to do things they should not do. [29] They are filled with every kind of sin, evil, selfishness, and hatred. They are full of jealousy, murder, fighting, lying, and thinking the worst about each other. They gossip [30] and say evil things about each other. They hate God. They are rude and conceited and brag about themselves. They invent ways of doing evil. They do not obey their parents. [31] They are foolish, they do not keep their promises, and they show no kindness or

mercy to others. [32] They know God's law says that those who live like this should die. But they themselves not only continue to do these evil things, they applaud others who do them.

YOU PEOPLE ALSO ARE SINFUL

2 If you think you can judge others, you are wrong. When you judge them, you are really judging yourself guilty, because you do the same things they do. [2] God judges those who do wrong things, and we know that his judging is right. [3] You judge those who do wrong, but you do wrong yourselves. Do you think you will be able to escape the judgment of God? [4] He has been very kind and patient, waiting for you to change, but you think nothing of his kindness. Perhaps you do not understand that God is kind to you so you will change your hearts and lives. [5] But you are stubborn and refuse to change, so you are making your own punishment even greater on the day he shows his anger. On that day everyone will see God's right judgments. [6] God will reward or punish every person for what that person has done. [7] Some people, by always continuing to do good, live for God's glory, for honor, and for life that has no end. God will give them life forever. [8] But other people are selfish. They refuse to follow truth and, instead, follow evil. God will give them his punishment and anger. [9] He will give trouble and suffering to everyone who does evil—to the Jews first and also to those who are not Jews. [10] But he will give glory, honor, and peace to everyone who does good—to the Jews first and also to those who are not Jews. [11] For God judges all people in the same way.

[12] People who do not have the law and who are sinners will be lost, although they do not have the law. And, in the same way, those who have the law and are sinners will be judged by the law. [13] Hearing the law does not make people right with God. It is those who obey the law who will be right with him. [14] (Those who are not Jews do not have the law, but when they freely do what the law commands, they are the law for themselves. This is true even though they do not have the law. [15] They show that in their hearts they know what is right and wrong, just as the law commands. And they show this by their consciences. Sometimes their thoughts tell them they did wrong, and sometimes their thoughts tell them they did right.) [16] All these things will happen on the day when God, through Christ Jesus, will judge people's secret thoughts. The Good News that I preach says this.

THE JEWS AND THE LAW

[17] What about you? You call yourself a Jew. You trust in the law of Moses and brag that you are close to God. [18] You know what he wants you to do and what is important, because you have learned the law. [19] You think you are a guide for the blind and a light for those who are in darkness. [20] You think you can show foolish people what is right and teach those who know nothing. You have the law; so you think you know everything and have all truth. [21] You teach others, so why don't you teach yourself? You tell others not to steal, but you steal. [22] You say that others must not take part in adultery, but you are guilty of that sin. You hate idols, but you steal from temples. [23] You brag about having God's law, but you bring shame to God by breaking his law, [24] just as the Scriptures say: "Those who are not Jews speak against God's name because of you."[n]

[25] If you follow the law, your circumcision has meaning. But if you break the law, it is as if you were never circumcised. [26] People who are not Jews are not circumcised, but if they do what the law says, it is as if they were circumcised.

HOLY SPIRIT

The Holy Spirit is God's Spirit who lives inside every Christian. Before Jesus came, the Holy Spirit only came to certain people and for a certain amount of time. When Jesus' followers were sad that he was leaving them, he gave them a special promise: he would send God's Spirit to live inside each one of them! A few weeks after Jesus returned to heaven, the followers received the Holy Spirit (Acts 2). Ever since then, the Holy Spirit comes to live inside a person as soon as he becomes a Christian.

The Holy Spirit reminds us about Jesus and the things he taught. And if you've ever heard a silent voice tell you not to sin, you've heard the Holy Spirit!

⭐ **2:24** "Those . . . you." Quotation from Isaiah 52:5; Ezekiel 36:20.

first JOB

Do you daydream of becoming an astronaut or owning a big company? What about fighting fires or being a doctor? There will be lots of training and preparation for whatever job or career you imagine yourself doing when you're older. The first step toward your goal is finding your first job, and this can be an intimidating task!

Beginning to work is a big change for most young people, but your first job is an opportunity to learn new skills and gain life experience. Many people start working when they are still in high school, but you may not begin until after you graduate. Either way, there are a few important things to know about getting your first job so you aren't a mess of stress!

When you begin your job search, dress nicely and be polite when you ask for an application. Even if you are getting a job from a family friend or your buddy's parents, it's important to show that you're taking it seriously!

You'll probably have to prepare a résumé when you apply, which means writing down all the things you have been involved with. Great things to include on your résumé are descriptions of volunteering or other work you have done (paid or unpaid). Get an adult's help writing your résumé; you will want it to look professional.

If you have an interview for a job, be sure to speak slowly and clearly and make eye contact with the person interviewing you. Answer questions honestly and don't be scared of messing up—it's your first time!

When you get your first job, you won't know how to do everything, but that's no reason to get frustrated. Be patient with yourself and others, and ask questions when you're unsure. You'll keep learning as you work, and it's important to keep improving, too.

Businesses appreciate employees who work hard to do their best and who respect others. You'll be paid to work, so make sure you are earning it by giving your job your full attention while you are there. Colossians 3:23 says, "In all the work you are doing, work the best you can. Work as if you were doing it for the Lord, not for people." If you do your best and work hard, *you'll* feel good, too!

²⁷You Jews have the written law and circumcision, but you break the law. So those who are not circumcised in their bodies, but still obey the law, will show that you are guilty. ²⁸They can do this because a person is not a true Jew if he is only a Jew in his physical body; true circumcision is not only on the outside of the body. ²⁹A person is a Jew only if he is a Jew inside; true circumcision is done in the heart by the Spirit, not by the written law. Such a person gets praise from God rather than from people.

3 So, do Jews have anything that other people do not have? Is there anything special about being circumcised? ²Yes, of course, there is in every way. The most important thing is this: God trusted the Jews with his teachings. ³If some Jews were not faithful to him, will that stop God from doing what he promised? ⁴No! God will continue to be true even when every person is false. As the Scriptures say:

"So you will be shown to be right when you
        speak,
and you will win your case." *Psalm 51:4*

⁵When we do wrong, that shows more clearly that God is right. So can we say that God is wrong to punish us? (I am talking as people might talk.) ⁶No! If God could not punish us, he could not judge the world.

⁷A person might say, "When I lie, it really gives him glory, because my lie shows God's truth. So why am I judged a sinner?" ⁸It would be the same to say, "We should do evil so that good will come." Some people find fault with us and say we teach this, but they are wrong and deserve the punishment they will receive.

ALL PEOPLE ARE GUILTY

⁹So are we Jews better than others? No! We have already said that Jews and those who are not Jews are all guilty of sin. ¹⁰As the Scriptures say:

"There is no one who always does what is
        right,
    not even one.
¹¹There is no one who understands.
    There is no one who looks to God for
        help.
¹²All have turned away.
    Together, everyone has become useless.

There is no one who does anything good;
    there is not even one." *Psalm 14:1–3*
¹³"Their throats are like open graves;
    they use their tongues for telling lies."
                                    Psalm 5:9
"Their words are like snake poison."
                                    Psalm 140:3
¹⁴ "Their mouths are full of cursing and
        hate." *Psalm 10:7*
¹⁵"They are always ready to kill people.
¹⁶ Everywhere they go they cause ruin and
        misery.
¹⁷They don't know how to live in peace."
                                    Isaiah 59:7–8
¹⁸ "They have no fear of God." *Psalm 36:1*

¹⁹We know that the law's commands are for those who have the law. This stops all excuses and brings the whole world under God's judgment, ²⁰because no one can be made right with God by following the law. The law only shows us our sin.

HOW GOD MAKES PEOPLE RIGHT

²¹But God has a way to make people right with him without the law, and he has now shown us that way which the law and the prophets told us about. ²²God makes people right with himself through their faith in Jesus Christ. This is true for all who believe in Christ, because all people are the same: ²³Everyone has sinned and fallen short of God's glorious standard, ²⁴and all need to be made right with God by his grace, which is a free gift. They need to be made free from sin through Jesus Christ. ²⁵God sent him to die in our place to take away our sins. We receive forgiveness through faith in the blood of Jesus' death. This showed that God always does what is right and fair, as in the past when he was patient and did not punish people for their sins. ²⁶And God gave Jesus to show today that he does what is right. God did this so he could judge rightly and so he could make right any person who has faith in Jesus.

²⁷So do we have a reason to brag about ourselves? No! And why not? It is the way of faith that stops all bragging, not the way of trying to obey the law. ²⁸A person is made right with God through faith, not through obeying the law. ²⁹Is God only the God of the Jews? Is he not also the God of those who are not Jews? ³⁰Of course he is, because there is only one God. He will make Jews right with him by their faith, and he will also make those who are not Jews right with him through their faith. ³¹So do we destroy the law by following the way of faith? No! Faith causes us to be what the law truly wants.

Romans 3:22

A lot of people spend their whole lives trying to get right with God. Different religions are all about this big question: how does someone get right with God? People put all kinds of different systems together, like doing the right thing in order to make God happy in the end.

Eternity isn't something you want to play games with. We're talking about the rest of your existence; you don't want to die not being sure of what's next. This may be the most important moment of your life—don't miss it.

Romans 3:22 tells us how to get right with God: "God makes people right with himself through their faith in Jesus Christ." Religion will tell you all the things you have to do. But God himself says to just believe. God knew you weren't good enough to get to him, so he came down to get you!

Faith in Jesus Christ is what makes you right with God, period. Take the first step: you can't believe in someone you don't know, so get to know him. Begin with the Book of Matthew and read the New Testament all the way through. It's all about him.

Don't wait to start the rest of your life.

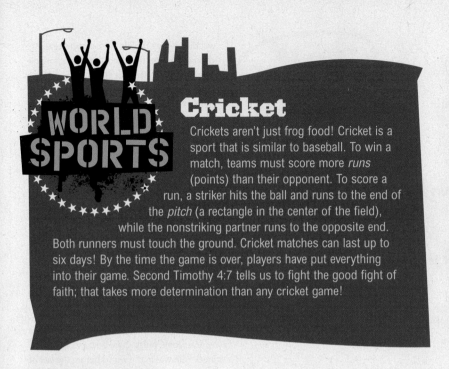

Cricket

Crickets aren't just frog food! Cricket is a sport that is similar to baseball. To win a match, teams must score more *runs* (points) than their opponent. To score a run, a striker hits the ball and runs to the end of the *pitch* (a rectangle in the center of the field), while the nonstriking partner runs to the opposite end. Both runners must touch the ground. Cricket matches can last up to six days! By the time the game is over, players have put everything into their game. Second Timothy 4:7 tells us to fight the good fight of faith; that takes more determination than any cricket game!

THE EXAMPLE OF ABRAHAM

4 So what can we say that Abraham," the father of our people, learned about faith? [2]If Abraham was made right by the things he did, he had a reason to brag. But this is not God's view, [3]because the Scripture says, "Abraham believed God, and God accepted Abraham's faith, and that faith made him right with God."[n]

[4]When people work, their pay is not given as a gift, but as something earned. [5]But people cannot do any work that will make them right with God. So they must trust in him, who makes even evil people right in his sight. Then God accepts their faith, and that makes them right with him. [6]David said the same thing. He said that people are truly blessed when God, without paying attention to their deeds, makes people right with himself.

[7]"Blessed are they
whose sins are forgiven,
whose wrongs are pardoned.
[8]Blessed is the person
whom the Lord does not consider
guilty."   *Psalm 32:1–2*

[9]Is this blessing only for those who are circumcised or also for those who are not circumcised? We have already said that God accepted Abraham's faith and that faith made him right with God. [10]So how did this happen? Did God accept Abraham before or after he was circumcised? It was before his circumcision. [11]Abraham was circumcised to show that he was right with God through faith before he was circumcised. So Abraham is the father of all those who believe but are not circumcised; he is the father of all believers who are accepted as being right with God. [12]And Abraham is also the father of those who have been circumcised and who live following the faith that our father Abraham had before he was circumcised.

GOD KEEPS HIS PROMISE

[13]Abraham[n] and his descendants received the promise that they would get the whole world. He did not receive that promise through the law, but through being right with God by his faith. [14]If people could receive what God promised by following the law, then faith is worthless. And God's promise to Abraham is worthless, [15]because the law can only bring God's anger. But if there is no law, there is nothing to disobey.

[16]So people receive God's promise by having faith. This happens so the promise can be a free gift. Then all of Abraham's children can have that promise. It is not only for those who live under the law of Moses but for anyone who lives with faith like that of Abraham, who is the father of us all. [17]As it is written in the Scriptures: "I am making you a father of many nations."[n] This is true before God, the God Abraham believed, the God who gives life to the dead and who creates something out of nothing.

[18]There was no hope that Abraham would have children. But Abraham believed God and continued hoping, and so he became the father of many nations. As God told him, "Your descendants also will be too many to count."[n] [19]Abraham was almost a hundred years old, much past the age for having children, and Sarah could not have children. Abraham thought about all this, but his faith in God did not become weak. [20]He never doubted that God would keep his promise, and he never stopped believing. He grew stronger in his faith and gave praise to God. [21]Abraham felt sure that God was able to do what he had promised.

dare to do

Romans 6:1
Read It: The fact that God forgives us should not become an excuse to keep sinning.
Do It: Don't let any sin "slide by." When God forgives you, he expects you to change your ways.

Romans 6:12
Read It: Don't let the desire to sin control you.
Do It: When you are tempted to do something wrong, ask God to help you make a better choice.

Romans 6:18
Read It: As a believer in Jesus, you have new desires to live and act in the right way!
Do It: Take the time to listen what God is telling you to do. Then do it!

4:1, 13 **Abraham** Most respected ancestor of the Jews. Every Jew hoped to see Abraham.   4:3 "**Abraham . . . God.**" Quotation from Genesis 15:6.   4:17 "**I . . . nations.**" Quotation from Genesis 17:5.
4:18 "**Your . . . count.**" Quotation from Genesis 15:5.

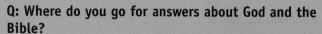

Q: What skill do you wish you had?
A: "I wish I could invent things better." (James, 9)

Q: Where do you go for answers about God and the Bible?
A: "My parents." (Andy, 11)

Q: What's the most important lesson you've learned?
A: "Treat others as you want to be treated." (Daniel, 10)

will die to save the life of someone else. Although perhaps for a good person someone might possibly die. [8]But God shows his great love for us in this way: Christ died for us while we were still sinners.

[9]So through Christ we will surely be saved from God's anger, because we have been made right with God by the blood of Christ's death. [10]While we were God's enemies, he made us his friends through the death of his Son. Surely, now that we are his friends, he will save us through his Son's life. [11]And not only that, but now we are also very happy in God through our Lord Jesus Christ. Through him we are now God's friends again.

ADAM AND CHRIST COMPARED

[12]Sin came into the world because of what one man did, and with sin came death. This is why everyone must die—because everyone sinned. [13]Sin was in the world before the law of Moses, but sin is not counted against us as breaking a command when there is no law. [14]But from the time of Adam to the time of Moses, everyone had to die, even those who had not sinned by breaking a command, as Adam had.

Adam was like the One who was coming in the future. [15]But God's free gift is not like Adam's sin. Many people died because of the sin of that one man. But the grace from God was much greater; many people received God's gift of life by the grace of the one man, Jesus Christ. [16]After Adam sinned once, he was judged guilty. But the gift of God is different. God's free gift came after many sins, and it makes people right with God. [17]One man

[22]So, "God accepted Abraham's faith, and that faith made him right with God."[n] [23]Those words ("God accepted Abraham's faith") were written not only for Abraham [24]but also for us. God will accept us also because we believe in the One who raised Jesus our Lord from the dead. [25]Jesus was given to die for our sins, and he was raised from the dead to make us right with God.

RIGHT WITH GOD

5 Since we have been made right with God by our faith, we have[n] peace with God. This happened through our Lord Jesus Christ, [2]who through our faith[n] has brought us into that blessing of God's grace that we now enjoy. And we are happy because of the hope we have of sharing God's glory. [3]We also have joy with our troubles, because we know that these troubles produce patience. [4]And patience produces character, and character produces hope. [5]And this hope will never disappoint us, because God has poured out his love to fill our hearts. He gave us his love through the Holy Spirit, whom God has given to us.

[6]When we were unable to help ourselves, at the right time, Christ died for us, although we were living against God. [7]Very few people

Romans 5:3–4

Have you ever gone through something really painful? Maybe your parents got a divorce or someone in your family died. Those things can hurt so badly and take a lot of time to work through.

If you've never experienced really tough times, there's a good chance you will sometime in the future. When you do, read Romans 5:3–4: "We also have joy with our troubles, because we know that these troubles produce patience. And patience produces character, and character produces hope."

This is amazing! Paul says that you can not only make it through troubles, but also have joy in them! Why? Because God is doing all these things in you. Like an artist, he's making you into a masterpiece. Hard times aren't random; they're his tools for making you powerful in him.

If you're going through something so painful you can hardly see through the tears, ask him, "Lord, show me what you're doing in my life." Keep coming back to these verses in Romans 5. God wrote them so that you could make it through times like these.

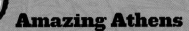

Amazing Athens

Athens is the birthplace of democracy, the city where theater was invented, and the home of the great philosophers Socrates, Plato, and Aristotle.

The first Olympics were held there in 776 B.C. There was only one event—a 200-meter sprint. The city hosted the first modern Olympics in 1896.

Athens was a proud and snobbish city. Paul preached there, but only a few people believed (Acts 17). They thought they were too smart for God. How dumb!

sinned, and so death ruled all people because of that one man. But now those people who accept God's full grace and the great gift of being made right with him will surely have true life and rule through the one man, Jesus Christ.

[18]So as one sin of Adam brought the punishment of death to all people, one good act that Christ did makes all people right with God. And that brings true life for all. [19]One man disobeyed God, and many became sinners. In the same way, one man obeyed God, and many will be made right. [20]The law came to make sin worse. But when sin grew worse, God's grace increased. [21]Sin once used death to rule us, but God gave people more of his grace so that grace could rule by making

people right with him. And this brings life forever through Jesus Christ our Lord.

DEAD TO SIN BUT ALIVE IN CHRIST

6 So do you think we should continue sinning so that God will give us even more grace? [2]No! We died to our old sinful lives, so how can we continue living with sin? [3]Did you forget that all of us became part of Christ when we were baptized? We shared his death in our baptism. [4]When we were baptized, we were buried with Christ and shared his death. So, just as Christ was raised from the dead by the wonderful power of the Father, we also can live a new life.

[5]Christ died, and we have been joined with him by dying too. So we will also be joined

with him by rising from the dead as he did. [6]We know that our old life died with Christ on the cross so that our sinful selves would have no power over us and we would not be slaves to sin. [7]Anyone who has died is made free from sin's control.

[8]If we died with Christ, we know we will also live with him. [9]Christ was raised from the dead, and we know that he cannot die again. Death has no power over him now. [10]Yes, when Christ died, he died to defeat the power of sin one time—enough for all time. He now has a new life, and his new life is with God. [11]In the same way, you should see yourselves as being dead to the power of sin and alive with God through Christ Jesus.

[12]So, do not let sin control your life here on earth so that you do what your sinful self wants to do. [13]Do not offer the parts of your

GET **CONNECTED**

LIFE HURTS!

Imagine that you have a bad sunburn—and you're standing in a swarm of bees! Double ouch! Sometimes life hurts. It might be because of something you've done (you hit your brother; he punched you back), but sometimes we don't understand why we suffer. The Bible says that sometimes pain has a purpose. "We are hurt sometimes...*so that* the life of Jesus can also be seen" (2 Corinthians 4:9–10). Get it? When you're hurting, let others see Jesus in you—it'll soothe the burn and numb the sting.

body to serve sin, as things to be used in doing evil. Instead, offer yourselves to God as people who have died and now live. Offer the parts of your body to God to be used in doing good. [14]Sin will not be your master, because you are not under law but under God's grace.

BE SLAVES OF RIGHTEOUSNESS

[15]So what should we do? Should we sin because we are under grace and not under law? No! [16]Surely you know that when you give yourselves like slaves to obey someone, then you are really slaves of that person. The person you obey is your master. You can follow sin, which brings spiritual death, or you can obey God, which makes you right with him. [17]In the past you were slaves to sin—sin controlled you. But thank God, you fully obeyed the things that you were taught. [18]You were made free from sin, and now you are slaves to goodness. [19]I use this example because this is hard for you to understand. In the past you offered the parts of your body to be slaves to sin and evil; you lived only for evil. In the same way now you must give yourselves to be slaves of goodness. Then you will live only for God.

[20]In the past you were slaves to sin, and goodness did not control you. [21]You did evil things, and now you are ashamed of them. Those things only bring death. [22]But now you are free from sin and have become slaves of God. This brings you a life that is only for God, and this gives you life forever. [23]The payment

SMART TIPS!

Wear Deodorant

Starting each day by applying your deodorant can keep you from offending anyone sitting next to you in class. In the same way, starting each day by reading your Bible will give you the sweet aroma of Jesus Christ. So don't forget to do both!

for sin is death. But God gives us the free gift of life forever in Christ Jesus our Lord.

AN EXAMPLE FROM MARRIAGE

7 Brothers and sisters, all of you understand the law of Moses. So surely you know that the law rules over people only while they are alive. [2]For example, a woman must

stay married to her husband as long as he is alive. But if her husband dies, she is free from the law of marriage. [3]But if she marries another man while her husband is still alive, the law says she is guilty of adultery. But if her husband dies, she is free from the law of marriage. Then if she marries another man, she is not guilty of adultery.

[4]In the same way, my brothers and sisters, your old selves died, and you became free from the law through the body of Christ. This happened so that you might belong to someone else—the One who was raised from the dead—and so that we might be used in service to God. [5]In the past, we were ruled by our sinful selves. The law made us want to do sinful things that controlled our bodies, so the things we did were bringing us death. [6]In the past, the law held us like prisoners, but our old selves died, and we were made free from the law. So now we serve God in a new way with the Spirit, and not in the old way with written rules.

OUR FIGHT AGAINST SIN

[7]You might think I am saying that sin and the law are the same thing. That is not true. But the law was the only way I could learn what sin meant. I would never have known what it means to want to take something belonging to someone else if the law had not said, "You must not want to take your neighbor's things."[n] [8]And sin found a way to use that command and cause me to want all kinds of things I

BIBLE SUPERHEROES

Barnabas
See Acts 13—15.

Joseph of Cyprus was such a people person that his friends called him *Barnabas,* which means "the encourager."

Barnabas always looked for the best in others. When Saul of Tarsus, a man who had put many Christians in jail, claimed to have become a believer, Barnabas stood up for him. Saul went on to become the apostle Paul. The two men went on a preaching trip together and did great things for God.

When Barnabas stood up for John Mark, another man who needed someone to believe in him, Paul got mad and the two split up. Later on, Paul admitted that Barnabas had been right.

Barnabas was a loyal friend, the kind who sticks by you. He was the kind of friend we should all try to be. What do your friends call *you*?

⭐ **7:7 "You . . . things."** Quotation from Exodus 20:17.

COOL!

The Search for Truth

According to the *Encyclopaedia Brittanica Book of the Year 2005,* at the start of the twenty-first century, here's how the major world religions compared to one another:

Religion	Number of followers	Percentage
Christian	2,106,962,000	32.84
Muslims	1,283,424,000	19.90
Hindus	851,291,000	13.29
Buddhists	375,440,000	5.92
Sikhs	24,989,000	0.39
Jews	14,990,000	0.23
Other religions		12.63
Nonreligious		12.44
Atheists		2.36

These different religions are all looking for the truth. But Jesus said, "I am the way, and the truth, and the life. The only way to the Father is through me" (John 14:6). Truth isn't a set of beliefs; it's a person—Jesus!

should not want. But without the law, sin has no power. [9]I was alive before I knew the law. But when the law's command came to me, then sin began to live, [10]and I died. The command was meant to bring life, but for me it brought death. [11]Sin found a way to fool me by using the command to make me die.

[12]So the law is holy, and the command is holy and right and good. [13]Does this mean that something that is good brought death to me? No! Sin used something that is good to bring death to me. This happened so that I could see what sin is really like; the command was used to show that sin is very evil.

THE WAR WITHIN US

[14]We know that the law is spiritual, but I am not spiritual since sin rules me as if I were its slave. [15]I do not understand the things I do. I do not do what I want to do, and I do the things I hate. [16]And if I do not want to do the hated things I do, that means I agree that the law is good. [17]But I am not really the one who is doing these hated things; it is sin living in me that does them. [18]Yes, I know that nothing good lives in me—I mean nothing good lives in the part of me that is earthly and sinful. I want to do the things that are good, but I do not do

them. [19]I do not do the good things I want to do, but I do the bad things I do not want to do. [20]So if I do things I do not want to do, then I am not the one doing them. It is sin living in me that does those things.

[21]So I have learned this rule: When I want to do good, evil is there with me. [22]In my mind, I am happy with God's law. [23]But I see another law working in my body, which makes war against the law that my mind accepts. That other law working in my body is the law of sin,

Romans 12:1
Read It: Give yourself to God.
Do It: Ask yourself: "What does God want me to be when I grow up?" Pray that he will help you glorify him no matter what you do.

Romans 12:2
Read It: You need to change the way you think.
Do It: Fill your head with God's truth from the Bible instead of thinking about TV shows, music, and video games that do not honor God.

Romans 12:3
Read It: Don't become arrogant and proud. Be aware of your own weaknesses.
Do It: Bragging is childish. You should always remember that without God, you would be lost.

trustables

Romans 8:10–14

When you think about athletic power, what comes to mind? Running a marathon? Winning a long-distance bicycle race? But even the most gifted sports stars lose their strength and stamina over time. In the end, they all die—right?

"A local man cheats death…" This might have been the headline story if television news had existed when God raised Jesus Christ from the dead. Talk about supernatural power! Romans 8:10–14 explains that God's power is working in our lives, too.

Romans 8:11 says, "God raised Jesus from the dead…and he will give life through his Spirit that lives in you." Amazingly, if you're a Christian, the same Holy Spirit is living in you. You do not have to resist evil desires with your own strength. The power of God resides within you. It is surely strong enough to help you stop doing wrong things. What's more, God gives you the power to do what is right.

So the next time you want to do something you know is wrong, stop and ask God to work in you. Do not give in to your evil desires, but let them die. Let God's Spirit give you resurrection life!

---

and it makes me its prisoner. [24]What a miserable man I am! Who will save me from this body that brings me death? [25]I thank God for saving me through Jesus Christ our Lord!

So in my mind I am a slave to God's law, but in my sinful self I am a slave to the law of sin.

BE RULED BY THE SPIRIT

8 So now, those who are in Christ Jesus are not judged guilty.[n] [2]Through Christ Jesus the law of the Spirit that brings life made you[n] free from the law that brings sin and death. [3]The law was without power, because the law was made weak by our sinful selves. But God did what the law could not do. He sent his own Son to earth with the same human life that others use for sin. By sending his Son to be an offering for sin, God used a human life to destroy sin. [4]He did this so that we could be the kind of people the law correctly wants us to be. Now we do not live following our sinful selves, but we live following the Spirit.

[5]Those who live following their sinful selves think only about things that their sinful selves want. But those who live following the Spirit are thinking about the things the Spirit wants them to do. [6]If people's thinking is controlled by the sinful self, there is death. But if their thinking is controlled by the Spirit, there

is life and peace. [7]When people's thinking is controlled by the sinful self, they are against God, because they refuse to obey God's law and really are not even able to obey God's law. [8]Those people who are ruled by their sinful selves cannot please God.

[9]But you are not ruled by your sinful selves. You are ruled by the Spirit, if that Spirit of God really lives in you. But the person who does not have the Spirit of Christ does not belong to Christ. [10]Your body will always be dead because of sin. But if Christ is in you, then the Spirit gives you life, because Christ made you right with God. [11]God raised Jesus from the dead, and if God's Spirit is living in you, he will also give life to your bodies that die. God is the One who raised Christ from the dead, and he will give life through[n] his Spirit that lives in you.

[12]So, my brothers and sisters, we must not be ruled by our sinful selves or live the way our sinful selves want. [13]If you use your lives to do the wrong things your sinful selves want, you will die spiritually. But if you use the Spirit's help to stop doing the wrong things you do with your body, you will have true life. [14]The true children of God are those who let God's Spirit lead them. [15]The Spirit we received does not make us slaves again to fear; it makes us children of God. With that Spirit we

cry out, "Father."[n] [16]And the Spirit himself joins with our spirits to say we are God's children. [17]If we are God's children, we will receive blessings from God together with Christ. But we must suffer as Christ suffered so that we will have glory as Christ has glory.

OUR FUTURE GLORY

[18]The sufferings we have now are nothing compared to the great glory that will be shown to us. [19]Everything God made is waiting with excitement for God to show his children's glory completely. [20]Everything God made was changed to become useless, not by its own wish but because God wanted it and because all along there was this hope: [21]that everything God made would be set free from ruin to have the freedom and glory that belong to God's children.

[22]We know that everything God made has been waiting until now in pain, like a woman ready to give birth. [23]Not only the world, but we also have been waiting with pain inside us. We have the Spirit as the first part of God's promise. So we are waiting for God to finish making us his own children, which means our bodies will be made free. [24]We were saved, and we have this hope. If we see what we are waiting for, that is not really hope. People do not hope for something

---

⭐ **8:1 guilty** Some Greek copies continue, "those who do not live in the power of their sinful selves, but in the power of the Spirit." **8:2 you** Some Greek copies read "me." **8:11 through** Some Greek copies read "because of." **8:15 "Father"** Literally, "Abba, Father." Jewish children called their fathers "Abba."

they already have. [25]But we are hoping for something we do not have yet, and we are waiting for it patiently.

[26]Also, the Spirit helps us with our weakness. We do not know how to pray as we should. But the Spirit himself speaks to God for us, even begs God for us with deep feelings that words cannot explain. [27]God can see what is in people's hearts. And he knows what is in the mind of the Spirit, because the Spirit speaks to God for his people in the way God wants.

[28]We know that in everything God works for the good of those who love him.[n] They are the people he called, because that was his plan. [29]God knew them before he made the world, and he chose them to be like his Son so that Jesus would be the firstborn[n] of many brothers and sisters. [30]God planned for them to be like his Son; and those he planned to be like his Son, he also called; and those he called, he also made right with him; and those he made right, he also glorified.

GOD'S LOVE IN CHRIST JESUS

[31]So what should we say about this? If God is for us, no one can defeat us. [32]He did not spare his own Son but gave him for us all. So with Jesus, God will surely give us all things. [33]Who can accuse the people God has chosen? No one, because God is the One who makes them right. [34]Who can say God's people are guilty? No one, because Christ Jesus died, but he was also raised from the dead, and now he is on God's right side, appealing to God for us. [35]Can anything separate us from the love Christ has for us? Can troubles or problems or sufferings or hunger or nakedness or danger or violent death? [36]As it is written in the Scriptures:

"For you we are in danger of death all the
time.
People think we are worth no more than
sheep to be killed."   *Psalm 44:22*

[37]But in all these things we are completely victorious through God who showed his love for us. [38]Yes, I am sure that neither death, nor life, nor angels, nor ruling spirits, nothing now, nothing in the future, no powers, [39]nothing above us, nothing below us, nor anything else in the whole world will ever be able to separate us from the love of God that is in Christ Jesus our Lord.

GOD AND THE JEWISH PEOPLE

9 I am in Christ, and I am telling you the truth; I do not lie. My conscience is ruled by the Holy Spirit, and it tells me I am not lying. [2]I have great sorrow and always feel much sadness. [3]I wish I could help my Jewish brothers and sisters, my people. I would even wish that I were cursed and cut off from Christ if that would help them. [4]They are the people of Israel, God's chosen children. They have seen the glory of God, and they have the agreements that God made between himself and his people. God gave them the law of Moses and the right way of worship and his promises. [5]They are the descendants of our great ancestors, and they are the earthly family into which Christ was born, who is God over all. Praise him forever![n] Amen.

[6]It is not that God failed to keep his promise to them. But only some of the people of Israel are truly God's people,[n] [7]and only some of Abraham's[n] descendants are true children of Abraham. But God said to Abraham: "The descendants I promised you will be from Isaac."[n] [8]This means that not all of Abraham's descendants are God's true children. Abraham's true children are those who become God's children because of the promise God made to Abraham. [9]God's promise to Abraham was this: "At the right time I will return, and Sarah will have a son."[n] [10]And that is not all. Rebekah's sons had the same father, our father Isaac. [11-12]But before the two boys were born, God told Rebekah, "The older will serve the younger."[n] This was before the boys had done anything good or bad. God said this so that the one chosen would be chosen because of God's own plan. He was chosen because he was the one God wanted to call, not because of anything he did. [13]As the Scripture says, "I loved Jacob, but I hated Esau."[n]

[14]So what should we say about this? Is God unfair? In no way. [15]God said to Moses, "I will show kindness to anyone to whom I want to show kindness, and I will show mercy to anyone to whom I want to show mercy."[n] [16]So God will choose the one to whom he decides to show mercy; his choice does not depend on what people want or try to do. [17]The Scripture says to the king of Egypt: "I made you king for this reason: to show my power in you so that my name will be talked about in all the earth."[n] [18]So God shows mercy where he wants to show mercy, and he makes stubborn the people he wants to make stubborn.

[19]So one of you will ask me: "Then why does God blame us for our sins? Who can fight his will?" [20]You are only human, and human

ROCK SOLID

Romans 8:35

Jesus Christ has the strongest hand in the world—once he has you in his hand, nothing can pull you away! Once you belong to him, nothing can break that bond.

Romans 8:35 says, "Can anything separate us from the love Christ has for us? Can troubles or problems or sufferings or hunger or nakedness or danger or violent death?" This is a rhetorical question with a resounding *no!* for an answer. There's absolutely nothing that can break your relationship with Jesus once you have it. Even if you wander off, he will keep pulling you back to himself and renewing the relationship.

This is one of the most awesome things about belonging to Jesus Christ. He will protect you no matter what and make sure that you join him in heaven someday. No problems on this earth can take you from him—he's the man with the strongest hand.

"Make A Difference"

"You get the clipboard and I'll get the whistles." Chris handed Josh his Conflict Manager's vest and they headed to the playground. Conflict managers at elementary schools across the nation have the privilege of making a difference.

Twice each week Chris and Josh patrol the playground with a teacher to help settle arguments, make sure kids aren't getting picked on and, ultimately, make sure everyone has fun. It's a great opportunity for guys and girls to help younger kids learn how to treat each other with kindness.

When asked about his job, Chris said, "I learned that the younger kids looked up to me as a Conflict Manager. That gave me a chance to show them how much fun games can be if everyone's trying to make it fun for everyone else. At first, I thought it was just a job, but now I know it's a great way for me to make a difference at my school."

But you don't have to be a conflict manager to make a difference. Just show some kindness—and kick it all over the playground.

beings have no right to question God. An object should not ask the person who made it, "Why did you make me like this?" ²¹The potter can make anything he wants to make. He can use the same clay to make one thing for special use and another thing for daily use.

²²It is the same way with God. He wanted to show his anger and to let people see his power. But he patiently stayed with those people he was angry with—people who were made ready to be destroyed. ²³He waited with patience so that he could make known his rich glory to the people who receive his mercy. He has prepared these people to have his glory, ²⁴and we are those people whom God called. He called us not from the Jews only but also from those who are not Jews. ²⁵As the Scripture says in Hosea:

"I will say, 'You are my people'
    to those I had called 'not my people.'
And I will show my love
    to those people I did not love."
                                        Hosea 2:1, 23

²⁶"They were called,
    'You are not my people,'
but later they will be called
    'children of the living God.' " *Hosea 1:10*
²⁷And Isaiah cries out about Israel:
"The people of Israel are many,
    like the grains of sand by the sea.
But only a few of them will be saved,
²⁸   because the Lord will quickly and
        completely punish the people on
        the earth."   *Isaiah 10:22–23*
²⁹It is as Isaiah said:

"The Lord All-Powerful
    allowed a few of our descendants to
        live.
Otherwise we would have been completely
        destroyed
    like the cities of Sodom and
        Gomorrah.'"   *Isaiah 1:9*

³⁰So what does all this mean? Those who are not Jews were not trying to make themselves right with God, but they were made right with God because of their faith. ³¹The people of Israel tried to follow a law to make themselves right with God. But they did not succeed, ³²because they tried to make themselves right by the things they did instead of trusting in God to make them right. They stumbled over the stone that causes people to stumble. ³³As it is written in the Scripture:

"I will put in Jerusalem a stone that causes
        people to stumble,
    a rock that makes them fall.
Anyone who trusts in him will never be
        disappointed."   *Isaiah 8:14; 28:16*

10 Brothers and sisters, the thing I want most is for all the Jews to be saved. That is my prayer to God. ²I can say this about them: They really try to follow God, but they do not know the right way. ³Because they did not know the way that God makes people right with him, they tried to make themselves right in their own way. So they did not accept God's way of making people right. ⁴Christ ended the law so that everyone who believes in him may be right with God.

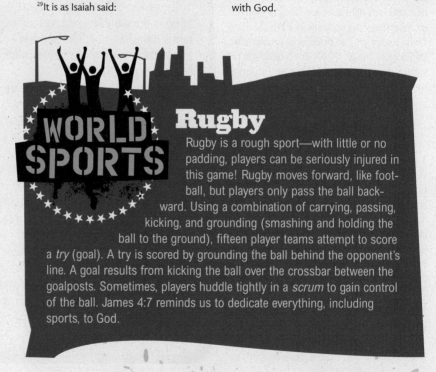

Rugby

Rugby is a rough sport—with little or no padding, players can be seriously injured in this game! Rugby moves forward, like football, but players only pass the ball backward. Using a combination of carrying, passing, kicking, and grounding (smashing and holding the ball to the ground), fifteen player teams attempt to score a *try* (goal). A try is scored by grounding the ball behind the opponent's line. A goal results from kicking the ball over the crossbar between the goalposts. Sometimes, players huddle tightly in a *scrum* to gain control of the ball. James 4:7 reminds us to dedicate everything, including sports, to God.

[5]Moses writes about being made right by following the law. He says, "A person who obeys these things will live because of them."[n] [6]But this is what the Scripture says about being made right through faith: "Don't say to yourself, 'Who will go up into heaven?' " (That means, "Who will go up to heaven and bring Christ down to earth?") [7]"And do not say, 'Who will go down into the world below?' " (That means, "Who will go down and bring Christ up from the dead?") [8]This is what the Scripture says: "The word is near you; it is in your mouth and in your heart."[n] That is the teaching of faith that we are telling. [9]If you declare with your mouth, "Jesus is Lord," and if you believe in your heart that God raised Jesus from the dead, you will be saved. [10]We believe with our hearts, and so we are made right with God. And we declare with our mouths that we believe, and so we are saved. [11]As the Scripture says, "Anyone who trusts in him will never be disappointed."[n] [12]That Scripture says "anyone" because there is no difference between those who are Jews and those who are not. The same Lord is the Lord of all and gives many blessings to all who trust in him, [13]as the Scripture says, "Anyone who calls on the Lord will be saved."[n]

[14]But before people can ask the Lord for help, they must believe in him; and before they can believe in him, they must hear about him; and for them to hear about the Lord, someone must tell them; [15]and before someone can go and tell them, that person must be sent. It is written, "How beautiful is the person who comes to bring good news."[n] [16]But not all the Jews accepted the good news. Isaiah said, "Lord, who believed what we told them?"[n] [17]So faith comes from hearing the Good News, and people hear the Good News when someone tells them about Christ.

[18]But I ask: Didn't people hear the Good News? Yes, they heard—as the Scripture says:

"Their message went out through all the world;
    their words go everywhere on earth."

Psalm 19:4

[19]Again I ask: Didn't the people of Israel understand? Yes, they did understand. First, Moses says:

"I will use those who are not a nation to make you jealous.
    I will use a nation that does not understand to make you angry."

Deuteronomy 32:21

[20]Then Isaiah is bold enough to say:

"I was found by those who were not asking me for help.
    I made myself known to people who were not looking for me."

Isaiah 65:1

[21]But about Israel God says,

"All day long I stood ready to accept people who disobey and are stubborn."

Isaiah 65:2

GOD SHOWS MERCY TO ALL PEOPLE

11 So I ask: Did God throw out his people? No! I myself am an Israelite from the family of Abraham, from the tribe of Benjamin. [2]God chose the Israelites to be his people before they were born, and he has not thrown his people out. Surely you know what the Scripture says about Elijah, how he prayed to God against the people of Israel. [3]"Lord," he said, "they have killed your prophets, and they have destroyed your altars. I am the only prophet left, and now they are trying to kill me, too."[n] [4]But what answer did God give Elijah? He said, "But I have left seven thousand people in Israel who have never bowed down before Baal."[n] [5]It is the

---

Q: I hate taking piano lessons because I'm not very good at it. Is there something in the Bible that says you have to take music lessons?

A: No. While the Bible talks about how good it is to make music (especially in the Book of Psalms in the Old Testament), it never says you have to take music lessons. But it does say to obey your parents in everything because it pleases God (Colossians 3:20). Piano lessons might not seem fun, but you should do your best anyway. One day you might be thankful to know how to play—even if you're not that good yet.

Q: Is the world really like what they show on the TV news?

A: Not always. Billions of things are happening around the world every single day, and the news channels can only pick a few to show on TV. Since viewers are more likely to watch scary or tragic news, that's what you see. The news doesn't usually cover many of the good things God has done that day.

Q: Is TV good or bad?

A: It can be both good and bad, depending on what it's used for. Many people have heard about Jesus for the first time by watching TV. But TV becomes bad when it makes sin look fun or when it becomes a waste of time. If you're not praying or reading your Bible every day, but you *are* watching hours of TV, you need to make a change.

10:5 "A person . . . them." Quotation from Leviticus 18:5.   **10:6–8** But . . . heart." Quotations from Deuteronomy 9:4; 30:12–14; Psalm 107:26.   **10:11** "Anyone . . . disappointed." Quotation from Isaiah 28:16.   **10:13** "Anyone . . . saved." Quotation from Joel 2:32.   **10:15** "How . . . news." Quotation from Isaiah 52:7.   **10:16** "Lord, . . . them?" Quotation from Isaiah 53:1.   **11:3** "they . . . too" Quotation from 1 Kings 19:10, 14.   **11:4** "But . . . Baal." Quotation from 1 Kings 19:18.

trustables

Romans 8:38–39

Nothing lasts forever. Your shiny new bike is starting to rust. Last year's school clothes are probably worn out. Your best friend doesn't want to hang out much anymore. Not even your "permanent" teeth will stick around forever! Man, what does last?

Things change so much, it's hard to get attached to anything. But the Bible tells us about one thing we can always count on: God's love. Now there are a lot of things that cause human love to fade: death, divorce, even just moving away. But God's love is *permanent*!

Romans 8:38–39 says *nothing* can separate us from God's love. Not death, not life, not any spiritual power. Time and distance can't take it away. The government can't take it away. And just to drive the point home, the Bible promises that nothing else in the whole universe can take it away. That about covers everything!

When you begin a relationship with Jesus Christ, you are making a friend who is always there no matter what you do and no matter where you go. He's not only there, but he loves you and has big plans for your life!

Your life will change. People and plans will sometimes bring disappointment. But through it all, remember that God's love for you is constant, unchanging, and will last forever!

---

same now. There are a few people that God has chosen by his grace. [6]And if he chose them by grace, it is not for the things they have done. If they could be made God's people by what they did, God's gift of grace would not really be a gift.

[7]So this is what has happened: Although the Israelites tried to be right with God, they did not succeed, but the ones God chose did become right with him. The others were made stubborn and refused to listen to God. [8]As it is written in the Scriptures:

> "God gave the people a dull mind so they
> could not understand."
>
> *Isaiah 29:10*

"He closed their eyes so they could not see and their ears so they could not hear. This continues until today."

Deuteronomy 29:4

[9]And David says:

> "Let their own feasts trap them and cause
> their ruin;
> let their feasts cause them to stumble
> and be paid back.

BIBLE SUPERHEROES

David
See 1 Samuel.

David was Israel's second king and the standard by which all other kings were judged. He was willing to put his life on the line for God. As a teen, he killed Goliath the giant. He went on to lead Israel's armies to many victories.

David was also a skilled musician. Check out his songs in the Book of Psalms.

God said, "I have found in David son of Jesse the kind of man I want. He will do all I want him to do" (Acts 13:22). But David sometimes did things God did *not* want him to do—like steal another man's wife and have the man murdered.

David later admitted his sin and begged God for forgiveness. His life was one of great faith, great failure, great forgiveness...and a Great God!

[10]Let their eyes be closed so they cannot see
and their backs be forever weak from
troubles."   *Psalm 69:22–23*

[11]So I ask: When the Jews fell, did that fall destroy them? No! But their failure brought salvation to those who are not Jews, in order to make the Jews jealous. [12]The Jews' failure brought rich blessings for the world, and the Jews' loss brought rich blessings for the non-Jewish people. So surely the world will receive much richer blessings when enough Jews become the kind of people God wants.

[13]Now I am speaking to you who are not Jews. I am an apostle to those who are not Jews, and since I have that work, I will make the most of it. [14]I hope I can make my own people jealous and, in that way, help some of them to be saved. [15]When God turned away from the Jews, he became friends with other people in the world. So when God accepts the Jews, surely that will bring them life after death.

[16]If the first piece of bread is offered to God, then the whole loaf is made holy. If the roots of a tree are holy, then the tree's branches are holy too.

[17]It is as if some of the branches from an olive tree have been broken off. You non-Jewish people are like the branch of a wild olive tree that has been joined to that first tree. You now share the strength and life of the first tree, the Jews. [18]So do not brag about those branches that were broken off. If you brag, remember that you do not support the root, but the root supports you. [19]You will say, "Branches were broken off so that I could be joined to their tree." [20]That is true. But those branches were broken off because they did not believe, and you continue to be part of the tree only because you believe. Do not be proud, but be afraid. [21]If God did not let the natural branches of that tree stay, then he will not let you stay if you don't believe.

[22]So you see that God is kind and also very strict. He punishes those who stop following him. But God is kind to you, if you continue following in his kindness. If you do not, you will be cut off from the tree. [23]And if the Jews will believe in God again, he will accept them back. God is able to put them back where they were. [24]It is not natural for a wild branch to be part of a good tree. And you who are not Jews are like a branch cut from a wild olive tree and joined to a good olive tree. But since those Jews are like a branch that grew from the good tree, surely they can be joined to their own tree again.

[25]I want you to understand this secret, brothers and sisters, so you will understand that you do not know everything: Part of Israel has been made stubborn, but that will change when many who are not Jews have come to God. [26]And that is how all Israel will be saved. It is written in the Scriptures:

"The Savior will come from Jerusalem;
he will take away all evil from the family
of Jacob."
[27]And I will make this agreement
with those people
when I take away their sins."
       Isaiah 59:20–21; 27:9

[28]The Jews refuse to accept the Good News, so they are God's enemies. This has happened to help you who are not Jews. But the Jews are still God's chosen people, and he loves them very much because of the promises he made to their ancestors. [29]God never changes his mind about the people he calls and the things he gives them. [30]At one time you refused to obey God. But now you have received mercy, because those people refused to obey. [31]And now the Jews refuse to obey, because God showed mercy to you. But this happened so that they also can" receive mercy from him. [32]God has given all people over to their stubborn ways so that he can show mercy to all.

PRAISE TO GOD

[33]Yes, God's riches are very great, and his wisdom and knowledge have no end! No one can explain the things God decides or understand his ways. [34]As the Scripture says,
"Who has known the mind of the Lord,
or who has been able to give him
advice?"   *Isaiah 40:13*
[35]"No one has ever given God anything
that he must pay back."   *Job 41:11*
[36]Yes, God made all things, and everything continues through him and for him. To him be the glory forever! Amen.

GIVE YOUR LIVES TO GOD

12 So brothers and sisters, since God has shown us great mercy, I beg you to offer your lives as a living sacrifice to him. Your offering must be only for God and

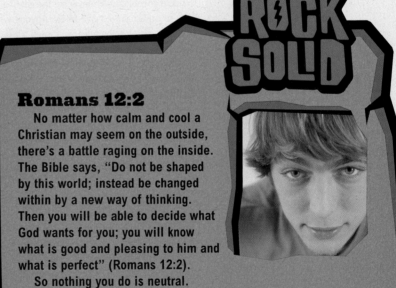

Romans 12:2

No matter how calm and cool a Christian may seem on the outside, there's a battle raging on the inside. The Bible says, "Do not be shaped by this world; instead be changed within by a new way of thinking. Then you will be able to decide what God wants for you; you will know what is good and pleasing to him and what is perfect" (Romans 12:2).

So nothing you do is neutral. You're living for God or giving in to the world, either becoming more like Jesus Christ or more bent out of shape. When you do what is right, like telling the truth, you're changing for the good. When you lie to get out of trouble, you're doing the opposite of what God considers good and pleasing to him.

Do you want to be more like Christ? Spend time reading and thinking about God's Word. Memorize this verse, and when you're tempted to do what you know is wrong, choose what is right and good.

11:26 Jacob Father of the twelve family groups of Israel, the people God chose to be his people.   **11:31 can** Some Greek copies read "can now."

pleasing to him, which is the spiritual way for you to worship. [2]Do not be shaped by this world; instead be changed within by a new way of thinking. Then you will be able to decide what God wants for you; you will know what is good and pleasing to him and what is perfect. [3]Because God has given me a special gift, I have something to say to everyone among you. Do not think you are better than you are. You must decide what you really are by the amount of faith God has given you. [4]Each one of us has a body with many parts, and these parts all have different uses. [5]In the same way, we are many, but in Christ we are all one body. Each one is a part of that body, and each part belongs to all the other parts. [6]We all have different gifts, each of which came because of the grace God gave us. The person who has the gift of prophecy should use that gift in agreement with the faith. [7]Anyone who

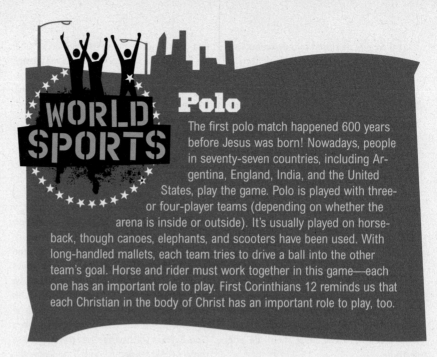

Polo

The first polo match happened 600 years before Jesus was born! Nowadays, people in seventy-seven countries, including Argentina, England, India, and the United States, play the game. Polo is played with three- or four-player teams (depending on whether the arena is inside or outside). It's usually played on horseback, though canoes, elephants, and scooters have been used. With long-handled mallets, each team tries to drive a ball into the other team's goal. Horse and rider must work together in this game—each one has an important role to play. First Corinthians 12 reminds us that each Christian in the body of Christ has an important role to play, too.

Romans 12:17
Read It: When someone does something mean to you, don't try to get even.
Do It: If someone does something to you, don't react immediately; cool down and get advice from someone you trust.

Romans 12:18
Read It: As much as you can, keep things cool between you and everyone else.
Do It: If a friend is mad at you, do everything you can to make it right as soon as possible.

Romans 13:1
Read It: God wants you to obey the authorities, because he put them there.
Do It: Obey the law, because when you do, you are also obeying God.

has the gift of serving should serve. Anyone who has the gift of teaching should teach. [8]Whoever has the gift of encouraging others should encourage. Whoever has the gift of giving to others should give freely. Anyone who has the gift of being a leader should try hard when he leads. Whoever has the gift of showing mercy to others should do so with joy.

[9]Your love must be real. Hate what is evil, and hold on to what is good. [10]Love each other like brothers and sisters. Give each other more honor than you want for yourselves. [11]Do not be lazy but work hard, serving the Lord with all your heart. [12]Be joyful because you have hope. Be patient when trouble comes, and pray at all times. [13]Share with God's people who need help. Bring strangers in need into your homes.

[14]Wish good for those who harm you; wish them well and do not curse them. [15]Be happy with those who are happy, and be sad with those who are sad. [16]Live in peace with each other. Do not be proud, but make friends with those who seem unimportant. Do not think how smart you are.

[17]If someone does wrong to you, do not pay him back by doing wrong to him. Try to do what everyone thinks is right. [18]Do your best to live in peace with everyone. [19]My friends, do not try to punish others when they wrong you, but wait for God to punish them with his anger. It is written: "I will punish those who do wrong; I will repay them,"[n] says the Lord. [20]But you should do this:

"If your enemy is hungry, feed him;
    if he is thirsty, give him a drink.

Doing this will be like pouring burning coals on his head."   *Proverbs 25:21–22*
[21]Do not let evil defeat you, but defeat evil by doing good.

CHRISTIANS SHOULD OBEY THE LAW

13 All of you must yield to the government rulers. No one rules unless God has given him the power to rule, and no one rules now without that power from God. [2]So those who are against the government are really against what God has commanded. And they will bring punishment on themselves. [3]Those who do right do not have to fear the rulers; only those who do wrong fear them. Do you want to be unafraid of the rulers? Then do what is right, and they will praise you. [4]The ruler is God's servant to help you. But if you do wrong, then be afraid. He has the power to punish; he is God's servant to punish those who do wrong. [5]So you must yield to the government, not only because you might be punished, but because you know it is right.

[6]This is also why you pay taxes. Rulers are working for God and give their time to their work. [7]Pay everyone, then, what you owe. If you owe any kind of tax, pay it. Show respect and honor to them all.

LOVING OTHERS

[8]Do not owe people anything, except always owe love to each other, because the person who loves others has obeyed all the law. [9]The law says, "You must not be guilty of adultery. You must not murder anyone. You must

LOOKING AHEAD

high School

tarting high school is one of the most exciting things about being a teenager, but it's also a big adjustment! Walking down the halls of a high school is enough to frighten most people. Changing classes five to seven times a day can also be hard to figure out, and you're probably not looking forward to final exams, either.

Before you start imagining the worst about high school, take time to learn about the changes that you'll be making. And don't worry—everyone understands that it takes time to adjust. There will be teachers and older students who can answer your questions and help you find your classrooms as you settle in. If you're scared, read Philippians 4:6, "Do not worry about anything, but pray and ask God for everything you need, always giving thanks."

You might have heard stories about difficult teachers in high school. If you're scared that teachers won't like you, or will give you too much homework—relax! Your teachers aren't out to make life impossible or stressful for you; they are there to challenge you so you can grow. If you do your best, you'll have no problem getting along in your classes. And don't be scared to talk to teachers. Put away those scary thoughts and fears *before* you walk into the classroom, and give your new teacher a chance!

Taking high school exams is another stressful subject. But the tests you'll take are designed to see what you know, not to torture you. There are many ways to prepare for an exam so that you won't have butterflies in your stomach. Pay attention in class and take notes so you can study before the test. It's also a wise idea to get enough sleep the night before and to eat a healthy breakfast. You might not get an "A," but you can do your best!

High school is a place where you will meet many new people—so don't be concerned if you don't know anyone yet. And you won't be bored; there will be lots of opportunities to get involved and try new things! If you have older siblings, talk to them about their favorite part of high school and things you can do to get ready for the change. By preparing a positive attitude about high school, it will be easier to start when it's time.

not steal. You must not want to take your neighbor's things."[n] All these commands and all others are really only one rule: "Love your neighbor as you love yourself."[n] [10]Love never hurts a neighbor, so loving is obeying all the law.

[11]Do this because we live in an important time. It is now time for you to wake up from your sleep, because our salvation is nearer now than when we first believed. [12]The "night"[n] is almost finished, and the "day"[n] is almost here. So we should stop doing things that belong to darkness and take up the weapons used for fighting in the light. [13]Let us live in a right way, like people who belong to the day. We should not have wild parties or get drunk. There should be no sexual sins of any kind, no fighting or jealousy. [14]But clothe yourselves with the Lord Jesus Christ and forget about satisfying your sinful self.

DO NOT CRITICIZE OTHER PEOPLE

14 Accept into your group someone who is weak in faith, and do not argue about opinions. [2]One person believes it is right to eat all kinds of food.[n] But another, who is weak, believes it is right to eat only vegetables. [3]The one who knows that it is right to eat any kind of food must not reject the one who eats only vegetables. And the person who eats only vegetables must not think that the one who eats all foods is wrong, because God has accepted that person. [4]You cannot judge another person's servant. The master decides if the servant is doing well or not. And the Lord's servant will do well because the Lord helps him do well.

[5]Some think that one day is more important than another, and others think that every day is the same. Let all be sure in their own mind. [6]Those who think one day is more important than other days are doing that for the Lord. And those who eat all kinds of food are doing that for the Lord, and they give thanks to God. Others who refuse to eat some foods do that for the Lord, and they give thanks to God. [7]We do not live or die for ourselves. [8]If we live, we are living for the Lord, and if we die, we are dying for the Lord. So living or dying, we belong to the Lord.

[9]The reason Christ died and rose from the dead to live again was so he would be Lord over both the dead and the living. [10]So why do you judge your brothers or sisters in Christ? And why do you think you are better than they are? We will all stand before God to be judged, [11]because it is written in the Scriptures:

" 'As surely as I live,' says the Lord,

Secrets to Become Better at Sports

1. When you watch sports, take notes on what the athletes do.
2. Push yourself to your limit at every practice.
3. Ask your coaches what you can work on.
4. Keep practicing off-season.
5. When you play sports-related video games, look for the strategies that work.
6. Listen to more experienced athletes.
7. Exercise to gain strength and speed.
8. Learn the rules.
9. Rest when you're injured.
10. Practice, practice, practice!

'Everyone will bow before me;
everyone will say that I am God.' "

Isaiah 45:23

[12]So each of us will have to answer to God.

DO NOT CAUSE OTHERS TO SIN

[13]For that reason we should stop judging each other. We must make up our minds not to do anything that will make another Christian sin. [14]I am in the Lord Jesus, and I know that there is no food that is wrong to eat. But if a person believes something is wrong, that thing is wrong for him. [15]If you hurt your brother's or sister's faith because of something you eat, you are not really following the way of love. Do not destroy someone's faith by eating food he thinks is wrong, because Christ died for him. [16]Do not allow what you think is good to become what others say is evil. [17]In the kingdom of God, eating and drinking are not important. The important things are living right with God, peace, and joy in the Holy Spirit. [18]Anyone who

ROCK SOLID

Romans 14:17–19

One of the questions parents often ask their kids is "What on earth were you thinking?" as if there should be a logical explanation for some of the stupid things kids do. In reality, the correct answer to this question is usually, "I wasn't thinking!"

Sound familiar? You're not alone. In fact, you're in pretty good company. Your parents might not say so, but everyone does things they don't understand and don't even want to do. Like telling white lies. Gossiping about other people. Wanting what others have. Being greedy. Hating. We all do these things, no matter how much we think they are wrong.

Not even the apostle Paul, the guy who wrote most of the books in the New Testament, could avoid sinning. He said, "The important things are living right with God, peace, and joy in the Holy Spirit....So let us *try* to do what makes peace and helps one another" (Acts 14:17–19).

We'll never get it perfect, but we need to keep trying. The important thing is to remember that everyone struggles and God loves us enough to keep forgiving us. What do you struggle with the most? Talk to God about it. He wants to help you kick your bad habits!

13:9 "You . . . things." Quotation from Exodus 20:13–15, 17.   **13:9 "Love . . . yourself."** Quotation from Leviticus 19:18.   **13:12 "night"** This is used as a symbol of the sinful world we live in. This world will soon end.   **13:12 "day"** This is used as a symbol of the good time that is coming, when we will be with God.   **14:2 all . . . food** The Jewish law said there were some foods Jews should not eat. When Jews became Christians, some of them did not understand they could now eat all foods.

serves Christ by living this way is pleasing God and will be accepted by other people.

[19] So let us try to do what makes peace and helps one another. [20] Do not let the eating of food destroy the work of God. All foods are all right to eat, but it is wrong to eat food that causes someone else to sin. [21] It is better not to eat meat or drink wine or do anything that will cause your brother or sister to sin.

[22] Your beliefs about these things should be kept secret between you and God. People are happy if they can do what they think is right without feeling guilty. [23] But those who eat something without being sure it is right are wrong because they did not believe it was right. Anything that is done without believing it is right is a sin.

15 We who are strong in faith should help the weak with their weaknesses, and not please only ourselves. [2] Let each of us please our neighbors for their good, to help them be stronger in faith. [3] Even Christ did not live to please himself. It was as the Scriptures said: "When people insult you, it hurts me."[n] [4] Everything that was written in the past was written to teach us. The Scriptures give us patience and encouragement so that we can have hope. [5] May the patience and encouragement that come from God allow you to live in harmony with each other the way Christ Jesus wants. [6] Then you will all be joined together, and you will give glory to God the Father of our Lord Jesus Christ. [7] Christ accepted you, so you should accept each other, which will bring glory to God. [8] I tell you that Christ became a servant of the Jews to show that God's promises to the Jewish ancestors are true. [9] And he also did this so that those who are not Jews could give glory to God for the mercy he gives to them. It is written in the Scriptures:

"So I will praise you among the non-Jewish
people.
I will sing praises to your name."
Psalm 18:49

[10] The Scripture also says,

"Be happy, you who are not Jews, together
with his people."
Deuteronomy 32:43

[11] Again the Scripture says,

"All you who are not Jews, praise the Lord.
All you people, sing praises to him."
Psalm 117:1

[12] And Isaiah says,

"A new king will come from the family of
Jesse."
He will come to rule over the
non-Jewish people,

DID YOU KNOW?

29% of boys hope to run their own business someday.

Trends & Tudes. Harris Interactive. January 2003.

and they will have hope because of him."
Isaiah 11:10

[13] I pray that the God who gives hope will fill you with much joy and peace while you trust in him. Then your hope will overflow by the power of the Holy Spirit.

PAUL TALKS ABOUT HIS WORK

[14] My brothers and sisters, I am sure that you are full of goodness. I know that you have

all the knowledge you need and that you are able to teach each other. [15] But I have written to you very openly about some things I wanted you to remember. I did this because God gave me this special gift: [16] to be a minister of Christ Jesus to those who are not Jews. I served God by teaching his Good News, so that the non-Jewish people could be an offering that God would accept—an offering made holy by the Holy Spirit.

[17] So I am proud of what I have done for God in Christ Jesus. [18] I will not talk about anything except what Christ has done through me in leading those who are not Jews to obey God. They have obeyed God because of what I have said and done, [19] because of the power of miracles and the great things they saw, and because of the power of the Holy Spirit. I preached the Good News from Jerusalem all the way around to Illyricum, and so I have finished that part of my work. [20] I always want to preach the Good News in places where people have never heard of Christ, because I do not want to build on the work someone else has already started. [21] But it is written in the Scriptures:

"Those who were not told about him will
see,
and those who have not heard about
him will understand." *Isaiah 52:15*

PAUL'S PLAN TO VISIT ROME

[22] This is the reason I was stopped many times from coming to you. [23] Now I have

dare to do

Romans 14:13
Read It: Don't do anything that could help another Christian sin.
Do It: Do friends come over to your house to watch movies they aren't allowed to watch at home? If so, don't share them, because you're helping your friends to sin!

Romans 14:19
Read It: Do things that create peace and help others.
Do It: If you see someone getting picked on or hurt, try to help or tell an adult.

Romans 15:7
Read It: Accept people just like Jesus accepted you.
Do It: Invite people into your group of friends, especially if they're alone. Remember how Jesus died for us even though we didn't deserve it.

15:3 *"When . . . me."* Quotation from Psalm 69:9.   **15:12 Jesse** Jesse was the father of David, king of Israel. Jesus was from their family.

finished my work here. Since for many years I have wanted to come to you, [24]I hope to visit you on my way to Spain. After I enjoy being with you for a while, I hope you can help me on my trip. [25]Now I am going to Jerusalem to help God's people. [26]The believers in Macedonia and Southern Greece were happy to give their money to help the poor among God's people at Jerusalem. [27]They were happy to do this, and really they owe it to them. These who are not Jews have shared in the Jews' spiritual blessings, so they should use their material possessions to help the Jews. [28]After I am sure the poor in Jerusalem get the money that has been given for them, I will leave for Spain and stop and visit you. [29]I know that when I come to you I will bring Christ's full blessing.

[30]Brothers and sisters, I beg you to help me in my work by praying to God for me. Do this because of our Lord Jesus and the love that the Holy Spirit gives us. [31]Pray that I will be saved from the nonbelievers in Judea and that this help I bring to Jerusalem will please God's people there. [32]Then, if God wants me to, I will come to you with joy, and together you and I will have a time of rest. [33]The God who gives peace be with you all. Amen.

GREETINGS TO THE CHRISTIANS

16 I recommend to you our sister Phoebe, who is a helper" in the church in Cenchrea. [2]I ask you to accept her in the Lord in the way God's people should. Help her with anything she needs, because she has helped me and many other people also.

[3]Give my greetings to Priscilla and Aquila, who work together with me in Christ Jesus [4]and who risked their own lives to save my life. I am thankful to them, and all the non-Jewish churches are thankful as well. [5]Also, greet for me the church that meets at their house.

Greetings to my dear friend Epenetus, who was the first person in Asia to follow Christ. [6]Greetings to Mary, who worked very

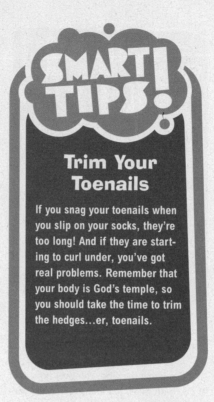

Trim Your Toenails

If you snag your toenails when you slip on your socks, they're too long! And if they are starting to curl under, you've got real problems. Remember that your body is God's temple, so you should take the time to trim the hedges...er, toenails.

hard for you. [7]Greetings to Andronicus and Junia, my relatives, who were in prison with me. They are very important apostles. They were believers in Christ before I was. [8]Greetings to Ampliatus, my dear friend in the Lord. [9]Greetings to Urbanus, a worker together with me for Christ. And greetings to my dear friend Stachys. [10]Greetings to Apelles, who was tested and proved that he truly loves Christ. Greetings to all those who are in the family of Aristobulus. [11]Greetings to Herodion, my fellow citizen. Greetings to all those in the family of Narcissus who belong to the Lord. [12]Greetings to Tryphena and Tryphosa, women who work very hard for the Lord. Greetings to my dear friend Persis, who also has worked very hard for the Lord. [13]Greetings to Rufus, who is a special person in the Lord, and to his

mother, who has been like a mother to me also. [14]Greetings to Asyncritus, Phlegon, Hermes, Patrobas, Hermas, and all the brothers and sisters who are with them. [15]Greetings to Philologus and Julia, Nereus and his sister, and Olympas, and to all God's people with them. [16]Greet each other with a holy kiss. All of Christ's churches send greetings to you.

[17]Brothers and sisters, I ask you to look out for those who cause people to be against each other and who upset other people's faith. They are against the true teaching you learned, so stay away from them. [18]Such people are not serving our Lord Christ but are only doing what pleases themselves. They use fancy talk and fine words to fool the minds of those who do not know about evil. [19]All the believers have heard that you obey, so I am very happy because of you. But I want you to be wise in what is good and innocent in what is evil.

[20]The God who brings peace will soon defeat Satan and give you power over him.

The grace of our Lord Jesus be with you.

[21]Timothy, a worker together with me, sends greetings, as well as Lucius, Jason, and Sosipater, my relatives.

[22]I am Tertius, and I am writing this letter from Paul. I send greetings to you in the Lord.

[23]Gaius is letting me and the whole church here use his home. He also sends greetings to you, as do Erastus, the city treasurer, and our brother Quartus. [[24]The grace of our Lord Jesus Christ be with all of you. Amen.]"

[25]Glory to God who can make you strong in faith by the Good News that I tell people and by the message about Jesus Christ. The message about Christ is the secret that was hidden for long ages past but is now made known. [26]It has been made clear through the writings of the prophets. And by the command of the eternal God it is made known to all nations that they might believe and obey.

[27]To the only wise God be glory forever through Jesus Christ! Amen.

16:1 helper Literally, "deaconess." This might mean the same as one of the special women helpers in 1 Timothy 3:11.   **16:24 The . . . Amen.** Some Greek copies do not contain the bracketed text.

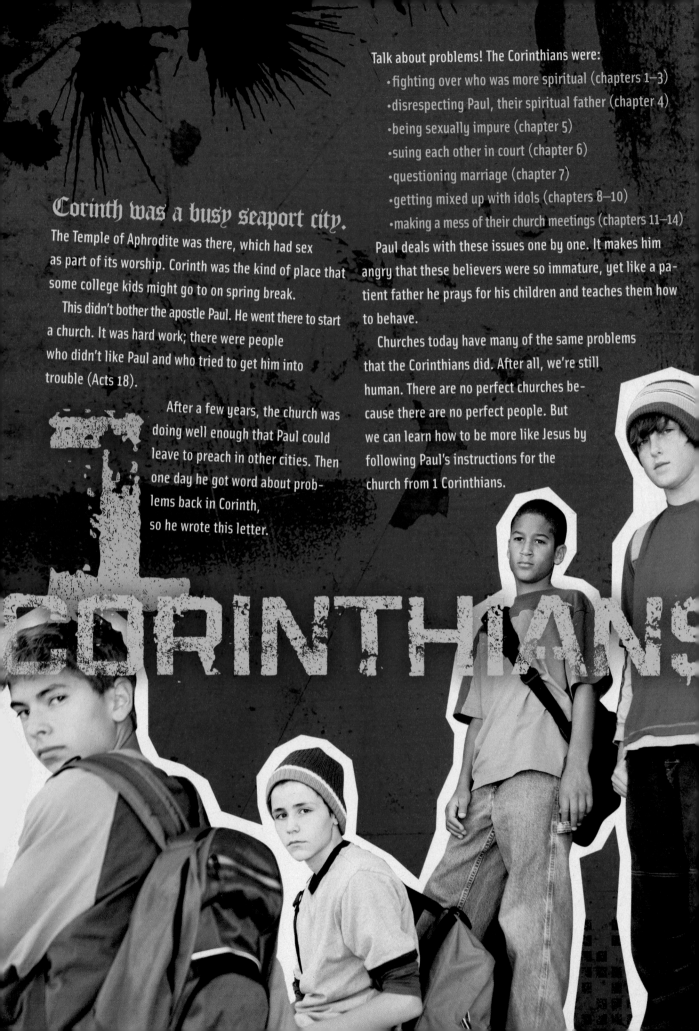

Corinth was a busy seaport city.

The Temple of Aphrodite was there, which had sex as part of its worship. Corinth was the kind of place that some college kids might go to on spring break.

This didn't bother the apostle Paul. He went there to start a church. It was hard work; there were people who didn't like Paul and who tried to get him into trouble (Acts 18).

After a few years, the church was doing well enough that Paul could leave to preach in other cities. Then one day he got word about problems back in Corinth, so he wrote this letter.

Talk about problems! The Corinthians were:

- fighting over who was more spiritual (chapters 1–3)
- disrespecting Paul, their spiritual father (chapter 4)
- being sexually impure (chapter 5)
- suing each other in court (chapter 6)
- questioning marriage (chapter 7)
- getting mixed up with idols (chapters 8–10)
- making a mess of their church meetings (chapters 11–14)

Paul deals with these issues one by one. It makes him angry that these believers were so immature, yet like a patient father he prays for his children and teaches them how to behave.

Churches today have many of the same problems that the Corinthians did. After all, we're still human. There are no perfect churches because there are no perfect people. But we can learn how to be more like Jesus by following Paul's instructions for the church from 1 Corinthians.

1 CORINTHIANS

1 From Paul. God called me to be an apostle of Christ Jesus because that is what God wanted. Also from Sosthenes, our brother in Christ.

²To the church of God in Corinth, to you who have been made holy in Christ Jesus. You were called to be God's holy people with all people everywhere who pray in the name of the Lord Jesus Christ—their Lord and ours:

³Grace and peace to you from God our Father and the Lord Jesus Christ.

PAUL GIVES THANKS TO GOD

⁴I always thank my God for you because of the grace God has given you in Christ Jesus. ⁵I thank God because in Christ you have been made rich in every way, in all your speaking and in all your knowledge. ⁶Just as our witness about Christ has been guaranteed to you, ⁷so you have every gift from God while you wait for our Lord Jesus Christ to come again. ⁸Jesus will keep you strong until the end so that there will be no wrong in you on the day our Lord Jesus Christ comes again. ⁹God, who has called you into fellowship with his Son, Jesus Christ our Lord, is faithful.

PROBLEMS IN THE CHURCH

¹⁰I beg you, brothers and sisters, by the name of our Lord Jesus Christ that all of you agree with each other and not be split into groups. I beg that you be completely joined together by having the same kind of thinking and the same purpose. ¹¹My brothers and sisters, some people from Chloe's family have told me quite plainly that there are quarrels among you. ¹²This is what I mean: One of you says, "I follow Paul"; another says, "I follow Apollos"; another says, "I follow Peter"; and another says, "I follow Christ." ¹³Christ has been divided up into different groups! Did Paul die on the cross for you? No! Were you baptized in the name of Paul? No! ¹⁴I thank God I did not baptize any of you except Crispus and Gaius ¹⁵so that now no one can say you were baptized in my name. ¹⁶(I also baptized the family of Stephanas, but I do not remember that I baptized anyone else.) ¹⁷Christ did not send me to baptize people but to preach the Good News. And he sent me to preach the Good News without using words of human wisdom so that the crossⁿ of Christ would not lose its power.

CHRIST IS GOD'S POWER AND WISDOM

¹⁸The teaching about the cross is foolishness to those who are being lost, but to us who are being saved it is the power of God. ¹⁹It is written in the Scriptures:

"I will cause the wise to lose their wisdom;
    I will make the wise unable to
        understand."   *Isaiah 29:14*

²⁰Where is the wise person? Where is the educated person? Where is the skilled talker of this world? God has made the wisdom of the world foolish. ²¹In the wisdom of God the world did not know God through its own wisdom. So God chose to use the message that sounds foolish to save those who believe. ²²The Jews ask for miracles, and the Greeks want wisdom. ²³But we preach a crucified Christ. This causes the Jews to stumble and is foolishness to non-Jews. ²⁴But Christ is the power of God and the wisdom of God to those people God has called—Jews and Greeks. ²⁵Even the foolishness of God is wiser than human wisdom, and the weakness of God is stronger than human strength.

²⁶Brothers and sisters, look at what you

Q: My dad hates hip-hop music, especially rap. But that's the only kind of music I really like. What's wrong with listening to it on my own if he never finds out?

A: It's wrong if you know he doesn't want you to do it. God wants you to obey your parents (Ephesians 6:1). Your dad's job is to make sure he does what's best for you, even if you don't like it. You might ask him what he doesn't like about hip-hop. If it's the violent lyrics, respectfully ask if you could listen to Christian hip-hop. But if he still says no, you must respect his decision.

Q: Why don't the most popular movies seem to be about the Bible?

A: There have been a few successful movies about Bible stories, like Mel Gibson's *The Passion of the Christ*. The reason there haven't been more is that many people in Hollywood don't like the Bible's message. They want to make movies about having a good time and succeeding by the world's standards. The stories in the Bible are about living by God's standards. To people who've never experienced God's love, that doesn't sound like much fun.

Q: Why do prices usually end in .99 or .97?

A: Prices end with uneven amounts to make you think you're paying less. Something priced at $19.99 doesn't *seem* as expensive as something that costs a whole $20 bill. Stores use it as a trick to get you to buy something you might not buy if you saw the higher price. As a Christian, you can use the wisdom God gives you to see through any of the world's tricks.

1:17 cross Paul uses the cross as a picture of the Good News, the story of Christ's death and rising from the dead for people's sins. The cross, or Christ's death, was God's way to save people.

were when God called you. Not many of you were wise in the way the world judges wisdom. Not many of you had great influence. Not many of you came from important families. [27]But God chose the foolish things of the world to shame the wise, and he chose the weak things of the world to shame the strong. [28]He chose what the world thinks is unimportant and what the world looks down on and thinks is nothing in order to destroy what the world thinks is important. [29]God did this so that no one can brag in his presence. [30]Because of God you are in Christ Jesus, who has become for us wisdom from God. In Christ we are put right with God, and have been made holy, and have been set free from sin. [31]So, as the Scripture says, "If people want to brag, they should brag only about the Lord."[n]

THE MESSAGE OF CHRIST'S DEATH

2 Dear brothers and sisters, when I came to you, I did not come preaching God's secret[n] with fancy words or a show of human wisdom. [2]I decided that while I was with you I would forget about everything except Jesus Christ and his death on the cross. [3]So when I came to you, I was weak and fearful and trembling. [4]My teaching and preaching were not with words of human wisdom that persuade people but with proof of the power that the Spirit gives. [5]This was so that your faith would be in God's power and not in human wisdom.

GOD'S WISDOM

[6]However, I speak a wisdom to those who are mature. But this wisdom is not from this world or from the rulers of this world, who are losing their power. [7]I speak God's secret wisdom, which he has kept hidden. Before the world began, God planned this wisdom for our glory. [8]None of the rulers of this world understood it. If they had, they would not have crucified the Lord of glory. [9]But as it is written in the Scriptures:

"No one has ever seen this,
and no one has ever heard about it.
No one has ever imagined
what God has prepared for those who
love him." Isaiah 64:4

[10]But God has shown us these things through the Spirit.

The Spirit searches out all things, even the deep secrets of God. [11]Who knows the thoughts that another person has? Only a person's spirit that lives within him knows his thoughts. It is the same with God. No one knows the thoughts of God except the Spirit of God. [12]Now we did not receive the spirit of the world, but we received the Spirit that is from God so that we can know all that God has given us. [13]And we speak about these things, not with words taught us by human wisdom but with words taught us by the Spirit. And so we explain spiritual truths to spiritual people. [14]A person who does not have the Spirit does not accept the truths that come from the Spirit of God. That person thinks they are foolish and cannot understand them, because they can only be judged to be true by the Spirit. [15]The spiritual person is able to judge all things, but no one can judge him. The Scripture says:

[16]"Who has known the mind of the Lord?
Who has been able to teach him?"
Isaiah 40:13

But we have the mind of Christ.

FOLLOWING PEOPLE IS WRONG

3 Brothers and sisters, in the past I could not talk to you as I talk to spiritual people. I had to talk to you as I would to people without the Spirit—babies in Christ. [2]The teaching I gave you was like milk, not solid food, because you were not able to take solid food. And even now you are not ready. [3]You are still not spiritual, because there is jealousy and quarreling among you, and this shows that you are not spiritual. You are acting like people of the world. [4]One of you says, "I belong to Paul," and another says, "I belong to Apollos."

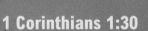

1 Corinthians 1:30

Have you ever tried out for a sport or a musical? You just can't wait to find out if you made the team or got a lead role. A lot of people feel this way about heaven, too! They think life is an audition for one day getting into heaven. They believe that if they perform well, and be as good as they can, they just might make the cut.

The truth is, performing well on earth won't get you into heaven. What matters is that you know the secret to getting in! Don't panic. It's not a "secret" secret. It's been given to everyone. The Bible says,

"In Christ we are put right with God, and have been made holy, and have been set free from sin" (1 Corinthians 1:30).

The secret of getting into heaven is being "in Christ"! That means you must invite Jesus Christ into your heart. If you do that, you're in! Here's the catch: when you invite Christ in, he changes your heart and you want to live for him! When you know the secret to getting into heaven, you start learning to act like you deserve to go there. Then the things you do on earth will bring you rewards in heaven.

1:31 "If . . . Lord." Quotation from Jeremiah 9:24.   2:1 God's secret Some Greek copies read "God's message."

Ways to Get Girls to Leave You Alone

1. Don't tease them.
2. Don't chase them when they tease you.
3. Play sports with your guy friends at recess.
4. Treat all girls the same.
5. Sit with your guy friends at church and at lunch.
6. Don't ask your guy friends questions about any specific girls.
7. Let all the girls know you just want to be "a friend."
8. Tell them you're not dating until college (if it's true).
9. Hang out where the girls don't go.
10. Do gross stuff.

When you say things like this, you are acting like people of the world.

⁵Is Apollos important? No! Is Paul important? No! We are only servants of God who helped you believe. Each one of us did the work God gave us to do. ⁶I planted the seed, and Apollos watered it. But God is the One who made it grow. ⁷So the one who plants is not important, and the one who waters is not important. Only God, who makes things grow, is important. ⁸The one who plants and the one who waters have the same purpose, and each will be rewarded for his own work. ⁹We are God's workers, working together; you are like God's farm, God's house.

¹⁰Using the gift God gave me, I laid the foundation of that house like an expert builder. Others are building on that foundation, but all people should be careful how they build on it. ¹¹The foundation that has already been laid is Jesus Christ, and no one can lay down any other foundation. ¹²But if people build on that foundation, using gold, silver, jewels, wood, grass, or straw, ¹³their work will be clearly seen, because the Day of Judgment" will make it visible. That Day will appear with fire, and the fire will test everyone's work to show what sort of work it was. ¹⁴If the building that has been put on the foundation still stands, the builder will get a reward. ¹⁵But if the building is burned up, the builder will suffer loss. The builder will be saved, but it will be as one who escaped from a fire.

¹⁶Don't you know that you are God's temple and that God's Spirit lives in you? ¹⁷If anyone destroys God's temple, God will destroy that person, because God's temple is holy and you are that temple.

¹⁸Do not fool yourselves. If you think you are wise in this world, you should become a fool so that you can become truly wise, ¹⁹because the wisdom of this world is foolishness with God. It is written in the Scriptures, "He catches those who are wise in their own clever traps."" ²⁰It is also written in the Scriptures, "The Lord knows what wise people think. He knows their thoughts are just a puff of wind."" ²¹So you should not brag about human leaders. All things belong to you: ²²Paul, Apollos, and Peter; the world, life, death, the present, and the future—all these belong to you. ²³And you belong to Christ, and Christ belongs to God.

APOSTLES ARE SERVANTS OF CHRIST

4 People should think of us as servants of Christ, the ones God has trusted with his secrets. ²Now in this way those who are trusted with something valuable must show they are worthy of that trust. ³As for myself, I do not care if I am judged by you or by any human court. I do not even judge myself. ⁴I know of no wrong I have done, but this does not make me right before the Lord. The Lord is the One who judges me. ⁵So do not judge before the right time; wait until the Lord comes. He will bring to light things that are now hidden in darkness, and will make known the secret purposes of people's hearts. Then God will praise each one of them.

⁶Brothers and sisters, I have used Apollos and myself as examples so you could learn through us the meaning of the saying, "Follow only what is written in the Scriptures." Then you will not be more proud of one person than another. ⁷Who says you are better than others? What do you have that was not given to you? And if it was given to you, why do you brag as if you did not receive it as a gift?

⁸You think you already have everything you need. You think you are rich. You think you have become kings without us. I wish you really were kings so we could be kings together with you. ⁹But it seems to me that God has put us apostles in last place, like those sentenced to die. We are like a show for the whole world to see—angels and people. ¹⁰We are fools for Christ's sake, but you are very wise in Christ. We are weak, but you are strong. You receive honor, but we are shamed. ¹¹Even to this very hour we do not have enough to eat or drink or to wear. We are often beaten, and we have no homes in which to live. ¹²We work hard with

1 Corinthians 1:10
Read It: Be unified with other believers in the church.
Do It: Be friendly with everyone in your youth group or Sunday school class. This is no place for cliques that exclude people.

1 Corinthians 1:27
Read It: God uses average, ordinary people to do great things.
Do It: Don't get down about what you can't do. Ask God to work through you! He will help you accomplish great things with your life.

1 Corinthians 1:31
Read It: Your bragging should be about God alone.
Do It: Don't talk big about yourself; tell people about the greatness of God!

3:13 Day of Judgment The day Christ will come to judge all people and take his people home to live with him.   **3:19 "He . . . traps."** Quotation from Job 5:13.   **3:20 "The Lord . . . wind."** Quotation from Psalm 94:11.

1 Corinthians 5:11–13

Who do you eat lunch with? What kind of people are they? You may not think it matters, but God cares about those you eat with! That's because to him, eating is an important part of our lives that we share with other people. When you share a meal with someone, you are deepening your connection to him.

There's one type of person God wants you to avoid eating with. No, it's not the sinful unbeliever. You might do him some good! It's the person who calls himself a Christian but who does not act that way. The Bible says, "I am writing to tell you that you must not associate with those who call themselves believers in Christ but who sin sexually, or are greedy, or worship idols, or abuse others with words, or get drunk, or cheat people. Do not even eat with people like that" (1 Corinthians 5:11–12).

It's one thing to behave badly and drag your own name through the dirt. But when self-proclaimed Christians behave badly, they drag God's name through the dirt! And you shouldn't eat with them because they may drag you down with them. So next time you head for the lunchroom, pick your table wisely. God is watching.

our own hands for our food. When people curse us, we bless them. When they hurt us, we put up with it. [13]When they tell evil lies about us, we speak nice words about them. Even today, we are treated as though we were the garbage of the world—the filth of the earth.

[14]I am not trying to make you feel ashamed. I am writing this to give you a warning as my own dear children. [15]For though you may have ten thousand teachers in Christ, you do not have many fathers. Through the Good News I became your father in Christ Jesus, [16]so I beg you, please follow my example. [17]That is why I am sending to you Timothy, my son in the Lord. I love Timothy, and he is faithful. He will help you remember my way of life in Christ Jesus, just as I teach it in all the churches everywhere.

[18]Some of you have become proud, thinking that I will not come to you again. [19]But I will come to you very soon if the Lord wishes. Then I will know what the proud ones do, not what they say, [20]because the kingdom of God is present not in talk but in power. [21]Which do you want: that I come to you with punishment or with love and gentleness?

WICKEDNESS IN THE CHURCH

5 It is actually being said that there is sexual sin among you. And it is a kind that does not happen even among people who do not know God. A man there has his father's wife. [2]And you are proud! You should have been filled with sadness so that the man who did this should be put out of your group. [3]I am not there with you in person, but I am with you in spirit. And I have already judged the man who did that sin as if I were really there. [4]When you meet together in the name of our Lord Jesus, and I meet with you in spirit with the power of our Lord Jesus, [5]then hand this man over to Satan. So his sinful self[n] will be destroyed, and his spirit will be saved on the day of the Lord.

[6]Your bragging is not good. You know the saying, "Just a little yeast makes the whole batch of dough rise." [7]Take out all the old yeast so that you will be a new batch of dough without yeast, which you really are. For Christ, our Passover lamb, has been sacrificed. [8]So let us celebrate this feast, but not with the bread that has the old yeast—the yeast of sin and wickedness. Let us celebrate this feast with the bread that has no yeast—the bread of goodness and truth.

[9]I wrote you in my earlier letter not to associate with those who sin sexually. [10]But I did not

60% of boys plan to go to college someday.

Trends & Tudes. Harris Interactive. January 2003.

mean you should not associate with those of this world who sin sexually, or with the greedy, or robbers, or those who worship idols. To get away from them you would have to leave this world. [11]I am writing to tell you that you must not associate with those who call themselves believers in Christ but who sin sexually, or are greedy, or worship idols, or abuse others with words, or get drunk, or cheat people. Do not even eat with people like that.

[12-13]It is not my business to judge those who are not part of the church. God will judge them. But you must judge the people who are part of the church. The Scripture says, "You must get rid of the evil person among you."[n]

JUDGING PROBLEMS AMONG CHRISTIANS

6 When you have something against another Christian, how can you bring yourself to go before judges who are not right with God? Why do you not let God's people decide who is right? [2]Surely you know that God's people will judge the world. So if you are to judge the world, are you not able to judge small cases as well? [3]You know that in the future we will judge angels, so surely we can judge the ordinary things of this life. [4]If you have ordinary cases that must be judged, are you going to appoint people as judges who mean nothing to the church? [5]I say this to shame you. Surely there is someone among you wise enough to judge a complaint between believers? [6]But now one believer goes to court against another believer—and you do this in front of unbelievers!

[7]The fact that you have lawsuits against each other shows that you are already defeated. Why not let yourselves be wronged?

5:5 sinful self Literally, "flesh." This could also mean his body.   **5:12–13 "You . . . you."** Quotation from Deuteronomy 17:7; 19:19; 22:21, 24; 24:7.

June

1

2 Get ready for a brain freeze! Today is *"Rocky Road Day."*

3

4 Pray for a person of influence: actress Angelina Jolie adds another candle to her cake today.

5

6 You're almost done! Thank your teacher for the school year.

7 Are you full of joy? Or do you worry all the time? Either way, read Philippians 4:4–8.

8 Celebrate friendship… hang out with your best friend today.

9 Pray for a person of influence: it's actor Michael J. Fox's birthday.

10 Give yourself more room; pack your winter clothes under your bed until fall.

11

12

13 Pray for people of influence: the Olsen twins—actresses Mary Kate and Ashley—share their birthday today.

14

15 Today is *"Smile Power Day."* Grin at everyone to see how much power your smile has!

17

18 Stick a cup of yogurt in the freezer before bed. It'll make a yummy breakfast in the morning!

19 Tell your dad you love him this Father's Day. And thank God for being your heavenly Father.

21 Pray for a person of influence: Prince William of Great Britain has a birthday today.

22 Be a tourist in your own city! Go see the sights that make your town unique.

25 Are you holding a grudge? Ask God to help you forgive the person.

27 Pray for a person of influence: *Spiderman* actor Tobey Maguire gets older today.

30 Ask permission first, then take a blanket outside and watch the stars.

Why not let yourselves be cheated? [8]But you yourselves do wrong and cheat, and you do this to other believers!

[9-10]Surely you know that the people who do wrong will not inherit God's kingdom. Do not be fooled. Those who sin sexually, worship idols, take part in adultery, those who are male prostitutes, or men who have sexual relations with other men, those who steal, are greedy, get drunk, lie about others, or rob—these people will not inherit God's kingdom. [11]In the past, some of you were like that, but you were washed clean. You were made holy, and you were made right with God in the name of the Lord Jesus Christ and in the Spirit of our God.

USE YOUR BODIES FOR GOD'S GLORY

[12]"I am allowed to do all things," but not all things are good for me to do. "I am allowed to do all things," but I will not let anything make me its slave. [13]"Food is for the stomach, and the stomach for food," but God will destroy them both. The body is not for sexual sin but for the Lord, and the Lord is for the body. [14]By his power God has raised the Lord from the dead and will also raise us from the dead. [15]Surely you know that your bodies are parts of Christ himself. So I must never take the parts of Christ and join them to a prostitute! [16]It is written in the Scriptures, "The two will become one body."[n] So you should know that anyone who joins with a prostitute becomes one body with the prostitute. [17]But the one who joins with the Lord is one spirit with the Lord.

[18]So run away from sexual sin. Every other sin people do is outside their bodies, but those who sin sexually sin against their own bodies. [19]You should know that your body is a temple for the Holy Spirit who is in you. You have received the Holy Spirit from God. So you do not belong to yourselves, [20]because you were bought by God for a price. So honor God with your bodies.

ABOUT MARRIAGE

7 Now I will discuss the things you wrote me about. It is good for a man not to have sexual relations with a woman. [2]But because sexual sin is a danger, each man should have his own wife, and each woman should have her own husband. [3]The husband should give his wife all that he owes her as his wife. And the wife should give her husband all that she owes him as her husband. [4]The wife does not have full rights over her own body; her husband shares them. And the husband does not have full rights over his own body; his wife shares them. [5]Do not refuse to give your bodies to each other, unless you both agree to stay away from sexual relations for a time so you can give your time to prayer. Then come together again so Satan cannot tempt you because of a lack of self-control. [6]I say this to give you permission to stay away from sexual relations for a time. It is not a command to do so. [7]I wish that everyone were like me, but each person has his own gift from God. One has one gift, another has another gift.

[8]Now for those who are not married and for the widows I say this: It is good for them to stay unmarried as I am. [9]But if they cannot control themselves, they should marry. It is better to marry than to burn with sexual desire.

[10]Now I give this command for the married people. (The command is not from me; it is from the Lord.) A wife should not leave her husband. [11]But if she does leave, she must not marry again, or she should make up with her husband. Also the husband should not divorce his wife.

[12]For all the others I say this (I am saying this, not the Lord): If a Christian man has a wife who is not a believer, and she is happy to live with him, he must not divorce her. [13]And if a Christian woman has a husband who is not a believer, and he is happy to live with her, she must not divorce him. [14]The husband who is not a believer is made holy through his believing wife. And the wife who is not a believer is made holy through her believing husband. If this were not true, your children would not be clean, but now your children are holy.

[15]But if those who are not believers decide to leave, let them leave. When this happens, the Christian man or woman is free. But God called us[n] to live in peace. [16]Wife, you don't know; maybe you will save your husband. And husband, you don't know; maybe you will save your wife.

LIVE AS GOD CALLED YOU

[17]But in any case each one of you should continue to live the way God has given you to live—the way you were when God called you. This is a rule I make in all the churches. [18]If a man was already circumcised when he was

Cool!

Special Forces

The Air Force's Combat Search and Rescue teams are the Special Forces you never hear of. The parajumpers on these teams—PJs for short—are sent on difficult rescue missions in the worst conditions.

It takes longer to train a PJ than a Navy SEAL or a Green Beret. They have to parachute from helicopters, dive with SCUBA gear, and scale mountains.

God's Special Forces are the missionaries who go to the ends of the world and risk their lives to share the Good News. You may not hear much about them now, but you will in heaven.

6:16 "The two . . . body." Quotation from Genesis 2:24.   **7:15 us** Some Greek copies read "you."

called, he should not undo his circumcision. If a man was without circumcision when he was called, he should not be circumcised. ¹⁹It is not important if a man is circumcised or not. The important thing is obeying God's commands. ²⁰Each one of you should stay the way you were when God called you. ²¹If you were a slave when God called you, do not let that bother you. But if you can be free, then make good use of your freedom. ²²Those who were slaves when the Lord called them are free persons who belong to the Lord. In the same way, those who were free when they were called are now Christ's slaves. ²³You all were bought at a great price, so do not become slaves of people. ²⁴Brothers and sisters, each of you should stay as you were when you were called, and stay there with God.

QUESTIONS ABOUT GETTING MARRIED

²⁵Now I write about people who are not married. I have no command from the Lord about this; I give my opinion. But I can be trusted, because the Lord has shown me mercy. ²⁶The present time is a time of trouble, so I think it is good for you to stay the way you are. ²⁷If you have a wife, do not try to become free from her. If you are not married, do not try to find a wife. ²⁸But if you decide to marry, you have not sinned. And if a girl who has never married decides to marry, she has not sinned. But those who marry will have trouble in this life, and I want you to be free from trouble.

²⁹Brothers and sisters, this is what I mean: We do not have much time left. So starting now, those who have wives should live as if they had no wives. ³⁰Those who are crying should live as if they were not crying. Those who are happy should live as if they were not happy. Those who buy things should live as if they own nothing. ³¹Those who use the things of the world should live as if they were not using them, because this world in its present form will soon be gone.

³²I want you to be free from worry. A man who is not married is busy with the Lord's work, trying to please the Lord. ³³But a man who is married is busy with things of the world, trying to please his wife. ³⁴He must think about two things—pleasing his wife and pleasing the Lord. A woman who is not married or a girl who has never married is busy with the Lord's work. She wants to be holy in body and spirit. But a married woman is busy with things of the world, as to how she can please her husband. ³⁵I am saying this to help you, not to limit you. But I want you to live in the right way, to give

50% of preteens wish they had more friends.

Trends & Tudes. Harris Interactive. January 2003.

yourselves fully to the Lord without concern for other things.

³⁶If a man thinks he is not doing the right thing with the girl he is engaged to, if she is almost past the best age to marry and he feels he should marry her, he should do what he wants. They should get married. It is no sin. ³⁷But if a man is sure in his mind that there is no need for marriage, and has his own desires under control, and has decided not to marry the one to whom he is engaged, he is doing the right thing. ³⁸So the man who marries his girl does right, but the man who does not marry will do better.

³⁹A woman must stay with her husband as long as he lives. But if her husband dies, she is free to marry any man she wants, but she must marry another believer. ⁴⁰The woman is happier if she does not marry again. This is my opinion, but I believe I also have God's Spirit.

ABOUT FOOD OFFERED TO IDOLS

8 Now I will write about meat that is sacrificed to idols. We know that "we all have knowledge." Knowledge puffs you up with pride, but love builds up. ²If you think you know something, you do not yet know anything as you should. ³But if any person loves God, that person is known by God.

⁴So this is what I say about eating meat sacrificed to idols: We know that an idol is really nothing in the world, and we know there is only one God. ⁵Even though there are things called gods, in heaven or on earth (and there are many "gods" and "lords"), ⁶for us there is only one God—our Father. All things came from him, and we live for him. And there is only one Lord—Jesus Christ. All things were made through him, and we also were made through him.

⁷But not all people know this. Some people are still so used to idols that when they eat meat, they still think of it as being sacrificed to an idol. Because their conscience is weak, when they eat it, they feel guilty. ⁸But food will not bring us closer to God. Refusing to eat does not make us less pleasing to God, and eating does not make us better in God's sight.

⁹But be careful that your freedom does not cause those who are weak in faith to fall into

KNOW THE WORD!

RELIGION

Religions are ways that people try to please God (or "gods"). There are hundreds of religions—Buddhism, Hinduism, Mormonism, and Christianity are just a few of the better known ones.

James 1:27 says, "Religion that God accepts as pure and without fault is this: caring for orphans or widows who need help, and keeping yourself free from the world's evil influence." In other words, if you want to follow the world's only genuine religion, you should take care of other people and keep away from sin.

Even more than being a religion, Christianity is about having a personal relationship with God. If you are his child and are trying to please him, you will be "religious" in the way he loves!

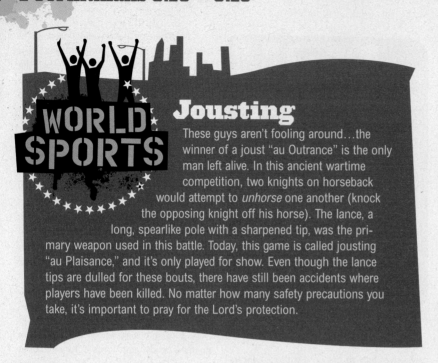

WORLD SPORTS

Jousting

These guys aren't fooling around...the winner of a joust "au Outrance" is the only man left alive. In this ancient wartime competition, two knights on horseback would attempt to *unhorse* one another (knock the opposing knight off his horse). The lance, a long, spearlike pole with a sharpened tip, was the primary weapon used in this battle. Today, this game is called jousting "au Plaisance," and it's only played for show. Even though the lance tips are dulled for these bouts, there have still been accidents where players have been killed. No matter how many safety precautions you take, it's important to pray for the Lord's protection.

sin. [10]Suppose one of you who has knowledge eats in an idol's temple.[*] Someone who is weak in faith might see you eating there and be encouraged to eat meat sacrificed to idols while thinking it is wrong to do so. [11]This weak believer for whom Christ died is ruined because of your "knowledge." [12]When you sin against your brothers and sisters in Christ like this and cause them to do what they feel is wrong, you are also sinning against Christ. [13]So if the food I eat causes them to fall into sin, I will never eat meat again so that I will not cause any of them to sin.

PAUL IS LIKE THE OTHER APOSTLES

9 I am a free man. I am an apostle. I have seen Jesus our Lord. You people are all an example of my work in the Lord. [2]If others do not accept me as an apostle, surely you do, because you are proof that I am an apostle in the Lord.

[3]This is the answer I give people who want to judge me: [4]Do we not have the right to eat and drink? [5]Do we not have the right to bring a believing wife with us when we travel as do the other apostles and the Lord's brothers and Peter? [6]Are Barnabas and I the only ones who must work to earn our living? [7]No soldier ever serves in the army and pays his own salary. No one ever plants a vineyard without eating some of the grapes. No person takes care of a flock without drinking some of the milk.

[8]I do not say this by human authority; God's law also says the same thing. [9]It is written in the law of Moses: "When an ox is working in the grain, do not cover its mouth to keep it from eating."[*] When God said this, was he thinking only about oxen? No. [10]He was really talking about us. Yes, that Scripture was written for us, because it goes on to say: "The one who plows and the one who works in the grain should hope to get some of the grain for their work." [11]Since we planted spiritual seed among you, is it too much if we should harvest material things? [12]If others have the right to get something from you, surely we have this right, too. But we do not use it. No, we put up with everything ourselves so that we will not keep anyone from believing the Good News of Christ. [13]Surely you know that those who work at the Temple get their food from the Temple, and those who serve at the altar get part of what is offered at the altar. [14]In the same way, the Lord has commanded that those who tell the Good News should get their living from this work.

[15]But I have not used any of these rights. And I am not writing this now to get anything from you. I would rather die than to have my

BIBLE SUPERHEROES

John
See Matthew 4:21–22.

John and his brother, James, were fishermen. Along with their partners, Peter and Andrew, they left their boats when Jesus called them to "fish for people" (Matthew 4:19, 21–22).

Over the next few years, they saw and heard things that blew their minds. They became sure that Jesus was God's Son, and they spent the rest of their lives convincing others.

John wrote a book about his time with Jesus: the Gospel of John. He also wrote a few letters and Revelation, the last book in the Bible.

John was a hothead by nature. Jesus once gave him and James the nickname "Sons of Thunder" (Mark 3:17). But by the time of his death, John was known as "The Apostle of Love."

What made the difference? Spending time with Jesus.

⭐ **8:10 idol's temple** Building where a god is worshiped.　**9:9 "When an ox . . . eating."** Quotation from Deuteronomy 25:4.

reason for bragging taken away. ¹⁶Telling the Good News does not give me any reason for bragging. Telling the Good News is my duty—something I must do. And how terrible it will be for me if I do not tell the Good News. ¹⁷If I preach because it is my own choice, I have a reward. But if I preach and it is not my choice to do so, I am only doing the duty that was given to me. ¹⁸So what reward do I get? This is my reward: that when I tell the Good News I can offer it freely. I do not use my full rights in my work of preaching the Good News.

¹⁹I am free and belong to no one. But I make myself a slave to all people to win as many as I can. ²⁰To the Jews I became like a Jew to win the Jews. I myself am not ruled by the law. But to those who are ruled by the law I became like a person who is ruled by the law. I did this to win those who are ruled by the law. ²¹To those who are without the law I became like a person who is without the law. I did this to win those people who are without the law. (But really, I am not without God's law—I am ruled by Christ's law.) ²²To those who are weak, I became weak so I could win the weak. I have become all things to all people so I could save some of them in any way possible. ²³I do all this because of the Good News and so I can share in its blessings.

²⁴You know that in a race all the runners run, but only one gets the prize. So run to win! ²⁵All those who compete in the games use self-control so they can win a crown. That crown is an earthly thing that lasts only a short time, but our crown will never be destroyed. ²⁶So I do not run without a goal. I fight like a boxer who is hitting something—not just the air. ²⁷I treat my body hard and make it my slave so

that I myself will not be disqualified after I have preached to others.

WARNINGS FROM ISRAEL'S PAST

10 Brothers and sisters, I want you to know what happened to our ancestors who followed Moses. They were all under the cloud and all went through the sea. ²They were all baptized as followers of Moses in the cloud and in the sea. ³They all ate the same spiritual food, ⁴and all drank the same spiritual drink. They drank from that spiritual rock that followed them, and that rock was Christ. ⁵But God was not pleased with most of them, so they died in the desert.

⁶And these things happened as examples for us, to stop us from wanting evil things as those people did. ⁷Do not worship idols, as some of them did. Just as it is written in the

ROCK SOLID

1 Corinthians 9:27

You probably want your life to make a difference in the world, but you won't just wake up one morning and find that, presto, you're ready.

Do you think Michael Jordan or Lance Armstrong just woke up one morning as the best in the world at what they did? No. And neither did the apostle Paul, who was probably the greatest missionary of all time. He says, "I treat my body hard and make it my slave so that I myself will not be disqualified after I have preached to others" (1 Corinthians 9:27).

Shooting baskets or riding a bike every single day can get boring. Jordan and Armstrong probably didn't jump out of bed with a big smile every time the alarm clock went off. But they treated their bodies hard to make them do what they wanted them to.

Being a follower of Jesus Christ is no different. You have to be rough on yourself, even when it doesn't feel good. A Christian who lived a long time ago, Martin Luther, got up early every morning to pray for hours at a time, and he changed the world.

Want to be a great Christian—a Christian who makes a difference? Take the challenge; commit to spend time praying every morning. God will make sure your life will count for eternity.

"Would you be my Valentine?"

Holidays are great times to make a difference in the lives of your friends. Take Valentine's Day, for example. You have your Superman cards, your NFL cards, your cartoon cards—all kinds of ways to say "Have a happy Valentine's Day!" to your friends.

Devon and his friends from church decided to use Valentine's Day to share about Jesus! Almost every holiday has a holy day behind it— some event that inspired the holiday in the first place. Most of these events are related to God's love. Devon and his friends found that typing a short explanation of the meaning behind a holiday and including it in their cards caused their friends to ask questions about things like God's love, forgiveness, and heaven.

Valentine's Day is only one example of a way to turn a holiday into a holy day—a day that can be used to make a difference in the lives of your friends.

Scriptures: "They sat down to eat and drink, and then they got up and sinned sexually."[n] [8] We must not take part in sexual sins, as some of them did. In one day twenty-three thousand of them died because of their sins. [9] We must not test Christ as some of them did; they were killed by snakes. [10] Do not complain as some of them did; they were killed by the angel that destroys.

[11] The things that happened to those people are examples. They were written down to teach us, because we live in a time when all these things of the past have reached their goal. [12] If you think you are strong, you should be careful not to fall. [13] The only temptation that has come to you is that which everyone has. But you can trust God, who will not permit you to be tempted more than you can stand. But when you are tempted, he will also give you a way to escape so that you will be able to stand it.

[14] So, my dear friends, run away from the worship of idols. [15] I am speaking to you as to reasonable people; judge for yourselves what I say. [16] We give thanks for the cup of blessing,[n] which is a sharing in the blood of Christ. And the bread that we break is a sharing in the body of Christ. [17] Because there is one loaf of bread, we who are many are one body, because we all share that one loaf.

[18] Think about the Israelites: Do not those who eat the sacrifices share in the altar? [19] I do not mean that the food sacrificed to an idol is important. I do not mean that an idol is anything at all. [20] But I say that what is sacrificed to idols is offered to demons, not to God. And I do not want you to share anything with demons. [21] You cannot drink the cup of the Lord and the cup of demons also. You cannot share in the Lord's table and the table of demons. [22] Are we trying to make the Lord jealous? We are not stronger than he is, are we?

HOW TO USE CHRISTIAN FREEDOM

[23] "We are allowed to do all things," but not all things are good for us to do. "We are allowed to do all things," but not all things help others grow stronger. [24] Do not look out only for yourselves. Look out for the good of others also.

[25] Eat any meat that is sold in the meat market. Do not ask questions about it. [26] You may eat it, "because the earth belongs to the Lord, and everything in it."[n]

[27] Those who are not believers may invite you to eat with them. If you want to go, eat anything that is put before you. Do not ask questions about it. [28] But if anyone says to you, "That food was offered to idols," do not eat it.

Do not eat it because of that person who told you and because eating it might be thought to be wrong. [29] I don't mean you think it is wrong, but the other person might. But why, you ask, should my freedom be judged by someone else's conscience? [30] If I eat the meal with thankfulness, why am I criticized because of something for which I thank God?

[31] The answer is, if you eat or drink, or if you do anything, do it all for the glory of God. [32] Never do anything that might hurt others— Jews, Greeks, or God's church— [33] just as I, also, try to please everybody in every way. I am not trying to do what is good for me but what is good for most people so they can be saved.

11 Follow my example, as I follow the example of Christ.

93% of kids feel their parents love them.

Sonna, Linda, Ph.D. *The Everything Tween Book*, p. 51.

BEING UNDER AUTHORITY

[2] I praise you because you remember me in everything, and you follow closely the teachings just as I gave them to you. [3] But I want you to understand this: The head of every man is Christ, the head of a woman is the man,[n] and the head of Christ is God. [4] Every man who prays or prophesies with his head covered brings shame to his head. [5] But every woman who prays or prophesies with her head uncovered brings shame to her head. She is the same as a woman who has her head shaved. [6] If a woman does not cover her head, she should have her hair cut off. But since it is shameful for a woman to cut off her hair or to shave her head, she should cover her head. [7] But a man should not cover his head, because he is the likeness and glory of God. But

trustables

1 Corinthians 10:13

Ever feel *tempted* to do something wrong? Sure, we all are. So what did you do?

Giving in to temptation is too easy, and resisting is too hard. God actually has made that part of life a little easier. First Corinthians 10:13 says, "The only temptation that has come to you is that which everyone has. But you can trust God, who will not permit you to be tempted more than you can stand. But when you are tempted, he will also give you a way to escape so that you will be able to stand it."

God doesn't allow us to be tempted by more than we can handle. What's more, he always makes a way out for us.

God knows our limitations better than we do, so anytime we are tempted to sin, God knows that we can handle it. He believes in you! And not only does he believe you can resist, but he also makes a way out of every temptation. All you have to do is ask him to show you the way out; he always will.

Next time you're tempted beyond what you think you can bear, remember to ask God for the way out!

---

woman is man's glory. [8]Man did not come from woman, but woman came from man. [9]And man was not made for woman, but woman was made for man. [10]So that is why a woman should have a symbol of authority on her head, because of the angels.

[11]But in the Lord women are not independent of men, and men are not independent of women. [12]This is true because woman came from man, but also man is born from woman. But everything comes from God. [13]Decide this for yourselves: Is it right for a woman to pray to God with her head uncovered? [14]Even nature itself teaches you that wearing long hair is shameful for a man. [15]But long hair is a woman's glory. Long hair is given to her as a covering. [16]Some people may still want to argue about this, but I would add that neither we nor the churches of God have any other practice.

THE LORD'S SUPPER

[17]In the things I tell you now I do not praise you, because when you come together you do more harm than good. [18]First, I hear that when

---

Hell on Earth

Death Valley, California, has been called "Hell on Earth"—for good reason:

★ It's the lowest point in the western hemisphere—282 feet below sea level.
★ It's recorded the hottest temperature in the U.S. and the second hottest in the world—134°F.
★ It's one of the driest places on the planet—it rains less than two inches each year.
★ As awful as Death Valley is, it doesn't compare to the real hell, or "lake of fire" (Revelation 20:14–15).

Jesus died to save us from hell. If you believe in him, you'll go to heaven!

you meet together as a church you are divided, and I believe some of this. [19](It is necessary to have differences among you so that it may be clear which of you really have God's approval.) [20]When you come together, you are not really eating the Lord's Supper." [21]This is because when you eat, each person eats without waiting for the others. Some people do not get enough to eat, while others have too much to drink. [22]You can eat and drink in your own homes! You seem to think God's church is not important, and you embarrass those who are poor. What should I tell you? Should I praise you? I do not praise you for doing this.

[23]The teaching I gave you is the same teaching I received from the Lord: On the night when the Lord Jesus was handed over to be killed, he took bread [24]and gave thanks for it. Then he broke the bread and said, "This is my body; it is" for you. Do this to remember me." [25]In the same way, after they ate, Jesus took the cup. He said, "This cup is the new agreement that is sealed with the blood of

dare to do

1 Corinthians 11:4
Read It: Don't pray with your head covered.
Do It: Show respect when you are praying and remove your hat.

1 Corinthians 11:27
Read It: Don't participate in communion if you don't mean it or if you have not confessed your sins.
Do It: When you take communion, first confess your sins and remember the sacrifice of our Lord Jesus. Eat and drink in a solemn and respectful way.

1 Corinthians 11:33
Read It: If you are supposed to be communing with other believers, don't rush to take the bread and cup ahead of the rest.
Do It: When you take communion at your church, thank God that he has given you a group to gather with.

my death. When you drink this, do it to remember me." [26]Every time you eat this bread and drink this cup you are telling others about the Lord's death until he comes.

[27]So a person who eats the bread or drinks the cup of the Lord in a way that is not worthy of it will be guilty of sinning against the body and the blood of the Lord. [28]Look into your own hearts before you eat the bread and drink the cup, [29]because all who eat the bread and drink the cup without recognizing the body eat and drink judgment against themselves. [30]That is why many in your group are sick and weak, and some of you have died. [31]But if we judged ourselves in the right way, God would not judge us. [32]But when the Lord judges us, he disciplines us so that we will not be destroyed along with the world.

[33]So my brothers and sisters, when you come together to eat, wait for each other. [34]Anyone who is too hungry should eat at home so that in meeting together you will not bring God's judgment on yourselves. I will tell you what to do about the other things when I come.

GIFTS FROM THE HOLY SPIRIT

12 Now, brothers and sisters, I want you to understand about spiritual gifts. [2]You know the way you lived before you were believers. You let yourselves be influenced and led away to worship idols—things that could not speak. [3]So I want you to understand that no one who is speaking with the help of God's Spirit says, "Jesus be cursed." And no one can say, "Jesus is Lord," without the help of the Holy Spirit.

ROCK SOLID

1 Corinthians 10:31

What have you done for God lately? A lot of people would have a hard time answering this question. They might scratch their heads and say, "Well, I gave some money to the church not too long ago." Or, "I bought a Christian music CD."

Well, would you believe the Bible says we should do *everything* for God? That means brushing our teeth, walking our dog, and doing our homework...all for God. Really! The Bible says, "If you eat or drink, or if you do anything, do it all for the glory of God" (1 Corinthians 10:31).

So how do you do your homework for the glory of God? you ask. By doing the best job you possibly can. When you strive for excellence, God delights in your efforts and others can see God working through you. When we do things for God, it makes life so much more interesting! A walk with your dog becomes a special time enjoying God's creation. Brushing your teeth becomes a moment to appreciate the ability to chow down on delicious food.

Don't go through life just doing things for yourself. Do things for the glory of God and see what living really means!

 11:20 Lord's Supper The meal Jesus told his followers to eat to remember him (Luke 22:14–20).   **11:24 it is** Some Greek copies read "it is broken."

home rules

How often do you hear yourself saying, "But, Mom, all my friends get to"? Do you ever get frustrated that your family's rules are different from everyone else's? It can be hard when you feel like others get to do things you don't. House rules are unique in each family, and the sooner you understand that, the easier it will be!

What rules do you have at your house? Maybe you have a rule about how much time you can spend over at a friend's house or how long you can play computer games. When you get older, you will still have rules and sometimes you might still get frustrated with them. The rules will probably change a bit—and there will be new ones added, too! No matter what, remember Ephesians 6:2, which tells you to "honor your father and mother." That means obeying with a good attitude!

Remember that rules are designed to help you and protect you. Instead of focusing on your disappointment about what you *can't* do, think about what you *can* do! Making a list of all the things you *can* do will cheer you up.

There will probably be rules that you don't understand, and if that's the case, talk to your parents. Understanding *why* you have a rule will help you have a good attitude about following it. And if you are unsure about what your home rules are in a situation, check with your parents *before* making your decision.

Even if your friends don't have the rules you do, there's no reason to get upset. When you move out of your house, you won't have family rules for your life anymore. You'll have to make the decision about what is right and wrong. Don't worry, though; you won't be all the way on your own! Read the Bible to learn about what God wants for your life. Right now is a good time to start following God's rules so you will have them with you always.

The next time you feel like complaining to your parents about a rule, remember that they are doing what's best for you. Be thankful that someone is looking out for you and cares about you very much!

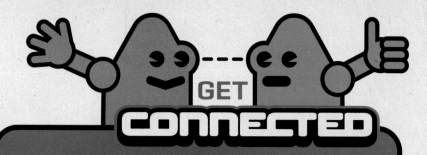

GET **CONNECTED**

[4]There are different kinds of gifts, but they are all from the same Spirit. [5]There are different ways to serve but the same Lord to serve. [6]And there are different ways that God works through people but the same God. God works in all of us in everything we do. [7]Something from the Spirit can be seen in each person, for the common good. [8]The Spirit gives one person the ability to speak with wisdom, and the same Spirit gives another the ability to speak with knowledge. [9]The same Spirit gives faith to one person. And, to another, that one Spirit gives gifts of healing. [10]The Spirit gives to another person the power to do miracles, to another the ability to prophesy. And he gives to another the ability to know the difference between good and evil spirits. The Spirit gives one person the ability to speak in different kinds of languages" and to another the ability to interpret those languages. [11]One Spirit, the same Spirit, does all these things, and the Spirit decides what to give each person.

ALONE OR LONELY?

Being alone is not necessarily a bad thing—unless you don't want to be. If you find yourself alone and feeling lonely—or maybe even feeling that way in a crowd—you may want to see what you can do to change your situation.

Pray that God will open the way to new relationships. Show a genuine curiosity about others—really listening to them and asking about what they like and what they're doing. And if you discover you have common interests, you may be able to use those interests as a foot in the door to great friendships.

THE BODY OF CHRIST WORKS TOGETHER

[12]A person's body is one thing, but it has many parts. Though there are many parts to a body, all those parts make only one body. Christ is like that also. [13]Some of us are Jews, and some are Greeks. Some of us are slaves, and some are free. But we were all baptized into one body through one Spirit. And we were all made to share in the one Spirit.

[14]The human body has many parts. [15]The foot might say, "Because I am not a hand, I am not part of the body." But saying this would not stop the foot from being a part of the body. [16]The ear might say, "Because I am not an eye, I am not part of the body." But saying this would not stop the ear from being a part of the body. [17]If the whole body were an eye, it would not be able to hear. If the whole body were an ear, it would not be able to smell. [18-19]If each part of the body were the same part, there would be no body. But truly

trustables

1 Corinthians 12:31

The deepest part of the Pacific Ocean is 36,200 feet deep. Mount Everest is more than 29,000 feet high. The Nile River is 4,145 miles long. The Grand Canyon is more than 18 miles wide. But God's love is deeper, higher, longer, and wider than these things. Can you imagine? Now imagine your life full of God and his love. It can happen to you.

Look in 1 Corinthians 13. It's the best description of love anyone has ever penned. God longs for us to be filled with his great, magnificent love. Why? Because what is said and done in love is "the best way of all" (1 Corinthians 12:31).

Anything done without love is here today, gone tomorrow. Yet what you say and do in love can last forever! The key is being filled with God's kind of love.

It's a love so vast, so amazing, that we'll never comprehend its full greatness. Swim the deepest ocean, climb the highest mountain, navigate the longest river, and cross the widest canyon—God's love is still greater.

God can do more than you can ask, so ask him for a little help. After all, he wants to do more in and through your life—that lasts forever—than you could ever dream. It's hard to imagine!

12:10 languages This can also be translated "tongues."

God put all the parts, each one of them, in the body as he wanted them. [20]So then there are many parts, but only one body.

[21]The eye cannot say to the hand, "I don't need you!" And the head cannot say to the foot, "I don't need you!" [22]No! Those parts of the body that seem to be the weaker are really necessary. [23]And the parts of the body we think are less deserving are the parts to which we give the most honor. We give special respect to the parts we want to hide. [24]The more respectable parts of our body need no special care. But God put the body together and gave more honor to the parts that need it [25]so our body would not be divided. God wanted the different parts to care the same for each other. [26]If one part of the body suffers, all the other parts suffer with it. Or if one part of our body is honored, all the other parts share its honor.

[27]Together you are the body of Christ, and each one of you is a part of that body. [28]In the church God has given a place first to apostles, second to prophets, and third to teachers. Then God has given a place to those who do miracles, those who have gifts of healing, those who can help others, those who are able to govern, and those who can speak in different languages." [29]Not all are apostles. Not all are prophets. Not all are teachers. Not all do miracles. [30]Not all have gifts of healing. Not all speak in different languages. Not all interpret those languages. [31]But you should truly want to have the greater gifts.

LOVE IS THE GREATEST GIFT

And now I will show you the best way of all.

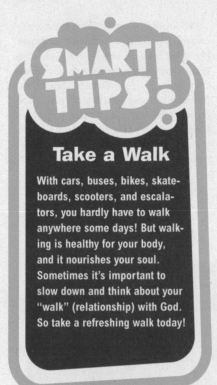

SMART TIPS!

Take a Walk

With cars, buses, bikes, skateboards, scooters, and escalators, you hardly have to walk anywhere some days! But walking is healthy for your body, and it nourishes your soul. Sometimes it's important to slow down and think about your "walk" (relationship) with God. So take a refreshing walk today!

13 I may speak in different languages" of people or even angels. But if I do not have love, I am only a noisy bell or a crashing cymbal. [2]I may have the gift of prophecy. I may understand all the secret things of God and have all knowledge, and I may have faith so great I can move mountains. But even with all these things, if I do not have love, then I am nothing. [3]I may give away everything I have, and I may even give my body as an offering to be burned." But I gain nothing if I do not have love.

[4]Love is patient and kind. Love is not jealous, it does not brag, and it is not proud. [5]Love is not rude, is not selfish, and does not get upset with others. Love does not count up wrongs that have been done. [6]Love takes no pleasure in evil but rejoices over the truth. [7]Love patiently accepts all things. It always trusts, always hopes, and always endures.

[8]Love never ends. There are gifts of prophecy, but they will be ended. There are gifts of speaking in different languages, but those gifts will stop. There is the gift of knowledge, but it will come to an end. [9]The reason is that our knowledge and our ability to prophesy are not perfect. [10]But when perfection comes, the things that are not perfect will end. [11]When I was a child, I talked like a child, I thought like a child, I reasoned like a child. When I became a man, I stopped those childish ways. [12]It is the same with us. Now we see a dim reflection, as if we were looking into a mirror, but then we shall see clearly. Now I know only a part, but then I will know fully, as God has known me. [13]So these three things continue forever: faith, hope, and love. And the greatest of these is love.

DESIRE SPIRITUAL GIFTS

14 You should seek after love, and you should truly want to have the spiritual gifts, especially the gift of prophecy. [2]I will explain why. Those who have the gift of speak-

BIBLE SUPERHEROES

Mary and Martha
See Luke 10:38–42.

Mary and Martha were sisters who lived with their brother, Lazarus, in the town of Bethany. They were good friends of Jesus. One day, when he was visiting their home, Martha was doing all the work while Mary sat listening to him talk.

Martha got very upset about doing all the work. She asked Jesus to tell Mary to help!

This sounds like a fair request, but the Lord answered, "Martha, Martha, you are worried and upset about many things. Only one thing is important. Mary has chosen the better thing, and it will never be taken away from her" (Luke 10:41–42).

It's easy to get so busy doing things "for" Jesus that we don't spend enough time "with" him. Don't make Martha's mistake. Be like Mary by spending time with Jesus in his Word.

12:28; 13:1 **languages** This can also be translated "tongues." 13:3 **give . . . burned** Other Greek copies read "hand over my body in order that I may brag."

ing in different languages[n] are not speaking to people; they are speaking to God. No one understands them; they are speaking secret things through the Spirit. [3]But those who prophesy are speaking to people to give them strength, encouragement, and comfort. [4]The ones who speak in different languages are helping only themselves, but those who prophesy are helping the whole church. [5]I wish all of you had the gift of speaking in different kinds of languages, but more, I wish you would prophesy. Those who prophesy are greater than those who can only speak in different languages—unless someone is there who can explain what is said so that the whole church can be helped.

[6]Brothers and sisters, will it help you if I come to you speaking in different languages? No! It will help you only if I bring you a new truth or some new knowledge, or prophecy, or teaching. [7]It is the same as with lifeless things that make sounds—like a flute or a harp. If they do not make clear musical notes, you will not know what is being played. [8]And in a war, if the trumpet does not give a clear sound, who will prepare for battle? [9]It is the same with you.

Unless you speak clearly with your tongue, no one can understand what you are saying. You will be talking into the air! [10]It may be true that there are all kinds of sounds in the world, and none is without meaning. [11]But unless I understand the meaning of what someone says to me, we will be like foreigners to each other. [12]It is the same with you. Since you want spiritual gifts very much, seek most of all to have the gifts that help the church grow stronger.

[13]The one who has the gift of speaking in a different language should pray for the gift to interpret what is spoken. [14]If I pray in a different language, my spirit is praying, but my mind does nothing. [15]So what should I do? I will pray with my spirit, but I will also pray with my mind. I will sing with my spirit, but I will also sing with my mind. [16]If you praise God with your spirit, those persons there without understanding cannot say amen[n] to your prayer of thanks, because they do not know what you are saying. [17]You may be thanking God in a good way, but the other person is not helped.

[18]I thank God that I speak in different kinds of languages more than all of you. [19]But in the church meetings I would rather speak five words I understand in order to teach others than thousands of words in a different language.

[20]Brothers and sisters, do not think like children. In evil things be like babies, but in your thinking you should be like adults. [21]It is written in the Scriptures:

"With people who use strange words and
        foreign languages
    I will speak to these people.
    But even then they will not listen to me,"

Isaiah 28:11–12

says the Lord.

[22]So the gift of speaking in different kinds of languages is a sign for those who do not believe, not for those who do believe. And prophecy is for people who believe, not for those who do not believe. [23]Suppose the whole church meets together and everyone speaks in different languages. If some people come in who do not understand or do not believe, they will say you are crazy. [24]But suppose everyone is prophesying and some people come in who do not believe or do not understand. If everyone is prophesying, their sin will be shown to them, and they will be judged by all that they hear. [25]The secret things in their hearts will be made known. So they will bow down and worship God saying, "Truly, God is with you."

Q: I have a stepbrother I can't stand. He seems to hate me, too. What can I do?

A: It can be tough when two families try to blend together. Suddenly you've got a brother you didn't grow up with, and it's the same for him, too. Jesus told us that we should treat each other the way we'd like to be treated (Matthew 7:12). He also said that when somebody does something hurtful to us, we should not try to hurt them back (Matthew 5:39). Treat your new brother the way Jesus would treat him, and pray that his heart will change toward you.

Q: Our whole family is overweight. Is there a diet I should tell my mom about?

A: The Bible says that we should take care of our bodies because they belong to God (1 Corinthians 6:19–20). That means keeping them in good shape. Your mom is probably aware of your family's extra weight (especially her own). And she's probably already tried lots of diets that haven't worked. Ask your mom how you can help your whole family eat healthier food every day.

Q: My Sunday school teacher said that our neighborhood is our mission field. What did he mean?

A: Jesus told us to tell everybody in the world the Good News about him (Matthew 28:19). Missionaries go out to the far corners of the world to reach groups of people who haven't heard about Jesus. But you may have people living right next door who don't know Jesus. Pray that God would give you the chance to tell them—and you'll be a missionary in your own neighborhood!

14:2 **languages** This can also be translated "tongues."   14:16 **amen** To say amen means to agree with the things that were said.

MEETINGS SHOULD HELP THE CHURCH

[26]So, brothers and sisters, what should you do? When you meet together, one person has a song, and another has a teaching. Another has a new truth from God. Another speaks in a different language," and another person interprets that language. The purpose of all these things should be to help the church grow strong. [27]When you meet together, if anyone speaks in a different language, it should be only two, or not more than three, who speak. They should speak one after the other, and someone should interpret. [28]But if there is no interpreter, then those who speak in a different language should be quiet in the church meeting. They should speak only to themselves and to God.

[29]Only two or three prophets should speak, and the others should judge what they say. [30]If a message from God comes to another person who is sitting, the first speaker should stop. [31]You can all prophesy one after the other. In this way all the people can be taught and encouraged. [32]The spirits of prophets are under the control of the prophets themselves. [33]God is not a God of confusion but a God of peace.

As is true in all the churches of God's people, [34]women should keep quiet in the church meetings. They are not allowed to speak, but they must yield to this rule as the law says. [35]If they want to learn something, they should ask their own husbands at home. It is shameful for a woman to speak in the church meeting. [36]Did God's teaching come from you? Or are you the only ones to whom it has come?

[37]Those who think they are prophets or spiritual persons should understand that what I am writing to you is the Lord's command. [38]Those who ignore this will be ignored by God."

[39]So my brothers and sisters, you should truly want to prophesy. But do not stop people from using the gift of speaking in different kinds of languages. [40]But let everything be done in a right and orderly way.

THE GOOD NEWS ABOUT CHRIST

15 Now, brothers and sisters, I want you to remember the Good News I brought to you. You received this Good News and continue strong in it. [2]And you are being saved by it if you continue believing what I told you. If you do not, then you believed for nothing.

[3]I passed on to you what I received, of which this was most important: that Christ died for our sins, as the Scriptures say; [4]that he was buried and was raised to life on the third day as the Scriptures say; [5]and that he was seen by Peter and then by the twelve apostles. [6]After that, Jesus was seen by more than five hundred of the believers at the same time. Most of them are still living today, but some have died. [7]Then he was seen by James and later by all the apostles. [8]Last of all he was seen by me—as by a person not born at the normal time. [9]All the other apostles are greater than I am. I am not even good enough to be called an apostle, because I persecuted the church of God. [10]But God's grace has made me what I am, and his grace to me was not wasted. I worked harder than all the other apostles. (But it was not I really; it was God's grace that was with me.) [11]So if I preached to you or the other apostles preached to you, we all preach the same thing, and this is what you believed.

WE WILL BE RAISED FROM THE DEAD

[12]Now since we preached that Christ was raised from the dead, why do some of you say that people will not be raised from the dead? [13]If no one is ever raised from the dead, then Christ has not been raised. [14]And if Christ has not been raised, then our preaching is worth nothing, and your faith is worth nothing. [15]And also, we are guilty of lying about God, because we testified of him that he raised Christ from the dead. But if people are not raised from the dead, then God never raised Christ. [16]If the dead are not raised, Christ has not been raised either. [17]And if Christ has not been raised, then your faith has nothing to it; you are still guilty of your sins. [18]And those in Christ who have already died are lost. [19]If our hope in Christ is for this life only, we should be pitied more than anyone else in the world.

[20]But Christ has truly been raised from the dead—the first one and proof that those who sleep in death will also be raised. [21]Death has come because of what one man did, but the rising from death also comes because of one man. [22]In Adam all of us die. In the same way, in Christ all of us will be made alive again. [23]But everyone will be raised to life in the right order. Christ was first to be raised. When Christ comes again, those who belong to him will be raised to life, [24]and then the end will come. At that time Christ will destroy all rulers, authorities, and powers, and he will hand over the kingdom to God the Father. [25]Christ must rule until he puts all enemies under his control. [26]The last enemy to be destroyed will be death. [27]The Scripture says that God put all things under his control." When it says "all things" are under him, it is clear this does not include God himself. God is the One who put everything under his control. [28]After everything has been put under the Son, then he will put himself under God, who had put all things

14:26 language This can also be translated "tongue." **14:38 Those . . . God.** Some Greek copies read "Those who are ignorant of this will stay ignorant." **15:27 God put . . . control.** From Psalm 8:6.

under him. Then God will be the complete ruler over everything.

[29]If the dead are never raised, what will people do who are being baptized for the dead? If the dead are not raised at all, why are people being baptized for them?

[30]And what about us? Why do we put ourselves in danger every hour? [31]I die every day. That is true, brothers and sisters, just as it is true that I brag about you in Christ Jesus our Lord. [32]If I fought wild animals in Ephesus only with human hopes, I have gained nothing. If the dead are not raised, "Let us eat and drink, because tomorrow we will die."[n]

[33]Do not be fooled: "Bad friends will ruin good habits." [34]Come back to your right way of thinking and stop sinning. Some of you do not know God—I say this to shame you.

WHAT KIND OF BODY WILL WE HAVE?

[35]But someone may ask, "How are the dead raised? What kind of body will they have?" [36]Foolish person! When you sow a seed, it must die in the ground before it can live and grow. [37]And when you sow it, it does not have the same "body" it will have later. What you sow is only a bare seed, maybe wheat or something else. [38]But God gives it a body that he has planned for it, and God gives each kind of seed its own body. [39]All things made of flesh are not the same: People have one kind of flesh, animals have another, birds have another, and fish have another. [40]Also there are heavenly bodies and earthly bodies. But the beauty of the heavenly bodies is one kind, and the beauty of the earthly bodies is another. [41]The sun has one kind of beauty, the moon has another beauty, and the stars have another. And each star is different in its beauty.

[42]It is the same with the dead who are raised to life. The body that is "planted" will ruin and decay, but it is raised to a life that cannot be destroyed. [43]When the body is "planted," it is without honor, but it is raised in glory. When the body is "planted," it is weak, but when it is raised, it is powerful. [44]The body that is "planted" is a physical body. When it is raised, it is a spiritual body.

There is a physical body, and there is also a spiritual body. [45]It is written in the Scriptures: "The first man, Adam, became a living person."[n] But the last Adam became a spirit that gives life. [46]The spiritual did not come first, but the physical and then the spiritual. [47]The first man came from the dust of the earth. The second man came from heaven. [48]People who belong to the earth are like the first man of earth. But those people who belong to heaven are like the man of heaven. [49]Just as we were made like the man of earth, so we will[n] also be made like the man of heaven.

[50]I tell you this, brothers and sisters: Flesh and blood cannot have a part in the kingdom of God. Something that will ruin cannot have a part in something that never ruins. [51]But look! I tell you this secret: We will not all sleep in death, but we will all be changed. [52]It will take only a second—as quickly as an eye blinks—when the last trumpet sounds. The trumpet will sound, and those who have died will be raised to live forever, and we will all be changed. [53]This body that can be destroyed must clothe itself with something that can never be destroyed. And this body that dies must clothe itself with something that can never die. [54]So this body that can be destroyed will clothe itself with that which can never be destroyed, and this body that dies will clothe itself with that which can never die. When this happens, this Scripture will be made true:

"Death is destroyed forever in victory."

Isaiah 25:8

[55]"Death, where is your victory?

ROCK SOLID

1 Corinthians 15:33

Whether you know it or not, you become like the people you spend the most time with. This is a serious thing. Do you want to be like your friends? Think about what their lives are like, what's important to them, and where they're going in life. Now, is that what you want to be like?

Paul writes, "Do not be fooled: 'Bad friends will ruin good habits'" (1 Corinthians 15:33). "Don't be fooled" means that some people have been fooled. Some people have been tricked into hanging with the wrong crowd. They may say, "My friends don't affect me" or "I hang out with them, but I don't do the things they do." Guess what? They've been fooled! People who say things like that show that they don't know what they're talking about.

What about your friends? Do you like the direction their lives are going? Do you want to be like them? If not, now's the time to get out.

Death, where is your pain?"   *Hosea 13:14*
[56]Death's power to hurt is sin, and the power of sin is the law. [57]But we thank God! He gives us the victory through our Lord Jesus Christ.

[58]So my dear brothers and sisters, stand strong. Do not let anything move you. Always give yourselves fully to the work of the Lord, because you know that your work in the Lord is never wasted.

THE GIFT FOR OTHER BELIEVERS

16 Now I will write about the collection of money for God's people. Do the same thing I told the Galatian churches to do: [2]On the first day of every week, each one of you should put aside money as you have been blessed. Save it up so you will not have to collect money after I come. [3]When I arrive, I will send whomever you approve to take your gift to Jerusalem. I will send them with letters of introduction, [4]and if it seems good for me to go also, they will go along with me.

PAUL'S PLANS

[5]I plan to go through Macedonia, so I will come to you after I go through there. [6]Perhaps I will stay with you for a time or even all winter. Then you can help me on my trip, wherever I go. [7]I do not want to see you now just in passing. I hope to stay a longer time with you if the Lord allows it. [8]But I will stay at Ephesus until Pentecost, [9]because a good opportunity for a great and growing work has been given to me now. And there are many people working against me.

[10]If Timothy comes to you, see to it that he has nothing to fear with you, because he is working for the Lord just as I am. [11]So none of you should treat Timothy as unimportant, but help him on his trip in peace so that he can come back to me. I am expecting him to come with the brothers.

[12]Now about our brother Apollos: I strongly encouraged him to visit you with the other brothers. He did not at all want to come now; he will come when he has the opportunity.

PAUL ENDS HIS LETTER

[13]Be alert. Continue strong in the faith. Have courage, and be strong. [14]Do everything in love.

[15]You know that the family of Stephanas were the first believers in Southern Greece and that they have given themselves to the service of God's people. I ask you, brothers and sisters, [16]to follow the leading of people like these and anyone else who works and serves with them.

[17]I am happy that Stephanas, Fortunatus, and Achaicus have come. You are not here, but they have filled your place. [18]They have refreshed my spirit and yours. You should recognize the value of people like these.

[19]The churches in Asia send greetings to you. Aquila and Priscilla greet you in the Lord, as does the church that meets in their house. [20]All the brothers and sisters here send greetings. Give each other a holy kiss when you meet.

[21]I, Paul, am writing this greeting with my own hand.

[22]If anyone does not love the Lord, let him be separated from God—lost forever!

Come, O Lord!

[23]The grace of the Lord Jesus be with you.

[24]My love be with all of you in Christ Jesus."

COOL!

New Testament E-mail

If the New Testament were written today, many of its letters would probably be sent as e-mails. E-mail is used more all the time; here's how it's currently used:

★ Number of e-mail users worldwide: 651 million
★ Total messages sent daily: 76.8 billion
★ Number of e-mails the average user sends daily: 34
★ Number of e-mails the average user gets daily: 99
★ Percentage of e-mail that is spam: 77

Of course, you can communicate with the God of the universe quicker than you could send an e-mail—just start talking!

16:24 My . . . Jesus. Some Greek copies add "Amen."

A short time after writing his first letter to the Corinthians, Paul had to write them again.

In between letters he visited them face-to-face, but their problems only got worse.

It didn't help that some false teachers were trying to get the Christians in Corinth to follow the old Jewish ways. These intruders were dissing Paul and trying to turn the church against him (11:1–4).

This is the most personal of Paul's letters. It drips with emotions. The Corinthians had moved him to tears of both joy and anger.

In the first seven chapters, Paul talks about the hard times the church has been through. Then he brings up the collection for the poor in Jerusalem. This important work had been forgotten in all the confusion. Paul urges them to finish what they had started (chapters 8 and 9).

Because of the personal attacks, Paul adds a final section to defend his ministry (chapters 10–13). These chapters show just how much it cost him to be the "Apostle to the Gentiles." (An "apostle" is someone with special authority to speak on behalf of a country or a ruler. The word we use for this today is "ambassador.")

If you catch some flack for being a Christian, it's nothing compared to what Paul went through. Telling others about Jesus may get you into trouble with some people—but it will also get you in good with God.

Who would you rather please?

2 CORINTHIANS

1 From Paul, an apostle of Christ Jesus. I am an apostle because that is what God wanted. Also from Timothy our brother in Christ.

To the church of God in Corinth, and to all of God's people everywhere in Southern Greece:

²Grace and peace to you from God our Father and the Lord Jesus Christ.

PAUL GIVES THANKS TO GOD

³Praise be to the God and Father of our Lord Jesus Christ. God is the Father who is full of mercy and all comfort. ⁴He comforts us every time we have trouble, so when others have trouble, we can comfort them with the same comfort God gives us. ⁵We share in the many sufferings of Christ. In the same way, much comfort comes to us through Christ. ⁶If we have troubles, it is for your comfort and salvation, and if we have comfort, you also have comfort. This helps you to accept patiently the same sufferings we have. ⁷Our hope for you is strong, knowing that you share in our sufferings and also in the comfort we receive.

⁸Brothers and sisters, we want you to know about the trouble we suffered in Asia. We had great burdens there that were beyond our own strength. We even gave up hope of living. ⁹Truly, in our own hearts we believed we would die. But this happened so we would not trust in ourselves but in God, who raises people from the dead. ¹⁰God saved us from these great dangers of death, and he will continue to save us. We have put our hope in him, and he will save us again. ¹¹And you can help us with your prayers. Then many people will give thanks for us—that God blessed us because of their many prayers.

THE CHANGE IN PAUL'S PLANS

¹²This is what we are proud of, and I can say it with a clear conscience: In everything we have done in the world, and especially with you, we have had an honest" and sincere heart from God. We did this by God's grace, not by the kind of wisdom the world has. ¹³⁻¹⁴We write to you only what you can read and understand. And I hope that as you have understood some things about us, you may come to know everything about us. Then you can be proud of us, as we will be proud of you on the day our Lord Jesus Christ comes again.

¹⁵I was so sure of all this that I made plans to visit you first so you could be blessed twice. ¹⁶I planned to visit you on my way to Macedonia and again on my way back. I wanted to get help from you for my trip to Judea. ¹⁷Do you think that I made these plans without really meaning it? Or maybe you think I make plans as the world does, so that I say yes, yes and at the same time no, no.

¹⁸But since you can believe God, you can believe that what we tell you is never both yes and no. ¹⁹The Son of God, Jesus Christ, that Silas and Timothy and I preached to you, was not yes and no. In Christ it has always been yes. ²⁰The yes to all of God's promises is in Christ, and through Christ we say yes to the glory of God. ²¹Remember, God is the One who makes you and us strong in Christ. God made us his chosen people. ²²He put his mark on us to show that we are his, and he put his Spirit in our hearts to be a guarantee for all he has promised.

²³I tell you this, and I ask God to be my witness that this is true: The reason I did not come back to Corinth was to keep you from being punished or hurt. ²⁴We are not trying to control your faith. You are strong in faith. But we are workers with you for your own joy.

2 So I decided that my next visit to you would not be another one to make you sad. ²If I make you sad, who will make me glad? Only you can make me glad—particularly the person whom I made sad. ³I wrote you a letter for this reason: that when I came to you I would not be made sad by the people who should make me happy. I felt sure of all of you, that you would share my joy. ⁴When I wrote to you before, I was very troubled and unhappy in my heart, and I wrote with many tears. I did not write to make you sad, but to let you know how much I love you.

FORGIVE THE SINNER

⁵Someone there among you has caused sadness, not to me, but to all of you. I mean he caused sadness to all in some way. (I do not want to make it sound worse than it really is.) ⁶The punishment that most of you gave him is enough for him. ⁷But now you should forgive him and comfort him to keep him from having too much sadness and giving up completely. ⁸So I beg you to show that you love him. ⁹I wrote you to test you and to see if you

ROCK SOLID

2 Corinthians 1:4

If you've ever had to stay in a hospital, you know it's not always the nicest place to be. What encouraged you while you were there? The people who visited you?

When you are hurting, God is there to comfort you. The apostle Paul tells us, "He comforts us every time we have trouble, so when others have trouble, we can comfort them with the same comfort God gives us" (2 Corinthians 1:4).

God's comfort comes in all situations when it's needed, not just in a hospital. And God is so wise that when he comforts you it's for two reasons: first, so you'll feel better, and second, so you can comfort and encourage other people.

If someone needs encouragement, remember what encouraged you when you were hurting. Just be there to let the person know you care. And even if you don't know what to say, you have the best words in the world you can share: God's words in the Bible. Open your Bible and read a verse that's been important to you and let God encourage your friend through you.

1:12 **honest** Some Greek copies read "holy."

BIBLE SUPERHEROES

Lazarus
See John 11.

Lazarus, a good friend of Jesus, died one day when Jesus was out of town. Jesus heard about it and went to Lazarus's hometown. He went straight to where Lazarus was buried—not to pay his respects, but to cheat death.

Lazarus had been in the tomb for four days when Jesus showed up. But he hopped out wrapped up like a mummy when Jesus called his name!

Many people believed in Jesus because of this miracle. Others went to tattle to the religious leaders. The leaders decided he was getting too popular. "That day they started planning to kill Jesus" (John 11:53).

The leaders also decided to kill Lazarus (John 12:10–11). Rather than believe the "living proof" that Jesus was God's Son, they wanted to destroy it!

Lazarus was *living* evidence that Jesus is God!

obey in everything. [10]If you forgive someone, I also forgive him. And what I have forgiven—if I had anything to forgive—I forgave it for you, as if Christ were with me. [11]I did this so that Satan would not win anything from us, because we know very well what Satan's plans are.

PAUL'S CONCERN IN TROAS

[12]When I came to Troas to preach the Good News of Christ, the Lord gave me a good opportunity there. [13]But I had no peace, because I did not find my brother Titus. So I said good-bye to them at Troas and went to Macedonia.

VICTORY THROUGH CHRIST

[14]But thanks be to God, who always leads us as captives in Christ's victory parade. God

COOL!

Some Like It Hot

God loves variety. Just look at all the different foods he's created for us to enjoy, including spicy foods. The "hotness" in peppers and chilies is counted in Scoville units, which tell the level of capsaicins in food. Capsaicins have no flavor; but they do react with pain receptors in your mouth and throat.

Here's how some well-known peppers rate:

Pepper	Scoville units
Bell	0
Jalapeno	2,500 – 10,000
Serrano	5,000 – 23,000
Cayenne	30,000 – 50,000
Habañeros	80,000 – 300,000

Try some new foods for a change. See how much of God's "hot creations" you can take!

uses us to spread his knowledge everywhere like a sweet-smelling perfume. [15]Our offering to God is this: We are the sweet smell of Christ among those who are being saved and among those who are being lost. [16]To those who are lost, we are the smell of death that brings death, but to those who are being saved, we are the smell of life that brings life. So who is able to do this work? [17]We do not sell the word of God for a profit as many other people do. But in Christ we speak the truth before God, as messengers of God.

SERVANTS OF THE NEW AGREEMENT

3 Are we starting to brag about ourselves again? Do we need letters of introduction to you or from you, like some other people? [2]You yourselves are our letter, written on our hearts, known and read by everyone. [3]You show that you are a letter from Christ sent through us. This letter is not written with ink but with the Spirit of the living God. It is not written on stone tablets[n] but on human hearts.

[4]We can say this, because through Christ we feel certain before God. [5]We are not saying that we can do this work ourselves. It is God who makes us able to do all that we do. [6]He made us able to be servants of a new agreement from himself to his people. This new agreement is not a written law, but it is of the Spirit. The written law brings death, but the Spirit gives life.

[7]The law that brought death was written in words on stone. It came with God's glory, which made Moses' face so bright that the Israelites could not continue to look at it. But that glory later disappeared. [8]So surely the new way that brings the Spirit has even more glory. [9]If the law that judged people guilty of sin had glory, surely the new way that makes people right with God has much greater glory. [10]That old law had glory, but it really loses its glory when it is compared to the much greater glory of this new way. [11]If that law which disappeared came with glory, then this new way which continues forever has much greater glory.

[12]We have this hope, so we are very bold. [13]We are not like Moses, who put a covering over his face so the Israelites would not see it. The glory was disappearing, and Moses did not want them to see it end. [14]But their minds were closed, and even today that same covering hides the meaning when they read the old agreement. That covering is taken away only through Christ. [15]Even today, when they read the law of Moses, there is a covering over their minds. [16]But when a person changes and follows the Lord, that covering is taken away. [17]The Lord is the Spirit, and where the Spirit of the Lord is, there is freedom. [18]Our faces, then, are not covered. We all show the Lord's glory, and we are being changed to be like him. This change in us brings ever greater glory, which comes from the Lord, who is the Spirit.

PREACHING THE GOOD NEWS

4 God, with his mercy, gave us this work to do, so we don't give up. [2]But we have turned away from secret and shameful ways. We use no trickery, and we do not change the teaching of God. We teach the truth plainly, showing everyone who we are. Then they can know in their hearts what kind of people we are in God's sight. [3]If the Good News that we preach is hidden, it is hidden only to those who are lost. [4]The devil who rules this world has blinded the minds of those who do not believe. They cannot see the light of the Good News—the Good News about the glory of Christ, who is exactly like God. [5]We do not preach about ourselves, but we preach that Jesus Christ is Lord and that we are your servants for Jesus. [6]God once said, "Let the light shine out of the darkness!" This is the same God who made his light shine in our hearts by letting us know the glory of God that is in the face of Christ.

dare to do

1 Corinthians 13:2
Read It: Talents without love are meaningless.
Do It: Pray that God would give you love for him and for other people.

1 Corinthians 13:4
Read It: Love is others-centered; it's not me-centered.
Do It: When you talk to your friends, does what you say make you look better or does it make them look better?

1 Corinthians 13:5
Read It: Love doesn't count up the bad things that have been done against it.
Do It: Are you still angry or hurt by something that happened a long time ago? Ask God to take away your pain or anger.

SPIRITUAL TREASURE IN CLAY JARS

[7]We have this treasure from God, but we are like clay jars that hold the treasure. This shows that the great power is from God, not from us. [8]We have troubles all around us, but we are not defeated. We do not know what to do, but we do not give up the hope of living. [9]We are persecuted, but God does not leave us. We are hurt sometimes, but we are not destroyed. [10]We carry the death of Jesus in our own bodies so that the life of Jesus can also be

SMART TIPS!

Do Laundry

There's nothing worse than realizing you don't have any clean underwear because you've let your laundry pile up too long. It will start smelling bad. The same is true when we let our sins pile up. God promises that if we confess our sins he will forgive us. It's time to wash up!

3:3 **stone tablets** Meaning the Law of Moses that was written on stone tablets (Exodus 24:12; 25:16).

seen in our bodies. [11]We are alive, but for Jesus we are always in danger of death so that the life of Jesus can be seen in our bodies that die. [12]So death is working in us, but life is working in you.

[13]It is written in the Scriptures, "I believed, so I spoke."[n] Our faith is like this, too. We believe, and so we speak. [14]God raised the Lord Jesus from the dead, and we know that God will also raise us with Jesus. God will bring us together with you, and we will stand before him. [15]All these things are for you. And so the grace of God that is being given to more and more people will bring increasing thanks to God for his glory.

LIVING BY FAITH

[16]So we do not give up. Our physical body is becoming older and weaker, but our spirit inside us is made new every day. [17]We have small troubles for a while now, but they are helping us gain an eternal glory that is much greater than the troubles. [18]We set our eyes not on what we see but on what we cannot see. What we see will last only a short time, but what we cannot see will last forever.

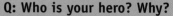

Q: Who is your hero? Why?
A: "Jesus, because he saved us."
(Benjamin, 9)

Q: How should guys treat girls?
A: "With kindness and respect." (David, 12)

Q: What does it mean to be a man?
A: "It means to not be a scaredy-cat and face life."
(Christian, 12)

5 We know that our body—the tent we live in here on earth—will be destroyed. But when that happens, God will have a house for us. It will not be a house made by human hands; instead, it will be a home in heaven that will last forever. [2]But now we groan in this tent. We want God to give us our heavenly home, [3]because it will clothe us so we will not be naked. [4]While we live in this body, we have burdens, and we groan. We do not want to be naked, but we want to be clothed with our heavenly home. Then this body that dies will be fully covered with life. [5]This is what God made us for, and he has given us the Spirit to be a guarantee for this new life.

[6]So we always have courage. We know that while we live in this body, we are away from the Lord. [7]We live by what we believe, not by what we can see. [8]So I say that we have courage. We really want to be away from this body and be at home with the Lord. [9]Our only goal is to please God whether we live here or there, [10]because we must all stand before Christ to be judged. Each of us will receive what we should get—good or bad—for the things we did in the earthly body.

BECOMING FRIENDS WITH GOD

[11]Since we know what it means to fear the Lord, we try to help people accept the truth about us. God knows what we really are, and I hope that in your hearts you know, too. [12]We are not trying to prove ourselves to you again, but we are telling you about ourselves so you will be proud of us. Then you will have an answer for those who are proud about things that can be seen rather than what is in the heart. [13]If we are out of our minds, it is for God. If we have our right minds, it is for you. [14]The love of Christ controls us, because we know that One died for all, so all have died. [15]Christ died for all so that those who live would not continue to live for themselves. He died for them and was raised from the dead so that they would live for him.

[16]From this time on we do not think of

ROCK SOLID

2 Corinthians 4:7

You are a ceramic pot.

If you're a Christian, your purpose in life is to hold God's treasure. The apostle Paul explains, "We have this treasure from God, but we are like clay jars that hold the treasure" (2 Corinthians 4:7).

You're not a perfect pot; you have some chips and cracks. But that makes you all the better for God to use. Look at the rest of the verse: "This shows that the great power is from God, not from us."

So when people look at the jar, they never say, "Wow! That's a really cool pot!" because then it would be the clay jar that is being praised. Instead, they look at you and say, "You're just a pot, but there is something really cool inside you!"

Don't show off to make yourself look good. Let people see the shine of Jesus in your life. After all, they have cracks and chips, too, and need Jesus as much as you do.

 4:13 "I . . . spoke." Quotation from Psalm 116:10.

anyone as the world does. In the past we thought of Christ as the world thinks, but we no longer think of him in that way. [17]If anyone belongs to Christ, there is a new creation. The old things have gone; everything is made new! [18]All this is from God. Through Christ, God made peace between us and himself, and God gave us the work of telling everyone about the peace we can have with him. [19]God was in Christ, making peace between the world and himself. In Christ, God did not hold the world guilty of its sins. And he gave us this message of peace. [20]So we have been sent to speak for Christ. It is as if God is calling to you through us. We speak for Christ when we beg you to be at peace with God. [21]Christ had no sin, but God made him become sin so that in Christ we could become right with God.

6 We are workers together with God, so we beg you: Do not let the grace that you received from God be for nothing. [2]God says,

> "At the right time I heard your prayers.
> On the day of salvation I helped you."
>
> *Isaiah 49:8*

I tell you that the "right time" is now, and the "day of salvation" is now.

[3]We do not want anyone to find fault with our work, so nothing we do will be a problem for anyone. [4]But in every way we show we are servants of God: in accepting many hard things, in troubles, in difficulties, and in great problems. [5]We are beaten and thrown into prison. We meet those who become upset with us and start riots. We work hard, and sometimes we get no sleep or food. [6]We show we are servants of God by our pure lives, our understanding, patience, and kindness, by the Holy Spirit, by true love, [7]by speaking the truth, and by God's power. We use our right living to defend ourselves against everything. [8]Some people honor us, but others blame us. Some people say evil things about us, but others say good things. Some people say we are liars, but we speak the truth. [9]We are not known, but we are well known. We seem to be dying, but we continue to live. We are punished, but we are not killed. [10]We have much sadness, but we are always rejoicing. We are poor, but we are making many people rich in faith. We have nothing, but really we have everything.

[11]We have spoken freely to you in Corinth and have opened our hearts to you. [12]Our feelings of love for you have not stopped, but you have stopped your feelings of love for us. [13]I speak to you as if you were my children. Do to us as we have done—open your hearts to us.

WARNING ABOUT NON-CHRISTIANS

[14]You are not the same as those who do not believe. So do not join yourselves to them. Good and bad do not belong together. Light and darkness cannot share together. [15]How can Christ and Belial, the devil, have any agreement? What can a believer have together with a nonbeliever? [16]The temple of God cannot have any agreement with idols, and we are the temple of the living God. As God said: "I will live with them and walk with them. And I will be their God, and they will be my people."[n]

[17]"Leave those people,
and be separate, says the Lord.

Touch nothing that is unclean,
and I will accept you."

Isaiah 52:11; Ezekiel 20:34, 41

[18]"I will be your father,
and you will be my sons and
daughters,
says the Lord Almighty."   *2 Samuel 7:14*

7 Dear friends, we have these promises from God, so we should make ourselves pure—free from anything that makes body or

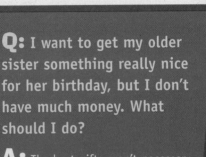

Q: I want to get my older sister something really nice for her birthday, but I don't have much money. What should I do?

A: The best gifts aren't necessarily expensive. Really good gifts show that you know the person. Pay attention to the kinds of things your sister likes. For instance, does she have any hobbies? One thing everybody appreciates is being served by someone else. Make your sister a coupon book of certificates for household chores you agree to do for her. Be generous and she'll love it.

Q: Does caffeine really stunt your growth?

A: No. According to www.KidsHealth.org, the theory that caffeine stunts growth has never been supported by research. Caffeine can make you jittery, dehydrated, and unable to sleep, but your height will be fine.

Q: Is it okay for Christians to be rock stars? That's what I want to be when I grow up!

A: Christians can have any job that glorifies and honors God. There are some Christian musicians who write and sing rock music, like the group Third Day and artist Jeremy Camp. But, like any other job, becoming a music star can be dangerous if you depend on yourself instead of God. So make sure that you are putting him first and then pursuing your career goals. Follow the Bible's advice: "If you eat or drink, or if you do anything, do it all for the glory of God" (1 Corinthians 10:31).

6:16 "I . . . people." Quotation from Leviticus 26:11–12; Jeremiah 32:38; Ezekiel 37:27.

soul unclean. We should try to become holy in the way we live, because we respect God.

PAUL'S JOY

²Open your hearts to us. We have not done wrong to anyone, we have not ruined the faith of anyone, and we have not cheated anyone. ³I do not say this to blame you. I told you before that we love you so much we would live or die with you. ⁴I feel very sure of you and am very proud of you. You give me much comfort, and in all of our troubles I have great joy.

⁵When we came into Macedonia, we had no rest. We found trouble all around us. We had fighting on the outside and fear on the inside. ⁶But God, who comforts those who are troubled, comforted us when Titus came. ⁷We were comforted, not only by his coming but also by the comfort you gave him. Titus told us about your wish to see me and that you are very sorry for what you did. He also told me about your great care for me, and when I heard this, I was much happier.

⁸Even if my letter made you sad, I am not sorry I wrote it. At first I was sorry, because it made you sad, but you were sad only for a short time. ⁹Now I am happy, not because you were made sad, but because your sorrow made you change your lives. You became sad in the way God wanted you to, so you were not hurt by us in any way. ¹⁰The kind of sorrow God wants makes people change their hearts and lives. This leads to salvation, and you cannot be sorry for that. But the kind of sorrow the world has brings death. ¹¹See what this sorrow—the sorrow God wanted you to have—has done to you: It has made you very serious. It made you want to restore yourselves. It made you angry and afraid. It made you want to see me. It made you care.

ROCK SOLID

2 Corinthians 6:14

Are you different? Is there something about you that just isn't like other kids? Being different is usually the last thing a kid wants to be! You want to fit in. You want acceptance. That's perfectly normal. In fact, it's not just kids that feel that way; adults want to belong, too!

But if you're a believer in Jesus you should know that you *are* different. Deep down, you have something that unbelievers don't. That's because God has given you a new heart!

One of the big reasons we go to church is to gather with people who think as we do because God's Spirit is opening their eyes, as well. It is in your church that you'll find a deep sense of belonging and acceptance.

The Bible cautions us about this difference from unbelievers. Second Corinthians 6:14 says, "You are not the same as those who do not believe. So do not join yourselves to them." It's not that you can't have non-Christian friends. But be careful about the things you do together. Whether it's a club, a sport, a band, or even a girlfriend, these relationships can short-circuit your walk with God because they aren't really like you.

The best thing you can do is expose unbelievers to Jesus Christ—that way you won't be distracted from following him.

It made you want to do the right thing. In every way you have regained your innocence. ¹²I wrote that letter, not because of the one who did the wrong or because of the person who was hurt. I wrote the letter so you could see, before God, the great care you have for us. ¹³That is why we were comforted.

Not only were we very comforted, we were even happier to see that Titus was so happy. All of you made him feel much better. ¹⁴I bragged to Titus about you, and you showed that I was right. Everything we said to you was true, and you have proved that what we bragged about to Titus is true. ¹⁵And his love for you is stronger when he remembers that you were all ready to obey. You welcomed him with respect and fear. ¹⁶I am very happy that I can trust you fully.

CHRISTIAN GIVING

8 And now, brothers and sisters, we want you to know about the grace God gave the churches in Macedonia. ²They have been tested by great troubles, and they are very poor. But they gave much because of their great joy. ³I can tell you that they gave as much as they were able and even more than they could afford. No one told them to do it. ⁴But they begged and pleaded with us to let them share in this service for God's people. ⁵And they gave in a way we did not expect: They

know that Christ was rich, but for you he became poor so that by his becoming poor you might become rich.

[10]This is what I think you should do: Last year you were the first to want to give, and you were the first who gave. [11]So now finish the work you started. Then your "doing" will be equal to your "wanting to do." Give from what you have. [12]If you want to give, your gift will be accepted. It will be judged by what you have, not by what you do not have. [13]We do not want you to have troubles while other people are at ease, but we want everything to be equal. [14]At this time you have plenty. What you have can help others who are in need. Then later, when they have plenty, they can help you when you are in need, and all will be equal. [15]As it is written in the Scriptures, "The person who gathered more did not have too much, nor did the person who gathered less have too little."[n]

TITUS AND HIS COMPANIONS HELP

[16]I thank God because he gave Titus the same love for you that I have. [17]Titus accepted what we asked him to do. He wanted very much to go to you, and this was his own idea. [18]We are sending with him the brother who is praised by all the churches because of his service in preaching the Good News. [19]Also, this brother was chosen by the churches to go with

first gave themselves to the Lord and to us. This is what God wants. [6]So we asked Titus to help you finish this special work of grace since he is the one who started it. [7]You are rich in everything—in faith, in speaking, in knowledge, in truly wanting to help, and in the love you learned from us.[n] In the same way, be strong also in the grace of giving.

[8]I am not commanding you to give. But I want to see if your love is true by comparing you with others that really want to help. [9]You know the grace of our Lord Jesus Christ. You

FAITH

Faith means believing something without having all of the proof that it's true. "Placing your faith" in Jesus means trusting that Jesus is who he says he is (the Son of God!) and that his death on the cross is enough to get rid of your sin.

Faith is "being sure of the things we hope for and knowing that something is real even if we do not see it" (Hebrews 11:1). We have faith that God is real and powerful—though we haven't seen or touched him. We also have faith that Jesus is coming back to take us to live in heaven with him. If you have trouble believing something from the Bible, then ask God to strengthen your faith!

trustables

2 Corinthians 6:16

Why are you holding the Word of God in your hands? Did you have the good sense to buy it? If it was a gift, are you the one who chose to open it up and read it?

Well, you may not be as "in charge" as you think. The Bible says you have been picked for this special assignment out of all the people in the world. And not only have you been picked, but God has special plans for you! Scripture says, "We are the temple of the living God. As God said: 'I will live with them and walk with them. And I will be their God, and

they will be my people'" (2 Corinthians 6:16).

Did you catch that? You are a part of God's temple! You probably don't even own a white robe! Actually, the outfit has nothing to do with it. If God has called you to be his servant, and enabled you to believe in his Son, then you *are* part of God's temple on earth.

You have been put where you are, and have been given God's Word, to represent Jesus Christ. There is no greater honor that could be bestowed on someone. So count yourself really lucky! And go—be a blessing to your world.

8:7 in . . . us Some Greek copies read "in your love for us."   **8:15 "The person . . . little."** Quotation from Exodus 16:18.

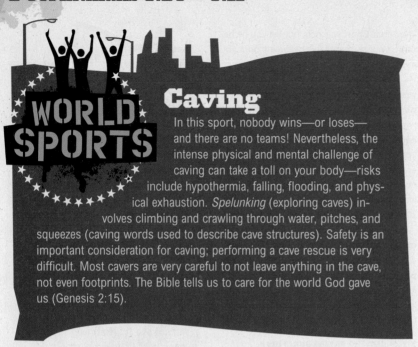

WORLD SPORTS

Caving

In this sport, nobody wins—or loses—and there are no teams! Nevertheless, the intense physical and mental challenge of caving can take a toll on your body—risks include hypothermia, falling, flooding, and physical exhaustion. *Spelunking* (exploring caves) involves climbing and crawling through water, pitches, and squeezes (caving words used to describe cave structures). Safety is an important consideration for caving; performing a cave rescue is very difficult. Most cavers are very careful to not leave anything in the cave, not even footprints. The Bible tells us to care for the world God gave us (Genesis 2:15).

us when we deliver this gift of money. We are doing this service to bring glory to the Lord and to show that we really want to help.

20We are being careful so that no one will criticize us for the way we are handling this large gift. 21We are trying hard to do what the Lord accepts as right and also what people think is right.

22Also, we are sending with them our brother, who is always ready to help. He has proved this to us in many ways, and he wants to help even more now, because he has much faith in you.

23Now about Titus—he is my partner who is working with me to help you. And about the other brothers—they are sent from the churches, and they bring glory to Christ. 24So show these men the proof of your love and the reason we are proud of you. Then all the churches can see it.

HELP FOR FELLOW CHRISTIANS

9 I really do not need to write you about this help for God's people. 2I know you want to help. I have been bragging about this to the people in Macedonia, telling them that you in Southern Greece have been ready to give since last year. And your desire to give has made most of them ready to give also. 3But I am sending the brothers to you so that our bragging about you in this will not be empty words. I want you to be ready, as I said you would be. 4If any of the people from Macedonia come with me and find that you are not ready, we will be ashamed that we were so sure of you. (And you will be ashamed, too!) 5So I thought I should ask these brothers to go to you before we do. They will finish getting in order the generous gift you promised so it will be ready when we come. And it will be a generous gift—not one that you did not want to give.

6Remember this: The person who plants a little will have a small harvest, but the person who plants a lot will have a big harvest. 7Each of you should give as you have decided in your heart to give. You should not be sad when you give, and you should not give because you feel forced to give. God loves the person who gives happily. 8And God can give you more blessings than you need. Then you will always have plenty of everything—enough to give to every good work. 9It is written in the Scriptures:

"He gives freely to the poor.
The things he does are right and will
continue forever."   *Psalm 112:9*

10God is the One who gives seed to the farmer and bread for food. He will give you all the seed you need and make it grow so there will be a great harvest from your goodness. 11He will

BIBLE SUPERHEROES

Priscilla and Aquila
See Acts 18.

Priscilla and her husband, Aquila, were tent makers. The apostle Paul, who was also a tent maker, met them in the city of Corinth. Together they started a church that met in Priscilla and Aquila's home (1 Corinthians 16:19).

The couple went on to help churches in cities like Ephesus and Rome. When Paul wrote about them in his letter to the Romans, he praised their courage. "Give my greetings to Priscilla and Aquila, who work together with me in Christ Jesus and who risked their own lives to save my life. I am thankful to them, and all the non-Jewish churches are thankful as well" (Romans 16:3–4).

Priscilla was not just her husband's shadow; she was his able coworker and teammate. In fact, whenever they are mentioned in the Bible, Priscilla's name usually comes first.

mission trips

Imagine yourself building shelters for the homeless or serving meals at a rescue mission. Can you see yourself helping lead Vacation Bible School or being a counselor at a youth camp? These are just a few of the activities that you may have the chance to be involved with if your church or youth group does missions or ministry trips.

If you like to travel and are interested in serving God in different places, look for opportunities that may open up when you are in high school. But before you start packing your bags, there are a few things you should know.

Mission trips usually take place in another city or even another country. It can be frightening to be in an unfamiliar place, and getting out of your "comfort zone" is hard. If you are going to another country, try to learn a few key phrases before you go. Learning how to say "hello," "good-bye," and "where is the bathroom?" will take you a long way!

If you've never traveled before, then talk with someone who knows about the culture or area you'll be in. It's important to understand the customs of the people so that you aren't rude. Remember, you're the stranger, so be polite. If the food is different from what you are used to eating, don't make a bad face; eating is a learning experience, too!

Mission trips involve working with people and communities—talking with them about Jesus while helping improve their situation. Some of the time you may be working very hard and getting tired, but the trip is not just about getting dirty and sweaty. Most importantly, you will be sharing your faith and love for God.

Your youth leader or pastor will help you prepare for talking about Jesus Christ with the people you meet. By spending time praying and reading the Bible, you will be ready. And nothing is more exciting than sharing the Good News of salvation! Paul says in Romans 1:16 that the Good News "is the power God uses to save everyone who believes." Wow! The Bible says to "serve each other with love" (Galatians 5:13). Mission trips are a great place to put this verse into practice. You'll have the opportunity to help others and see God working in a different place. Talk to your youth leaders to find out how you can be involved.

make you rich in every way so that you can always give freely. And your giving through us will cause many to give thanks to God. ¹²This service you do not only helps the needs of God's people, it also brings many more thanks to God. ¹³It is a proof of your faith. Many people will praise God because you obey the Good News of Christ—the gospel you say you believe—and because you freely share with them and with all others. ¹⁴And when they pray, they will wish they could be with you because of the great grace that God has given you. ¹⁵Thanks be to God for his gift that is too wonderful for words.

PAUL DEFENDS HIS MINISTRY

10 I, Paul, am begging you with the gentleness and the kindness of Christ. Some people say that I am easy on you when I am with you and bold when I am away. ²They think we live in a worldly way, and I plan to be very bold with them when I come. I beg you that when I come I will not need to use that same boldness with you. ³We do live in the world, but we do not fight in the same way the world fights. ⁴We fight with weapons that are different from those the world uses. Our weapons have power from God that can destroy the enemy's strong places. We destroy people's arguments ⁵and every proud thing that raises itself against the knowledge of God. We capture every thought and make it give up and obey Christ. ⁶We are ready to punish anyone there who does not obey, but first we want you to obey fully.

⁷You must look at the facts before you. If you feel sure that you belong to Christ, you must remember that we belong to Christ just as you do. ⁸It is true that we brag freely about the authority the Lord gave us. But this authority is to build you up, not to tear you down. So I will not be ashamed. ⁹I do not want you to think I am trying to scare you with my letters. ¹⁰Some people say, "Paul's letters are powerful and sound important, but when he is with us, he is weak. And his speaking is nothing." ¹¹They should know this: We are not there with you now, so we say these things in letters. But when we are there with you, we will show the same authority that we show in our letters.

¹²We do not dare to compare ourselves with those who think they are very important. They use themselves to measure themselves, and they judge themselves by what they themselves are. This shows that they know nothing.

BIBLE SUPERHEROES

Ruth
See Book of Ruth.

Ruth is one of only four women who are listed in the family tree of Jesus Christ (Matthew 1:5). This is a great privilege because official *genealogies* (lists of family ancestors) usually only give the fathers' names.

What had Ruth done to be so honored? Find out by reading the book named after her in the Old Testament.

Ruth was a loving and loyal person who caught the eye of a rich man named Boaz. They married and had children. One of her grandsons became the famous King David (Ruth 4:16–17). Her great-great- (times some!) grandson was Jesus Christ.

Ruth, a non-Jew, was accepted into God's family because of her kindness toward her own family. How we treat our family members says a lot about the kind of people we are. And you can be sure God notices.

GET CONNECTED

ANGER

Think about the last time you were really mad at someone or something. Guess what? It's okay to be mad sometimes! God wants you to love what he loves and hate what he hates. That means some things, like abuse, are going to make you mad. But just as God forgives those who make him mad, we have to control our anger. Ephesians 4:26 says, "When you are angry, do not sin, and be sure to stop being angry before the end of the day." It's not the anger that's wrong—but it matters what we do about it!

[13]But we will not brag about things outside the work that was given us to do. We will limit our bragging to the work that God gave us, and this includes our work with you. [14]We are not bragging too much, as we would be if we had not already come to you. But we have come to you with the Good News of Christ. [15]We limit our bragging to the work that is ours, not what others have done. We hope that as your faith continues to grow, you will help our work to grow much larger. [16]We want to tell the Good News in the areas beyond your city. We do not want to brag about work that has already been done in another person's area. [17]But, "If people want to brag, they should brag only about the Lord."[n] [18]It is not those who say they are good who are accepted but those the Lord thinks are good.

PAUL AND THE FALSE APOSTLES

11 I wish you would be patient with me even when I am a little foolish, but you are already doing that. [2]I am jealous over you with a jealousy that comes from God. I promised to give you to Christ, as your only husband. I want to give you as his pure bride. [3]But I am afraid that your minds will be led away from your true and pure following of Christ just as Eve was tricked by the snake with his evil ways. [4]You are very patient with anyone who comes to you and preaches a different Jesus from the one we preached. You are very willing to accept a spirit or gospel that is different from the Spirit and Good News you received from us.

[5]I do not think that those "great apostles" are any better than I am. [6]I may not be a trained speaker, but I do have knowledge. We have shown this to you clearly in every way.

[7]I preached God's Good News to you without pay. I made myself unimportant to make you important. Do you think that was wrong? [8]I accepted pay from other churches, taking their money so I could serve you. [9]If I needed something when I was with you, I did not trouble any of you. The brothers who came from Macedonia gave me all that I needed. I did not allow myself to depend on you in any way, and I will never depend on you.

[10]No one in Southern Greece will stop me from bragging about that. I say this with the truth of Christ in me. [11]And why do I not depend on you? Do you think it is because I do not love you? God knows that I love you.

[12]And I will continue doing what I am doing now, because I want to stop those people from

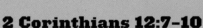

ROCK SOLID

2 Corinthians 12:7–10

Just about everyone wonders why God allows bad things to happen to good people. Some people even refuse to believe in God because they don't think he would let good people suffer. But maybe God has a very good reason for it. One reason is that during the tough times, God can show his love and power the best!

The apostle Paul was having a hard time once and he prayed three times, begging God to help him. Instead of taking away his pain, God said to him, "My grace is enough for you. When you are weak, my power is made perfect in you" (2 Corinthians 12:9). You see, if we didn't have tough times, we never would have to cry out to God and depend on him for help. But when we have troubles and we turn to God, he can help us and prove his love and power. People with no problems are often the people who question, "Who needs God?"

Next time you're in pain or in a difficult situation, it's fine to pray for God to take it away. But also remember that God may prefer to walk with you for a while to teach you about himself.

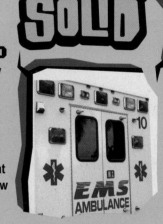

⭐ 10:17 "If . . . Lord." Quotation from Jeremiah 9:24.

having a reason to brag. They would like to say that the work they brag about is the same as ours. [13]Such men are not true apostles but are workers who lie. They change themselves to look like apostles of Christ. [14]This does not surprise us. Even Satan changes himself to look like an angel of light." [15]So it does not surprise us if Satan's servants also make themselves look like servants who work for what is right. But in the end they will be punished for what they do.

PAUL TELLS ABOUT HIS SUFFERINGS

[16]I tell you again: No one should think I am a fool. But if you think so, accept me as you would accept a fool. Then I can brag a little, too. [17]When I brag because I feel sure of myself, I am not talking as the Lord would talk but as a fool. [18]Many people are bragging about their lives in the world. So I will brag too. [19]You are wise, so you will gladly be patient with fools! [20]You are even patient with those who order you around, or use you, or trick you, or think they are better than you, or hit you in the face. [21]It is shameful to me to say this, but we were too "weak" to do those things to you!

But if anyone else is brave enough to brag, then I also will be brave and brag. (I am talking as a fool.) [22]Are they Hebrews?" So am I. Are

Share What You Have

When you share, you might not remember it for long, but the other person will never forget it. The Bible says we get back as much as we give. So don't be greedy about your money and stuff, but give it to God and he'll remember for all of eternity.

they Israelites? So am I. Are they from Abraham's family? So am I. [23]Are they serving Christ? I am serving him more. (I am crazy to talk like this.) I have worked much harder than

they. I have been in prison more often. I have been hurt more in beatings. I have been near death many times. [24]Five times the Jews have given me their punishment of thirty-nine lashes with a whip. [25]Three different times I was beaten with rods. One time I was almost stoned to death. Three times I was in ships that wrecked, and one of those times I spent a night and a day in the sea. [26]I have gone on many travels and have been in danger from rivers, thieves, my own people, the Jews, and those who are not Jews. I have been in danger in cities, in places where no one lives, and on the sea. And I have been in danger with false Christians. [27]I have done hard and tiring work, and many times I did not sleep. I have been hungry and thirsty, and many times I have been without food. I have been cold and without clothes. [28]Besides all this, there is on me every day the load of my concern for all the churches. [29]I feel weak every time someone is weak, and I feel upset every time someone is led into sin.

[30]If I must brag, I will brag about the things that show I am weak. [31]God knows I am not lying. He is the God and Father of the Lord

Q: My brothers and I fight all the time. How did Jesus get along with his brothers?

A: The Bible doesn't say how they got along. We know that Jesus lived without sinning (Hebrews 4:15). But we don't know if this perfection rubbed his brothers the wrong way. You can imagine that if Jesus treated his four brothers (Matthew 13:55–56) with the same respect and compassion he showed to other people he met, they would have loved him. We know that at least two of his brothers, James and Judas, were members of the early church.

Q: Are cigarettes really as dangerous as they tell us?

A: Cigarettes are definitely bad for you. If you get hooked on them, it's very hard to quit. And long-term smoking causes thousands of people to die every year. There are many other addictions and lifestyles that will cause you to die early, but everybody agrees that smoking is bad for your health, so

it gets the attention. Smoking a cigarette is not a sin, but it can lead to an addiction that will destroy your body, which God wants you to take care of (1 Corinthians 6:19).

Q: Next year in PE everybody is going to have to shower together. I can't think of anything more embarrassing. How do I get out of this?

A: Talk to your parents about it. They can go with you to talk to next year's PE teacher about other options for showering. If you do have to shower with the other guys, be quick and don't make anyone else feel uncomfortable—that way, there will be less reason for other guys to notice you.

⭐ **11:14 angel of light** Messenger from God. The devil fools people so that they think he is from God.   **11:22 Hebrews** A name for the Jews that some Jews were very proud of.

trustables

2 Corinthians 12:9

In 1501, Michelangelo, one of the greatest sculptors in history, cut a fourteen-foot-tall statue called *The David* out of a damaged piece of marble. He finished the project in 1504—that's three years chipping on one rock. It is still one of the greatest sculptures in the world.

A slab of uncut stone or blob of clay would be a good way to describe your life in God's hands. You're not perfect—you don't have to be. Like a blob of clay, you're not what you will be yet. When you believe that Jesus Christ died for your sins, God forgives the things you've done wrong. He wipes the canvas of your life clean so that he can begin a great work in you.

God is at work in you just as you are. He could tell the apostle Paul, "My grace is enough for you. When you are weak, my power is made perfect in you" (2 Corinthians 12:9).

God is doing a great work in your life. If Michelangelo can use a damaged piece of marble to create a masterpiece in three years, then think of what the one who gave Michelangelo his talents can do with you in a lifetime. After all, your life is in God's hands. Don't worry—he's not finished with you yet!

Jesus Christ, and he is to be praised forever. 32 When I was in Damascus, the governor under King Aretas wanted to arrest me, so he put guards around the city. 33 But my friends lowered me in a basket through a hole in the city wall. So I escaped from the governor.

A SPECIAL BLESSING IN PAUL'S LIFE

12 I must continue to brag. It will do no good, but I will talk now about visions and revelations" from the Lord. ²I know a man in Christ who was taken up to the third heaven fourteen years ago. I do not know whether the man was in his body or out of his body, but God knows. ³⁻⁴And I know that this man was taken up to paradise." I don't know if he was in his body or away from his body, but God knows. He heard things he is not able to

COOL!

What Are the Odds?

What are the odds that life on Earth happened by chance? Not too likely.

Mathematician Fred Hoyle said the probability of evolution happening by chance is as likely as "a tornado sweeping through a junk yard [and] assembling a Boeing 747."

It makes more sense to believe that the universe—and everyone and everything in it—happened on purpose. The "intelligent designer" who made life is none other than the God of the Bible! (Colossians 1:16).

12:1 revelations Revelation is making known a truth that was hidden.   **12:3-4 paradise** Another word for heaven.

TOP 10

Mother's Day Gifts

1. **Something homemade**
2. **CD with her favorite music**
3. **Framed picture of you**
4. **Dinner you've made for her**
5. **Devotional book**
6. **Magazine subscription**
7. **Handwritten letter or card**
8. **Bath soaps**
9. **Perfume**
10. **Flowers**

explain, things that no human is allowed to tell. [5]I will brag about a man like that, but I will not brag about myself, except about my weaknesses. [6]But if I wanted to brag about myself, I would not be a fool, because I would be telling the truth. But I will not brag about myself. I do not want people to think more of me than what they see me do or hear me say.

[7]So that I would not become too proud of the wonderful things that were shown to me, a painful physical problem[n] was given to me. This problem was a messenger from Satan, sent to beat me and keep me from being too proud. [8]I begged the Lord three times to take this problem away from me. [9]But he said to me, "My grace is enough for you. When you are weak, my power is made perfect in you." So I am very happy to brag about my weaknesses. Then Christ's power can live in me. [10]For this reason I am happy when I have weaknesses, insults, hard times, sufferings, and all kinds of troubles for Christ. Because when I am weak, then I am truly strong.

PAUL'S LOVE FOR THE CHRISTIANS

[11]I have been talking like a fool, but you made me do it. You are the ones who should say good things about me. I am worth nothing, but those "great apostles" are not worth any more than I am!

[12]When I was with you, I patiently did the things that prove I am an apostle—signs, wonders, and miracles. [13]So you received everything that the other churches have received. Only one thing was different: I was not a burden to you. Forgive me for this!

[14]I am now ready to visit you the third time, and I will not be a burden to you. I want nothing from you, except you. Children should not have to save up to give to their parents. Parents should save to give to their children. [15]So I am happy to give everything I have for you, even myself. If I love you more, will you love me less?

[16]It is clear I was not a burden to you, but you think I was tricky and lied to catch you. [17]Did I cheat you by using any of the messengers I sent to you? No, you know I did not. [18]I asked Titus to go to you, and I sent our brother with him. Titus did not cheat you, did he? No, you know that Titus and I did the same thing and with the same spirit.

[19]Do you think we have been defending ourselves to you all this time? We have been speaking in Christ and before God. You are our dear friends, and everything we do is to make you stronger. [20]I am afraid that when I come, you will not be what I want you to be, and I will not be what you want me to be. I am afraid that among you there may be arguing, jealousy, anger, selfish fighting, evil talk, gossip, pride, and confusion. [21]I am afraid that when I come to you again, my God will make me ashamed before you. I may be saddened by many of those who have sinned because they have not changed their hearts or turned from their sexual sins and the shameful things they have done.

FINAL WARNINGS AND GREETINGS

13 I will come to you for the third time. "Every case must be proved by two or three witnesses."[n] [2]When I was with you the second time, I gave a warning to those who had sinned. Now I am away from you, and I give a warning to all the others. When I come to you again, I will not be easy with them. [3]You want proof that Christ is speaking through me.

My proof is that he is not weak among you, but he is powerful. [4]It is true that he was weak when he was killed on the cross, but he lives now by God's power. It is true that we are weak in Christ, but for you we will be alive in Christ by God's power.

[5]Look closely at yourselves. Test yourselves to see if you are living in the faith. You know that Jesus Christ is in you—unless you fail the test. [6]But I hope you will see that we ourselves have not failed the test. [7]We pray to God that you will not do anything wrong. It is not important to see that we have passed the test, but it is important that you do what is right, even if it seems we have failed. [8]We cannot do anything against the truth, but only for the truth. [9]We are happy to be weak, if you are strong, and we pray that you will become complete. [10]I am writing this while I am away from you so that when I come I will not have to be harsh in my use of authority. The Lord gave me this authority to build you up, not to tear you down.

[11]Now, brothers and sisters, I say goodbye. Live in harmony. Do what I have asked you to do. Agree with each other, and live in peace. Then the God of love and peace will be with you.

[12]Greet each other with a holy kiss. [13]All of God's holy people send greetings to you.

[14]The grace of the Lord Jesus Christ, the love of God, and the fellowship of the Holy Spirit be with you all.

DID YOU KNOW?

On average, preteens only spend 15 minutes a day with their parents.

Sonna, Linda, Ph.D. *The Everything Tween Book*, p. 96.

⭐ **12:7 painful physical problem** Literally, "thorn in the flesh." **13:1 "Every . . . witnesses."** Quotation from Deuteronomy 19:15.

Imagine you just shared great news with your best friends.

How would you feel if they didn't pay any attention? You would probably be upset, right?

That's how Paul felt about the Galatians. The Galatians were a group of Christians who needed some harsh reminders about the truth. They weren't using their heads, and some of them believed lies. It made Paul mad! Paul wrote this letter to clue the Galatians in to their foolish mistakes.

Think about a time when someone in authority told you that you were heading down the wrong road. If you've experienced that, you can understand how the Galatians felt when they got Paul's letter.

GALATIANS

Though he didn't cut the Galatians any slack, Paul did encourage them. He wanted them to remember to follow Jesus Christ; nothing else is as important!

Some of the most famous verses in this letter can change your life today. Paul said that the Holy Spirit produces spiritual "fruit" (good attitudes and actions) in our lives that proves we know and love Jesus. Better than strawberries or watermelon, this fruit—love, joy, peace, patience, kindness, goodness, faithfulness, gentleness, and self-control—won't let you down! Pick a fruit of the Spirit that's weak in your life. Are you always ready to fight when someone gets up in your face? Ask the Holy Spirit to produce peace and gentleness in your life (and check out Galatians 5:22–26).

Watch for Paul's instructions for living an ideal Christian life in the Book of Galatians.

From Paul, an apostle. I was not chosen to be an apostle by human beings, nor was I sent from human beings. I was made an apostle through Jesus Christ and God the Father who raised Jesus from the dead. [2]This letter is also from all those of God's family" who are with me.

To the churches in Galatia:"

[3]Grace and peace to you from God our Father and the Lord Jesus Christ. [4]Jesus gave himself for our sins to free us from this evil world we live in, as God the Father planned. [5]The glory belongs to God forever and ever. Amen.

THE ONLY GOOD NEWS

[6]God, by his grace through Christ, called you to become his people. So I am amazed that you are turning away so quickly and believing something different than the Good News. [7]Really, there is no other Good News. But some people are confusing you; they want to change the Good News of Christ. [8]We preached to you the Good News. So if we ourselves, or even an angel from heaven, should preach to you something different, we should be judged guilty! [9]I said this before, and now I say it again: You have already accepted the Good News. If anyone is preaching something different to you, let that person be judged guilty!

[10]Do you think I am trying to make people accept me? No, God is the One I am trying to please. Am I trying to please people? If I still wanted to please people, I would not be a servant of Christ.

PAUL'S AUTHORITY IS FROM GOD

[11]Brothers and sisters, I want you to know that the Good News I preached to you was not made up by human beings. [12]I did not get it from humans, nor did anyone teach it to me, but Jesus Christ showed it to me. [13]You have heard about my past life in the Jewish religion. I attacked the church of God and tried to destroy it. [14]I was becoming a leader in the Jewish religion, doing better than most other Jews of my age. I tried harder than anyone else to follow the teachings handed down by our ancestors. [15]But God had special plans for me and set me apart for his work even before I was born. He called me through his grace [16]and showed his son to me so that I might tell the Good News about him to those who are not Jewish. When God called me, I did not get advice or help from any person. [17]I did not go to Jerusalem to see those who were apostles be-

fore I was. But, without waiting, I went away to Arabia and later went back to Damascus.

[18]After three years I went to Jerusalem to meet Peter and stayed with him for fifteen days. [19]I met no other apostles, except James, the brother of the Lord. [20]God knows that these things I write are not lies. [21]Later, I went to the areas of Syria and Cilicia.

[22]In Judea the churches in Christ had never met me. [23]They had only heard it said, "This man who was attacking us is now preaching the same faith that he once tried to destroy." [24]And these believers praised God because of me.

OTHER APOSTLES ACCEPTED PAUL

After fourteen years I went to Jerusalem again, this time with Barnabas. I also took Titus with me. [2]I went because God showed me I should go. I met with the believers there, and in private I told their leaders the Good News that I preach to the non-Jewish people. I did not want my past work and the work I am now doing to be wasted. [3]Titus was with me, but he was not forced to be circumcised, even though he was a Greek. [4]We talked about this problem because some false believers had come into our group secretly. They came in like spies to overturn the freedom we have in Christ Jesus. They wanted to make us slaves. [5]But we did not give in to those false believers for a minute. We wanted the truth of the Good News to continue for you.

[6]Those leaders who seemed to be important did not change the Good News that I preach. (It doesn't matter to me if they were "important" or not. To God everyone is the same.) [7]But these leaders saw that I had been given the work of telling the Good News to those who are not Jewish, just as Peter had the work of telling the Jews. [8]God gave Peter the power to work as an apostle for the Jewish people. But he also gave me the power to work as an apostle for those who are not Jews. [9]James, Peter, and John, who seemed to be the leaders, understood that God had given me this special grace, so they accepted Barnabas and me. They agreed that they would go

ROCK SOLID

Galatians 2:20

If you stay up really late, you can usually catch some ridiculous zombie movie on cable. It's always the same plot: a town gets invaded by the undead (those who were once dead but came back to life). Zombies are always starving for brains and once bitten, live people become zombies themselves.

It sounds crazy, but would you believe that the Bible describes Christians in a very zombielike way (without the brain-eating)? Galatians 2:20 says, "I do not live anymore—it is Christ who lives in me. I still live in my body, but I live by faith in the Son of God..."

Pretty amazing, huh? But instead of walking around moaning all day, Christians are moved by Jesus Christ's love to do good works. And instead of biting people to make converts, Christians simply share the good news about Jesus with them.

So don't be ashamed to be a zombie for Jesus! Now go out into the world and capture people's brains, er...hearts for Christ.

1:2 those . . . family The Greek text says "brothers."   1:2 Galatia Probably the same country where Paul preached and began churches on his first missionary trip. Read the Book of Acts, chapters 13 and 14.

to the Jewish people and that we should go to those who are not Jewish. [10]The only thing they asked us was to remember to help the poor—something I really wanted to do.

PAUL SHOWS THAT PETER WAS WRONG

[11]When Peter came to Antioch, I challenged him to his face, because he was wrong. [12]Peter ate with the non-Jewish people until some Jewish people sent from James came to Antioch. When they arrived, Peter stopped eating with those who weren't Jewish, and he separated himself from them. He was afraid of the Jews. [13]So Peter was a hypocrite, as were the other Jewish believers who joined with him. Even Barnabas was influenced by what these Jewish believers did. [14]When I saw they were not following the truth of the Good News, I spoke to Peter in front of them all. I said, "Peter, you are a Jew, but you are not living like a Jew. You are living like those who are not Jewish. So why do you now try to force those who are not Jewish to live like Jews?"

[15]We were not born as non-Jewish "sinners," but as Jews. [16]Yet we know that a person is made right with God not by following the law, but by trusting in Jesus Christ. So we, too, have put our faith in Christ Jesus, that we might be made right with God because we trusted in Christ. It is not because we followed the law, because no one can be made right with God by following the law.

[17]We Jews came to Christ, trying to be made right with God, and it became clear that we are sinners, too. Does this mean that Christ encourages sin? No! [18]But I would really be wrong to begin teaching again those things that I gave up. [19]It was the law that put me to death, and I died to the law so that I can now live for God. [20]I was put to death on the cross with Christ, and I do not live anymore—it is Christ who lives in me. I still live in my body, but I live by faith in the Son of God who loved me and gave himself to save me. [21]By saying these things I am not going against God's grace. Just the opposite, if the law could make us right with God, then Christ's death would be useless.

BLESSING COMES THROUGH FAITH

3 You people in Galatia were told very clearly about the death of Jesus Christ on the cross. But you were foolish; you let someone trick you. [2]Tell me this one thing: How did you receive the Holy Spirit? Did you receive the Spirit by following the law? No, you received the Spirit because you heard the Good News and believed it. [3]You began your life in Christ by the Spirit. Now are you trying to make it complete by your own power? That is foolish. [4]Were all your experiences wasted? I hope not! [5]Does God give you the Spirit and work miracles among you because you follow the law? No, he does these things because you heard the Good News and believed it.

[6]The Scriptures say the same thing about Abraham: "Abraham believed God, and God accepted Abraham's faith, and that faith made him right with God."[n] [7]So you should know that the true children of Abraham are those who have faith. [8]The Scriptures, telling what would happen in the future, said that God would make the non-Jewish people right through their faith. This Good News was told to Abraham beforehand, as the Scripture says: "All nations will be blessed through you."[n] [9]So all who believe as Abraham

KNOW THE WORD!

PRAYER

Prayer is a two-way conversation with God. The pray-er (you!) tells God about his worries, doubts, needs, victories, excitements—anything that's on his heart. But it doesn't just stop with talking! God actively listens to everything you say to him, and he always answers. Sometimes God says yes. Other times he says no or wait.

If you need encouragement, watch to see how God uses other people to answer your prayers. If you're excited about something, tell God about it...your happiness will become even deeper! Prayer is the key to having a growing relationship with God. It doesn't take fancy formulas or special words; just talk with God!

3:6 "Abraham . . . God." Quotation from Genesis 15:6.   3:8 "All . . . you." Quotation from Genesis 12:3 and 18:18.

July

1

2 Tell your sister a joke; it's *"International Joke Day."*

3 Pray for a person of influence: actor Tom Cruise adds another year today.

4 Pray for the leaders of your country today.

5 It's *"Anti-Boredom Month."* Find one interesting thing to do every day!

6 Pray for a person of influence: rapper 50 Cent will be humming "Happy Birthday" today.

7 It's Ringo Starr's birthday. Ask your dad to put on an old Beatles' album.

8

9 Pray for the classmates you'll meet this fall.

10

11 Call a friend; it's *"Cheer Up the Lonely Day."*

12

13 Play your favorite "geeky" game; it's *"Embrace Your Geekiness Day"!*

14

15 Be adventurous! Try a new ice cream flavor today.

16 Look through old photo albums with your family.

17 Offer to do a chore without being asked.

18 Pray for a person of influence: it's actor Vin Diesel's birthday.

19 Read 1 Timothy 4 today—and learn how to become a young man of influence!

20

21 Grab the kids in your neighborhood; it's *"Tug-of-War Tournament Day."*
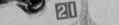

22

23 Read 1 Corinthians 12. What's your spiritual gift?

24 Pray for a person of influence: it's actress Jennifer Lopez's birthday.

25 With your parents' permission, put a sprinkler in your yard and invite your neighbors to cool down.

26 Call your favorite aunt or uncle to catch up.

27

28 Check out a Garfield cartoon book at the library. It's Garfield's creator Jim Davis's birthday.

29

30 Help your parents make dinner tonight.

believed are blessed just as Abraham was. [10]But those who depend on following the law to make them right are under a curse, because the Scriptures say, "Anyone will be cursed who does not always obey what is written in the Book of the Law."[n] [11]Now it is clear that no one can be made right with God by the law, because the Scriptures say, "Those who are right with God will live by faith."[n] [12]The law is not based on faith. It says, "A person who obeys these things will live because of them."[n] [13]Christ took away the curse the law put on us. He changed places with us and put himself under that curse. It is written in the Scriptures, "Anyone whose body is displayed on a tree[n] is cursed." [14]Christ did this so that God's blessing promised to Abraham might come through Jesus Christ to those who are not Jews. Jesus died so that by our believing we could receive the Spirit that God promised.

THE LAW AND THE PROMISE

[15]Brothers and sisters, let us think in human terms: Even an agreement made between two persons is firm. After that agreement is accepted by both people, no one can stop it or add anything to it. [16]God made promises both to Abraham and to his descendant. God did not say, "and to your descendants." That would mean many people. But God said, "and to your descendant." That means only one person; that person is Christ. [17]This is what I mean: God had an agreement with Abraham and promised to keep it. The law, which came four hundred thirty years later, cannot change that agreement and so destroy

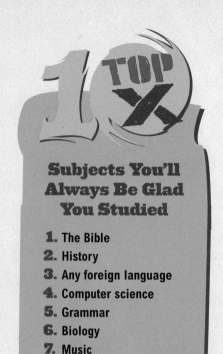

Subjects You'll Always Be Glad You Studied

1. The Bible
2. History
3. Any foreign language
4. Computer science
5. Grammar
6. Biology
7. Music
8. Auto mechanics
9. Wood shop
10. Martial arts

God's promise to Abraham. [18]If the law could give us Abraham's blessing, then the promise would not be necessary. But that is not possi-

ble, because God freely gave his blessings to Abraham through the promise he had made.

[19]So what was the law for? It was given to show that the wrong things people do are against God's will. And it continued until the special descendant, who had been promised, came. The law was given through angels who used Moses for a mediator[n] to give the law to people. [20]But a mediator is not needed when there is only one side, and God is only one.

THE PURPOSE OF THE LAW OF MOSES

[21]Does this mean that the law is against God's promises? Never! That would be true only if the law could make us right with God. But God did not give a law that can bring life. [22]Instead, the Scriptures showed that the whole world is bound by sin. This was so the promise would be given through faith to people who believe in Jesus Christ.

[23]Before this faith came, we were all held prisoners by the law. We had no freedom until God showed us the way of faith that was coming. [24]In other words, the law was our guardian leading us to Christ so that we could be made right with God through faith. [25]Now the way of faith has come, and we no longer live under a guardian.

[26-27]You were all baptized into Christ, and so you were all clothed with Christ. This means that you are all children of God through faith in Christ Jesus. [28]In Christ, there is no difference between Jew and Greek, slave and free person, male and female. You are all the same in Christ Jesus. [29]You belong to Christ, so you are Abraham's descendants. You will inherit all of

COOL! The Blogosphere

Blogs—short for "Web logs"—are a modern way for people to share their thoughts and lives online. Some experts believe that there were more than nine million bloggers (people who use blogs) in the world in 2005 and that the "blogosphere" doubles in size every six months.

Whether you keep a blog or not, God knows everything that happens in your life. He knows every thought and sees every deed. He not only watches you, he watches out for you night and day (Matthew 10:29–31).

3:10 "Anyone . . . Law." Quotation from Deuteronomy 27:26. **3:11** "Those . . . faith." Quotation from Habakkuk 2:4. **3:12** "A person . . . them." Quotation from Leviticus 18:5. **3:13 displayed on a tree** Deuteronomy 21:22–23 says that when a person was killed for doing wrong, the body was hung on a tree to show shame. Paul means that the cross of Jesus was like that. **3:19 mediator** A person who helps one person talk to or give something to another person.

God's blessings because of the promise God made to Abraham.

4 I want to tell you this: While those who will inherit their fathers' property are still children, they are no different from slaves. It does not matter that the children own everything. [2] While they are children, they must obey those who are chosen to care for them. But when the children reach the age set by their fathers, they are free. [3] It is the same for us. We were once like children, slaves to the useless rules of this world. [4] But when the right time came, God sent his Son who was born of a woman and lived under the law. [5] God did this so he could buy freedom for those who were under the law and so we could become his children.

[6] Since you are God's children, God sent the Spirit of his Son into your hearts, and the Spirit cries out, "Father."[n] [7] So now you are not a slave; you are God's child, and God will give you the blessing he promised, because you are his child.

PAUL'S LOVE FOR THE CHRISTIANS

[8] In the past you did not know God. You were slaves to gods that were not real. [9] But now you know the true God. Really, it is God who knows you. So why do you turn back to those weak and useless rules you followed before?

DID YOU KNOW?

46% of preteen boys have their own cell phones.

Shopping In America Survey, April 2005. "What's in the Bag for Tween Shoppers."

Do you want to be slaves to those things again? [10] You still follow teachings about special days, months, seasons, and years. [11] I am afraid for you, that my work for you has been wasted.

[12] Brothers and sisters, I became like you, so I beg you to become like me. You were very good to me before. [13] You remember that it was because of an illness that I came to you the first time, preaching the Good News.

[14] Though my sickness was a trouble for you, you did not hate me or make me leave. But you welcomed me as an angel from God, as if I were Jesus Christ himself! [15] You were very happy then, but where is that joy now? I am ready to testify that you would have taken out your eyes and given them to me if that were possible. [16] Now am I your enemy because I tell you the truth?

[17] Those people[n] are working hard to persuade you, but this is not good for you. They want to persuade you to turn against us and follow only them. [18] It is good for people to show interest in you, but only if their purpose is good. This is always true, not just when I am with you. [19] My little children, again I feel the pain of childbirth for you until you truly become like Christ. [20] I wish I could be with you now and could change the way I am talking to you, because I do not know what to think about you.

THE EXAMPLE OF HAGAR AND SARAH

[21] Some of you still want to be under the law. Tell me, do you know what the law says? [22] The Scriptures say that Abraham had two sons. The mother of one son was a slave woman, and the mother of the other son was a free woman. [23] Abraham's son from the slave woman was born in the normal human way.

trustables

Galatians 4:7

Shoes, clothes, food, a place to sleep—we need stuff, and none of it is free. The apostle Paul was doing God's work, telling everyone about God's love for them, and he wasn't paid for doing it. He helped to provide for himself by making tents; but fortunately, Christians in cities like Antioch and Philippi also supported Paul and his mission efforts.

You need money for things in your life: school, sports, and music, to name a few. Most kids don't have a job to earn the money it takes to pay for such things. Even more than Paul, you depend on someone else to support you.

Don't worry! If you're doing what God wants you to do, he will give you everything you need. The Bible says, "You are God's child, and God will give you the blessing he promised, because you are his child" (Galatians 4:7). You're part of God's family! So, if you need anything, God knows—and will provide. That's a small part of his blessing on your life.

It's a good idea to thank your parents for what you have and what you are able to do because they support you. But remember that it all comes from God. The next time you are worried about things you need, stop, remember this promise, and ask him for a little help.

4:6 "Father" Literally, "Abba, Father." Jewish children called their fathers "Abba." **4:17 Those people** They are the false teachers who were bothering the believers in Galatia (Galatians 1:7).

But the son from the free woman was born because of the promise God made to Abraham.

24This story teaches something else: The two women are like the two agreements between God and his people. One agreement is the law that God made on Mount Sinai," and the people who are under this agreement are like slaves. The mother named Hagar is like that agreement. 25She is like Mount Sinai in Arabia and is a picture of the earthly city of Jerusalem. This city and its people are slaves to the law. 26But the heavenly Jerusalem, which is above, is like the free woman. She is our mother. 27It is written in the Scriptures:

"Be happy, Jerusalem.

You are like a woman who never gave
    birth to children.
Start singing and shout for joy.
You never felt the pain of giving birth,
but you will have more children
    than the woman who has a husband."

Isaiah 54:1

28My brothers and sisters, you are God's children because of his promise, as Isaac was then. 29The son who was born in the normal way treated the other son badly. It is the same today. 30But what does the Scripture say? "Throw out the slave woman and her son. The son of the slave woman should not inherit anything. The son of the free woman should receive it all."[n] 31So, my brothers and sisters, we are not children of the slave woman, but of the free woman.

KEEP YOUR FREEDOM

5 We have freedom now, because Christ made us free. So stand strong. Do not change and go back into the slavery of the law. 2Listen, I Paul tell you that if you go back to the law by being circumcised, Christ does you no good. 3Again, I warn every man: If you allow yourselves to be circumcised, you must follow all the law. 4If you try to be made right with God through the law, your life with Christ is over—you have left God's grace. 5But we have the true hope that comes from being made right with God, and by the Spirit we wait eagerly for this hope. 6When we are in Christ Jesus, it is not important if we are circumcised or not. The important thing is faith—the kind of faith that works through love.

7You were running a good race. Who stopped you from following the true way? 8This change did not come from the One who chose you. 9Be careful! "Just a little yeast makes the whole batch of dough rise." 10But I trust in the Lord that you will not believe those different ideas. Whoever is confusing you with such ideas will be punished.

11My brothers and sisters, I do not teach that a man must be circumcised. If I teach circumcision, why am I still being attacked? If I still taught circumcision, my preaching about the cross would not be a problem. 12I wish the people who are bothering you would castrate" themselves!

13My brothers and sisters, God called you to be free, but do not use your freedom as an excuse to do what pleases your sinful self. Serve each other with love. 14The whole law is made complete in this one command: "Love your neighbor as you love yourself."[n] 15If you go on hurting each other and tearing each other apart, be careful, or you will completely destroy each other.

THE SPIRIT AND HUMAN NATURE

16So I tell you: Live by following the Spirit. Then you will not do what your sinful selves want. 17Our sinful selves want what is against the Spirit, and the Spirit wants what is against our sinful selves. The two are against each other, so you cannot do just what you

---

Q&A

Q: I have to share a room with my little brother and he's constantly into my stuff, which drives me crazy. How do I get this into his thick, little skull?

A: Little kids look up to their older brothers and want to imitate them. This can be annoying when it includes using your things without asking. Try setting aside a few things that he is free to use any time he likes. Since he might not take care of your stuff the way you do, agree with your parents on which of your valuables are off-limits. Treat him the way that you want to be treated, and your little brother may grow up to be one of your best friends.

Q: How come the Bible doesn't have any science in it?

A: Science is a special type of study where you make a prediction and then gather physical evidence to support it. The Bible is history, prophecy, poems, and letters on how to live like a Christian. It was not written to make scientific claims or predictions. But sciences like archeology and biology have confirmed many things in the Bible.

Q: My best friend used to live next door, but he moved out of the state. When will I stop feeling bummed out all the time?

A: It's natural to feel depressed when a friend leaves. You'll eventually make new friends, but waiting for that sad feeling to go away can seem to take forever. Write to your friend and tell him how much you miss him. It'll cheer him up; he's probably feeling lonely, too.

4:24 Mount Sinai Mountain in Arabia where God gave his Law to Moses (Exodus 19 and 20).   **4:30 "Throw . . . all."** Quotation from Genesis 21:10.   **5:12 castrate** To cut off part of the male sex organ. Paul uses this word because it is similar to "circumcision." Paul wanted to show that he is very upset with the false teachers.   **5:14 "Love . . . yourself."** Quotation from Leviticus 19:18.

please. [18]But if the Spirit is leading you, you are not under the law.

[19]The wrong things the sinful self does are clear: being sexually unfaithful, not being pure, taking part in sexual sins, [20]worshiping gods, doing witchcraft, hating, making trouble, being jealous, being angry, being selfish, making people angry with each other, causing divisions among people, [21]feeling envy, being drunk, having wild and wasteful parties, and doing other things like these. I warn you now as I warned you before: Those who do these things will not inherit God's kingdom. [22]But the Spirit produces the fruit of love, joy, peace, patience, kindness, goodness, faithfulness, [23]gentleness, self-control. There is no law that says these things are wrong. [24]Those who belong to Christ Jesus have crucified their own sinful selves. They have given up their old selfish feelings and the evil things they wanted to do. [25]We get our new life from the Spirit, so we should follow the Spirit. [26]We must not be proud or make trouble with each other or be jealous of each other.

HELP EACH OTHER

6 Brothers and sisters, if someone in your group does something wrong, you who are spiritual should go to that person and gently help make him right again. But be careful, because you might be tempted to sin, too. [2]By helping each other with your troubles, you truly obey the law of Christ. [3]If anyone thinks he is important when he really is not, he is only

77% of kids dream of traveling the world someday.

Exploring How to Motivate Behavior Change Among Tweens in America.

fooling himself. [4]Each person should judge his own actions and not compare himself with others. Then he can be proud for what he himself has done. [5]Each person must be responsible for himself.

[6]Anyone who is learning the teaching of God should share all the good things he has with his teacher.

LIFE IS LIKE PLANTING A FIELD

[7]Do not be fooled: You cannot cheat God. People harvest only what they plant. [8]If they plant to satisfy their sinful selves, their sinful selves will bring them ruin. But if they plant to please the Spirit, they will receive eternal life from the Spirit. [9]We must not become tired of doing good. We will receive our harvest of eternal life at the right time if we do not give up. [10]When we have the opportunity to help anyone, we should do it. But we should give special attention to those who are in the family of believers.

PAUL ENDS HIS LETTER

[11]See what large letters I use to write this myself. [12]Some people are trying to force you to be circumcised so the Jews will accept them. They are afraid they will be attacked if they follow only the cross of Christ.[n] [13]Those who are circumcised do not obey the law themselves, but they want you to be circumcised so they can brag about what they forced you to do. [14]I hope I will never brag about things like that. The cross of our Lord Jesus Christ is my only reason for bragging. Through the cross of Jesus my world was crucified, and I died to the world. [15]It is not important if a man is circumcised or uncircumcised. The important thing is being the new people God has made. [16]Peace and mercy to those who follow this rule—and to all of God's people.

[17]So do not give me any more trouble. I have scars on my body that show[n] I belong to Christ Jesus.

[18]My brothers and sisters, the grace of our Lord Jesus Christ be with your spirit. Amen.

BIBLE SUPERHEROES

Peter

See Matthew 16, 26; John 21; Acts 2.

Simon was a fisherman whom Jesus called to "fish for people." Jesus changed Simon's name to Peter—which means "the rock"—because of his rough edges.

Peter became the leader of the Twelve Apostles, the men Jesus chose to start his church. For three years, Peter followed the Master. He made a lot of mistakes, but always learned from them.

Peter became a powerful preacher. One of his sermons caused 3,000 people to become Christians. Shortly after this, he was thrown in jail; but an angel set him free so he could go on preaching, which he did for the rest of his life.

Finally, the Romans had enough. They arrested Peter and crucified him. Tradition says that Peter asked to be hung upside-down because he wasn't worthy to die the same way Jesus had.

6:12 cross of Christ Paul uses the cross as a picture of the Good News, the story of Christ's death and rising from the dead to pay for our sins. The cross, or Christ's death, was God's way to save us.
6:17 that show Many times Paul was beaten and whipped by people who were against him because he was teaching about Christ. The scars were from these beatings.

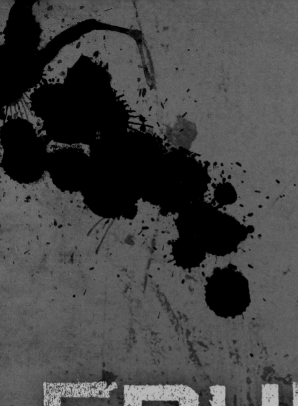

Paul wrote this letter when he was in prison, probably in Rome.

It's written to the churches around Ephesus, a leading city in Asia where Paul had spent a lot of time (Acts 19 and 20).

Paul opens and closes this letter with thankful prayers. In between, he lists many of the great things God has done for us (chapters 1–3). Then he tells us how we should act out of thankfulness for these blessings (chapters 4–6).

The order is important. When we know what God has given us in Jesus Christ—a new life now and a future home in heaven—we will want to please him in everything we do.

EPHESIANS

Paul talks a lot about the church. Back then it was a big deal for Jews and non-Jews to worship together. They never had anything to do with each other, but now Paul says, "You are like a building that was built on the foundation of the apostles and prophets. . . . [Christ] makes it grow and become a holy temple in the Lord" (2:20–21).

The Holy Spirit comes to live inside Christians to help us become more like Jesus. He makes parents more loving, children more obedient, bosses more kind, and workers better at their jobs (chapters 5 and 6).

Because Satan fights against the church, Paul explains the spiritual armor we have been given to protect ourselves (6:10–18). Learn how to put this on and you will be able to defeat the devil!

1 From Paul, an apostle of Christ Jesus. I am an apostle because that is what God wanted.

To God's holy people living in Ephesus," believers in Christ Jesus:

²Grace and peace to you from God our Father and the Lord Jesus Christ.

SPIRITUAL BLESSINGS IN CHRIST

³Praise be to the God and Father of our Lord Jesus Christ. In Christ, God has given us every spiritual blessing in the heavenly world. ⁴That is, in Christ, he chose us before the world was made so that we would be his holy people—people without blame before him. ⁵Because of his love, God had already decided to make us his own children through Jesus Christ. That was what he wanted and what pleased him, ⁶and it brings praise to God because of his wonderful grace. God gave that grace to us freely, in Christ, the One he loves. ⁷In Christ we are set free by the blood of his death, and so we have forgiveness of sins. How rich is God's grace, ⁸which he has given to us so fully and freely. God, with full wisdom and understanding, ⁹let us know his secret purpose. This was what God wanted, and he planned to do it through Christ. ¹⁰His goal was to carry out his plan, when the right time came, that all things in heaven and on earth would be joined together in Christ as the head.

¹¹In Christ we were chosen to be God's people, because from the very beginning God

58% of boys say they have a lot of friends.

Trends & Tudes. Harris Interactive. January 2003.

had decided this in keeping with his plan. And he is the One who makes everything agree with what he decides and wants. ¹²We are the first people who hoped in Christ, and we were chosen so that we would bring praise to God's glory. ¹³So it is with you. When you heard the true teaching—the Good News about your salvation—you believed in Christ. And in Christ, God put his special mark of ownership on you by giving you the Holy Spirit that he had promised. ¹⁴That Holy Spirit is the guarantee that we will receive what God promised for his people until God gives full freedom to

those who are his—to bring praise to God's glory.

PAUL'S PRAYER

¹⁵That is why since I heard about your faith in the Lord Jesus and your love for all God's people, ¹⁶I have not stopped giving thanks to God for you. I always remember you in my prayers, ¹⁷asking the God of our Lord Jesus Christ, the glorious Father, to give you a spirit of wisdom and revelation so that you will know him better. ¹⁸I pray also that you will have greater understanding in your heart so you will know the hope to which he has called us and that you will know how rich and glorious are the blessings God has promised his holy people. ¹⁹And you will know that God's power is very great for us who believe. That power is the same as the great strength ²⁰God used to raise Christ from the dead and put him at his right side in the heavenly world. ²¹God has put Christ over all rulers, authorities, powers, and kings, not only in this world but also in the next. ²²God put everything under his power and made him the head over everything for the church, ²³which is Christ's body. The church is filled with Christ, and Christ fills everything in every way.

WE NOW HAVE LIFE

2 In the past you were spiritually dead because of your sins and the things you did against God. ²Yes, in the past you lived the way the world lives, following the ruler of the evil powers that are above the earth. That

ROCK SOLID

Ephesians 1:16–17

A person can never have too much of God in his life. No matter how mature you become as a Christian, you can always grow more.

In New Testament times, a church in the city of Ephesus was really strong spiritually because it was filled with growing Christians. What do Christians like that need when it seems like they've already got it all together?

This is what the apostle Paul prayed for them: "I always remember you in my prayers, asking the God of our Lord Jesus Christ, the glorious Father, to give you a spirit of wisdom and revelation so that you will know him better" (Ephesians 1:16–17).

A spirit of wisdom and revelation? What's that? Well, it isn't the Holy Spirit, because these Christians already had him in their lives. Paul is telling us that our spirit can always be learning new things about God—constantly!

Do you have that kind of spirit? If not, how do you get it? Simple! Do what Paul did for the Ephesians—pray for it. Pray the words of this prayer for yourself, that God would give you this kind of spirit—so that you are constantly learning new things about him.

1:1 in Ephesus Some Greek copies do not have this phrase.

same spirit is now working in those who refuse to obey God. [3]In the past all of us lived like them, trying to please our sinful selves and doing all the things our bodies and minds wanted. We should have suffered God's anger because we were sinful by nature. We were the same as all other people.

[4]But God's mercy is great, and he loved us very much. [5]Though we were spiritually dead because of the things we did against God, he gave us new life with Christ. You have been saved by God's grace. [6]And he raised us up with Christ and gave us a seat with him in the heavens. He did this for those in Christ Jesus [7]so that for all future time he could show the very great riches of his grace by being kind to us in Christ Jesus. [8]I mean that you have been saved by grace through believing. You did not save yourselves; it was a gift from God. [9]It was not the result of your own efforts, so you cannot brag about it. [10]God has made us what we are. In Christ Jesus, God made us to do good works, which God planned in advance for us to live our lives doing.

ONE IN CHRIST

[11]You were not born Jewish. You are the people the Jews call "uncircumcised."[n] Those who call you "uncircumcised" call themselves "circumcised." (Their circumcision is only something they themselves do on their bodies.) [12]Remember that in the past you were without Christ. You were not citizens of Israel, and you had no part in the agreements[n] with the promise that God made to his people. You had no

DID YOU KNOW?

82% of kids say they believe in God.

Faith Factors. Review of the Literature on Tweens.

hope, and you did not know God. [13]But now in Christ Jesus, you who were far away from God are brought near through the blood of Christ's death. [14]Christ himself is our peace. He made both Jewish people and those who are not Jews one people. They were separated as if there were a wall between them, but Christ broke down that wall of hate by giving his own body. [15]The Jewish law had many commands and rules, but Christ ended that law. His purpose was to make the two groups of people become one new people in him and in this way make peace. [16]It was also

Christ's purpose to end the hatred between the two groups, to make them into one body, and to bring them back to God. Christ did all this with his death on the cross. [17]Christ came and preached peace to you who were far away from God, and to those who were near to God. [18]Yes, it is through Christ we all have the right to come to the Father in one Spirit.

[19]Now you who are not Jewish are not foreigners or strangers any longer, but are citizens together with God's holy people. You belong to God's family. [20]You are like a building that was built on the foundation of the apostles and prophets. Christ Jesus himself is the most important stone[n] in that building, [21]and that whole building is joined together in Christ. He makes it grow and become a holy temple in the Lord. [22]And in Christ you, too, are being built together with the Jews into a place where God lives through the Spirit.

PAUL'S WORK IN TELLING THE GOOD NEWS

3 So I, Paul, am a prisoner of Christ Jesus for you who are not Jews. [2]Surely you have heard that God gave me this work to tell you about his grace. [3]He let me know his secret by showing it to me. I have already written a little about this. [4]If you read what I wrote then, you can see that I truly understand the secret about the Christ. [5]People who lived in other times were not told that secret. But now, through the Spirit, God has shown that secret to his holy apostles and prophets. [6]This is that secret: that through the Good News those who are not Jews will share with the Jews in

COOL!

Elephants Never Forget

The saying "Elephants never forget" is based on fact. When an elephant leaves the herd for a long time and then returns, it is welcomed back with a special ritual. That's amazing to think about, isn't it?!?

Elephants not only remember, they play, laugh, and cry. God gave them emotions in addition to size. (A bull elephant can weigh 12,000 pounds!)

God made elephants with a great memory and great size, but he made humans with something even greater. We have the ability to believe in Jesus Christ and have a personal relationship with the God of the universe! Don't forget about that!

2:11 "uncircumcised" People not having the mark of circumcision as the Jews had.   **2:12 agreements** The agreements that God gave to his people in the Old Testament.   **2:20 most important stone** Literally, "cornerstone." The first and most important stone in a building.

SALVATION

Have you ever had someone ask if you are "saved"? *Saved from what?* you might have wondered. The Bible says, "Jesus is the only One who can save people. No one else in the world is able to save us" (Acts 4:12).

In the Bible, *salvation* refers to God's great rescue plan for people like us. Without God sending Jesus to live, die, and rise to life again, we would not have any way to be saved from our sin. We would have no hope of living forever in God's perfect heaven.

God's rescue plan includes a way for us to be saved *from* sin and its harmful consequences now, and saved *for* right living and eternity with him!

God's blessing. They belong to the same body, and they share together in the promise that God made in Christ Jesus.

⁷By God's special gift of grace given to me through his power, I became a servant to tell that Good News. ⁸I am the least important of all God's people, but God gave me this gift—to tell those who are not Jews the Good News about the riches of Christ, which are too great to understand fully. ⁹And God gave me the work of telling all people about the plan for his secret, which has been hidden in him since the beginning of time. He is the One who created everything. ¹⁰His purpose was that through the church all the rulers and powers in the heavenly world will now know God's wisdom, which has so many forms. ¹¹This agrees with the purpose God had since the beginning of time, and he carried out his plan through Christ Jesus our Lord. ¹²In Christ we can come before God with freedom and without fear. We can do this through faith in Christ. ¹³So I ask you not to become discouraged because of the sufferings I am having for you. My sufferings are for your glory.

THE LOVE OF CHRIST

¹⁴So I bow in prayer before the Father ¹⁵from whom every family in heaven and on earth gets its true name. ¹⁶I ask the Father in his great glory to give you the power to be strong inwardly through his Spirit. ¹⁷I pray that Christ will live in your hearts by faith and that your life will be strong in love and be built on love. ¹⁸And I pray that you and all God's holy people will have the power to understand the greatness of Christ's love—how wide and how long and how high and how deep that love is. ¹⁹Christ's love is greater than anyone can ever know, but I pray that you will be able to know that love. Then you can be filled with the fullness of God.

²⁰With God's power working in us, God can do much, much more than anything we can ask or imagine. ²¹To him be glory in the church and in Christ Jesus for all time, forever and ever. Amen.

THE UNITY OF THE BODY

4 I am in prison because I belong to the Lord. Therefore I urge you who have been chosen by God to live up to the life to which God called you. ²Always be humble, gentle, and patient, accepting each other in love. ³You are joined together with peace through the Spirit, so make every effort to continue together in this way. ⁴There is one body and one Spirit, and God called you to have one hope. ⁵There is one Lord, one faith, and one baptism. ⁶There is one God and Father of everything. He rules everything and is everywhere and is in everything.

⁷Christ gave each one of us the special gift of grace, showing how generous he is. ⁸That is why it says in the Scriptures,

"When he went up to the heights,
    he led a parade of captives,
    and he gave gifts to people."   *Psalm 68:18*

⁹When it says, "He went up," what does it mean? It means that he first came down to the earth. ¹⁰So Jesus came down, and he is the same One who went up above all the heaven. Christ did that to fill everything with his presence. ¹¹And Christ gave gifts to people—he made some to be apostles, some to be prophets, some to go and tell the Good News, and some to have the work of caring for and teaching God's people. ¹²Christ gave those gifts to prepare God's holy people for the work of serving, to make the body of Christ stronger. ¹³This work must continue until we are all joined together in the same faith and in the same knowledge of the Son of

God. We must become like a mature person, growing until we become like Christ and have his perfection.

¹⁴Then we will no longer be babies. We will not be tossed about like a ship that the waves carry one way and then another. We will not be influenced by every new teaching we hear from people who are trying to fool us. They make plans and try any kind of trick to fool people into following the wrong path. ¹⁵No! Speaking the truth with love, we will grow up in every way into Christ, who is the head. ¹⁶The whole body depends on Christ, and all the

Galatians 5:26
Read It: Don't be jealous of others.
Do It: If you're feeling bad because you don't have something, pray and thank God for what you do have. You'll be amazed at how much better you feel!

Galatians 6:2
Read It: Help each other out when you're in trouble.
Do It: If one of your friends or relatives is in the hospital, go and visit them.

Galatians 6:10
Read It: Help everyone, but especially other Christians.
Do It: If you're a Christian, other Christians are your family. Take care of them like you would your mom or little brother.

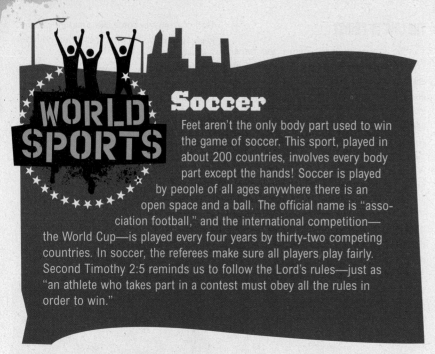

Soccer

Feet aren't the only body part used to win the game of soccer. This sport, played in about 200 countries, involves every body part except the hands! Soccer is played by people of all ages anywhere there is an open space and a ball. The official name is "association football," and the international competition—the World Cup—is played every four years by thirty-two competing countries. In soccer, the referees make sure all players play fairly. Second Timothy 2:5 reminds us to follow the Lord's rules—just as "an athlete who takes part in a contest must obey all the rules in order to win."

parts of the body are joined and held together. Each part does its own work to make the whole body grow and be strong with love.

THE WAY YOU SHOULD LIVE

[17]In the Lord's name, I tell you this. Do not continue living like those who do not believe. Their thoughts are worth nothing. [18]They do not understand, and they know nothing, because they refuse to listen. So they cannot have the life that God gives. [19]They have lost all feeling of shame, and they use their lives for doing evil. They continually want to do all kinds of evil. [20]But what you learned in Christ was not like this. [21]I know that you heard about him, and you are in him, so you were taught the truth that is in Jesus. [22]You were taught to leave your old self—to stop living the evil way you lived before. That old self becomes worse, because people are fooled by the evil things they want to do. [23]But you were taught to be made new in your hearts, [24]to become a new person. That new person is made to be like God—made to be truly good and holy.

[25]So you must stop telling lies. Tell each other the truth, because we all belong to each other in the same body.[n] [26]When you are angry, do not sin, and be sure to stop being angry before the end of the day. [27]Do not give the devil a way to defeat you. [28]Those who are stealing must stop stealing and start working. They should earn an honest living for themselves. Then they will have something to share with those who are poor.

[29]When you talk, do not say harmful things, but say what people need—words that will help others become stronger. Then what you say will do good to those who listen to you. [30]And do not make the Holy Spirit sad. The Spirit is God's proof that you belong to him. God gave you the Spirit to show that God will make you free when the final day comes. [31]Do not be bitter or angry or mad. Never shout angrily or say things to hurt others. Never do anything evil. [32]Be kind and loving to each other, and forgive each other just as God forgave you in Christ.

LIVING IN THE LIGHT

5 You are God's children whom he loves, so try to be like him. [2]Live a life of love just as Christ loved us and gave himself for us as a sweet-smelling offering and sacrifice to God.

[3]But there must be no sexual sin among you, or any kind of evil or greed. Those things are not right for God's holy people. [4]Also, there must be no evil talk among you, and you

COOL! ETs

Do you believe in ETs—Extraterrestrials? You should. They're mentioned over 270 times in the Bible. But they aren't alien beings—they're angels! Since angels aren't from Earth, they are true *extra*terrestrials. They come from heaven to do special assignments for God. They're not human, though they can look like us. Angels are sexless (neither male nor female). They don't get older, don't get married, and don't have baby angels.

So what *do* angels do? "All the angels are spirits who serve God and are sent to help those who will receive salvation" (Hebrews 1:14). That's us!

must not speak foolishly or tell evil jokes. These things are not right for you. Instead, you should be giving thanks to God. ⁵You can be sure of this: No one will have a place in the kingdom of Christ and of God who sins sexually, or does evil things, or is greedy. Anyone who is greedy is serving a false god.

⁶Do not let anyone fool you by telling you things that are not true, because these things will bring God's anger on those who do not obey him. ⁷So have nothing to do with them. ⁸In the past you were full of darkness, but now you are full of light in the Lord. So live like children who belong to the light. ⁹Light brings every kind of goodness, right living, and truth. ¹⁰Try to learn what pleases the Lord. ¹¹Have nothing to do with the things done in darkness, which are not worth anything. But show that they are wrong. ¹²It is shameful even to talk about what those people do in secret. ¹³But the light makes all things easy to see, ¹⁴and everything that is made easy to see can become light. This is why it is said:

"Wake up, sleeper!
Rise from death,
and Christ will shine on you."

¹⁵So be very careful how you live. Do not live like those who are not wise, but live wisely. ¹⁶Use every chance you have for doing good,

39% of kids say they pray every day.

Faith Factors. Review of the Literature on Tweens.

because these are evil times. ¹⁷So do not be foolish but learn what the Lord wants you to do. ¹⁸Do not be drunk with wine, which will ruin you, but be filled with the Spirit. ¹⁹Speak to each other with psalms, hymns, and spiritual songs, singing and making music in your hearts to the

Lord. ²⁰Always give thanks to God the Father for everything, in the name of our Lord Jesus Christ.

WIVES AND HUSBANDS

²¹Yield to obey each other as you would to Christ.

²²Wives, yield to your husbands, as you do to the Lord, ²³because the husband is the head of the wife, as Christ is the head of the church. And he is the Savior of the body, which is the church. ²⁴As the church yields to Christ, so you wives should yield to your husbands in everything.

²⁵Husbands, love your wives as Christ loved the church and gave himself for it ²⁶to make it belong to God. Christ used the word to make the church clean by washing it with water. ²⁷He died so that he could give the church to himself like a bride in all her beauty. He died so that the church could be pure and without fault, with no evil or sin or any other wrong thing in it. ²⁸In the same way, husbands should love their wives as they love their own bodies. The man who loves his wife loves himself. ²⁹No one ever hates his own body, but feeds and takes care of it. And that is what Christ does for the church, ³⁰because we are

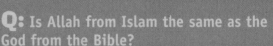

Q: People say that the Bible was written by God, but how can I know it's not just another book?

A: The Bible was written by specially chosen men who were *inspired* by God, which means that God gave them the message to write. Each of the sixty-six books in the Bible has the style of the author, and each has a different story about how it came to be in the Bible. For instance, people recognized that the prophecies written by Isaiah, Jeremiah, and Daniel were from God, because what they predicted came true. The more you look into the history of the Bible, the more convinced you'll be that it is God's message to us (2 Timothy 3:16).

Q: Why are missionaries supposed to go to every part of the world?

A: One of the last things that Jesus said before he returned to heaven was, "Go and make followers of all people in the world" (Matthew 28:19). When

Jesus died, he died for the *whole* world. Missionaries are people who take part in God's plan to bring the Good News to every group of people on earth. Not every Christian has to move to another country, but we do all need to share about Jesus where we live. You can start with your neighborhood!

Q: Is Allah from Islam the same as the God from the Bible?

A: No. Muslims will tell you that Allah does not have a son, that he has never become a man, and that when you die you will be judged completely on the things you've done. That's certainly not the God that the Bible tells us about!

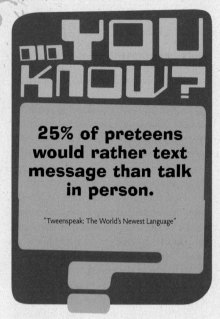

parts of his body. [31] The Scripture says, "So a man will leave his father and mother and be united with his wife, and the two will become one body."[n] [32] That secret is very important—I am talking about Christ and the church. [33] But each one of you must love his wife as he loves himself, and a wife must respect her husband.

CHILDREN AND PARENTS

6 Children, obey your parents as the Lord wants, because this is the right thing to do. [2] The command says, "Honor your father and mother."[n] This is the first command that has a promise with it— [3] "Then everything will be well with you, and you will have a long life on the earth."[n]

[4] Fathers, do not make your children angry, but raise them with the training and teaching of the Lord.

SLAVES AND MASTERS

[5] Slaves, obey your masters here on earth with fear and respect and from a sincere heart, just as you obey Christ. [6] You must do this not only while they are watching you, to please them. With all your heart you must do what God wants as people who are obeying Christ. [7] Do your work with enthusiasm. Work as if you were serving the Lord, not as if you were serving only men and women. [8] Remember that the Lord will give a reward to everyone, slave or free, for doing good.

[9] Masters, in the same way, be good to your slaves. Do not threaten them. Remember that

the One who is your Master and their Master is in heaven, and he treats everyone alike.

WEAR THE FULL ARMOR OF GOD

[10] Finally, be strong in the Lord and in his great power. [11] Put on the full armor of God so that you can fight against the devil's evil tricks. [12] Our fight is not against people on earth but against the rulers and authorities and the powers of this world's darkness, against the spiritual powers of evil in the heavenly world. [13] That is why you need to put on God's full armor. Then on the day of evil you will be able to stand strong. And when you have finished the whole fight, you will still be standing. [14] So stand strong, with the belt of truth tied around your waist and the protection of right living on your chest. [15] On your feet wear the Good News of peace to help you stand strong. [16] And also use the shield of faith with which you can stop all the burning arrows of the Evil One. [17] Accept God's salvation as your helmet, and take the sword of the Spirit, which is the word of God. [18] Pray in the Spirit at all times with all kinds of prayers, asking for everything you need. To do this you must always be

ready and never give up. Always pray for all God's people.

[19] Also pray for me that when I speak, God will give me words so that I can tell the secret of the Good News without fear. [20] I have been sent to preach this Good News, and I am doing that now, here in prison. Pray that when I preach the Good News I will speak without fear, as I should.

FINAL GREETINGS

[21] I am sending to you Tychicus, our brother whom we love and a faithful servant of the Lord's work. He will tell you everything that is happening with me. Then you will know how I am and what I am doing. [22] I am sending him to you for this reason—so that you will know how we are, and he can encourage you.

[23] Peace and love with faith to you brothers and sisters from God the Father and the Lord Jesus Christ. [24] Grace to all of you who love our Lord Jesus Christ with love that never ends.

ROCK SOLID

Ephesians 6:10–17

Today there are boys in uniform just a few years older than you who spend every hour risking their lives to protect our freedoms. They wear body armor to guard against explosives. They wear helmets to protect them from bullets. They drive around in armor-plated Humvees taking enemy fire. They are very familiar with the absolute necessity of these tools to protect them physically.

But this high-tech gear won't protect us spiritually and there's a spiritual war going on right now! Satan is on the attack and he's got armies to spare. That's why we need something the Bible calls "the armor of God." We need to begin each day getting suited up and ready for battle! That means prayer. That means time in God's Word. That means seeking to follow God's guidance.

Ephesians 6:10–17 lists the different pieces of armor. If we put on this armor of God, the Bible makes us this promise: "Then on the day of evil you will be able to stand strong. And when you have finished the whole fight, you will still be standing" (Ephesians 6:13). It's a war out there! Don't go out unprotected.

5:31 "So . . . body." Quotation from Genesis 2:24.   **6:2** "Honor . . . mother." Quotation from Exodus 20:12; Deuteronomy 5:16.   **6:3** "Then . . . earth." Quotation from Exodus 20:12; Deuteronomy 5:16.

Philippians is a joy-filled letter Paul wrote from prison to the church in the city of Philippi.

You might think the great apostle would be discouraged about being in jail. But his heart was filled with praise, and it spilled out in this letter.

The church at Philippi was the first European church Paul started (Acts 16). When they heard he was in prison, they sent him some money and a man named Epaphroditus to help him. This is Paul's "thank you" note.

In chapter 1, Paul gives thanks for the Philippians and tells them how the Good News is spreading around the world.

PHILIPPIANS

In chapter 2, he encourages them to be humble and loving, like Jesus Christ. He also holds up his fellow workers Timothy and Epaphroditus as role models.

In chapter 3, Paul warns about false teachers and looks ahead to the hope of heaven.

The letter ends (chapter 4) with the command to "be full of joy in the Lord always" and the promise that "God's peace, which is so great we cannot understand it, will keep your hearts and minds in Christ Jesus" (4:4, 7).

Pay special attention to the things Paul says to think about in 4:8. Memorize this verse, and use it to decide what kind of video games to play, or music to listen to, or movies to watch. Forget the Hollywood rating system—use this one instead!

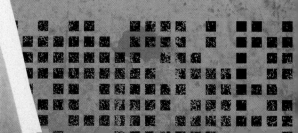

1 From Paul and Timothy, servants of Christ Jesus.

To all of God's holy people in Christ Jesus who live in Philippi, including your overseers and deacons:

[2]Grace and peace to you from God our Father and the Lord Jesus Christ.

PAUL'S PRAYER

[3]I thank my God every time I remember you, [4]always praying with joy for all of you. [5]I thank God for the help you gave me while I preached the Good News—help you gave from the first day you believed until now. [6]God began doing a good work in you, and I am sure he will continue it until it is finished when Jesus Christ comes again.

[7]And I know that I am right to think like this about all of you, because I have you in my heart. All of you share in God's grace with me while I am in prison and while I am defending and proving the truth of the Good News. [8]God knows that I want to see you very much, because I love all of you with the love of Christ Jesus.

[9]This is my prayer for you: that your love will grow more and more; that you will have knowledge and understanding with your love; [10]that you will see the difference between good and bad and will choose the good; that

Did YOU KNOW?

Bike riding is the favorite free-time activity for 12% of boys.

ytvmedia.com . Tween Report.

you will be pure and without wrong for the coming of Christ; [11]that you will be filled with the good things produced in your life by Christ to bring glory and praise to God.

PAUL'S TROUBLES HELP THE WORK

[12]I want you brothers and sisters to know that what has happened to me has helped to spread the Good News. [13]All the palace guards and everyone else knows that I am in prison because I am a believer in Christ. [14]Because I am in prison, most of the believers have become more bold in Christ and are not afraid to speak the word of God.

[15]It is true that some preach about Christ because they are jealous and ambitious, but others preach about Christ because they want to help. [16]They preach because they have love, and they know that God gave me the work of defending the Good News. [17]But the others preach about Christ for selfish and wrong reasons, wanting to make trouble for me in prison.

[18]But it doesn't matter. The important thing is that in every way, whether for right or wrong reasons, they are preaching about Christ. So I am happy, and I will continue to be happy. [19]Because you are praying for me and the Spirit of Jesus Christ is helping me, I know this trouble will bring my freedom. [20]I expect and hope that I will not fail Christ in anything but that I will have the courage now, as always, to show the greatness of Christ in my life here on earth, whether I live or die. [21]To me the only important thing about living is Christ, and dying would be profit for me. [22]If I continue living in my body, I will be able to work for the Lord. I do not know what to choose—living or dying. [23]It is hard to choose between the two.

trustables

Philippians 3:21

Okay, so you're not Mr. Universe with muscles bulging out all over your body. So what? Does it really matter what you look like, anyway? Besides, have you ever seen those big bodybuilding guys walk? It's just not natural. It's true that many people have something about their bodies that they wish they could change.

In fact, you've probably seen some kind of extreme makeover show where a person will go through a cosmetic surgery and eat according to a radical diet, and put their bodies through harsh workouts. The people on these shows are desperate to make a change no matter what the cost.

According to the Bible, Jesus is coming back, and when he does, he's going to make some changes to our bodies. Philippians 3:21 says, "By his power to rule all things, he will change our humble bodies and make them like his own glorious body." Yes! Okay, so maybe you don't like something about your physique. Do your best to take care of yourself. Make your mom happy and eat your vegetables. Get outside and kick the soccer ball around a little, toss the pigskin, shoot a few hoops, launch a model rocket and chase it down. But don't stress out about it, because when Jesus comes back it's all going to change.

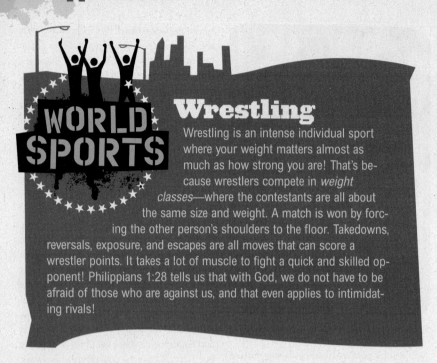

Wrestling

Wrestling is an intense individual sport where your weight matters almost as much as how strong you are! That's because wrestlers compete in *weight classes*—where the contestants are all about the same size and weight. A match is won by forcing the other person's shoulders to the floor. Takedowns, reversals, exposure, and escapes are all moves that can score a wrestler points. It takes a lot of muscle to fight a quick and skilled opponent! Philippians 1:28 tells us that with God, we do not have to be afraid of those who are against us, and that even applies to intimidating rivals!

I want to leave this life and be with Christ, which is much better, ²⁴but you need me here in my body. ²⁵Since I am sure of this, I know I will stay with you to help you grow and have joy in your faith. ²⁶You will be very happy in Christ Jesus when I am with you again.

²⁷Only one thing concerns me: Be sure that you live in a way that brings honor to the Good News of Christ. Then whether I come and visit you or am away from you, I will hear that you are standing strong with one purpose, that you work together as one for the faith of the Good News, ²⁸and that you are not afraid of those who are against you. All of this is proof that your enemies will be destroyed but that you will be saved by God. ²⁹God gave you the honor not only of believing in Christ but also of suffering for him, both of which bring glory to Christ. ³⁰When I was with you, you saw the struggles I had, and you hear about the struggles I am having now. You yourselves are having the same kind of struggles.

2 Does your life in Christ give you strength? Does his love comfort you? Do we share together in the spirit? Do you have mercy and kindness? ²If so, make me very happy by having the same thoughts, sharing the same love, and having one mind and purpose. ³When you do things, do not let selfishness or pride be your guide. Instead, be humble and give more honor to others than to yourselves. ⁴Do not be interested only in your own life, but be interested in the lives of others.

BE UNSELFISH LIKE CHRIST

⁵In your lives you must think and act like Christ Jesus.
⁶Christ himself was like God in everything.
But he did not think that being equal
with God was something to be
used for his own benefit.
⁷But he gave up his place with God and
made himself nothing.
He was born as a man
and became like a servant.
⁸And when he was living as a man,
he humbled himself and was fully
obedient to God,
even when that caused his death—
death on a cross.
⁹So God raised him to the highest place.
God made his name greater than every
other name
¹⁰so that every knee will bow to the name of
Jesus—
everyone in heaven, on earth, and under
the earth.

COOL!

Different Dragons

There are different kinds of dragons in mythology. *Eastern* dragons are kind, wise, and friendly. They eat sparrows, not humans.

Western dragons are fire-breathing serpents with wings. They hoard treasure in caves and are always hungry for human flesh.

But the fiercest dragon of all is no myth. Revelation 12:7–9 says:

"Michael and his angels fought against the dragon, and the dragon and his angels fought back....The giant dragon was thrown down out of heaven. (He is that old snake called the devil or Satan)" (Revelation 12:7–9).

Good thing for us that God and his forces are stronger than the devil and his!

¹¹And everyone will confess that Jesus Christ is Lord
and bring glory to God the Father.

BE THE PEOPLE GOD WANTS YOU TO BE

¹²My dear friends, you have always obeyed God when I was with you. It is even more important that you obey now while I am away from you. Keep on working to complete your salvation with fear and trembling, ¹³because God is working in you to help you want to do and be able to do what pleases him.

¹⁴Do everything without complaining or arguing. ¹⁵Then you will be innocent and without any wrong. You will be God's children without fault. But you are living with crooked and mean people all around you, among whom you shine like stars in the dark world. ¹⁶You offer the teaching that gives life. So when Christ comes again, I can be happy because my work was not wasted. I ran the race and won.

¹⁷Your faith makes you offer your lives as a sacrifice in serving God. If I have to offer my own blood with your sacrifice, I will be happy and full of joy with all of you. ¹⁸You also should be happy and full of joy with me.

TIMOTHY AND EPAPHRODITUS

¹⁹I hope in the Lord Jesus to send Timothy to you soon. I will be happy to learn how you are. ²⁰I have no one else like Timothy, who truly cares for you. ²¹Other people are interested only in their own lives, not in the work of Jesus Christ. ²²You know the kind of person Timothy is. You know he has served with me in telling the Good News, as a son serves his father. ²³I plan to send him to you quickly when I know what will happen to me. ²⁴I am sure that the Lord will help me to come to you soon.

²⁵Epaphroditus, my brother in Christ, works and serves with me in the army of Christ. When I needed help, you sent him to me. I think now that I must send him back to you, ²⁶because he wants very much to see all of you. He is worried because you heard that he was sick. ²⁷Yes, he was sick, and nearly died, but God had mercy on him and me too so that I would not have more sadness. ²⁸I want very much to send him to you so that when you see him you can be happy, and I can stop worrying about you. ²⁹Welcome him in the Lord with much joy. Give honor to people like him, ³⁰because he almost died for the work of Christ. He risked his life to give me the help you could not give in your service to me.

THE IMPORTANCE OF CHRIST

3 My brothers and sisters, be full of joy in the Lord. It is no trouble for me to write the same things to you again, and it will help you to be more ready. ²Watch out for those who do evil, who are like dogs, who demand to cut" the body. ³We are the ones who are truly circumcised. We worship God through his Spirit, and our pride is in Christ Jesus. We do not put trust in ourselves or anything we can do, ⁴although I might be able to put trust in myself. If anyone thinks he has a reason to trust in himself, he should know that I have greater reason for trusting in myself. ⁵I was circumcised eight days after my birth. I am from the people of Israel and the tribe of Benjamin. I am a Hebrew, and my parents were Hebrews. I had a strict view of the law, which is why I became a Pharisee. ⁶I was so enthusiastic I tried to hurt the church. No one could find fault with the way I obeyed the law of Moses. ⁷Those things were important to me, but now I think they are worth nothing because of Christ. ⁸Not only those things, but I think that all things are worth nothing compared with the greatness of knowing Christ Jesus my Lord. Because of him,

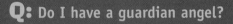

Q: I've heard people talk about being friends with God. If you can't see or hear him, how does that work?

A: If you believe in Jesus, you will one day see him face-to-face. Until then, he has promised to be with you all the time—and he is! As you talk with him every day, you can feel his responses in your heart and read them in the Bible. As your friendship with Jesus grows, you will realize that God is right by your side! This means you are friends!

Q: Do I have a guardian angel?

A: The Bible says that God sends angels to protect his children (Hebrews 1:14), but it doesn't say if each person gets a particular angel who follows him around like a bodyguard. Angels are powerful servants of God who work behind the scenes. When they appeared to people in Bible times, they looked like regular men, not like rock stars with giant wings.

Q: Is there life on other planets?

A: The Bible doesn't tell us. God has given us a curiosity that has caused explorers to sail the oceans, land on the moon, and now try to figure out how to get to other planets. He has left *us* to discover if life is on other planets. However, when you study the way God created the earth and his special relationship with humans, it's hard to imagine there's life somewhere else in the universe. That's a question to ask him when you get to heaven!

3:2 cut The word in Greek is like the word "circumcise," but it means "to cut completely off."

I have lost all those things, and now I know they are worthless trash. This allows me to have Christ ⁹and to belong to him. Now I am right with God, not because I followed the law, but because I believed in Christ. God uses my faith to make me right with him. ¹⁰I want to know Christ and the power that raised him from the dead. I want to share in his sufferings and become like him in his death. ¹¹Then I have hope that I myself will be raised from the dead.

CONTINUING TOWARD OUR GOAL

¹²I do not mean that I am already as God wants me to be. I have not yet reached that goal, but I continue trying to reach it and to make it mine. Christ wants me to do that, which is the reason he made me his. ¹³Brothers and sisters, I know that I have not yet reached that goal, but there is one thing I always do. Forgetting the past and straining toward what is ahead, ¹⁴I keep trying to reach the goal and

get the prize for which God called me through Christ to the life above.

¹⁵All of us who are spiritually mature should think this way, too. And if there are things you do not agree with, God will make them clear to you. ¹⁶But we should continue following the truth we already have.

¹⁷Brothers and sisters, all of you should try to follow my example and to copy those who live the way we showed you. ¹⁸Many people live like enemies of the cross of Christ. I have often told you about them, and it makes me cry to tell you about them now. ¹⁹In the end, they will be destroyed. They do whatever their bodies want, they are proud of their shameful acts, and they think only about earthly things. ²⁰But our homeland is in heaven, and we are waiting for our Savior, the Lord Jesus Christ, to come from heaven. ²¹By his power to rule all things, he will change our humble bodies and make them like his own glorious body.

WHAT THE CHRISTIANS ARE TO DO

4 My dear brothers and sisters, I love you and want to

ROCK SOLID

Philippians 4:13

You're standing by your locker at school when that really annoying kid walks by. Since you just failed your English test, you're already feeling bad enough. Then this kid calls you stupid. How do you keep from thrashing him, from folding him up and stuffing him into his own locker?

From a human standpoint, doing the right thing seems impossible. But it's at moments like that when you are most able to shine for Jesus Christ. When everything's cool, it's not hard to be a nice guy; but when it's impossible to do the right thing, and somehow you're able to do it anyway, that's when people see Jesus in you.

Jesus taught us to do all kinds of impossible things, like loving our enemies and doing good things for people who do bad things against us. What was he thinking? Why did he put us out on a limb?

Philippians 4:13 says, "I can do all things through Christ, because he gives me strength." When Jesus asks us to do impossible things, he gives us supernatural power to do it. Do you want people to know you have God living in you? It's simple—just do things that aren't possible.

see you. You bring me joy and make me proud of you, so stand strong in the Lord as I have told you.

²I ask Euodia and Syntyche to agree in the Lord. ³And I ask you, my faithful friend, to help these women. They served with me in telling the Good News, together with Clement and others who worked with me, whose names are written in the book of life."

⁴Be full of joy in the Lord always. I will say again, be full of joy.

⁵Let everyone see that you are gentle and kind. The Lord is coming soon. ⁶Do not worry about anything, but pray and ask God for everything you need, always giving thanks. ⁷And God's peace, which is so great we cannot understand it, will keep your hearts and minds in Christ Jesus.

⁸Brothers and sisters, think about the things that are good and worthy of praise. Think about the things that are true and honorable and right and pure and beautiful and respected. ⁹Do what you learned and received from me, what I told you, and what you saw me do. And the God who gives peace will be with you.

PAUL THANKS THE CHRISTIANS

¹⁰I am very happy in the Lord that you have shown your care for me again. You continued to care about me, but there was no way for you to show it. ¹¹I am not telling you this because I need anything. I have learned to be satisfied with the things I have and with everything that happens. ¹²I know how to live when I am poor, and I know how to live when

⭐ **4:3 book of life** God's book that has the names of all God's chosen people (Revelation 3:5; 21:27).

I have plenty. I have learned the secret of being happy at any time in everything that happens, when I have enough to eat and when I go hungry, when I have more than I need and when I do not have enough. [13] I can do all things through Christ, because he gives me strength.

[14] But it was good that you helped me when I needed it. [15] You Philippians remember when I first preached the Good News there. When I left Macedonia, you were the only church that gave me help. [16] Several times you sent me things I needed when I was in Thessalonica. [17] Really, it is not that I want to receive gifts from you, but I want you to have the good that comes from giving. [18] And now I have everything, and more. I have all I need, because Epaphroditus brought your gift to me. It is like a sweet-smelling sacrifice offered to God, who accepts that sacrifice and is pleased with it. [19] My God will use his wonderful riches in Christ Jesus to give you everything you need. [20] Glory to our God and Father forever and ever! Amen.

[21] Greet each of God's people in Christ Jesus. Those who are with me send greetings to you. [22] All of God's people greet you, particularly those from the palace of Caesar.

[23] The grace of the Lord Jesus Christ be with you all.

This letter was written around the same time as the letter of Ephesians.

That's why they sound alike in spots. It was sent from a Roman jail to the churches in the small town of Colossae.

As in most of his letters, Paul starts out with prayer and thanksgiving (1:1–14). Then he talks about the greatness of Jesus and how "he ranks higher than everything that has been made" (1:15).

Paul has a lot to say about Jesus. Among other things, he is:

- God's Son (1:14)
- Lord of creation (1:15)
- Head of the church (1:18)
- Conqueror of the powers of evil (2:15)

Paul also tells the Colossians how much he's suffered on their behalf (1:24–2:7), to encourage them as they face sufferings of their own.

After warning about false teachers who can cause great harm, Paul spells out the old habits that Christians are to put off and the new habits we are to put on instead (2:8–3:17).

Out with the old: "sexual sinning, doing evil, letting evil thoughts control you, wanting things that are evil, and greed . . . anger, bad temper, doing or saying things to hurt others, and using evil words when you talk" (3:5–8).

In with the new: "mercy, kindness, humility, gentleness, and patience. Bear with each other, and forgive each other. . . . Even more than all this, clothe yourself in love" (3:12–14).

Dressing like a Christian isn't about T-shirts with catchy slogans; it's about wearing the character of Christ.

COLOSSIANS

1 From Paul, an apostle of Christ Jesus. I am an apostle because that is what God wanted. Also from Timothy, our brother.

²To the holy and faithful brothers and sisters in Christ that live in Colossae:

Grace and peace to you from God our Father."

³In our prayers for you we always thank God, the Father of our Lord Jesus Christ, ⁴because we have heard about the faith you have in Christ Jesus and the love you have for all of God's people. ⁵You have this faith and love because of your hope, and what you hope for is kept safe for you in heaven. You learned about this hope when you heard the message about the truth, the Good News ⁶that was told to you. Everywhere in the world that Good News is bringing blessings and is growing. This has

9% of kids have their own Web site.

RAB Instant Background Report for Kids and Tweens Market.

happened with you, too, since you heard the Good News and understood the truth about the grace of God. ⁷You learned about God's grace from Epaphras, whom we love. He works together with us and is a faithful servant of Christ for us." ⁸He also told us about the love you have from the Holy Spirit.

⁹Because of this, since the day we heard about you, we have continued praying for you, asking God that you will know fully what he wants. We pray that you will also have great wisdom and understanding in spiritual things ¹⁰so that you will live the kind of life that honors and pleases the Lord in every way. You will produce fruit in every good work and grow in the knowledge of God. ¹¹God will strengthen you with his own great power so that you will not give up when troubles come, but you will be patient. ¹²And you will joyfully give thanks to the Father

who has made you" able to have a share in all that he has prepared for his people in the kingdom of light. ¹³God has freed us from the power of darkness, and he brought us into the kingdom of his dear Son. ¹⁴The Son paid for our sins," and in him we have forgiveness.

THE IMPORTANCE OF CHRIST

¹⁵No one can see God, but Jesus Christ is exactly like him. He ranks higher than everything that has been made. ¹⁶Through his power all things were made—things in heaven and on earth, things seen and unseen, all powers, authorities, lords, and rulers. All things were made through Christ and for Christ. ¹⁷He was there before anything was made, and all things continue because of him. ¹⁸He is the head of the body, which is the church. Everything comes from him. He is the first one who was raised from the dead. So in all things Jesus has first place. ¹⁹God was pleased for all of himself to live in Christ. ²⁰And through Christ, God has brought all things back to himself again—things on earth and things in heaven. God made peace through the blood of Christ's death on the cross.

²¹At one time you were separated from God. You were his enemies in your minds, and the evil things you did were against God. ²²But now God has made you his friends again. He did this through Christ's death in the body so that he might bring you into God's presence as people who are holy, with no wrong, and with nothing of which God can judge you guilty. ²³This will happen if you continue strong and sure in your faith. You must not be moved away from the hope brought to you by the Good News that you heard. That same Good News has been told to everyone in the world, and I, Paul, help in preaching that Good News.

PAUL'S WORK FOR THE CHURCH

²⁴I am happy in my sufferings for you. There are things that Christ must still suffer through his body, the church. I am accepting, in my body, my part of these things that must be suffered. ²⁵I became a servant of the church because God gave me a special work to do that helps you, and that work is to tell fully the message of God. ²⁶This message is the secret that was hidden from everyone since the beginning of time, but now it is made known to God's holy people. ²⁷God decided to let his people know this rich and glorious secret which he has for all people. This secret is Christ himself, who is in you. He is our only hope for glory. ²⁸So we continue to preach Christ to

ROCK SOLID

Colossians 1:15–17

You may have heard that Jesus was a carpenter, but did you know he also made the universe? Imagine the tool belt he must have worn to do that!

It's a pretty deep concept, but the Bible says that before Jesus became a man, he was a spiritual force who was always there with God the Father. And this "force" was what God used to breathe life into the universe. Eventually this "force" would take the form of a man named Jesus, born as a baby in Bethlehem. Now that's deep!

Need more proof? Check out Colossians 1:16 where it says, "Through his [Jesus'] power all things were made—things in heaven and on earth, things seen and unseen, all powers, authorities, lords, and rulers. All things were made through Christ and for Christ."

It wasn't a big bang. It wasn't millions of years of evolution. It was the power of Jesus Christ! Your teacher may not accept it as a correct answer on a science test, but it's true anyway.

So the next time you hear that Jesus was a carpenter, politely remind that person that he's also the builder of the universe!

each person, using all wisdom to warn and to teach everyone, in order to bring each one into God's presence as a mature person in Christ. [29]To do this, I work and struggle, using Christ's great strength that works so powerfully in me.

2 I want you to know how hard I work for you, those in Laodicea, and others who have never seen me. [2]I want them to be strengthened and joined together with love so that they may be rich in their understanding. This leads to their knowing fully God's secret, that is, Christ himself. [3]In him all the treasures of wisdom and knowledge are safely kept.

[4]I say this so that no one can fool you by arguments that seem good, but are false. [5]Though I am absent from you in my body, my heart is with you, and I am happy to see your good lives and your strong faith in Christ.

CONTINUE TO LIVE IN CHRIST

[6]As you received Christ Jesus the Lord, so continue to live in him. [7]Keep your roots deep in him and have your lives built on him. Be strong in the faith, just as you were taught, and always be thankful.

[8]Be sure that no one leads you away with false and empty teaching that is only human,

DID YOU KNOW?

50% of students worry about getting bad grades in school.

Exploring How to Motivate Behavior Change Among Tweens in America.

which comes from the ruling spirits of this world, and not from Christ. [9]All of God lives fully in Christ (even when Christ was on earth), [10]and you have a full and true life in Christ, who is ruler over all rulers and powers.

[11]Also in Christ you had a different kind of circumcision, a circumcision not done by hands. It was through Christ's circumcision, that is, his death, that you were made free from the power of your sinful self. [12]When you were baptized, you were buried with Christ, and you were raised up with him through your faith in God's power that was shown when he raised Christ from the dead. [13]When you were spiritually dead because of your sins and because you were not free from the power of your sinful self, God made you alive with Christ, and he forgave all our sins. [14]He canceled the debt, which listed all the rules we failed to follow. He took away that record with its rules and nailed it to the cross. [15]God stripped the spiritual rulers and powers of their authority. With the cross, he won the victory and showed the world that they were powerless.

DON'T FOLLOW PEOPLE'S RULES

[16]So do not let anyone make rules for you about eating and drinking or about a religious feast, a New Moon Festival, or a Sabbath day. [17]These things were like a shadow of what was to come. But what is true and real has come and is found in Christ. [18]Do not let anyone disqualify

Q & A

Q: My older sister is dating a guy I really don't like. What should I do?

A: If you don't like him just because he looks goofy or drives a rusty car, you don't need to do anything. But if you don't like him because he seems disrespectful to your sister or she acts mean to you when he's around, you should tell her. Pray for the right words and then talk to her in private. She will probably not like what you say at the time, but if she sees that you really care for her, she'll at least think about it.

Q: Which sport is the toughest?

A: It depends....Rugby is like playing tackle football without pads. The Ironman Triathalon takes superhuman endurance. Even golf can be tough if your cart goes into the lake!

Q: I really want to play football, but I'm small for my age. What can I do?

A: There's really nothing you can do to make yourself bigger. But skill and effort can beat size any day. God has done amazing things with little guys like King David, in the Old Testament, who killed bears, lions, and even a giant when he was still a teenager (1 Samuel 17). Practice playing the position you want and make sure you're in good shape before football practice even starts. If you give it all you've got on every play, your coach will notice.

you by making you humiliate yourself and worship angels. Such people enter into visions, which fill them with foolish pride because of their human way of thinking. [19] They do not hold tightly to Christ, the head. It is from him that all the parts of the body are cared for and held together. So it grows in the way God wants it to grow.

[20] Since you died with Christ and were made free from the ruling spirits of the world, why do you act as if you still belong to this world by following rules like these: [21]"Don't handle this," "Don't taste that," "Don't even touch that thing"? [22] These rules refer to earthly things that are gone as soon as they are used. They are only human commands and teachings. [23] They seem to be wise, but they are only part of a human religion. They make people pretend not to be proud and make them punish their bodies, but they do not really control the evil desires of the sinful self.

YOUR NEW LIFE IN CHRIST

3 Since you were raised from the dead with Christ, aim at what is in heaven, where Christ is sitting at the right hand of God. [2] Think only about the things in heaven, not the things on earth. [3] Your old sinful self has died, and your new life is kept with Christ in God.

TOP 10

Things Worth Collecting

1. **Sports cards**
2. **Action figures**
3. **Mint coins**
4. **Comic books**
5. **Marbles**
6. **Autographs**
7. **Stamps**
8. **Bottle caps**
9. **Train sets**
10. **Fossils**

[4] Christ is your[n] life, and when he comes again, you will share in his glory.

[5] So put all evil things out of your life: sexual sinning, doing evil, letting evil thoughts control you, wanting things that are evil, and greed. This is really serving a false god. [6] These things make God angry.[n] [7] In your past, evil life you also did these things.

[8] But now also put these things out of your life: anger, bad temper, doing or saying things to hurt others, and using evil words when you talk. [9] Do not lie to each other. You have left your old sinful life and the things you did before. [10] You have begun to live the new life, in which you are being made new and are becoming like the One who made you. This new life brings you the true knowledge of God. [11] In the new life there is no difference between Greeks and Jews, those who are circumcised and those who are not circumcised, or people who are foreigners, or Scythians.[n] There is no difference between slaves and free people. But Christ is in all believers, and Christ is all that is important.

[12] God has chosen you and made you his holy people. He loves you. So you should always clothe yourselves with mercy, kindness, humility, gentleness, and patience. [13] Bear with each other, and forgive each other. If someone does wrong to you, forgive that person because the Lord forgave you. [14] Even more than

trustables

Colossians 3:12

Being chosen last when you and your friends are making teams can be a real downer. You feel like the captains thought everyone else they picked before you was better. The only thing worse than being picked last is not being chosen at all.

The good news? God chose you! Colossians 3:12 says, "God has chosen you and made you his holy people. He loves you. So you should always clothe yourselves with mercy, kindness, humility, gentleness, and patience." Not only did God choose you, but he also thinks you're cool. God loves you. He thinks you make a good addition to his team. Cool!

Knowing that God has chosen you should give you a sense of hope, great joy, and responsibility. You're on God's team now, and he has chosen you to be one of his holy people. You don't get dressed in the morning by accident. Sure, you might put a shirt on backward once in a while, but you get dressed on purpose.

It's the same way with wearing "mercy, kindness, humility, gentleness, and patience." These aren't hard things to understand, but they won't be in our lives by accident. Just like getting dressed, we must choose to be kind and humble on purpose.

God believes you can do it, or he wouldn't have chosen *you*.

SMART TIPS!

Defragment Your Hard Drive

Is your computer running a little slow? Are things just not working like they should? If you defragment your hard drive, you'll better organize your system and help it run much smoother. Likewise, if we organize our priorities in life and put God at the front, everything else runs smoothly, too!

all this, clothe yourself in love. Love is what holds you all together in perfect unity. ¹⁵Let the peace that Christ gives control your thinking, because you were all called together in one body" to have peace. Always be thankful.

¹⁶Let the teaching of Christ live in you richly. Use all wisdom to teach and instruct each other by singing psalms, hymns, and spiritual songs with thankfulness in your hearts to God. ¹⁷Everything you do or say should be done to obey Jesus your Lord. And in all you do, give thanks to God the Father through Jesus.

YOUR NEW LIFE WITH OTHER PEOPLE

¹⁸Wives, yield to the authority of your husbands, because this is the right thing to do in the Lord.

¹⁹Husbands, love your wives and be gentle with them.

²⁰Children, obey your parents in all things, because this pleases the Lord.

²¹Fathers, do not nag your children. If you are too hard to please, they may want to stop trying.

²²Slaves, obey your masters in all things. Do not obey just when they are watching you, to gain their favor, but serve them honestly, because you respect the Lord. ²³In all the work you are doing, work the best you can. Work as if you were doing it for the Lord, not for people. ²⁴Remember that you will receive your reward from the Lord, which he promised to his people. You are serving the Lord Christ. ²⁵But remember that anyone who does wrong will be punished for that wrong, and the Lord treats everyone the same.

4 Masters, give what is good and fair to your slaves. Remember that you have a Master in heaven.

KNOW THE WORD!

CHURCH

The *church* can refer to the whole group of Christians, living and dead—that's billions of people! The *church* can also be the smaller group you meet with to learn about God every Sunday. The people in these smaller groups live near each other, typically speak the same language, and love to worship God in similar ways. Every Christian is part of the larger church...but should also be involved in a small church group. Churches are part of God's plan. Through spending time with other Christians, remembering what Jesus has done for us, learning about the Bible, and worshiping God, we honor him!

WHAT THE CHRISTIANS ARE TO DO

²Continue praying, keeping alert, and always thanking God. ³Also pray for us that God will give us an opportunity to tell people his message. Pray that we can preach the secret that God has made known about Christ. This is why I am in prison. ⁴Pray that I can speak in a way that will make it clear, as I should.

⁵Be wise in the way you act with people who are not believers, making the most of every opportunity. ⁶When you talk, you should always be kind and pleasant so you will be able to answer everyone in the way you should.

NEWS ABOUT THE PEOPLE WITH PAUL

⁷Tychicus is my dear brother in Christ and a faithful minister and servant with me in the Lord. He will tell you all the things that are happening to me. ⁸This is why I am sending him: so you may know how we are" and he may encourage you. ⁹I send him with Onesimus, a faithful and dear brother in Christ, and one of your group. They will tell you all that has happened here.

dare to do

Ephesians 4:2
Read It: Be humble, gentle, and patient.
Do It: Don't "trash talk" when you play sports. Try to be a positive influence by cheering people on.

Ephesians 4:25
Read It: Don't lie; instead, work extra hard to tell the truth.
Do It: Cheating in school is just like telling a lie. Make sure you are doing all your own schoolwork.

Ephesians 4:27
Read It: Don't give the devil the chance to defeat you.
Do It: What area of your life causes you the most problems? Satan is using that area to trip you up. Pray and ask God for protection.

3:15 body The spiritual body of Christ, meaning the church or his people.   **4:8 so . . . are** Some Greek copies read "so he may know how you are."

[10]Aristarchus, a prisoner with me, and Mark, the cousin of Barnabas, greet you. (I have already told you what to do about Mark. If he comes, welcome him.) [11]Jesus, who is called Justus, also greets you. These are the only Jewish believers who work with me for the kingdom of God, and they have been a comfort to me.

[12]Epaphras, a servant of Jesus Christ, from your group, also greets you. He always prays for you that you will grow to be spiritually mature and have everything God wants for you. [13]I know he has worked hard for you and the people in Laodicea and in Hierapolis. [14]Demas and our dear friend Luke, the doctor, greet you.

[15]Greet the brothers and sisters in Laodicea. And greet Nympha and the church that meets in her house. [16]After this letter is read to you, be sure it is also read to the church in Laodicea. And you read the letter that I wrote to Laodicea. [17]Tell Archippus, "Be sure to finish the work the Lord gave you."

[18]I, Paul, greet you and write this with my own hand. Remember me in prison. Grace be with you.

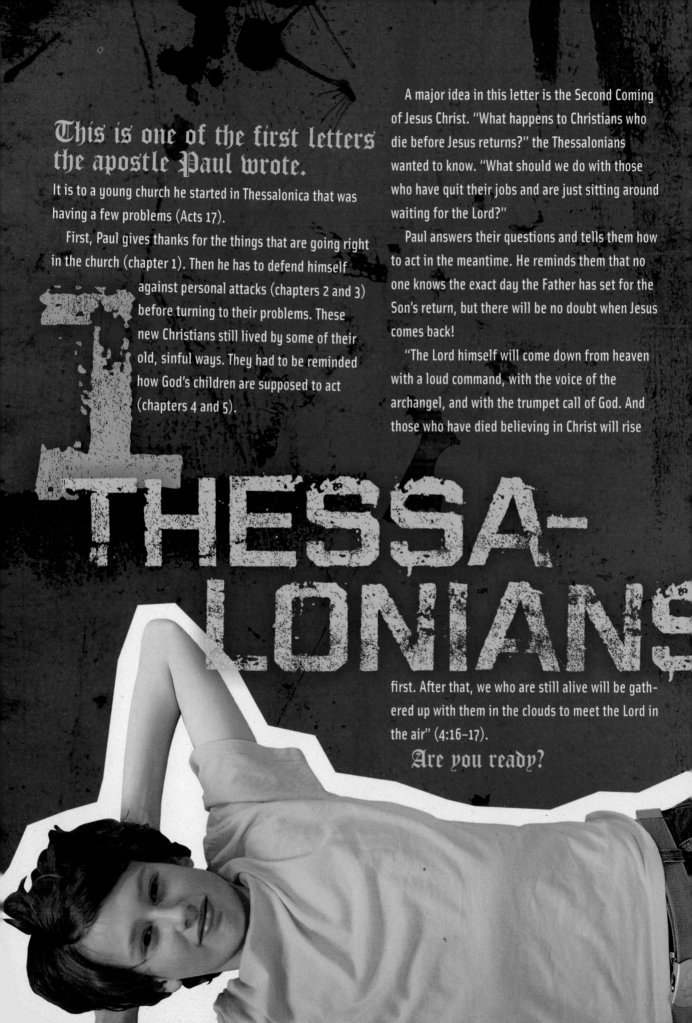

This is one of the first letters the apostle Paul wrote.

It is to a young church he started in Thessalonica that was having a few problems (Acts 17).

First, Paul gives thanks for the things that are going right in the church (chapter 1). Then he has to defend himself against personal attacks (chapters 2 and 3) before turning to their problems. These new Christians still lived by some of their old, sinful ways. They had to be reminded how God's children are supposed to act (chapters 4 and 5).

A major idea in this letter is the Second Coming of Jesus Christ. "What happens to Christians who die before Jesus returns?" the Thessalonians wanted to know. "What should we do with those who have quit their jobs and are just sitting around waiting for the Lord?"

Paul answers their questions and tells them how to act in the meantime. He reminds them that no one knows the exact day the Father has set for the Son's return, but there will be no doubt when Jesus comes back!

"The Lord himself will come down from heaven with a loud command, with the voice of the archangel, and with the trumpet call of God. And those who have died believing in Christ will rise first. After that, we who are still alive will be gathered up with them in the clouds to meet the Lord in the air" (4:16-17).

Are you ready?

1 THESSA-LONIANS

1 From Paul, Silas, and Timothy.

To the church in Thessalonica, the church in God the Father and the Lord Jesus Christ:

Grace and peace to you.

THE FAITH OF THE THESSALONIANS

[2]We always thank God for all of you and mention you when we pray. [3]We continually recall before God our Father the things you have done because of your faith and the work you have done because of your love. And we thank him that you continue to be strong because of your hope in our Lord Jesus Christ.

[4]Brothers and sisters, God loves you, and we know he has chosen you, [5]because the Good News we brought to you came not only with words, but with power, with the Holy Spirit, and with sure knowledge that it is true. Also you know how we lived when we were with you in order to help you. [6]And you became like us and like the Lord. You suffered much, but still you accepted the teaching with the joy that comes from the Holy Spirit. [7]So you became an example to all the believers in Macedonia and Southern Greece. [8]And the Lord's teaching spread from you not only into

39% of boys collect rocks.

KidScreen Magazine. "KidThink: What Today's Kids are Thinking: Most kids are avid collectors."

Macedonia and Southern Greece, but now your faith in God has become known everywhere. So we do not need to say anything about it. [9]People everywhere are telling about the way you accepted us when we were there with you. They tell how you stopped worshiping idols and began serving the living and true

God. [10]And you wait for God's Son, whom God raised from the dead, to come from heaven. He is Jesus, who saves us from God's angry judgment that is sure to come.

PAUL'S WORK IN THESSALONICA

2 Brothers and sisters, you know our visit to you was not a failure. [2]Before we came to you, we suffered in Philippi. People there insulted us, as you know, and many people were against us. But our God helped us to be brave and to tell you his Good News. [3]Our appeal does not come from lies or wrong reasons, nor were we trying to trick you. [4]But we speak the Good News because God tested us and trusted us to do it. When we speak, we are not trying to please people, but God, who tests our hearts. [5]You know that we never tried to influence you by saying nice things about you. We were not trying to get your money; we had no selfishness to hide from you. God knows that this is true. [6]We were not looking for human praise, from you or anyone else, [7]even though as apostles of Christ we could have used our authority over you.

Q: Why is my brother so good at basketball and I can't hit the backboard to save my life?

A: God made each of us for a different purpose. If God didn't make you to be a basketball star, then he has something even better in mind. The Bible says that everything we're given and everything that happens to us is for our good (Romans 8:28).

Q: My grandma says that "gluttony" is a sin. What on earth is she talking about?

A: "Gluttony" means "eating too much." God does not want us to be addicted to anything, including food. With so much super-sized fast food around, it's funny that Christians don't talk about this sin very much. Especially since the Bible warns us to not make our physical appetites a replacement for God (Philippians 3:19). You might ask your grandma for some advice to avoid being a glutton!

Q: I really like a girl in my class. Is it okay to have a girlfriend?

A: It's okay to be special friends with a girl. But having a girlfriend can be really complicated. She might expect you to spend all your time with her or spend a lot of money buying stuff for her. Remember, God wants you to treat girls your age like they are your sisters (1 Timothy 5:2).

Have you ever tried to whistle with your mouth full of peanut butter and crackers? Sometimes you can feel the same way when a friend asks a hard question about God. It's embarrassing! But it doesn't have to be.

Eddie and Caleb, two football players, were putting their helmets away after practice when Andrew asked how all the animals fit into the ark, a big survival boat God had a man named Noah build before a world flood. Although they were a bit embarrassed, they told him the truth—they didn't really know how, they just believed it happened. Two weeks later, Andrew came to youth group with them. He didn't ask Jesus into his heart that night, but at least he came—he came because Eddie and Caleb impressed him with their honesty. (Andrew did become a Christian, later, in high school.)

God doesn't expect you to know all the answers—and none of your friends do. They might ask questions to stump you or to make you feel stupid, but they're listening more to your faith than to your answers. Be honest about what you don't know and God will use what you do know—how real he is in your life—to make a difference.

But we were very gentle with you," like a mother caring for her little children. [8]Because we loved you, we were happy to share not only God's Good News with you, but even our own lives. You had become so dear to us! [9]Brothers and sisters, I know you remember our hard work and difficulties. We worked night and day so we would not burden any of you while we preached God's Good News to you.

[10]When we were with you, we lived in a holy and honest way, without fault. You know this is true, and so does God. [11]You know that we treated each of you as a father treats his own children. [12]We encouraged you, we urged you, and we insisted that you live good lives for God, who calls you to his glorious kingdom.

[13]Also, we always thank God because when you heard his message from us, you accepted it as the word of God, not the words of humans. And it really is God's message which works in you who believe. [14]Brothers and sisters, your experiences have been like those of God's churches in Christ that are in Judea." You suffered from the people of your own country, as they suffered from the Jews [15]who killed both the Lord Jesus and the prophets and forced us to leave that country. They do not please God and are against all people. [16]They try to stop us from teaching those who are not Jews so they may be saved. By doing this, they are increasing their sins to the limit. The anger of God has come to them at last.

PAUL WANTS TO VISIT THEM AGAIN

[17]Brothers and sisters, though we were separated from you for a short time, our thoughts were still with you. We wanted very much to see you and tried hard to do so. [18]We wanted to come to you. I, Paul, tried to come more than once, but Satan stopped us. [19]You are our hope, our joy, and the crown we will take pride in when our Lord Jesus Christ comes. [20]Truly you are our glory and our joy.

3 When we could not wait any longer, we decided it was best to stay in Athens alone [2]and send Timothy to you. Timothy, our brother, works with us for God and helps us tell people the Good News about Christ. We sent him to strengthen and encourage you in your faith [3]so none of you would be upset by these troubles. You yourselves know that we must face these troubles. [4]Even when we were with you, we told you we all would have to suffer, and you know it has happened. [5]Because of this, when I could wait no longer, I sent Timo-

thy to you so I could learn about your faith. I was afraid the devil had tempted you, and perhaps our hard work would have been wasted.

[6]But Timothy now has come back to us from you and has brought us good news about your faith and love. He told us that you always remember us in a good way and that you want to see us just as much as we want to see you. [7]So, brothers and sisters, while we have much trouble and suffering, we are encouraged about you because of your faith. [8]Our life is really full if you stand strong in the Lord. [9]We have so much joy before our God because of

Ephesians 5:4
Read It: Your joking should be completely clean.
Do It: Don't laugh if your friends are telling dirty jokes. Change the subject or leave. If they are Christians, gently remind them what the Bible says.

Ephesians 5:6
Read It: People can talk a whole lot without ever saying anything.
Do It: Hang out with people whose talk has meaning and eternal value.

Ephesians 5:16
Read It: Do acts of kindness often; there's already enough evil in the world.
Do It: Keep your eyes open today for something good to do that you normally wouldn't.

August

Pray for a person of influence: it's hip-hop artist Coolio's birthday. **1**

With one month of summer left, what's still on your to-do list? **2**

Host a watermelon seed-spitting contest. **3**

This is *"Simplify Your Life Week."* Take it easy! **5**

Turn down the heat! Enjoy a pool or water park. **6**

Today is *"Sneak Some Zucchini onto Your Neighbor's Porch Night."* Have fun! **8**

Pray for peace. **9**

Ask your dad for help building a campfire. It's *"S'mores Day."* **10**

Read Romans 12:2. Ask God to help you resist giving in to peer pressure this school year. **11** **12**

13

How much can you buy with $5? Grab your spare change and head to a local thrift store. **14**

Go school shopping in honor of *"No. 2 Pencil Day."* **16**

18

It's *"Potato Day."* Eat as many types of potatoes as possible. **20**

Go for a hike with your siblings. **21**

Pull out your Super Soakers and challenge your buddies to an End of Summer Duel. **22**

23

Pray for a person of influence: it's comedian Dave Chappelle's birthday today. **25**

Be thankful for this invention—it's *"Toilet Paper Day"!* **26**

27

Pray for a person of influence: tennis player Andy Roddick serves up birthday cake today. **30**

OLD TESTAMENT

The *Old Testament* is the first part of a full-length Bible (this BibleZine is just the New Testament). The Old Testament has thirty-nine books, which contain everything from genealogies to miracles. The first book of the Old Testament (and the Bible) is Genesis, which tells the story of God creating the heavens and earth, how sin came into the world, and how God began his plan to make things right again. The Old Testament also has books of prophecy, history, and poetry (like the Psalms).

The Old Testament was written thousands of years ago and records the story of God's love for the Jewish nation. It also gives us a sneak peek at what's to come: a Savior (Jesus)! Though Christians now have the New Testament, the Old Testament is still God's Word and has important things to teach us.

you. We cannot thank him enough for all the joy we feel. [10]Night and day we continue praying with all our heart that we can see you again and give you all the things you need to make your faith strong.

[11]Now may our God and Father himself and our Lord Jesus prepare the way for us to come to you. [12]May the Lord make your love grow more and multiply for each other and for all people so that you will love others as we love you. [13]May your hearts be made strong so that you will be holy and without fault before our God and Father when our Lord Jesus comes with all his holy ones.

A LIFE THAT PLEASES GOD

4 Brothers and sisters, we taught you how to live in a way that will please God, and you are living that way. Now we ask and encourage you in the Lord Jesus to live that way even more. [2]You know what we told you to do by the authority of the Lord Jesus. [3]God wants you to be holy and to stay away from sexual sins. [4]He wants each of you to learn to control your own body" in a way that is holy and honorable. [5]Don't use your body for sexual sin like the people who do not know God. [6]Also, do not wrong or cheat another Christian in this way. The Lord will punish people who do those things as we have already told you and warned you. [7]God called us to be holy and does not want us to live in sin. [8]So the person who refuses to obey this teaching is disobeying God, not simply a human teaching. And God is the One who gives us his Holy Spirit.

[9]We do not need to write you about having love for your Christian family, because God has already taught you to love each other. [10]And truly you do love the Christians in all of Macedonia. Brothers and sisters, now we encourage you to love them even more.

[11]Do all you can to live a peaceful life. Take care of your own business, and do your own work as we have already told you. [12]If you do, then people who are not believers will respect you, and you will not have to depend on others for what you need.

THE LORD'S COMING

[13]Brothers and sisters, we want you to know about those Christians who have died so you will not be sad, as others who have no hope. [14]We believe that Jesus died and that he rose again. So, because of him, God will raise with Jesus those who have died. [15]What we tell you now is the Lord's own message. We

1 Thessalonians 5:23-24

God wants you to be righteous—living a life without sin. That's a lot of pressure! You are surrounded by temptations all the time, and it's impossible to make the right choice all the time, right? So does that mean you are disappointing God?

The Bible has some very interesting things to say about this. It's true that God wants you to be righteous. But he is *also* the one who will *make* you righteous. It's not something he expects you to do alone.

Scripture says, "May God himself...*make* you pure...You can trust the one who calls you to do that *for* you" (1 Thessalonians 5:23–24). So it's not just something God is demanding of you. It's something he wants to do *for* you if you allow him to!

If you feel pressure to be righteous, you're taking the wrong approach and you'll never succeed. You need to let go and look to God to transform your heart and guide your steps. That way he gets the credit and not you!

Becoming the person God wants you to be is a lifelong process. You won't change overnight! But if you continue to surrender to God, he'll finish the work he's started in you.

4:4 learn . . . body This might also mean "learn to live with your own wife."

who are living when the Lord comes again will not go before those who have already died. [16]The Lord himself will come down from heaven with a loud command, with the voice of the archangel,″ and with the trumpet call of God. And those who have died believing in Christ will rise first. [17]After that, we who are still alive will be gathered up with them in the clouds to meet the Lord in the air. And we will be with the Lord forever. [18]So encourage each other with these words.

BE READY FOR THE LORD'S COMING

5 Now, brothers and sisters, we do not need to write you about times and dates. [2]You know very well that the day the Lord comes again will be a surprise, like a thief that comes in the night. [3]While people are saying, "We have peace and we are safe," they will be destroyed quickly. It is like pains that come quickly to a woman having a baby. Those people will not escape. [4]But you, brothers and sisters, are not living in darkness, and so that day will not surprise you like a thief. [5]You are all people who belong to the light and to the day. We do not belong to the night or to darkness. [6]So we should not be like other people who are sleeping, but we should be alert and have self-control. [7]Those who sleep, sleep at night. Those who get drunk, get drunk at night. [8]But we belong to the day, so we should control ourselves. We should wear faith and love to protect us, and the

DID YOU KNOW?

39% of kids like vacations because they can have new adventures.

RAB Instant Background Report for Kids and Tweens Market.

hope of salvation should be our helmet. [9]God did not choose us to suffer his anger but to have salvation through our Lord Jesus Christ. [10]Jesus died for us so that we can live together with him, whether we are alive or dead when he comes. [11]So encourage each other and give each other strength, just as you are doing now.

FINAL INSTRUCTIONS AND GREETINGS

[12]Now, brothers and sisters, we ask you to appreciate those who work hard among you, who lead you in the Lord and teach you. [13]Respect them with a very special love because of the work they do.

Live in peace with each other. [14]We ask you, brothers and sisters, to warn those who do not work. Encourage the people who are afraid. Help those who are weak. Be patient with everyone. [15]Be sure that no one pays back wrong for wrong, but always try to do what is good for each other and for all people.

[16]Always be joyful. [17]Pray continually, [18]and give thanks whatever happens. That is what God wants for you in Christ Jesus.

[19]Do not hold back the work of the Holy Spirit. [20]Do not treat prophecy as if it were unimportant. [21]But test everything. Keep what is good, [22]and stay away from everything that is evil.

[23]Now may God himself, the God of peace, make you pure, belonging only to him. May your whole self—spirit, soul, and body—be kept safe and without fault when our Lord Jesus Christ comes. [24]You can trust the One who calls you to do that for you.

[25]Brothers and sisters, pray for us. [26]Give each other a holy kiss when you meet. [27]I tell you by the authority of the Lord to read this letter to all the believers.

[28]The grace of our Lord Jesus Christ be with you.

COOL!

Lost at Sea

The Bermuda Triangle is a 1,500,000-square-mile wedge of the southeastern Atlantic Ocean. It is infamous for the many ships, planes, and people who have been lost there.

Some believe these disappearances are caused by supernatural forces. But the U.S. Coast Guard says all the tragic incidents were due to bad weather or human error.

Some things *are* lost at sea due to a supernatural cause. The Bible says that God "will throw away *all our sins* into the deepest part of the sea" (Micah 7:19). And when God throws something away, it will *never* be found!

⭐ **4:16 archangel** The leader among God's angels or messengers.

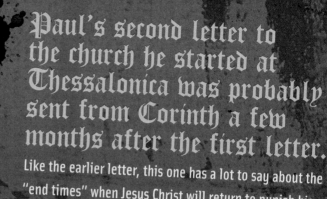

Paul's second letter to the church he started at Thessalonica was probably sent from Corinth a few months after the first letter. Like the earlier letter, this one has a lot to say about the "end times" when Jesus Christ will return to punish his enemies and to rescue his children (chapter 1).

2 THESSALONIANS

The Thessalonians were suffering for following Jesus—and Paul wanted them to understand why. Satan and his forces are active in the world. They constantly fight against Jesus and his church. They can cause a lot of trouble—for now. But Satan's works will be exposed and destroyed when Jesus returns with his army of angels. The ungodly will be judged and the godly will be rewarded for their faithful service (chapter 2).

Paul doesn't want Christians to sit on their hands and wait for Jesus to come back. They are to keep working and taking care of their own needs and the needs of others (chapter 3).

Paul reminds the Thessalonians—and us—that God's great blessings are freely given and totally undeserved. We are only spared from judgment because "God chose you from the beginning to be saved . . . so you can share in the glory of our Lord Jesus Christ" (2:13–14).

Many popular books talk about the end times, but if you really want to know what's going to happen, then read the letters to the Thessalonians.

2 Thessalonians 1:5

Astronauts have one of the most amazing jobs in the world. But it's not an easy ride; astronauts go through a really tough training program.

Being a disciple, or follower, of Jesus Christ is the greatest thing on earth, but it's also one of the hardest. The best things in life do not come easily.

Being a disciple of Christ is way cooler than being an astronaut, so it has an even tougher training program. God wants you "to be counted worthy of his kingdom for which you are suffering," the apostle Paul writes in 2 Thessalonians 1:5. So suffering is part of his training program to sharpen you for the greatest assignment in history.

But because of the greatness of the assignment, we have the hardest of all instructions. Jesus uses hard times to sharpen us and make us even better at what we do. Becoming a Christian didn't mean that your life would be easier; it meant that it would be of much greater value. So the next time something really tough hits your life, remember that you're in training.

1 From Paul, Silas, and Timothy.

To the church in Thessalonica in God our Father and the Lord Jesus Christ:

²Grace and peace to you from God the Father and the Lord Jesus Christ.

PAUL TALKS ABOUT GOD'S JUDGMENT

³We must always thank God for you, brothers and sisters. This is only right, because your faith is growing more and more, and the love that every one of you has for each other is increasing. ⁴So we brag about you to the other churches of God. We tell them about the way you continue to be strong and have faith even though you are being treated badly and are suffering many troubles.

⁵This is proof that God is right in his judgment. He wants you to be counted worthy of his kingdom for which you are suffering. ⁶God will do what is right. He will give trouble to those who trouble you. ⁷And he will give rest to you who are troubled and to us also when the Lord Jesus appears with burning fire from heaven with his powerful angels. ⁸Then he will punish those who do not know God and who do not obey the Good News about our Lord Jesus Christ. ⁹Those people will be punished with a destruction that continues forever. They will be kept away from the Lord and from his great power. ¹⁰This will happen on the day when the Lord Jesus comes to receive glory because of his holy people. And all the people who have believed will be amazed at Jesus. You will be in that group, because you believed what we told you.

¹¹That is why we always pray for you, asking our God to help you live the kind of life he called you to live. We pray that with his power God will help you do the good things you want and perform the works that come from

O Little Town of Bethlehem

Bethlehem is several miles south of Jerusalem in the Holy Land. It was where Ruth and Boaz met. Their grandson, David, became king of Israel. His direct descendant Jesus Christ was also born in Bethlehem (Luke 2).

Jesus' birth in Bethlehem was foretold by the prophet Micah hundreds of years before it happened (5:2). When he was born, angels announced the good news to shepherds in the nearby fields. They were the first to come and worship Jesus.

Thousands still flock to Bethlehem every Christmas to worship Jesus—God's greatest gift to the human race.

your faith. 12We pray all this so that the name
of our Lord Jesus Christ will have glory in you,
and you will have glory in him. That glory
comes from the grace of our God and the Lord
Jesus Christ.

EVIL THINGS WILL HAPPEN

2 Brothers and sisters, we have something
to say about the coming of our Lord
Jesus Christ and the time when we will meet
together with him. 2Do not become easily
upset in your thinking or afraid if you hear that
the day of the Lord has already come. Someone may have said this in a prophecy or in a
message or in a letter as if it came from us. 3Do
not let anyone fool you in any way. That day of
the Lord will not come until the turning away*
from God happens and the Man of Evil,* who
is on his way to hell, appears. 4He will be
against and put himself above any so-called
god or anything that people worship. And that
Man of Evil will even go into God's Temple and
sit there and say that he is God.
5I told you when I was with you that all this
would happen. Do you not remember? 6And
now you know what is stopping that Man of
Evil so he will appear at the right time. 7The secret power of evil is already working in the
world, but there is one who is stopping that
power. And he will continue to stop it until he
is taken out of the way. 8Then that Man of Evil
will appear, and the Lord Jesus will kill him with
the breath that comes from his mouth and will
destroy him with the glory of his coming. 9The
Man of Evil will come by the power of Satan.
He will have great power, and he will do many
different false miracles, signs, and wonders.
10He will use every kind of evil to trick those
who are lost. They will die, because they refused to love the truth. (If they loved the truth,
they would be saved.) 11For this reason God
sends them something powerful that leads

dare to do

Philippians 2:3
Read It: Give other people more honor than yourself.
Do It: Don't brag about how great you are. Instead, compliment others on the good qualities you see in them.

Philippians 2:4
Read It: Think about others' needs before your own.
Do It: Don't rush to get the best seat on the bus or in class. Slow down and offer the best seat to someone else. You'll blow his mind!

Philippians 2:12
Read It: If you have been saved by God, show your gratitude by serving him.
Do It: Pray to God and offer him your life. Be prepared to do whatever he asks of you.

trustables

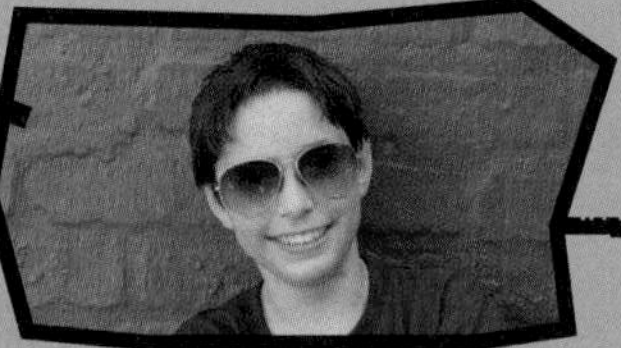

2 Thessalonians 1:11

Did you know the creator of the universe is working in your life?

The Bible says, "We always pray for you, asking our God to help you live the kind of life he called you to live. We pray that with his power God will help you do the good things you want" (2 Thessalonians 1:11). How cool is that? God is helping you not only to do what pleases him, but also to *want* to do it.

We know that we please God when we bless our enemies, but *wanting to* can be difficult. Last week Billy Bob, who is not cool, stole five bucks from you and got away with it. Your teacher just busted him in class again. You know God wants you to pray for him, but you're glad he got in trouble because he deserves it. The Bible tells us, however, that God is working in our hearts to help us *want* to bless him. In our own strength, we can't be perfect. That's why *he* is working in our hearts.

Wow! That changes everything, doesn't it? You may be thinking that you'll never want to pray for a person like Billy Bob, but you are not alone. God himself is working in your life so that you can do what is right with his help.

2:3 turning away Or "the rebellion." **2:3 Man of Evil** Some Greek copies read "Man of Sin."

parents

Luke 15:11–32 tells the story of a son who was very selfish. He wanted his dad to give him money so he could leave home and start partying. He did everything wrong and wasted the money, yet his dad threw him a big party when he finally came home! This dad's love was unconditional, just like God's love. That meant he loved his son no matter what!

If you worry about disappointing your parents, it's time to rethink your relationship with them. If you worry about getting good enough grades or being the perfect son, you're in for a big surprise—parents don't expect you to be perfect! Sometimes it might seem like your parents expect too much from you, and it feels unfair. Don't stress yourself out by trying to do everything exactly as you think they want it . . . just do your best.

Someday you won't live with your parents. You might be excited about the day you get to leave home, or you might be scared silly of being on your own. Either way, the reality is that for now your parents are in charge. It's important to obey and follow our parents; it's also important to realize that we will make mistakes and there will be times we need to ask for forgiveness. Don't be scared to admit when you are wrong to your parents—they will appreciate your honesty!

If your parents seem like they are always embarrassing you when you're with your friends, don't get mad at them—parents aren't perfect. If you are upset or angry with your parents, the best thing to do is to wait until you've cooled off and then go directly to them to work it out. If something is clearly wrong (if the situation is unsafe for you or your family members), then get outside help. Otherwise, remember that God wants you to obey your parents; he's put them in charge of you. Colossians 3:20 says, "Children, obey your parents in all things, because this pleases the Lord."

No matter what frustrations you have with your family, remember that they love you. Thank God for your family!

them away from the truth so they will believe a lie. [12]So all those will be judged guilty who did not believe the truth, but enjoyed doing evil.

YOU ARE CHOSEN FOR SALVATION

[13]Brothers and sisters, whom the Lord loves, God chose you from the beginning[n] to be saved. So we must always thank God for you. You are saved by the Spirit that makes you holy and by your faith in the truth. [14]God used the Good News that we preached to call you to be saved so you can share in the glory of our Lord Jesus Christ. [15]So, brothers and sisters, stand strong and continue to believe the teachings we gave you in our speaking and in our letter.

[16-17]May our Lord Jesus Christ himself and God our Father encourage you and strengthen you in every good thing you do and say. God loved us, and through his grace he gave us a good hope and encouragement that continues forever.

PRAY FOR US

3 And now, brothers and sisters, pray for us that the Lord's teaching will continue to spread quickly and that people will give honor to that teaching, just as happened with you. [2]And pray that we will be protected from stubborn and evil people, because not all people believe.

[3]But the Lord is faithful and will give you strength and will protect you from the Evil One. [4]The Lord makes us feel sure that you are doing and will continue to do the things we told you. [5]May the Lord lead your hearts into God's love and Christ's patience.

THE DUTY TO WORK

[6]Brothers and sisters, by the authority of our Lord Jesus Christ we command you to stay away from any believer who refuses to work and does not follow the teaching we gave you. [7]You yourselves know that you should live as we live. We were not lazy when we were with you. [8]And when we ate another person's food, we always paid for it. We worked very hard night and day so we would not be an expense to any of you. [9]We had the right to ask you to help us, but we worked to take care of ourselves so we would be an example for you to follow. [10]When we were with you, we gave you this rule: "Anyone who refuses to work should not eat."

[11]We hear that some people in your group refuse to work. They do nothing but busy themselves in other people's lives. [12]We command those people and beg them in the Lord Jesus Christ to work quietly and earn their own food. [13]But you, brothers and sisters, never become tired of doing good.

[14]If some people do not obey what we tell you in this letter, then take note of them. Have nothing to do with them so they will feel ashamed. [15]But do not treat them as enemies. Warn them as fellow believers.

FINAL WORDS

[16]Now may the Lord of peace give you peace at all times and in every way. The Lord be with all of you.

[17]I, Paul, end this letter now in my own handwriting. All my letters have this to show they are from me. This is the way I write.

[18]The grace of our Lord Jesus Christ be with you all.

Q&A

Q: My older brother is really disrespectful to my mom. What should I do?

A: If you confront him openly, you may get the same disrespect. First, pray that God would give you the right words, then go and talk to him one-on-one. Be respectful and use a quiet voice even if you feel like yelling at him. He may not realize that he is being disrespectful. Older brothers usually don't like to take advice from little brothers, but God can use what you say if you tell the truth with love (Ephesians 4:15).

Q: Jesus says we're supposed to be a "light to the world." How can *I* do that?

A: You should treat people in your neighborhood, school, and church the way that Jesus would treat them (Acts 10:38). Always ask forgiveness if you do something wrong and quickly forgive others. Pray for the people in your life and ask God to show you ways to reflect his light to them.

Q: Does the Bible say anything about saving the environment?

A: Back when the Bible was written, everybody lived much closer to nature than we do now. Humans "saving the environment" would have been an odd idea. In the Old Testament, God told Adam to take good care of the earth (Genesis 1:28), and he told Noah to save the animals from the flood (Genesis 6:19). And we know that God watches each animal that he creates (Matthew 10:29). So we should respect his creation, too.

1 TIMOTHY

First Timothy, 2 Timothy, and Titus are sometimes called *pastoral letters* because they say a lot about a pastor's duties in the local church.

The letters were written by Paul to men he had trained and sent to help the churches in the city of Ephesus and the island of Crete.

The church in Ephesus was having problems with false teachers (chapter 1). Paul tells Timothy how to deal with those who claimed to be religious experts but who didn't know what they were talking about. In chapter 2, he talks about prayer and worship. In chapter 3, he explains about church leaders and how to pick them. In chapter 4, he gives more details on dealing with *apostasy* (Christians falling away from the faith) and false teaching.

Chapters 5 and 6 tell us how to act toward certain groups in the church like widows, elders, and slaves. There's a warning about the dangers of money and Paul's final words of advice to Timothy: "Guard what God has trusted to you. Stay away from foolish, useless talk and from the arguments of what is falsely called 'knowledge'" (1 Timothy 6:20).

These details may not seem important, but Paul is very concerned about the local church. It is the one place where people should be able to find Jesus and be trained to be like him. You can tell if you are in a good church if it follows the rules Paul sets down here.

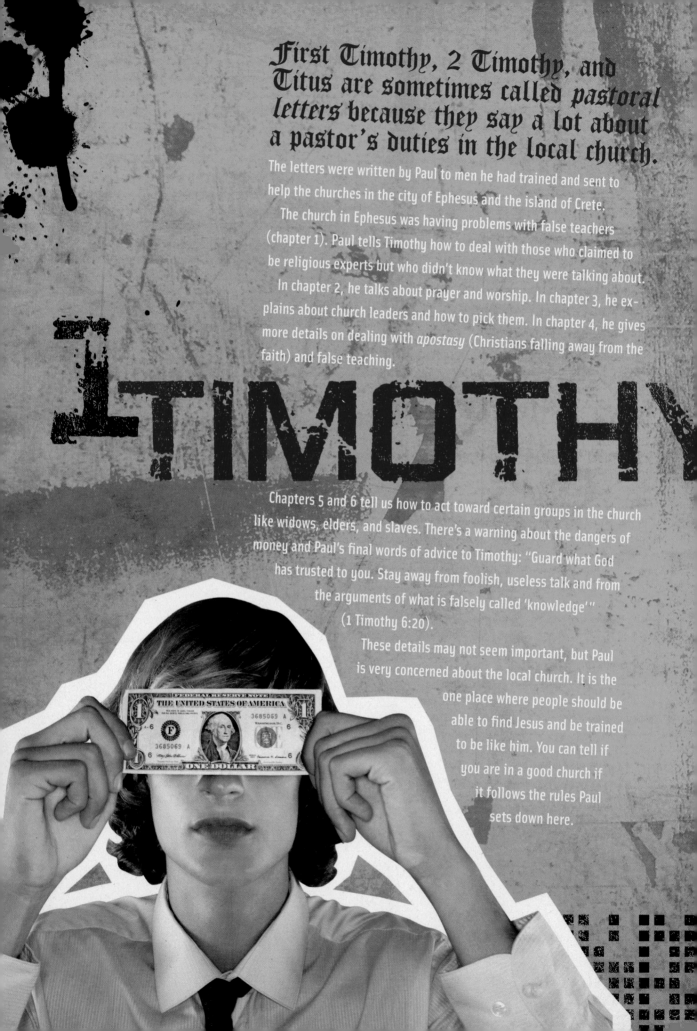

GET **CONNECTED**

NO ONE UNDERSTANDS!

Jordan plopped on his bed, trying to ignore his parents. *How could they understand?* he thought. *They don't know what it's like to be pushed around.*

When Jordan finally told his parents about the bully at school, he was surprised to find out that they did understand—they'd faced bullies before, too! They reminded Jordan that Jesus was a kid once, and bullies were probably mean to him sometimes.

Hebrews 4:15 tells us that Jesus knows and understands what we go through. The next time you feel like no one understands, remember that Jesus was a boy, too!

1 From Paul, an apostle of Christ Jesus, by the command of God our Savior and Christ Jesus our hope.

²To Timothy, a true child to me because you believe:

Grace, mercy, and peace from God the Father and Christ Jesus our Lord.

WARNING AGAINST FALSE TEACHING

³I asked you to stay longer in Ephesus when I went into Macedonia so you could command some people there to stop teaching false things. ⁴Tell them not to spend their time on stories that are not true and on long lists of names in family histories. These things only bring arguments; they do not help God's work, which is done in faith. ⁵The purpose of this command is for people to have love, a love that comes from a pure heart and a good conscience and a true faith. ⁶Some people have missed these things and turned to useless talk. ⁷They want to be teachers of the law, but they do not understand either what they are talking about or what they are sure about.

⁸But we know that the law is good if someone uses it lawfully. ⁹We also know that the law is not made for good people but for those who are against the law and for those who refuse to follow it. It is for people who are against God and are sinful, who are unholy and ungodly, who kill their fathers and mothers, who murder, ¹⁰who take part in sexual sins, who have sexual relations with people of the same sex, who sell slaves, who tell lies, who speak falsely, and who do anything against the true teaching of God. ¹¹That teaching is part of the Good News of the blessed God that he gave me to tell.

THANKS FOR GOD'S MERCY

¹²I thank Christ Jesus our Lord, who gave me strength, because he trusted me and gave me this work of serving him. ¹³In the past I spoke against Christ and persecuted him and did all kinds of things to hurt him. But God showed me mercy, because I did not know what I was doing. I did not believe. ¹⁴But the grace of our Lord was fully given to me, and with that grace came the faith and love that are in Christ Jesus.

God Loves Music

God loves music; here's the proof:

★ When he created the heavens and the earth, the angels sang along.
★ God included a whole book of songs in the Bible (the Psalms).
★ Jesus sang with his followers before he died (Matthew 26:30).
★ The Holy Spirit fills our hearts with "psalms, hymns, and spiritual songs" (Ephesians 5:18–20).

Heaven's inhabitants will certainly enjoy singing and playing instruments! (Revelation 5:8–14; 15:1–4). Why? Because God loves music; he invented it!

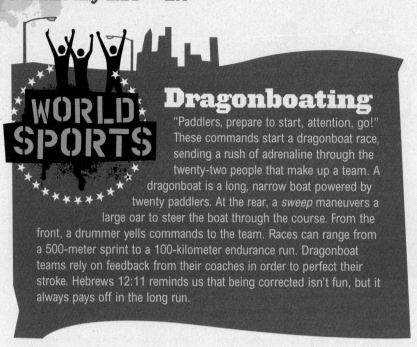

WORLD SPORTS

Dragonboating

"Paddlers, prepare to start, attention, go!" These commands start a dragonboat race, sending a rush of adrenaline through the twenty-two people that make up a team. A dragonboat is a long, narrow boat powered by twenty paddlers. At the rear, a *sweep* maneuvers a large oar to steer the boat through the course. From the front, a drummer yells commands to the team. Races can range from a 500-meter sprint to a 100-kilometer endurance run. Dragonboat teams rely on feedback from their coaches in order to perfect their stroke. Hebrews 12:11 reminds us that being corrected isn't fun, but it always pays off in the long run.

¹⁵What I say is true, and you should fully accept it: Christ Jesus came into the world to save sinners, of whom I am the worst. ¹⁶But I was given mercy so that in me, the worst of all sinners, Christ Jesus could show that he has patience without limit. His patience with me made me an example for those who would believe in him and have life forever. ¹⁷To the King that rules forever, who will never die, who cannot be seen, the only God, be honor and glory forever and ever. Amen.

¹⁸Timothy, my child, I am giving you a command that agrees with the prophecies that were given about you in the past. I tell you this so you can follow them and fight the good fight. ¹⁹Continue to have faith and do what you know is right. Some people have rejected this, and their faith has been shipwrecked. ²⁰Hymenaeus and Alexander have done that, and I have given them to Satan so they will learn not to speak against God.

SOME RULES FOR MEN AND WOMEN

2 First, I tell you to pray for all people, asking God for what they need and being thankful to him. ²Pray for rulers and for all who have authority so that we can have quiet and peaceful lives full of worship and respect for God. ³This is good, and it pleases God our Savior, ⁴who wants all people to be saved and to know the truth. ⁵There is one God and one mediator so that human beings can reach God. That way is through Christ Jesus, who is himself human. ⁶He gave himself as a payment to free all people. He is proof that came at the right time. ⁷That is why I was chosen to tell the Good News and to be an

Q: What does it mean to love others as I love myself?

A: Nobody has to teach you how to love yourself. We're all born selfish and without the Holy Spirit working in our hearts, so we naturally look out for our own interests first (Philippians 2:3–4). Since self-love is so natural, Jesus said to love *others* that way, too (Mark 12:31). You love yourself without thinking about it; you should love other people in the same way!

Q: Who was the most evil man who ever lived?

A: Since all humans are born with the ability to do evil, there are thousands of examples of horribly wicked people. Some evil men like Hitler or Stalin actually killed millions of innocent people. Still others would have done the same if given half the chance. The Bible says that it would have been better if Judas Iscariot (who betrayed Jesus) had never been born (Mark 14:21). We all sometimes experience evil temptations and desires—only Jesus can take away our wrong thoughts and actions.

Q: Is God really going to destroy the whole world?

A: Yes. Our entire world is living under the curse of sin. And there's only one way to fix it forever. God has promised that one day our entire universe will be destroyed and he will make a new earth and a new heaven for us to live in (2 Peter 3:10–13). If you are a Christian, you don't have to worry about the world being destroyed—you'll be safe in heaven!

September

It's still hot! Head to the local pool and invent five new ways to dive. **1**

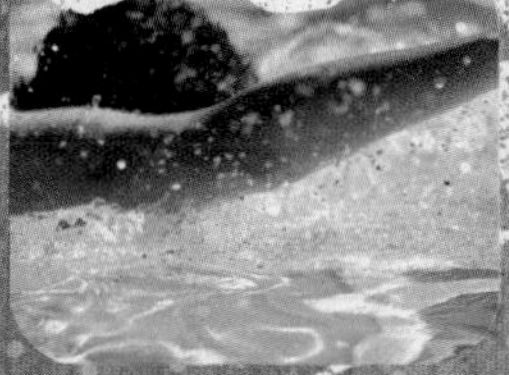

Pray for a person of influence: snowboarder Shaun White will open birthday presents today. **3**

Pray for a person of influence: it's singer Beyoncé Knowles's birthday. **4**

Be a DJ for a day… spin CDs from your favorite Christian artists. **5**

In honor of *"Fight Procrastination Day,"* do something you've been putting off. **6**

7

Stick some frozen berries and yogurt in the blender and make a smoothie. Mmmm! **8**

Pray for a person of influence: actor Adam Sandler has a birthday today. **9**

When you're tempted to judge your friends, read James 4:11–12. **10**

It's *"Make Your Bed Day."* Come on, just do it—it's a holiday! **11**

Pray for a person of influence: it's singer Ruben Studdard's birthday. **12**

Read *James and the Giant Peach*. Author Roald Dahl was born on this day. **13**

14

Pray for a person of influence: actor Tommy Lee Jones will open birthday presents today. **15**

Draw a picture of heaven and stick it in your Bible at Revelation 21:1–4. **16**

18

Ahoy, mateys—it's *"Talk Like a Pirate Day"*! Try it! **19**

Is life getting rough? Read 1 Peter 1:5–7 for Peter's encouragement. **22**

23

24

Pray for people of influence: actors Will Smith and Catherine Zeta-Jones have birthdays today. **25**

It's getting cold… pray for the Lord's comfort for the homeless. **29**

30

dare to do

Colossians 3:2
Read It: Think about your eternal life in heaven, not always about life on earth.
Do It: In heaven, you'll be rewarded for the good you do for Jesus Christ on earth. So start building up your heavenly rewards by serving Christ today!

Colossians 3:5
Read It: Get rid of anything evil in your life.
Do It: Do you have any music, comic books, or video games that glorify evil instead of God? Toss them out! They will do you no good.

Colossians 3:9
Read It: Don't lie to anyone.
Do It: When you screw up, tell your parents. It's better to be honest about your sins than to make things worse by lying!

apostle. (I am telling the truth; I am not lying.) I was chosen to teach those who are not Jews to believe and to know the truth.

[8] So, I want the men everywhere to pray, lifting up their hands in a holy manner, without anger and arguments.

[9] Also, women should wear proper clothes that show respect and self-control, not using braided hair or gold or pearls or expensive clothes. [10] Instead, they should do good deeds, which is right for women who say they worship God.

[11] Let a woman learn by listening quietly and being ready to cooperate in everything.

[12] But I do not allow a woman to teach or to have authority over a man, but to listen quietly, [13] because Adam was formed first and then Eve. [14] And Adam was not tricked, but the woman was tricked and became a sinner. [15] But she will be saved through having children if she continues in faith, love, and holiness, with self-control.

ELDERS IN THE CHURCH

3 What I say is true: Anyone wanting to become an overseer desires a good work. [2] An overseer must not give people a reason to criticize him, and he must have only one wife. He must be self-controlled, wise, respected by others, ready to welcome guests, and able to teach. [3] He must not drink too much wine or like to fight, but rather be gentle and peaceable, not loving money. [4] He must be a good family leader, having children who cooperate with full respect. [5] (If someone does not know how to lead the family, how can that person take care of God's church?) [6] But an elder must not be a new believer, or he might be too proud of himself and be judged guilty just as the devil was. [7] An elder must also have the respect of people who are not in the church so he will not be criticized by others and caught in the devil's trap.

DEACONS IN THE CHURCH

[8] In the same way, deacons must be respected by others, not saying things they do not

ROCK SOLID

1 Timothy 4:12

Chances are pretty good that you're not the pastor of your church, but what's holding you back from doing the work of a pastor? That question isn't as far out as it sounds.

A pastor encourages people who are going through tough times. A pastor visits people who are sick. A pastor shows people how to live for Jesus Christ. What's keeping you from encouraging your friends, from visiting a friend who is sick, and from showing kids at school what it means to live for the Lord? Isn't that possible for someone your age?

Your ability to minister to other people has nothing to do with how old you are. Timothy was a pretty young guy, but he was a pastor and Paul wrote to him, "Do not let anyone treat you as if you are unimportant because you are young. Instead, be an example to the believers with your words, your actions, your love, your faith, and your pure life."

That's amazing! No matter how young you are, you can be an example for the whole church. Leadership isn't having a position; it's who you are—your character. So what's holding you back from being a leader at your church? What's keeping you from showing other Christians twice your age how it's done?

He was proclaimed to the nations,
believed in by the world,
and taken up in glory.

A WARNING ABOUT FALSE TEACHERS

4 Now the Holy Spirit clearly says that in the later times some people will stop believing the faith. They will follow spirits that lie and teachings of demons. ²Such teachings come from the false words of liars whose consciences are destroyed as if by a hot iron. ³They forbid people to marry and tell them not to eat certain foods which God created to be eaten with thanks by people who believe and know the truth. ⁴Everything God made is good, and nothing should be refused if it is accepted with thanks, ⁵because it is made holy by what God has said and by prayer.

BE A GOOD SERVANT OF CHRIST

⁶By telling these things to the brothers and sisters, you will be a good servant of Christ Jesus. You will be made strong by the words of the faith and the good teaching which you have been following. ⁷But do not follow foolish

TOP 10 X

Fun Summertime Activities

1. Summer camp
2. Family vacation
3. Building forts
4. Bike riding
5. Skateboarding
6. Pool parties
7. Camping
8. County/state fair
9. Sleepovers
10. Water balloon fights

mean. They must not drink too much wine or try to get rich by cheating others. ⁹With a clear conscience they must follow the secret of the faith that God made known to us. ¹⁰Test them first. Then let them serve as deacons if you find nothing wrong in them. ¹¹In the same way, women* must be respected by others. They must not speak evil of others. They must be self-controlled and trustworthy in everything. ¹²Deacons must have only one wife and be good leaders of their children and their own families. ¹³Those who serve well as deacons are making an honorable place for themselves, and they will be very bold in their faith in Christ Jesus.

THE SECRET OF OUR LIFE

¹⁴Although I hope I can come to you soon, I am writing these things to you now. ¹⁵Then, even if I am delayed, you will know how to live in the family of God. That family is the church of the living God, the support and foundation of the truth. ¹⁶Without doubt, the secret of our life of worship is great:

He* was shown to us in a human body,
proved right in spirit,
and seen by angels.

Q&A

Q: My grandma seems so strict all the time. Don't people her age like to have fun?

A: Older people do like to have fun. But because their bodies have aged, a lot of the things they enjoyed when they were young have been taken away. Your grandma may be feeling this. Pray that God will help with these changes. Also, she may have grown up in a time when people were more serious and she's wondering just what's gotten into you. Ask her to tell you stories about when she was your age. You'll enjoy hearing about this fun side of grandma!

Q: Sometimes I feel like I'm not good at anything. Is there such a thing as a completely worthless human?

A: No. God has an important purpose for each person—including you. Many people who have gone on to do great things have felt at one time that they were worthless. They were wrong! Jesus loves you so much that he thinks you were worth dying for. His story of the shepherd who goes and looks for one lost sheep is an illustration of how God values each person (check it out in Luke 15:3–7).

Q: My mom says that things are a lot more expensive now than when she was a kid. What happened?

A: Prices go up over time. It's called inflation. Fortunately, people's wages have also gone up, so it evens out. When you're grown up, you'll remember being able to buy a candy bar for less than a dollar. And it'll be *your* kids giving you funny looks.

stories that disagree with God's truth, but train yourself to serve God. [8]Training your body helps you in some ways, but serving God helps you in every way by bringing you blessings in this life and in the future life, too. [9]What I say is true, and you should fully accept it. [10]This is why we work and struggle:[n] We hope in the living God who is the Savior of all people, especially of those who believe.

[11]Command and teach these things. [12]Do not let anyone treat you as if you are unimportant because you are young. Instead, be an example to the believers with your words, your actions, your love, your faith, and your pure life. [13]Until I come, continue to read the Scriptures to the people, strengthen them, and teach them. [14]Use the gift you have, which was given to you through prophecy when the group of elders laid their hands on[n] you. [15]Continue to do those things; give your life to doing them so your progress may be seen by everyone. [16]Be careful in your life and in your teaching. If you continue to live and teach rightly,

you will save both yourself and those who listen to you.

RULES FOR LIVING WITH OTHERS

5 Do not speak angrily to an older man, but plead with him as if he were your father. Treat younger men like brothers, [2]older women like mothers, and younger women like sisters. Always treat them in a pure way.

[3]Take care of widows who are truly widows. [4]But if a widow has children or grandchildren, let them first learn to do their duty to their own family and to repay their parents or grandparents. That pleases God. [5]The true widow, who is all alone, puts her hope in God and continues to pray night and day for God's help. [6]But the widow who uses her life to please herself is really dead while she is alive. [7]Tell the believers to do these things so that no one can criticize them. [8]Whoever does not care for his own relatives, especially his own family members, has turned against the faith and is worse than someone who does not believe in God.

[9]To be on the list of widows, a woman must be at least sixty

years old. She must have been faithful to her husband. [10]She must be known for her good works—works such as raising her children, welcoming strangers, washing the feet of God's people, helping those in trouble, and giving her life to do all kinds of good deeds.

[11]But do not put younger widows on that list. After they give themselves to Christ, they are pulled away from him by their physical desires, and then they want to marry again. [12]They will be judged for not doing what they first promised to do. [13]Besides that, they learn to waste their time, going from house to house. And they not only waste their time but also begin to gossip and busy themselves with other people's lives, saying things they should not say. [14]So I want the younger widows to marry, have children, and manage their homes. Then no enemy will have any reason to criticize them. [15]But some have already turned away to follow Satan.

[16]If any woman who is a believer has widows in her family, she should care for them herself. The church should not have to care for them. Then it will be able to take care of those who are truly widows.

[17]The elders who lead the church well should receive double honor, especially those who work hard by speaking and teaching, [18]because the Scripture says: "When an ox is working in the grain, do not cover its mouth to keep it from eating,"[n] and "A worker should be given his pay."[n]

[19]Do not listen to someone who accuses an elder, without two or three witnesses. [20]Tell those who continue sinning that they are

ROCK SOLID

1 Timothy 6:10

Some people think Christians shouldn't earn a lot of money and be wealthy. They like to quote the popular verse, "Money causes all kinds of evil." But this verse often gets misused—and they leave out the most important part! It says, "The *love* of money causes all kinds of evil" (1 Timothy 6:10). Money itself isn't bad. But loving it is.

Like any addiction, loving money will distract you from the really important things in life like family, faith, and bringing people to Jesus Christ. But there are plenty of rich people who do this incredibly well! Since God has blessed them, they are able to support ministries all around the world. They build hospitals and schools. And if they lost all their money, their faith in Christ would sustain them and they would still be happy.

That is what every believer should strive for. Because no matter how big our bank account or paycheck is, when we have Christ, we are all multimillionaires!

4:10 struggle Some Greek copies read "suffer."   **4:14 laid their hands on** The laying on of hands had many purposes, including the giving of a blessing, power, or authority.   **5:18 "When . . . eating."** Quotation from Deuteronomy 25:4.   **5:18 "A worker . . . pay."** Quotation from Luke 10:7.

wrong. Do this in front of the whole church so
that the others will have a warning.
21Before God and Christ Jesus and the
chosen angels, I command you to do these
things without showing favor of any kind to
anyone.
22Think carefully before you lay your hands
on[n] anyone, and don't share in the sins of others. Keep yourself pure.
23Stop drinking only water, but drink a little
wine to help your stomach and your frequent
sicknesses.
24The sins of some people are easy to see
even before they are judged, but the sins of
others are seen only later. 25So also good deeds
are easy to see, but even those that are not
easily seen cannot stay hidden.

6 All who are slaves under a yoke should
show full respect to their masters so no
one will speak against God's name and our
teaching. 2The slaves whose masters are believers should not show their masters any less
respect because they are believers. They
should serve their masters even better, because they are helping believers they love.
You must teach and preach these things.

FALSE TEACHING AND TRUE RICHES

3Anyone who has a different teaching does
not agree with the true teaching of our Lord
Jesus Christ and the teaching that shows the
true way to serve God. 4This person is full of
pride and understands nothing, but is sick with
a love for arguing and fighting about words.
This brings jealousy, fighting, speaking against
others, evil mistrust, 5and constant quarrels
from those who have evil minds and have lost
the truth. They think that serving God is a way
to get rich.
6Serving God does make us very rich, if we
are satisfied with what we have. 7We brought
nothing into the world, so we can take nothing
out. 8But, if we have food and clothes, we will
be satisfied with that. 9Those who want to become rich bring temptation to themselves and
are caught in a trap. They want many foolish
and harmful things that ruin and destroy people. 10The love of money causes all kinds of
evil. Some people have left the faith, because
they wanted to get more money, but they
have caused themselves much sorrow.

SOME THINGS TO REMEMBER

11But you, man of God, run away from all
those things. Instead, live in the right way, serve
God, have faith, love, patience, and gentleness.
12Fight the good fight of faith, grabbing hold of
the life that continues forever. You were called
to have that life when you confessed the good
confession before many witnesses. 13In the

KNOW THE WORD!

GOOD WORKS

Mowing your neighbor's lawn while he's on vacation. Saying kind words to your little sister even though she's driving you crazy. These things are called *good works*—doing right things.

Some people feel that they need to do enough good works in order to make God happy. Many religions teach that good works are what gets a person into heaven. But the Bible says something totally different. Not even ten million good works could make our sin go away. The only thing that can get us right with God—and save our spot in heaven—is trusting that Jesus paid for our sins.

It's still important to obey God and love other people. But don't think that good works alone will make God smile.

trustables

1 Timothy 6:18–19

If you are an American or Canadian, you are rich. In fact, you're loaded. You have more than do ninety percent of the rest of the people on earth. It wasn't by chance that you came to occupy this privileged position. God has a plan for you. He wants you, who are rich, to share with the poor.

Here's the beauty of this situation: the more you give away now, the more you have in the afterlife! Have you started an eternal savings account? This is how you fill it up! Scripture says, "Tell the rich people to do good, to be rich in doing good deeds, to be generous and ready to share. By doing that, they will be saving a treasure for themselves as a strong foundation for the future. Then they will be able to have the life that is true life."

If you think this life is good, just wait until you see what's coming next! And you can make it even better by sharing the abundance you have right now. It could be money. It could be time. It could be your things. By being willing to share them, you are racking up credits in heaven!

5:22 lay your hands on The laying on of hands had many purposes, including the giving of a blessing, power, or authority.

SMART TIPS!

Give Your Thumbs a Rest

Look at your fingers. Are they calloused and blistered? Is your neck sore? Then maybe it's time to put the video games away and look around. Jesus told his followers to look up and see that the harvest was ready. He meant that people were ready to accept Jesus Christ, so pay attention!

sight of God, who gives life to everything, and of Christ Jesus, I give you a command. Christ Jesus made the good confession when he stood before Pontius Pilate. ¹⁴Do what you were commanded to do without wrong or blame until our Lord Jesus Christ comes again. ¹⁵God will make that happen at the right time. He is the blessed and only Ruler, the King of all kings and the Lord of all lords. ¹⁶He is the only One who never dies. He lives in light so bright no one can go near it. No one has ever seen God, or can see him. May honor and power belong to God forever. Amen.

¹⁷Command those who are rich with things of this world not to be proud. Tell them to hope in God, not in their uncertain riches. God richly gives us everything to enjoy. ¹⁸Tell the rich people to do good, to be rich in doing good deeds, to be generous and ready to share. ¹⁹By doing that, they will be saving a treasure for themselves as a strong foundation for the future. Then they will be able to have the life that is true life.

²⁰Timothy, guard what God has trusted to you. Stay away from foolish, useless talk and from the arguments of what is falsely called "knowledge." ²¹By saying they have that "knowledge," some have missed the true faith.

Grace be with you.

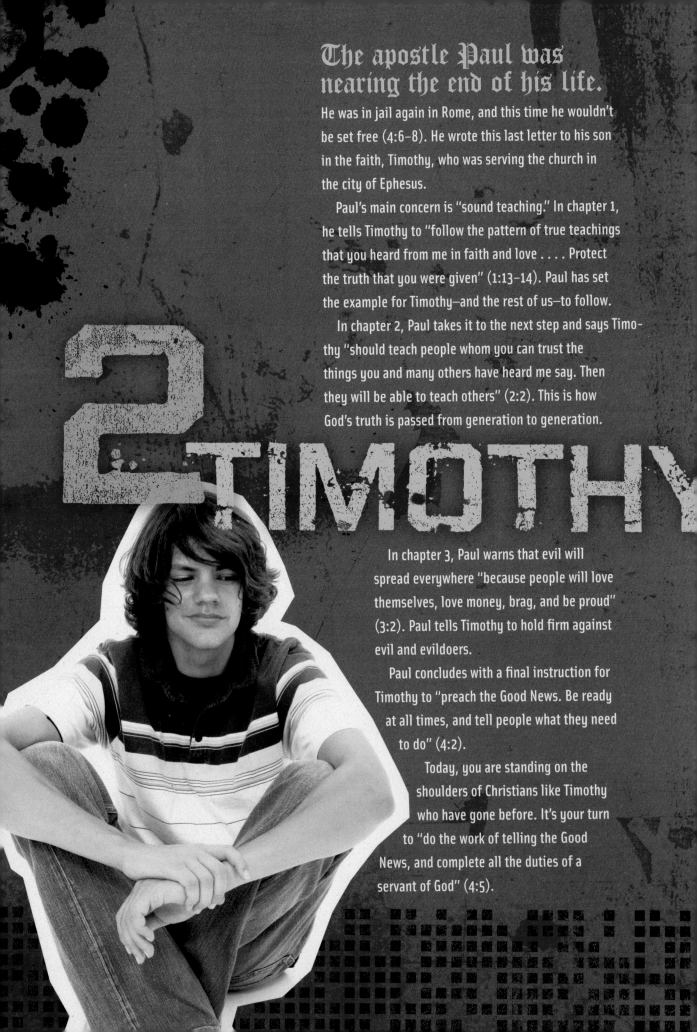

The apostle Paul was nearing the end of his life.

He was in jail again in Rome, and this time he wouldn't be set free (4:6–8). He wrote this last letter to his son in the faith, Timothy, who was serving the church in the city of Ephesus.

Paul's main concern is "sound teaching." In chapter 1, he tells Timothy to "follow the pattern of true teachings that you heard from me in faith and love . . . . Protect the truth that you were given" (1:13–14). Paul has set the example for Timothy—and the rest of us—to follow.

In chapter 2, Paul takes it to the next step and says Timothy "should teach people whom you can trust the things you and many others have heard me say. Then they will be able to teach others" (2:2). This is how God's truth is passed from generation to generation.

2 TIMOTHY

In chapter 3, Paul warns that evil will spread everywhere "because people will love themselves, love money, brag, and be proud" (3:2). Paul tells Timothy to hold firm against evil and evildoers.

Paul concludes with a final instruction for Timothy to "preach the Good News. Be ready at all times, and tell people what they need to do" (4:2).

Today, you are standing on the shoulders of Christians like Timothy who have gone before. It's your turn to "do the work of telling the Good News, and complete all the duties of a servant of God" (4:5).

1 From Paul, an apostle of Christ Jesus by the will of God. God sent me to tell about the promise of life that is in Christ Jesus. ²To Timothy, a dear child to me:

Grace, mercy, and peace to you from God the Father and Christ Jesus our Lord.

ENCOURAGEMENT FOR TIMOTHY

³I thank God as I always mention you in my prayers, day and night. I serve him, doing what I know is right as my ancestors did. ⁴Remembering that you cried for me, I want very much to see you so I can be filled with joy. ⁵I remember your true faith. That faith first lived in your grandmother Lois and in your mother Eunice, and I know you now have that same faith. ⁶This is why I remind you to keep using the gift God gave you when I laid my hands on" you. Now let it grow, as a small flame grows into a fire. ⁷God did not give us a spirit that makes us afraid but a spirit of power and love and self-control.

⁸So do not be ashamed to tell people about our Lord Jesus, and do not be ashamed of me, in prison for the Lord. But suffer with me for the Good News. God, who gives us the strength to do that, ⁹saved us and made us his holy people. That was not because of anything we did ourselves but because of God's purpose and grace. That grace was given to us through Christ Jesus before time began, ¹⁰but it is now shown to us by the coming of our Savior Christ Jesus. He destroyed death, and through the Good News he showed us the way to have life that cannot be destroyed. ¹¹I was chosen to tell that Good News and to be

an apostle and a teacher. ¹²I am suffering now because I tell the Good News, but I am not ashamed, because I know Jesus, the One in whom I have believed. And I am sure he is able to protect what he has trusted me with until that day." ¹³Follow the pattern of true teachings that you heard from me in faith and love, which are in Christ Jesus. ¹⁴Protect the truth that you were given; protect it with the help of the Holy Spirit who lives in us.

DID YOU KNOW?

11% of boys who play sports want to become professional athletes.

Taylor KidsPulse 2004 Report. Taylor Research & Consulting Group.

¹⁵You know that everyone in Asia has left me, even Phygelus and Hermogenes. ¹⁶May the Lord show mercy to the family of Onesiphorus, who has often helped me and was not ashamed that I was in prison. ¹⁷When he came to Rome, he looked eagerly for me until he found me. ¹⁸May the Lord allow him to find mercy from the Lord on that day. You know how many ways he helped me in Ephesus.

A LOYAL SOLDIER OF CHRIST JESUS

2 You then, Timothy, my child, be strong in the grace we have in Christ Jesus. ²You should teach people whom you can trust the things you and many others have heard me say. Then they will be able to teach others. ³Share in the troubles we have like a good soldier of Christ Jesus. ⁴A soldier wants to please the enlisting officer, so no one serving in the army wastes time with everyday matters. ⁵Also an athlete who takes part in a contest must obey all the rules in order to win. ⁶The farmer who works hard should be the first person to get some of the food that was grown. ⁷Think about what I am saying, because the Lord will give you the ability to understand everything.

⁸Remember Jesus Christ, who was raised from the dead, who is from the family of David. This is the Good News I preach, ⁹and I am suffering because of it to the point of being bound with chains like a criminal. But God's teaching is not in chains. ¹⁰So I patiently accept all these troubles so that those whom God has chosen can have the salvation that is in Christ Jesus. With that salvation comes glory that never ends.

COOL!

Qin's Tomb

The ruler who united China also built one of the grandest tombs of all time. Emperor Qin Shih Huang died in 210 B.C. His enormous tomb took 750,000 workers thirty-seven years to complete.

Buried a short distance from the central tomb are more than 8,000 clay soldiers, along with chariots and horses. The life-size warriors are all unique. They are armed and ready to protect their emperor in the next life.

No clay soldiers were buried around the tomb of Jesus Christ near Jerusalem. He didn't need protection. Besides, he didn't stay dead!

1:6 laid my hands on The laying on of hands had many purposes, including the giving of a blessing, power, or authority.   **1:12 day** The day Christ will come to judge all people and take his people to live with him.

¹¹ This teaching is true:
If we died with him, we will also live with him.
¹² If we accept suffering, we will also rule with him.
If we say we don't know him, he will say he doesn't know us.
¹³ If we are not faithful, he will still be faithful, because he must be true to who he is.

A WORKER PLEASING TO GOD

¹⁴ Continue teaching these things, warning people in God's presence not to argue about words. It does not help anyone, and it ruins those who listen. ¹⁵ Make every effort to give yourself to God as the kind of person he will approve. Be a worker who is not ashamed and who uses the true teaching in the right way. ¹⁶ Stay away from foolish, useless talk, because that will lead people further away from God. ¹⁷ Their evil teaching will spread like a sickness inside the body. Hymenaeus and Philetus are like that. ¹⁸ They have left the true teaching, saying that the rising from the dead has already taken place, and so they are destroying the faith of some people. ¹⁹ But God's strong foundation continues to stand. These words are written on the seal: "The Lord knows those who belong to him,"ⁿ and "Everyone who wants to belong to the Lord must stop doing wrong."

²⁰ In a large house there are not only things made of gold and silver, but also things made of wood and clay. Some things are used for special purposes, and others are made for ordinary jobs. ²¹ All who make themselves clean from evil will be used for special purposes. They will be made holy, useful to the Master, ready to do any good work.

²² But run away from the evil desires of youth. Try hard to live right and to have faith, love, and peace, together with those who trust in the Lord from pure hearts. ²³ Stay away from foolish and stupid arguments, because you know they grow into quarrels. ²⁴ And a servant of the Lord must not quarrel but must be kind to everyone, a good teacher, and patient. ²⁵ The Lord's servant must gently teach those who disagree. Then maybe God will let them change their minds so they can accept the truth. ²⁶ And they may wake up and escape from the trap of the devil, who catches them to do what he wants.

THE LAST DAYS

3 Remember this! In the last days there will be many troubles, ² because people

Q: There's stuff I can talk to my uncle about that I can't tell my dad. Is this okay?

A: Some subjects are tough to talk about with your parents. If your uncle is somebody you can trust, then it's okay to talk with him instead of your dad. If he believes in Jesus, it's even better. But even though you don't discuss certain things with your parents, you shouldn't keep secrets from them or ask your uncle to either.

Q: Do pets go to heaven?

A: Nobody knows for sure. The Bible only talks about people going to heaven if they are saved by Jesus. But since the new earth will have everything we need to be happy, it may include our special animals from this world. That's just one of the things we'll get to find out about when we get to heaven.

Q: Our pastor is always saying, "It's not about you." Isn't this hurting people's self-esteem?

A: It might be hurting their self-esteem in a good way! Part of being a Christian is realizing that God is the only one who holds the universe in his hand, and he's the only one who deserves our worship. God tells us in Psalm 46:10, "Be still and know that I am God." One of the reasons we should pray every day is that it reminds us that God is the only one who is in control.

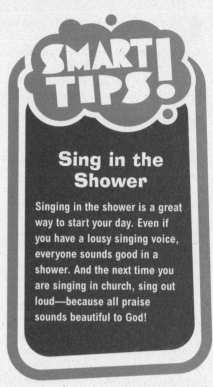

SMART TIPS!

Sing in the Shower

Singing in the shower is a great way to start your day. Even if you have a lousy singing voice, everyone sounds good in a shower. And the next time you are singing in church, sing out loud—because all praise sounds beautiful to God!

October

1 Pray for a person of influence: it's baseball player Mark McGwire's birthday.

2 Gandhi said, "Be the change you want to see in the world." Think about it.

3 Help change the oil in your parent's car. When you have your own, you'll be glad to know how!

4

5 It's "Do Something Nice Day." Think of five nice things you can do today—and do them!

6

7

8 Get a huge tag tournament going at recess.

9 Pray for a person of influence: it's snowboarder Travis Rice's birthday.

10

11 After church on Sunday, thank your pastor for the way he leads you.

12 Pray for a person of influence: it's track athlete Marion Jones's birthday.

13 Read about God's love in Romans 3:21–31. Thank him for caring about you unconditionally.

14 Pray for a person of influence: musician Usher will be humming "Happy Birthday" today.

15

16 Pray for a person of influence: singer-songwriter John Mayer gets older today.

17

18 Wild goose chase! Race your pets to see which one is the leader of the pack.

19

20 Pray for a person of influence: rapper Snoop Dogg celebrates his birthday today.

21 It's "Popcorn Poppin' Month"—Watch a fun movie with friends, and eat lots of popcorn!

22

23

24

25

26 Can you find 100 people to say "hey" to today?

27

28

29 Finally, a reason to surf the Web. It's the Internet's birthday!

30

31 Witness to trick-or-treaters: tape a Bible verse to the candy you hand out.

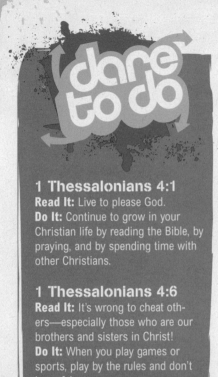

1 Thessalonians 4:1
Read It: Live to please God.
Do It: Continue to grow in your Christian life by reading the Bible, by praying, and by spending time with other Christians.

1 Thessalonians 4:6
Read It: It's wrong to cheat others—especially those who are our brothers and sisters in Christ!
Do It: When you play games or sports, play by the rules and don't be unfair.

1 Thessalonians 4:7
Read It: God has asked you to be holy.
Do It: Don't compare yourself to your friends and think you're doing all right. Instead, try to live and be more ike Jesus.

ined, and they have failed in trying to follow the faith. [9]But they will not be successful in what they do, because as with Jannes and Jambres, everyone will see that they are foolish.

OBEY THE TEACHINGS

[10]But you have followed what I teach, the way I live, my goal, faith, patience, and love. You know I never give up. [11]You know how I have been hurt and have suffered, as in Antioch, Iconium, and Lystra. I have suffered, but the Lord saved me from all those troubles. [12]Everyone who wants to live as God desires, in Christ Jesus, will be persecuted. [13]But people who are evil and cheat others will go from bad to worse. They will fool others, but they will also be fooling themselves.

[14]But you should continue following the teachings you learned. You know they are true, because you trust those who taught you. [15]Since you were a child you have known the Holy Scriptures which are able to make you wise. And that wisdom leads to salvation through faith in Christ Jesus. [16]All Scripture is inspired by God and is useful for teaching, for showing people what is wrong in their lives, for correcting faults, and for teaching how to live right. [17]Using the Scriptures, the person who serves God will be capable, having all that is needed to do every good work.

4 I give you a command in the presence of God and Christ Jesus, the One who will judge the living and the dead, and by his coming and his kingdom: [2]Preach the Good News. Be ready at all times, and tell people what they need to do. Tell them when they are wrong. Encourage them with great patience and careful teaching, [3]because the time will come when people will not listen to the true teaching but will find many more teachers who please them by saying the things they want to hear. [4]They will stop listening to the truth and will begin to follow false stories. [5]But you should control yourself at all times, accept troubles, do the work of telling the Good News, and complete all the duties of a servant of God.

[6]My life is being given as an offering to God, and the time has come for me to leave this life. [7]I have fought the good fight, I have

ROCK SOLID

2 Timothy 3:5

Have you ever checked your horoscope? Do you know what your sign is? It's hard to believe, but there are people who base their entire life on what they see "in the stars." Astrology is one of the fake "faiths" the Bible warns us about.

Since we are spiritual beings, we all have a drive to understand that part of ourselves. But without the revealed truth of God's Word, we are left to crazy ideas and confusion. Scripture itself warns us that in these last days, people will "act as if they serve God but will not have his power" (2 Timothy 3:5). That's what astrology is! God's advice in this passage is to "stay away from those people."

Satan has invented hundreds of "counterfeits" to distract people from the truth. The best ones are those that most closely resemble the true good news of Jesus Christ. But make no mistake, they do not have God's power and will lead you astray. So don't fall for silly hoaxes like astrology or other spiritual silliness. Stick with the Bible! Test what you see and hear against God's revealed truth in scripture.

will love themselves, love money, brag, and be proud. They will say evil things against others and will not obey their parents or be thankful or be the kind of people God wants. [3]They will not love others, will refuse to forgive, will gossip, and will not control themselves. They will be cruel, will hate what is good, [4]will turn against their friends, and will do foolish things without thinking. They will be conceited, will love pleasure instead of God, [5]and will act as if they serve God but will not have his power. Stay away from those people. [6]Some of them go into homes and get control of silly women who are full of sin and are led by many evil desires. [7]These women are always learning new teachings, but they are never able to understand the truth fully. [8]Just as Jannes and Jambres were against Moses, these people are against the truth. Their thinking has been ru-

finished the race, I have kept the faith. [8]Now, a crown is being held for me—a crown for being right with God. The Lord, the judge who judges rightly, will give the crown to me on that day[n]—not only to me but to all those who have waited with love for him to come again.

PERSONAL WORDS

[9]Do your best to come to me as soon as you can, [10]because Demas, who loved this world, left me and went to Thessalonica. Crescens went to Galatia, and Titus went to Dalmatia. [11]Luke is the only one still with me. Get Mark and bring him with you when you come, because he can help me in my work here. [12]I sent Tychicus to Ephesus. [13]When I was in Troas, I left my coat there with Carpus. So when you come, bring it to me, along with my books, particularly the ones written on parchment.[n]

[14]Alexander the metalworker did many harmful things against me. The Lord will punish him for what he did. [15]You also should be careful that he does not hurt you, because he fought strongly against our teaching.

[16]The first time I defended myself, no one helped me; everyone left me. May they be forgiven. [17]But the Lord stayed with me and gave me strength so I could fully tell the Good News to all those who are not Jews. So I was saved from the lion's mouth. [18]The Lord will save me when anyone tries to hurt me, and he will bring me safely to his heavenly kingdom. Glory forever and ever be the Lord's. Amen.

FINAL GREETINGS

[19]Greet Priscilla and Aquila and the family of Onesiphorus. [20]Erastus stayed in Corinth, and I left Trophimus sick in Miletus. [21]Try as hard as you can to come to me before winter.

Eubulus sends greetings to you. Also Pudens, Linus, Claudia, and all the brothers and sisters in Christ greet you.

[22]The Lord be with your spirit. Grace be with you.

Cures for Boredom

1. Build a bike/skateboard jump.
2. Build a tree house.
3. Play the drums/guitar.
4. Make a home movie.
5. Make crazy foods.
6. Play street hockey.
7. Catch a caterpillar and watch it make a cocoon.
8. Fix up your bike.
9. Go fishing.
10. Draw cool pictures.

4:8 day The day Christ will come to judge all people and take his people to live with him.   **4:13 parchment** A writing paper made from the skins of sheep.

Titus was one of Paul's "trainees."

He was a good learner who became a trusted coworker. He was a Greek by birth and may have become a Christian through Paul's preaching, for Paul calls him "my true child in the faith" (1:4).

Paul gave Titus a lot of on-the-job training to be a pastor. When Titus was ready, Paul sent him to the island of Crete to work with the church there (1:4–5).

This assignment was no picnic. The Cretans were so bad that they inspired a popular saying: "Cretans are always liars, evil animals, and lazy people who do nothing but eat" (1:12).

Paul doesn't expect Titus to do everything himself. He wants him to pick mature men to be "elders" in the church (chapter 1). Then he tells Titus what key truths to teach to different groups of people (chapters 2 and 3).

Want to know how to act toward those who are older than you are? Those who are younger? Girls and women? Teachers and others in authority? The answers are in here.

"This teaching is true," Paul says at the end of this letter, "and I want you to be sure the people understand these things. Then those who believe in God will be careful to use their lives for doing good" (3:8).

If you want to be a good person, pay close attention to what you are about to read!

TITUS

The Ten Commandments

Here are three things you must know about the Ten Commandments:

1. They are based on love. You can obey all of God's laws by loving God and loving other people (Matthew 22:37–40).
2. They were given to the Jewish people in the Old Testament. Christians are not required to obey these laws in order to be saved. Instead, we obey out of love! (Romans 13:8–10).
3. They can't save you. The commandments prove that we can't get it all right and we need a savior, Jesus (Galatians 2:15–16).

1 From Paul, a servant of God and an apostle of Jesus Christ. I was sent to help the faith of God's chosen people and to help them know the truth that shows people how to serve God. [2] That faith and that knowledge come from the hope for life forever, which God promised to us before time began. And God cannot lie. [3] At the right time God let the world know about that life through preaching. He trusted me with that work, and I preached by the command of God our Savior.

[4] To Titus, my true child in the faith we share: Grace and peace from God the Father and Christ Jesus our Savior.

TITUS' WORK IN CRETE

[5] I left you in Crete so you could finish doing the things that still needed to be done and so you could appoint elders in every town, as I directed you. [6] An elder must not be guilty of doing wrong, must have only one wife, and must have believing children. They must not be known as children who are wild and do not cooperate. [7] As God's managers, overseers must not be guilty of doing wrong, being selfish, or becoming angry quickly. They must not drink too much wine, like to fight, or try to get rich by

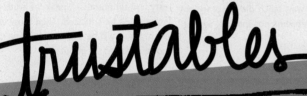

Titus 2:14

Secret sins are like invisible bricks tied around our neck. We may manage to carry a few without being too bothered. But once they start adding up, the weight will drag us down and cause more and more discomfort and pain. There is only one way to cut the ropes that hold these bricks: confess your sins to God. If you pray to the Lord, are honest about the sin in your life, and ask for his mercy, God takes that load from you and gives you freedom and relief!

Want proof? The Bible promises that Jesus Christ "gave himself for us so he might pay the price to free us from all evil and to make us pure people who belong only to him—people who are always wanting to do good deeds" (Titus 2:14).

What an amazing God we have! He doesn't want to punish us. Instead, he wants to free us! Do you have some secret sins in your life? Are you feeling weighed down? Even just a little bit? You don't have to be. Have that heart-to-heart talk with God right now. Tell him everything—after all, he already knows. Then ask him to forgive you and release your burden today.

Things That Should Stay Out of Style

1. Mullet haircuts
2. Penny loafers
3. Speedo swimsuits
4. Disco
5. El Caminos
6. Parachute pants
7. Smurfs
8. Chia Pets
9. Vanilla Ice
10. Barney

it, overseers can help people by using true teaching, and they can show those who are against the true teaching that they are wrong.

[10]There are many people who refuse to co-operate, who talk about worthless things and lead others into the wrong way—mainly those who insist on circumcision to be saved. [11]These people must be stopped, because they are upsetting whole families by teaching things they should not teach, which they do to get rich by cheating people. [12]Even one of their own prophets said, "Cretans are always liars, evil animals, and lazy people who do nothing but eat." [13]The words that prophet said are true. So firmly tell those people they are wrong so they may become strong in the faith, [14]not accepting Jewish false stories and the commands of people who reject the truth. [15]To those who are pure, all things are pure, but to those who are full of sin and do not believe, nothing is pure. Both their minds and their consciences have been ruined. [16]They say they know God, but their actions show they do not accept him. They are hateful people, they refuse to obey, and they are useless for doing anything good.

FOLLOWING THE TRUE TEACHING

2 But you must tell everyone what to do to follow the true teaching. [2]Teach older men to be self-controlled, serious, wise, strong in faith, in love, and in patience.

[3]In the same way, teach older women to be holy in their behavior, not speaking against

DID YOU KNOW?

66% of boys who play sports play to have fun.

Taylor KidsPulse 2004 Report. Taylor Research & Consulting Group.

others or enslaved to too much wine, but teaching what is good. [4]Then they can teach the young women to love their husbands, to love their children, [5]to be wise and pure, to be good workers at home, to be kind, and to yield to their husbands. Then no one will be able to criticize the teaching God gave us.

[6]In the same way, encourage young men to be wise. [7]In every way be an example of doing good deeds. When you teach, do it with honesty and seriousness. [8]Speak the truth so that you cannot be criticized. Then those who are against you will be ashamed because there is nothing bad to say about us.

cheating others. [8]Overseers must be ready to welcome guests, love what is good, be wise, live right, and be holy and self-controlled. [9]By holding on to the trustworthy word just as we teach

Titus 3:9

Watch out for people who like to argue! There are people like that—whatever anyone says, they voice their opinion against it. You probably know someone—maybe at your school, maybe at your church—who would disagree with you if you said the sky is blue.

Titus 3:9 says, "But stay away from those who have foolish arguments and talk about useless family histories and argue and quarrel about the law. Those things are worth nothing and will not help anyone."

Arguing simply for the sake of arguing doesn't do anyone any good. Are there people at your church who only want to argue about points in the sermon or Sunday school lesson? Be careful, because the Word of God isn't for starting debates; it's for growing in love, faith, and life.

Watch out if you're trying to talk to someone about life in Jesus and all he wants to do is argue. If he's not ready to listen, move on and find someone who is. Jesus says not to throw your pearls before pigs (Matthew 7:6). That means don't waste the best news of all time on someone who won't even listen.

SMART TIPS!

Mix It Up

Do you always eat the same snack after school? Then mix things up and make something new, like your own minipizzas. Keep your times with God fresh, too, by trying new things like writing a praise song, reading a new Christian book, or going on a prayer walk.

[9]Slaves should yield to their own masters at all times, trying to please them and not arguing with them. [10]They should not steal from them but should show their masters they can be fully trusted so that in everything they do they will make the teaching of God our Savior attractive.

[11]That is the way we should live, because God's grace that can save everyone has come. [12]It teaches us not to live against God nor to do the evil things the world wants to do. Instead, that grace teaches us to live in the present age in a wise and right way and in a way that shows we serve God. [13]We should live like that while we wait for our great hope and the coming of the glory of our great God and Savior Jesus Christ. [14]He gave himself for us so he might pay the price to free us from all evil and to make us pure people who belong only to him—people who are always wanting to do good deeds.

[15]Say these things and encourage the people and tell them what is wrong in their lives, with all authority. Do not let anyone treat you as if you were unimportant.

THE RIGHT WAY TO LIVE

3 Remind the believers to yield to the authority of rulers and government leaders, to obey them, to be ready to do good, [2]to speak no evil about anyone, to live in peace, and to be gentle and polite to all people.

[3]In the past we also were foolish. We did not obey, we were wrong, and we were slaves to many things our bodies wanted and enjoyed. We spent our lives doing evil and being jealous. People hated us, and we hated each other. [4]But when the kindness and love of God our Savior was shown, [5]he saved us because of his mercy. It was not because of good deeds we did to be right with him. He saved us through the washing that made us new people through the Holy Spirit. [6]God poured out richly upon us that Holy Spirit through Jesus Christ our Savior. [7]Being made right with God by his grace, we could have the hope of receiving the life that never ends.

[8]This teaching is true, and I want you to be sure the people understand these things. Then those who believe in God will be careful to use their lives for doing good. These things are good and will help everyone.

[9]But stay away from those who have foolish arguments and talk about useless family histories and argue and quarrel about the law. Those things are worth nothing and will not help anyone. [10]After a first and second warning, avoid someone who causes arguments. [11]You can know that such people are evil and sinful; their own sins prove them wrong.

SOME THINGS TO REMEMBER

[12]When I send Artemas or Tychicus to you, make every effort to come to me at Nicopolis, because I have decided to stay there this winter. [13]Do all you can to help Zenas the lawyer and Apollos on their journey so that they have everything they need. [14]Our people must learn to use their lives for doing good deeds to provide what is necessary so that their lives will not be useless.

[15]All who are with me greet you. Greet those who love us in the faith.

Grace be with you all.

dare to do

1 Thessalonians 5:16
Read It: Be joyful all the time.
Do It: It sounds crazy, but God wouldn't command it if it weren't possible. Ask him for joy even in tough situations.

1 Thessalonians 5:17
Read It: Pray all the time.
Do It: Even when you're not actively praying, keep turning your thoughts and heart back toward God. Remember, a prayer can be as quick as, "Lord, help me!"

1 Thessalonians 5:19
Read It: Don't keep the Holy Spirit from working.
Do It: Sin keeps the Holy Spirit from working in and through you. Ask him to show you what's blocking him in your life, and he will!

Philemon, Paul's shortest letter, was probably written from prison in Rome at the same time Paul wrote the letter to the Colossians.

It concerns a runaway slave named Onesimus and is addressed to his owner, a man named Philemon.

Onesimus had run away from his home in Colossae. He must have done some other bad things, too, because he winds up in prison, where he meets Paul. Onesimus also learns about Jesus in jail through Paul's preaching, and Onesimus becomes a Christian (verse 10).

PHILEMON

After Onesimus does his time and is released, Paul urges him to go back to his master and confess his crimes. This is very risky because Roman law allowed masters to put runaway slaves to death if they were caught.

Do you believe in coincidences? Just wait till you find out "the rest of the story." Philemon—the man who holds Onesimus's life in his hands—is one of Paul's best friends!

So does Philemon listen to Paul and forgive Onesimus? Does he pardon his slave and accept him back as a brother in Christ? Or does he have Onesimus executed on the spot?

As you read this letter, put yourself in Philemon's sandals. What would you do?

1 Timothy 4:7
Read It: Don't listen to ungodly stories.
Do It: Don't fall for stories about ghosts and magic. It's all part of Satan's attempts to confuse the truth.

1 Timothy 4:12
Read It: Even though you are young, you can be an example to everyone.
Do It: Become a leader in your youth group and show others how to have a strong faith.

1 Timothy 5:1
Read It: If you have a complaint against someone, treat him with respect.
Do It: Don't be a brat! Show older people you respect them by sharing your concerns calmly and peacefully.

[1]From Paul, a prisoner of Christ Jesus, and from Timothy, our brother.

To Philemon, our dear friend and worker with us; [2]to Apphia, our sister; to Archippus, a worker with us; and to the church that meets in your home:

[3]Grace and peace to you from God our Father and the Lord Jesus Christ.

PHILEMON'S LOVE AND FAITH

[4]I always thank my God when I mention you in my prayers, [5]because I hear about the love you have for all God's holy people and the faith you have in the Lord Jesus. [6]I pray that the faith you share may make you understand every blessing we have in Christ. [7]I have great joy and comfort, my brother, because the love you have shown to God's people has refreshed them.

ACCEPT ONESIMUS AS A BROTHER

[8]So, in Christ, I could be bold and order you to do what is right. [9]But because I love you, I am pleading with you instead. I, Paul, an old man now and also a prisoner for Christ Jesus, [10]am pleading with you for my child Onesimus, who became my child while I was in prison. [11]In the past he was useless to you, but now he has become useful for both you and me.

[12]I am sending him back to you, and with him I am sending my own heart. [13]I wanted to keep him with me so that in your place he might help me while I am in prison for the Good News. [14]But I did not want to do anything without asking you first so that any good you do for me will be because you want to do it, not because I forced you. [15]Maybe Onesimus was separated from you for a short time so you could have him back forever— [16]no longer as a slave, but better than a slave, as a loved brother. I love him very much, but you will love him even more, both as a person and as a believer in the Lord.

[17]So if you consider me your partner, welcome Onesimus as you would welcome me.

Q: My cousin told me about some bad stuff going on in her family. She asked me to keep it a secret. Should I tell my parents?

A: Ask God for wisdom and pray for your cousin. Encourage her to talk with an adult who can help her. If keeping it a secret will cause somebody to get hurt, you should tell your parents. Even if the truth is uncomfortable and embarrassing for your cousin's family, it's better to have it out in the open where it can be dealt with.

Q: What makes Jesus better than Buddha?

A: Buddha was a man who taught people to live in a "moral" way. He never claimed to be anything more than a man and now he's still dead. Jesus is the God of the universe who, because he loves us, became a man and allowed himself to be killed as the perfect sacrifice for sin (1 Corinthians 15:3). Jesus came back from the dead and made a way for us to defeat death, as well (Acts 2:24). Buddha was a good moral teacher. But Jesus is the Savior who died out of love for the world (John 3:16) and lives on.

Q: If I'm angry with someone, does it mean I have to forgive him?

A: Yes. God has forgiven you for many wrong things that he has every right to be angry about. You must be willing to forgive others in the same way that God forgives you. Jesus said that holding a grudge against somebody and not forgiving him is very serious (Matthew 6:14–15).

Ask for Advice

Did you know that you never really experience anything new? Someone else has been there before. If you're struggling with a spiritual question or problem, there's certainly someone you know who's been through it, too—the worst thing is not asking.

[18]If he has done anything wrong to you or if he owes you anything, charge that to me. [19]I, Paul, am writing this with my own hand. I will pay it back, and I will say nothing about what you owe me for your own life. [20]So, my brother, I ask that you do this for me in the Lord: Refresh my heart in Christ. [21]I write this letter, knowing that you will do what I ask you and even more.

[22]One more thing—prepare a room for me in which to stay, because I hope God will answer your prayers and I will be able to come to you.

FINAL GREETINGS

[23]Epaphras, a prisoner with me for Christ Jesus, sends greetings to you. [24]And also Mark, Aristarchus, Demas, and Luke, workers together with me, send greetings.

[25]The grace of our Lord Jesus Christ be with your spirit.

We don't know who wrote this letter to the Hebrews (another word for "Jews").

Whoever did wanted to help Jewish Christians understand that Jesus Christ was the *Messiah*, the "Promised One" they had been expecting.

The Old Testament laws that were so important to the Jews had ended. Jesus has made a New Testament and sealed it with his blood. Gone are the laws, the priests, the Temple, and the animal sacrifices. Jesus has made them all unnecessary!

He has done away with the law. He has become our new high priest. He has offered the perfect sacrifice for our sins—himself.

Hebrews holds up Jesus like a diamond to the light and points out the different sides of his awesome glory. Jesus is:

- fully God and fully man
- superior to angels
- more important than Moses
- the Creator
- the undying high priest
- the spotless lamb—acceptable payment for our sins

The letter is also full of strong warnings for those who don't believe in Jesus (2:1–4; 3:7–4:13).

HEBREWS

The last chapters (10–13) encourage Christians to stick with it, even when times get tough. They contain many examples of faithful people who have gone before and who are now cheering us on from heaven (12:1–3).

"In the past God spoke to our ancestors through the prophets. . . . But now in these last days God has spoken to us through his Son" (1:1–2).

Listen up!

GOD SPOKE THROUGH HIS SON

1 In the past God spoke to our ancestors through the prophets many times and in many different ways. [2]But now in these last days God has spoken to us through his Son. God has chosen his Son to own all things, and through him he made the world. [3]The Son reflects the glory of God and shows exactly what God is like. He holds everything together with his powerful word. When the Son made people clean from their sins, he sat down at the right side of God, the Great One in heaven. [4]The Son became much greater than the angels, and God gave him a name that is much greater than theirs.

[5]This is because God never said to any of the angels,

"You are my Son.
Today I have become your Father."
Psalm 2:7

Nor did God say of any angel,

"I will be his Father,
and he will be my Son." *2 Samuel 7:14*

[6]And when God brings his firstborn Son into the world, he says,

"Let all God's angels worship him."[n]
Psalm 97:7

[7]This is what God said about the angels:

"God makes his angels become like winds.
He makes his servants become like
flames of fire." *Psalm 104:4*

[8]But God said this about his Son:

"God, your throne will last forever and ever.
You will rule your kingdom with fairness.
[9]You love right and hate evil,
so God has chosen you from among
your friends;
he has set you apart with much joy."
Psalm 45:6–7

[10]God also says,

"Lord, in the beginning you made the
earth,
and your hands made the skies.
[11]They will be destroyed, but you will
remain.
They will all wear out like clothes.
[12]You will fold them like a coat.
And, like clothes, you will change them.
But you never change,
and your life will never end."
Psalm 102:25–27

[13]And God never said this to an angel:

"Sit by me at my right side
until I put your enemies under your
control."[n] *Psalm 110:1*

[14]All the angels are spirits who serve God and are sent to help those who will receive salvation.

KNOW THE WORD!

CHRISTIAN

Christian means "little Christ." A Christian is a person who chooses to give his heart to Jesus and let him be in control of his life. Christians know that they can't please God on their own. They believe that Jesus died for their sins, came back to life, and lives in heaven. Becoming a Christian is as easy as saying yes to Jesus and admitting that you aren't good enough on your own. The benefits are huge—a relationship with God, a future in heaven, and God's promise that he will always take care of you.

Christians show their thankfulness for what Jesus did by sharing the Good News with other people. They also love and obey God and love other people. Are you a "little Christ"?

COOL!

Boneless Sharks

Sharks are the most efficient killers on the planet. They have no natural enemies—except humans—and are immune to all diseases.

Sharks have no bones; their skeletons are made of cartilage. But they have *lots* of teeth. A shark grows up to 30,000 teeth in a lifetime, replacing them about once a week.

How deadly are these fearsome hunters to humans? Not very. Dogs, pigs, and deer kill more people every year than sharks do.

Sharks are beautiful creatures in their own way. God didn't make them to terrify us. Just don't pick a fight with one!

1:6 "Let . . . him." These words are found in Deuteronomy 32:43 in the Septuagint, the Greek version of the Old Testament, and in a Hebrew copy among the Dead Sea Scrolls. **1:13 until . . . control** Literally, "until I make your enemies a footstool for your feet."

OUR SALVATION IS GREAT

2 So we must be more careful to follow what we were taught. Then we will not stray away from the truth. [2]The teaching God spoke through angels was shown to be true, and anyone who did not follow it or obey it received the punishment that was earned. [3]So surely we also will be punished if we ignore this great salvation. The Lord himself first told about this salvation, and those who heard him testified it was true. [4]God also testified to the truth of the message by using wonders, great signs, many kinds of miracles, and by giving people gifts through the Holy Spirit, just as he wanted.

CHRIST BECAME LIKE HUMANS

[5]God did not choose angels to be the rulers of the new world that was coming, which is what we have been talking about. [6]It is written in the Scriptures,

"Why are people even important to you?
Why do you take care of human beings?
[7]You made them a little lower than the angels
and crowned them with glory and honor."
[8]You put all things under their control."

Psalm 8:4–6

When God put everything under their control, there was nothing left that they did not rule. Still, we do not yet see them ruling over everything. [9]But we see Jesus, who for a short time was made lower than the angels. And now he is wearing a crown of glory and honor because he suffered and died. And by God's grace, he died for everyone.

[10]God is the One who made all things, and all things are for his glory. He wanted to have many children share his glory, so he made the One who leads people to salvation perfect through suffering.

[11]Jesus, who makes people holy, and those who are made holy are from the same family. So he is not ashamed to call them his brothers and sisters. [12]He says,

"Then, I will tell my brothers and sisters about you;
I will praise you in the public meeting."

Psalm 22:22

[13]He also says,

"I will trust in God." *Isaiah 8:17*

And he also says,

"I am here, and with me are the children God has given me." *Isaiah 8:18*

dare to do

2 Timothy 2:2
Read It: Teach others what you have learned from God.
Do It: Don't keep your faith to yourself. Talk to the other kids at church about what God is doing in your life!

2 Timothy 2:15
Read It: Prepare yourself to be approved by God.
Do It: Start your training! Life is a test and you must work out to be spiritually fit. This begins by knowing God's Word. As a first step, commit to reading the entire New Testament.

2 Timothy 2:22
Read It: Run away from bad youthful desires.
Do It: Kids get into all kinds of trouble. Don't join in when "everyone else" wants you to smoke, drink, steal, or vandalize. Run away!

Cool!

"Christian" Money

Americans are willing to spend a lot of money to be close to God. Religious books made up 7 percent of all book sales in 2004 (that's 3.7 billion dollars!).

Christian music sales topped $700 million in 2004. That's about 6 percent of all music sold; more than classical and jazz combined.

Yet no amount of religious books, Christian music, or even Bibles can make a person right with God. Jesus told a rich, young man to leave behind all of his money and things—so the man could follow him! (Mark 10:21–22).

⭐ **2:7 You . . . honor.** Some Greek copies continue, "You put them in charge of everything you made." See Psalm 8:6.

[8]Do not be stubborn as in the past
when you turned against God,
when you tested God in the desert.
[9]There your ancestors tried me and tested me
and saw the things I did for forty years.
[10]I was angry with them.
I said, 'They are not loyal to me
and have not understood my ways.'
[11]I was angry and made a promise,
'They will never enter my rest.' "[n]

Psalm 95:7–11

[12]So brothers and sisters, be careful that none of you has an evil, unbelieving heart that will turn you away from the living God. [13]But encourage each other every day while it is "today."[n] Help each other so none of you will become hardened because sin has tricked you. [14]We all share in Christ if we keep till the end the sure faith we had in the beginning. [15]This is what the Scripture says:

"Today listen to what he says.
Do not be stubborn as in the past
when you turned against God."

Psalm 95:7–8

[16]Who heard God's voice and was against him? It was all those people Moses led out of Egypt. [17]And with whom was God angry for forty years? He was angry with those who sinned, who died in the desert. [18]And to whom was God talking when he promised that they would never enter his rest? He was talking to those who did not obey him. [19]So we see they were not allowed to enter and have God's rest, because they did not believe.

4 Now, since God has left us the promise that we may enter his rest, let us be very careful so none of you will fail to enter. [2]The Good News was preached to us just as it was to them. But the teaching they heard did not

[14]Since these children are people with physical bodies, Jesus himself became like them. He did this so that, by dying, he could destroy the one who has the power of death— the devil— [15]and free those who were like slaves all their lives because of their fear of death. [16]Clearly, it is not angels that Jesus helps, but the people who are from Abraham.[n] [17]For this reason Jesus had to be made like his brothers and sisters in every way so he could be their merciful and faithful high priest in service to God. Then Jesus could die in their place to take away their sins. [18]And now he can help those who are tempted, because he himself suffered and was tempted.

JESUS IS GREATER THAN MOSES

3 So all of you holy brothers and sisters, who were called by God, think about Jesus, who was sent to us and is the high priest of our faith. [2]Jesus was faithful to God as Moses was in God's family. [3]Jesus has more honor than Moses, just as the builder of a house has more honor than the house itself. [4]Every house is built by someone, but the builder of everything is God himself. [5]Moses was faithful in God's family as a servant, and he told what God would say in the future. [6]But Christ is faithful as a Son over God's house. And we are God's house if we confidently maintain our hope.

WE MUST CONTINUE TO FOLLOW GOD

[7]So it is as the Holy Spirit says:
"Today listen to what he says.

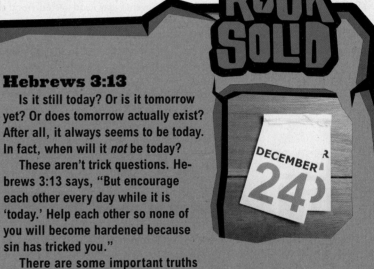

ROCK SOLID

Hebrews 3:13

Is it still today? Or is it tomorrow yet? Or does tomorrow actually exist? After all, it always seems to be today. In fact, when will it *not* be today?

These aren't trick questions. Hebrews 3:13 says, "But encourage each other every day while it is 'today.' Help each other so none of you will become hardened because sin has tricked you."

There are some important truths in this verse. First, we need to be encouraging each other as long as it's "today." When does "today" end? When Jesus comes back. Until then we should be encouraging each other every single day.

Second, the reason to encourage each other is that sin can harden us and trick us. Encouragement is there so that we don't get hardened or tricked by sin, so if encouragement is not there, that's exactly what will happen.

We have to be there for each other like a soldier covering his friend's back from the bullets of sin. We're getting shot at all the time. If we don't encourage each other to keep going and not to turn away from God, sin could get us. We're in the thick of battle, with bullets flying all over the place. If we're not watching out for each other, we're all going down.

2:16 Abraham Most respected ancestor of the Jews. Every Jew hoped to see Abraham.   **3:11 rest** A place of rest God promised to give his people.   **3:13 "today"** This word is taken from verse 7. It means that it is important to do these things now.

help them, because they heard it but did not accept it with faith." [3]We who have believed are able to enter and have God's rest. As God has said,

"I was angry and made a promise,
'They will never enter my rest.'"

Psalm 95:11

But God's work was finished from the time he made the world. [4]In the Scriptures he talked about the seventh day of the week: "And on the seventh day God rested from all his works."[n] [5]And again in the Scripture God said, "They will never enter my rest."

[6]It is still true that some people will enter God's rest, but those who first heard the way to be saved did not enter, because they did not obey. [7]So God planned another day, called "today." He spoke about that day through David a long time later in the same Scripture used before:

"Today listen to what he says.
Do not be stubborn." *Psalm 95:7–8*

[8]We know that Joshua[n] did not lead the people into that rest, because God spoke later about another day. [9]This shows that the rest[n] for God's people is still coming. [10]Anyone who enters God's rest will rest from his work as God did. [11]Let us try as hard as we can to enter God's rest so that no one will fail by following the example of those who refused to obey.

[12]God's word is alive and working and is sharper than a double-edged sword. It cuts all the way into us, where the soul and the spirit are joined, to the center of our joints and bones. And it judges the thoughts and feelings in our hearts. [13]Nothing in all the world can be hidden from God. Everything is clear and lies open before him, and to him we must explain the way we have lived.

JESUS IS OUR HIGH PRIEST

[14]Since we have a great high priest, Jesus the Son of God, who has gone into heaven, let us hold on to the faith we have. [15]For our high priest is able to understand our weaknesses. He was tempted in every way that we are, but he did not sin. [16]Let us, then, feel very sure that we can come

trustables

Hebrews 4:12

If you ask the average person what the Bible is, you'll probably get a less than satisfactory answer. Some will say "a historical book." Some will say "a poetic book." Some will say "a book of wonderful mythical tales." But only a few will know what it really is: a weapon!

Scripture says, "God's word is alive and working and is sharper than a double-edged sword. It cuts all the way into us, where the soul and the spirit are joined, to the center of our joints and bones. And it judges the thoughts and feelings in our hearts"

(Hebrews 4:12). Wow, that's quite a weapon! It sure doesn't sound like a book of poetry anymore!

It's possible to read the Bible without it having this effect. Some people aren't ready to hear the truth about themselves. But for those who are, scripture can tell you things about yourself you didn't think anyone else knew. It can strip you down to nothing and then show you how to begin again the right way! If you haven't already done so, ask God to reveal himself to you and to open your mind to the truth of his Word. Then read!

GET CONNECTED

LITTLE BROTHERS

Does your little brother bug you? Is he always hanging out with *your* friends and getting in the way of *your* fun? If your answer is "Yes!" here are two ideas that can help.

1. Think of three things you've enjoyed doing with your brother. Then the next time he starts hanging around, tell him you'd like to do those three things again soon, but ask if you can hang with just your friends this time.
2. Remind yourself that the best "friends" are the ones who become friends with your whole family—little brother included!

before God's throne where there is grace. There we can receive mercy and grace to help us when we need it.

5 Every high priest is chosen from among other people. He is given the work of going before God for them to offer gifts and sacrifices for sins. [2]Since he himself is weak, he is able to be gentle with those who do not understand and who are doing wrong things. [3]Because he is weak, the high priest must offer sacrifices for his own sins and also for the sins of the people.

[4]To be a high priest is an honor, but no one chooses himself for this work. He must be called by God as Aaron" was. [5]So also Christ did not choose himself to have the honor of being a high priest, but God chose him. God said to him,

"You are my Son.
  Today I have become your Father."

Psalm 2:7

[6]And in another Scripture God says,
"You are a priest forever,
  a priest like Melchizedek."" *Psalm 110:4*

[7]While Jesus lived on earth, he prayed to God and asked God for help. He prayed with loud cries and tears to the One who could save him from death, and his prayer was heard because he trusted God. [8]Even though Jesus was the Son of God, he learned obedience by what he suffered. [9]And because his obedience was perfect, he was able to give eternal salvation to all who obey him. [10]In this way God made Jesus a high priest, a priest like Melchizedek.

WARNING AGAINST FALLING AWAY

[11]We have much to say about this, but it is hard to explain because you are so slow to understand. [12]By now you should be teachers, but you need someone to teach you again the first lessons of God's message. You still need the teaching that is like milk. You are not ready for solid food. [13]Anyone who lives on milk is still a baby and knows nothing about right teaching. [14]But solid food is for those who are grown up. They are mature enough to know the difference between good and evil.

6 So let us go on to grown-up teaching. Let us not go back over the beginning lessons we learned about Christ. We should not again start teaching about faith in God and about turning away from those acts that lead to death. [2]We should not return to the teaching

Hebrews 5:13–14

When you were a baby, your mom picked you up and carried you into the kitchen where she set you in your high chair. She tied a bib around your neck and then fed you green goop from a jar.

Growing up makes a big difference in the food we eat! Babies get something mushy out of a jar, but as they get older, they get more "real" food. Pretty soon they learn to eat by themselves with a spoon. And once they've really grown up, they learn to prepare their own meals.

It would look ridiculous for a grown man to be sitting in a high chair with his mom feeding him baby food. But that is what some people's spiritual lives are like. Hebrews 5:13–14 says, "Anyone who lives on milk is still a baby and knows nothing about right teaching. But solid food is for those who are grown up. They are mature enough to know the difference between good and evil."

You don't eat baby food anymore; and as you grow as a Christian, you don't want to be spoon-fed God's Word. Your youth group leaders and other adults at your church want to help you grow spiritually; but if you're not opening your Bible and learning to feed yourself, you're not really growing up as a Christian.

5:4 Aaron Moses' brother and the first Jewish high priest. **5:6 Melchizedek** A priest and king who lived in the time of Abraham. (Read Genesis 14:17–24.)

"MAKE A DIFFERENCE"

Every day after school, ten-year-old Michael waited near his fence for Big John to walk by. And every day, Big John stopped to talk to Michael about superheroes, cartoons, toys, and other guys and girls in the neighborhood. But no matter how often Michael tried to talk to him about God, Big John always changed the subject. Sound familiar?

It's hard to be patient with someone who doesn't seem to care. Sometimes you just want to stop waiting by the fence. You want so much for your friend to accept Jesus Christ as his Savior, but you get frustrated by the way he always changes the subject. But if you don't give up, God might surprise you. That's what happened to Michael. One day Big John stopped by the fence and told him that he'd gone to a youth event in town and accepted Jesus Christ into his heart!

Maybe you have a friend or family member you've been praying for and talking to. Just keep waiting. Sometimes waiting makes all the difference!

about baptisms,"[n] about laying on of hands,"[n] about the raising of the dead and eternal judgment. [3]And we will go on to grown-up teaching if God allows.

[4]Some people cannot be brought back again to a changed life. They were once in God's light, and enjoyed heaven's gift, and shared in the Holy Spirit. [5]They found out how good God's word is, and they received the powers of his new world. [6]But they fell away from Christ. It is impossible to bring them back to a changed life again, because they are nailing the Son of God to a cross again and are shaming him in front of others.

[7]Some people are like land that gets plenty of rain. The land produces a good crop for those who work it, and it receives God's blessings. [8]Other people are like land that grows thorns and weeds and is worthless. It is about to be cursed by God and will be destroyed by fire.

[9]Dear friends, we are saying this to you, but we really expect better things from you that will lead to your salvation. [10]God is fair; he will not forget the work you did and the love you showed for him by helping his people. And he will remember that you are still helping them. [11]We want each of you to go on with the same hard work all your lives so you will surely get what you hope for. [12]We do not want you to become lazy. Be like those who through faith and patience will receive what God has promised.

[13]God made a promise to Abraham. And as there is no one greater than God, he used himself when he swore to Abraham, [14]saying, "I will surely bless you and give you many descendants."[n] [15]Abraham waited patiently for this to happen, and he received what God promised.

[16]People always use the name of someone greater than themselves when they swear. The oath proves that what they say is true, and this ends all arguing. [17]God wanted to prove that his promise was true to those who would get what he promised. And he wanted them to understand clearly that his purposes never change, so he made an oath. [18]These two things cannot change: God cannot lie when he makes a promise, and he cannot lie when he makes an oath. These things encourage us who came to God for safety. They give us strength to hold on to the hope we have been given. [19]We have this hope as an anchor for the soul, sure and strong. It enters behind the curtain in the Most Holy Place in heaven, [20]where Jesus has gone ahead of us and for us. He has become

the high priest forever, a priest like Melchizedek."

THE PRIEST MELCHIZEDEK

7 Melchizedek" was the king of Salem and a priest for God Most High. He met Abraham when Abraham was coming back after defeating the kings. When they met, Melchizedek blessed Abraham, [2]and Abraham gave him a tenth of everything he had brought back from the battle. First, Melchizedek's name means "king of goodness," and he is king

dare to do

Titus 2:7
Read It: Be a positive example to everyone by doing good deeds.
Do It: Offer to volunteer at church doing yard work or another important task. See if you can get your friends involved, too!

Titus 3:1
Read It: Obey the authorities.
Do It: Be cooperative and helpful to your teachers. Obey people who are in charge, like police officers or other leaders where you live.

Titus 3:2
Read It: Don't speak evil about others, but try to live in peace
Do It: If you hear someone "bad-mouthing" someone else, try pointing out the positive things about that person.

6:2 baptisms The word here may refer to Christian baptism, or it may refer to the Jewish ceremonial washings.   **6:2 laying on of hands** The laying on of hands had many purposes, including the giving of a blessing, power, or authority.   **6:14 "I . . . descendants."** Quotation from Genesis 22:17.   **6:20; 7:1 Melchizedek** A priest and king who lived in the time of Abraham. (Read Genesis 14:17–24.)

of Salem, which means "king of peace." ³No one knows who Melchizedek's father or mother was,ⁿ where he came from, when he was born, or when he died. Melchizedek is like the Son of God; he continues being a priest forever.

⁴You can see how great Melchizedek was. Abraham, the great father, gave him a tenth of everything that he won in battle. ⁵Now the law says that those in the tribe of Levi who become priests must collect a tenth from the people—their own people—even though the priests and the people are from the family of Abraham. ⁶Melchizedek was not from the tribe of Levi, but he collected a tenth from Abraham. And he blessed Abraham, the man who had God's promises. ⁷Now everyone knows that the more important person blesses the less important person. ⁸Priests receive a tenth, even though they are only men who live and then die. But Melchizedek, who received a tenth from Abraham, continues living, as the Scripture says. ⁹We might even say that Levi, who receives a tenth, also paid it when Abraham paid Melchizedek a tenth. ¹⁰Levi was not yet born, but he was in the body of his ancestor when Melchizedek met Abraham.

¹¹The people were given the lawⁿ concerning the system of priests from the tribe

Cool Sports Terms

1. **Gridiron**
2. **Sudden-death overtime**
3. **Shotgun formation**
4. **Blitz**
5. **Slam-dunk**
6. **Spike**
7. **Hail Mary**
8. **Alley-oop**
9. **Bogey**
10. **Slap shot**

of Levi, but they could not be made perfect through that system. So there was a need for another priest to come, a priest like Melchizedek, not Aaron. ¹²And when a different kind of priest comes, the law must be changed, too. ¹³We are saying these things about Christ, who belonged to a different tribe. No one from that tribe ever served as a priest at the altar. ¹⁴It is clear that our Lord came from the tribe of Judah, and Moses said nothing about priests belonging to that tribe.

JESUS IS LIKE MELCHIZEDEK

¹⁵And this becomes even more clear when we see that another priest comes who is like Melchizedek.ⁿ ¹⁶He was not made a priest by human rules and laws but through the power of his life, which continues forever. ¹⁷It is said about him,

"You are a priest forever,
a priest like Melchizedek."   *Psalm 110:4*

¹⁸The old rule is now set aside, because it was weak and useless. ¹⁹The law of Moses could not make anything perfect. But now a

---

Q: My grandpa is a nice guy, but he says that the Bible is just a bunch of made-up stories. I'm worried about where he'll go when he dies. Will God send him to hell?

A: Jesus clearly told us that he is the only way to eternal life (John 14:6). All of us are born with a natural desire to do wrong; and when we die, we'll simply get what we deserve. Through the death of Jesus, God has provided a way out of that. But if someone chooses to *not* follow Jesus, then he is choosing hell. Pray for your grandpa, and ask God to open his eyes to the truth.

Q: Is there anything wrong with having a lot of money?

A: No. Having a lot of money may be a sign that God has blessed a person's hard work. But being wealthy can be spiritually dangerous. When you have a lot of money, you may be tempted to trust money instead of God. Jesus warns us that it's hard for rich people to enter God's kingdom (Mark 10:25). So while being wealthy isn't wrong, it isn't as wonderful as the world would have us believe.

Q: Why do movie stars get treated like they're the most important people in the world?

A: If a visitor from another planet arrived here, he might think that our official religion was celebrity worship! Movie stars get a lot of attention because they are rich, attractive, and famous. People usually judge others by their looks, but God cares about what's inside a person's heart.

7:3 No . . . was Literally, "Melchizedek was without father, without mother, without genealogy."   **7:11 The . . . law** This refers to the people of Israel who were given the Law of Moses.   **7:15 Melchizedek** A priest and king who lived in the time of Abraham. (Read Genesis 14:17–24.)

SMART TIPS!

Take Pictures

Taking pictures is an awesome way to capture moments in your life. One of the best ways to use photos is to put them in a journal. You can make a "God journal" that is all about your relationship with God. You may even want to add prayers, favorite verses, and thoughts.

better hope has been given to us, and with this hope we can come near to God. [20]It is important that God did this with an oath. Others became priests without an oath, [21]but Christ became a priest with God's oath. God said:

"The Lord has made a promise
and will not change his mind.
'You are a priest forever.' "   *Psalm 110:4*

[22]This means that Jesus is the guarantee of a better agreement" from God to his people.

[23]When one of the other priests died, he could not continue being a priest. So there were many priests. [24]But because Jesus lives forever, he will never stop serving as priest. [25]So he is able always to save those who come to God through him because he always lives, asking God to help them.

[26]Jesus is the kind of high priest we need. He is holy, sinless, pure, not influenced by sinners, and he is raised above the heavens. [27]He is not like the other priests who had to offer sacrifices every day, first for their own sins, and then for the sins of the people. Christ offered his sacrifice only once and for all time when he offered himself. [28]The law chooses high priests who are people with weaknesses, but the word of God's oath came later than the law. It made God's Son to be the high priest, and that Son has been made perfect forever.

JESUS IS OUR HIGH PRIEST

8 Here is the point of what we are saying: We have a high priest who sits on the right side of God's throne in heaven. [2]Our high priest serves in the Most Holy Place, the true place of worship that was made by God, not by humans.

[3]Every high priest has the work of offering gifts and sacrifices to God. So our high priest must also offer something to God. [4]If our high priest were now living on earth, he would not be a priest, because there are already priests here who follow the law by offering gifts to God. [5]The work they do as priests is only a copy and a shadow of what is in heaven. This is why God warned Moses when he was ready to build the Holy Tent: "Be very careful to make everything by the plan I showed you on the mountain."" [6]But the priestly work that has been given to Jesus is much greater than the work that was given to the other priests. In the same way, the new agreement that Jesus brought from God to his people is much greater than the old one. And the new agreement is based on promises of better things.

[7]If there had been nothing wrong with the first agreement," there would have been no need for a second agreement. [8]But God found something wrong with his people. He says:"

"Look, the time is coming, says the Lord,
    when I will make a new agreement
with the people of Israel
    and the people of Judah.
[9]It will not be like the agreement
    I made with their ancestors
when I took them by the hand
    to bring them out of Egypt.
But they broke that agreement,
    and I turned away from them, says the
        Lord.
[10]This is the agreement I will make
    with the people of Israel at that time,
        says the Lord.
I will put my teachings in their minds
    and write them on their hearts.
I will be their God,
    and they will be my people.

COOL! Story Time

A *parable* is an earthly story with a heavenly meaning. It was Jesus' favorite way to teach. About forty of his parables are found in the Gospels (Matthew through John). Many are now world famous. (Can you name some?)

Jesus used stories because they are easier to remember than just ideas. Also, parables have a way of showing truth to the open-minded while hiding it from people who doubt or who don't believe.

Jesus' parables are like arrows. Each one is skillfully crafted to drive home a point. They prick people's minds in ways that make them think about how they should act.

7:22 agreement God gives a contract or agreement to his people. For the Jews, this agreement was the Law of Moses. But now God has given a better agreement to his people through Christ. **8:5 "Be . . . mountain."** Quotation from Exodus 25:40. **8:7 first agreement** The contract God gave the Jewish people when he gave them the Law of Moses. **8:8 But . . . says** Some Greek copies read "But God found something wrong and says to his people."

November

It's Election Day in the U.S. Pray that elected leaders will ask God to guide their decisions. **2**

3

Pray for a person of influence: it's entrepreneur P. Diddy's birthday. **4**

Write down one thing you're thankful for every day until Thanksgiving. **5**

If you hear a rumor, don't repeat it. Pray that God will comfort those affected by it. **6**

Pray for a person of influence: it's evangelist Billy Graham's birthday. **7**

Do you have a crazy family? Thank God for their weirdness on *"Chaos Never Dies Day."* **9**

Pray for a person of influence: it's actor Leonardo DiCaprio's birthday. **11**

Suggest pizza for dinner—it's *"Pizza with the Works Except Anchovies Day."* **12**

Read 1 Thessalonians 5:16–18. **13**

14

If your family doesn't recycle, set up a recycling system. **15**

Do the Web sites you're visiting honor God? If you're not sure, pray for God to make it clear. **16**

17

Look back on all the things you're thankful for. Praise God for blessing you! **18**

God calls us to love people, even when they don't live by his standards. Practice being non-judgmental. **19**

20

Pray for a person of influence: actress Scarlett Johansson celebrates her birthday today. **22**

Now that it's really getting cold, get your buddies together for an intense game of hockey. **24**

25

Wear 'em proudly! It's *"Freckle Pride Day."*

Read *The Adventures of Huck Finn*; its author (Mark Twain) was born on this day. **30**

[11]People will no longer have to teach their
neighbors and relatives
to know the Lord,
because all people will know me,
from the least to the most important.
[12]I will forgive them for the wicked things
they did,
and I will not remember their sins
anymore." *Jeremiah 31:31–34*
[13]God called this a new agreement, so he
has made the first agreement old. And anything that is old and worn out is ready to disappear.

THE OLD AGREEMENT

9 The first agreement[n] had rules for worship and a place on earth for worship.
[2]The Holy Tent was set up for this. The first
area in the Tent was called the Holy Place. In it
were the lamp and the table with the bread
that was made holy for God. [3]Behind the second curtain was a room called the Most Holy
Place. [4]In it was a golden altar for burning incense and the Ark covered with gold that held
the old agreement. Inside this Ark was a
golden jar of manna, Aaron's rod that once
grew leaves, and the stone tablets of the old
agreement. [5]Above the Ark were the creatures
that showed God's glory, whose wings reached
over the lid. But we cannot tell everything
about these things now.

[6]When everything in the Tent was made
ready in this way, the priests went into the first
room every day to worship. [7]But only the high
priest could go into the second room, and he
did that only once a year. He could never enter
the inner room without taking blood with him,
which he offered to God for himself and for
sins the people did without knowing they did
them. [8]The Holy Spirit uses this to show that
the way into the Most Holy Place was not
open while the system of the old Holy Tent
was still being used. [9]This is an example for the
present time. It shows that the gifts and sacrifices offered cannot make the conscience of
the worshiper perfect. [10]These gifts and sacrifices were only about food and drink and special washings. They were rules for the body, to
be followed until the time of God's new way.

THE NEW AGREEMENT

[11]But when Christ came as the high priest
of the good things we now have,[n] he entered
the greater and more perfect tent. It is not
made by humans and does not belong to this
world. [12]Christ entered the Most Holy Place
only once—and for all time. He did not take
with him the blood of goats and calves. His
sacrifice was his own blood, and by it he set us
free from sin forever. [13]The blood of goats and
bulls and the ashes of a cow are sprinkled on
the people who are unclean, and this makes
their bodies clean again. [14]How much more is
done by the blood of Christ. He offered himself through the eternal Spirit[n] as a perfect sac-

rifice to God. His blood will make our consciences pure from useless acts so we may
serve the living God.

[15]For this reason Christ brings a new
agreement from God to his people. Those
who are called by God can now receive the
blessings he has promised, blessings that will
last forever. They can have those things because Christ died so that the people who
lived under the first agreement could be set
free from sin.

[16]When there is a will,[n] it must be proven
that the one who wrote that will is dead. [17]A
will means nothing while the person is alive;
it can be used only after the person dies.
[18]This is why even the first agreement could
not begin without blood to show death.
[19]First, Moses told all the people every command in the law. Next he took the blood of
calves and mixed it with water. Then he used
red wool and a branch of the hyssop plant to
sprinkle it on the book of the law and on all
the people. [20]He said, "This is the blood that
begins the Agreement that God commanded you to obey."[n] [21]In the same way,

END TIMES

The *End Times* refer to the end of
this world as we know it—and the
beginning of a perfect new world.
Jesus will come back to take all
Christians to live with him in
heaven. He'll judge each person's
life—the good and the bad. The
End Times will be the end of evil,
Satan, and death. Satan and his
demons will be defeated once and
for all!

At that time, God will make a
new heaven and a new earth
where all of his people will live
forever. People have lots of questions about what will happen at the
end of time. Only God has all the
answers (but you can find out more
in the last book of the Bible, Revelation).

Hebrews 5:14
Read It: To understand the "deep" things about
God's Word, you need to practice the basics.
Do It: Give your faith a test. Jesus said "love
your enemy." Pick the person you have the
hardest time getting along with. Now go show
him God's love.

Hebrews 6:7
Read It: Land that produces fruit is what pleases
God.
Do It: Are you good soil or hard rock? God is trying
to create a harvest in your life. Why not start by
choosing one person in your life to invite to church!

Hebrews 6:19
Read It: God's promises make us secure in our position with him just as an
anchor secures a boat's position in calm or rough waters.
Do It: Memorize verses to help you when you find yourself in difficult situations.

Moses sprinkled the blood on the Holy Tent and over all the things used in worship. [22]The law says that almost everything must be made clean by blood, and sins cannot be forgiven without blood to show death.

CHRIST'S DEATH TAKES AWAY SINS

[23]So the copies of the real things in heaven had to be made clean by animal sacrifices. But the real things in heaven need much better sacrifices. [24]Christ did not go into the Most Holy Place made by humans, which is only a copy of the real one. He went into heaven itself and is there now before God to help us. [25]The high priest enters the Most Holy Place once every year with blood that is not his own. But Christ did not offer himself many times. [26]Then he would have had to suffer many times since the world was made. But Christ came only once and for all time at just the right time to take away all sin by sacrificing himself. [27]Just as everyone must die once and then be judged, [28]so Christ was offered as a sacrifice one time to take away the sins of many people. And he will come a second time, not to offer himself for sin, but to bring salvation to those who are waiting for him.

10 The law is only an unclear picture of the good things coming in the future; it is not the real thing. The people under the law offer the same sacrifices every year, but these sacrifices can never make perfect those who come near to worship God. [2]If the law could make them perfect, the sacrifices would have already stopped. The worshipers would be made clean, and they would no longer have a sense of sin. [3]But these sacrifices remind them of their sins every year, [4]because it is impossible for the blood of bulls and goats to take away sins.

[5]So when Christ came into the world, he said:

"You do not want sacrifices and offerings,
    but you have prepared a body for me.
[6]You do not ask for burnt offerings
    and offerings to take away sins.
[7]Then I said, 'Look, I have come.
    It is written about me in the book.
    God, I have come to do what you want.'"

Psalm 40:6–8

[8]In this Scripture he first said, "You do not want sacrifices and offerings. You do not ask for burnt offerings and offerings to take away sins." (These are all sacrifices that the law commands.) [9]Then he said, "Look, I have come to do what you want." God ends the first system of sacrifices so he can set up the new system. [10]And because of this, we are made holy through the sacrifice Christ made in his body once and for all time.

[11]Every day the priests stand and do their religious service, often offering the same sacrifices. Those sacrifices can never take away sins. [12]But after Christ offered one sacrifice for sins, forever, he sat down at the right side of God. [13]And now Christ waits there for his enemies to be put under his power. [14]With one sacrifice he made perfect forever those who are being made holy.

[15]The Holy Spirit also tells us about this. First he says:
[16]"This is the agreement" I will make
    with them at that time, says the Lord.
I will put my teachings in their hearts
    and write them on their minds."

Jeremiah 31:33

[17]Then he says:
"Their sins and the evil things they do—
    I will not remember anymore."

Jeremiah 31:34

[18]Now when these have been forgiven, there is no more need for a sacrifice for sins.

CONTINUE TO TRUST GOD

[19]So, brothers and sisters, we are completely free to enter the Most Holy Place without fear because of the blood of Jesus' death. [20]We can enter through a new and living way

DID YOU KNOW?

93% of kids watch TV every day.

Taylor KidsPulse 2004 Report. Taylor Research & Consulting Group.

ROCK SOLID

Hebrews 10:25

There's no such thing as private faith. Faith grows and develops best within a community.

Hebrews 10:25 says, "You should not stay way from the church meetings, as some are doing, but you should meet together and encourage each other." If you're not going to church, there's a good chance you don't have a strong spiritual life. You need other believers to build up your faith, and they need you. The more community you can get the better.

Get hooked up with the different gatherings at your church. Go to youth group, even if you don't know anyone. Friendships come in time. Go to the Sunday morning service, as well as to other activities that are offered.

Why? The rest of Hebrews 10:25 says, "Do this even more as you see the day coming." What day? The day Jesus tears open the skies and comes back. That will the most awesome day in history and we want to be ready.

Christianity is a community thing. God created us to need each other. Look for ways that you can get involved, and see what happens!

10:16 agreement God gives a contract or agreement to his people. For the Jews, this agreement was the Law of Moses. But now God has given a better agreement to his people through Christ.

that Jesus opened for us. It leads through the curtain—Christ's body. ²¹And since we have a great priest over God's house, ²²let us come near to God with a sincere heart and a sure faith, because we have been made free from a guilty conscience, and our bodies have been washed with pure water. ²³Let us hold firmly to the hope that we have confessed, because we can trust God to do what he promised.

²⁴Let us think about each other and help each other to show love and do good deeds. ²⁵You should not stay away from the church meetings, as some are doing, but you should meet together and encourage each other. Do this even more as you see the dayⁿ coming.

²⁶If we decide to go on sinning after we have learned the truth, there is no longer any sacrifice for sins. ²⁷There is nothing but fear in waiting for the judgment and the terrible fire that will destroy all those who live against God. ²⁸Anyone who refused to obey the law of Moses was found guilty from the proof given by two or three witnesses. He was put to death without mercy. ²⁹So what do you think should be done to those who do not respect the Son of God, who look at the blood of the agreement that made them holy as no different from others' blood, who insult the Spirit of God's grace? Surely they should have a much

worse punishment. ³⁰We know that God said, "I will punish those who do wrong; I will repay them."ⁿ And he also said, "The Lord will judge his people."ⁿ ³¹It is a terrible thing to fall into the hands of the living God.

³²Remember those days in the past when you first learned the truth. You had a hard struggle with many sufferings, but you continued strong. ³³Sometimes you were hurt and attacked before crowds of people, and sometimes you shared with those who were being treated that way. ³⁴You helped the prisoners. You even had joy when all that you owned was taken from you, because you knew you had something better and more lasting.

³⁵So do not lose the courage you had in the past, which has a great reward. ³⁶You must hold on, so you can do what God wants and receive what he has promised. ³⁷For in a very short time,

"The One who is coming will come
    and will not be delayed.
³⁸Those who are right with me
    will live by faith.
But if they turn back with fear,
    I will not be pleased with them."

Habakkuk 2:3–4

³⁹But we are not those who turn back and are lost. We are people who have faith and are saved.

WHAT IS FAITH?

11 Faith means being sure of the things we hope for and knowing that something is real even if we do not see it. ²Faith is the reason we remember great people who lived in the past.

³It is by faith we understand that the whole world was made by God's command so what we see was made by something that cannot be seen.

⁴It was by faith that Abel offered God a better sacrifice than Cain did. God said he was pleased with the gifts Abel offered and called Abel a good man because of his faith. Abel died, but through his faith he is still speaking.

⁵It was by faith that Enoch was taken to heaven so he would not die. He could not be found, because God had taken him away. Before he was taken, the Scripture says that he was a man who truly pleased God. ⁶Without faith no one can please God. Anyone who comes to God must believe that he is real and that he rewards those who truly want to find him.

⁷It was by faith that Noah heard God's warnings about things he could not yet see.

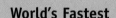

World's Fastest

When God told Job (an Old Testament character) about the animals he'd made, he pointed out a funny-looking bird and said, "When the ostrich gets up to run, it is so fast that it laughs at the horse and its rider" (Job 39:18).

An ostrich can run 43 miles an hour, but it's not the swiftest of God's creatures. Here are the world's other fastest flyers, swimmers, and runners:

Fastest	Miles Per Hour
Bird: peregrine falcon	200
Land animal: cheetah	70
Fish: sailfish	68
Insect: dragonfly	36
Marine mammal: blue whale	30
Human	21

10:25 day The day Christ will come to judge all people and take his people to live with him.   **10:30 "I . . . them."** Quotation from Deuteronomy 32:35.   **10:30 "The Lord . . . people."** Quotation from Deuteronomy 32:36; Psalm 135:14.

Paul
See Book of Acts.

Saul of Tarsus was a Jewish rabbi (teacher) who fought against the early Christians. He even helped put some of them to death. All that changed when Jesus Christ appeared to him. Saul the murderer became Paul the preacher (Acts 9).

The Book of Acts tells about Paul's long trips around the Roman Empire. He spoke without fear and did many miracles to prove his message was from God. In many cities, he was beaten or jailed. He suffered a lot yet was always thankful for the privilege of serving Jesus.

To stay in touch with the churches he started, Paul wrote them letters. Many of his letters are now part of the Bible.

Paul was beheaded in Rome almost two thousand years ago, but you can still learn from him by reading his letters (1 Corinthians through Philemon).

He obeyed God and built a large boat to save his family. By his faith, Noah showed that the world was wrong, and he became one of those who are made right with God through faith.

[8]It was by faith Abraham obeyed God's call to go to another place God promised to give him. He left his own country, not knowing where he was to go. [9]It was by faith that he lived like a foreigner in the country God promised to give him. He lived in tents with Isaac and Jacob, who had received that same promise from God. [10]Abraham was waiting for the city[n] that has real foundations—the city planned and built by God.

[11]He was too old to have children, and Sarah could not have children. It was by faith that Abraham was made able to become a father, because he trusted God to do what he had promised."

Q: Every Sunday I see a lot of money go into the offering plate. What does the pastor do with all of it?

A: It takes a lot of money to run a church, and your pastor doesn't get all the money. A group of people known as the church board, deacons, elders, or the vestry determines how your church spends its money. Just like employees in many organizations, your pastor receives a salary for his work. Some of the money is used for paying bills like keeping the church warm or cool, and some is used for missions and other good things. God wants people to give cheerfully (2 Corinthians 9:7). Decide a certain amount to give to God every week, and then give it with a smile!

Q: Why did God make some people handicapped?

A: Jesus' followers thought that God made people handicapped to punish sin. But Jesus straight-ened them out. The blind man who Jesus healed was born blind so that people could see God's power (John 9:2–3). Because we live in a "fallen" world, we all have things that go wrong with us—sometimes including handicaps. God takes those things and turns them into good for his glory—even though in some cases we'll only understand in heaven.

Q: Why do old people get so mad when your basketball goes into their yard?

A: Imagine that you spent a lot of money on plants and then spent hours carefully planting them in the ground. If a basketball bounced through and knocked a few over, and then the kid who owned the basketball stepped on a few more plants getting his ball back, it might make you a little irritated. Be careful with your ball, because whatever we do, God wants us to think of other people first (Philippians 2:3).

11:10 city The spiritual "city" where God's people live with him. Also called "the heavenly Jerusalem." (See Hebrews 12:22.) **11:11 It . . . promised.** Some Greek copies refer to Sarah's faith, rather than Abraham's.

"MAKE A DIFFERENCE"

Jason's youth pastor read, "Religion that God accepts as pure and without fault is this: caring for orphans or widows who need help" (James 1:27). Jason knew his church raised money for orphans in Nepal, but Jason was puzzled about the widow part.

"What's a widow?" he asked. Jason's youth pastor smiled and named a couple of women in the church whose husbands had died. "Oh!" Jason nodded. "What do we do for them?" His pastor's smile changed to a frown. "Not much, Jason. Not much at all."

Two months later, Jason and some of his church friends were standing next to a greenhouse on Mrs. Boeder's farm. "Her husband died and left her with this farm. Now she makes her living selling these flowers." Jason's pastor pointed through the mud-caked glass at the rows of plants.

Three hours later, the group was sitting under an old oak tree, devouring Mrs. Boeder's famous peach cobbler. "Well, you sure made a difference on those lonely, old windows," she smiled, "and on my peach cobbler, too!"

Making a difference in the life of a widow can be as simple and significant as washing a window. Think of some other ways you can help!

¹²This man was so old he was almost dead, but from him came as many descendants as there are stars in the sky. Like the sand on the seashore, they could not be counted.

¹³All these great people died in faith. They did not get the things that God promised his people, but they saw them coming far in the future and were glad. They said they were like visitors and strangers on earth. ¹⁴When people say such things, they show they are looking for a country that will be their own. ¹⁵If they had been thinking about the country they had left, they could have gone back. ¹⁶But they were waiting for a better country—a heavenly country. So God is not ashamed to be called their God, because he has prepared a city for them.

¹⁷It was by faith that Abraham, when God tested him, offered his son Isaac as a sacrifice. God made the promises to Abraham, but Abraham was ready to offer his own son as a sacrifice. ¹⁸God had said, "The descendants I promised you will be from Isaac."[n] ¹⁹Abraham believed that God could raise the dead, and really, it was as if Abraham got Isaac back from death.

²⁰It was by faith that Isaac blessed the future of Jacob and Esau. ²¹It was by faith that Jacob, as he was dying, blessed each one of Joseph's sons. Then he worshiped as he leaned on the top of his walking stick.

²²It was by faith that Joseph, while he was dying, spoke about the Israelites leaving Egypt and gave instructions about what to do with his body.

²³It was by faith that Moses' parents hid him for three months after he was born. They saw that Moses was a beautiful baby, and they were not afraid to disobey the king's order.

²⁴It was by faith that Moses, when he grew up, refused to be called the son of the king of Egypt's daughter. ²⁵He chose to suffer with God's people instead of enjoying sin for a short time. ²⁶He thought it was better to suffer for the Christ than to have all the treasures of Egypt, because he was looking for God's reward. ²⁷It was by faith that Moses left Egypt and was not afraid of the king's anger. Moses continued strong as if he could see the God that no one can see. ²⁸It was by faith that Moses prepared the Passover and spread the

ROCK SOLID

Hebrews 12:1

If you grew up in church, you've probably heard many of the Bible stories from long ago. You've heard about Noah and Moses and Jonah and Daniel more times than you can count. If you didn't grow up in church, you might wonder what the point is of reading about people who lived thousands of years ago in a far-off place. Their names are hard to pronounce and you don't expect you'll ever get swallowed by a giant fish!

But faith is faith no matter what century you live in. Our struggles and temptations are the same. And God is unchanging. We can learn from these people's mistakes and copy their successes. The Bible says, "We are surrounded by a great cloud of people whose lives tell us what faith means. So let us run the race that is before us and never give up" (Hebrews 12:1).

We are running the same race all believers have run since the beginning of time. If we want to finish strong, we have to learn how others have overcome the roadblocks that trip us up.

So learn all you can about the "heroes" of the faith. They weren't perfect. But they all teach us something unique about being human and about God's ways.

11:18 "The descendants . . . Isaac." Quotation from Genesis 21:12.

trustables

Hebrews 12:11

The best thing that can happen to you when you break the rules is to get caught. Sure, it's no fun staying after school to write "I won't throw things in class" a hundred times in a row. But it sure can be effective!

Discipline is important for us in our homes, in school, and in our spiritual lives. The Bible promises that we will be disciplined by God. Maybe he'll make you endure some tough times. Maybe he'll take something of yours away. Whatever he does, it's because he's trying to teach you something!

But you can be certain that God doesn't punish you for the fun of it. He has a goal in mind. Hebrews 12:11 says, "We do not enjoy being disciplined. It is painful at the time, but later, after we have learned from it, we have peace, because we start living in the right way." Once you start living right, you won't need the discipline any longer and you'll be a better person!

So don't be surprised when it seems like God's disciplining you. Just like your parents, he does it because he loves you. Ask him to help you be patient and learn from it!

---

blood on the doors so the one who brings death would not kill the firstborn sons of Israel.

[29]It was by faith that the people crossed the Red Sea as if it were dry land. But when the Egyptians tried it, they were drowned.

[30]It was by faith that the walls of Jericho fell after the people had marched around them for seven days.

[31]It was by faith that Rahab, the prostitute, welcomed the spies and was not killed with those who refused to obey God.

[32]Do I need to give more examples? I do not have time to tell you about Gideon, Barak, Samson, Jephthah, David, Samuel, and the prophets. [33]Through their faith they defeated kingdoms. They did what was right, received God's promises, and shut the mouths of lions. [34]They stopped great fires and were saved from being killed with swords. They were weak, and yet were made strong. They were powerful in battle and defeated other armies. [35]Women received their dead relatives raised back to life. Others were tortured and refused to accept their freedom so they could be raised from the dead to a better life. [36]Some were laughed at and beaten. Others were put in chains and thrown into prison. [37]They were stoned to death, they were cut in half,* and they were killed with swords. Some wore the skins of sheep and goats. They were poor,

abused, and treated badly. [38]The world was not good enough for them! They wandered in deserts and mountains, living in caves and holes in the earth.

[39]All these people are known for their faith, but none of them received what God had promised. [40]God planned to give us something better so that they would be made perfect, but only together with us.

FOLLOW JESUS' EXAMPLE

12 We are surrounded by a great cloud of people whose lives tell us what faith means. So let us run the race that is before us and never give up. We should remove from our lives anything that would get in the way and the sin that so easily holds us back. [2]Let us look only to Jesus, the One who began our faith and who makes it perfect. He suffered death on the cross. But he accepted the shame as if it were nothing because of the joy that God put before him. And now he is sitting at the right side of God's throne. [3]Think about Jesus' example. He held on while wicked people were doing evil things to him. So do not get tired and stop trying.

GOD IS LIKE A FATHER

[4]You are struggling against sin, but your struggles have not yet caused you to be killed.

[5]You have forgotten the encouraging words that call you his children:

"My child, don't think the Lord's discipline
    is worth nothing,
    and don't stop trying when he corrects
        you.
[6]The Lord disciplines those he loves,
    and he punishes everyone he accepts as
        his child."   *Proverbs 3:11–12*

[7]So hold on through your sufferings, because they are like a father's discipline. God is treating you as children. All children are disciplined by their fathers. [8]If you are never disciplined (and every child must be disciplined), you are not true children. [9]We have all had fathers here on earth who disciplined us, and we respected them. So it is even more important that we accept discipline from the Father of our spirits so we will have life. [10]Our fathers on earth disciplined us for a short time in the way they thought was best. But God disciplines us to help us, so we can become holy as he is. [11]We do not enjoy being disciplined. It is painful at the time, but later, after we have learned from it, we have peace, because we start living in the right way.

BE CAREFUL HOW YOU LIVE

[12]You have become weak, so make yourselves strong again. [13]Keep on the right path,

---

⭐ **11:37 they were cut in half** Some Greek copies also include, "they were tested."

so the weak will not stumble but rather be strengthened.

¹⁴Try to live in peace with all people, and try to live free from sin. Anyone whose life is not holy will never see the Lord. ¹⁵Be careful that no one fails to receive God's grace and begins to cause trouble among you. A person like that can ruin many of you. ¹⁶Be careful that no one takes part in sexual sin or is like Esau and never thinks about God. As the oldest son, Esau would have received everything from his father, but he sold all that for a single meal. ¹⁷You remember that after Esau did this, he wanted to get his father's blessing, but his father refused. Esau could find no way to change what he had done, even though he wanted the blessing so much that he cried.

¹⁸You have not come to a mountain that can be touched and that is burning with fire. You have not come to darkness, sadness, and storms. ¹⁹You have not come to the noise of a trumpet or to the sound of a voice like the one the people of Israel heard and begged not to hear another word. ²⁰They did not want to hear the command: "If anything, even an animal, touches the mountain, it must be put to death with stones."ⁿ ²¹What they saw was so terrible that Moses said, "I am shaking with fear."ⁿ

²²But you have come to Mount Zion,ⁿ to the city of the living God, the heavenly Jerusalem. You have come to thousands of angels gathered together with joy. ²³You have come to the meeting of God's firstbornⁿ children whose names are written in heaven. You have come to God, the judge of all people, and to the spirits of good people who have been made perfect. ²⁴You have come to Jesus, the One who brought the new agreement from God to his people, and you have come to the sprinkled bloodⁿ that has a better message than the blood of Abel.ⁿ

²⁵So be careful and do not refuse to listen when God speaks. Others refused to listen to him when he warned them on earth, and they did not escape. So it will be worse for us if we refuse to listen to God who warns us from heaven. ²⁶When he spoke before, his voice shook the earth, but now he has promised, "Once again I will shake not only the earth but also the heavens."ⁿ ²⁷The words "once again" clearly show us that everything that was made—things that can be shaken—will be destroyed. Only the things that cannot be shaken will remain.

²⁸So let us be thankful, because we have a kingdom that cannot be shaken. We should worship God in a way that pleases him with respect and fear, ²⁹because our God is like a fire that burns things up.

13 Keep on loving each other as brothers and sisters. ²Remember to welcome strangers, because some who have done this have welcomed angels without knowing it. ³Remember those who are in prison as if you were in prison with them. Remember those who are suffering as if you were suffering with them.

⁴Marriage should be honored by everyone, and husband and wife should keep their marriage pure. God will judge as guilty those who take part in sexual sins. ⁵Keep your lives free from the love of money, and be satisfied with what you have. God has said,

"I will never leave you;
　I will never abandon you."

Deuteronomy 31:6

⁶So we can be sure when we say,

"I will not be afraid, because the Lord is my
　helper.
People can't do anything to me."

Psalm 118:6

⁷Remember your leaders who taught God's message to you. Remember how they lived and died, and copy their faith. ⁸Jesus

---

Q: When I'm older I want to go skydiving and do other dangerous things. Does God care about things like that?

A: If you go skydiving, God would want you to use a parachute! There is nothing wrong with going on adventures unless you are selfish about it. Being reckless and putting your life in danger just so you can say "I did it" is not okay. Maybe God made you a risk taker for some special assignments to bring the Good News to others. Bungee jumping gives you a thirty-second rush. Facing danger so that someone can hear about Jesus will give you a rush that lasts forever.

Q: I don't understand a lot of things from the Bible. Will I still go to heaven?

A: Anybody who says he understands everything in the Bible is either mistaken or lying! The mystery of how Jesus was fully God and fully man is something we'll never figure out. There are lots of other mysteries, too. You don't have to understand everything to receive God's gift of life. Jesus made the Good News simple enough that even little kids can understand it: if you believe in him, you *will* go to heaven (John 3:16).

Q: Which athlete has the greatest comeback story?

A: It's a tough call, but Laura Wilkinson had an amazing comeback at the 2000 Olympics. She competed in the high dive event with a partially healed broken foot that still needed surgery. Coming from eighth place, she performed two perfect dives to win the gold medal. Afterward, she quoted Philippians 4:13, "I can do all things through Christ, because he gives me strength."

12:20 "If . . . stones." Quotation from Exodus 19:12–13. **12:21** "I . . . fear." Quotation from Deuteronomy 9:19. **12:22 Mount Zion** Another name for Jerusalem, here meaning the spiritual city of God's people. **12:23 firstborn** The first son born in a Jewish family was given the most important place in the family and received special blessings. All of God's children are like that. **12:24 sprinkled blood** The blood of Jesus' death. **12:24 Abel** The son of Adam and Eve, who was killed by his brother Cain (Genesis 4:8). **12:26** "Once . . . heavens." Quotation from Haggai 2:6, 21.

Christ is the same yesterday, today, and forever.

[9]Do not let all kinds of strange teachings lead you into the wrong way. Your hearts should be strengthened by God's grace, not by obeying rules about foods, which do not help those who obey them.

[10]We have a sacrifice, but the priests who serve in the Holy Tent cannot eat from it. [11]The high priest carries the blood of animals into the Most Holy Place where he offers this blood for sins. But the bodies of the animals are burned outside the camp. [12]So Jesus also suffered outside the city to make his people holy with his own blood. [13]So let us go to Jesus outside the camp, holding on as he did when we are abused.

[14]Here on earth we do not have a city that lasts forever, but we are looking for the city that we will have in the future. [15]So through Jesus let us always offer to God our sacrifice of praise, coming from lips that speak his name. [16]Do not forget to do good to others, and share with them, because such sacrifices please God.

[17]Obey your leaders and act under their authority. They are watching over you, because they are responsible for your souls. Obey them so that they will do this work with joy, not sadness. It will not help you to make their work hard.

[18]Pray for us. We are sure that we have a clear conscience, because we always want to do the right thing. [19]I especially beg you to pray so that God will send me back to you soon.

[20-21]I pray that the God of peace will give you every good thing you need so you can do what he wants. God raised from the dead our Lord Jesus, the Great Shepherd of the sheep, because of the blood of his death. His blood began the eternal agreement that God made with his people. I pray that God will do in us what pleases him, through Jesus Christ, and to him be glory forever and ever. Amen.

[22]My brothers and sisters, I beg you to listen patiently to this message I have written to encourage you, because it is not very long. [23]I want you to know that our brother Timothy has been let out of prison. If he arrives soon, we will both come to see you.

[24]Greet all your leaders and all of God's people. Those from Italy send greetings to you.

[25]Grace be with you all.

There are several men named James in the New Testament.

The one who wrote this letter was probably Jesus' younger brother (Matthew 13:55). James didn't believe Jesus was the Son of God until after Jesus rose from the dead.

James was a holy man who prayed so much he got the nickname "Camel-knees." He was a leader in the church at Jerusalem. He's writing to Jewish-Christians around the world (1:1), but what he says applies to all believers.

James has the passion of a stern father who wants his children to behave because he loves them. He tells them to expect hard times ("troubles") and to "do" the Word, not just listen to it (chapter 1). He encourages them to live their faith, not just talk about it (chapter 2). He warns them to watch what they say and to seek true wisdom (chapter 3).

James is on a roll now. In chapter 4, he scolds shallow Christians for their greed and lust. He blasts them for making foolish plans for the future without thinking about God.

In chapter 5, he warns rich people not to trust in money. Finally, he closes with a reminder of the power of prayer and the joy of serving the Lord.

There's a lot of "heat" in this letter because James wants us to take our faith as seriously as he does. Use it like a torch to check your own life.

1 From James, a servant of God and of the Lord Jesus Christ.

To all of God's people who are scattered everywhere in the world:

Greetings.

FAITH AND WISDOM

[2]My brothers and sisters, when you have many kinds of troubles, you should be full of joy, [3]because you know that these troubles test your faith, and this will give you patience. [4]Let your patience show itself perfectly in what you do. Then you will be perfect and complete and will have everything you need. [5]But if any of you needs wisdom, you should ask God for it. He is generous to everyone and will give you wisdom without criticizing you. [6]But when you ask God, you must believe and not doubt. Anyone who doubts is like a wave in the sea, blown up and down by the wind. [7-8]Such doubters are thinking two different things at the same time, and they cannot decide about anything they do. They should not think they will receive anything from the Lord.

TRUE RICHES

[9]Believers who are poor should take pride that God has made them spiritually rich. [10]Those who are rich should take pride that God has shown them that they are spiritually poor. The rich will die like a wild flower in the grass. [11]The sun rises with burning heat and dries up the plants. The flower falls off, and its beauty is gone. In the same way the rich will die while they are still taking care of business.

TEMPTATION IS NOT FROM GOD

[12]When people are tempted and still continue strong, they should be happy. After they have proved their faith, God will reward them with life forever. God promised this to all those who love him. [13]When people are tempted, they should not say, "God is tempting me." Evil cannot tempt God, and God himself does not tempt anyone. [14]But people are tempted when their own evil desire leads them away and traps them. [15]This desire leads to sin, and then the sin grows and brings death.

[16]My dear brothers and sisters, do not be fooled about this. [17]Every good action and every perfect gift is from God. These good gifts come down from the Creator of the sun, moon, and stars, who does not change like their shifting shadows. [18]God decided to give us life through the word of truth so we might be the most important of all the things he made.

LISTENING AND OBEYING

[19]My dear brothers and sisters, always be willing to listen and slow to speak. Do not become angry easily, [20]because anger will not

---

SMART TIPS!

Trustworthy Friends

You probably want friends that you can trust to not make fun of you or talk trash when you aren't around. Of course, all your friends will mess up now and then. But there's one friend who won't. Hang with God; he's the only one you can totally trust!

Q&A

Q: How much money should I get for my allowance?

A: If you get any spending money from your parents, you should be grateful. Lots of kids get nothing. Whatever your parents decide to give you is the right amount. God does not want getting more money to be the goal of your life. Instead, be content with whatever he's given you! (Hebrews 13:5).

Q: My cousin smokes pot. He says that it's not a big deal. Is he right?

A: No. People smoke pot because it gives them a temporary escape from life's problems and helps them feel good. But pretty soon they want to feel good all the time and the main goal of their lives becomes figuring out how to get the next joint. Eventually pot slows down your brain and could make you sick. God wants us to take our troubles to him instead (Titus 2:12).

Q: Is Jesus coming back really soon?

A: The followers asked Jesus when he would come back again. He told them about the events that would happen right before he returned (Matthew 24). There will be wars, famines, and earthquakes—all of which are happening today. But he also said that nobody will be able to predict his exact return, so we have to be ready all the time (Matthew 24:42–44). You can be ready by asking God to forgive your sins and make you his son.

Making a difference isn't always about leading a friend to Jesus Christ. Sometimes it's just about being yourself wherever nonbelievers are—even on the bench at a basketball game.

John was on the bench for the third game in a row when Nick sat down next to him. Nick, the best player on their middle school basketball team, had twisted his ankle and was out for the rest of the game.

"What are you doing this weekend?" Nick asked. "I'm going to a party with my dad— he'll probably get drunk and I'll end up watching videos all weekend."

"My dad's taking me to the sports warehouse after the game, then..."

"Does your dad always spend time with you?" Nick interrupted. "He's at every game, even though you sit on the bench."

John didn't lead Nick to Christ that day, but he did share with Nick a little of what it means to be a dad, just by telling Nick about his own family! God may use John's few short words to help Nick when he becomes a dad someday. Like John, you can make a difference for Jesus Christ— sometimes by just being there.

help you live the right kind of life God wants. [21]So put out of your life every evil thing and every kind of wrong. Then in gentleness accept God's teaching that is planted in your hearts, which can save you.

[22]Do what God's teaching says; when you only listen and do nothing, you are fooling yourselves. [23]Those who hear God's teaching and do nothing are like people who look at themselves in a mirror. [24]They see their faces and then go away and quickly forget what they looked like. [25]But the truly happy people are those who carefully study God's perfect law that makes people free, and they continue to study it. They do not forget what they heard, but they obey what God's teaching says. Those who do this will be made happy.

THE TRUE WAY TO WORSHIP GOD

[26]People who think they are religious but say things they should not say are just fooling themselves. Their "religion" is worth nothing. [27]Religion that God accepts as pure and without fault is this: caring for orphans or widows who need help, and keeping yourself free from the world's evil influence.

LOVE ALL PEOPLE

2 My dear brothers and sisters, as believers in our glorious Lord Jesus Christ, never think some people are more important than others. [2]Suppose someone comes into your church meeting wearing nice clothes and a gold ring. At the same time a poor person comes in wearing old, dirty clothes. [3]You show special attention to the one wearing nice clothes and say, "Please, sit here in this good seat." But you say to the poor person, "Stand over there," or, "Sit on the floor by my feet." [4]What are you doing? You are making some people more important than others, and with evil thoughts you are deciding that one person is better.

[5]Listen, my dear brothers and sisters! God chose the poor in the world to be rich with faith and to receive the kingdom God promised to those who love him. [6]But you show no respect to the poor. The rich are always trying to control your lives. They are the ones who take you to court. [7]And they are the ones who speak against Jesus, who owns you.

[8]This royal law is found in the Scriptures: "Love your neighbor as you love yourself."[n] If you obey this law, you are doing right. [9]But if you treat one person as being more important than another, you are sinning. You are guilty of breaking God's law. [10]A person who follows all of God's law but fails to obey even one com-

mand is guilty of breaking all the commands in that law. [11]The same God who said, "You must not be guilty of adultery,"[n] also said, "You must not murder anyone."[n] So if you do not take part in adultery but you murder someone, you are guilty of breaking all of God's law. [12]In everything you say and do, remember that you will be judged by the law that makes people free. [13]So you must show mercy to others, or God will not show mercy to you when he judges you. But the person who shows mercy can stand without fear at the judgment.

90% of boys receive about $90 on their birthdays!

http://www.youthography.com/aboutus/press/news/32.html

FAITH AND GOOD WORKS

[14]My brothers and sisters, if people say they have faith, but do nothing, their faith is worth nothing. Can faith like that save them? [15]A brother or sister in Christ might need clothes or food. [16]If you say to that person, "God be with you! I hope you stay warm and get plenty to eat," but you do not give what that person needs, your words are worth nothing. [17]In the same way, faith by itself—that does nothing—is dead.

[18]Someone might say, "You have faith, but I have deeds." Show me your faith without doing anything, and I will show you my faith by what I do. [19]You believe there is one God. Good! But the demons believe that, too, and they tremble with fear.

[20]You foolish person! Must you be shown that faith that does nothing is worth nothing? [21]Abraham, our ancestor, was made right with God by what he did when he offered his son Isaac on the altar. [22]So you see that Abraham's

2:8 "Love . . . yourself." Quotation from Leviticus 19:18. **2:11** "You . . . adultery." Quotation from Exodus 20:14 and Deuteronomy 5:18. **2:11** "You . . . anyone." Quotation from Exodus 20:13 and Deuteronomy 5:17.

faith and the things he did worked together. His faith was made perfect by what he did. [23]This shows the full meaning of the Scripture that says: "Abraham believed God, and God accepted Abraham's faith, and that faith made him right with God."[n] And Abraham was called God's friend."[n] [24]So you see that people are made right with God by what they do, not by faith only.

[25]Another example is Rahab, a prostitute, who was made right with God by something she did. She welcomed the spies into her home and helped them escape by a different road.

[26]Just as a person's body that does not have a spirit is dead, so faith that does nothing is dead!

CONTROLLING THE THINGS WE SAY

3 My brothers and sisters, not many of you should become teachers, because you know that we who teach will be judged more strictly. [2]We all make many mistakes. If people never said anything wrong, they would be perfect and able to control their entire selves, too. [3]When we put bits into the mouths of horses to make them obey us, we can control their whole bodies. [4]Also a ship is very big, and it is pushed by strong winds. But a very small rudder controls that big ship, making it go wherever the pilot wants. [5]It is the same with the tongue. It is a small part of the body, but it brags about great things.

A big forest fire can be started with only a little flame. [6]And the tongue is like a

James 5:7
Read It: Be patient for the return of Christ.
Do It: You don't know when Jesus will return, so do all that you can to bring people to faith in Jesus Christ until he does!

James 5:12
Read It: Don't make promises by swearing on things like the Bible, to God, or on someone's grave.
Do It: Your word alone should be strong and trustworthy. Make a promise by saying "yes" or "no."

James 5:15
Read It: Prayer can make sick people well.
Do It: Visit the hospital sometime and pray for the patients there. You just may help heal someone!

fire. It is a whole world of evil among the parts of our bodies. The tongue spreads its evil through the whole body. The tongue is set on fire by hell, and it starts a fire that influences all of life. [7]People can tame every kind of wild animal, bird, reptile, and fish, and they have tamed them, [8]but no one can tame the tongue. It is wild and evil and full of deadly poison. [9]We use our tongues to praise our Lord and Father, but then we curse people, whom God made like himself. [10]Praises and curses come from the same mouth! My brothers and sisters, this should not happen. [11]Do good and bad water flow from the same spring? [12]My brothers and sisters, can a fig tree make olives, or can a grapevine make figs? No! And a well full of salty water cannot give good water.

COOL!

Party Town

Corinth was an important Roman city in the first century. At its peak, it probably had 200,000 citizens, plus half a million slaves.

Corinth had lots of pagan temples and shrines. It even had a theater that could seat 18,000. The temple of Poseidon hosted the wild Isthmian Games every other year.

Corinth was the Las Vegas of its time. The apostle Paul started a church there because he wanted these people to know that God was far better than their wild times!

2:23 **"Abraham . . . God."** Quotation from Genesis 15:6.   2:23 **God's friend** These words about Abraham are found in 2 Chronicles 20:7 and Isaiah 41:8.

TRUE WISDOM

[13]Are there those among you who are truly wise and understanding? Then they should show it by living right and doing good things with a gentleness that comes from wisdom. [14]But if you are selfish and have bitter jealousy in your hearts, do not brag. Your bragging is a lie that hides the truth. [15]That kind of "wisdom" does not come from God but from the world. It is not spiritual; it is from the devil. [16]Where jealousy and selfishness are, there will be confusion and every kind of evil. [17]But the wisdom that comes from God is first of all pure, then peaceful, gentle, and easy to please. This wisdom is always ready to help those who are troubled and to do good for others. It is always fair and honest. [18]People who work for peace in a peaceful way plant a good crop of right-living.

GIVE YOURSELVES TO GOD

4 Do you know where your fights and arguments come from? They come from the selfish desires that war within you. [2]You want things, but you do not have them. So you are ready to kill and are jealous of other people, but you still cannot get what you want. So you argue and fight. You do not get what you want, because you do not ask God. [3]Or when you ask, you do not receive because the reason you ask is wrong. You want things so you can use them for your own pleasures.

[4]So, you are not loyal to God! You should know that loving the world is the same as hating God. Anyone who wants to be a friend of the world becomes God's enemy. [5]Do you think the Scripture means nothing that says, "The Spirit that God made to live in us wants us for himself alone"?[n] [6]But God gives us even more grace, as the Scripture says,

"God is against the proud,
but he gives grace to the humble."

Proverbs 3:34

[7]So give yourselves completely to God. Stand against the devil, and the devil will run from you. [8]Come near to God, and God will come near to you. You sinners, clean sin out of your lives. You who are trying to follow God and the world at the same time, make your thinking pure. [9]Be sad, cry, and weep! Change your laughter into crying and your joy into sadness. [10]Humble yourself in the Lord's presence, and he will honor you.

YOU ARE NOT THE JUDGE

[11]Brothers and sisters, do not tell evil lies about each other. If you speak against your fellow believers or judge them, you are judging and speaking against the law they follow. And when you are judging the law, you are no longer a follower of the law. You have become a judge. [12]God is the only Lawmaker and Judge. He is the only One who can save and destroy. So it is not right for you to judge your neighbor.

LET GOD PLAN YOUR LIFE

[13]Some of you say, "Today or tomorrow we will go to some city. We will stay there a year, do business, and make money." [14]But you do not know what will happen tomorrow! Your life is like a mist. You can see it for a short time, but then it goes away. [15]So you should say, "If the Lord wants, we will live and do this or that." [16]But now you are proud and you brag. All of this bragging is wrong. [17]Anyone who knows the right thing to do, but does not do it, is sinning.

A WARNING TO THE RICH

5 You rich people, listen! Cry and be very sad because of the troubles that are coming to you. [2]Your riches have rotted, and your clothes have been eaten by moths. [3]Your gold and silver have rusted, and that rust will be a proof that you were wrong. It will eat your bodies like fire. You saved your treasure for the last days. [4]The pay you did not give the workers who mowed your fields cries out against you, and the cries of the workers have been heard by the Lord All-Powerful. [5]Your life on earth was full of rich living and pleasing yourselves with everything you wanted. You made yourselves fat, like an animal ready to be killed. [6]You have judged guilty and then murdered innocent people, who were not against you.

BE PATIENT

[7]Brothers and sisters, be patient until the Lord comes again. A farmer patiently waits for his valuable crop to grow from the earth and for it to receive the autumn and spring rains. [8]You, too, must be patient. Do not give up hope, because the Lord is coming soon. [9]Brothers and sisters, do not complain against each other or you will be judged guilty. And the Judge is ready to come! [10]Brothers and sisters, follow the example of the prophets who

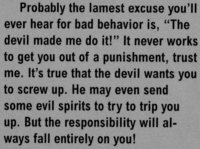

ROCK SOLID

James 4:1

Probably the lamest excuse you'll ever hear for bad behavior is, "The devil made me do it!" It never works to get you out of a punishment, trust me. It's true that the devil wants you to screw up. He may even send some evil spirits to try to trip you up. But the responsibility will always fall entirely on you!

We try to blame our sins on a lot of things, but the Bible makes it clear what the real cause is. It says that our sins "come from the selfish desires that war within you" (James 4:1). So it's not the devil. Even though he may tempt you, the choice to sin or not isn't his. And it's definitely not God's. It's yours. Deep within you are evil desires that want to take control. Even if you are a believer in Jesus and the Holy Spirit has changed you from within, you still have some of those old desires lurking around.

It's important that we take responsibility for our sin and that we don't point the finger at anyone else. When we own up to our sin and confess it, God wants to forgive us and help us do better the next time!

 4:5 "The Spirit . . . alone." These words may be from Exodus 20:5.

spoke for the Lord. They suffered many hard things, but they were patient. [11]We say they are happy because they did not give up. You have heard about Job's patience, and you know the Lord's purpose for him in the end. You know the Lord is full of mercy and is kind.

BE CAREFUL WHAT YOU SAY

[12]My brothers and sisters, above all, do not use an oath when you make a promise. Don't use the name of heaven, earth, or anything else to prove what you say. When you mean yes, say only yes, and when you mean no, say only no so you will not be judged guilty.

THE POWER OF PRAYER

[13]Anyone who is having troubles should pray. Anyone who is happy should sing praises. [14]Anyone who is sick should call the church's elders. They should pray for and pour oil on the person" in the name of the

DID YOU KNOW?

90% of middle and high school boys play sports.

Youth University Newsflash. Vol. 27.

Lord. [15]And the prayer that is said with faith will make the sick person well; the Lord will heal that person. And if the person has sinned, the sins will be forgiven. [16]Confess your sins to each other and pray for each other so God can heal you. When a believing person prays, great things happen. [17]Elijah was a human being just like us. He prayed that it would not rain, and it did not rain on the land for three and a half years! [18]Then Elijah prayed again, and the rain came down from the sky, and the land produced crops again.

SAVING A SOUL

[19]My brothers and sisters, if one of you wanders away from the truth, and someone helps that person come back, [20]remember this: Anyone who brings a sinner back from the wrong way will save that sinner's soul from death and will cause many sins to be forgiven.

trustables

James 4:7

Thanks to Hollywood, we all know how to fend off the most classic evil creatures of the night: vampires. They can be repelled by garlic, a crucifix, and, of course, holy water. But to eliminate them completely requires a stab in the heart with a wooden stake. All this would be very helpful information if there actually were such things as vampires!

So what about our *real* enemy, the devil? Scripture tells us he is prowling around like a lion trying to get us. Is there any known defense against this force of darkness? The Bible says, "Give yourselves completely to God. Stand against the devil, and the devil will run from you" (James 4:7).

You see, the devil cannot *make* you do anything. He requires cooperation. Therefore, the way you defeat him is by not believing his lies, not giving him any place in your life, and actually ordering him away from you! Just like Jesus said, "Go away from me, Satan!" (Matthew 16:23).

It sounds easy, but many people don't follow this simple rule. The devil makes things sound fun and exciting. He knows how to make us desire things. Always think twice before you take part in anything. Pray and ask God to direct you. Then, if you suspect you are being tempted by the devil, stand against it!

 5:14 pour oil on the person Oil was used in the name of the Lord as a sign that the person was now set apart for God's special attention and care.

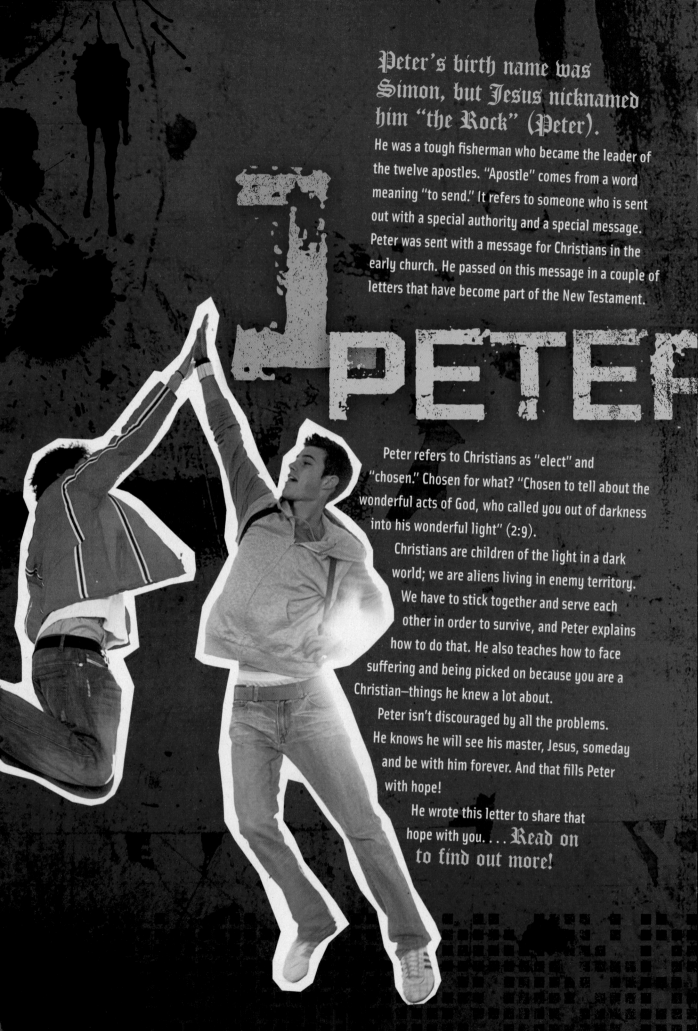

Peter's birth name was Simon, but Jesus nicknamed him "the Rock" (Peter).

He was a tough fisherman who became the leader of the twelve apostles. "Apostle" comes from a word meaning "to send." It refers to someone who is sent out with a special authority and a special message. Peter was sent with a message for Christians in the early church. He passed on this message in a couple of letters that have become part of the New Testament.

1 PETER

Peter refers to Christians as "elect" and "chosen." Chosen for what? "Chosen to tell about the wonderful acts of God, who called you out of darkness into his wonderful light" (2:9).

Christians are children of the light in a dark world; we are aliens living in enemy territory. We have to stick together and serve each other in order to survive, and Peter explains how to do that. He also teaches how to face suffering and being picked on because you are a Christian—things he knew a lot about.

Peter isn't discouraged by all the problems. He knows he will see his master, Jesus, someday and be with him forever. And that fills Peter with hope!

He wrote this letter to share that hope with you. . . . Read on to find out more!

1 From Peter, an apostle of Jesus Christ.
To God's chosen people who are away from their homes and are scattered all around Pontus, Galatia, Cappadocia, Asia, and Bithynia. [2]God planned long ago to choose you by making you his holy people, which is the Spirit's work. God wanted you to obey him and to be made clean by the blood of the death of Jesus Christ.

Grace and peace be yours more and more.

WE HAVE A LIVING HOPE

[3]Praise be to the God and Father of our Lord Jesus Christ. In God's great mercy he has caused us to be born again into a living hope, because Jesus Christ rose from the dead. [4]Now we hope for the blessings God has for his children. These blessings, which cannot be destroyed or be spoiled or lose their beauty, are kept in heaven for you. [5]God's power protects you through your faith until salvation is shown to you at the end of time. [6]This makes you very happy, even though now for a short time different kinds of troubles may make you sad. [7]These troubles come to prove that your faith is pure. This purity of faith is worth more than gold, which can be proved to be pure by fire but will ruin. But the purity of your faith will

22% of kids like to drink milk at dinner.

RAB Instant Background Report for Kids and Tweens Market.

bring you praise and glory and honor when Jesus Christ is shown to you. [8]You have not seen Christ, but still you love him. You cannot see him now, but you believe in him. So you are filled with a joy that cannot be explained, a joy full of glory. [9]And you are receiving the goal of your faith—the salvation of your souls.

[10]The prophets searched carefully and tried to learn about this salvation. They prophesied about the grace that was coming to you. [11]The Spirit of Christ was in the prophets, telling in advance about the sufferings of Christ and about the glory that would follow those sufferings. The prophets tried to learn about what the Spirit was showing them, when those things would happen, and what the world would be like at that time. [12]It was shown them that their service was not for themselves but for you, when they told about the truths you have now heard. Those who preached the Good News to you told you those things with the help of the Holy Spirit who was sent from heaven—things into which angels desire to look.

A CALL TO HOLY LIVING

[13]So prepare your minds for service and have self-control. All your hope should be for the gift of grace that will be yours when Jesus Christ is shown to you. [14]Now that you are obedient children of God do not live as you did in the past. You did not understand, so you

Q: Our youth leader said, "God doesn't have any grandchildren." What did he mean by that?

A: He meant that you can't get to heaven on your parents' faith. You have to believe in Jesus for yourself. The Jews living in Jesus' time thought that God would be happy with them just because they were descendants of Abraham. Jesus told them that their family history didn't count for anything (Luke 3:8). Don't rely on your parents' faith to get you right with God; it has to be your own faith.

Q: My grandpa says that money is the root of all evil. Is he exaggerating just a little?

A: He's quoting just a part of 1 Timothy 6:10 from an older version of the Bible. In the New Century Version, the translation used in *Explore,* this verse says, "The *love of* money causes all kinds of evil." People do all kinds of bad things to get

money. In this verse, Paul warned Timothy to not get caught up in a desire to get rich. He knew people who had given up their faith over it. Money can be used for many good things, but be careful that you don't start to love money more than you love God.

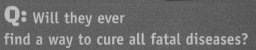

Q: Will they ever find a way to cure all fatal diseases?

A: No. It's kind of depressing, but each time scientists have found cures for old diseases, people start dying of new ones. Ever since the first man rebelled against God, all humans have faced physical death (Romans 5:12). So it's a good idea to know where we're going. Are you sure that you're going to heaven?

"MAKE A DIFFERENCE"

Making a difference for Jesus Christ can be really cool! Take one church's snowboard event. Over forty guys and girls help plan, advertise, pray, and clean donated equipment—all to have some fun and to share God's love.

Every November more than one hundred kids take four buses to a nearby ski area. Snowboarding, inner-tubing, and fun talks highlight the weekend. At the evening meeting, their pastor, Brian, tells the horrifying story of falling into an ice cave while snowboarding. He explains how God saved his life and then shares how God saved his life again—when he became a Christian.

The best part is when the large group breaks into smaller ones and some share how they came to Christ. Often others come to Christ while talking in the small groups, and more continue to attend events at the church and believe in Jesus later.

This group makes a difference through planning, praying, and inviting friends to an event they'll always remember—an event you and others like you can help put together. Ask your pastor if you could help plan an "outreach event" to "reach out" to your community by doing something fun and sharing about Jesus!

did the evil things you wanted. [15]But be holy in all you do, just as God, the One who called you, is holy. [16]It is written in the Scriptures: "You must be holy, because I am holy."[n]

[17]You pray to God and call him Father, and he judges each person's work equally. So while you are here on earth, you should live with respect for God. [18]You know that in the past you were living in a worthless way, a way passed down from the people who lived before you. But you were saved from that useless life. You were bought, not with something that ruins like gold or silver, [19]but with the precious blood of Christ, who was like a pure and perfect lamb. [20]Christ was chosen before the world was made, but he was shown to the world in these last times for your sake. [21]Through Christ you believe in God, who raised Christ from the dead and gave him glory. So your faith and your hope are in God.

[22]Now that your obedience to the truth has purified your souls, you can have true love for your Christian brothers and sisters. So love each other deeply with all your heart.[n] [23]You have been born again, and this new life did not come from something that dies, but from something that cannot die. You were born again through God's living message that continues forever. [24]The Scripture says,

"All people are like the grass,
and all their glory is like the flowers of
the field.
The grass dies and the flowers fall,

[25] but the word of the Lord will live
forever."
Isaiah 40:6–8

And this is the word that was preached to you.

JESUS IS THE LIVING STONE

2 So then, rid yourselves of all evil, all lying, hypocrisy, jealousy, and evil speech. [2]As newborn babies want milk, you should want the pure and simple teaching. By it you can mature in your salvation, [3]because you have already examined and seen how good the Lord is.

[4]Come to the Lord Jesus, the "stone"[n] that lives. The people of the world did not want this stone, but he was the stone God chose, and he was precious. [5]You also are like living stones, so let yourselves be used to build a spiritual temple—to be holy priests who offer spiritual sacrifices to God. He will accept those sacrifices through Jesus Christ. [6]The Scripture says:

"I will put a stone in the ground in
Jerusalem.
Everything will be built on this
important and precious rock.
Anyone who trusts in him
will never be disappointed."
Isaiah 28:16

[7]This stone is worth much to you who believe. But to the people who do not believe,

"the stone that the builders rejected
has become the cornerstone."
Psalm 118:22

GET CONNECTED

BIG BROTHERS

Does your brother boss you around? Does he make you feel like the last dog on an Eskimo sled team?

If you've felt bossed out of your brain, try this: Tell your parents you'd like to have a better relationship with your brother. Ask them to drop the two of you off at your brother's favorite ice-cream or fast-food place. Then tell your brother you'd like to be his friend and that you're taking him to his favorite place.

You won't be just his *little brother* anymore, and he'll be less likely to boss you around.

1:16 "You must be . . . holy." Quotation from Leviticus 11:45; 19:2; 20:7. **1:22 with all your heart** Some Greek copies read "with a pure heart." **2:4 "stone"** The most important stone in God's spiritual temple or house (his people).

peer pressure

Everywhere you look, there are people who seem to be in the "inside group" of cool people. Every person on earth wants to be accepted and liked by others; it's just natural! It feels good to be invited to go with others, or to be complimented by those we see as popular. And it feels bad to be excluded, ignored, or put down.

If you think peer pressure is just about drugs and alcohol—think again! You'll probably experience it in many ways, including the pressure to be popular. Because we all love to be included, popularity can seem important in order to be happy. But there are a few things you should think about before you try to get into that "inside group."

To gain popularity, some people change the way they dress and act. They could even treat others hurtfully in order to become popular. By acting as if they are better than everyone else, these people can confuse others into thinking that they actually *are* better.

People may accept you when you are pretending to be someone you are not—but it won't bring you happiness. True friends are the ones who accept you and love you for who you really are—not for the things you do to be popular.

If some of your friends begin changing themselves in order to become more popular, encourage them by reminding them that you like them just the way they are! And if you feel pressured to change, too, remember that you're in charge of yourself and your actions; you don't have to give in! Romans 12:2 says, "Do not be shaped by this world; instead be changed within by a new way of thinking. Then you will be able to decide what God wants for you; you will know what is good and pleasing to him and what is perfect." You will earn respect and true friends when you stick to what is right and don't give in to the pressure.

No matter who your friends are, or if you don't have many right now, remember that Jesus is the friend who will always be with you and accept you despite what others think. His opinion is what matters—and he thinks you're very cool!

1 Peter 3:15

If you are a believer in Jesus, you should be able to share your testimony. Don't worry, this has nothing to do with a judge and jury. A testimony is just the story of how you decided to put your faith in Jesus.

The Bible says, "Always be ready to answer everyone who asks you to explain about the hope you have" (1 Peter 3:15). You didn't realize there was going to be a test, did you? Well, don't get too concerned about it. If you've put your trust in Jesus Christ, there must have been reasons, right? Were there Bible verses that made a lot of sense to you? Did you see God answer prayer? Was there someone in your life who showed you what Christianity meant? What are your reasons now?

If you actively live your faith, people will ask questions. They'll want to know what led you to your beliefs. If all you can say is "I don't know," that won't seem very convincing. So think about it and even practice your answer so you can be prepared when that first question comes. Who knows, maybe you'll end up being part of someone else's testimony!

---

[8]Also, he is

"a stone that causes people to stumble,
    a rock that makes them fall."

Isaiah 8:14

They stumble because they do not obey what God says, which is what God planned to happen to them.

[9]But you are a chosen people, royal priests, a holy nation, a people for God's own possession. You were chosen to tell about the wonderful acts of God, who called you out of darkness into his wonderful light. [10]At one time you were not a people, but now you are God's people. In the past you had never received mercy, but now you have received God's mercy.

LIVE FOR GOD

[11]Dear friends, you are like foreigners and strangers in this world. I beg you to avoid the evil things your bodies want to do that fight against your soul. [12]People who do not believe are living all around you and might say that you are doing wrong. Live such good lives that they will see the good things you do and will give glory to God on the day when Christ comes again.

YIELD TO EVERY HUMAN AUTHORITY

[13]For the Lord's sake, yield to the people who have authority in this world: the king, who is the highest authority, [14]and the leaders who are sent by him to punish those who do wrong and to praise those who do right. [15]It is God's desire that by doing good you should stop foolish people from saying stupid things about you. [16]Live as free people, but do not use your freedom as an excuse to do evil. Live as servants of God. [17]Show respect for all people: Love the brothers and sisters of God's family, respect God, honor the king.

FOLLOW CHRIST'S EXAMPLE

[18]Slaves, yield to the authority of your masters with all respect, not only those who are good and kind, but also those who are dishonest. [19]A person might have to suffer even when it is unfair, but if he thinks of God and can stand the pain, God is pleased. [20]If you are beaten for doing wrong, there is no reason to praise you for being patient in your punishment. But if you suffer for doing good, and you are patient, then God is pleased. [21]This is what you were called to do, because Christ suffered for you and gave

---

you an example to follow. So you should do as he did.

[22]"He had never sinned,
    and he had never lied."   *Isaiah 53:9*

[23]People insulted Christ, but he did not insult them in return. Christ suffered, but he did not threaten. He let God, the One who judges rightly, take care of him. [24]Christ carried our sins in his body on the cross so we would stop living for sin and start living for what is right. And you are healed because of his wounds. [25]You were like sheep that wandered away, but now you have come back to the Shepherd and Overseer of your souls.

WIVES AND HUSBANDS

3 In the same way, you wives should yield to your husbands. Then, if some husbands do not obey God's teaching, they will be

1 Peter 2:1
Read It: Get rid of any mean thoughts or talk about someone else.
Do It: The next time someone starts ripping on someone else at school, stand up for him!

1 Peter 2:11
Read It: Don't take part in sinful behavior.
Do It: Kids often vandalize and destroy other people's property. Have the guts not to go along with the crowd! Stand up for what you believe.

1 Peter 2:16
Read It: Don't abuse the goodness of God by living badly and expecting forgiveness.
Do It: When you are tempted to sin, don't think, *Oh, it's OK, God will forgive me.* Remember, you will answer to God for what you do with your life.

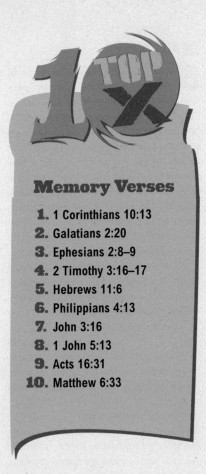

Memory Verses

1. 1 Corinthians 10:13
2. Galatians 2:20
3. Ephesians 2:8–9
4. 2 Timothy 3:16–17
5. Hebrews 11:6
6. Philippians 4:13
7. John 3:16
8. 1 John 5:13
9. Acts 16:31
10. Matthew 6:33

persuaded to believe without anyone's saying a word to them. They will be persuaded by the way their wives live. [2]Your husbands will see the pure lives you live with your respect for God. [3]It is not fancy hair, gold jewelry, or fine clothes that should make you beautiful. [4]No, your beauty should come from within you—the beauty of a gentle and quiet spirit that will never be destroyed and is very precious to God. [5]In this same way the holy women who lived long ago and followed God made themselves beautiful, yielding to their own husbands. [6]Sarah obeyed Abraham, her husband, and called him her master. And you women are true children of Sarah if you always do what is right and are not afraid.

[7]In the same way, you husbands should live with your wives in an understanding way, since they are weaker than you. But show them respect, because God gives them the same blessing he gives you—the grace that gives true life. Do this so that nothing will stop your prayers.

SUFFERING FOR DOING RIGHT

[8]Finally, all of you should be in agreement, understanding each other, loving each other as family, being kind and humble. [9]Do not do wrong to repay a wrong, and do not insult to repay an insult. But repay with a blessing, because you yourselves were called to do this so that you might receive a blessing. [10]The Scripture says,

"A person must do these things
to enjoy life and have many happy days.
He must not say evil things,
and he must not tell lies.
[11]He must stop doing evil and do good.
He must look for peace and work for it.
[12]The Lord sees the good people
and listens to their prayers.
But the Lord is against
those who do evil."   *Psalm 34:12–16*

[13]If you are trying hard to do good, no one can really hurt you. [14]But even if you suffer for doing right, you are blessed.

"Don't be afraid of what they fear;
do not dread those things."
                              Isaiah 8:12–13

[15]But respect Christ as the holy Lord in your hearts. Always be ready to answer everyone who asks you to explain about the hope you have, [16]but answer in a gentle way and with respect. Keep a clear conscience so that those who speak evil of your good life in Christ will be made ashamed. [17]It is better to suffer for doing good than for doing wrong if that is what God wants. [18]Christ himself suffered for sins once. He was not guilty, but he suffered for those who are guilty to bring you to God. His body was killed, but he was made alive in the spirit. [19]And in the spirit he went and preached to the spirits in prison [20]who refused to obey God long ago in the time of Noah. God was waiting patiently for them while Noah was building the boat. Only a few people—eight in all—were saved by water. [21]And that water is like baptism that now saves you—not the washing of dirt from the body, but the promise made to God from a good conscience. And this is because Jesus Christ was raised from the dead. [22]Now Jesus has gone into heaven and is at God's right side ruling over angels, authorities, and powers.

CHANGE YOUR LIVES

4 Since Christ suffered while he was in his body, strengthen yourselves with the same way of thinking Christ had. The person who has suffered in the body is finished with sin. [2]Strengthen yourselves so that you will live here on earth doing what God wants, not the evil things people want. [3]In the past you wasted too much time doing what nonbelievers enjoy. You were guilty of sexual sins, evil desires, drunkenness, wild and drunken parties, and hateful idol worship. [4]Nonbelievers think it is strange that you do not do the many wild and wasteful things they do, so they insult you. [5]But they will have to explain this to God, who is ready to judge the living and the dead. [6]For this reason the Good News was preached to those who are now dead. Even though they were judged like all people, the Good News was preached to them so they could live in the spirit as God lives.

USE GOD'S GIFTS WISELY

[7]The time is near when all things will end. So think clearly and control yourselves so you will be able to pray. [8]Most importantly, love each other deeply, because love will cause people to forgive each other for many sins. [9]Open your homes to each other, without complaining. [10]Each of you has received a gift to use to serve others. Be good servants of God's various gifts of grace. [11]Anyone who speaks should speak words from God. Anyone who serves should serve with the strength God gives so that in everything God will be praised through Jesus Christ. Power and glory belong to him forever and ever. Amen.

SUFFERING AS A CHRISTIAN

[12]My friends, do not be surprised at the terrible trouble which now comes to test

Turn Up the Noise

Want to give your movies some real *wow*!?! Ask your dad to help you plug your TV or DVD player into the stereo for some great sound. And if you really want to be heard, write an article that tells how you feel about God for a magazine or newspaper!

you. Do not think that something strange is happening to you. [13]But be happy that you are sharing in Christ's sufferings so that you will be happy and full of joy when Christ comes again in glory. [14]When people insult you because you follow Christ, you are blessed, because the glorious Spirit, the Spirit of God, is with you. [15]Do not suffer for murder, theft, or any other crime, nor because you trouble other people. [16]But if you suffer because you are a Christian, do not be ashamed. Praise God because you wear that name. [17]It is time for judgment to begin with God's family. And if that judging begins with us, what will happen to those people who do not obey the Good News of God?

[18]"If it is very hard for a good person to be saved,
the wicked person and the sinner will surely be lost!"[n]

[19]So those who suffer as God wants should trust their souls to the faithful Creator as they continue to do what is right.

DID YOU KNOW?

70% of boys have helped their parents learn to use electronics.

Youth University Newsflash. Vol. 21.

KNOW THE WORD!

ISRAEL

Israel is a modern-day country...but when the Bible talks about Israel, it means the Jews. The Old Testament tells the story of the Israelites, God's special chosen people. He had a unique relationship with this race of people. The Israelites are the ones who were saved from Egyptian slavery, received the Ten Commandments, and were taken care of by God himself!

Jesus was an Israelite (his family was Jewish). When he came, there was a big change! God wanted to have a special relationship with every person of every race.

The early Jewish Christians had a hard time believing that God would accept non-Jews (Gentiles) into his family. Yet because of Jesus, *anyone* can know God as long as they believe in his Son.

THE FLOCK OF GOD

5 Now I have something to say to the elders in your group. I also am an elder. I have seen Christ's sufferings, and I will share in the glory that will be shown to us. I beg you to [2]shepherd God's flock, for whom you are responsible. Watch over them because you want to, not because you are forced. That is how God wants it. Do it because you are happy to serve, not because you want money. [3]Do not be like a ruler over people you are responsible for, but be good examples to them. [4]Then when Christ, the Chief Shepherd, comes, you will get a glorious crown that will never lose its beauty.

[5]In the same way, younger people should be willing to be under older people. And all of you should be very humble with each other.

"God is against the proud,
but he gives grace to the humble."

Proverbs 3:34

[6]Be humble under God's powerful hand so he will lift you up when the right time comes. [7]Give all your worries to him, because he cares about you.

[8]Control yourselves and be careful! The devil, your enemy, goes around like a roaring lion looking for someone to eat. [9]Refuse to give in to him, by standing strong in your faith. You know that your Christian family all over the world is having the same kinds of suffering.

[10]And after you suffer for a short time, God, who gives all grace, will make everything right. He will make you strong and support you and keep you from falling. He called you to share in his glory in Christ, a glory that will continue forever. [11]All power is his forever and ever. Amen.

FINAL GREETINGS

[12]I wrote this short letter with the help of Silas, who I know is a faithful brother in Christ. I wrote to encourage you and to tell you that this is the true grace of God. Stand strong in that grace.

[13]The church in Babylon, who was chosen like you, sends you greetings. Mark, my son in Christ, also greets you. [14]Give each other a kiss of Christian love when you meet.

Peace to all of you who are in Christ.

Peter sent this second letter to the same Christians in Asia Minor he had written to before (2 Peter 3:1).

In 1 Peter, he encourages the church to stand firm against suffering and persecution. In 2 Peter, he deals with the threat of apostasy from inside. "Apostasy" means falling away from the faith.

Peter says the way to avoid being tricked by those who have fallen away is to know the truth. He uses the words "know" and "knowledge"—not head knowledge, but *heart* knowledge, which comes from a personal relationship with Jesus.

Such knowledge produces:
- grace and peace (1:2)
- fruitfulness (1:8)
- freedom from evil (2:20)
- spiritual growth (3:18)

2 PETER

In chapter 1, Peter explains what spiritual knowledge is all about. In chapter 2, he talks about the danger of apostasy and false teachers. In chapter 3, he looks ahead to the "Day of the Lord," which will bring doom to the ungodly (verses 1–7) and reward to the godly (verses 8–13).

Peter was probably in prison when he wrote these words. He expected to be killed any time. "I know I must soon leave this body, as our Lord Jesus Christ has shown me. I will try my best so that you may be able to remember these things even after I am gone" (1:14–15).

Peter is gone now, but his knowledge is still here. You're holding it in your hands. Now "hide it in your heart" by remembering what you read!

1 From Simon Peter, a servant and apostle of Jesus Christ.

To you who have received a faith as valuable as ours, because our God and Savior Jesus Christ does what is right.

²Grace and peace be given to you more and more, because you truly know God and Jesus our Lord.

GOD HAS GIVEN US BLESSINGS

³Jesus has the power of God, by which he has given us everything we need to live and to serve God. We have these things because we know him. Jesus called us by his glory and goodness. ⁴Through these he gave us the very great and precious promises. With these gifts you can share in God's nature, and the world will not ruin you with its evil desires.

⁵Because you have these blessings, do your best to add these things to your lives: to your faith, add goodness; and to your goodness, add knowledge; ⁶and to your knowledge, add self-control; and to your self-control, add patience; and to your patience, add service for God; ⁷and to your service for God, add kindness for your brothers and sisters in Christ; and to this kindness, add love. ⁸If all these things are in you and are growing, they will help you to be useful and productive in your knowledge of our Lord Jesus Christ. ⁹But anyone who does not have these things cannot see clearly. He is blind and has forgotten that he was made clean from his past sins.

SMART TIPS!

Learn from the Talented

The best way to really get good at something is to watch someone else who's already great at it. Watch what they do, study their moves, do what they do. This can really help you in your Christian life, too. Find someone you really respect—then watch and learn.

¹⁰My brothers and sisters, try hard to be certain that you really are called and chosen by God. If you do all these things, you will never fall. ¹¹And you will be given a very great welcome into the eternal kingdom of our Lord and Savior Jesus Christ.

¹²You know these things, and you are very strong in the truth, but I will always help you remember them. ¹³I think it is right for me to help you remember as long as I am in this body. ¹⁴I know I must soon leave this body, as our Lord Jesus Christ has shown me. ¹⁵I will try my best so that you may be able to remember these things even after I am gone.

WE SAW CHRIST'S GLORY

¹⁶When we told you about the powerful coming of our Lord Jesus Christ, we were not telling just clever stories that someone invented. But we saw the greatness of Jesus with our own eyes. ¹⁷Jesus heard the voice of God, the Greatest Glory, when he received honor and glory from God the Father. The voice said, "This is my Son, whom I love, and I am very pleased with him." ¹⁸We heard that voice from heaven while we were with Jesus on the holy mountain.

¹⁹This makes us more sure about the message the prophets gave. It is good for you to follow closely what they said as you would follow a light shining in a dark place, until the day

trustables

2 Peter 1:20–21

Sing along! "Jesus loves me this I know, for the Bible tells me so..." Right? Well, when you start to get older, things get a little more complicated.

Around about the time you hit junior high, you might start asking tough questions like "You say the Bible is the word of God, but it was written by men. So how can we believe that it's true?" It's an excellent question! It shows you are thinking seriously.

So, how *do* we know the Bible is true? The answer is found in 2 Peter 1:20–21. It says, "No prophecy in the Scriptures ever comes from the prophet's own interpretation. No prophecy ever came from what a person wanted to say, but people led by the Holy Spirit spoke words from God." So even though it was men who did the writing, the author was God himself!

Another amazing fact is that more than thirty-five people wrote the Bible over a span of 1,500 years. And yet God's plan and his nature are consistently described all through it! If men alone had done all that writing on their own, apart from God's leading, the Bible would be wildly random and inconsistent. Instead, if it's in the Bible, God said it—and you can believe it!

Thrill rides, animals, music, and food draw thousands to state fairs every year—among them kids who are hot and thirsty and ready for anything that's free!

"Would you like a cup of cool, free water?" young Christians shout above the roar of the rides. They always find others who are glad to step into the shade for a cold cup of refreshment. While there, the Christian youth ask the other kids if they'd like to hear about the water of eternal life. They hand the non-Christians a card and read through it with them.

Then they listen. "They listen to stories of broken homes and missing parents. They listen to lots of loneliness," says Ed, the volunteer who started the event. Many who read the cards bow their heads right there to ask Jesus to fill their empty hearts with his living water! It's the highlight of the year for the kids who participate. And it all starts over a simple cup of cool water.

You could hold the same kind of event or dream up one of your own—then you can make a difference the way these guys and girls do.

begins and the morning star rises in your hearts. [20]Most of all, you must understand this: No prophecy in the Scriptures ever comes from the prophet's own interpretation. [21]No prophecy ever came from what a person wanted to say, but people led by the Holy Spirit spoke words from God.

FALSE TEACHERS

2 There used to be false prophets among God's people, just as you will have some false teachers in your group. They will secretly teach things that are wrong—teachings that will cause people to be lost. They will even refuse to accept the Master, Jesus, who bought their freedom. So they will bring quick ruin on themselves. [2]Many will follow their evil ways and say evil things about the way of truth. [3]Those false teachers only want your money, so they will use you by telling you lies. Their judgment spoken against them long ago is still coming, and their ruin is certain.

[4]When angels sinned, God did not let them go free without punishment. He sent them to hell and put them in caves" of darkness where they are being held for judgment. [5]And God punished the world long ago when he brought a flood to the world that was full of people who were against him. But God saved Noah, who preached about being right with God, and seven other people with him. [6]And God also destroyed the evil cities of Sodom and Gomorrah" by burning them until they were ashes. He made those cities an example of what will happen to those who are against God. [7]But he saved Lot from those cities. Lot, a good man, was troubled because of the filthy lives of evil people. [8](Lot was a good man, but because he lived with evil people every day, his good heart was hurt by the evil things he saw and heard.) [9]So the Lord knows how to save those who serve him when troubles come. He will hold evil people and punish them, while waiting for the Judgment Day. [10]That punishment is especially for those who live by doing the evil things their sinful selves want and who hate authority.

These false teachers are bold and do anything they want. They are not afraid to speak against the angels. [11]But even the angels, who are much stronger and more powerful than false teachers, do not accuse them with insults before" the Lord. [12]But these people speak against things they do not understand. They are like animals that act without thinking, animals born to be caught and killed. And, like animals, these false teachers will be destroyed. [13]They have caused many people to suffer, so

they themselves will suffer. That is their pay for what they have done. They take pleasure in openly doing evil, so they are like dirty spots and stains among you. They delight in deceiving you while eating meals with you. [14]Every time they look at a woman they want her, and their desire for sin is never satisfied. They lead weak people into the trap of sin, and they have taught their hearts to be greedy. God will punish them! [15]These false teachers left the right road and lost their way, following the way Balaam went. Balaam was the son of Beor, who loved being paid for doing wrong. [16]But a donkey, which cannot talk, told Balaam he was sinning. It spoke with a man's voice and stopped the prophet's crazy thinking.

[17]Those false teachers are like springs without water and clouds blown by a storm. A place in the blackest darkness has been kept

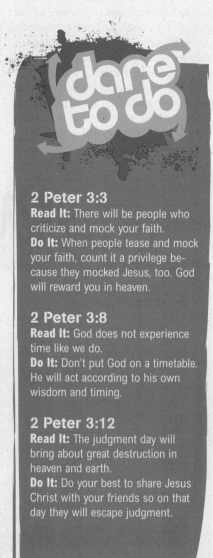

2 Peter 3:3
Read It: There will be people who criticize and mock your faith.
Do It: When people tease and mock your faith, count it a privilege because they mocked Jesus, too. God will reward you in heaven.

2 Peter 3:8
Read It: God does not experience time like we do.
Do It: Don't put God on a timetable. He will act according to his own wisdom and timing.

2 Peter 3:12
Read It: The judgment day will bring about great destruction in heaven and earth.
Do It: Do your best to share Jesus Christ with your friends so on that day they will escape judgment.

YOU SPEAK OUT!

Q: What is the grossest thing you've ever done?
A: "I like Squirtbeer floats—chocolate peanut butter ice cream and Diet Squirt." (Sam, 10)

Q: What makes you feel close to God?
A: "Going to Vacation Bible School." (Sam, 10)

Q: What does it mean to pray?
A: "It means that you thank God for his creations, thank him for how he's helped you in difficult times, confess to him the things you've done that are bad, and ask him to help you in the future." (Matthew, 11)

for them. [18] They brag with words that mean nothing. By their evil desires they lead people into the trap of sin—people who are just beginning to escape from others who live in error. [19] They promise them freedom, but they themselves are not free. They are slaves of things that will be destroyed. For people are slaves of anything that controls them. [20] They were made free from the evil in the world by knowing our Lord and Savior Jesus Christ. But if they return to evil things and those things control them, then it is worse for them than it was before. [21] Yes, it would be better for them to have never known the right way than to know it and to turn away from the holy teaching that was given to them. [22] What they did is like this true saying: "A dog goes back to what it has thrown up,"[n] and, "After a pig is washed, it goes back and rolls in the mud."

JESUS WILL COME AGAIN

3 My friends, this is the second letter I have written you to help your honest minds remember. [2] I want you to think about the words the holy prophets spoke in the past, and remember the command our Lord and Savior gave us through your apostles. [3] It is most important for you to understand what will happen in the last days. People will laugh at you. They will live doing the evil things they want to do. [4] They will say, "Jesus promised to come again. Where is he? Our fathers have died, but the world continues the way it has been since it was made." [5] But they do not want to remember what happened long ago. By the word of God heaven was made, and the earth was made from water and with water. [6] Then the world was flooded and destroyed with water. [7] And that same word of God is keeping heaven and earth that we now have in order to be destroyed by fire. They are being

Q&A

Q: I've heard people say that school isn't like the real world. What do they mean by that?

A: They mean that, believe it or not, a lot of the things that kids worry about in school turn out to be not very important in adult life. In the working world, the brand of shoes you wear or the kind of skateboard you have don't matter all that much. Also, when you're in school, your home, food, and clothes are paid for by somebody else. When you're an adult, it's all up to you—that's what they mean by the "real world."

Q: Why do kids get bored when there's nothing to do—but adults seem to like doing nothing?

A: As a kid, you get a lot of time each day to do your own thing. But adults have bosses, bills to pay, errands to run, and then they have to get din-

ner on the table. There's always something to do. Kids are always looking for something new to do to occupy their free time. Most adults are looking for the opposite: a few minutes when they don't have to *do* anything.

Q: I want to carry a knife to protect myself, but my dad won't let me. Why not?

A: Instead of protecting you, a knife is more likely to hurt you. It's also illegal for kids to carry weapons to school. If you regularly run into people who make you feel so unsafe that you want a knife, then you need to talk to your parents about your safety.

2:22 "A dog . . . up." Quotation from Proverbs 26:11.

kept for the Judgment Day and the destruction of all who are against God.

⁸But do not forget this one thing, dear friends: To the Lord one day is as a thousand years, and a thousand years is as one day. ⁹The Lord is not slow in doing what he promised—the way some people understand

ROCK SOLID

2 Peter 3:18

When you stand before the throne of the indescribably wonderful Creator of the universe—and look back over everything you have done—you don't want to regret your life. So how can you live in such a way that your life is totally full *now*, and was totally worth it *later*?

Here's one way: "grow in the grace and knowledge of our Lord and Savior Jesus Christ" (2 Peter 3:18). Growing as a Christian begins the minute you trust Jesus Christ and ask him to come into your life. And it never stops. You are never too young, too old, or too smart to grow as a Christian…and to help other Christians grow with you.

Don't just sit there—grow! Read your Bible every day, and go to church to learn how to stand strong in the Lord. Pray every day, and get together with a few Christian friends to pray for one another.

Helping other Christians grow is called *discipleship*. It's one of the most rewarding activities for any Christian. When you help people grow in the Lord, you feel great. And when you stand before the throne of God, you'll know you made your life a worthy investment for eternity.

slowness. But God is being patient with you. He does not want anyone to be lost, but he wants all people to change their hearts and lives.

¹⁰But the day of the Lord will come like a thief. The skies will disappear with a loud noise. Everything in them will be destroyed by fire, and the earth and everything in it will be exposed." ¹¹In that way everything will be destroyed. So what kind of people should you be? You should live holy lives and serve God, ¹²as you wait for and look forward to the coming of the day of God. When that day comes, the skies will be destroyed with fire, and everything in them will melt with heat. ¹³But God made a promise to us, and we are waiting for a new heaven and a new earth where goodness lives.

¹⁴Dear friends, since you are waiting for this to happen, do your best to be without sin and without fault. Try to be at peace with God. ¹⁵Remember that we are saved because our Lord is patient. Our dear brother Paul told you the same thing when he wrote to you with the wisdom that God gave him. ¹⁶He writes about this in all his letters. Some things in Paul's letters are hard to understand, and people who are ignorant and weak in faith explain these things falsely. They also falsely explain the other Scriptures, but they are destroying themselves by doing this.

¹⁷Dear friends, since you already know about this, be careful. Do not let those evil people lead you away by the wrong they do. Be careful so you will not fall from your strong faith. ¹⁸But grow in the grace and knowledge of our Lord and Savior Jesus Christ. Glory be to him now and forever! Amen.

The apostle John wrote the Gospel of John, the Book of Revelation, and three short letters. He had spent time with "God in the flesh" (Jesus), and he wrote to those who had not seen Jesus in person to "announce to you what we have seen and heard, because we want you also to have fellowship with us. Our fellowship is with God the Father and with his Son, Jesus Christ" (1:3).

Many false teachers had come along since Jesus had returned to heaven. They were saying things that weren't true and doing things that weren't right. John sets the record straight about what it means to "know" God.

God Is Light, and his true children walk in the light (1:5–2:28). This means obeying his commands and not being taken in by false teachers or "Antichrists."

God Is Righteous, and his faithful followers do what is right (2:29–4:6). This means taking care of

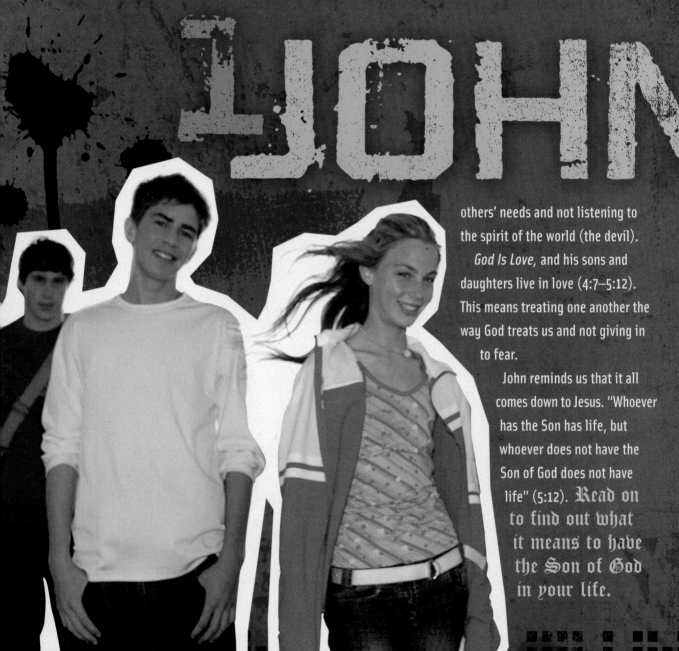

1 JOHN

others' needs and not listening to the spirit of the world (the devil).

God Is Love, and his sons and daughters live in love (4:7–5:12). This means treating one another the way God treats us and not giving in to fear.

John reminds us that it all comes down to Jesus. "Whoever has the Son has life, but whoever does not have the Son of God does not have life" (5:12). Read on to find out what it means to have the Son of God in your life.

1 We write you now about what has always existed, which we have heard, we have seen with our own eyes, we have looked at, and we have touched with our hands. We write to you about the Word[n] that gives life. [2]He who gives life was shown to us. We saw him and can give proof about it. And now we announce to you that he has life that continues forever. He was with God the Father and was shown to us. [3]We announce to you what we have seen and heard, because we want you also to have fellowship with us. Our fellowship is with God the Father and with his Son, Jesus Christ. [4]We write this to you so we may be full of joy.[n]

GOD FORGIVES OUR SINS

[5]Here is the message we have heard from Christ and now announce to you: God is light,[n] and in him there is no darkness at all. [6]So if we say we have fellowship with God, but we continue living in darkness, we are liars and do not follow the truth. [7]But if we live in the light, as God is in the light, we can share fellowship with each other. Then the blood of Jesus, God's Son, cleanses us from every sin.

DID YOU KNOW?

12% of kids think they will join the military someday.

RAB Instant Background Report for Kids and Tweens Market.

[8]If we say we have no sin, we are fooling ourselves, and the truth is not in us. [9]But if we confess our sins, he will forgive our sins, because we can trust God to do what is right. He will cleanse us from all the wrongs we have done. [10]If we say we have not sinned, we make God a liar, and we do not accept God's teaching.

JESUS IS OUR HELPER

2 My dear children, I write this letter to you so you will not sin. But if anyone does sin, we have a helper in the presence of the Father—Jesus Christ, the One who does what is right. [2]He died in our place to take away our sins, and not only our sins but the sins of all people.

[3]We can be sure that we know God if we obey his commands. [4]Anyone who says, "I know God," but does not obey God's commands is a liar, and the truth is not in that person. [5]But if someone obeys God's teaching, then in that person God's love has truly reached its goal. This is how we can be sure we are living in God: [6]Whoever says that he lives in God must live as Jesus lived.

THE COMMAND TO LOVE OTHERS

[7]My dear friends, I am not writing a new command to you but an old command you have had from the beginning. It is the teaching you have already heard. [8]But also I am writing a new command to you, and you can see its truth in Jesus and in you, because the darkness

Q: What should I do to get smart?

A: Being smart these days means knowing a lot of facts and having a lot of college degrees. There's nothing wrong with this but God wants you to aim for something better: being wise. Wisdom is knowing how to use your "smartness" for the most good. You don't have to go to school to get wisdom. You just have to be humble enough to know that you need it. Ask for wisdom from God—he promises to make you wise (James 1:5).

Q: My friends steal candy from the convenience store in our neighborhood. What should I do?

A: You should tell them it's wrong. God said so in the Ten Commandments (see Exodus 20:15 in the Old Testament). Stealing candy is the same as taking money from the store's owner. The best thing for your friends to do is to apologize to the store owner and offer to pay for what they've taken. If they confess to God, then he will take away their guilt (Ephesians 4:28). No matter what they choose to do, you can choose to do the right thing by not stealing.

Q: Is it okay to be angry?

A: Anger and other emotions are like the weather. You can't control when they show up. But you *can* control what you do about them. The Bible talks about a holy anger that comes from God. This is very rare; most of the time we're angry because someone or something has irritated us. Jesus said we should forgive other people as soon as we can (Matthew 5:22)—and that means we choose to not be angry anymore.

is passing away, and the true light is already shining.

[9] Anyone who says, "I am in the light,"[n] but hates a brother or sister, is still in the darkness. [10] Whoever loves a brother or sister lives in the light and will not cause anyone to stumble in his faith. [11] But whoever hates a brother or sister is in darkness, lives in darkness, and does not know where to go, because the darkness has made that person blind.

[12] I write to you, dear children,
because your sins are forgiven through Christ.
[13] I write to you, fathers,
because you know the One who existed from the beginning.
I write to you, young people,
because you have defeated the Evil One.
[14] I write to you, children,
because you know the Father.
I write to you, fathers,
because you know the One who existed from the beginning.
I write to you, young people,
because you are strong;
the teaching of God lives in you,
and you have defeated the Evil One.

[15] Do not love the world or the things in the world. If you love the world, the love of the Father is not in you. [16] These are the ways of the world: wanting to please our sinful selves, wanting the sinful things we see, and being too proud of what we have. None of these come from the Father, but all of them come from the world. [17] The world and everything that people want in it are passing away, but the person who does what God wants lives forever.

REJECT THE ENEMIES OF CHRIST

[18] My dear children, these are the last days. You have heard that the enemy of Christ is coming, and now many enemies of Christ are already here. This is how we know that these are the last days. [19] These enemies of Christ were in our fellowship, but they left us. They never really belonged to us; if they had been a part of us, they would have stayed with us. But they left, and this shows that none of them really belonged to us.

[20] You have the gift[n] that the Holy One gave you, so you all know the truth.[n] [21] I do not write to you because you do not know the truth but because you do know the truth. And you know that no lie comes from the truth.

[22] Who is the liar? It is the person who does not accept Jesus as the Christ. This is the enemy of Christ: the person who does not accept the Father and his Son. [23] Whoever does not accept the Son does not have the Father. But whoever confesses the Son has the Father, too.

[24] Be sure you continue to follow the teaching you heard from the beginning. If you continue to follow what you heard from the beginning, you will stay in the Son and in the Father. [25] And this is what the Son promised to us—life forever.

[26] I am writing this letter about those people who are trying to lead you the wrong way. [27] Christ gave you a special gift that is still in you, so you do not need any other teacher. His gift teaches you about everything, and it is true, not false. So continue to live in Christ, as his gift taught you.

[28] Yes, my dear children, live in him so that when Christ comes back, we can be without fear and not be ashamed in his presence. [29] Since you know that Christ is righteous, you know that all who do right are God's children.

WE ARE GOD'S CHILDREN

3 The Father has loved us so much that we are called children of God. And we really are his children. The reason the people in the world do not know us is that they have not known him. [2] Dear friends, now we are children of God, and we have not yet been shown what we will be in the future. But we know that

Beyond the Grave

According to Barna Research, here's what Americans believe about the afterlife:

★ 81 percent believe in life after death.
★ 76 percent believe in heaven—64 percent expect to go there.
★ 71 percent believe in hell—0.5 percent think they might go there.
★ 24 percent have no idea what will happen when they die.
★ 18 percent believe in reincarnation (coming back to life in another body or form).

Of those who expect to be in heaven:

★ 43 percent say it's because they've accepted Jesus as their Savior.
★ 15 percent say it's because they've tried to keep the Ten Commandments.
★ 15 percent say it's because they're good people.

Accepting Jesus as your Savior means that *you* will be in heaven after you die!

2:9 light Here, it is used as a symbol of God's goodness or truth.   **2:20 gift** This might mean the Holy Spirit, or it might mean teaching or truth as in verse 24.   **2:20 you . . . truth** Some Greek copies read "so you know all things."

dare to do

2 Peter 3:13
Read It: God promised us a new world where goodness rules.
Do It: Make a list of the things that will be better when we get to heaven and we don't sin anymore.

2 Peter 3:14
Read It: Since you're not living for this world, stay pure!
Do It: Strain your brain to live beyond the moment. Otherwise, you'll forget why you're on earth.

2 Peter 3:18
Read It: Grow into the grace and knowledge of Jesus.
Do It: Having a lot of conversations with God (we call it praying) will help you to grow spiritually.

when Christ comes again, we will be like him, because we will see him as he really is. ³Christ is pure, and all who have this hope in Christ keep themselves pure like Christ.

⁴The person who sins breaks God's law. Yes, sin is living against God's law. ⁵You know that Christ came to take away sins and that there is no sin in Christ. ⁶So anyone who lives in Christ does not go on sinning. Anyone who goes on sinning has never really understood Christ and has never known him.

⁷Dear children, do not let anyone lead you the wrong way. Christ is righteous. So to be like Christ a person must do what is right. ⁸The devil has been sinning since the beginning, so anyone who continues to sin belongs to the devil. The Son of God came for this purpose: to destroy the devil's work.

⁹Those who are God's children do not continue sinning, because the new life from God remains in them. They are not able to go on sinning, because they have become children of God. ¹⁰So we can see who God's children are and who the devil's children are: Those who do not do what is right are not God's children, and those who do not love their brothers and sisters are not God's children.

WE MUST LOVE EACH OTHER

¹¹This is the teaching you have heard from the beginning: We must love each other. ¹²Do not be like Cain who belonged to the Evil One and killed his brother. And why did he kill him? Because the things Cain did were evil, and the things his brother did were good.

¹³Brothers and sisters, do not be surprised when the people of the world hate you. ¹⁴We know we have left death and have come into life because we love each other. Whoever does not love is still dead. ¹⁵Everyone who hates a brother or sister is a murderer,ⁿ and you know that no murderers have eternal life in them. ¹⁶This is how we know what real love is: Jesus gave his life for us. So we should give our lives for our brothers and sisters. ¹⁷Suppose some-one has enough to live and sees a brother or sister in need, but does not help. Then God's love is not living in that person. ¹⁸My children, we should love people not only with words and talk, but by our actions and true caring.

¹⁹⁻²⁰This is the way we know that we belong to the way of truth. When our hearts make us feel guilty, we can still have peace before God. God is greater than our hearts, and he knows everything. ²¹My dear friends, if our hearts do not make us feel guilty, we can come without fear into God's presence. ²²And God gives us what we ask for because we obey God's commands and do what pleases him. ²³This is what God commands: that we believe in his Son, Jesus Christ, and that we love each other, just as he commanded. ²⁴The people who obey God's commands live in God, and God lives in them. We know that God lives in us because of the Spirit God gave us.

WARNING AGAINST FALSE TEACHERS

4 My dear friends, many false prophets have gone out into the world. So do

ROCK SOLID

1 John 4:20
One of the biggest challenges for guys your age is to getting along with siblings. Some fight so much they just stop trying to get along. They don't talk to each other and try to avoid any contact. It's a very sad situation and one that people should take very seriously.

Scripture says, "If people say, 'I love God,' but hate their brothers or sisters, they are liars. Those who do not love their brothers and sisters, whom they have seen, cannot love God, whom they have never seen" (1 John 4:20). If you've given up trying to love your siblings, then you'll never have the ability to love God!

Are your brothers or sisters really hard to be around? Do they bug the heck out of you? Just remember, you weren't exactly a perfect person when God chose to love you. He overlooked all your faults and made you his child. Can't you muster up the kindness to love your annoying siblings? When you can do that, your love for God will start to overflow.

3:15 Everyone . . . murderer If one person hates a brother or sister, then in the heart that person has killed that brother or sister. Jesus taught about this sin to his followers (Matthew 5:21–26).

COOL!

Busy Bees

God sometimes uses small things to do big jobs. Take bees for instance. They do a lot more than make honey; they pollinate most of the flowers, fruit trees, and crops in the world!

As many as 60,000 bees can live in one hive. A queen bee lays 1,500 eggs a day and lives up to two years. Worker bees—all females who can't lay eggs—work themselves to death within forty days by collecting pollen and nectar in the summer.

No matter how small you are, God can use you to do a big job for him!

not believe every spirit, but test the spirits to see if they are from God. [2] This is how you can know God's Spirit: Every spirit who confesses that Jesus Christ came to earth as a human is from God. [3] And every spirit who refuses to say this about Jesus is not from God. It is the spirit of the enemy of Christ, which you have heard is coming, and now he is already in the world.

[4] My dear children, you belong to God and have defeated them; because God's Spirit, who is in you, is greater than the devil, who is in the world. [5] And they belong to the world, so what they say is from the world, and the world listens to them. [6] But we belong to God, and those who know God listen to us. But those who are not from God do not listen to us. That is how we know the Spirit that is true and the spirit that is false.

LOVE COMES FROM GOD

[7] Dear friends, we should love each other, because love comes from God. Everyone who loves has become God's child and knows God.

trustables

1 John 5:14

It's true: the God of the universe likes to listen to you. Check out 1 John 5:14, which says, "And this is the boldness we have in God's presence: that if we ask God for anything that agrees with what he wants, he hears us." He's listening!

Praying is not like going to the principal's office when you've messed up. It's more like going to the most powerful being in the world who also happens to be your dad. Through Jesus' death and rising again, we are right with God. So we can pray to God with confidence. We don't have to worry about what we've done wrong.

When your birthday gets close, you make sure your parents know what you want. More than likely, they would prefer to get something for you that you really want. You are asking them to do something for you that *they* want to do. It's the same way with God. When we ask him to save people, we are asking him to do something he wants to do. He wants to do great things in our lives, and he wants us to ask him what we'd like him to do.

So let us pray boldly—asking God to do great things. He likes to hear—and answer—those kinds of prayers.

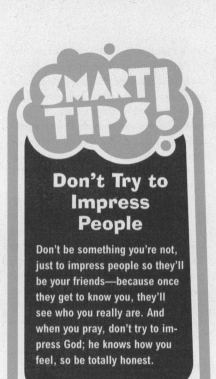

SMART TIPS!

Don't Try to Impress People

Don't be something you're not, just to impress people so they'll be your friends—because once they get to know you, they'll see who you really are. And when you pray, don't try to impress God; he knows how you feel, so be totally honest.

---

ers or sisters, they are liars. Those who do not love their brothers and sisters, whom they have seen, cannot love God, whom they have never seen. [21]And God gave us this command: Those who love God must also love their brothers and sisters.

FAITH IN THE SON OF GOD

5 Everyone who believes that Jesus is the Christ is God's child, and whoever loves the Father also loves the Father's children. [2]This is how we know we love God's children: when we love God and obey his commands. [3]Loving God means obeying his commands. And God's commands are not too hard for us, [4]because everyone who is a child of God conquers the world. And this is the victory that conquers the world—our faith. [5]So the one who conquers the world is the person who believes that Jesus is the Son of God.

[6]Jesus Christ is the One who came by water" and blood." He did not come by water only, but by water and blood. And the Spirit says that this is true, because the Spirit is the truth. [7]So there are three witnesses:" [8]the

---

[8]Whoever does not love does not know God, because God is love. [9]This is how God showed his love to us: He sent his one and only Son into the world so that we could have life through him. [10]This is what real love is: It is not our love for God; it is God's love for us. He sent his Son to die in our place to take away our sins.

[11]Dear friends, if God loved us that much we also should love each other. [12]No one has ever seen God, but if we love each other, God lives in us, and his love is made perfect in us.

[13]We know that we live in God and he lives in us, because he gave us his Spirit. [14]We have seen and can testify that the Father sent his Son to be the Savior of the world. [15]Whoever confesses that Jesus is the Son of God has God living inside, and that person lives in God. [16]And so we know the love that God has for us, and we trust that love.

God is love. Those who live in love live in God, and God lives in them. [17]This is how love is made perfect in us: that we can be without fear on the day God judges us, because in this world we are like him. [18]Where God's love is, there is no fear, because God's perfect love drives out fear. It is punishment that makes a person fear, so love is not made perfect in the person who fears.

[19]We love because God first loved us. [20]If people say, "I love God," but hate their broth-

---

Q & A

Q: Kids at school can be so mean sometimes. What makes them act like that?

A: Most all of us want to be popular, and we can achieve that if we appear to be really special—even if it means putting someone else down. It seems cruel that it's the weakest and loneliest kids who get picked on at school, but they're the easiest targets. God wants you to stick up for the kids who get picked on, even if it hurts your popularity (1 Thessalonians 5:14). If you're getting picked on, talk privately with your teacher or parents.

Q: I want to earn some money by doing work, but I get bored quickly. How do people stand working eight hours a day?

A: There are a lot of people who do not like their jobs and wonder how they're going to get through the eight hours each day. It's a great blessing to find a job that matches your skills and makes the time fly by. Before you start working a full-time job, think about the kinds of things that you would enjoy doing every day. Whatever kind of work you do, do it to obey the Lord (Colossians 3:17).

Q: Is there anybody in the Bible who was angry in a good way?

A: Anger in itself is not a sin. It's what you do about it. Jesus was angry with how the money changers in the Temple were ripping people off and he turned their tables over. He was right to be angry because they were stealing from God (Matthew 21:12–13). Ephesians 4:26 says, "When you are angry, do not sin." That means that you shouldn't be violent or use hurtful words.

 5:6 water This probably means the water of Jesus' baptism.   **5:6 blood** This probably means the blood of Jesus' death.   **5:7–8 So . . . witnesses** A few very late Greek copies and the Latin Vulgate continue, "in heaven: the Father, the Word, and the Holy Spirit, and these three witnesses agree. [8]And there are three witnesses on earth:"

"MAKE A DIFFERENCE"

Some think there's little *fun* in making a difference for Jesus Christ. But that isn't the case! Meet the Fishers of Men club—a group of young guys and their dads who use fishing trips as a way to make a difference.

Once each month from May to September, the Fishers pray about and advertise a fishing trip to the mountains or a local river or pond. No matter what a guest's level of fishing skill, this group is prepared. Some of the members work with beginners on casting, others work with types of bait, and others with the art of fly fishing. No one is left out.

After an exciting day of fishing, the participants devour fish and s'mores around the campfire. In its bright red glow, they share stories about the fish they caught and the ones that got away. Then, before they settle down for the night, one of the young Fishers of Men shares the story of how he became a Christian. And every month, other youth respond to the simple story of God's love.

What do you love to do? Can you think of a way to use it to share Jesus with your friends?

Spirit, the water, and the blood; and these three witnesses agree. [9]We believe people when they say something is true. But what God says is more important, and he has told us the truth about his own Son. [10]Anyone who believes in the Son of God has the truth that God told us. Anyone who does not believe makes God a liar, because that person does not believe what God told us about his Son. [11]This is what God told us: God has given us eternal life, and this life is in his Son. [12]Whoever has the Son has life, but whoever does not have the Son of God does not have life.

WE HAVE ETERNAL LIFE NOW

[13]I write this letter to you who believe in the Son of God so you will know you have eternal life. [14]And this is the boldness we have in God's presence: that if we ask God for anything that agrees with what he wants, he hears us. [15]If we know he hears us every time we ask him, we know we have what we ask from him.

[16]If anyone sees a brother or sister sinning (sin that does not lead to eternal death), that person should pray, and God will give the sinner life. I am talking about people whose sin does not lead to eternal death. There is sin that leads to death. I do not mean that a person should pray about that sin. [17]Doing wrong is always sin, but there is sin that does not lead to eternal death.

[18]We know that those who are God's children do not continue to sin. The Son of God keeps them safe, and the Evil One cannot touch them. [19]We know that we belong to God, but the Evil One controls the whole world. [20]We also know that the Son of God has come and has given us understanding so that we can know the True One. And our lives are in the True One and in his Son, Jesus Christ. He is the true God and the eternal life.

[21]So, dear children, keep yourselves away from false gods.

The "Elder" who writes this postcard of faith is probably the apostle John, who was now an old man.

The "chosen lady and her children" refers to a church, although we don't know which one.

2 JOHN

This letter is so short because John was planning to visit this church soon and would have a lot more to say in person. Until then, he offers a word of encouragement (verses 4–6) and a word of warning (verses 7–11), squeezed between his greeting and his closing.

The word of encouragement is to "love," which means "living the way God commanded us to live" (verse 6).

The word of warning is against "false teachers . . . who do not confess that Jesus Christ came to earth as a human" (verse 7).

Many groups today claim to be Christians but teach that Jesus Christ is not fully God and fully human. If a group is right about everything else but wrong about Jesus Christ, John says they do not have the truth and are not from God.

Study what the Bible teaches about Jesus Christ, and you will not be taken in by the clever lies of the Enemy.

¹From the Elder."

To the chosen lady" and her children:

I love all of you in the truth," and all those who know the truth love you. ²We love you because of the truth that lives in us and will be with us forever.

³Grace, mercy, and peace from God the Father and his Son, Jesus Christ, will be with us in truth and love.

⁴I was very happy to learn that some of your children are following the way of truth, as the Father commanded us. ⁵And now, dear lady, this is not a new command but is the same command we have had from the beginning. I ask you that we all love each other. ⁶And love means living the way God commanded us to live. As you have heard from the beginning, his command is this: Live a life of love.

⁷Many false teachers are in the world now who do not confess that Jesus Christ came to earth as a human. Anyone who does not confess this is a false teacher and an enemy of Christ. ⁸Be careful yourselves that you do not lose everything you" have worked for, but that you receive your full reward.

⁹Anyone who goes beyond Christ's teaching and does not continue to follow only his teaching does not have God. But whoever continues to follow the teaching of Christ has both the Father and the Son. ¹⁰If someone comes to you and does not bring this teaching, do not welcome or accept that person into your house. ¹¹If you welcome such a person, you share in the evil work.

¹²I have many things to write to you, but I do not want to use paper and ink. Instead, I hope to come to you and talk face to face so we can be full of joy. ¹³The children of your chosen sister" greet you.

dare to do

1 John 1:8
Read It: If we say we don't sin, we're fooling ourselves.
Do It: Even if no one sees you sin, God sees it. If you know of any sins you've been trying to hide, tell God about them right now and he will forgive you.

1 John 2:4
Read It: If you say "I know God" but you don't obey him, you're a liar.
Do It: Make a list of any of God's commandments that you have trouble obeying and ask him to help you keep them.

1 John 2:6
Read It: If you're truly a Christian, you will live like Jesus did.
Do It: Read through the Gospel of Matthew to see what Jesus says about being his follower.

Q & A

Q: I like chatting online because no one knows who I am and I can say things I wouldn't normally say. Is this okay?

A: Anything you say in a chat room, even though you're there anonymously, is still coming from your mouth. A good test is this: if you type things that you wouldn't dare let your parents read, it's wrong. Jesus said that expressing ourselves in sinful language makes us filthy inside (Mark 7:20). The chat room may be a fantasy world, but the bad effects are totally real.

Q: What did Jesus say about animals?

A: Jesus said that God watches over what happens to each little bird, and yet people are far more important to God than animals. And speaking of birds, Jesus also said we should be more like our little feathered friends. They live without worrying all the time (Matthew 6:25–26)—and so should we!

Q: How do I know God is always with me?

A: God has promised that he will always be with you (Hebrews 13:5). If you don't feel like he is, then ask God to give you confidence that he is right by your side. God has many different ways of showing that he is with you and he wants your faith in him to be strong. Remember: your feelings aren't as "true" as the reality that God won't ever leave you!

---

1 Elder "Elder" means an older person. It can also mean a special leader in the church (as in Titus 1:5).   **1 lady** This might mean a woman, or in this letter it might mean a church. If it is a church, then "her children" would be the people of the church.   **1 truth** The truth or "Good News" about Jesus Christ that joins all believers together.   **8 you** Some Greek copies read "we."   **13 sister** Sister of the "lady" in verse 1. This might be another woman or another church.

Third John is similar in tone and ideas to 1 and 2 John.

These short letters were written by John the Elder to his spiritual children. This is the same John who wrote the Gospel of John and the Book of Revelation.

This letter is about people (three men in particular):

- *"Gaius,* whom John praises for walking in the truth and for taking care of traveling Christians (verses 1–8)
- *"Diotrephes,* whom John blasts for being selfish and for trying to control the church (verses 9–10)
- *"Demetrius,* whom John holds up as a shining example of what Christians should be like (verses 11–12)

Although John names specific people in this letter, it is filled with good advice for all Christians:

- "Help the brothers and sisters, even those you do not know" (verse 5).
- "We should help such people [missionaries]; when we do, we share in their work for the truth" (verse 8).
- "Do not follow what is bad; follow what is good" (verse 11).

John closes by saying he plans to visit the church in the near future and will have more to say then (verses 13–15).

If John were writing to your church today, what would he write about you?

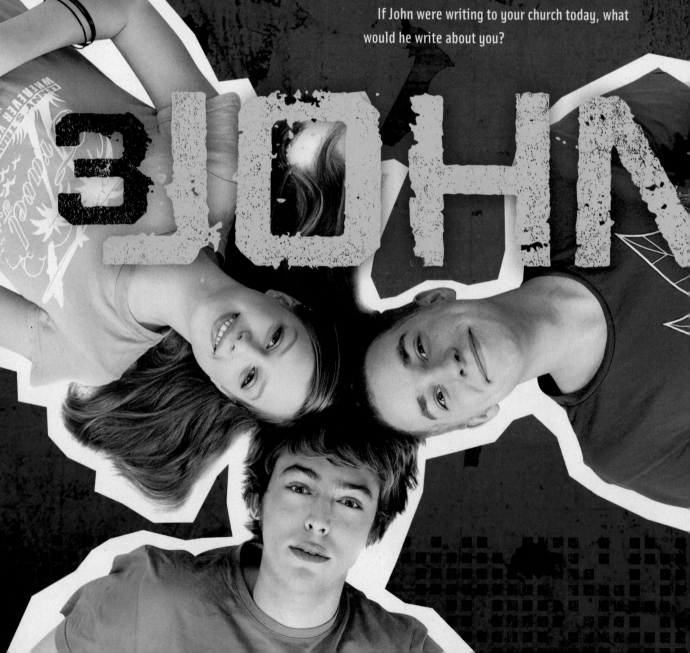

[1]From the Elder.[a]

To my dear friend Gaius, whom I love in the truth:[b]

[2]My dear friend, I know your soul is doing fine, and I pray that you are doing well in every way and that your health is good. [3]I was very happy when some brothers and sisters came and told me about the truth in your life and how you are following the way of truth. [4]Nothing gives me greater joy than to hear that my children are following the way of truth.

[5]My dear friend, it is good that you help the brothers and sisters, even those you do not know. [6]They told the church about your love. Please help them to continue their trip in a way worthy of God. [7]They started out in service to Christ, and they have been accepting nothing from nonbelievers. [8]So we should help such people; when we do, we share in their work for the truth.

[9]I wrote something to the church, but Diotrephes, who loves to be their leader, will not listen to us. [10]So if I come, I will talk about what Diotrephes is doing, about how he lies and says evil things about us. But more than that, he refuses to accept the other brothers and sisters; he even stops those who do want to accept them and puts them out of the church.

[11]My dear friend, do not follow what is bad; follow what is good. The one who does good belongs to God. But the one who does evil has never known God.

[12]Everyone says good things about Demetrius, and the truth agrees with what they say. We also speak well of him, and you know what we say is true.

[13]I have many things I want to write you, but I do not want to use pen and ink. [14]I hope to see you soon and talk face to face. [15]Peace to you. The friends here greet you. Please greet each friend there by name.

ROCK SOLID

3 John 3

Your teacher rambles on in a monotone about the politics of the French monarchy during the Middle Ages, but you're daydreaming. Or your friend moved out of town last weekend and you just realized he was your closest friend so you feel depressed.

Do you ever feel trapped by your thoughts? Well, here's some good news: you can take control of them. Yes, you have complete control over what you think, instead of your thoughts controlling you.

The apostle John sent a brief letter to one of his friends, Gaius. In it, he wrote: "I was very happy when some brothers and sisters came and told me about the truth in your life and how you are following the way of truth" (3 John 3). John urged his friend to never stop thinking about the truth.

Like Gaius, you can choose what you think about. This is great news, especially if you are struggling with more than daydreaming. If you are having trouble not thinking about things that are clearly sin, read the Bible. It can be a sword of truth in your hand.

Every time your thoughts start going somewhere they shouldn't, hack up those sinful thoughts, open your Bible, and renew your mind with the truth.

dare to do

1 John 3:17
Read It: God's love is in your heart when you help people in need.
Do It: If there's a poor family in your church, ask your youth group leader to help you organize a group project to pay for something they need.

1 John 3:18
Read It: "Love" is a verb. You don't just talk about it—you do it.
Do It: Do something nice for your brother or your dad, like helping with the chores.

1 John 3:21
Read It: Come before God with a clear conscience.
Do It: Before you pray for things you want, make sure you've confessed all your sins to God (see Matthew 5:23-24).

---

1 Elder "Elder" means an older person. It can also mean a special leader in the church (as in Titus 1:5). **1 truth** The truth or "Good News" about Jesus Christ that joins all believers together.

Jude was the brother of James (verse 1) and the half brother of Jesus Christ (Mark 6:3).

He wrote this short letter "to encourage you to fight hard for the faith that was given the holy people of God once and for all time" (verse 3).

Already in the early church, false teachers were causing problems. God had dealt with false prophets in the past, Jude reminds his readers, and he will deal with this current batch of troublemakers, as well (verses 5–19).

For their part, the Christians were to "use your most holy faith to build yourselves up, praying in the Holy Spirit. Keep yourselves in God's love as you wait for the Lord Jesus Christ with his mercy to give you life forever" (verses 20–23).

JUDE

There are still lots of false teachers today. They give sermons, write books, and attract thousands of followers. How can you tell who to trust? How can you know who's telling the truth and who's lying?

Jude says to rely on the teaching of the apostles. Jesus handpicked these men and trained them to be the foundation of his church. Their words live on in the New Testament. It is the standard by which everything else should be judged.

That's why you should constantly read and study your Bible—to keep from being tricked.

¹From Jude, a servant of Jesus Christ and a brother of James.

To all who have been called by God. God the Father loves you, and you have been kept safe in Jesus Christ:

²Mercy, peace, and love be yours richly.

GOD WILL PUNISH SINNERS

³Dear friends, I wanted very much to write you about the salvation we all share. But I felt the need to write you about something else: I want to encourage you to fight hard for the faith that was given the holy people of God once and for all time. ⁴Some people have secretly entered your group. Long ago the prophets wrote about these people who will be judged guilty. They are against God and have changed the grace of our God into a reason for sexual sin. They also refuse to accept Jesus Christ, our only Master and Lord.

⁵I want to remind you of some things you already know: Remember that the Lord" saved his people by bringing them out of the land of Egypt. But later he destroyed all those who did not believe. ⁶And remember the angels who did not keep their place of power but left their proper home. The Lord has kept these angels in darkness, bound with everlasting chains, to

be judged on the great day. ⁷Also remember the cities of Sodom and Gomorrah" and the other towns around them. In the same way they were full of sexual sin and people who desired sexual relations that God does not allow. They suffer the punishment of eternal fire, as an example for all to see.

⁸It is the same with these people who have entered your group. They are guided by dreams and make themselves filthy with sin. They reject God's authority and speak against the angels. ⁹Not even the archangel" Michael, when he argued with the devil about who would have the body of Moses, dared to judge the devil guilty. Instead, he said, "The Lord punish you." ¹⁰But these people speak against things they do not understand. And what they do know, by feeling, as dumb animals know things, are the very things that destroy them. ¹¹It will be terrible for them. They have followed the way of Cain, and for money they have given themselves to doing the wrong that Balaam did. They have fought against God as Korah did, and like Korah, they surely will be destroyed. ¹²They are like dirty spots in your special Christian meals you share. They eat with you and have no fear, caring only for themselves. They are clouds without rain, which the wind blows around. They are autumn trees

SMART TIPS!

Be a Team Player

Many sports are team sports—the point is to win by playing and working together. The better you play together, the better the chance of winning. Likewise, living out your Christian faith is often more successful when you depend on other Christians to help you out.

COOL!

All Those Animals!

When God created the world, he said, "'Let there be tame animals and small crawling animals and wild animals, and let each produce more of its kind.' And it happened" (Genesis 1:24).

And it's *still* happening! Today there are more than a million animal species on the planet, including:

★ 9,000 kinds of birds
★ 6,000 species of reptiles
★ 4,600 kinds of mammals

And when it comes to insects, there are about:

★ 73,000 species of spiders
★ 3,000 types of lice

For every person on Earth—all 6.5 billion of us—there are about 200 million insects.

5 the Lord Some Greek copies read "Jesus."   **7 Sodom and Gomorrah** Two cities God destroyed because they were so evil.   **9 archangel** The leader among God's angels or messengers.

Jude 20
Read It: Pray in the Holy Spirit
Do It: When you pray, ask the Holy Spirit to communicate for you about things you don't even understand.

Jude 22
Read It: Be merciful to those who doubt.
Do It: Everyone needs time to consider God's truth. Be patient when they need more time. But never give up praying and sharing about Jesus with them!

Jude 23
Read It: Save people from the coming fire.
Do It: Some of your friends are ready to become Christians and you don't even know it. Be bold and ask them if they are ready to take that important step!

without fruit that are pulled out of the ground. So they are twice dead. [13] They are like wild waves of the sea, tossing up their own shameful actions like foam. They are like stars that wander in the sky. A place in the blackest darkness has been kept for them forever.

[14] Enoch, the seventh descendant from Adam, said about these people: "Look, the Lord is coming with many thousands of his holy angels to [15] judge every person. He is coming to punish all who are against God for all the evil they have done against him. And he will punish the sinners who are against God for all the evil they have said against him."

[16] These people complain and blame others, doing the evil things they want to do. They brag about themselves, and they flatter others to get what they want.

A WARNING AND THINGS TO DO

[17] Dear friends, remember what the apostles of our Lord Jesus Christ said before. [18] They said to you, "In the last times there will be people who laugh about God, following their own evil desires which are against God." [19] These are the people who divide you, people whose thoughts are only of this world, who do not have the Spirit.

[20] But dear friends, use your most holy faith to build yourselves up, praying in the Holy Spirit. [21] Keep yourselves in God's love as you wait for the Lord Jesus Christ with his mercy to give you life forever.

[22] Show mercy to some people who have doubts. [23] Take others out of the fire, and save them. Show mercy mixed with fear to others, hating even their clothes which are dirty from sin.

PRAISE GOD

[24] God is strong and can help you not to fall. He can bring you before his glory without any wrong in you and can give you great joy. [25] He is the only God, the One who saves us. To him be glory, greatness, power, and authority through Jesus Christ our Lord for all time past, now, and forever. Amen.

The Book of Revelation is sometimes called the *Apocalypse,* which means "unveiling."

It is filled with visions of the end times. These "revelations" were shown to John—the same man who wrote the Gospel and letters of John—while he was exiled on the island of Patmos (1:9).

The book revolves around four great visions:

- The *first vision* (1:9–3:22) pictures the risen Lord Jesus judging seven churches. These churches probably stand for all churches throughout history. Jesus praises what is good and tells them how to correct what needs fixing.

REVELATION

- The *second vision* (4:1–19:10) deals with the Seven Seals, Trumpets, and Bowls of God's judgment. These are poured out on the world because of the sinful acts of humankind. After God destroys the wicked governments (referred to as "Babylon"), there will be a joyful Wedding Feast of the Lamb.

- The *third vision* (19:11–20:15) shows the return of Jesus and the final events of history: the binding of Satan, the thousand-year reign of Jesus on Earth, the final rebellion, and the Great White Throne Judgment.

- The *fourth vision* (21:1–22:5) reveals the New Heaven, the New Earth, and the New Jerusalem. This eternal city will be the home of all who love God.

Because this book is full of symbols and mysteries, it's not always easy to understand. But the central message is clear: Jesus is coming back to destroy his enemies and set up his perfect kingdom.

It's time to get ready!

JOHN TELLS ABOUT THIS BOOK

1 This is the revelation" of Jesus Christ, which God gave to him, to show his servants what must soon happen. And Jesus sent his angel to show it to his servant John, ²who has told everything he has seen. It is the word of God; it is the message from Jesus Christ. ³Blessed is the one who reads the words of God's message, and blessed are the people who hear this message and do what is written in it. The time is near when all of this will happen.

JESUS' MESSAGE TO THE CHURCHES

⁴From John.

To the seven churches in Asia:

Grace and peace to you from the One who is and was and is coming, and from the seven spirits before his throne, ⁵and from Jesus Christ. Jesus is the faithful witness, the first among those raised from the dead. He is the ruler of the kings of the earth.

He is the One who loves us, who made us free from our sins with the blood of his death. ⁶He made us to be a kingdom of priests who serve God his Father. To Jesus Christ be glory and power forever and ever! Amen.

⁷Look, Jesus is coming with the clouds, and everyone will see him, even those who stabbed him. And all peoples of the earth will cry loudly because of him. Yes, this will happen! Amen.

⁸The Lord God says, "I am the Alpha and the Omega." I am the One who is and was and is coming. I am the Almighty."

DID YOU KNOW?

Preteens grow more than two inches a year.

Sonna, Linda, Ph.D. *The Everything Tween Book*, p. 178.

⁹I, John, am your brother. All of us share with Christ in suffering, in the kingdom, and in patience to continue. I was on the island of Patmos," because I had preached the word of God and the message about Jesus. ¹⁰On the Lord's day I was in the Spirit, and I heard a loud voice behind me that sounded like a trumpet. ¹¹The voice said, "Write what you see in a book and send it to the seven churches: to Ephesus, Smyrna, Pergamum, Thyatira, Sardis, Philadelphia, and Laodicea."

¹²I turned to see who was talking to me. When I turned, I saw seven golden lampstands ¹³and someone among the lampstands who was "like a Son of Man."" He was dressed in a long robe and had a gold band around his chest. ¹⁴His head and hair were white like wool, as white as snow, and his eyes were like flames of fire. ¹⁵His feet were like bronze that glows hot in a furnace, and his voice was like the noise of flooding water. ¹⁶He held seven stars in his right hand, and a sharp double-edged sword came out of his mouth. He looked like the sun shining at its brightest time.

¹⁷When I saw him, I fell down at his feet like a dead man. He put his right hand on me and said, "Do not be afraid. I am the First and the Last. ¹⁸I am the One who lives; I was dead, but look, I am alive forever and ever! And I hold the keys to death and to the place of the dead. ¹⁹So write the things you see, what is now and what will happen later. ²⁰Here is the secret of the seven stars that you saw in my right hand and the seven golden lampstands: The seven lampstands are the seven churches, and the seven stars are the angels of the seven churches.

TO THE CHURCH IN EPHESUS

2 "Write this to the angel of the church in Ephesus:

"The One who holds the seven stars in his right hand and walks among the seven golden lampstands says this: ²I know what you do, how you work hard and never give up. I know you do not put up with the false teachings of

BIBLE SUPERHEROES

Titus

See 2 Corinthians 8:16-24; Titus.

Titus was a friend and helper of the apostle Paul. He became an important part of the early church.

The church had started among the Jewish people. When non-Jews like Titus joined, some Jews wanted them to keep the Jewish law. Keeping the law was like earning your way to heaven.

Paul was dead set against this. He said that Jews or non-Jews (called Gentiles) only had to believe in Jesus Christ. Being saved was by faith, not works. He went to a meeting in Jerusalem to argue about it—and he won the day! (Acts 15).

Titus served the Lord for many years after that. He helped churches in places like Corinth, the island of Crete, and the province of Dalmatia. This brave man stood up for truth, even when it wasn't popular.

1:1 revelation Making known truth that has been hidden.   **1:8 Alpha and the Omega** The first and last letters of the Greek alphabet. This means "the beginning and the end."   **1:9 Patmos** A small island in the Aegean Sea, near the coast of Asia Minor (modern Turkey).   **1:13 "like . . . Man"** "Son of Man" is a name Jesus called himself.

Every difference a person makes is huge in God's eyes. Lisa, a twelve-year-old in Dallas, Texas, uses the word "HEART" to remember how:

H – Hear what people need. Lisa has discovered that those who hear what people need often can meet that need (like mowing a lawn or telling someone about God).

E – Entertain. Lisa knows she can make a difference by inviting people over (or inviting them to sit next to her at lunch).

A – Ask questions. Lisa works hard to ask good questions. She gives other people a chance to talk about what's happening in their lives. Often they just need a friend.

R – Respond. Lisa responds when she sees something that needs to be done (like helping a friend with a project).

T – Touch. Lisa enjoys giving a hug to a relative or friend who needs affirmation or a physical expression of love. And she feels better, too!

Loving with all your HEART always make a huge difference!

evil people. You have tested those who say they are apostles but really are not, and you found they are liars. ³You have patience and have suffered troubles for my name and have not given up.

⁴"But I have this against you: You have left the love you had in the beginning. ⁵So remember where you were before you fell. Change your hearts and do what you did at first. If you do not change, I will come to you and will take away your lampstand from its place. ⁶But there is something you do that is right: You hate what the Nicolaitans" do, as much as I.

⁷"Every person who has ears should listen to what the Spirit says to the churches. To those who win the victory I will give the right to eat the fruit from the tree of life, which is in the garden of God.

TO THE CHURCH IN SMYRNA

⁸"Write this to the angel of the church in Smyrna:

"The One who is the First and the Last, who died and came to life again, says this: ⁹I know your troubles and that you are poor, but really you are rich! I know the bad things some people say about you. They say they are Jews, but they are not true Jews. They are a synagogue that belongs to Satan. ¹⁰Do not be afraid of what you are about to suffer. I tell you, the devil will put some of you in prison to test you, and you will suffer for ten days. But be faithful, even if you have to die, and I will give you the crown of life.

¹¹"Everyone who has ears should listen to what the Spirit says to the churches. Those who win the victory will not be hurt by the second death.

TO THE CHURCH IN PERGAMUM

¹²"Write this to the angel of the church in Pergamum:

"The One who has the sharp, double-edged sword says this: ¹³I know where you live. It is where Satan has his throne. But you are true to me. You did not refuse to tell about your faith in me even during the time of Antipas, my faithful witness who was killed in your city, where Satan lives.

¹⁴"But I have a few things against you: You have some there who follow the teaching of Balaam. He taught Balak how to cause the people of Israel to sin by eating food offered to idols and by taking part in sexual sins. ¹⁵You also have some who follow the teaching of the Nicolaitans." ¹⁶So change your hearts and lives. If you do not, I will come to you quickly and fight against them with the sword that comes out of my mouth.

¹⁷"Everyone who has ears should listen to what the Spirit says to the churches.

"I will give some of the hidden manna to everyone who wins the victory. I will also give to each one who wins the victory a white stone with a new name written on it. No one knows this new name except the one who receives it.

TO THE CHURCH IN THYATIRA

¹⁸"Write this to the angel of the church in Thyatira:

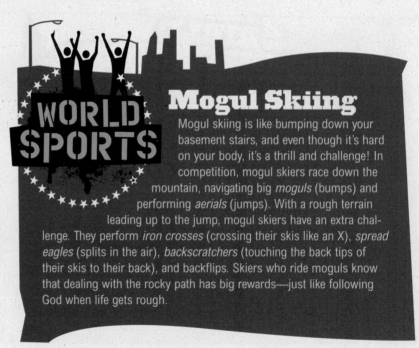

Mogul Skiing

Mogul skiing is like bumping down your basement stairs, and even though it's hard on your body, it's a thrill and challenge! In competition, mogul skiers race down the mountain, navigating big *moguls* (bumps) and performing *aerials* (jumps). With a rough terrain leading up to the jump, mogul skiers have an extra challenge. They perform *iron crosses* (crossing their skis like an X), *spread eagles* (splits in the air), *backscratchers* (touching the back tips of their skis to their back), and backflips. Skiers who ride moguls know that dealing with the rocky path has big rewards—just like following God when life gets rough.

2:6, 15 **Nicolaitans** This is the name of a religious group that followed false beliefs and ideas.

varsity Sports

What sports are you passionate about? Do you remember when you got your first baseball mitt, basketball, or hockey stick? The dream of becoming a professional sports player can start at a very young age and stay with you for a lifetime. There is a drive in each of us for competition and challenging ourselves—and also to have fun doing something we love!

In high school, the sports will probably get more competitive than any team you've been on before. The teams can be difficult to get on and tryouts can be scary. Don't worry! Practicing the sport at home or school will prepare you. Then give it your best! At tryouts, don't compare yourself to others; that will only cause you more nervousness. Instead, have a good attitude toward every player. Coaches appreciate good skills, but they appreciate a good attitude, too. You may or may not make it onto the team; just do your best and don't beat yourself up if you get cut.

Playing on a varsity or high school sports team is hard work, as well as fun. But life isn't just about sports! You still have schoolwork, friends, and family, and they are important, too. Playing sports requires focus, organization, and the ability to balance practices and games with the rest of your life. In fact, playing sports is a lot like the Christian life—you have to keep practicing and focusing in order to improve. Ask your parents to help you plan a schedule so you don't get behind on your homework or miss an important family event.

The focus of your high school sports teams may be on winning only. If you are excited about playing a sport but don't like the competitiveness, try recreational sports—where the goal is to have fun rather than to win. These leagues are made up of players from all over a community. On a recreational sports team, your coach will care most about the players.

You may never make it to the big leagues, but sports can be a part of your life if you get involved in high school or community teams. Playing sports is good for your health. And a positive attitude is good for you, too! Playing on sports teams can be a great way to meet friends and have fun while exercising.

trustables

Revelation 3:12

Did you know that if you put your faith in Jesus you get a special tattoo? Tell that to your parents and see if they freak out! Then once they calm down, show them this verse: Revelation 3:12. Jesus says, "I will write on them [Christians] the name of my God and the name of the city of my God, the new Jerusalem...I will also write on them my new name."

Cool, huh? Do you think these three tattoos are on your head? Or maybe on your hand? Probably they're somewhere under the surface like on your heart. We have no way of knowing because they're invisible.

But even if we can't see them, the important thing is that God can. And they are the tattoos that give you special treatment when the judgment day comes. They mean you get to live in heaven. Most importantly, these tattoos will never fade and can't be removed. They're permanent. That's guaranteed by Jesus himself. Isn't that amazing?

So if you've always wanted a tattoo, I highly recommend these three. And unlike those tattoos that many people end up regretting, like a movie star's name or a goofy picture, you'll never regret these. In fact, you'll be enjoying the privileges they give you *forever*!

"The Son of God, who has eyes that blaze like fire and feet like shining bronze, says this: [19] I know what you do. I know about your love, your faith, your service, and your patience. I know that you are doing more now than you did at first.

[20] "But I have this against you: You let that woman Jezebel spread false teachings. She says she is a prophetess, but by her teaching she leads my people to take part in sexual sins and to eat food that is offered to idols. [21] I have given her time to change her heart and turn away from her sin, but she does not want to change. [22] So I will throw her on a bed of suffering. And all those who take part in adultery with her will suffer greatly if they do not turn away from the wrongs she does. [23] I will also kill her followers. Then all the churches will know I am the One who searches hearts and minds, and I will repay each of you for what you have done.

COOL!

Lighting the Way

The oldest—and tallest—lighthouse ever was the *Pharos* in Alexandria, Egypt. It was built about 280 B.C. and stood as high as a forty-five-story skyscraper.

The first lighthouse in America was built on Little Brewster Island near Boston in 1716. About 1,500 lighthouses have been built in the U.S.

Lighthouses were built for one purpose: to keep ships and sailors safe.

Jesus said, "I am the light of the world. The person who follows me will never live in darkness" (John 8:12). Jesus is the ultimate "lighthouse"!

24"But others of you in Thyatira have not followed her teaching and have not learned what some call Satan's deep secrets. I say to you that I will not put any other load on you. 25Only continue in your loyalty until I come.

26"I will give power over the nations to everyone who wins the victory and continues to be obedient to me until the end.

27'You will rule over them with an iron rod,
  as when pottery is broken into pieces.'

Psalm 2:9

28This is the same power I received from my Father. I will also give him the morning star. 29Everyone who has ears should listen to what the Spirit says to the churches.

TO THE CHURCH IN SARDIS

3 "Write this to the angel of the church in Sardis:

"The One who has the seven spirits and the seven stars says this: I know what you do. People say that you are alive, but really you are dead. 2Wake up! Strengthen what you have left before it dies completely. I have found that what you are doing is less than what my God wants. 3So do not forget what you have received and heard. Obey it, and change your hearts and lives. So you must wake up, or I will come like a thief, and you will not know when I will come to you. 4But you have a few there in Sardis who have kept their clothes unstained, so they will walk with me and will wear white clothes, because they are worthy. 5Those who win the victory will be dressed in white clothes like them. And I will not erase their names from the book of life, but I will say they belong to me before my Father and before his angels. 6Everyone who has ears should listen to what the Spirit says to the churches.

TO THE CHURCH IN PHILADELPHIA

7"Write this to the angel of the church in Philadelphia:

"This is what the One who is holy and true, who holds the key of David, says. When he opens a door, no one can close it. And when he closes it, no one can open it. 8I know what you do. I have put an open door before you, which no one can close. I know you have little strength, but you have obeyed my teaching and were not afraid to speak my name. 9Those in the synagogue that belongs to Satan say they are Jews, but they are not true Jews; they are liars. I will make them come before you and bow at your feet, and they will know that I have loved you. 10You have obeyed my teaching about not giving up your faith. So I will

keep you from the time of trouble that will come to the whole world to test those who live on earth.

11"I am coming soon. Continue strong in your faith so no one will take away your crown. 12I will make those who win the victory pillars in the temple of my God, and they will never have to leave it. I will write on them the name of my God and the name of the city of my God, the new Jerusalem," that comes down out of heaven from my God. I will also write on them my new name. 13Everyone who has ears should listen to what the Spirit says to the churches.

TO THE CHURCH IN LAODICEA

14"Write this to the angel of the church in Laodicea:

"The Amen," the faithful and true witness, the ruler of all God has made, says this: 15I know what you do, that you are not hot or cold. I wish that you were hot or cold! 16But because you are lukewarm—neither hot, nor cold—I am ready to spit you out of my mouth. 17You say, 'I am rich, and I have become

Q: The jocks seem to run everything at my school. What do you do if you're not athletic?

A: Sometimes it seems that kids who are good at sports get all the attention, but there are lots of other great activities available! Find something you enjoy and *are* good at doing—like art, music, a foreign language, drama—and find a friend or two to join you. After checking out your options, you may discover your school offers more opportunities than you thought!

Q: Does the Bible say the future is going to be good or bad?

A: Both. It's going to get a lot worse and then it's going to get better than anything you could imagine. There is going to be a time called "the Tribulation" when awful things will happen all over the world, especially to Christians. But Jesus will return to reign on earth. Then everybody will be judged before God, and those who faithfully followed Jesus will be rewarded with eternal life (Luke 21:26–28).

Q: This guy in New Jersey says he used to be a pharaoh in a previous life. Is it possible for somebody to have lived before as someone else?

A: The idea that people live multiple lives is called *reincarnation*. The Bible says that this doesn't happen. We each live once, and then we stand before God to be judged (Hebrews 9:27). We have to make the most of our life—because we only get one!

3:12 **Jerusalem** This name is used to mean the spiritual city God built for his people. See Revelation 21–22.   3:14 **Amen** Used here as a name for Jesus; it means to agree fully that something is true.

wealthy and do not need anything.' But you do not know that you are really miserable, pitiful, poor, blind, and naked. [18]I advise you to buy from me gold made pure in fire so you can be truly rich. Buy from me white clothes so you can be clothed and so you can cover your shameful nakedness. Buy from me medicine to put on your eyes so you can truly see.

[19]"I correct and punish those whom I love. So be eager to do right, and change your hearts and lives. [20]Here I am! I stand at the door and knock. If you hear my voice and open the door, I will come in and eat with you, and you will eat with me.

[21]"Those who win the victory will sit with me on my throne in the same way that I won the victory and sat down with my Father on his throne. [22]Everyone who has ears should listen to what the Spirit says to the churches."

JOHN SEES HEAVEN

4 After the vision of these things I looked, and there before me was an open door in heaven. And the same voice that spoke to me before, that sounded like a trumpet, said, "Come up here, and I will show you what must happen after this." [2]Immediately I was in the Spirit, and before me was a throne in heaven, and someone was sitting on it. [3]The One who sat on the throne looked like precious stones, like jasper and carnelian. All around the throne was a rainbow the color of an emerald. [4]Around the throne there were twenty-four other thrones with twenty-four elders sitting on them. They were dressed in white and had golden crowns on their heads. [5]Lightning flashes and noises and thunder came from the throne. Before the throne seven lamps were burning, which are the seven spirits of God. [6]Also before the throne there was something that looked like a sea of glass, clear like crystal.

In the center and around the throne were four living creatures with eyes all over them, in front and in back. [7]The first living creature was like a lion. The second was like a calf. The third had a face like a man. The fourth was like a flying eagle. [8]Each of these four living creatures had six wings and was covered all over with eyes, inside and out. Day and night they never stop saying:

"Holy, holy, holy is the Lord God Almighty.
He was, he is, and he is coming."

[9]These living creatures give glory, honor,

Things to Do When the Power Goes Out

1. Use flashlights to make silhouettes on the wall.
2. Read (if it's daylight).
3. Talk with your family.
4. Play a card game.
5. Make no-bake cookies.
6. Ride your bike.
7. Tell scary stories.
8. Take the dog or cat for a walk.
9. Sleep.
10. Wrestle with your siblings.

Revelation 5:9–10

What do you want to be when you grow up? What is the coolest possible thing someone could become? How's this for a job description: *be like Jesus.*

Followers of Jesus Christ have the most fabulous ending you could possibly imagine!

In heaven Jesus receives the worship of God's people. They declare: "with the blood of your death you bought people for God from every tribe, language, people, and nation. You made them to be a kingdom of priests for our God, and they will rule on the earth" (Revelation 5:9–10).

Right now we're God's children; but when Jesus Christ comes back, he's going to take us to a whole new level. When Jesus takes us to be with him, we will become *like* him!

While we don't know what exactly what that means, if we're like Jesus Christ, it will be mind blowing. We have the coolest possible future!

and thanks to the One who sits on the throne, who lives forever and ever. [10]Then the twenty-four elders bow down before the One who sits on the throne, and they worship him who lives forever and ever. They put their crowns down before the throne and say:

[11]"You are worthy, our Lord and God,
to receive glory and honor and power,
because you made all things.
Everything existed and was made,
because you wanted it."

5 Then I saw a scroll in the right hand of the One sitting on the throne. The scroll had writing on both sides and was kept closed with seven seals. [2]And I saw a powerful angel calling in a loud voice, "Who is worthy to break the seals and open the scroll?" [3]But there was no one in heaven or on earth or under the earth who could open the scroll or look inside it. [4]I cried bitterly because there was no one who was worthy to open the scroll or look inside. [5]But one of the elders said to me, "Do not cry! The Lion" from the tribe of Judah, David's descendant, has won the victory so that he is able to open the scroll and its seven seals."

5:5 **Lion** Here refers to Christ.

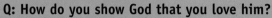

⁶Then I saw a Lamb standing in the center of the throne and in the middle of the four living creatures and the elders. The Lamb looked as if he had been killed. He had seven horns and seven eyes, which are the seven spirits of God that were sent into all the world. ⁷The Lamb came and took the scroll from the right hand of the One sitting on the throne. ⁸When he took the scroll, the four living creatures and the twenty-four elders bowed down before the Lamb. Each one of them had a harp and golden bowls full of incense, which are the prayers of God's holy people. ⁹And they all sang a new song to the Lamb:

"You are worthy to take the scroll
    and to open its seals,
because you were killed,
    and with the blood of your death you
        bought people for God
    from every tribe, language, people, and
        nation.
¹⁰You made them to be a kingdom of priests
        for our God,
    and they will rule on the earth."

¹¹Then I looked, and I heard the voices of many angels around the throne, and the four living creatures, and the elders. There were thousands and thousands of angels, ¹²saying in a loud voice:

"The Lamb who was killed is worthy
    to receive power, wealth, wisdom, and
        strength,
    honor, glory, and praise!"

¹³Then I heard all creatures in heaven and on earth and under the earth and in the sea saying:

"To the One who sits on the throne
    and to the Lamb

be praise and honor and glory and power
    forever and ever."

¹⁴The four living creatures said, "Amen," and the elders bowed down and worshiped.

6 Then I watched while the Lamb opened the first of the seven seals. I heard one of the four living creatures say with a voice like thunder, "Come!" ²I looked, and there before me was a white horse. The rider on the horse held a bow, and he was given a crown, and he rode out, determined to win the victory.

³When the Lamb opened the second seal, I heard the second living creature say, "Come!"

⁴Then another horse came out, a red one. Its rider was given power to take away peace from the earth and to make people kill each other, and he was given a big sword.

⁵When the Lamb opened the third seal, I heard the third living creature say, "Come!" I looked, and there before me was a black horse, and its rider held a pair of scales in his hand. ⁶Then I heard something that sounded like a voice coming from the middle of the four living creatures. The voice said, "A quart of wheat for a day's pay, and three quarts of barley for a day's pay, and do not damage the olive oil and wine!"

⁷When the Lamb opened the fourth seal, I heard the voice of the fourth living creature say, "Come!" ⁸I looked, and there before me was a pale horse. Its rider was named death, and Hades" was following close behind him. They were given power over a fourth of the earth to kill people by war, by starvation, by disease, and by the wild animals of the earth.

⁹When the Lamb opened the fifth seal, I saw under the altar the souls of those who had been killed because they were faithful to the word of God and to the message they had received. ¹⁰These souls shouted in a loud voice, "Holy and true Lord, how long until you judge the people of the earth and punish them for killing us?" ¹¹Then each one of them was given a white robe and was told to wait a short time longer. There were still some of their fellow

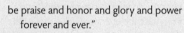

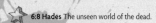

6:8 Hades The unseen world of the dead.

servants and brothers and sisters in the service of Christ who must be killed as they were. They had to wait until all of this was finished.

¹²Then I watched while the Lamb opened the sixth seal, and there was a great earthquake. The sun became black like rough black cloth, and the whole moon became red like blood. ¹³And the stars in the sky fell to the earth like figs falling from a fig tree when the wind blows. ¹⁴The sky disappeared as a scroll when it is rolled up, and every mountain and island was moved from its place.

¹⁵Then the kings of the earth, the rulers, the generals, the rich people, the powerful people, the slaves, and the free people hid themselves in caves and in the rocks on the mountains. ¹⁶They called to the mountains and the rocks, "Fall on us. Hide us from the face of the One who sits on the throne and from the anger of the Lamb! ¹⁷The great day for their anger has come, and who can stand against it?"

THE 144,000 PEOPLE OF ISRAEL

7 After the vision of these things I saw four angels standing at the four corners of the earth. The angels were holding the four winds of the earth to keep them from blowing on the land or on the sea or on any tree. ²Then I saw another angel coming up from the east who had the seal of the living God. And he called out in a loud voice to the four angels to whom God had given power to harm the earth and the sea. ³He said to them, "Do not harm the land or the sea or the trees until we mark with a sign the foreheads of the people who serve our God." ⁴Then I heard how many people were marked with the sign. There were one hundred forty-four thousand from every tribe of the people of Israel.

⁵From the tribe of Judah twelve thousand were marked with the sign,
 from the tribe of Reuben twelve thousand,
 from the tribe of Gad twelve thousand,
⁶from the tribe of Asher twelve thousand,
 from the tribe of Naphtali twelve thousand,
 from the tribe of Manasseh twelve thousand,

SMART TIPS!

Earn Your Own Money

Your parents won't always be there to pay for everything, so it's good to get an early start on earning your own money. Also, don't just depend on your parents and church in order to be a good Christian—pray and read the Bible on your own.

⁷from the tribe of Simeon twelve thousand,
 from the tribe of Levi twelve thousand,
 from the tribe of Issachar twelve thousand,
⁸from the tribe of Zebulun twelve thousand,
 from the tribe of Joseph twelve thousand,
 and from the tribe of Benjamin twelve thousand were marked with the sign.

THE GREAT CROWD WORSHIPS GOD

⁹After the vision of these things I looked, and there was a great number of people, so many that no one could count them. They were from every nation, tribe, people, and language of the earth. They were all standing before the throne and before the Lamb, wearing white robes and holding palm branches in their hands. ¹⁰They were shouting in a loud voice, "Salvation belongs to our God, who sits on the throne, and to the Lamb." ¹¹All the angels were standing around the throne and the elders and the four living creatures. They all bowed down on their faces before the throne and worshiped God, ¹²saying, "Amen! Praise, glory, wisdom, thanks, honor, power, and strength belong to our God forever and ever. Amen!"

¹³Then one of the elders asked me, "Who are these people dressed in white robes? Where did they come from?"

¹⁴I answered, "You know, sir."

And the elder said to me, "These are the people who have come out of the great distress.

ROCK SOLID

Revelation 7:16–17

We face a lot of junk on this earth, a lot of hurt and pain and awful things. People kill other people, moms abort their babies, and men beat up their wives and kids. Even if you haven't experienced any of these things yourself, you probably know someone who has.

All of these things are a product of sin, and a time is coming when all of these things will disappear. Can you imagine a place where everything that caused you pain and hurt is gone forever and everything you loved the most is magnified a million times?

Revelation 7:16–17 describes God with his people in heaven by saying, "Those people will never be hungry again, and they will never be thirsty again. The sun will not hurt them, and no heat will burn them, because the Lamb at the center of the throne will be their shepherd. He will lead them to springs of water that give life. And God will wipe away every tear from their eyes."

No more junk, just happiness in huge volumes. It will be so overwhelmingly good that we will spend all of eternity enjoying it.

December

The countdown begins...24 days until Christmas! **1**	Pray for a person of influence: singer Britney Spears celebrates her birthday today. **2**	Today is *"Roof-Over-Your-Head Day."* Pray for those who don't have a home. **3**	**4**	**5**
DECEMBER **24** **6**	Pray for a person of influence: singer Aaron Carter has a birthday today. **7**	**8**	**9**	**10**
Build a snowman! No snow? Cut one out of paper and tape it in a window. **11**	**12**	Read the Christmas story in Matthew 1:18–2:23; then share in your own words with a younger neighbor. **13**	**14**	**15**
Who doesn't love this? It's *"Chocolate Covered Anything Day"!* **16**	**17**	Show your Christmas spirit: dress in red and green from head to toe. **18**	Go caroling up and down your block tonight. Pray for those who hear your carols. **19**	**20**
21	**22**	**23**	It's *"Eggnog Day."* Give it a try with some whipped cream on top. **24**	*Christmas Day—* Sing "Happy Birthday" to Jesus! **25**
26	**27**	Pray for a person of influence: it's snowboarder Todd Richards's birthday. **28**	If you write thank-you notes today, you'll have more time to play with your gifts later! **29**	**30**
Invite your buddies over, watch the ball drop, make lots of noise, and celebrate the new year! **31**				

They have washed their robes" and made them white in the blood of the Lamb. [15]Because of this, they are before the throne of God. They worship him day and night in his temple. And the One who sits on the throne will be present with them. [16]Those people will never be hungry again, and they will never be thirsty again. The sun will not hurt them, and no heat will burn them, [17]because the Lamb at the center of the throne will be their shepherd. He will lead them to springs of water that give life. And God will wipe away every tear from their eyes."

THE SEVENTH SEAL

8 When the Lamb opened the seventh seal, there was silence in heaven for about half an hour. [2]And I saw the seven angels who stand before God and to whom were given seven trumpets.

[3]Another angel came and stood at the altar, holding a golden pan for incense. He was given much incense to offer with the prayers of all God's holy people. The angel put this offering on the golden altar before the throne. [4]The smoke from the incense went up from the angel's hand to God with the prayers of God's people. [5]Then the angel filled the incense pan with fire from the altar and threw it on the

DID YOU KNOW?

Strong religious faith helps kids resist dangerous temptations like drugs and sex.

Sonna, Linda, Ph.D. *The Everything Tween Book,* p. 240.

earth, and there were flashes of lightning, thunder and loud noises, and an earthquake.

THE SEVEN ANGELS AND TRUMPETS

[6]Then the seven angels who had the seven trumpets prepared to blow them.

[7]The first angel blew his trumpet, and hail and fire mixed with blood were poured down on the earth. And a third of the earth, and all the green grass, and a third of the trees were burned up.

[8]Then the second angel blew his trumpet, and something that looked like a big mountain, burning with fire, was thrown into the sea. And a third of the sea became blood, [9]a third of the living things in the sea died, and a third of the ships were destroyed.

[10]Then the third angel blew his trumpet, and a large star, burning like a torch, fell from the sky. It fell on a third of the rivers and on the springs of water. [11]The name of the star is Wormwood." And a third of all the water became bitter, and many people died from drinking the water that was bitter.

[12]Then the fourth angel blew his trumpet, and a third of the sun, and a third of the moon, and a third of the stars were struck. So a third of them became dark, and a third of the day was without light, and also the night.

[13]While I watched, I heard an eagle that was flying high in the air cry out in a loud voice,

Q: I'm falling further and further behind in math. I just don't get it. My parents are going to kill me when they see my report card. What should I do?

A: First, talk to your teacher and find out what your current grade is. There may be a way to still catch up and avoid failing the class. Then talk to your parents about it. They probably won't be happy about it; but between your teacher and your parents, you should get some help. Don't hide from problems like this, but ask God to help you face them.

Q: Can I do something so bad that I'm not a Christian anymore?

A: No. The sacrifice Jesus made on the cross was enough to pay for all the bad acts anyone could ever commit. God forgave Saul (who later became the apostle Paul)—and Saul had hunted down and killed Christians! God also forgave King David (from the Old Testament), who murdered a man so he could steal his wife. He forgave the apostle Peter for denying that he ever knew Jesus. These shocking sinners had one thing in common: they turned away from doing wrong and asked for God's forgiveness. If you ask him, he'll do the same for you (1 John 1:9).

Q: Why did God make annoying bugs like mosquitoes?

A: After Adam and Eve rebelled against God, a lot of things changed. God cursed the environment; that's when some animals that had eaten plants started eating each other. Blood-sucking bugs like mosquitoes are part of that curse.

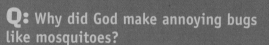

⭐ **7:14 washed their robes** This means they believed in Jesus so that their sins could be forgiven by Christ's blood.　**8:11 Wormwood** Name of a very bitter plant; used here to give the idea of bitter sorrow.

BIBLE SUPERHEROES

Mary, Mother of Jesus
See Luke 1:26–45.

Mary was a teenager when the angel Gabriel told her she would give birth to God's Son. She was engaged to Joseph but they weren't married yet. There was no natural way Mary could have a son, but God did a supernatural thing and Jesus was born nine months later.

Mary was a good mother. She watched her boy grow up to become a great teacher and miracle-worker. She was so proud of him. It hurt her deeply when the Romans nailed him to a cross, but she rejoiced when she saw him come back from the dead!

Mary was truly "blessed" among women. She was never worshiped in the early church, but she has always been honored for her faith in God and her faithfulness in raising Jesus.

"Trouble! Trouble! Trouble for those who live on the earth because of the remaining sounds of the trumpets that the other three angels are about to blow!"

9 Then the fifth angel blew his trumpet, and I saw a star fall from the sky to the earth. The star was given the key to the deep hole that leads to the bottomless pit. [2] Then it opened up the hole that leads to the bottomless pit, and smoke came up from the hole like smoke from a big furnace. Then the sun and sky became dark because of the smoke from the hole. [3] Then locusts came down to the earth out of the smoke, and they were given the power to sting like scorpions." [4] They were told not to harm the grass on the earth or any plant or tree. They could harm only the people who did not have the sign of God on their foreheads. [5] These locusts were not given the power to kill anyone, but to cause pain to the people for five months. And the pain they felt was like the pain a scorpion gives when it stings someone. [6] During those days people will look for a way to die, but they will not find it. They will want to die, but death will run away from them.

[7] The locusts looked like horses prepared for battle. On their heads they wore what looked like crowns of gold, and their faces looked like human faces. [8] Their hair was like women's hair, and their teeth were like lions' teeth. [9] Their chests looked like iron breastplates, and the sound of their wings was like the noise of many horses and chariots hurrying into battle. [10] The locusts had tails with stingers like scorpions, and in their tails was their power to hurt people for five months. [11] The locusts had a king who was the angel of the bottomless pit. His name in the Hebrew language is Abaddon and in the Greek language is Apollyon."

[12] The first trouble is past; there are still two other troubles that will come.

COOL!

Fallen Angels

Demons are fallen angels who chose to serve Satan rather than God. These "evil spirits" are referred to more than one hundred times in the Bible. Jesus cast demons out of people to show that he was stronger than the devil. He gave his followers the power to do the same thing (Matthew 10:1). Demons work hard to keep people from believing in Jesus. They fight against God's plans and create problems in the church. But they won't cause trouble forever; one day they will be thrown into the lake of fire along with their master, Satan (Matthew 25:41).

9:3 scorpions A scorpion is an insect that stings with a bad poison.   **9:11 Abaddon, Apollyon** Both names mean "Destroyer."

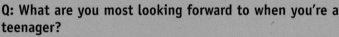

[20] The other people who were not killed by these terrible disasters still did not change their hearts and turn away from what they had made with their own hands. They did not stop worshiping demons and idols made of gold, silver, bronze, stone, and wood—things that cannot see or hear or walk. [21] These people did not change their hearts and turn away from murder or evil magic, from their sexual sins or stealing.

THE ANGEL AND THE SMALL SCROLL

10 Then I saw another powerful angel coming down from heaven dressed in a cloud with a rainbow over his head. His face was like the sun, and his legs were like pillars of fire. [2] The angel was holding a small scroll open in his hand. He put his right foot on the sea and his left foot on the land. [3] Then he shouted loudly like the roaring of a lion. And when he shouted, the voices of seven thunders spoke. [4] When the seven thunders spoke, I started to write. But I heard a voice from heaven say, "Keep hidden what the seven thunders said, and do not write them down."

[5] Then the angel I saw standing on the sea and on the land raised his right hand to heaven, [6] and he made a promise by the power of the One who lives forever and ever. He is the One who made the skies and all that is in them, the earth and all that is in it, and the sea and all that is in it. The angel promised, "There

[13] Then the sixth angel blew his trumpet, and I heard a voice coming from the horns on the golden altar that is before God. [14] The voice said to the sixth angel who had the trumpet, "Free the four angels who are tied at the great river Euphrates." [15] And they let loose the four angels who had been kept ready for this hour and day and month and year so they could kill a third of all people on the earth. [16] I heard how many troops on horses were in their army—two hundred million.

[17] The horses and their riders I saw in the vision looked like this: They had breastplates that were fiery red, dark blue, and yellow like sulfur. The heads of the horses looked like heads of lions, with fire, smoke, and sulfur coming out of their mouths. [18] A third of all the people on earth were killed by these three terrible disasters coming out of the horses' mouths: the fire, the smoke, and the sulfur. [19] The horses' power was in their mouths and in their tails; their tails were like snakes with heads, and with them they hurt people.

Revelation 11:15

Are your prayers boring? Not to God—he never gets tired of listening to you. But maybe your prayers are boring to you, because you pretty much always pray the same thing with the same words in the same way.

Maybe it's time to inject some jet fuel into your prayer life.

First, pray in the Spirit. That means to pray in such a way that the Holy Spirit fully agrees with your prayer. How do you do that? Take a verse in the Bible, believe it, pray it, and you're praying in the Spirit.

Revelation 11:15 records an awesome prayer: "The power to rule the world now belongs to our Lord and his Christ, and he will rule forever and ever." Do you believe it? Then pray it back to God. He loves hearing the important truths of Scripture.

Second, pray using all kinds of different prayers. Yes, there is more than one way to pray. There are asking prayers, thanksgiving prayers, and praise prayers, just to mention a few.

Try thanksgiving prayer. You like people to thank you when you do something good for them. Think of some of the things you've forgotten to thank God for. Write them down, and then, one by one, thank God in prayer for each one.

Rev up your prayer life today!

GET
CONNECTED

SISTERS

Girls! Whoever said you can't live without them didn't have *your* sister, right? But just like playing a videogame helps you understand a real sport, learning from your sister helps you understand other girls—something you'll appreciate soon. As Proverbs 18:15 says, "The wise person listens to learn more." If you'll pay attention to what makes your sister different, you'll be way ahead of guys who don't have sisters in their families.

will be no more waiting! [7] In the days when the seventh angel is ready to blow his trumpet, God's secret will be finished. This secret is the Good News God told to his servants, the prophets."

[8] Then I heard the same voice from heaven again, saying to me: "Go and take the open scroll that is in the hand of the angel that is standing on the sea and on the land."

[9] So I went to the angel and told him to give me the small scroll. And he said to me, "Take the scroll and eat it. It will be sour in your stomach, but in your mouth it will be sweet as honey." [10] So I took the small scroll from the angel's hand and ate it. In my mouth it tasted sweet as honey, but after I ate it, it was sour in my stomach. [11] Then I was told, "You must prophesy again about many peoples, nations, languages, and kings."

THE TWO WITNESSES

11 I was given a measuring stick like a rod, and I was told, "Go and measure the temple of God and the altar, and count the people worshiping there. [2] But do not measure the yard outside the temple. Leave it alone, because it has been given to those who are not God's people. And they will trample on the holy city for forty-two months. [3] And I will give power to my two witnesses to prophesy for one thousand two hundred sixty days, and they will be dressed in rough cloth to show their sadness."

[4] These two witnesses are the two olive trees and the two lampstands that stand before the Lord of the earth. [5] And if anyone tries to hurt them, fire comes from their mouths and kills their enemies. And if anyone tries to hurt them in whatever way, in that same way that person will die. [6] These witnesses have the

power to stop the sky from raining during the time they are prophesying. And they have power to make the waters become blood, and they have power to send every kind of trouble to the earth as many times as they want.

[7] When the two witnesses have finished telling their message, the beast that comes up from the bottomless pit will fight a war against them. He will defeat them and kill them. [8] The bodies of the two witnesses will lie in the street of the great city where the Lord was killed. This city is named Sodom[n] and Egypt, which has a spiritual meaning. [9] Those from every race of people, tribe, language, and nation will look at the bodies of the two witnesses for three and one-half days, and they will refuse to bury them. [10] People who live on the earth will re-

joice and be happy because these two are dead. They will send each other gifts, because these two prophets brought much suffering to those who live on the earth.

[11] But after three and one-half days, God put the breath of life into the two prophets again. They stood on their feet, and everyone who saw them became very afraid. [12] Then the two prophets heard a loud voice from heaven saying, "Come up here!" And they went up into heaven in a cloud as their enemies watched.

[13] In the same hour there was a great earthquake, and a tenth of the city was destroyed. Seven thousand people were killed in the earthquake, and those who did not die were very afraid and gave glory to the God of heaven.

WORLD SPORTS

Curling

Brooms are usually used to clean, but curlers use them to win games. Curling is played on a long ice rink. The team with the most rocks near the center of the *house* (a bull's-eye-shaped goal) wins the game. The thrower spins the forty-four-pound *rock* (a granite stone) down the ice. If the rock *curls* (moves across the rink) too much, two team members adjust the rock's path by sweeping the ice with brooms. The *skip* (the team captain) stands by the house, yelling commands to the sweepers. The team is dependent on the skip for guidance—just like Christians depend on God for victory in life.

⭐ **11:8 Sodom** City that God destroyed because the people were so evil.

[14] The second trouble is finished. Pay attention: The third trouble is coming soon.

THE SEVENTH TRUMPET

[15] Then the seventh angel blew his trumpet. And there were loud voices in heaven, saying:

"The power to rule the world now belongs
　　to our Lord and his Christ,
　and he will rule forever and ever."

[16] Then the twenty-four elders, who sit on their thrones before God, bowed down on their faces and worshiped God. [17] They said:

"We give thanks to you, Lord God
　　Almighty,
　who is and who was,
　because you have used your great power
　　and have begun to rule!

[18] The people of the world were angry,
　but your anger has come.
The time has come to judge the dead,
　and to reward your servants the
　　prophets
and your holy people,
　all who respect you, great and small.
The time has come to destroy those who
　　destroy the earth!"

[19] Then God's temple in heaven was opened. The Ark that holds the agreement God gave to his people could be seen in his

TOP 10

Bible Names for Pets

1. **Moses**
2. **Melchizedek**
3. **Nebuchadnezzar**
4. **Shadrach**
5. **Meshach**
6. **Abednego**
7. **Noah**
8. **Gabriel**
9. **Ahab**
10. **Elijah**

temple. Then there were flashes of lightning, noises, thunder, an earthquake, and a great hailstorm.

THE WOMAN AND THE DRAGON

12 And then a great wonder appeared in heaven: A woman was clothed with the sun, and the moon was under her feet, and a crown of twelve stars was on her head. [2] She was pregnant and cried out with pain, because she was about to give birth. [3] Then another wonder appeared in heaven: There was a giant red dragon with seven heads and seven crowns on each head. He also had ten horns. [4] His tail swept a third of the stars out of the sky and threw them down to the earth. He stood in front of the woman who was ready to give birth so he could eat her baby as soon as it was born. [5] Then the woman gave birth to a son who will rule all the nations with an iron rod. And her child was taken up to God and to his throne. [6] The woman ran away into the desert to a place God prepared for her where she would be taken care of for one thousand two hundred sixty days.

[7] Then there was a war in heaven. Michael" and his angels fought against the dragon, and the dragon and his angels fought back. [8] But the dragon was not strong enough, and he and his angels lost their place in heaven. [9] The giant

trustables

Revelation 11:18

Have you ever heard someone say, "Hey, I'm a good person; isn't that enough?" Being a good person can help you get by in life and can even win you friends. But the fact is that you can never be good enough to earn your way into heaven.

Getting into heaven isn't a popularity contest, or an award you can earn for good behavior. Getting into heaven is a matter of faith. Faith means respecting God and believing what he says.

Believing what God tells us in the Bible matters big time!

At the end of history, God lets us know what will be announced in heaven: "The time has come to judge the dead, and to reward your servants the prophets and your holy people, all who respect you, great and small" (Revelation 11:18).

God doesn't want anyone to miss the rewards of heaven. Here's the best part: all we have to do is trust God and heaven is ours. It doesn't matter where you were born or where you live. It doesn't matter what you look like. It doesn't matter how much money you have. It doesn't matter how smart you are. It doesn't matter how cool you are.

When it comes to heaven, what matters is *who* you believe.

 12:7 Michael The archangel—leader among God's angels or messengers (Jude 9).

dragon was thrown down out of heaven. (He is that old snake called the devil or Satan, who tricks the whole world.) The dragon with his angels was thrown down to the earth.

[10]Then I heard a loud voice in heaven saying:

"The salvation and the power and the
  kingdom of our God
and the authority of his Christ have now
  come.
The accuser of our brothers and sisters,
  who accused them day and night before
  our God,
has been thrown down.
[11]And our brothers and sisters defeated him
  by the blood of the Lamb's death
  and by the message they preached.
They did not love their lives so much
  that they were afraid of death.
[12]So rejoice, you heavens
  and all who live there!
But it will be terrible for the earth and the
  sea,
  because the devil has come down to
  you!
He is filled with anger,
  because he knows he does not have
  much time."

[13]When the dragon saw he had been

50% of kids do chores every day.

Taylor KidsPulse 2004 Report. Taylor Research & Consulting Group.

thrown down to the earth, he hunted for the woman who had given birth to the son. [14]But the woman was given the two wings of a great eagle so she could fly to the place prepared for her in the desert. There she would be taken care of for three and one-half years, away from the snake. [15]Then the snake poured water out of its mouth like a

river toward the woman so the flood would carry her away. [16]But the earth helped the woman by opening its mouth and swallowing the river that came from the mouth of the dragon. [17]Then the dragon was very angry at the woman, and he went off to make war against all her other children—those who obey God's commands and who have the message Jesus taught.

[18]And the dragon" stood on the seashore.

THE TWO BEASTS

13 Then I saw a beast coming up out of the sea. It had ten horns and seven heads, and there was a crown on each horn. A name against God was written on each head. [2]This beast looked like a leopard, with feet like a bear's feet and a mouth like a lion's mouth. And the dragon gave the beast all of his power and his throne and great authority. [3]One of the heads of the beast looked as if it had been killed by a wound, but this death wound was healed. Then the whole world was amazed and followed the beast. [4]People worshiped the dragon because he had given his

Q: Is it okay to fight if I'm defending myself?

A: If you have to fight to get away from someone for your own safety, it's okay to hit. But if someone punches or shoves you just to try to start a fight, you should not hit back—that's exactly what he wants you to do. Jesus taught that we should not fight back. He said that if someone slaps you across one side of your face, you are to turn so he can slap the other side, too (Matthew 5:39). That may sound funny, but Jesus wants us to show love that is so different from the world that it makes people ask about God!

Q: Is littering a sin?

A: Yes. It's against the law to litter, and so littering is morally and legally wrong. But more than that, littering shows a selfish disrespect for other people and for God's creation.

Q: Of the 6.5 billion people in the world, how many are going to heaven?

A: People who study religion say that there are over a billion Christians in the world. But Jesus warned us that not everybody who claims to be a Christian is automatically going to heaven (Matthew 7:21–23). Only God knows each person's heart and how many of those billion really believe in Jesus. Many people have grown up in the church only to realize one day that they've never given their heart to the Lord. Make sure that you know where *you* are going!

In Avigliana, Italy, young people use Italian editions of video games to make a difference for Jesus Christ. The video games attract local kids to Avigliana's only youth center. Since Italians tend to be family-oriented and love soccer, the Italian Christians play family kinds of video games, like soccer.

Tournaments are held in which families can compete against other families. The young hosts arrive early to set up snacks and connect multiple game boxes so that large families can play together. The events create lively competition and lots of laughter. After the games are over, the church members invite the families to dinner. This helps them build friendships. For many Italians, this game night is the first time they have been in a Bible-teaching church.

Think through the kinds of games your neighbors would like play and the kinds of events (like tournaments) that would attract them. A video game event might be a great way to attract other young people to your church. Or maybe you could hold a sports tournament—get together with some Christian friends and start brainstorming!

power to the beast. And they also worshiped the beast, asking, "Who is like the beast? Who can make war against it?"

[5] The beast was allowed to say proud words and words against God, and it was allowed to use its power for forty-two months. [6] It used its mouth to speak against God, against God's name, against the place where God lives, and against all those who live in heaven. [7] It was given power to make war against God's holy people and to defeat them. It was given power over every tribe, people, language, and nation. [8] And all who live on earth will worship the beast—all the people since the beginning of the world whose names are not written in the Lamb's book of life. The Lamb is the One who was killed.

[9] Anyone who has ears should listen:
[10] If you are to be a prisoner,
    then you will be a prisoner.
  If you are to be killed with the sword,
    then you will be killed with the sword.
This means that God's holy people must have patience and faith.

[11] Then I saw another beast coming up out of the earth. It had two horns like a lamb, but it spoke like a dragon. [12] This beast stands before the first beast and uses the same power the first beast has. By this power it makes everyone living on earth worship the first beast, who had the death wound that was healed. [13] And the second beast does great miracles so that it even makes fire come down from heaven to earth while people are watching. [14] It fools those who live on earth by the miracles it has been given the power to do. It does these miracles to serve the first beast. The second beast orders people to make an idol to honor the first beast, the one that was wounded by the deadly sword but sprang to life again. [15] The second beast was given power to give life to the idol of the first one so that the idol could speak. And the second beast was given power to command all who will not worship the image of the beast to be killed. [16] The second beast also forced all people, small and great, rich and poor, free and slave, to have a mark on their right hand or on their forehead. [17] No one could buy or sell without this mark, which is the name of the beast or the number of its name. [18] This takes wisdom. Let the one who has understanding find the meaning of the number, which is the number of a person. Its number is 666."

THE SONG OF THE SAVED

14 Then I looked, and there before me was the Lamb standing on Mount Zion." With him were one hundred forty-four thousand people who had his name and his Father's name written on their foreheads. [2] And I heard a sound from heaven like the noise of flooding water and like the sound of loud thunder. The sound I heard was like people playing harps. [3] And they sang a new song before the throne and before the four living creatures and the elders. No one could learn the new song except the one hundred forty-four

71% of boys talk to their dads about problems.

"Fatherhood by the Numbers" by Steve Brearton.

Pay Attention

Having trouble staying awake on those warm lazy afternoons in the classroom? Remember, it's important to show respect to your teachers by paying attention. Sometimes concentrating in church isn't always easy, either. Try writing an outline of the sermon and giving your family a summary at lunch.

COOL!

Noble Centurions

Centurions were Roman officers who commanded one hundred men. Because they went into battle at the head of their troops, they were known for their courage—and short life spans!

The centurions in the Bible were noble men. Jesus praised one for his faith (Matthew 8:5–13). The centurion who watched Jesus die on the cross exclaimed, "This man really was the Son of God!" (Mark 15:39).

A centurion named Cornelius was among the first non-Jews to believe in Jesus (Acts 10). And Julius (the commander) protected the apostle Paul (Acts 27).

These tough men had tender hearts toward God.

---

thousand who had been bought from the earth. ⁴These are the ones who did not do sinful things with women, because they kept themselves pure. They follow the Lamb every place he goes. These one hundred forty-four thousand were bought from among the people of the earth as people to be offered to God and the Lamb. ⁵They were not guilty of telling lies; they are without fault.

THE THREE ANGELS

⁶Then I saw another angel flying high in the air. He had the eternal Good News to preach to those who live on earth—to every nation, tribe, language, and people. ⁷He preached in a loud voice, "Fear God and give him praise, because the time has come for God to judge all people. So worship God who made the heavens, and the earth, and the sea, and the springs of water."

⁸Then the second angel followed the first angel and said, "Ruined, ruined is the great city of Babylon! She made all the nations drink the wine of the anger of her adultery."

⁹Then a third angel followed the first two angels, saying in a loud voice: "If anyone worships the beast and his idol and gets the beast's

---

trustables

Revelation 14:13

When the Bible describes our life apart from Jesus Christ, it's not a pretty picture. Even our best deeds look bad to God.

Thankfully, God wants to come into our sinful lives and change everything for all time. We did not deserve such mercy and grace; we deserved death. That's what people mean when they say, "I am saved." God saves us from dying and gives us the gift of truly living.

Once we're saved, God gives us the ability to do things *he* considers good. Stories of the lives of Jesus and the apostles give us many examples of truly good deeds.

It's often been said that only two things will last forever: God's Word and God's people. Actually, the Bible also says that when people die in the Lord, "the reward of all they have done stays with them" (Revelation 14:13). That's a promise worth remembering!

After doing a few good works, you might be tempted to take a little credit for your life, but the Bible reminds us that our new life in Jesus Christ is a gift from God. We should thank God for saving us and then get back to the good works he's planned for us to do. After all, the rewards will last forever!

mark on the forehead or on the hand, [10]that one also will drink the wine of God's anger, which is prepared with all its strength in the cup of his anger. And that person will be put in pain with burning sulfur before the holy angels and the Lamb. [11]And the smoke from their burning pain will rise forever and ever. There will be no rest, day or night, for those who worship the beast and his idol or who get the mark of his name." [12]This means God's holy people must be patient. They must obey God's commands and keep their faith in Jesus.

[13]Then I heard a voice from heaven saying, "Write this: Blessed are the dead who die from now on in the Lord."

The Spirit says, "Yes, they will rest from their hard work, and the reward of all they have done stays with them."

THE EARTH IS HARVESTED

[14]Then I looked, and there before me was a white cloud, and sitting on the white cloud was One who looked like a Son of Man." He had a gold crown on his head and a sharp sickle" in his hand. [15]Then another angel came out of the temple and called out in a loud voice to the One who was sitting on the cloud, "Take your sickle and harvest from the earth, because the time to harvest has come, and the fruit of the earth is ripe." [16]So the One who was sitting on the cloud swung his sickle over the earth, and the earth was harvested.

[17]Then another angel came out of the temple in heaven, and he also had a sharp sickle. [18]And then another angel, who has power over the fire, came from the altar. This angel called to the angel with the sharp sickle, saying, "Take your sharp sickle and gather the bunches of grapes from the earth's vine, because its grapes are ripe." [19]Then the angel swung his sickle over the earth. He gathered the earth's grapes and threw them into the great winepress of God's anger. [20]They were trampled in the winepress outside the city, and blood flowed out of the winepress as high as horses' bridles for a distance of about one hundred eighty miles.

THE LAST TROUBLES

15 Then I saw another wonder in heaven that was great and amazing. There were seven angels bringing seven disasters. These are the last disasters, because after them, God's anger is finished.

[2]I saw what looked like a sea of glass mixed with fire. All of those who had won the victory over the beast and his idol and over the number of his name were standing by the sea of glass. They had harps that God had given them. [3]They sang the song of Moses, the servant of God, and the song of the Lamb:

"You do great and wonderful things,

Psalm 111:2

Lord God Almighty. *Amos 3:13*

Everything the Lord does is right and true,

Psalm 145:17

King of the nations."

[4]Everyone will respect you, Lord,

Jeremiah 10:7

and will honor you.

Only you are holy.

All the nations will come

and worship you, *Psalm 86:9–10*

because the right things you have done

are now made known."

Deuteronomy 32:4

[5]After this I saw that the temple (the Tent of the Agreement) in heaven was opened. [6]And the seven angels bringing the seven disasters came out of the temple. They were dressed in clean, shining linen and wore golden bands tied around their chests. [7]Then one of the four living creatures gave to the seven angels seven golden bowls filled with the anger of God, who lives forever and ever. [8]The temple was filled with smoke from the glory and the power of God, and no one could enter the temple until the seven disasters of the seven angels were finished.

THE BOWLS OF GOD'S ANGER

16 Then I heard a loud voice from the temple saying to the seven angels, "Go and pour out the seven bowls of God's anger on the earth."

[2]The first angel left and poured out his bowl on the land. Then ugly and painful sores came upon all those who had the mark of the beast and who worshiped his idol.

Revelation 15:3

Have you ever gone a whole day without complaining? It's hard! Maybe that's why most people don't even bother to try.

Philippians 2:14 tells us to do everything without complaining or arguing. That's a tall order. We are tempted to complain all the time. "I'm bored." "My homework is stupid." "I don't like those people." Sound familiar? We all have these thoughts. But saying them only makes things worse.

Instead of complaining, think of something good about your situation. Say it out loud. And then find a way to make things better. Cure your boredom by learning new hobbies, get help for your "stupid" homework, and get to know the kids you don't like...they may surprise you.

Just don't complain. Even at the end of the world, God's people will praise him: "You do great and wonderful things, Lord God Almighty. Everything the Lord does is right and true" (Revelation 15:3).

What do you usually complain about? Your parents' rules? Your little sister? That you don't have the cool new video game? You can stop complaining if you start to be thankful! Write down five things you're thankful for. Try to think of one new thing every day. Pretty soon, you'll be out of the habit of complaining—and in the habit of praising God.

14:14 Son of Man "Son of Man" is a name Jesus called himself.   **14:14 sickle** A farming tool with a curved blade. It was used to harvest grain.   **15:3 King . . . nations** Some Greek copies read "King of the ages."

[3] The second angel poured out his bowl on the sea, and it became blood like that of a dead man, and every living thing in the sea died.

[4] The third angel poured out his bowl on the rivers and the springs of water, and they became blood. [5] Then I heard the angel of the waters saying:

"Holy One, you are the One who is and who was.

You are right to decide to punish these evil people.

[6] They have poured out the blood of your holy people and your prophets.

So now you have given them blood to drink as they deserve."

[7] And I heard a voice coming from the altar saying:

"Yes, Lord God Almighty,

the way you punish evil people is right and fair."

[8] The fourth angel poured out his bowl on the sun, and he was given power to burn the people with fire. [9] They were burned by the great heat, and they cursed the name of God, who had control over these disasters. But the people refused to change their hearts and lives and give glory to God.

[10] The fifth angel poured out his bowl on the throne of the beast, and darkness covered its kingdom. People gnawed their tongues because of the pain. [11] They also cursed the God of heaven because of their pain and the sores they had, but they refused to change their hearts and turn away from the evil things they did.

Top 10 Things You'll Wish You'd Done When You're Older

1. **Learn a musical instrument.**
2. **Read the classics.**
3. **Learn a foreign language.**
4. **Travel abroad.**
5. **Keep up with friends.**
6. **Listen to your parents.**
7. **Be friends with your siblings.**
8. **Save money.**
9. **Play sports.**
10. **Trust God with your life.**

[12] The sixth angel poured out his bowl on the great river Euphrates so that the water in the river was dried up to prepare the way for the kings from the east to come. [13] Then I saw three evil spirits that looked like frogs coming out of the mouth of the dragon, out of the mouth of the beast, and out of the mouth of the false prophet. [14] These evil spirits are the spirits of demons, which have power to do miracles. They go out to the kings of the whole world to gather them together for the battle on the great day of God Almighty.

[15] "Listen! I will come as a thief comes! Blessed are those who stay awake and keep their clothes on so that they will not walk around naked and have people see their shame."

[16] Then the evil spirits gathered the kings together to the place that is called Armageddon in the Hebrew language.

[17] The seventh angel poured out his bowl into the air. Then a loud voice came out of the temple from the throne, saying, "It is finished!" [18] Then there were flashes of lightning, noises, thunder, and a big earthquake—the worst earthquake that has ever happened since people have been on earth. [19] The great city split into three parts, and the cities of the nations were destroyed. And God remembered the sins of Babylon the Great, so he gave that city the cup filled with the wine of his terrible anger. [20] Then every island ran away, and mountains disappeared. [21] Giant hailstones, each weighing about a hundred pounds, fell from the sky upon people. People cursed God

BIBLE SUPERHEROES

John Mark
See Acts 15:36-40.

John Mark grew up in a Christian home. There was even a church that met in his house (Acts 12:12). When the apostle Paul went on his first preaching trip, he took Mark along as a helper.

The trip started well, but Mark quit in the middle (Acts 13:13). Later, when he asked Paul for another chance, Paul said no. But Paul's partner, Barnabas, gave Mark a second shot.

Barnabas turned out to be right about Mark. He became a great witness for the Lord. Paul forgave him, and they even worked together again (2 Timothy 4:11). Mark went on to write one of the Gospels.

You don't have to be perfect to serve Jesus; you just have to persevere. It's not failure when you fall down—only when you don't get up.

Ever play flashlight tag or flashlight hide-and-seek at church? Games that involve flashlights are a lot of fun and allow everyone to be involved because almost every family owns at least one flashlight. Flashlight games can help shine the light of God's love into the hearts of others.

Once each summer, Derick and Dustin get the neighborhood together for an event they call "Night Games." After outdoor games like flashlight tag, the group gathers in the family garage for a game they call "Flashlight Follies." During this game, the participants act out, in the dark, scenes from their favorite movies while those who are watching quickly wave their flashlights over the actors. The flashlights create the look of an old-fashioned movie.

Toward the end of this game, Derick and Dustin act out a scene from the Bible that they've rehearsed ahead of time. The scene opens the door for future conversations about what it means to be a Christian.

Having a neighborhood game night is a great way to get everyone having fun together—and don't forget to take a few minutes to talk about what God has done for you!

for the disaster of the hail, because this disaster was so terrible.

THE WOMAN ON THE ANIMAL

17 Then one of the seven angels who had the seven bowls came and spoke to me. He said, "Come, and I will show you the punishment that will be given to the great prostitute, the one sitting over many waters. [2] The kings of the earth sinned sexually with her, and the people of the earth became drunk from the wine of her sexual sin."

[3] Then the angel carried me away by the Spirit to the desert. There I saw a woman sitting on a red beast. It was covered with names against God written on it, and it had seven heads and ten horns. [4] The woman was dressed in purple and red and was shining with the gold, precious jewels, and pearls she was wearing. She had a golden cup in her hand, a cup filled with evil things and the uncleanness of her sexual sin. [5] On her forehead a title was written that was secret. This is what was written:

THE GREAT BABYLON
MOTHER OF PROSTITUTES
AND OF THE EVIL THINGS OF THE EARTH

[6] Then I saw that the woman was drunk with the blood of God's holy people and with the blood of those who were killed because of their faith in Jesus.

When I saw the woman, I was very amazed. [7] Then the angel said to me, "Why are you amazed? I will tell you the secret of this woman and the beast she rides—the one with seven heads and ten horns. [8] The beast you saw was once alive but is not alive now. But soon it will come up out of the bottomless pit and go away to be destroyed. There are people who live on earth whose names have not been written in the book of life since the beginning of the world. They will be amazed when they see the beast, because he was once alive, is not alive now, but will come again.

[9] "You need a wise mind to understand this. The seven heads on the beast are seven mountains where the woman sits. [10] And they are seven kings. Five of the kings have already been destroyed, one of the kings lives now, and another has not yet come. When he comes, he must stay a short time. [11] The beast that was once alive, but is not alive now, is also an eighth king. He belongs to the first seven kings, and he will go away to be destroyed.

[12] "The ten horns you saw are ten kings who have not yet begun to rule, but they will receive power to rule with the beast for one hour. [13] All ten of these kings have the same purpose, and they will give their power and authority to the beast. [14] They will make war against the Lamb, but the Lamb will defeat them, because he is Lord of lords and King of kings. He will defeat them with his called, chosen, and faithful followers."

[15] Then the angel said to me, "The waters that you saw, where the prostitute sits, are peoples, races, nations, and languages. [16] The ten horns and the beast you saw will hate the prostitute. They will take everything she has and leave her naked. They will eat her body and burn her with fire. [17] God made the ten horns want to carry out his purpose by agreeing to give the beast their power to rule, until what God has said comes about. [18] The woman you saw is the great city that rules over the kings of the earth."

BABYLON IS DESTROYED

18 After the vision of these things, I saw another angel coming down from heaven. This angel had great power, and his glory made the earth bright. [2] He shouted in a powerful voice:

"Ruined, ruined is the great city of Babylon!
She has become a home for demons

THE CROSS

It's worn as jewelry, attached to the sides of church buildings, and used as a Christian symbol. What is it? The *cross*! In ancient times, criminals were not executed by firing squads or electric chairs; they were often slowly and painfully killed by being hung on wooden crosses.

Jesus was killed on a cross—but he wasn't a criminal! The religious leaders didn't like Jesus' message that anyone could know God if they believed in God's Son. They didn't believe that Jesus was God and they wanted him dead. Jesus was crucified (killed on the cross). Because he was the perfect Son of God, his death paid for our sins. He didn't stay dead, though. Three days later, he came back to life!

and a prison for every evil spirit,
and a prison for every unclean bird and
unclean beast.
[3]She has been ruined, because all the
peoples of the earth
have drunk the wine of the desire of her
sexual sin.
She has been ruined also because the kings
of the earth
have sinned sexually with her,
and the merchants of the earth
have grown rich from the great wealth
of her luxury."
[4]Then I heard another voice from heaven
saying:
"Come out of that city, my people,
so that you will not share in her sins,
so that you will not receive the disasters
that will come to her.
[5]Her sins have piled up as high as the sky,
and God has not forgotten the wrongs
she has done.
[6]Give that city the same as she gave to
others.
Pay her back twice as much as she did.
Prepare wine for her that is twice as strong
as the wine she prepared for others.
[7]She gave herself much glory and rich living.
Give her that much suffering and
sadness.
She says to herself, 'I am a queen sitting on
my throne.
I am not a widow; I will never be sad.'
[8]So these disasters will come to her in one
day:
death, and crying, and great hunger,
and she will be destroyed by fire,
because the Lord God who judges her is
powerful."
[9]The kings of the earth who sinned sexually with her and shared her wealth will see the smoke from her burning. Then they will cry and be sad because of her death. [10]They will be afraid of her suffering and stand far away and say:
"Terrible! How terrible for you, great city,
powerful city of Babylon,
because your punishment has come in one
hour!"
[11]And the merchants of the earth will cry and be sad about her, because now there is no one to buy their cargoes— [12]cargoes of gold, silver, jewels, pearls, fine linen, purple cloth, silk, red cloth; all kinds of citron wood and all kinds of things made from ivory, expensive wood, bronze, iron, and marble; [13]cinnamon, spice, incense, myrrh, frankincense, wine, olive oil, fine flour, wheat, cattle, sheep, horses, carriages, slaves, and human lives.

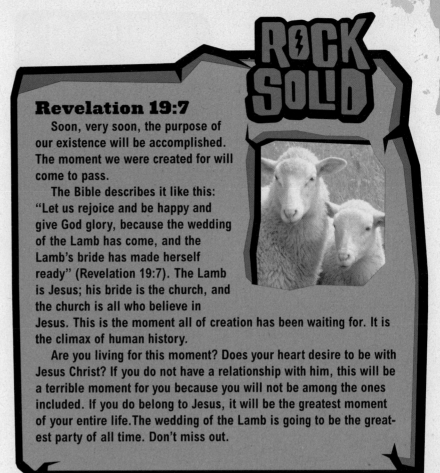

ROCK SOLID

Revelation 19:7

Soon, very soon, the purpose of our existence will be accomplished. The moment we were created for will come to pass.

The Bible describes it like this: "Let us rejoice and be happy and give God glory, because the wedding of the Lamb has come, and the Lamb's bride has made herself ready" (Revelation 19:7). The Lamb is Jesus; his bride is the church, and the church is all who believe in Jesus. This is the moment all of creation has been waiting for. It is the climax of human history.

Are you living for this moment? Does your heart desire to be with Jesus Christ? If you do not have a relationship with him, this will be a terrible moment for you because you will not be among the ones included. If you do belong to Jesus, it will be the greatest moment of your entire life. The wedding of the Lamb is going to be the greatest party of all time. Don't miss out.

[14]The merchants will say,
"Babylon, the good things you wanted are
gone from you.
All your rich and fancy things have
disappeared.
You will never have them again."
[15]The merchants who became rich from selling to her will be afraid of her suffering and will stand far away. They will cry and be sad [16]and say:
"Terrible! How terrible for the great city!
She was dressed in fine linen, purple and
red cloth,
and she was shining with gold, precious
jewels, and pearls!
[17]All these riches have been destroyed in
one hour!"
Every sea captain, every passenger, the sailors, and all those who earn their living from the sea stood far away from Babylon. [18]As they saw the smoke from her burning, they cried out loudly, "There was never a city like this great city!" [19]And they threw dust on their heads and cried out, weeping and being sad. They said:
"Terrible! How terrible for the great city!
All the people who had ships on the sea
became rich because of her wealth!
But she has been destroyed in one hour!
[20]Be happy because of this, heaven!
Be happy, God's holy people and
apostles and prophets!
God has punished her because of what she
did to you."
[21]Then a powerful angel picked up a large stone, like one used for grinding grain, and threw it into the sea. He said:
"In the same way, the great city of Babylon
will be thrown down,
and it will never be found again.
[22]The music of people playing harps and
other instruments, flutes, and
trumpets,
will never be heard in you again.
No workman doing any job
will ever be found in you again.
The sound of grinding grain
will never be heard in you again.
[23]The light of a lamp
will never shine in you again,
and the voices of a bridegroom and bride
will never be heard in you again.

Your merchants were the world's great
  people,
and all the nations were tricked by your
  magic.
²⁴You are guilty of the death of the prophets
  and God's holy people
and all who have been killed on earth."

PEOPLE IN HEAVEN PRAISE GOD

19 After this vision and announcement I heard what sounded like a great many people in heaven saying:
"Hallelujah!"
Salvation, glory, and power belong to our
  God,
² because his judgments are true and
  right.
He has punished the prostitute
  who made the earth evil with her sexual
  sin.
He has paid her back for the death of his
  servants."
³Again they said:
"Hallelujah!
She is burning, and her smoke will rise
  forever and ever."
⁴Then the twenty-four elders and the four living creatures bowed down and worshiped God, who sits on the throne. They said:

DID YOU KNOW?

42% of kids play video games on family road trips.

Youth University Newsflash. Vol. 2.

"Amen, Hallelujah!"
⁵Then a voice came from the throne, saying:
"Praise our God, all you who serve him
  and all you who honor him, both small
  and great!"
⁶Then I heard what sounded like a great many people, like the noise of flooding water, and like the noise of loud thunder. The people were saying:

"Hallelujah!
  Our Lord God, the Almighty, rules.
⁷Let us rejoice and be happy
  and give God glory,
because the wedding of the Lamb has
  come,
  and the Lamb's bride has made herself
  ready.
⁸Fine linen, bright and clean, was given to
  her to wear."
(The fine linen means the good things done by God's holy people.)
⁹And the angel said to me, "Write this: Blessed are those who have been invited to the wedding meal of the Lamb!" And the angel said, "These are the true words of God."
¹⁰Then I bowed down at the angel's feet to worship him, but he said to me, "Do not worship me! I am a servant like you and your brothers and sisters who have the message of Jesus. Worship God, because the message about Jesus is the spirit that gives all prophecy."

THE RIDER ON THE WHITE HORSE

¹¹Then I saw heaven opened, and there before me was a white horse. The rider on the horse is called Faithful and True, and he is right when he judges and makes war. ¹²His eyes are like burning fire, and on his head are many crowns. He has a name written on him, which

Q: Why do I have to go to school?

A: School helps to make you better prepared for the working world. If you go out looking for a job with a sixth-grade education, your choices will be very limited. The more schooling you've had, the better you'll be able to provide for your family and yourself. God doesn't love well-educated people more than he loves high school dropouts, but he does want you to use your mind to its full potential. No matter how far you get in school, you should be a life-long student of the Bible (2 Timothy 2:15).

Q: I pray all the time that my mom will win the lottery. Why hasn't it happened yet?

A: Sometimes God says no. The bad thing about the lottery is that it fools us into thinking money can solve our problems. Many lottery winners end up deep in debt and miserable just a few years after winning. If your family needs money, it's good for you to ask God to supply your needs; but he doesn't need to use the lottery to take care of you (Luke 11:9–13). And he will always do what's best for us in the long run.

Q: How does God know what's going to happen in the future?

A: This is kind of a mind-bender. God exists outside of time, so he sees everything that has happened and that will happen at the same time. He's in control of time! No matter what time in history it is, he is with you.

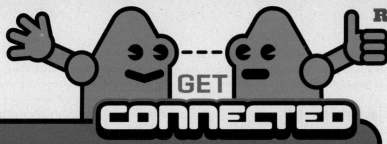

WHEN BAD THINGS HAPPEN

Jerry loved surfing in the ocean, but he'll probably never surf again. After a wave picked him up and threw him headfirst onto the sand, eleven-year-old Jerry was paralyzed from the waist down.

When something terrible changes your life, it sure doesn't seem fair. It seemed that way to Jerry. Then he read Romans 11:33: "No one can explain the things God decides or understand his ways." When life hurts, when it doesn't seem a bit fair, remember that God has a plan. In Jerry's case, God gave him a special way to share Jesus Christ with surfers.

no one but himself knows. [13]He is dressed in a robe dipped in blood, and his name is the Word of God. [14]The armies of heaven, dressed in fine linen, white and clean, were following him on white horses. [15]Out of the rider's mouth comes a sharp sword that he will use to defeat the nations, and he will rule them with a rod of iron. He will crush out the wine in the winepress of the terrible anger of God the Almighty. [16]On his robe and on his upper leg was written this name: KING OF KINGS AND LORD OF LORDS.

[17]Then I saw an angel standing in the sun, and he called with a loud voice to all the birds flying in the sky: "Come and gather together for the great feast of God [18]so that you can eat the bodies of kings, generals, mighty people, horses and their riders, and the bodies of all people—free, slave, small, and great."

[19]Then I saw the beast and the kings of the earth. Their armies were gathered together to make war against the rider on the horse and his army. [20]But the beast was captured and with him the false prophet who did the miracles for the beast. The false prophet had used these miracles to trick those who had the mark of the beast and worshiped his idol. The false prophet and the beast were thrown alive into the lake of fire that burns with sulfur. [21]And their armies were killed with the sword that came out of the mouth of the rider on the horse, and all the birds ate the bodies until they were full.

THE THOUSAND YEARS

20 I saw an angel coming down from heaven. He had the key to the bottomless pit and a large chain in his hand. [2]The angel grabbed the dragon, that old snake who is the devil and Satan, and tied him up for a thousand years. [3]Then he threw him into the bottomless pit, closed it, and locked it over him. The angel did this so he could not trick the people of the earth anymore until the thousand years were ended. After a thousand years he must be set free for a short time.

[4]Then I saw some thrones and people sitting on them who had been given the power to judge. And I saw the souls of those who had been killed because they were faithful to the message of Jesus and the message from God. They had not worshiped the beast or his idol, and they had not received the mark of the beast on their foreheads or on their hands. They came back to life and ruled with Christ for a thousand years. [5](The others that were dead did not live again until the thousand years were ended.) This is the first raising of the dead. [6]Blessed and holy are those who share in this first raising of the dead. The second death has no power over them. They will be priests

Sheep Need Shepherds

People have been raising sheep for a long time. One pound of wool from these gentle animals can make ten miles of yarn.

Moses took care of sheep before God called him to lead Israel. So did David before he became king. Both these Old Testament men knew that sheep need shepherds to watch them. If one falls on its back, it can't get up by itself. It will die.

We are like sheep in many ways. Jesus called himself the Good Shepherd who keeps us safe (John 10).

for God and for Christ and will rule with him for a thousand years.

[7]When the thousand years are over, Satan will be set free from his prison. [8]Then he will go out to trick the nations in all the earth—Gog and Magog—to gather them for battle. There are so many people they will be like sand on the seashore. [9]And Satan's army marched across the earth and gathered around the camp of God's people and the city God loves. But fire came down from heaven and burned them up. [10]And Satan, who tricked them, was thrown into the lake of burning sulfur with the beast and the false prophet. There they will be punished day and night forever and ever.

PEOPLE OF THE WORLD ARE JUDGED

[11]Then I saw a great white throne and the One who was sitting on it. Earth and sky ran away from him and disappeared. [12]And I saw the dead, great and small, standing before the throne. Then books were opened, and the book of life was opened. The dead were judged by what they had done, which was written in the books. [13]The sea gave up the dead who were in it, and Death and Hades" gave up the dead who were in them. Each person was judged by what he had done. [14]And Death and Hades were thrown into the lake of fire. The

lake of fire is the second death. [15]And anyone whose name was not found written in the book of life was thrown into the lake of fire.

THE NEW JERUSALEM

21 Then I saw a new heaven and a new earth. The first heaven and the first earth had disappeared, and there was no sea anymore. [2]And I saw the holy city, the new Jerusalem," coming down out of heaven from God. It was prepared like a bride dressed for her husband. [3]And I heard a loud voice from the throne, saying, "Now God's presence is with people, and he will live with them, and they will be his people. God himself will be with them and will be their God." [4]He will wipe away every tear from their eyes, and there will be no more death, sadness, crying, or pain, because all the old ways are gone."

[5]The One who was sitting on the throne said, "Look! I am making everything new!" Then he said, "Write this, because these words are true and can be trusted."

[6]The One on the throne said to me, "It is finished. I am the Alpha and the Omega," the Beginning and the End. I will give free water from the spring of the water of life to anyone who is thirsty. [7]Those who win the victory will receive this, and I will be their God, and they will be my

children. [8]But cowards, those who refuse to believe, who do evil things, who kill, who sin sexually, who do evil magic, who worship idols, and who tell lies—all these will have a place in the lake of burning sulfur. This is the second death."

[9]Then one of the seven angels who had the seven bowls full of the seven last troubles came to me, saying, "Come with me, and I will show you the bride, the wife of the Lamb." [10]And the angel carried me away by the Spirit to a very large and high mountain. He showed me the holy city, Jerusalem, coming down out of heaven from God. [11]It was shining with the glory of God and was bright like a very expensive jewel, like a jasper, clear as crystal. [12]The city had a great high wall with twelve gates with twelve angels at the gates, and on each gate was written the name of one of the twelve tribes of Israel. [13]There were three gates on the east, three on the north, three on the south, and three on the west. [14]The walls of the city were built on twelve foundation stones, and on the stones were written the names of the twelve apostles of the Lamb.

[15]The angel who talked with me had a measuring rod made of gold to measure the city, its gates, and its wall. [16]The city was built in a square, and its length was equal to its width. The angel measured the city with the rod. The city was 1,500 miles long, 1,500 miles

trustables

Revelation 22:12

Have you heard the old saying, "Eat, drink, and be merry, for tomorrow we will die"? It's used as an excuse to live for the moment and not worry about any long-term consequences. A lot of people live this way and think they are living the "good life." What they don't realize is that what they do now in their short earthly lives will determine what they do in their everlasting lives.

You've probably heard about the second coming of Jesus Christ. It's true—he's coming back! Only this time he won't come as a baby and he won't be

killed by men. He will come as the eternal King of glory. And every man and woman will get a chance to review his or her life with him. As Jesus said in Revelation 22:12, "Listen! I am coming soon! I will bring my reward with me, and I will repay each one of you for what you have done."

Everything you do in your life on earth will count for something in heaven! So what will your "repayment" be? You can't know the day or hour when Jesus will come back. But you can be certain that it *will* happen. Will you be ready?

20:13 Hades The place of the dead. · **21:2 new Jerusalem** The spiritual city where God's people live with him. · **21:3 and . . . God** Some Greek copies do not have this phrase. **21:6 Alpha and the Omega** The first and last letters of the Greek alphabet. This means "the beginning and the end."

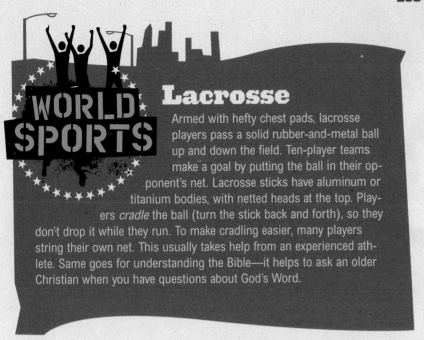

Lacrosse

Armed with hefty chest pads, lacrosse players pass a solid rubber-and-metal ball up and down the field. Ten-player teams make a goal by putting the ball in their opponent's net. Lacrosse sticks have aluminum or titanium bodies, with netted heads at the top. Players *cradle* the ball (turn the stick back and forth), so they don't drop it while they run. To make cradling easier, many players string their own net. This usually takes help from an experienced athlete. Same goes for understanding the Bible—it helps to ask an older Christian when you have questions about God's Word.

wide, and 1,500 miles high. ¹⁷The angel also measured the wall. It was 216 feet high, by human measurements, which the angel was using. ¹⁸The wall was made of jasper, and the city was made of pure gold, as pure as glass. ¹⁹The foundation stones of the city walls were decorated with every kind of jewel. The first foundation was jasper, the second was sapphire, the third was chalcedony, the fourth was emerald, ²⁰the fifth was onyx, the sixth was carnelian, the seventh was chrysolite, the eighth was beryl, the ninth was topaz, the tenth was chrysoprase, the eleventh was jacinth, and the twelfth was amethyst. ²¹The twelve gates were twelve pearls, each gate having been made from a single pearl. And the street of the city was made of pure gold as clear as glass.

²²I did not see a temple in the city, because the Lord God Almighty and the Lamb are the city's temple. ²³The city does not need the sun or the moon to shine on it, because the glory of God is its light, and the Lamb is the city's lamp. ²⁴By its light the people of the world will walk, and the kings of the earth will bring their glory into it. ²⁵The city's gates will never be shut on any day, because there is no night there. ²⁶The glory and the honor of the nations will be brought into it. ²⁷Nothing unclean and no one who does shameful things or tells lies will ever go into it. Only those whose names are written in the Lamb's book of life will enter the city.

22 Then the angel showed me the river of the water of life. It was shining like crystal and was flowing from the throne of God and of the Lamb ²down the middle of the street of the city. The tree of life was on each side of the river. It produces fruit twelve times a year, once each month. The leaves of the tree are for the healing of all the nations. ³Nothing that God judges guilty will be in that city. The throne of God and of the Lamb will be there, and God's servants will worship him. ⁴They will see his face, and his name will be written on their foreheads. ⁵There will never be night again. They will not need the light of a lamp or the light of the sun, because the Lord God will give them light. And they will rule as kings forever and ever.

⁶The angel said to me, "These words can be trusted and are true." The Lord, the God of the spirits of the prophets, sent his angel to show his servants the things that must happen soon.

⁷"Listen! I am coming soon! Blessed is the one who obeys the words of prophecy in this book."

⁸I, John, am the one who heard and saw these things. When I heard and saw them, I bowed down to worship at the feet of the angel who showed these things to me. ⁹But the angel said to me, "Do not worship me! I am a servant like you, your brothers the prophets, and all those who obey the words in this book. Worship God!"

¹⁰Then the angel told me, "Do not keep secret the words of prophecy in this book, because the time is near for all this to happen. ¹¹Let whoever is doing evil continue to do evil. Let whoever is unclean continue to be unclean. Let whoever is doing right continue to do right. Let whoever is holy continue to be holy."

¹²"Listen! I am coming soon! I will bring my reward with me, and I will repay each one of you for what you have done. ¹³I am the Alpha and the Omega," the First and the Last, the Beginning and the End.

¹⁴"Blessed are those who wash their robes" so that they will receive the right to eat the fruit from the tree of life and may go through the gates into the city. ¹⁵Outside the city are the evil people, those who do evil magic, who sin sexually, who murder, who worship idols, and who love lies and tell lies.

¹⁶"I, Jesus, have sent my angel to tell you these things for the churches. I am the descendant from the family of David, and I am the bright morning star."

¹⁷The Spirit and the bride say, "Come!" Let the one who hears this say, "Come!" Let whoever is thirsty come; whoever wishes may have the water of life as a free gift.

¹⁸I warn everyone who hears the words of the prophecy of this book: If anyone adds anything to these words, God will add to that person the disasters written about in this book. ¹⁹And if anyone takes away from the words of this book of prophecy, God will take away that one's share of the tree of life and of the holy city, which are written about in this book.

²⁰Jesus, the One who says these things are true, says, "Yes, I am coming soon."

Amen. Come, Lord Jesus!

²¹The grace of the Lord Jesus be with all. Amen.

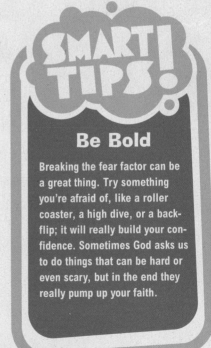

Be Bold

Breaking the fear factor can be a great thing. Try something you're afraid of, like a roller coaster, a high dive, or a backflip; it will really build your confidence. Sometimes God asks us to do things that can be hard or even scary, but in the end they really pump up your faith.

22:13 Alpha and the Omega The first and last letters of the Greek alphabet. This means "the beginning and the end." **22:14 wash their robes** This means they believed and obeyed Jesus so that their sins could be forgiven by Christ's blood. The "washing" may refer to baptism (Acts 22:16).

A 30 day journey with Jesus

1. John 1:1-51

2. Luke 2:1-52

3. Mark 1:1-11

4. Luke 4:1-44

5. John 3:1-36

6. Luke 5:1-39

7. John 4:1-54

8. Luke 6:1-49

9. Luke 7:1-50

10. Luke 8:1-56

11. Mark 8:1-38

12. Luke 10:1-42

13. Matthew 5:1-48

14. Matthew 6:1-34

15. Matthew 7:1-29

16. Luke 14:1-35

17. Luke 15:1-32

18. Luke 16:1-31

19. John 8:1-59

20. Luke 17:1-37

21. Luke 18:1-43

22. John 9:1-41

23. Luke 19:1-48

24. Luke 20:1-47

25. John 10:1-42

26. John 11:1-57

27. Mark 13:1-37

28. Luke 22:1-71

29. Matthew 27:1-66

30. Luke 24:1-53